murach's Visual Basic 2012

Anne Boehm

TRAINING & REFERENCE

murach's Visual Basic 2012

Anne Boehm

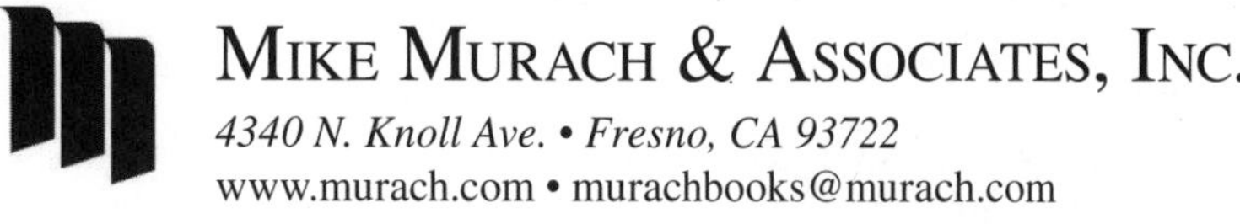
MIKE MURACH & ASSOCIATES, INC.
4340 N. Knoll Ave. • Fresno, CA 93722
www.murach.com • murachbooks@murach.com

Author: Anne Boehm

Editor: Mike Murach

Technical Consultant: Ged Mead

Cover design: Zylka Design

Production: Maria Spera

Books for .NET developers

Murach's Visual Basic 2012
Murach's ASP.NET 4.5 Web Programming with VB 2012

Murach's C# 2012
Murach's ASP.NET 4.5 Web Programming with C# 2012
Murach's ADO.NET Database Programming with C#

Murach's SQL Server 2012 for Developers

Books for web developers

Murach's Dreamweaver CC 2014
Murach's HTML5 and CSS3 (3rd Ed.)
Murach's JavaScript (2nd Ed.)
Murach's jQuery (2nd Ed.)
Murach's PHP and MySQL (2nd Ed.)
Murach's MySQL (2nd Ed.)

Books for Java programmers

Murach's Beginning Java with Eclipse
Murach's Beginning Java with NetBeans
Murach's Java Programming (4th Ed.)
Murach's Android Programming
Murach's Java Servlets and JSP (3rd Ed.)
Murach's Oracle SQL and PL/SQL (2nd Ed.)

Please check www.murach.com for the most up-to-date Murach books

Printed in the United States of America

10 9 8 7 6 5 4 3 2
ISBN: 978-1-890774-73-8

Contents

Expanded contents

Section 1 Introduction to Visual Basic programming

Chapter 5 How to code control structures

Chapter 6 How to code procedures and event handlers

Chapter 7 How to handle exceptions and validate data

Chapter 10 More skills for working with Windows forms and controls

Chapter 11 How to create and use classes

Introduction

Murach's Visual Basic 2012 is designed to teach you everything you need to know for developing Windows Forms applications with Visual Basic 2012. When you finish this book, you'll be able to develop and deploy object-oriented applications the way the best professionals do. And then, this book will become the on-the-job reference that you'll always turn to first.

Who this book is for

This book is for anyone who wants to learn how to use Visual Basic 2012 for developing professional Windows Forms applications or for anyone who wants a great reference book for doing that. That includes not only experienced Java, C#, and Visual Basic developers, but also programming novices.

To make that possible, this book uses a unique, topic-based approach that lets you set your own pace. In section 1, for example, you'll learn the basics of using Visual Studio 2012 and Visual Basic 2012. If you're a beginner, you'll work methodically through the chapters and do the exercises. If you're a Java or a C# programmer, you'll pick up the Visual Basic quickly and focus on the Visual Studio skills. And if you're a Visual Basic programmer who is already comfortable with Visual Studio, you'll skim this section to learn just the new 2012 features that it presents.

Section 2 uses the same approach to teach the Visual Basic essentials. Here again, if you're new to Visual Basic, you'll find that the material is broken down into manageable bites and organized in a logical sequence. That way, you can take as much time as you need to master one topic before moving on to the next.

When you complete section 2, you will have mastered the Visual Basic essentials, and you'll be ready to take your skills to a new level. That includes learning how to develop database applications in section 3 and how to use object-oriented features like inheritance and interfaces in section 4. Here again, all of the sections and chapters have a targeted, topic-based structure that lets you learn what you want to learn next, at the pace that's right for you.

What you'll learn in this book

- Section 1 tours the .NET Framework and teaches the basics of working with Microsoft's development environment, Visual Studio 2012. Here, you'll learn how to develop a simple Windows application. To do that, you'll use the Form Designer to design a Windows form, and you'll use the Code Editor to add and edit the Visual Basic code for the form.
- Section 2 presents the data types, control structures, and other essential elements of the Visual Basic language as well as the core .NET classes that you'll use to develop Windows applications. Along the way, you'll learn how to do the tasks that are required by professional business applications, like data validation. You'll also learn how to create and use your own business and database classes so your applications will be object-oriented.
- Section 3 teaches you the basic skills for developing database applications. To start, you'll learn how to use data sources to build database applications quicker than ever, with minimal code and without using any ADO.NET code. This is particularly useful for developing small, relatively simple applications and for prototyping larger applications. Then, you'll learn how to write ADO.NET code that directly accesses the database. You'll use these skills as your applications get more complicated.
- Section 4 teaches the object-oriented programming features of the Visual Basic language that weren't presented in section 2. Here, you'll learn how to use inheritance, polymorphism, interfaces, and much more. Although you may not need to use these features in typical business applications, they take you to a new level of understanding and expertise.
- Section 5 teaches you additional skills for working with data. That includes working with text, binary, and XML files. It also includes working with LINQ, a feature that lets you query most any data source using the Visual Basic language.
- Section 6 shows you how to enhance a Windows interface with a multiple-document interface (MDI), menus, toolbars, status bars, and help information…all the finishing touches that make your applications thoroughly professional. Then, to complete your training, you'll learn three ways to deploy your applications.
- As an added bonus in section 6, you'll be introduced to programming Windows 8 apps. This chapter starts off with the special design considerations that come into play for apps that can run on tablets and interact via touch screens. Then, it teaches you some of the basic skills for developing this type of app and submitting it to the Windows Store for public access.

Why you'll learn faster and better with this book

Like all our books, this one has features that you won't find in competing books. That's why we believe that you'll learn faster and better with our book than with any other. Here are five of those features.

- Unlike some Visual Basic books, this book shows you how to get the most from Visual Studio 2012 as you develop your applications. Since using the features of this IDE is one of the keys to development productivity, we illustrate the best use of Visual Studio throughout this book.
- The exercises for each chapter guide you through the development of the book applications and challenge you to apply what you've learned in new ways. Because you can download the starting points for these exercises for free from our web site, you get the maximum amount of practice in a minimum of time. And because you can also download the solutions, you can check your work and correct any misconceptions right away.
- Once you complete the first two sections of this book, you can continue with any of the other three sections. That's because you've already learned a complete subset of Visual Basic, including the skills you need for developing object-oriented applications. This means that you get to decide what you want to learn next without worrying about skipping something that's required. That makes this a great book for learning new skills whenever you need them.
- To help you develop applications at a professional level, this book presents 14 complete business applications. That way, you can see the relationships between the Visual Basic code, objects, properties, methods, and events that an application requires, which is essential to your understanding. In contrast, most competing books present trivial applications that have little resemblance to applications in the real world, and that limits your learning potential.
- All of the information in this book is presented in our unique paired-page format with the essential syntax, guidelines, and examples on the right page and the perspective and extra explanation on the left page. Programmers tell us that they love this format because they can learn new skills whenever they have a few minutes and because they can quickly get the information that they need when they use our books for reference.

What software you need

To develop Windows applications with Visual Basic 2012, you can use any of the full editions of Visual Studio 2012, including the Professional Edition, the Premium Edition, or the Ultimate Edition. As an alternative, you can use Visual Studio Express 2012 for Windows Desktop, which can be downloaded from Microsoft's web site for free. All of these editions come with everything you need to develop the Windows applications presented in this book, including the Visual Studio development environment, version 4.5 of the Microsoft .NET Framework, Visual Basic 2012, and a simplified version of SQL Server 2012 called SQL Server 2012 Express LocalDB.

If you use Visual Studio Express for Windows Desktop, you'll find that it has just a few minor differences from the Professional Edition of Visual Studio, which is the basis for this book. You'll also find that a few features aren't available from the Express Edition. To avoid any confusion, though, this book carefully notes these differences. The good news is that all of the skills you learn and all of the applications you develop with the Express Edition will still work with the full editions of Visual Studio.

Downloadable files that can help you learn

If you go to our web site at www.murach.com, you can download all the files that you need for getting the most from this book. These files include:

- all of the applications presented in this book
- the starting points for all of the exercises
- the solutions for all of the exercises
- the database and files that are used by the applications and exercises

The code for the book applications is especially valuable because it lets you run the applications on your own PC, view all of the source code, experiment with the code, and copy and paste any of the source code into your own applications.

Support materials for trainers and instructors

If you're a corporate trainer or a college instructor who would like to use this book for a course, we offer an Instructor's CD that includes: (1) a complete set of PowerPoint slides that you can use to review and reinforce the content of the book; (2) instructional objectives that describe the skills a student should have upon completion of each chapter; (3) test banks that measure mastery of those skills; (4) extra exercises and projects that prove mastery and that can be used for testing; and (5) solutions to the extra exercises and projects.

To learn more about this Instructor's CD and to find out how to get it, please go to our web site at www.murach.com and click on the *Trainers* link or the *Instructors* link. Or, if you prefer, you can call Kelly at 1-800-221-5528 or send an email to kelly@murach.com.

3 companion books that will enhance your skills

This book covers the Visual Basic language and skills that you can use as you develop *any* Visual Basic application. Then, we have 3 books that will help you build on those skills.

If you need to learn how to develop web applications with Visual Basic, we recommend that you get a copy of *Murach's ASP.NET 4.5 Web Programming with VB 2012*. By the time you finish the first five chapters, you'll know how to develop and test multi-form web applications. By the time you finish the book, you'll be able to develop commercial web applications at a professional level.

If you want to learn more about database programming after you complete this book, we recommend that you get a copy of *Murach's ADO.NET Database Programming with VB*. This book will teach you how to develop database applications the way the best professionals develop them. That includes developing three-layer applications that use parameters, stored procedures, transactions, and object data sources.

And because just about any business application you develop in Visual Basic is going to deal with database data, we recommend that you have a copy of *Murach's SQL Server 2012 for Developers* close at hand. Although most developers know some elementary SQL, they often stop there, never realizing all the power that SQL has to offer. But this book helps you code SQL queries for even complex retrievals. Beyond that, this book shows you how to design and implement databases and how to use advanced features like stored procedures, triggers, and functions.

Please let us know how this book works for you

This is the fifth edition of our Visual Basic.NET book. For each edition, we've added the new features of both Visual Studio and Visual Basic. But we've also tried to respond to the feedback that we've received and improve the content of the book.

Now that we're done with this book, we hope we've succeeded in making it as easy as possible to master Visual Basic, no matter what your background. So if you have any comments about our book, we would appreciate hearing from you. If you like our book, please tell a friend. And good luck with your Visual Basic programming.

Anne Boehm, Author
anne@murach.com

Mike Murach, Publisher
mike@murach.com

Section 1

Introduction to Visual Basic programming

This section introduces you to the Visual Studio 2012 components that support Visual Basic programming. To start, chapter 1 introduces you to the .NET Framework, the languages that work with the .NET Framework, and the Visual Studio development environment. Then, chapter 2 shows you how to use Visual Studio to design a form for a Windows Forms application. Finally, chapter 3 shows you how to use Visual Studio to enter and edit the code that determines how the form works.

When you complete this section, you should have a general understanding of how to use Visual Studio to develop a Windows Forms application. You should also have the skills that you need for designing a Windows form and entering the code for it. Then, the next section of this book will teach you the essentials of the Visual Basic language.

1

An introduction to Visual Studio

This chapter gets you started with Visual Studio 2012 by introducing the .NET Framework, the languages that work with the .NET Framework, and the Visual Studio development environment. It also provides a quick tour of this development environment. Along the way, you'll learn all of the concepts and terms that you need for developing .NET applications.

An introduction to .NET development

This section presents some of the concepts and terms that you need before you begin developing .NET applications. Although this section focuses on Visual Basic, most of these concepts and terms also apply to the other .NET programming languages.

.NET applications

The table in figure 1-1 summarizes some of the types of .NET applications that you can develop using Visual Studio. In this book, you'll learn Visual Basic by developing *Windows Forms applications* (or *WinForms apps*) like the one shown at the top of this figure. Keep in mind, though, that you can develop any of the types of applications listed in this figure using Visual Basic.

A Windows Forms application is a traditional *Windows application* that runs on the user's PC. Each *Windows form* (or just *form*) in the application provides a user interface that lets the user interact with the application. In the example in this figure, the application consists of a single form. Many applications, though, require more than one form.

As part of the user interface, a Windows Forms application uses *Windows Forms controls* like the ones shown in this figure. In the next chapter, you'll start learning how to develop Windows Forms applications.

Another type of application that you can develop with Visual Basic is an *ASP.NET Web Forms application*. A Web Forms application is a traditional *web application* that consists of one or more *web forms* that can contain *Web Forms controls*. Unlike Windows forms, web forms are accessed by and displayed in a *web browser* such as Microsoft's Internet Explorer. In addition, the code for a Web Forms application runs on a web server. As this code is executed, it passes the visual portion of the application to the browser running on the client in the form of HTML (Hypertext Markup Language). The browser then interprets the HTML and displays the form.

The last four types of applications listed in this figure provide the user with a more modern user interface than Windows Forms and Web Forms applications. To do that, the user interfaces for these applications is implemented using *XAML (Extensible Application Markup Language)*. With XAML (pronounced *zamel*), you can easily develop applications that include animation, enhanced graphics, touch processing, and much more.

One of the main differences between these types of applications is where they run. For example, *WPF (Windows Presentation Foundation) applications* are Windows applications that run on the user's PC. In contrast, *Silverlight applications* typically run in a browser, *Windows Store applications* run on a tablet or PC, and *Windows Phone 8 applications* run on a Windows 8 phone.

Note that you can only develop Windows Store and Windows Phone 8 applications if you have the Windows 8 operating system. In that case, you'll want to develop applications that follow the Windows 8 design principles. Chapter 26 introduces you to these principles and shows you how they can be applied to Windows Store applications.

A Windows Forms application running on the Windows desktop

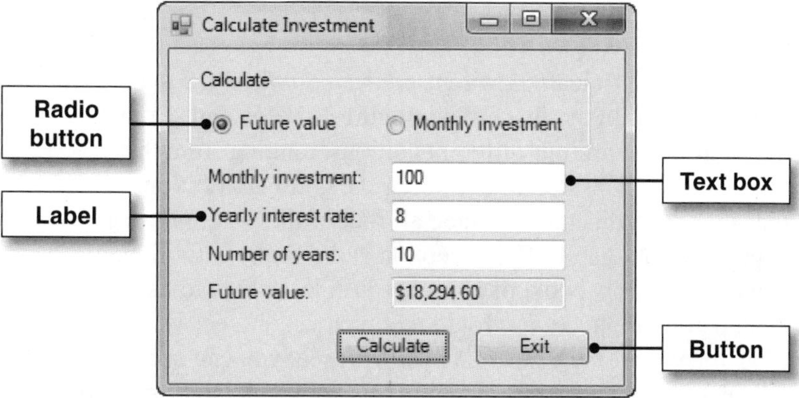

Common types of .NET applications

Type	Description
Windows Forms	Runs in its own window on the user's PC and consists of one or more Windows forms that provide the user interface for the application.
ASP.NET Web Forms	Runs on a web server and consists of one or more web forms. The web forms are displayed in a browser on the client machine and provide the user interface for the application.
WPF	Runs in windows on the user's PC and provides an enhanced user experience. Can also be made viewable in Internet Explorer.
Silverlight	Runs in a browser on a client machine and provides an enhanced user experience. Can also be hosted by an ASP.NET application.
Windows Store	Runs on a tablet or PC under the Windows 8 or Windows RT (runtime) operating system and provides an enhanced user experience.
Windows Phone 8	Runs on a Windows Phone under the Windows Phone 8 operating system and provides an enhanced user experience.

Description

- A *Windows Forms application* (or *WinForms app*) is a traditional *Windows application* that runs on the user's PC. The *Windows forms* that provide the user interface for this type of application contain *Windows Forms controls*, like labels, text boxes, buttons, and radio buttons, that let the user interact with the application.
- *Web Forms applications* are traditional *web applications* that run on a web server, but whose user interfaces are displayed in a browser on a client machine.
- The enhanced user experience that's provided by *WPF* (*Windows Presentation Foundation*), *Silverlight*, *Windows Store*, and *Windows Phone 8* applications developed using Visual Basic is implemented using *XAML* (*Extensible Application Markup Language*).

Figure 1-1 .NET applications

Visual Studio and the .NET programming languages

In this book, you're going to learn how to use *Visual Studio 2012* to develop Windows Forms applications. In the first table in figure 1-2, you can see that Visual Studio 2012 is available in four different editions, ranging from the free Express Edition for Windows Desktop to the expensive Ultimate Edition.

All four of the editions in this table include all four of the programming languages shown in the second table. The exception is the Express Edition, which doesn't include F#. In this book, of course, you'll learn how to use *Visual Basic 2012* to develop your applications. To do that, you need to get *Visual Studio Express 2012 for Windows Desktop*. As you will see, you can use this edition to do almost everything that's presented in this book, and we'll point out any limitations whenever they occur.

The three other languages that come with Visual Studio 2012 are C#, C++, and F#. Like Visual Basic, C# is a language that can be used for rapid application development. In contrast, Visual C++ is Microsoft's version of the C++ language. Visual F# is a relatively new language that provides functional programming in addition to object-oriented and procedural programming.

Although the four languages shown in this figure are the only languages that come with Visual Studio, it's possible for other vendors to develop languages for the .NET Framework. For example, Micro Focus has developed a version of COBOL for the .NET Framework.

Regardless of the language that's used, Visual Studio 2012 provides an *Integrated Development Environment* (*IDE*) that can be used for application development. Visual Studio also includes the *.NET Framework* (pronounced "dot net framework") that defines the environment that executes Visual Basic applications. You'll learn more about both as you progress through this chapter.

Visual Studio also includes *SQL Server 2012 Express LocalDB*. LocalDB is a new addition to the SQL Server family that's specifically designed for developers and doesn't require any management. Because of that, it's ideal for testing database applications on your own PC.

In this figure, you can see that Visual Studio 2012 can be used on any PC that runs Windows 7 or later. Then, the applications that are developed with Visual Studio 2012 can be run on any PC that runs Windows XP or later, depending on which .NET components are used by the application.

What about Visual Studio 2013?

At this writing, a new release of Visual Studio called *Visual Studio 2013* is promised for later this year. Note, however, that this release won't have any effect on the Visual Basic skills that are presented in this book. Instead, Visual Studio 2013 focuses on other types of enhancements, such as some minor improvements to the IDE. After Visual Studio 2013 is released, we will evaluate these enhancements to see whether any of them affect this book. If so, we will post that information to the FAQs for this book on our web site.

Visual Studio 2012 Editions

Edition	Description
Express Edition for Windows Desktop	A free, downloadable edition that supports the Visual Basic, C#, and C++ languages. It is appropriate for students and hobbyists.
Professional Edition	Designed for individual developers who want to build a wide variety of Windows, web, mobile, and Office-based solutions.
Premium Edition	Designed for individuals and teams who want to build scalable applications and includes standard testing tools, database deployment and change-management tools, and basic lifecycle management tools.
Ultimate Edition	Designed for teams and includes full testing, modeling, database, and lifecycle management tools.

Programming languages supported by Visual Studio 2012

Language	Description
Visual Basic	Designed for rapid application development
Visual C#	Combines the features of Java and C++ and is suitable for rapid application development
Visual C++	Microsoft's version of C++
Visual F#	Combines functional, procedural, and object-oriented programming

Platforms that can run Visual Studio 2012

- Windows 7, Windows 8, or later releases of Windows

Platforms that can run applications created with Visual Studio 2012

- Windows XP and later releases of Windows, depending on which .NET components the application uses

Description

- *Visual Studio 2012* is a suite of products that includes the .NET Framework and an *Integrated Development Environment (IDE)*.
- The *.NET Framework* provides a library of code that supports all four programming languages shown above.
- The *Visual Studio IDE* can be used to develop applications with any of the four programming languages.
- Visual Studio 2012 includes *SQL Server 2012 Express LocalDB*, which is a version of the Microsoft SQL Server 2012 database management system that is designed specifically for developers.

Figure 1-2 Visual Studio and the .NET programming languages

The .NET Framework

To give you a more detailed view of the .NET Framework, figure 1-3 presents its main components. As you can see, the .NET Framework provides a common set of services that application programs written in a .NET language such as Visual Basic can use to run on various operating systems and hardware platforms. The .NET Framework is divided into two main components: the .NET Framework Class Library and the Common Language Runtime.

The *.NET Framework Class Library* consists of segments of pre-written code called *classes* that provide many of the functions that you need for developing .NET applications. For instance, the Windows Forms classes are used for developing Windows Forms applications. The ASP.NET classes are used for developing Web Forms applications. And other classes let you work with databases, manage security, access files, and perform many other functions.

Although it's not apparent in this figure, the classes in the .NET Framework Class Library are organized in a hierarchical structure. Within this structure, related classes are organized into groups called *namespaces*. Each namespace contains the classes used to support a particular function. For example, the System.Windows.Forms namespace contains the classes used to create forms and the System.Data namespace contains the classes you use to access data.

The *Common Language Runtime* (*CLR*) provides the services that are needed for executing any application that's developed with one of the .NET languages. This is possible because all of the .NET languages compile to a common intermediate language, which you'll learn more about in figure 1-5. The CLR also provides the *Common Type System* that defines the data types that are used by all .NET languages. Because all of the .NET applications are managed by the CLR, they are sometimes referred to as *managed applications*.

If you're new to programming, you might not understand this diagram completely, but that's all right. For now, all you need to understand is the general structure of the .NET Framework and the terms that have been presented so far. As you progress through this book, this diagram will make more sense, and you will become more familiar with each of the terms.

The .NET Framework

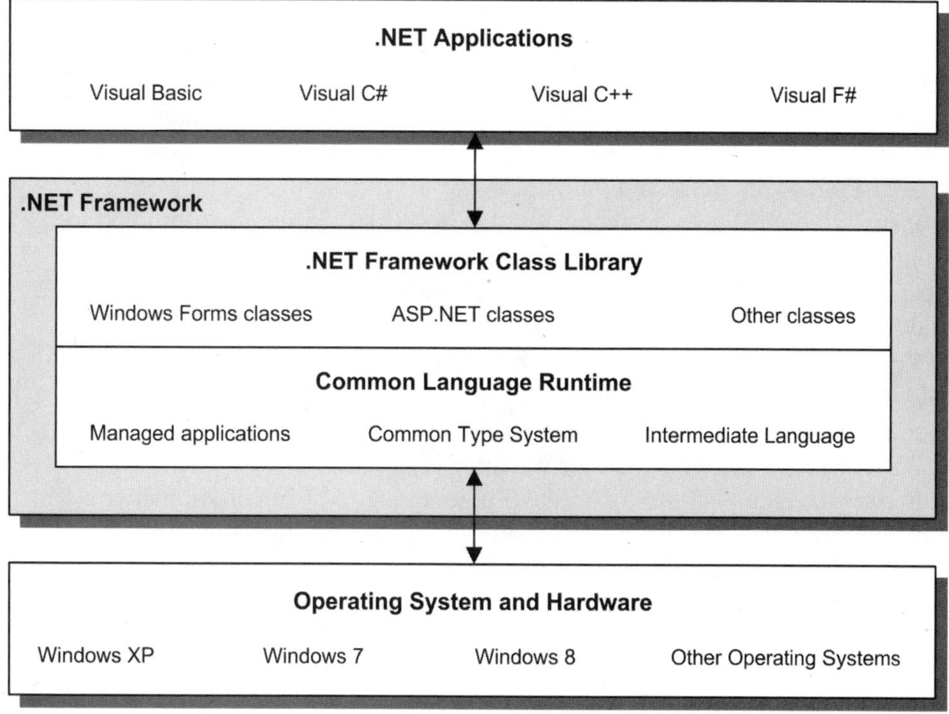

Description

- Windows Forms applications do not access the operating system or computer hardware directly. Instead, they use services of the .NET Framework, which in turn access the operating system and hardware.
- The .NET Framework consists of two main components: the .NET Framework Class Library and the Common Language Runtime.
- The *.NET Framework Class Library* provides files that contain pre-written code known as *classes* that are available to all of the .NET programming languages. This class library consists of thousands of classes, but you can create simple .NET applications once you learn how to use just a few of them.
- The *Common Language Runtime*, or *CLR*, manages the execution of .NET programs by coordinating essential functions such as memory management, code execution, security, and other services. Because .NET applications are managed by the CLR, they are called *managed applications*.
- The *Common Type System* is a component of the CLR that ensures that all .NET applications use the same basic data types no matter what programming languages are used to develop the applications.

Figure 1-3 The .NET Framework

The Visual Studio IDE

Figure 1-4 shows the Visual Studio IDE. In practice, this IDE is often referred to simply as *Visual Studio*, and that's how we'll refer to it throughout this book. By now, you already know that this IDE supports all four languages presented in figure 1-2. In addition, you should realize that this IDE works with the .NET Framework presented in figure 1-3.

Visual Studio includes designers that can be used to design the user interface for all of the types of applications you learned about in figure 1-1. These visual tools make this tough task much easier. You'll be introduced to the designer for Windows forms in figure 1-8.

Visual Studio also includes an editor that can be used to work with any of the four languages presented in figure 1-2 as well as HTML and XML. This editor contains many features that make it easy to enter and edit the code for an application. You'll be introduced to this editor in figure 1-9.

Before you take your tour of Visual Studio, though, it's important that you understand what happens when you use Visual Studio to compile and run an application.

The Visual Studio IDE

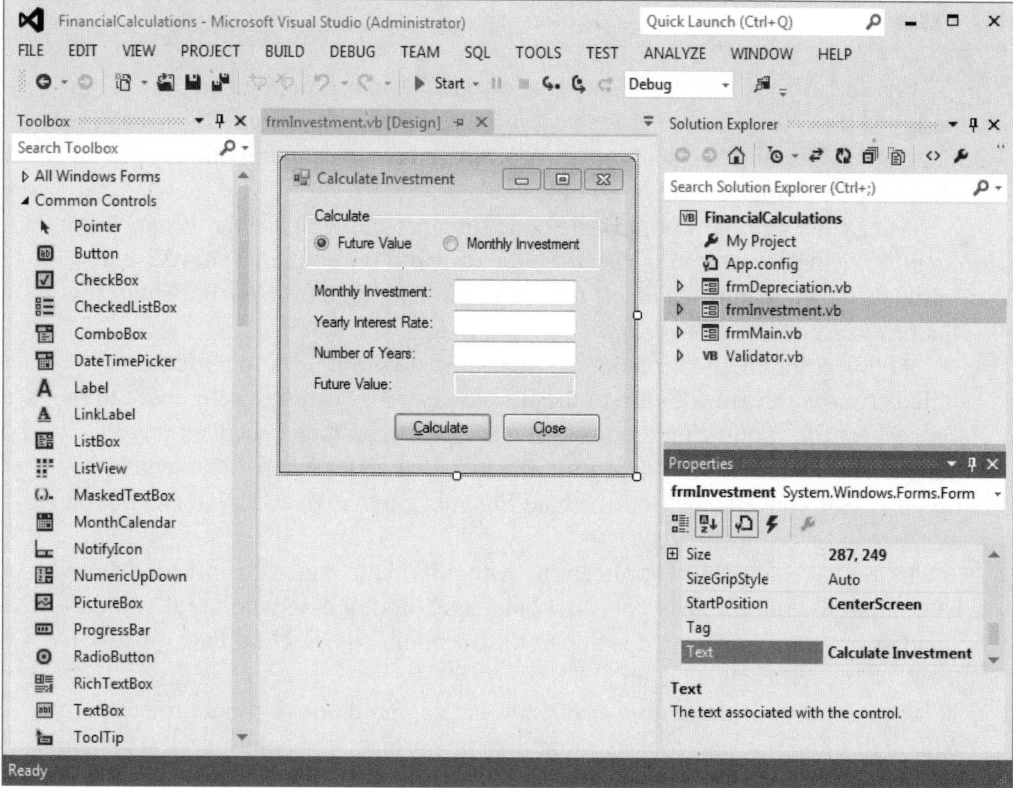

Description

- The Visual Studio IDE is often referred to as *Visual Studio*, even though that name is also used to refer to the entire suite of products, including the .NET Framework.
- Visual Studio supports all four languages presented in figure 1-2.
- Visual Studio includes designers that can be used to develop all of the application types presented in figure 1-1.
- Visual Studio includes a code editor that can be used to work with any of the four languages presented in figure 1-2 as well as HTML and XML.

Figure 1-4 The Visual Studio IDE

How a Visual Basic application is compiled and run

Figure 1-5 shows how a Visual Basic application is compiled and run. To start, you use Visual Studio to create a *project*, which is made up of *source files* that contain Visual Basic statements. A project may also contain other types of files, such as sound, image, or text files.

After you enter the Visual Basic code for a project, you use the *Visual Basic compiler*, which is built into Visual Studio, to *build* (or compile) your Visual Basic source code into *Microsoft Intermediate Language* (*MSIL*). For short, this can be referred to as *Intermediate Language* (*IL*).

At this point, the Intermediate Language is stored on disk in a file that's called an *assembly*. In addition to the IL, the assembly includes references to the classes that the application requires. The assembly can then be run on any PC that has the Common Language Runtime installed on it. When the assembly is run, the CLR converts the Intermediate Language to native code that can be run by the Windows operating system.

If you have developed applications with other languages, this process should be familiar to you. If this is your first language, though, you won't really understand this process until you develop your first applications. Until then, just try to focus on the terms and concepts.

Incidentally, a *solution* is a container that can hold one or more projects. Although a solution can contain more than one project, the solution for a simple application usually contains just one project. In that case, the solution and the project are essentially the same thing.

How Visual Basic differs from the other .NET languages

Visual Basic uses the same .NET Framework classes as the other .NET programming languages. These classes affect almost every aspect of programming, including creating and working with forms and controls, using databases, and working with basic language features such as arrays and strings. In addition, Visual Basic works with the same Visual Studio IDE as the other .NET languages. As a result, Visual Basic has many similarities to the other .NET languages. The main difference is the syntax of the language.

How a Visual Basic application is compiled and run

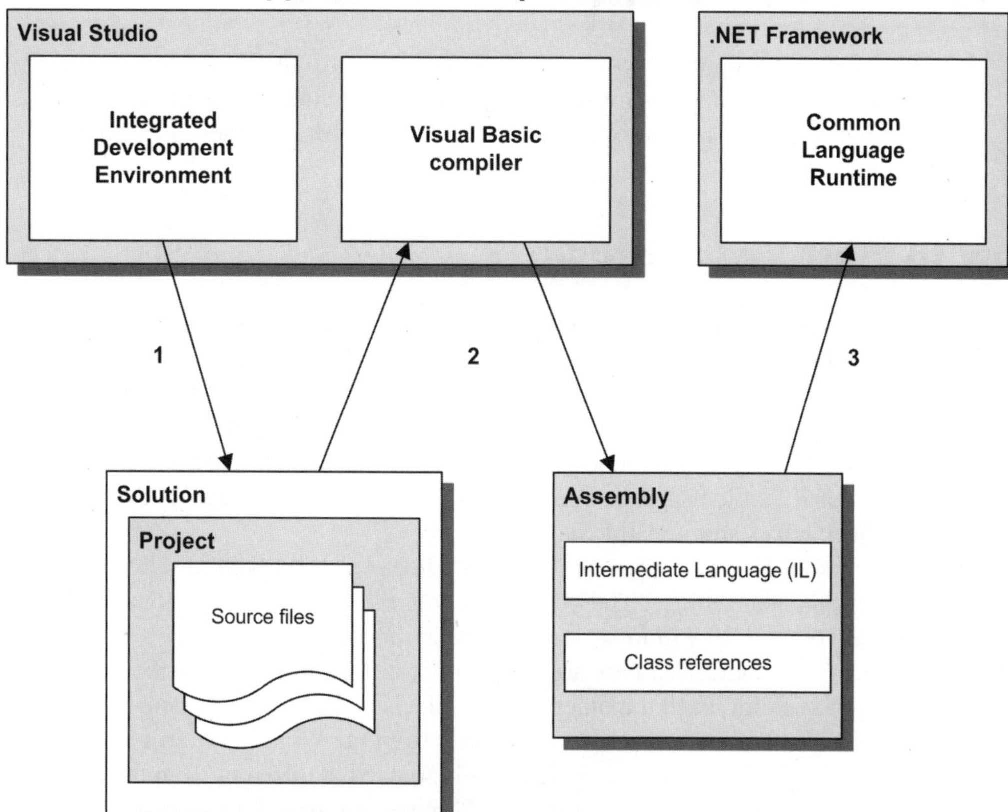

Operation

1. The programmer uses Visual Studio to create a *project*, which includes Visual Basic *source files*. In some cases, a project will also contain other types of files, such as graphic image or sound files.
2. The Visual Basic *compiler builds* (translates) the Visual Basic source code for a project into *Microsoft Intermediate Language* (*MSIL*), or just *Intermediate Language* (*IL*). This language is stored on disk in an *assembly* that also contains references to the required classes. An assembly is an executable file that has an *.exe* or *.dll* extension.
3. The assembly is run by the .NET Framework's Common Language Runtime. The CLR manages all aspects of how the assembly is run, including converting the Intermediate Language to native code that can be run by the operating system, managing memory for the assembly, and enforcing security.

About projects and solutions

- A *solution* is a container that can hold one or more projects.

Figure 1-5 How a Visual Basic application is compiled and run

A tour of the Visual Studio IDE

With that as background, you're ready to take a tour of the Visual Studio IDE. Along the way, you'll learn some of the basic techniques for working in this environment. You'll also see how some of the terms that you just learned are applied within the IDE.

How to start Visual Studio

Figure 1-6 shows how to start Visual Studio and what the opening view of the IDE looks like. In the main window within the IDE, a Start Page is displayed. This page lets you open recent projects, create new ones, and get news and information about Visual Studio. You can also control whether the Start Page is closed after you open a project and whether this page is shown each time you start Visual Studio using the check boxes in the lower left corner of the page. (These check boxes aren't visible here.)

Note that the first time you start Visual Studio, you'll be asked to select the default environment settings. Then, you can choose Visual Basic Development Settings so your menus will look like the ones in this book.

As this figure indicates, there are some minor differences between the Visual Studio Express Edition and the other editions of Visual Studio. In this case, you access Visual Studio Express a little differently from the Windows Start menu, and the Start Page for Visual Studio Express is somewhat different from the Start Page for the other editions. Both of these differences are trivial, though, as are most of the differences between Visual Studio Express and the other editions.

Throughout this book, all of the screen illustrations are based on the Professional Edition of Visual Studio 2012. Whenever the Express Edition varies in any way that is likely to confuse someone who's using it, though, we will carefully detail the differences. As you would expect, the Professional Edition also has some features that aren't available with the Express Edition, and we will of course point out those limitations too.

In general, though, using the Express Edition is an excellent way to get started with Visual Studio 2012. As you will see, you can develop professional applications with that edition. And both the skills that you learn and the applications that you develop will work whenever you want to upgrade to one of the other editions.

The Start Page that's displayed when you start Visual Studio

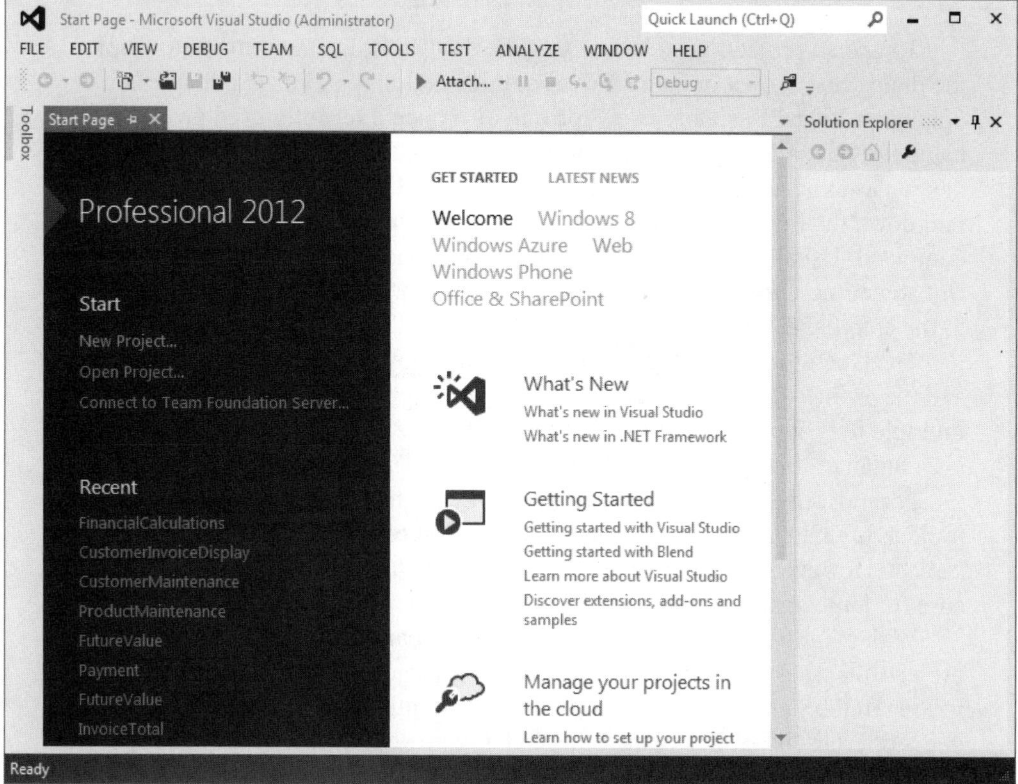

Description

- To start Visual Studio, open the Windows Start menu, then locate and select Visual Studio 2012. Typically, this item is in the Microsoft Visual Studio 2012 submenu of the All Programs menu.
- To make it easier to start Visual Studio, you may want to create a shortcut for Visual Studio 2012 or Visual Studio 2012 Express for Windows Desktop and place it on the desktop.
- When Visual Studio starts, a Start Page is displayed. You can use this page to open recent projects, create new ones, access resources, and so on.

Variations between the Professional and Express Editions

- In this book, all of the screen illustrations are from the Professional Edition of Visual Studio 2012. In general, these illustrations are the same for both the Professional Edition and the Express Edition.
- Whenever the Express Edition differs significantly from the Professional Edition, we'll point out the differences.

Express Edition difference

- To start Visual Studio, select VS Express for Desktop from the Windows Start menu.

Figure 1-6 How to start Visual Studio

How to open or close an existing project

To open a project, you can use the File→Open Project command to display the dialog box shown in figure 1-7. From this dialog box, you can locate and open your Visual Basic projects. You can also open a recently used project by using the File→Recent Projects and Solutions command.

In case you aren't familiar with this notation, File→Open Project means to pull down the File menu from the menu bar, and then select the Open Project command. Usually, you only need to pull down one menu and select a command. But sometimes, you need to go from a menu to one or more submenus and then to the command.

The Open Project dialog box in this figure shows both the *solution file* and the *project file* for a project. As this figure explains, a project can contain multiple files, including the files for source code. A solution, on the other hand, is a container that holds one or more projects.

For most of the applications in this book, a solution contains just a single project. In that case, there's not much distinction between a solution and a project. However, a solution can contain more than one project. This is often the case for large applications that are developed by teams of programmers.

With a multi-project solution, programmers can work independently on the projects that make up the solution. In fact, the projects don't even have to be written in the same language. For example, a solution can contain two projects, one written in Visual Basic, the other in C#.

At this point, you might wonder whether you should open a project or a solution. In this figure, for example, FinancialCalculations.sln is a solution and FinancialCalculations.vbproj is a Visual Basic project. In most cases, though, it doesn't matter whether you open the solution or the project. Either way, both the solution and the project files will be opened.

Some possible menu variations

Curiously, some of the menus vary slightly based on the option settings and the import and export settings. So don't be surprised if you find that you have to use the File→Open→Project/Solution command to open a project. Since these menu variations are trivial, you shouldn't have any trouble using menus even if the ones on your system are slightly different than the ones we specify. And in the next chapter, you'll learn how to set these options so your menus work the way they're described in this book.

The Open Project dialog box

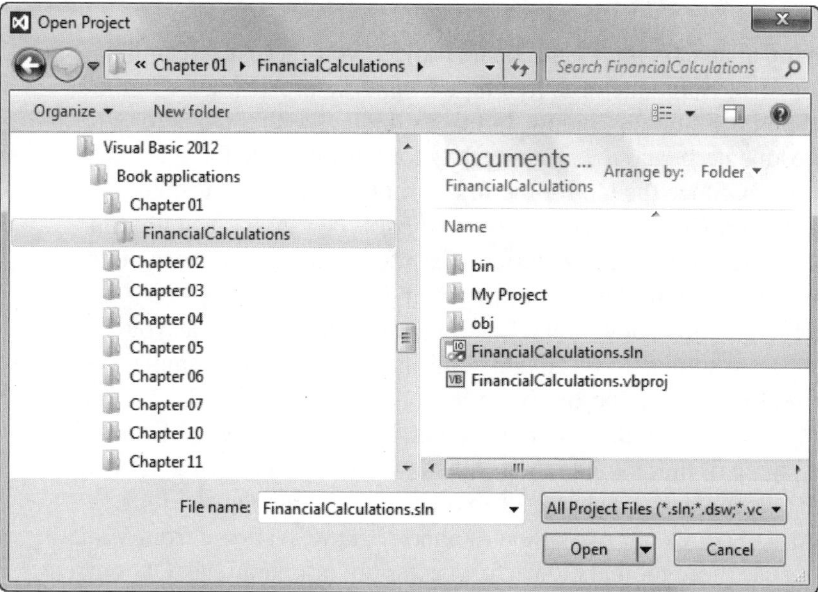

Project and solution concepts

- Every Visual Basic project has a *project file* with an extension of *vbproj* that keeps track of the files that make up the project and records various settings for the project. In this figure, the project file is just below the highlighted file.
- Every solution has a *solution file* with an extension of *sln* that keeps track of the projects that make up the solution. In this figure, the solution file is highlighted.
- When you open a project file, Visual Studio opens the solution that contains the project. And when you open a solution file, Visual Studio opens all the projects contained in the solution. So either way, both the project and the solution are opened.
- Sometimes the project and solution files are stored in the same directory. Sometimes the project file is stored in a subdirectory of the directory that contains the solution file.

How to open a project

- To open an existing project, use the File→Open Project command. Then, use the controls in the Open Project dialog box to locate and select the project or solution you want to open.
- After you've worked on one or more projects, their names will be listed in the File→Recent Projects and Solutions submenu. Then, you can click on a project name to open it.
- You can also use the links on the Start Page to open a project.

How to close a project or a solution

- Use the File→Close Project or File→Close Solution command.

Figure 1-7 How to open or close an existing project

How to use the Form Designer

When you open an existing Visual Basic project, you'll see a screen like the one in figure 1-8. Here, one or more *tabbed windows* are displayed in the main part of the Visual Studio window. In this example, the first tab is for a form named frmInvestment.vb, and the second tab is for a form named frmDepreciation.vb. Since the tab for the first form is selected, its form is displayed in the *Form Designer window* (or just *Form Designer*). You use the Form Designer to develop the user interface for a form, and you'll learn more about working with the Form Designer in chapter 2.

This figure also shows some of the other windows that you use as you develop Visual Basic applications. To add controls to a form, for example, you use the *Toolbox*. To set the properties of a form or control, you use the *Properties window*. And to manage the files that make up a solution, you use the *Solution Explorer*. If all three of these windows aren't shown when you open a project, you can use the techniques in figure 1-11 to open and arrange them.

This figure also points out two of the toolbars that are available from Visual Studio. You can use these toolbars to perform a variety of operations. Of course, you can also perform any operation by using the menus at the top of Visual Studio. And you can perform some operations by using the context-sensitive shortcut menu that's displayed when you right-click on an object within Visual Studio.

Visual Studio with the Form Designer window displayed

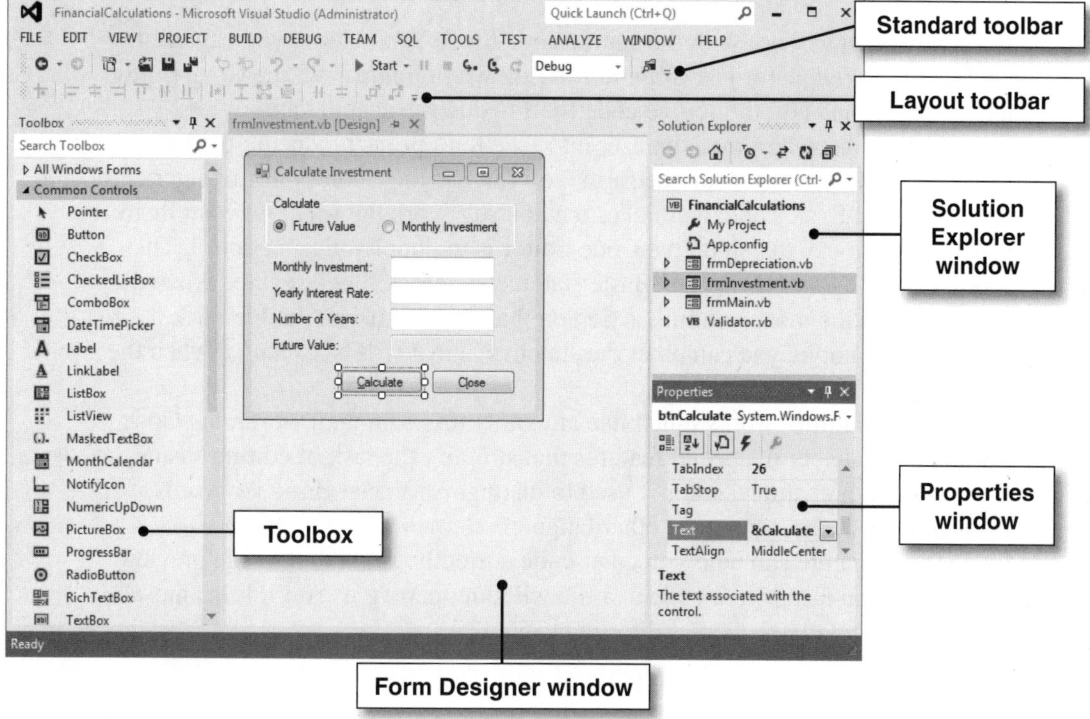

Description

- The main Visual Studio workspace contains one or more *tabbed windows*. To develop a form, you use the *Form Designer window* (or just *Form Designer*). To develop code, you use the Code Editor window that's shown in figure 1-9.
- To open the Form Designer, you can double-click on a form in the Solution Explorer, or you can select the form in the Solution Explorer and then use the View→Designer command.
- To add controls and other items to a form, you use the *Toolbox*. The Toolbox contains a variety of items organized into categories such as Common Controls, Containers, Menus & Toolbars, Data, and so on.
- To change the way a form or control looks or operates, you use the *Properties window*. This window displays the properties of the item that's selected in the Form Designer.
- You use the Solution Explorer window to manage project files. You'll learn more about the Solution Explorer in figure 1-10.
- Several toolbars are available from Visual Studio. The Standard toolbar includes standard Windows toolbar buttons such as Open, Save, Cut, Copy, and Paste, plus other buttons that you'll learn about as you progress through this book.
- To display any toolbar, right-click in an empty toolbar area and select the toolbar you want to display.

Figure 1-8 How to use the Form Designer

How to use the Code Editor

If you want to work with the source code for an application, you can use the *Code Editor window* (or just *Code Editor*) shown in figure 1-9. The Code Editor lets you enter and edit the source code for a Visual Basic application.

After you have designed the user interface for a project by using the Form Designer to place controls on the form, you can use the Code Editor to enter and edit the Visual Basic code that makes the controls work the way you want them to. The easiest way to call up the Code Editor is to double-click a control. Then, you can begin typing the Visual Basic statements that will be executed when the user performs the most common action on that control. If you double-click a button, for example, you can enter the statements that will be executed when the user clicks on that button.

The Code Editor works much like any other text editor. However, the Code Editor has a number of special features that simplify the task of editing Visual Basic code. For example, color is used to distinguish Visual Basic keywords from variables, comments, and other language elements. The improved IntelliSense feature can help you enter code correctly. And the new file preview feature lets you display the code in a file without opening it. You'll learn more about working with the Code Editor in chapter 3.

Visual Studio with the Code Editor window displayed

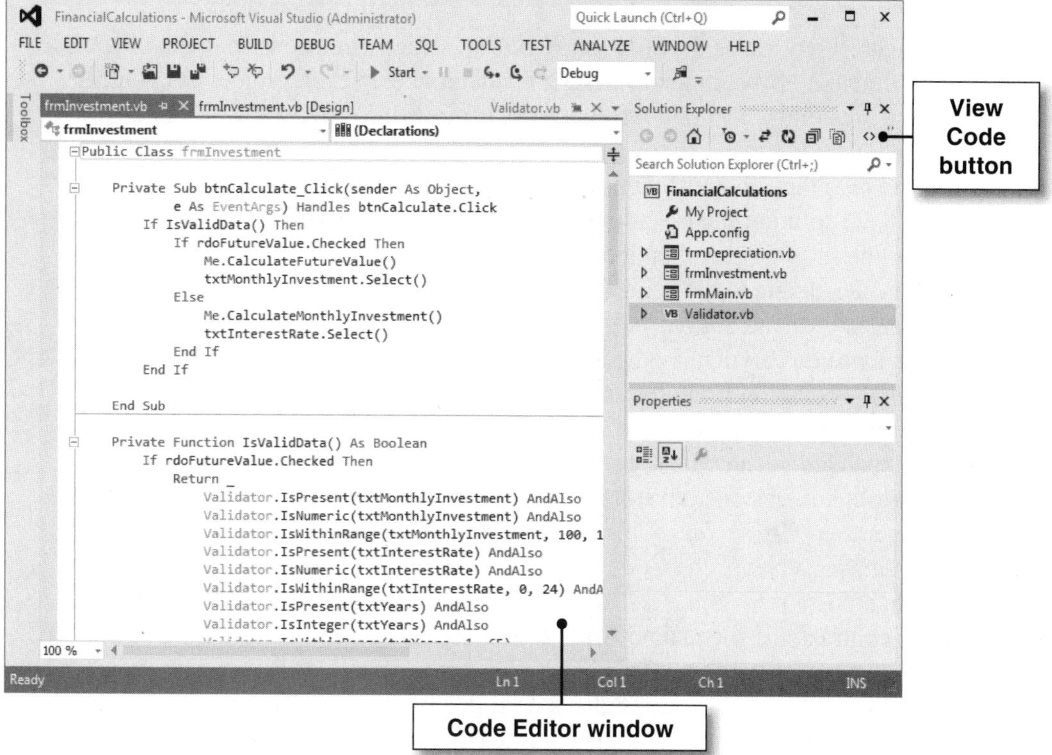

Description

- The *Code Editor window* (or just *Code Editor*) is where you create and edit the Visual Basic code that your application requires. The Code Editor works much like any other text editor, so you shouldn't have much trouble learning how to use it.
- You can display the Code Editor by double-clicking the form or one of the controls in the Form Designer window. Or, you can select the form in the Solution Explorer and click the View Code button.
- You can also preview the code in a file by selecting the file in the Solution Explorer. Then, a tab for the window appears at the right side of the Code Editor window as shown above. If you modify the file or click the Keep Open button in the tab, the file is opened.
- Once you've opened the Code Editor, you can return to the Form Designer by clicking the [Design] tab for that window. You can also move among these windows by pressing Ctrl+Tab or Shift+Ctrl+Tab, or by selecting a form from the Active Files drop-down list that's available to the right of the tabs.
- It's important to realize that the Form Designer and the Code Editor give you two different views of a form. The Form Designer gives you a visual representation of the form. The Code Editor shows you the Visual Basic code that makes the form work the way you want it to.

Figure 1-9 How to use the Code Editor

How to use the Solution Explorer

Figure 1-10 shows the *Solution Explorer*, which you use to manage the projects that make up a solution and the files that make up each project. As you can see, the files in the Solution Explorer are displayed in a tree view. If a node has a ▷ symbol next to it, you can click the symbol to display its contents. Conversely, you can hide the contents by clicking on the ◢ symbol next to it. Note that, by default, the solution file isn't displayed in the Solution Explorer. If, however, you set the option to display this file as shown in the next chapter, the project will appear subordinate to the solution in the Solution Explorer.

You can use the buttons at the top of the Solution Explorer to work with the files in a project. To display the code for a form, for example, you can select the form in the Solution Explorer and then click the View Code button.

In this figure, the form that's stored in the file named frmInvestment.vb has been expanded to show its supporting files. Here, the file named frmInvestment.Designer.vb stores most of the code that's generated by the Form Designer in a *partial class*. This code determines the appearance of the form. If you want, you can use the Code Editor to view this code, but you usually won't want to modify it.

In contrast, the file named frmInvestment.vb contains the Visual Basic code that you enter for the form. This is the code that determines how the controls on the form work. This code is also stored in a partial class, and the two partial classes are combined into a single class for the Investment form when the project is built. You'll learn a lot more about both classes and partial classes as you progress through this book.

As you develop a project, you can also create classes that contain Visual Basic code but don't define forms. In this figure, for example, the file named Validator.vb is a source file that contains a class that isn't for a form. In this case, you can display the code for the class in the Code Editor by selecting it and then clicking the View Code button or by double-clicking on it.

To identify the files that make up a project, you can look at the icon that's displayed to the left of the file name. The icon for a form file, for example, is a form, and the icon for a Visual Basic class file that isn't for a form has a VB icon on it. As you can see, this project consists of three form files and one class file that contains Visual Basic code.

Note, however, that all of the files except for the App.config file have the file extension vb regardless of their contents. Because of that, we recommend that you name your files in a way that identifies their contents. For example, we add the prefix frm to the names of our form files. That way, it's easy to identify the form files when you work with them outside of the Solution Explorer.

This project also includes two folders named My Project and References. The My Project folder contains information about the project, such as what form is displayed when the application starts. You can change this information by double-clicking on the folder to display the project's properties. You'll see examples of these properties later in this book.

The Solution Explorer

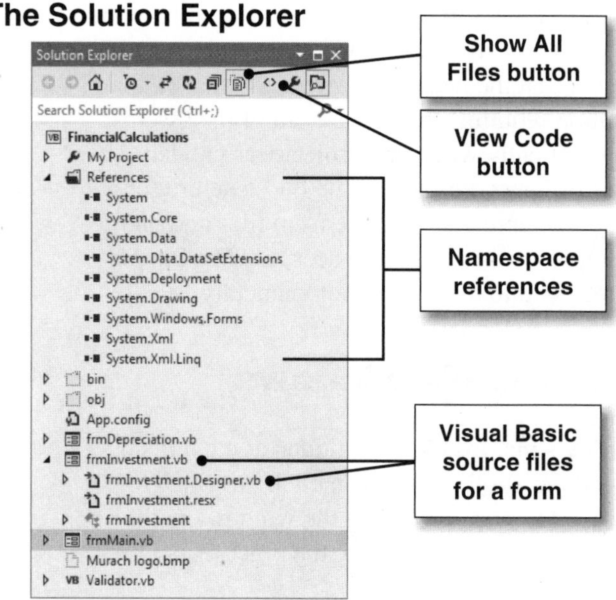

Description

- You use the *Solution Explorer* to manage and display the files and projects in a solution. The Solution Explorer lists all of the projects for the current solution, as well as all of the files that make up each project.
- The ▷ and ◢ symbols in the Solution Explorer indicate groups of files. You can click these signs to expand and collapse the groups.
- You can use the buttons at the top of the Solution Explorer window to perform a variety of functions, including viewing the code in a file in the Code Editor.

Project files

- The Solution Explorer uses different icons to distinguish between source code files that define forms and source code files that don't define forms.
- Each form is defined by two Visual Basic source files where each file contains a *partial class*. The file with the vb extension contains the code that's entered by the programmer, and the file with the Designer.vb extension contains the code that's generated when the programmer works with the Form Designer. When the project is compiled, these partial classes are combined into a single class.
- A source code file that doesn't define a form is usually stored in a single Visual Basic source file that contains a single class.
- My Project is a folder that contains information about the project. You can double-click on this folder to display and change the project information.
- The References folder contains references to the assemblies for the namespaces that the application can use.
- The App.config file contains configuration information for the application and is created automatically.

Figure 1-10 How to use the Solution Explorer

The References folder contains references to the assemblies that contain the namespaces that are available to the project. To display this folder, you can click the Show All Files button. Remember that the namespaces contain the .NET Framework classes that the application requires. In this case, all of the assemblies were added to the project automatically when this project was created.

This should give you some idea of how complicated the file structure for a project can be. For this relatively simple application, three form files and one class file were created by the developer. And nine namespaces, the My Project folder, and the App.config file were added to the project automatically.

How to work with Visual Studio's windows

In figure 1-11, the Toolbox isn't visible. Instead, it's hidden at the left side of the window. Then, when you need the Toolbox, you can click on its tab to display it. This is just one of the ways that you can adjust the windows in the IDE so it's easier to use. This figure also presents many of the other techniques that you can use.

By default, the Toolbox is docked at the edge of the application window and is hidden so it appears as a tab. To display a hidden window, you click on its tab. If you want the window to remain open when you click on another window, you can click the window's Auto Hide button. The Auto Hide button looks like a pushpin, as illustrated by the button near the upper right corner of the Properties window. To hide the window again, click its Auto Hide button.

You can also undock a window so it floats in the middle of the IDE, outside the IDE, or even on a separate monitor. That includes windows that are docked at the edge of the IDE, like the Toolbox and the Solution Explorer, as well as the tabbed windows in the middle of the IDE. To undock one of these windows, you drag it by its title bar or tab or double-click its title bar or tab. In this figure, for example, you can see that the Solution Explorer window that was docked at the right side of the IDE is now floating in the middle of the IDE. Although we don't recommend this arrangement of windows, it should give you an idea of the many ways that you can arrange them.

With Visual Studio 2012, you can also pin a window in the Form Designer so it's easy to access. This is illustrated by the tab for the frmInvestment.cs file in this figure. When a window is pinned, it's displayed at the left side of the Form Designer. That makes it easy to display the window if the tabs for all the windows you have open can't be displayed in the designer at the same time.

If you experiment with these techniques for a few minutes, you'll see that they're easy to master. Then, as you get more comfortable with Visual Studio, you can adjust the windows so they work best for you.

Two floating windows, a hidden window, and a pinned window

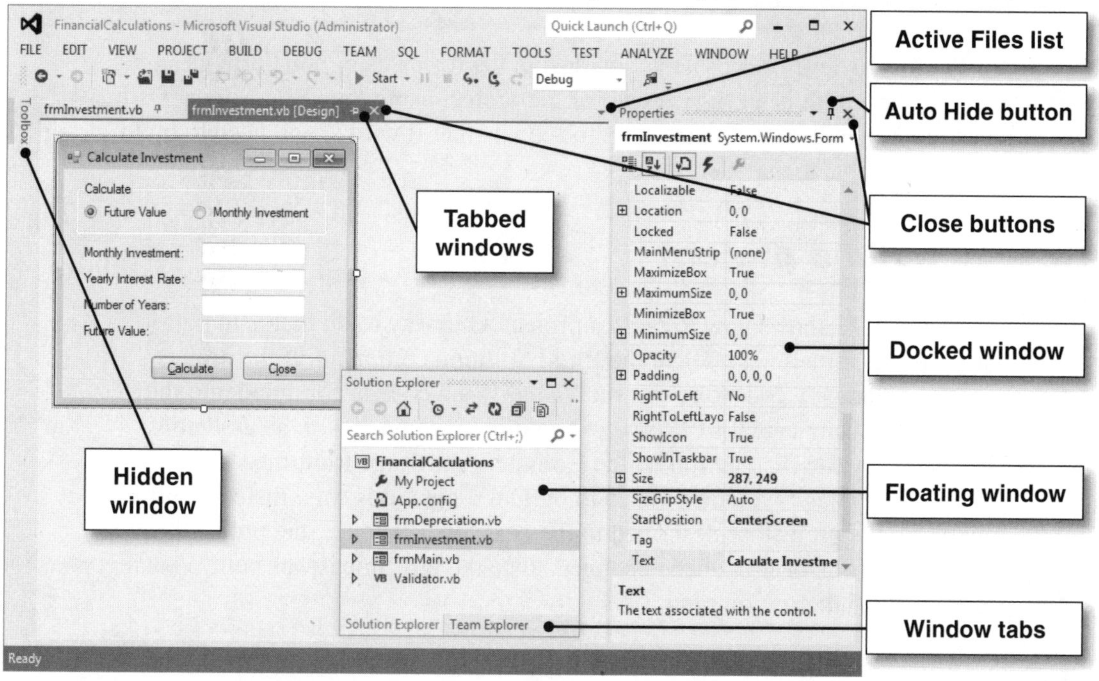

How to rearrange windows

- To close a window, click its Close button. To redisplay it, click its button in the Standard toolbar (if one is available) or select it from the View menu.
- To undock a *docked window* so it floats on the screen, drag it by its title bar away from the edge of the application window or double-click its title bar.
- To dock a floating window, drag it by its title bar onto one of the positioning arrows that become available. Or, hold down the Ctrl key and then double-click its title bar to return it to its previous docked location.
- To hide a docked window, click its Auto Hide button. Then, the window is displayed as a tab at the edge of the screen, and you can display it by clicking on the tab. To change it back, display it and then click the Auto Hide button again.
- To size a window, place the mouse pointer over an edge or a corner of the window and drag it.
- To display a window in a group of tabbed windows, click on its tab. To close a tabbed window, click on its Close button.
- If you dock, undock, hide, or unhide a tabbed window, all the windows in the group are docked, undocked, hidden, or unhidden.
- You can also use the commands in the Window menu to rearrange windows. In particular, you can use the Reset Window Layout command to return the windows to their default layout.

Figure 1-11 How to work with Visual Studio's windows

How to test a project

When you develop a project, you design the forms using the Form Designer, and you write the Visual Basic code for the project using the Code Editor. Then, when you're ready to test the project to see whether it works, you need to build and run the project.

How to build a project

Figure 1-12 shows how to *build* a project. One way to do that is to pull down the Build menu and select the Build Solution command. If the project doesn't contain any coding errors, the Visual Basic code is compiled into the Intermediate Language for the project and it is saved on disk in an assembly. This assembly can then be run by the Common Language Runtime.

Usually, though, you don't need to build a project this way. Instead, you can simply run the project, as described in the next topic. Then, if the project hasn't been built before, or if it's been changed since the last time it was built, Visual Studio builds it before running it.

How to run a project

The easiest way to *run* a project is to click the Start button that's identified in figure 1-12. Then, the project is built if necessary, the Intermediate Language is executed by the Common Language Runtime, and the first (or only) form of the project is displayed. In this figure, for example, you can see the first form that's displayed when the Financial Calculations project is run. This form contains two buttons that let you display the other forms of the project.

To test the project, you try everything that the application is intended to do. When data entries are required, you try ranges of data that test the limits of the application. When you're satisfied that the application works under all conditions, you can exit from it by clicking on the Close button in the upper right corner of the form or on a button control that has been designed for that purpose. If the application doesn't work, of course, you need to fix it, but you'll learn more about that in chapter 3.

The form that's displayed when the Financial Calculations project is run

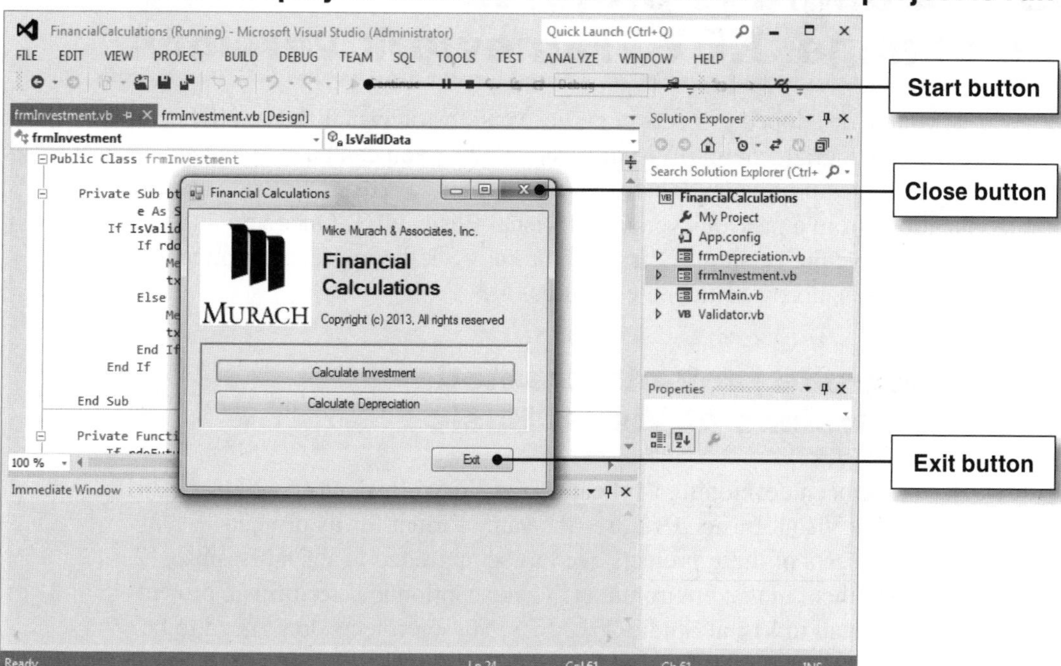

How to build a project without running it

- Use the Build→Build Solution command. Or, right-click the project in the Solution Explorer and select the Build command from the shortcut menu. This *builds* the Intermediate Language for the project and saves it in an assembly.

How to run a project

- You can *run* a project by clicking on the Start button in the Standard toolbar or by pressing F5. Then, the first form of the project is displayed on top of the Visual Studio window.
- If the project hasn't already been built, the project is first built and then run. As a result, it isn't necessary to use the Build command before you run the program.

Two ways to exit from a project that is running

- Click the Close button in the upper right corner of the startup form.
- Click the button control that's designed for exiting from the application. This is typically a button that is labeled Exit, Close, or Cancel.

How to upgrade projects and change .NET Framework versions

If you've developed projects in earlier versions of Visual Basic .NET, you may want to upgrade them to Visual Basic 2012 so you can take advantage of the new features it provides. That's why Visual Studio 2012 helps you upgrade applications from a previous version of Visual Basic .NET. Once you do that, you can change the version of the .NET Framework the upgraded applications use so you have access to the new features.

How to upgrade projects created in earlier versions of Visual Basic

If you've been developing applications in Visual Basic 2005, 2008, or 2010, you'll see that Visual Basic 2012 uses the same format for its projects. Even so, certain aspects of these projects need to be upgraded to Visual Basic 2012 to work with them in that environment. The exception is Visual Basic projects that were created in Visual Studio 2010 SP1. These projects don't need to be upgraded to open them in Visual Studio 2012, and they can continue to be opened in Visual Studio 2010 SP1 after they're opened in Visual Studio 2012.

Figure 1-13 shows how to upgrade Visual Basic projects that were created in a version of Visual Studio before 2010 SP1. When you open one of these projects, Visual Studio automatically displays a dialog box like the one shown in this figure. This dialog box indicates that a one-way upgrade is required, which means that after the upgrade, you will no longer be able to open the project in the version of Visual Studio where it was created. To upgrade the project and its solution, just click the OK button. When the upgrade is done, you can usually run the project without any further changes.

The dialog box for upgrading a project to Visual Studio 2012

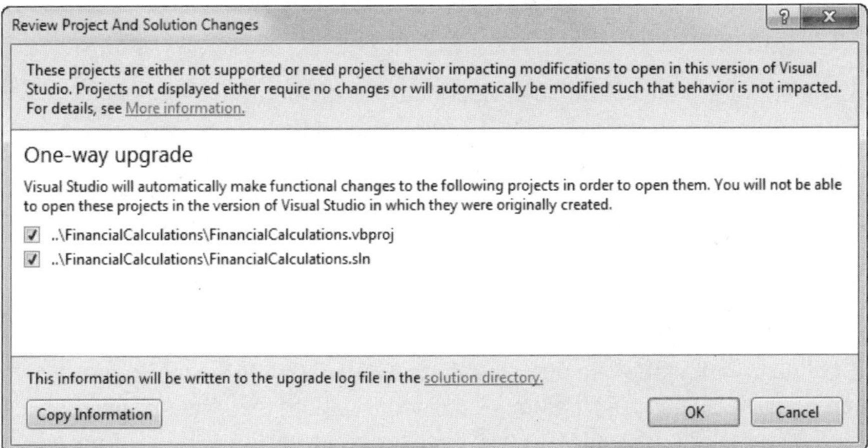

Description

- Windows Forms projects created in Visual Studio 2010 SP1 (Service Pack 1) are compatible with Visual Studio 2012 and do not need to be upgraded. Because of that, they can be opened in both versions of Visual Studio. This is referred to as *round-tripping*.
- To upgrade an older project to Visual Studio 2012, use the File→Open Project command to select the project or solution. A dialog box like the one above that indicates the type of upgrade that's required and lists the solution and projects to be upgraded is displayed.
- When the upgrade is complete, a migration report is displayed that indicates if the solution and each of its projects were updated successfully. If they weren't, you can review the messages in this report for additional information about the problems that were encountered.

Note

- Visual Studio 2012 doesn't provide for upgrading Visual Basic 6.0 projects. To do that, you will need to first convert the project to an earlier version of Visual Studio, such as Visual Studio 2008. Then, you can upgrade the 2008 project to 2012. For more information, see "How to: Upgrade a Project from Visual Basic 6.0" in online help.

Figure 1-13 How to upgrade projects created in earlier versions of Visual Basic

How to change the .NET Framework version used by a project

When you upgrade a Visual Basic project that was created in an earlier version of Visual Basic to Visual Basic 2012, the features that are provided by version 4.5 of the .NET Framework aren't automatically made available to the converted project. If you want to use any of these features, then, you'll need to change the version of the .NET Framework that's used by the project. Figure 1-14 shows you how to do that.

When you upgrade a project from Visual Basic 2005, the current .NET Framework, called the *target framework*, is .NET Framework 2.0. This version of the .NET Framework is the one that was made available with Visual Studio 2005. When you upgrade a project from Visual Studio 2008, the target framework is .NET Framework 3.5, unless it was changed to an earlier version. And when you upgrade a project from Visual Studio 2010, the target framework is .NET Framework 4, unless it was changed to an earlier version. If you want to use the features of version 4.5 of the .NET Framework, you can set the target framework to .NET Framework 4.5.

By the way, you'll notice that in addition to .NET Framework 3.5 and 4, the target framework list includes .NET Framework 3.5 and 4 Client Profile. These versions of the .NET Framework include some, but not all, of the features of the full framework. They were added to improve the deployment and installation of the .NET Framework by making it smaller. The Client Profile version has been discontinued with .NET 4.5, however.

The Application page of the Project Designer for a project

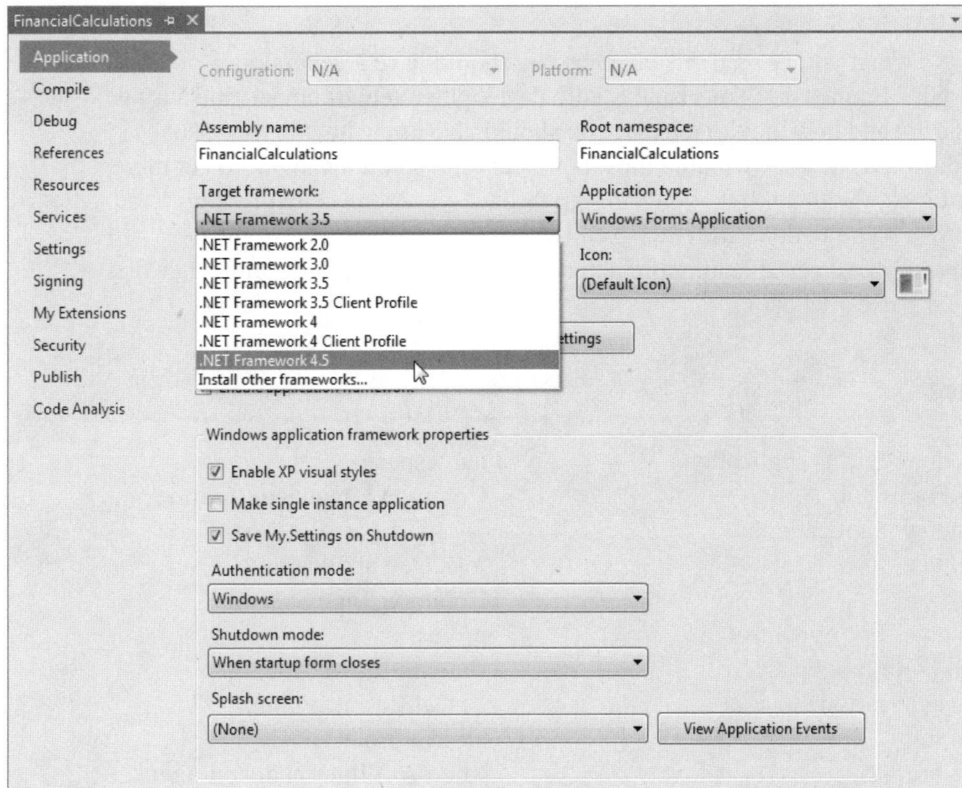

Description

- To change the version of the .NET Framework that's used by a project that you upgrade from an earlier version of Visual Basic, select the version you want to use from the Application page of the Project Designer for the project.
- To display the Project Designer, double-click on My Project in the Solution Explorer or use the Project→*ProjectName* Properties command.
- The .NET Framework version you choose determines the features you can use in the project.

Figure 1-14 How to change the .NET Framework version used by a project

Perspective

Now that you've read this chapter, you should have a general idea of what the .NET Framework, the Visual Studio development environment, and Visual Basic are and how they're related. You should also know how to use Visual Studio's IDE to work with the files in projects and solutions. Now, to get more comfortable with the IDE, you can step through the exercise that follows.

When you're done with this exercise, you should be ready for the next chapter. There, you'll learn more about using the IDE as you develop your first Visual Basic application.

Terms

Windows Forms application
WinForms app
Windows application
Windows form
form
Windows Forms control
Web Forms application
web application
web form
web browser
Web Forms control
XAML (Extensible Application Markup Language)
WPF (Windows Presentation Foundation) application
Silverlight application
Windows Store application
Windows Phone 8 application
Visual Studio 2012
Visual Basic 2012
Integrated Development Environment (IDE)
.NET Framework
Visual Studio IDE
SQL Server 2012 Express LocalDB
.NET Framework Class Library
class
namespace
Common Language Runtime (CLR)
managed applications
Common Type System
project
source file
Visual Basic compiler
build a project
Microsoft Intermediate Language (MSIL)
Intermediate Language (IL)
assembly
solution
project file
solution file
tabbed window
Form Designer
Toolbox
Properties window
Code Editor
Solution Explorer
partial class
docked window
run a project
round-tripping
target framework

Before you do the exercises in this book

Before you do any of the exercises in this book, you need to have Visual Studio installed on your system. You also need to download the folders and files for this book from our web site and install them on your PC in the C:\VB 2012 folder. For complete instructions, please refer to appendix A.

Exercise 1-1 Tour the Visual Studio IDE

This exercise guides you through the process of opening an existing Visual Basic project, working with the windows in the IDE, and building and running a project. When you're done, you should have a better feel for some of the techniques that you will use as you develop Visual Basic applications.

Start Visual Studio and open an existing project

1. Start Visual Studio as described in figure 1-6. If a dialog box that lets you select the default environment settings is displayed, select the Visual Basic Development Settings option.
2. Review the Start Page to see what it offers. When you're done, click on the Close button on the tab for this page to close it. To redisplay the Start Page, use the View→Start Page command.
3. Use the File menu to display the Open Project dialog box as described in figure 1-7. Next, locate the project file named FinancialCalculations.vbproj in the C:\VB 2012\Chapter 01\FinancialCalculations folder. Then, double-click the project file to open the project.

Experiment with the IDE

4. If the Form Designer window for the Calculate Investment form isn't displayed as shown in figure 1-8, double-click on the vb file for this form (frmInvestment.vb) in the Solution Explorer to display it.
5. Highlight the file for the Calculate Investment form (frmInvestment.vb) in the Solution Explorer and click the View Code button. A Code Editor window like the one shown in figure 1-9 should be displayed. This is the Visual Basic code that I developed for this form.
6. Click the tab for frmInvestment.vb [Design] to display the Form Designer again. Then, press Ctrl+Tab to move back to the Code Editor window, and do it again to move back to the Designer.
7. Click the Toggle Pin Status button in the frmInvestment.vb [Design] tab. That tab will move to the left of the other tab and will remain there when additional tabs are opened.
8. If the Toolbox is hidden, click on its tab along the left side of the window to display it. Then, click in the Designer to see that the Toolbox is hidden again. Display the Toolbox again, locate the pushpin near its upper right corner, and click it. Now when you click in another window, the Toolbox will remain displayed.

9. Undock the Solution Explorer window by dragging its title bar to the center of the screen. Notice that the Properties window expands to fill the space that was occupied by the docked Solution Explorer window. Hold down the Ctrl key and then double-click the title bar of the Solution Explorer window to return the window to its docked position.
10. Click the Show All Files button at the top of the Solution Explorer. Then, click the ▷ symbol next to the References folder to see the namespaces that are included in the project. When you're done, click the ◢ symbol next to the References folder to close it.
11. Click the ▷ symbol next to the frmInvestment.vb file to display the subordinate files. Then, click on the frmInvestment.Designer.vb file to preview its code. This is the code that was generated by the Form Designer.
12. Click on the Validator.vb file in the Solution Explorer, and note that its code replaces the code for the frmInvestment.Designer.vb file in the preview tab. Then, click the Keep Open button in the tab to open the code in the Code Editor. This is the code that I developed to validate the user entries. Now, close the tabbed window for this code.

Close and reopen the project

13. Select the File→Close Project (or Close Solution) command to close the project. If a dialog box is displayed that asks whether you want to save changes, click the No button.
14. Reopen the solution by using the File→Recent Projects and Solutions submenu to select the appropriate project file.

Build and run the application

15. Build the project by pulling down the Build menu and selecting the Build Solution (or Build FinancialCalculations) command. This assembles the project into Intermediate Language. It may also open another window, but you don't need to be concerned about that.
16. Run the application by clicking on the Start button in the Standard toolbar. When the first form is displayed, click the Calculate Investment button to go to the next form. Then, experiment with this form until you understand what it does. When you're done, close this form so you return to the first form.
17. Click the Calculate Depreciation button to go to another form. Then, experiment with that form to see what it does. When you close it, you will return to the first form.
18. Exit from the first form by clicking on either the Exit button or the Close button in the upper right corner of the form.

Close the project and exit from Visual Studio

19. Close the project the way you did in step 13.
20. Exit from Visual Studio by clicking on the Close button in the Visual Studio window or by using the File→Exit command.

2

How to design a Windows Forms application

In the last chapter, you learned the basic skills for working with Visual Studio, you toured a Windows Forms application, and you tested an application with three Windows forms. Now, in this chapter, you'll learn how to use Visual Studio to design the user interface for a Windows Forms application.

How to set options and create a new project

Before you start your first Windows Forms application with Visual Studio 2012, you probably should change a few of the Visual Studio options. You may also want to change the import and export settings.

How to set the Visual Studio options

To set the options for Visual Studio, you use the Options dialog box shown in figure 2-1. Once this dialog box is open, you can expand the Projects and Solutions group by clicking on the ▷ symbol to the left of that group, and you can click on the General group to display the options shown in this figure.

You can set the default project location by typing a path directly into the text box, or you can click the button to the right of the text box to display a dialog box that lets you navigate to the folder you want to use. This will set the default location for new projects, but you can always override the default when you create a new project.

By default, most of the options are set the way you want. However, if you want Visual Studio to work the way it's described in this book, you should check the Always Show Solution and the Save New Projects When Created options. Beyond that, it's worth taking a few minutes to review the other options that are available. Then, you can change them if Visual Studio isn't working the way you want it to. For instance, you may want to use the Startup group within the Environment group to change what's displayed when Visual Studio starts.

How to change the environment settings

The first time you start Visual Studio, you're asked what default environment settings you want to use. You can choose from several options including Visual Basic, Visual C#, Visual C++, and Web. Among other things, your choice affects what items are available from some menus and what buttons are available from the Standard toolbar. If, for example, you choose the Visual Basic settings, you open a project with the File→Open Project command. But if you choose the Visual C# settings, you open a project with the File→Open→Project/Solution command.

To change these settings, you use the Import and Export Settings Wizard as described in figure 2-1. In the first step of the wizard, choose the Reset All Settings option. In the second step, choose the Yes, Save My Current Settings option. And in the last step, if you want your menus to work as described in this book, choose the Visual Basic Development Settings option. Later, if you switch to C#, C++, or web development, you can change the settings again.

The Options dialog box for setting the project options

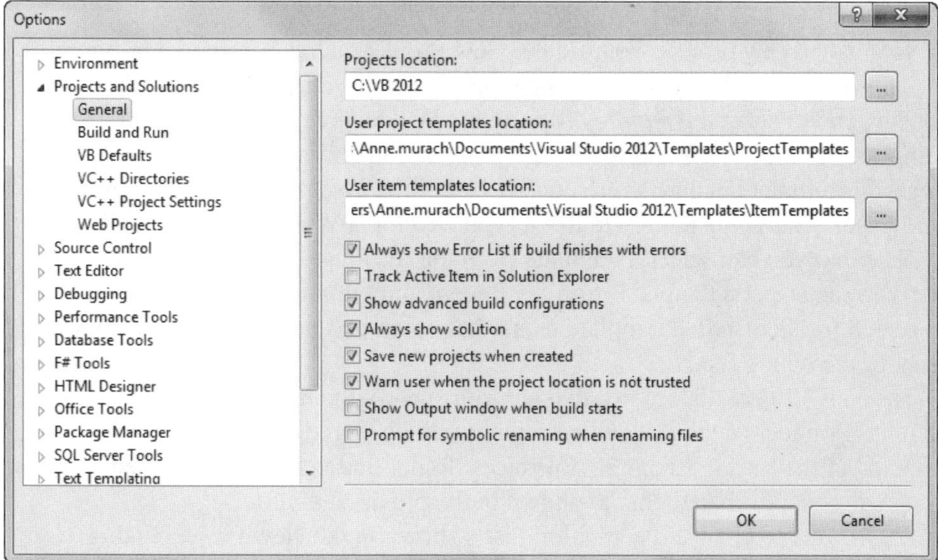

How to use the Options dialog box

- To display the Options dialog box, select the Tools→Options command.
- To expand and collapse a group of options, you can use the ▷ and ◢ symbols to the left of each group. To display the options for a group, click on the group.
- To set the default location for all projects that you start from Visual Studio, you can change the Projects Location as shown above.
- If you want Visual Studio to work the way this book describes it, check the Always Show Solution box and the Save New Projects When Created box.
- To change the color theme for Visual Studio, select the General category in the Environment group and then select an option from the Color Theme drop-down list.
- Although most of the options should be set the way you want them, you may want to review the options in each category so you know what's available.

How to set the enviroment settings

- The first time you start Visual Studio 2012, you are asked to choose the default environment settings. These settings affect how the menus work and what buttons are displayed on the Standard toolbar.
- To change the settings to the ones used for this book, use the Tools→Import and Export Settings command to start the Settings Wizard. Then, choose the Reset All Settings option, the Save My Current Settings option, and the Visual Basic Development Settings option as you step through the wizard.

Express Edition difference

- The Import and Export Settings Wizard doesn't have a third step because only one collection of settings is available.

Figure 2-1 How to set the Visual Studio options and enviroment settings

How to create a new project

To create a new project, you use the New Project dialog box shown in figure 2-2. This dialog box lets you select the type of project you want to create by choosing one of several *templates*. To create a Windows Forms application, for example, you select the Windows Forms Application template. Among other things, this template includes references to all of the assemblies that contain the namespaces you're most likely to use as you develop a Windows application.

Note that you can select a template from the Installed category as shown here. You can select a template from the Recent and Online categories. Or you can search for an installed template using the search text box in the upper right corner of the dialog box.

The New Project dialog box also lets you specify the name for the project, and it lets you identify the folder in which it will be stored. By default, projects are stored in the Visual Studio 2012\Projects folder under the My Documents folder, but you can change that as shown in the previous figure.

If you want to change the location that's shown in the New Project dialog box, you can click the Browse button to select a different location; display the Location drop-down list to select a location you've used recently; or type a path directly. If you specify a path that doesn't exist, Visual Studio will create the necessary folders for you.

When you click the OK button, Visual Studio automatically creates a new folder for the project using the project name you specify. In the dialog box in this figure, for example, InvoiceTotal is the project name and C:\VB 2012 is the location. By default, Visual Studio also creates a new folder for the solution, using the same name as the project. As a result, Visual Studio will create one folder for the solution, and a subfolder for the project. Then, you can add another project to the same solution by selecting Add To Solution from the Solution drop-down list in the New Project dialog box. (This list is displayed only if a solution is open.)

If a solution will contain a single project, though, you may want to store the project and solution in the same folder. To do that, you can deselect the Create Directory For Solution check box. Then, the solution is given the same name as the project. Because most of the solutions in this book contain only one project, that's the way most of the applications for this book are set up.

Incidentally, the terms *folder* and *directory* are used as synonyms throughout this book. With the introduction of Windows 95, Microsoft started referring to directories as folders. But most of the Visual Studio documentation still uses the term *directory*. That's why this book uses whichever term seems more appropriate at the time.

By default, the new projects you create target .NET Framework 4.5 so you can use the features it provides. If you use any of these features, however, any computer that you want to run the application on must also have .NET Framework 4.5. If that's not the case, you can change the target framework using the drop-down list at the top of the New Project dialog box. Then, only the features of the framework you choose will be available from Visual Studio.

The New Project dialog box

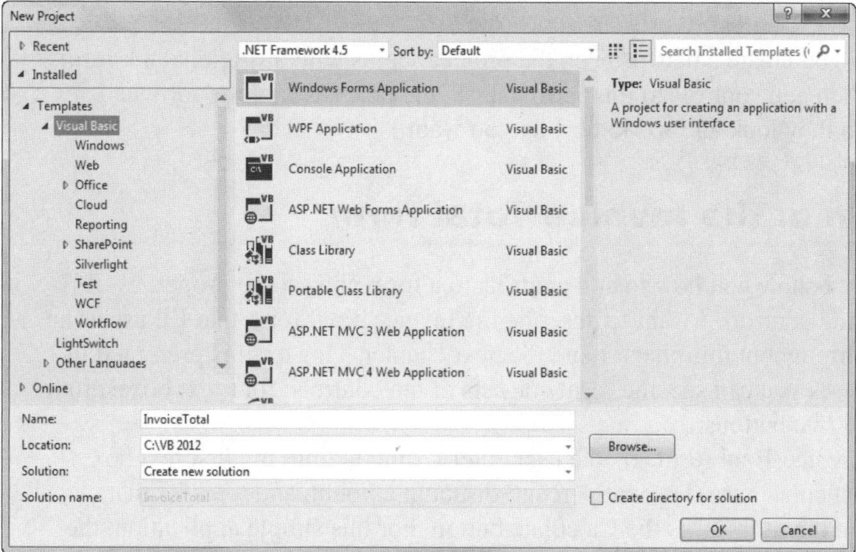

How to create a new Visual Basic project

1. Use the File→New Project command to open the New Project dialog box.
2. Choose Visual Basic from the Installed category, and choose the Windows Forms Application template for a Windows Forms application.
3. Enter a name for the project. Then, enter the location (folder) for the project (and solution).
4. If you want the solution file and the project file to be stored in the same directory, uncheck the Create Directory for Solution box.
5. Click the OK button to create the new project.

Description

- The project *template* that you select determines the initial files, assembly references, code, and property settings that are added to the project.
- If the Create Directory For Solution box is checked, Visual Studio creates a folder for the solution and a subfolder for the project. Otherwise, these files are stored in the same folder.
- If the Save New Projects When Created option is on as shown in the previous figure, the project is saved when it's created. Otherwise, the New Project dialog box only lets you select a template and enter a name for the project. Then, when you save the project, the Save Project dialog box asks for the other information shown above.
- If you want to target a version of the .NET Framework other than version 4.5, you can select the version from the drop-down list at the top of the dialog box.

Express Edition difference

- You can't change the version of the .NET Framework that's used by default.

Figure 2-2 How to create a new project

How to design a form

When you create a new project, the project begins with a single, blank form. You can then add controls to this form and set the properties of the form and controls so they look and work the way you want.

The design of the Invoice Total form

Before I show you how to add controls to a form and set the properties of the form and controls, I want to describe the Invoice Total form that I'll use as an example throughout this chapter and the next chapter. This form is presented in figure 2-3. As you can see, the form consists of ten controls: four text boxes, four labels, and two buttons.

The Invoice Total form lets the user enter a subtotal into the first text box, and then calculates the discount percent, discount amount, and total for that order when the user clicks the Calculate button. For this simple application, the discount percent is based upon the amount of the subtotal, and the results of the calculation are displayed in read-only text box controls.

After the results of the calculation are displayed, the user can enter a different subtotal and click the Calculate button again to perform another calculation. This cycle continues until the user clicks the Close button in the upper right corner of the form or clicks the Exit button. Then, the form is closed and the application ends.

This application also provides keystroke options for users who prefer using the keyboard to the mouse. In particular, the user can activate the Calculate button by pressing the Enter key and the Exit button by pressing the Esc key. The user can also activate the Calculate button by pressing Alt+C and the Exit button by pressing Alt+X.

In the early days of computing, it was a common practice to sketch the user interface for an application on paper before developing the application. That's because a programmer had to enter the code that defined the user interface, and the task of writing this code would have been error prone if the interface wasn't planned out first. As you'll see in this chapter, however, the Form Designer makes it easy to design a form at the same time that you implement it. Because of that, you usually don't need to sketch the layout of a form before you design it in Visual Studio.

As you use the Form Designer, Visual Studio automatically generates the Visual Basic code that's needed to define the form and its controls. In other words, the form that you see in the Form Designer is just a visual representation of the form that the Visual Basic code is going to display later on. Then, all you have to do is write the Visual Basic code that gives the form its functionality, and you'll learn how to do that in the next chapter.

The Invoice Total form

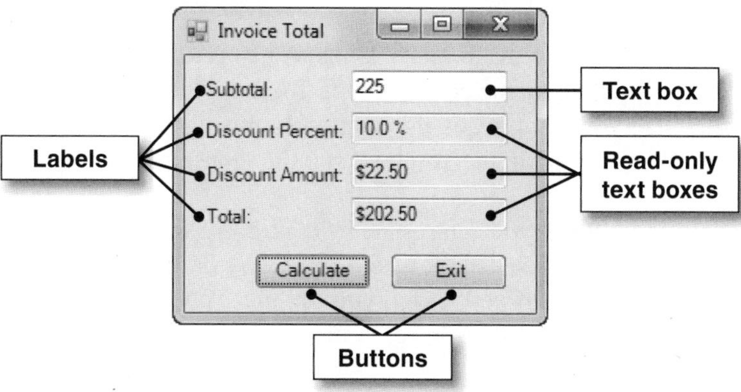

Description

- A text box is used to get the subtotal from the user. Read-only text boxes are used to display the discount percent, discount amount, and total. And label controls are used to identify the values that are in the text boxes on the form.
- After entering a subtotal, the user can click the Calculate button to calculate the discount percent, discount amount, and total. Alternatively, the user can press the Enter key to perform the calculation.
- To calculate another invoice total, the user can enter another subtotal and then click the Calculate button or press the Enter key again.
- To close the form and end the application, the user can click the Close button in the upper right corner of the form or click the Exit button. Alternatively, the user can press the Esc key to exit from the form.
- The user can press Alt+C to activate the Calculate button or Alt+X to activate the Exit button. On most systems, the letters that activate these buttons aren't underlined until the user presses the Alt key.

Three types of controls

- A *label* displays text on a form.
- A *text box* lets the user enter text on a form.
- A *button* initiates form processing when clicked.

Figure 2-3 The design of the Invoice Total form

How to add controls to a form

Figure 2-4 shows how you can use the Toolbox to add controls to a form. The easiest way to do that is to click on the control in the Toolbox, then click the form at the location where you want to add the control. In this figure, for example, the button control is selected in the Toolbox, and the mouse pointer is positioned over the form.

Once you add a control to a form, you can resize the control by selecting it and dragging one of its handles, and you can move the control by dragging the control to a new location on the form. If you prefer, you can place and size the control in a single operation by clicking the control in the Toolbox, then clicking and dragging in the form.

A second way to add a control is to drag the control from the Toolbox to the form. The control is placed wherever you drop it. You can then resize the control.

A third method for adding controls is to double-click the control you want to add in the Toolbox. This places the control in the upper left corner of the form. You can then move and resize the control.

If the AutoHide feature is activated for the Toolbox and you click on the Toolbox tab to display it, the display frequently obscures some or all of the form. This makes it difficult to add controls. As a result, it's a good idea to turn off the AutoHide feature when you're adding controls. To do that, just click the pushpin button in the upper right corner of the Toolbox.

After you have added controls to the form, you can work with several controls at once. For example, let's say that you have four text box controls on your form and you want to make them all the same size with the same alignment. To do that, first select all four controls by holding down the Ctrl or Shift key as you click on them or by using the mouse pointer to drag a dotted rectangular line around the controls. Then, use the commands in the Format menu or the buttons in the Layout toolbar to move, size, and align the controls relative to the *primary control*. If you select the controls one at a time, the primary control will be the first control you select. If you select the controls by dragging around them, the primary control will be the last control in the group. To change the primary control, just click on it. (The primary control will have different color handles so you can identify it.)

Although these techniques may be hard to visualize as you read about them, you'll find that they're relatively easy to use. All you need is a little practice, which you'll get in the exercise for this chapter.

A form after some controls have been added to it

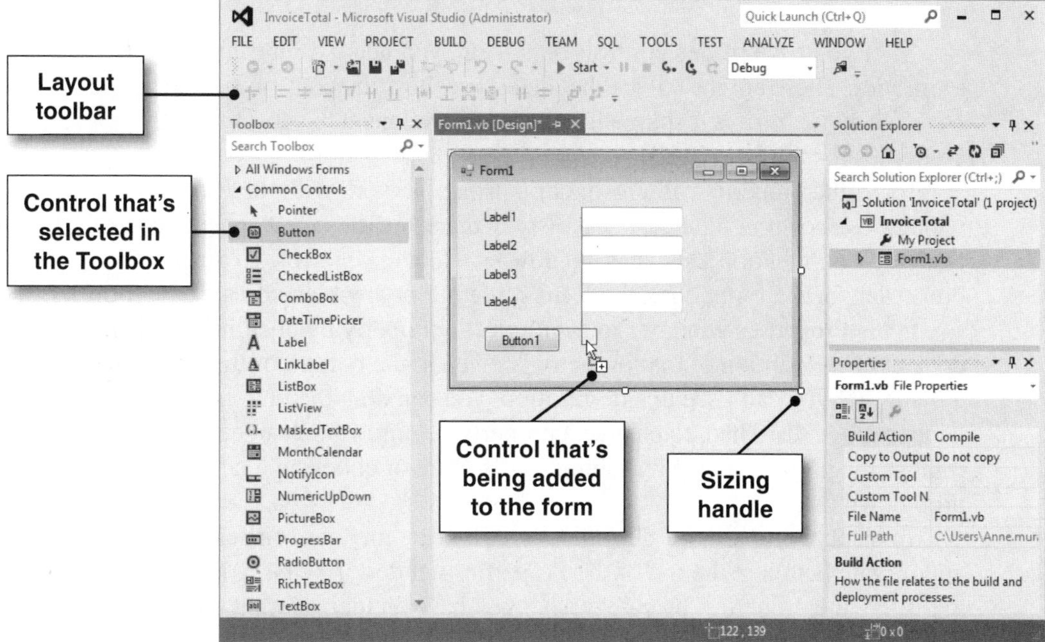

Three ways to add a control to a form

- Select the control in the Toolbox. Then, click in the form where you want to place the control. Or, drag the pointer on the form to place the control and size it at the same time.
- Double-click the control in the Toolbox. Then, the control is placed in the upper left corner of the form.
- Drag the control from the Toolbox and drop it on the form. Then, the control is placed wherever you drop it.

How to select and work with controls

- To select a control on the form, click it. To move a control, drag it.
- To size a selected control, drag one of its handles. Note, however, that a label is sized automatically based on the amount of text that it contains. As a result, you can't size a label by dragging its handles unless you change its AutoSize property to False.
- To select more than one control, hold down the Shift or Ctrl key as you click on each control. You can also select a group of controls by clicking on a blank spot in the form and then dragging around the controls.
- To align, size, or space a group of selected controls, click on a control to make it the *primary control*. Then, use the commands in the Format menu or the buttons on the Layout toolbar to align, size, or space the controls relative to the primary control.
- You can also size all of the controls in a group by sizing the primary control in the group. And you can drag any of the selected controls to move all the controls.
- To change the size of a form, click the form and drag one of its sizing handles.

Figure 2-4 How to add controls to a form

How to set properties

After you have placed controls on a form, you need to set each control's *properties*. These are the values that determine how the controls will look and work when the form is displayed. In addition, you need to set some of the properties for the form itself.

To set the properties of a form or control, you work with the Properties window as shown in figure 2-5. To display the properties for a specific control, click on it in the Form Designer window to select the control. To display the properties for the form, click the form's title bar or any blank area of the form.

In the Properties window, you can select a property by clicking it. When you do, a brief description of that property is given at the bottom of the Properties window. (If you can't see this description, you can drag the bottom line of the window upward.) Then, to change a property setting, you change the entry to the right of the property name by typing a new value or choosing a new value from a drop-down list.

To display properties alphabetically or by category, you can click the appropriate button at the top of the Properties window. At first, you may want to display the properties by category so you have an idea of what the different properties do. Once you become more familiar with the properties, though, you may be able to find the ones you're looking for faster if you display them alphabetically.

As you work with properties, you'll find that most are set the way you want them by default. In addition, some properties such as Height and Width are set interactively as you size and position the form and its controls in the Form Designer window. As a result, you usually only need to change a few properties for each object.

A form after the properties have been set

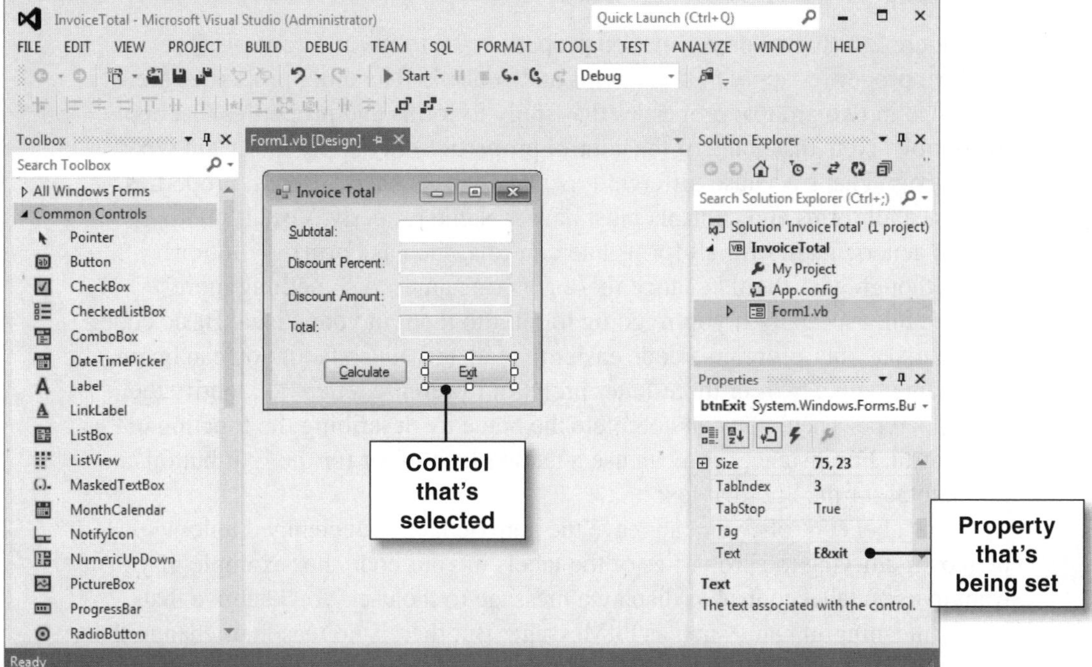

Description

- The Properties window displays the *properties* for the object that's currently selected in the Form Designer window. To display the properties for another object, click on that object or select the object from the drop-down list at the top of the Properties window.
- To change a property, enter a value into the text box or select a value from its drop-down list if it has one. If a button with an ellipsis (…) appears at the right side of a property's text box, you can click on the ellipsis to display a dialog box that lets you set options for the property.
- To change the properties for two or more controls at the same time, select the controls to display the common properties of the controls in the Properties window.
- When you click on a property in the Properties window, a brief explanation of the property appears in a pane at the bottom of the window. For more information, press F1 to display the help information for the property.
- If a description isn't displayed when you click on a property in the Properties window, right-click on the window and select Description from the shortcut menu.
- You can use the first two buttons at the top of the Properties window to sort the properties by category or alphabetically.
- You can use the plus (+) and minus (-) signs displayed to the left of some of the properties and categories in the Properties window to expand and collapse the list of properties.

Figure 2-5 How to set properties

Common properties for forms and controls

Figure 2-6 shows some common properties for forms and controls. The first two properties apply to both forms and controls. The other properties are presented in two groups: properties that apply to forms and properties that apply to controls. Note that some of the control properties only apply to certain types of controls. That's because different types of controls have different properties.

Since all forms and controls must have a Name property, Visual Studio creates generic names for all forms and controls, such as Form1 or Button1. Often, though, you should change these generic names to something more meaningful, especially if you're going to refer to them in your Visual Basic code.

To make your program's code easier to read and understand, you can begin each name with a two- or three-letter prefix in lowercase letters to identify the control's type. Then, you can complete the name by describing the function of the control. For instance, you can use a name like btnExit for the Exit button and txtSubtotal for the Subtotal text box.

For Label controls, you can leave the generic names unchanged unless you plan on modifying the properties of the labels in your code. For example, if you want to use a label control to display a message to the user, you can give that label a meaningful name such as lblMessage. But there's no reason to change the names for label controls that display text that won't be changed by the program.

Forms and most controls also have a Text property that is visible when the form is displayed. A form's Text property is displayed in the form's title bar. For a control, the Text property is usually displayed somewhere within the control. The Text property of a button, for example, is displayed on the button, and the Text property of a text box is displayed in the text box.

As you work with properties, you'll find that you can set some of them by selecting a value from a drop-down list. For example, you can select a True or False value for the TabStop property of a control. For other properties, you have to enter a number or text value. And for some properties, a button with an ellipsis (...) is displayed. Then, when you click this button, a dialog box appears that lets you set the property.

The Name property

- Sets the name you use to identify a control in your Visual Basic code.
- Can be changed to provide a more descriptive and memorable name for forms and controls that you will refer to when you write your code (such as text boxes and buttons).
- Doesn't need to be changed for controls that you won't refer to when you write your code (such as most labels).
- Can use a three-letter prefix to indicate whether the name refers to a form (frm), button (btn), label (lbl), or text box (txt).

The Text property

- Sets the text that's displayed on the form or control. Some controls such as forms and labels display the generic form or control name that's generated by Visual Studio, which you'll almost always want to change.
- For a form, the Text value is displayed in the title bar. For controls, the Text value is displayed directly on the control.
- For a text box, the Text value changes when the user types text into the control, and you can write code that uses the Text property to get the text that was entered by the user.

Other properties for forms

Property	Description
`AcceptButton`	Identifies the button that will be activated when the user presses the Enter key.
`CancelButton`	Identifies the button that will be activated when the user presses the Esc key.
`StartPosition`	Sets the position at which the form is displayed. To center the form, set this property to CenterScreen.

Other properties for controls

Property	Description
`Enabled`	Determines whether the control will be enabled or disabled.
`ReadOnly`	Determines whether the text in some controls like text boxes can be edited.
`TabIndex`	Indicates the control's position in the tab order, which determines the order in which the controls will receive the focus when the user presses the Tab key.
`TabStop`	Determines whether the control will accept the focus when the user presses the Tab key to move from one control to another. Some controls, like labels, don't have the TabStop property because they can't receive the focus.
`TextAlign`	Sets the alignment for the text displayed on a control.

Figure 2-6 Common properties for forms and controls

How to add navigation features

Windows forms have features that make it easier for users to move around in the forms without using the mouse. These navigation features are described in figure 2-7.

The *tab order* is the order in which the controls on a form receive the *focus* when the user presses the Tab key. The tab order should usually be set so the focus moves left-to-right and top-to-bottom, beginning at the top left of the form and ending at the bottom right. However, in some cases you'll want to deviate from that order. For example, if you have controls arranged in columns, you may want the tab order to move down each column.

The tab order is initially set based on the order in which you add controls to the form. So if you add the controls in the right order, you won't need to alter the tab order. But if you do need to change the tab order, you can do so by adjusting the TabIndex property settings. The TabIndex property is simply a number that represents the control's position in the tab order, beginning with zero. So, the first control in the tab order has a TabIndex of 0, the second control's TabIndex is 1, and so on.

Incidentally, chapter 10 will show you another way to set the tab order of the controls for a form. You can do that by using Tab Order view. When a form consists of more than a few controls, it is easier to use this view than to set the tab order for one control at a time.

Access keys are shortcut keys that let the user move the focus directly to a control. You set a control's access key by using the Text property. Just precede the letter in the Text property value that you want to use as the access key with an ampersand (&). Then, the user can move the focus to the control by pressing Alt plus the access key.

If you assign an access key to a control that can't receive the focus, such as a label control, pressing the access key causes the focus to move to the next control in the tab order. As a result, you can use an access key with a label control to create a shortcut for a text box control, which can't have an access key.

If you assign an access key to a button control, you should know that pressing Alt plus the access key doesn't simply move the focus to the control. Instead, it activates the control just as if it was clicked. Without an access key, a user would have to tab to the button control and then press the Enter key to activate it using the keyboard. The exception is if the button is selected for the AcceptButton or CancelButton property for the form.

The AcceptButton and CancelButton properties specify the buttons that are activated when the user presses the Enter and Esc keys. That can make it easier for a user to work with a form. If, for example, the AcceptButton property of the Invoice Total form in figure 2-3 is set to the Calculate button, the user can press the Enter key after entering a subtotal instead of using the mouse to click the Calculate button or using the access key to activate it.

How to adjust the tab order

- *Tab order* refers to the sequence in which the controls receive the *focus* when the user presses the Tab key. You should adjust the tab order so the Tab key moves the focus from one control to the next in a logical sequence.
- Each control has a TabIndex property that indicates the control's position in the tab order. You can change this property to change a control's tab order position.
- If you don't want a control to receive the focus when the user presses the Tab key, change that control's TabStop property to False.
- Label controls don't have a TabStop property so they can't receive the focus.

How to set access keys

- *Access keys* are shortcut keys that the user can use in combination with the Alt key to quickly move to individual controls on the form.
- You use the Text property to set the access key for a control by placing an ampersand immediately before the letter you want to use for the access key. For example, &Invoice sets the access key to *I*, but I&nvoice sets the access key to *n*.
- Since the access keys aren't case sensitive, &N and &n set the same access key.
- When you set access keys, make sure to use a unique letter for each control. If you don't, the user may have to press the access key two or more times to select a control.
- You can't set the access key for a text box. However, if you set an access key for a label that immediately precedes the text box in the tab order, the access key will take the user to the text box.
- If you assign an access key to a button, the button is activated when you press Alt plus the access key.

How to set the Enter and Esc keys

- The AcceptButton property of the form sets the button that will be activated if the user presses the Enter key.
- The CancelButton property of the form sets the button that will be activated if the user presses the Esc key. This property should usually be set to the Exit button.
- You set the AcceptButton or CancelButton values by choosing the button from a drop-down list that shows all of the buttons on the form. So be sure to create and name the buttons you want to use before you attempt to set these values.

Another way to set the tab order

- In chapter 10, you'll learn how to use Tab Order view to set the tab order of the controls on the form. If the form consists of more than a few controls, that is the best way to set that order.

Figure 2-7 How to add navigation features

The property settings for the Invoice Total form

Figure 2-8 shows the property settings for the Invoice Total form. As you can see, you don't need to change many properties to finish the design of this form. You only need to set four properties for the form, and you only use six of the properties (Name, Text, TextAlign, ReadOnly, TabStop, and TabIndex) for the controls. Depending on the order in which you create the controls, though, you may not need to change the TabIndex settings.

Notice that the three text boxes that display the form's calculation have their ReadOnly property set to True. This setting gives the text boxes a shaded appearance, as you saw in figure 2-3, and it prevents the user from entering text into these controls. In addition, the TabStop property for these text boxes has been set to False so the user can't use the Tab key to move the focus onto these controls.

Finally, the settings for the TabIndex properties of the text box and the two buttons are 1, 2, and 3. Since the label controls can't receive the focus, and since the TabStop property for the three read-only text boxes has been set to False, the user can press the Tab key to move the focus from the Subtotal text box to the Calculate button to the Exit button.

In addition, the Subtotal label has a TabIndex property of 0 and a Text property that includes an access key of S. As a result, the user can press Alt+S to move the focus to the control that has the next available tab index. In this case, that control is the Subtotal text box, which has a TabIndex property of 1.

Of course, this is just one way that the TabIndex properties could be set. If, for example, the TabIndex properties for the 10 controls were set from 0 through 9, from top to bottom in this summary, the tab order would work the same.

How to use Document Outline view

Document Outline view is a feature that first became available with Visual Studio 2005. To open the window for this view, you use the View→Other Windows→Document Outline command. This opens a window to the left of the Form Designer that lists the names of all of the controls that have been added to the current form.

This view makes it easy to check whether you've named all of the controls that you're going to refer to in your Visual Basic code. You can also select a control in the Form Designer by clicking on the name of the control in Document Outline view. Although these are minor benefits, it's worth experimenting with this view to see whether you're going to want to use it.

The property settings for the form

Default name	Property	Setting
Form1	Text	Invoice Total
	AcceptButton	btnCalculate
	CancelButton	btnExit
	StartPosition	CenterScreen

The property settings for the controls

Default name	Property	Setting
Label1	Text	&Subtotal:
	TextAlign	MiddleLeft
	TabIndex	0
Label2	Text	Discount percent:
	TextAlign	MiddleLeft
Label3	Text	Discount amount:
	TextAlign	MiddleLeft
Label4	Text	Total:
	TextAlign	MiddleLeft
TextBox1	Name	txtSubtotal
	TabIndex	1
TextBox2	Name	txtDiscountPercent
	ReadOnly	True
	TabStop	False
TextBox3	Name	txtDiscountAmount
	ReadOnly	True
	TabStop	False
TextBox4	Name	txtTotal
	ReadOnly	True
	TabStop	False
Button1	Name	btnCalculate
	Text	&Calculate
	TabIndex	2
Button2	Name	btnExit
	Text	E&xit
	TabIndex	3

Note

- To provide an access key for the Subtotal text box, you can set the TabIndex and Text properties for the Subtotal label as shown above.

Figure 2-8 The property settings for the Invoice Total form

How to name and save the files of a project

When you're working on a project, you may want to change the names of some of the files from their defaults. Then, you'll want to save the files with their new names.

How to name the files of a project

You may have noticed throughout this chapter that I didn't change the default name of the form (Form1.vb) that was added to the Invoice Total project when the project was created. In practice, though, you usually change the name of this form so it's more descriptive. For example, figure 2-9 shows how to use the Solution Explorer to change the name of the form file to frmInvoiceTotal.vb. When you do that, Visual Studio will also change the File Name property for the form from Form1 to frmInvoiceTotal and modify any of the code that's been generated for the form accordingly.

You may also want to change the name of the project. Or, you may want to change the name of the solution so it's different from the project name. If so, you can use the technique presented in this figure to do that too.

How to save the files of a project

Figure 2-9 also describes how to save the files of a project. Because Visual Studio saves any changes you make to the files in a project when you build the project, you won't usually need to save them explicitly. However, it's easy to do if you need to.

Notice in this figure that two factors determine which files are saved: what's selected in the Solution Explorer and the command you use to perform the save operation. If, for example, a single file is selected, you can use the Save command to save just that file, and you can use the Save All command to save the file along with the project and solution that contain the file. In contrast, if a project is selected in the Solution Explorer, the Save command causes the entire project to be saved, and the Save All command causes the entire solution to be saved.

If you haven't saved all of your recent changes when you close a project, Visual Studio will ask whether you want to save them. As a result, you don't need to worry that your changes will be lost.

The Solution Explorer as a form file is being renamed

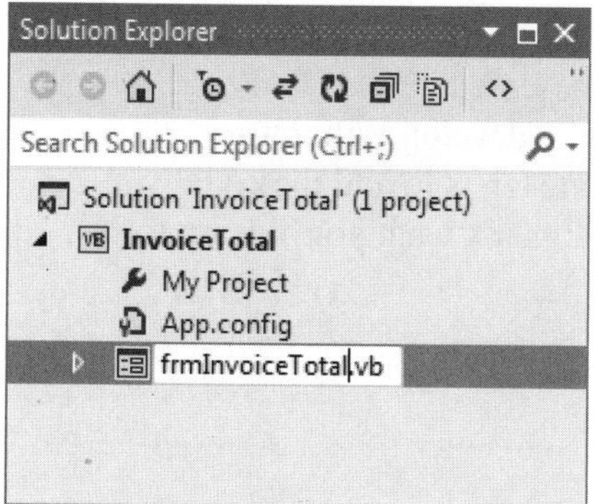

How to rename a file, project, or solution

- You can rename a file, project, or solution by right-clicking on it in the Solution Explorer window and selecting the Rename command from the shortcut menu. Or, you can select the file, project, or solution in the Solution Explorer and then change the appropriate property in the Properties window.
- Be sure not to change or omit the file extension when you rename a file. Remember too that using a three-letter prefix to indicate the contents of the file (like *frm* for a form file) makes it easier to tell what each file represents.
- When you change the name of a form file, Visual Studio will also change the Name property for the form and update any references within the existing code for the form, which is usually what you want.

How to save a file, project, or solution

- You can use the Save All button in the Standard toolbar or the Save All command in the File menu to save all files and projects in the solution.
- You can use the Save button in the Standard toolbar or the Save command in the File menu to save a file, project, or solution. The files that are saved depend on what's selected in the Solution Explorer window. If a single file is selected, just that file is saved. If a project is selected, the entire project and its solution are saved. And if a solution is selected, the entire solution and all its projects are saved.
- If you try to close a solution that contains modified files, a dialog box is displayed that asks you if you want to save those files.

Figure 2-9 How to name and save the files of a project

Perspective

If you can design the Invoice Total form that's presented in this chapter, you've taken a critical first step toward learning how to develop Windows Forms applications with Visual Studio 2012. The next step is to add the code that makes the form work the way you want it to, and that's what you'll learn to do in the next chapter.

Terms

template
label
text box
button
primary control
property
tab order
focus
access key

Exercise 2-1 Design the Invoice Total form

This exercise will guide you through the process of starting a new project and developing the user interface for the Invoice Total form shown in this chapter.

Set the default path and start a new project

1. Start Visual Studio. If you want to change the import and export settings to make sure your menus are the same as the ones in this book, use the Tools→Import and Export Settings command described in figure 2-1 to specify the default Visual Basic development settings.
2. Use the Tools→Options command to display the Options dialog box as shown in figure 2-1. Then, expand the Projects and Solutions group, select the General category, and change the projects location setting to C:\VB 2012.
3. If the Save New Projects When Created box and the Always Show Solution box aren't checked, check them.
4. If you want to stop the Start Page from being displayed each time you start Visual Studio, click on Startup within the Environment group. Then, select another option from the At Startup drop-down list.
5. If you're interested, take a few minutes to review the other options that are available in this dialog box. Then, close the dialog box.
6. Start a new project as shown in figure 2-2. The project should be named InvoiceTotal and it should be stored in the C:\VB 2012\Chapter 02 folder.

Add controls to the new form and set the properties

7. Use the techniques in figure 2-4 to add controls to the form so they have approximately the same sizes and locations as in figure 2-5. But don't worry about the size of the labels, just their locations.

8. Select groups of controls and use the buttons in the Layout toolbar to size and align the controls. But here again, let the labels automatically size themselves. Then, size the form so it looks like the one in figure 2-4.
9. Use the Properties window to set the properties for the form and its controls so it looks like the form in figure 2-3. These properties are summarized in figure 2-8.
10. Use the View→Other Windows→Document Outline command to open the window for Document Outline view. Next, use this window to check that you've named all of the controls that have Name properties in figure 2-8. Then, click on the controls in this view to see what happens, and close this window when you're done.

Test the user interface

11. Press F5 to build and run the project. That should display the form in the center of the screen, and it should look like the one in figure 2-3.
12. Experiment with the form to see what it can do. When you press the Tab key, notice how the focus moves from one control to another. When you click a button, notice how it indents and then pops back out just like any other Windows button control. Nothing else happens in response to these button clicks, though, because you haven't written the code for them yet.

    Notice that the Calculate button has a dark outline around it to indicate that its function will be executed if you press the Enter key. (If it doesn't have a dark outline, you haven't set the AcceptButton property of the form to the button.)

    When you press the Alt key, notice that an underline appears under the s in Subtotal, the first c in Calculate, and the x in Exit to indicate that you can use an access key to work with these controls. (If the underlines don't show, you haven't entered the Text properties correctly.)
13. If you notice that some of the properties are set incorrectly, click the Close button in the upper right corner of the form to close the form. Then, make the necessary changes and run the project again. When you're satisfied that the form is working right, close the form to return to the Form Designer.

Experiment with the properties for the form and its controls

14. In the Form Designer, click on the form so it is selected. Then, if necessary, adjust the Properties window so you can see the description for each property. To do that, drag the bottom boundary of the window up.
15. Click on the Categorized button at the top of the Properties window to display the properties by category. Then, review the properties in the Appearance, Behavior, Layout, and Window Style categories. Although you won't understand all of the descriptions, you should understand some of them.
16. In the Window Style category, change the settings for the MaximizeBox and MinimizeBox to False to see how that changes the form. Then, to undo those changes, click twice on the Undo button in the Standard toolbar or press Ctrl+Z twice.

17. Click on the first text box and review the Appearance, Behavior, and Layout properties for that control. Then, repeat this process for one of the labels and one of the buttons. Here again, you won't understand all of the descriptions, but you should understand some of them.
18. Select all four of the labels, click on the plus sign before the Font property in the Appearance group, and change the Bold setting to True to see how that changes the form. Then, undo that change.

Change the name of the form files

19. Use one of the techniques presented in figure 2-9 to change the name of the form file from Form1.vb to frmInvoiceTotal.vb.
20. Note in the Solution Explorer that this also changes the names of the Designer.vb and resx files subordinate to the .vb file. To see these files, you may have to click on the Show All Files button and then on the ▷ symbol for the frmInvoiceTotal.vb file.

Close the project and exit from Visual Studio

21. Use the File→Close Solution command to close the project. If you've made any changes to the project since the last time you tested it, a dialog box is displayed that asks whether you want to save the changes that you made. If you want to save those changes, click Yes.
22. Use the File→Exit command to exit from Visual Studio.

3

How to code and test a Windows Forms application

In the last chapter, you learned how to design a form for a Windows Forms application. In this chapter, you'll learn how to code and test a Windows Forms application. Here, the emphasis will be on the Visual Studio skills that you need for entering, editing, and testing the Visual Basic code for your applications. You'll learn how to write that code in the rest of this book.

An introduction to coding

Before you learn the mechanics of adding code to a form, it's important to understand some of the concepts behind object-oriented programming.

Introduction to object-oriented programming

Whether you know it or not, you are using *object-oriented programming* as you design a Windows form with Visual Studio's Form Designer. That's because each control on a form is an object, and the form itself is an object. These objects are derived from classes that are part of the .NET Class Library.

When you start a new project from the Windows Forms Application template, you are actually creating a new *class* that inherits the characteristics of the Form class that's part of the .NET Class Library. Later, when you run the form, you are actually creating an *instance* of your form class, and this instance is known as an *object*.

Similarly, when you add a control to a form, you are actually adding a control object to the form. Each control is an instance of a specific class. For example, a text box control is an object that is an instance of the TextBox class. Similarly, a label control is an object that is an instance of the Label class. This process of creating an object from a class can be called *instantiation*.

As you progress through this book, you will learn much more about classes and objects because Visual Basic is an *object-oriented language*. In chapter 11, for example, you'll learn how to use the Visual Basic language to create your own classes. At that point, you'll start to understand what's actually happening as you work with classes and objects. For now, though, you just need to get comfortable with the terms and accept the fact that a lot is going on behind the scenes as you design a form and its controls.

Figure 3-1 summarizes what I've just said about classes and objects. It also introduces you to the properties, methods, and events that are defined by classes and used by objects. As you've already seen, the *properties* of an object define the object's characteristics and data. For instance, the Name property gives a name to a control, and the Text property determines the text that is displayed within the control. In contrast, the *methods* of an object determine the operations that can be performed by the object.

An object's *events* are signals sent by the object to your application that something has happened that can be responded to. For example, a Button control object generates an event called Click if the user clicks the button. Then, your application can respond by running a Visual Basic procedure to handle the Click event.

By the way, the properties, methods, and events of an object or class are called the *members* of the object or class. You'll learn more about properties, methods, and events in the next three figures.

A form object and its ten control objects

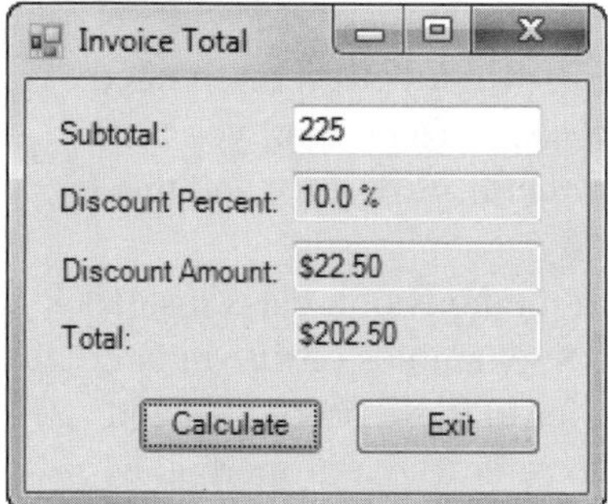

Class and object concepts

- An *object* is a self-contained unit that combines code and data. Two examples of objects you have already worked with are forms and controls.
- A *class* is the code that defines the characteristics of an object. You can think of a class as a template for an object.
- An object is an *instance* of a class, and the process of creating an object from a class is called *instantiation*.
- More than one object instance can be created from a single class. For example, a form can have several button objects, all instantiated from the same Button class. Each is a separate object, but all share the characteristics of the Button class.

Property, method, and event concepts

- *Properties* define the characteristics of an object and the data associated with an object.
- *Methods* are the operations that an object can perform.
- *Events* are signals sent by an object to the application telling it that something has happened that can be responded to.
- Properties, methods, and events can be referred to as *members* of an object.
- If you instantiate two or more instances of the same class, all of the objects have the same properties, methods, and events. However, the values assigned to the properties can vary from one instance to another.

Objects and forms

- When you use the Form Designer, Visual Studio automatically generates Visual Basic code that creates a new class based on the Form class. Then, when you run the project, a form object is instantiated from the new class.
- When you add a control to a form, Visual Studio automatically generates Visual Basic code in the class for the form that instantiates a control object from the appropriate class and sets the control's default properties. When you move and size a control, Visual Studio automatically sets the properties that specify the location and size of the control.

Figure 3-1 Introduction to object-oriented programming

How to refer to properties, methods, and events

As you enter the code for a form in the Code Editor window, you often need to refer to the properties, methods, and events of its objects. To do that, you type the name of the object, a period (also known as a *dot operator*, or *dot*), and the name of the member. This is summarized in figure 3-2.

In some cases, you will refer to the properties and methods of a class instead of an object that's instantiated from the class. You'll see examples of that in later chapters. For now, you just need to realize that you refer to these properties and methods using the same general syntax that you use to refer to the properties and methods of an object. You enter the class name, a dot, and the property or method name.

To make it easier for you to refer to the members of an object or class, Visual Studio's IntelliSense feature displays a list of the members that are available for that class or object after you type a class or object name and a period. Then, you can highlight the entry you want by clicking on it, typing one or more letters of its name, or using the arrow keys to scroll through the list. In most cases, you can then complete the entry by pressing the Tab or Enter key or entering a space. If the member name is followed by another character, such as a parenthesis, you can also complete the entry by typing that character.

To give you an idea of how properties, methods, and events are used in code, this figure shows examples of each. In the first example for properties, code is used to set the value that's displayed for a text box to 10. In the second example, code is used to set the ReadOnly property of a text box to True. Although you can also use the Properties window to set these values, that just sets the properties at the start of the application. By using code, you can change the properties as an application is running.

In the first example for methods, the Select method of a text box is used to move the focus to that text box. In the second example, the Close method of a form is used to close the active form. In this example, the Me keyword is used instead of the name of the form. Here, Me refers to the current instance of the active form. Note also that the names of the methods are followed by parentheses. If a method requires parentheses like these, they're added automatically when you press the Enter key after entering the method name.

As you progress through this book, you'll learn how to use the methods for many types of objects, and you'll learn how to supply *arguments* within the parentheses of a method. For now, though, just try to understand that you can call a method from a class or an object.

Although you'll frequently refer to properties and methods as you code an application, you'll rarely need to refer to an event. That's because Visual Studio automatically generates the code for working with events, as you'll see later in this chapter. To help you understand the code that Visual Studio generates, however, the last example in this figure shows how you refer to an event. In this case, the code refers to the Click event of a button named btnExit.

A member list that's displayed in the Code Editor window

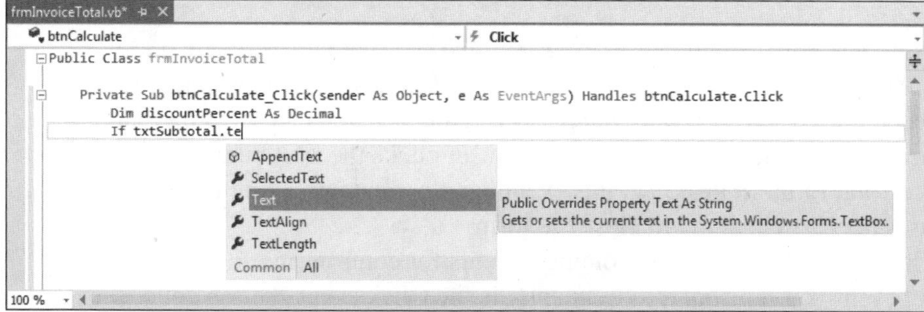

The syntax for referring to a member of a class or object

```
ClassName.MemberName
objectName.MemberName
```

Statements that refer to properties

txtTotal.Text = 10	Assigns the value 10 to the Text property of the text box named txtTotal.
txtTotal.ReadOnly = True	Assigns the True value to the ReadOnly property of the text box named txtTotal so the user can't change its contents.

Statements that refer to methods

txtMonthlyInvestment.Select()	Uses the Select method to move the focus to the text box named txtMonthlyInvestment.
Me.Close()	Uses the Close method to close the form that contains the statement. In this example, Me is a keyword that is used to refer to the current instance of the form class.

Code that refers to an event

btnExit.Click	Refers to the Click event of a button named btnExit.

How to enter member names when working in the Code Editor

- To display a list of the available members for a class or an object, type the class or object name followed by a period (called a *dot operator*, or just *dot*). Then, type one or more letters of the member name, and Visual Studio will filter the list so that only the members that start with those letters are displayed. You can also scroll through the list to select the member you want.
- You can display all the available members or just the common members in the list by using the tabs at the bottom of the list.
- If a member list isn't displayed, select the Tools→Options command to display the Options dialog box. Then, expand the Text Editor group, select the Basic group, and check the Auto List Members and Parameter Information boxes.

Figure 3-2 How to refer to properties, methods, and events

How an application responds to events

Windows Forms applications are *event-driven*. That means they work by responding to the events that occur on objects. To respond to an event, you code a procedure known as an *event handler*. In figure 3-3, you can see the event handler for the event that occurs when the user clicks the Exit button on the Invoice Total form. In this case, this event handler contains a single statement that uses the Close method to close the form.

This figure also lists some common events for controls and forms. One control event you'll respond to frequently is the Click event. This event occurs when the user clicks an object with the mouse. Similarly, the DoubleClick event occurs when the user double-clicks an object.

Although the Click and DoubleClick events are started by user actions, that's not always the case. For instance, the Enter and Leave events typically occur when the user moves the focus to or from a control, but they can also occur when code moves the focus to or from a control. Similarly, the Load event of a form occurs when a form is loaded into memory. For the first form of an application, this typically happens when the user starts the application. And the Closed event occurs when a form is closed. For the Invoice Total form in this figure, this happens when the user clicks the Exit button or the Close button in the upper right corner of the form.

In addition to the events shown here, most objects have many more events that the application can respond to. For example, events occur when the user positions the mouse over an object or when the user presses or releases a key. However, you don't typically respond to those events.

Event: The user clicks the Exit button

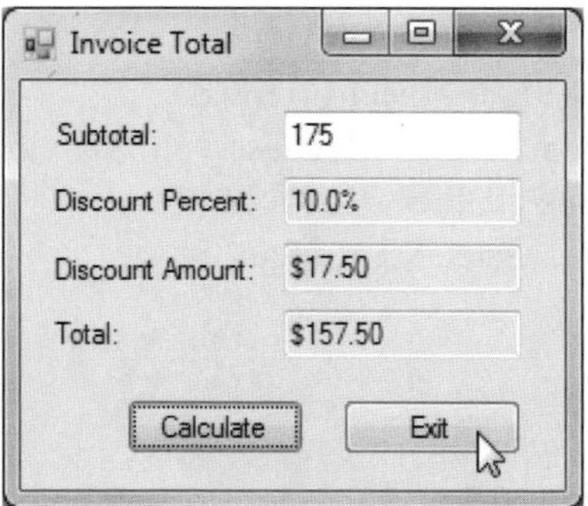

Response: The procedure for the Click event of the Exit button is executed

```
Private Sub btnExit_Click(sender As Object,
        e As EventArgs) Handles btnExit.Click
    Me.Close()
End Sub
```

Common control events

Event	Occurs when...
`Click`	...the user clicks the control.
`DoubleClick`	...the user double-clicks the control.
`Enter`	...the focus is moved to the control.
`Leave`	...the focus is moved from the control.

Common form events

Event	Occurs when...
`Load`	...the form is loaded into memory.
`Closing`	...the form is closing.
`Closed`	...the form is closed.

Concepts

- Windows Forms applications work by responding to events that occur on objects.
- To indicate how an application should respond to an event, you code an *event handler*, which is a Visual Basic procedure that handles the event.
- An event can be an action that's initiated by the user like the Click event, or it can be an action initiated by program code like the Closed event.

Figure 3-3 How an application responds to events

How to add code to a form

Now that you understand some of the concepts behind object-oriented programming, you're ready to learn how to add code to a form. Because you'll learn the essentials of the Visual Basic language in the chapters that follow, though, I won't focus on the coding details right now. Instead, I'll focus on the concepts and mechanics of adding the code to a form.

How to create an event handler for the default event of a form or control

Although you can create an event handler for any event of any object, you're most likely to create event handlers for the default event of a form or control. So that's what you'll learn to do in this chapter. Then, in chapter 6, you'll learn how to create event handlers for other events.

To create an event handler for the default event of a form or control, you double-click the object in the Form Designer. When you do that, Visual Studio opens the Code Editor, generates a *procedure declaration* for the default event of the object, and places the insertion point between the Sub and End Sub statements that it has generated. Then, you can enter the Visual Basic statements for the procedure between the Sub and End Sub statements.

To illustrate, figure 3-4 shows the Sub and End Sub statements that were generated when I double-clicked the Calculate button on the Invoice Total form. In the Sub statement, Visual Studio generated a *procedure name* that consists of the name of the object that the event occurred on (btnCalculate), an underscore, and the name of the event (Click).

This procedure name is followed by two arguments in parentheses that you'll learn more about later. And the arguments are followed by a Handles clause that says that the procedure is designed to handle the Click event of the button named btnCalculate. It is this clause, not the procedure name, that determines what event the procedure handles.

For now, you should avoid modifying the procedure declaration that's generated for you when you create an event handler. In chapter 6, though, you'll learn how to modify the declaration so a single procedure can provide for more than one event.

The procedure that handles the Click event of the Calculate button

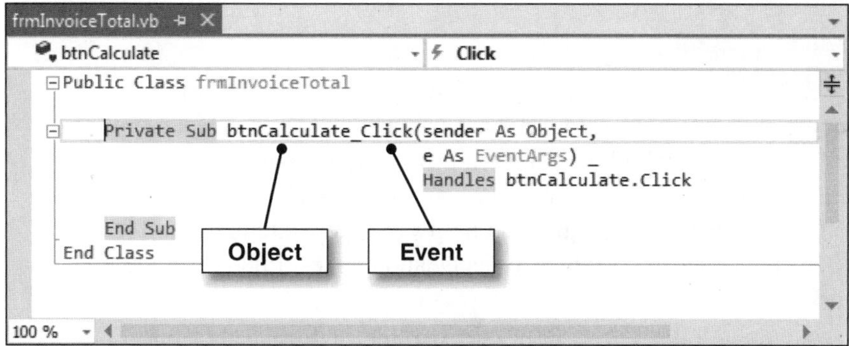

How to handle the Click event of a button

1. In the Form Designer, double-click the control. This opens the Code Editor, generates the declaration for the procedure that handles the event, and places the cursor within this declaration.
2. Type the Visual Basic code between the Sub statement and the End Sub statement.
3. When you finish entering the code, you can return to the Form Designer by clicking on its tab.

How to handle the Load event for a form

- Follow the procedure shown above, but double-click the form itself.

Description

- The *procedure declaration* for the event handler that's generated when you double-click on an object in the Form Designer includes a *procedure name* that consists of the object name, an underscore, and the event name.
- The Handles clause in the procedure declaration determines what event the procedure handles using the object name, dot, event name syntax.
- In chapter 6, you'll learn how to handle events other than the default event.

Figure 3-4 How to create an event handler for the default event of a form or control

How IntelliSense helps you enter the code for a form

In figure 3-2, you saw how IntelliSense displays a list of the available members for a class or an object. IntelliSense can also help you select a type for the variables you declare, which you'll learn how to do in chapter 4. It can help you use the correct syntax to call a procedure as shown in chapter 6 or to call a method as shown in chapter 11. And it can help you enter statements and functions as well as the names of variables, objects, and classes. Figure 3-5 illustrates how this works.

The first example in this figure shows the list that IntelliSense displays when you start to enter a new line of code. Here, because I entered the letter *d*, the list includes only those items that start with that letter. As described earlier in this chapter, you can enter as many letters as you want, and Visual Studio will continue to filter the list so it contains only the items that begin with those letters. You can also scroll through the list to select an item, and you can press the Tab or Enter key to insert the item into your code.

Note that when you select a keyword that begins a statement, a description of the statement is displayed in a *tool tip* along with the syntax of the statement. That can help you enter the statement correctly. In addition, as you enter the statement, you're prompted for any additional keywords that are required by the statement.

The second example in this figure shows the list that's displayed as you enter the code for an If statement. You'll learn more about this statement in chapter 5. For now, just notice that after I typed a space and the letter *t* following the If keyword, Visual Studio displayed a list of all the items that begin with the letter T. That made it easy to select the item I wanted, which in this case was the name of a control.

If you use these IntelliSense features, you'll see that they can help you avoid introducing errors into your code. For example, it's easy to forget the exact syntax of a statement or function, so the tool tip that's displayed when you select a statement or function can help refresh your memory. Similarly, it's easy to forget the names you've given to items such as controls and variables, so the list that's displayed can help you locate the appropriate name.

Although it's not shown here, Visual Studio also lets you see the code that's behind an IntelliSense list without closing the list. To do that, you simply press and hold the Ctrl key and the list is hidden until you release that key. This eliminates the frustration many programmers felt when code was hidden by an IntelliSense list in versions of Visual Studio before Visual Studio 2008.

The list that's displayed when you enter a letter at the beginning of a line of code

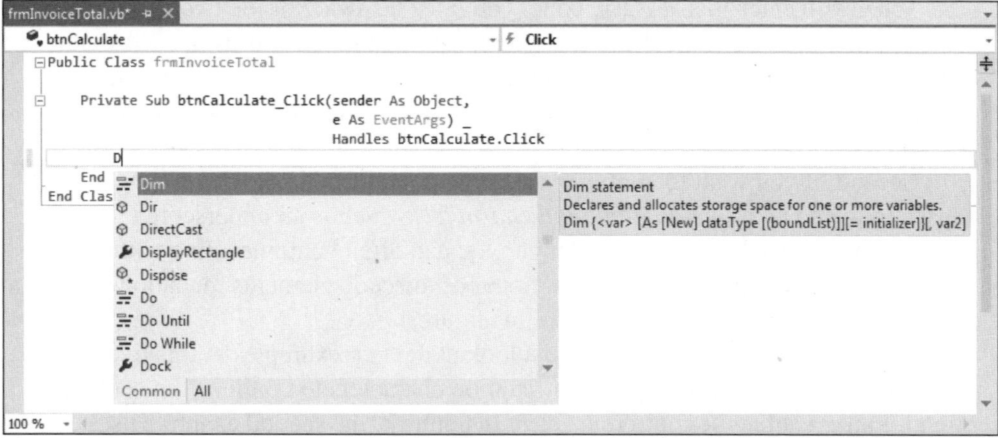

The list that's displayed as you enter code within a statement

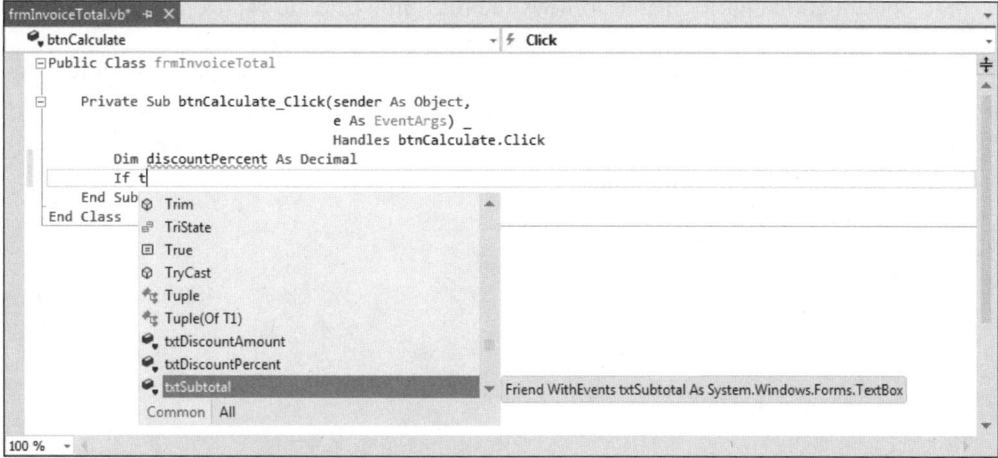

Description

- The IntelliSense that's provided for Visual Basic 2012 lists keywords, functions, variables, objects, and classes as you type so you can enter them correctly.
- When you highlight an item in a list, a tool tip is displayed with information about the item.
- If you need to see the code behind a list without closing the list, press and hold the Ctrl key. Then, the list is hidden until you release the Ctrl key.

Figure 3-5 How IntelliSense helps you enter the code for a form

Coding rules for Visual Basic statements

When you enter Visual Basic code, you must be aware of the two coding rules summarized in figure 3-6. First, you must separate the words in each statement by one or more spaces. Note, however, that you don't have to use spaces to separate the words from operators, although Visual Basic adds spaces for you by default.

Second, if you want to continue a statement, you can do that by coding a space followed by a *line-continuation character*, which is an underscore (_). Starting with Visual Basic 2010, though, you can often continue a line without using the line-continuation character. Some of the code elements that allow *implicit line continuation* are listed in this figure.

To illustrate how this works, take a look at the two examples in this figure. Here, the first example uses line-continuation characters to continue the declaration for an event handler onto four lines. In contrast, the second example uses implicit line continuation. Here, the line-continuation characters that followed the first two lines of code in the first example have been omitted. The line-continuation character that follows the third line of code is still required, though.

By the way, don't worry if you don't understand most of the code elements listed in this figure. You'll see how to use all of them later in this book. And when I present these elements, I'll show you how to use implicit line continuation with them whenever that makes sense.

Coding rules for Visual Basic statements

- Use spaces to separate the words in each statement.
- To continue a statement to the next line, you can type a space followed by an underscore (the *line-continuation character*). In the cases listed below, you can continue a statement without using a line-continuation character.

Common code elements that allow implicit line continuation

- After a comma
- After an open parenthesis or before a close parenthesis
- After a dot operator and before the member name
- After a concatenation operator
- After an assignment operator
- After a binary operator
- After the Is and IsNot operators
- After an open curly brace or before a close curly brace
- After the In keyword in a For Each statement
- After the From keyword in a collection initializer
- Before and after query operators

Code that uses line-continuation characters

```
Private Sub btnExit_Click( _
        sender As Object, _
        e As EventArgs) _
        Handles btnExit.Click
    Me.Close()
End Sub
```

Code that uses implicit line continuation

```
Private Sub btnExit_Click(
        sender As Object,
        e As EventArgs) _
        Handles btnExit.Click
    Me.Close()
End Sub
```

Description

- *Implicit line continuation* lets you continue a statement onto two or more lines without using the line-continuation character. This feature became available with Visual Basic 2010.
- You can't use implicit line continuation after a dot operator when it's coded within a With statement or within an object initialization list.

Figure 3-6 Coding rules for Visual Basic statements

The event handlers for the Invoice Total form

Figure 3-7 presents the two event handlers for the Invoice Total form. The code that's shaded in this example is the code that's generated when you double-click the Calculate and Exit buttons in the Form Designer. You have to enter the rest of the code yourself.

I'll describe this code briefly here so you have a general idea of how it works. If you're new to programming, however, you may not understand the code completely until after you read the next two chapters.

The event handler for the Click event of the Calculate button calculates the discount percent, discount amount, and invoice total based on the subtotal entered by the user. Then, it displays those calculations in the appropriate text box controls. For example, if the user enters a subtotal of $1000, the discount percent will be 20%, the discount amount will be $200, and the invoice total will be $800.

In contrast, the event handler for the Click event of the Exit button contains just one statement that executes the Close method of the form. As a result, when the user clicks this button, the form is closed, and the application ends.

In addition to the code that's generated when you double-click the Calculate and Exit buttons, Visual Studio generates other code that's hidden in the Designer.vb file. When the application is run, this is the code that implements the form and controls that you designed in the Form Designer. Although you may want to look at this code to see how it works, you shouldn't modify this code with the Code Editor as it may cause problems with the Form Designer.

The event handlers for the Invoice Total form

```
Public Class frmInvoiceTotal

    Private Sub btnCalculate_Click(sender As Object,
            e As EventArgs) Handles btnCalculate.Click

        Dim discountPercent As Decimal
        If txtSubtotal.Text >= 500 Then
            discountPercent = 0.2
        ElseIf txtSubtotal.Text >= 250 And txtSubtotal.Text < 500 Then
            discountPercent = 0.15
        ElseIf txtSubtotal.Text >= 100 And txtSubtotal.Text < 250 Then
            discountPercent = 0.1
        Else
            discountPercent = 0
        End If

        Dim discountAmount As Decimal =
            txtSubtotal.Text * discountPercent
        Dim invoiceTotal As Decimal = txtSubtotal.Text - discountAmount

        txtDiscountPercent.Text = FormatPercent(discountPercent, 1)
        txtDiscountAmount.Text = FormatCurrency(discountAmount)
        txtTotal.Text = FormatCurrency(invoiceTotal)

        txtSubtotal.Select()

    End Sub

    Private Sub btnExit_Click(sender As Object,
            e As EventArgs) Handles btnExit.Click
        Me.Close()
    End Sub

End Class
```

Description

- When you double-click the Calculate and Exit buttons in the Form Designer, Visual Studio generates the shaded code shown above. Then, you can enter the rest of the code within the event handlers.
- The first event handler for the Invoice Total form is executed when the user clicks the Calculate button. This procedure calculates and displays the discount percent, discount amount, and total based on the subtotal entered by the user.
- The second event handler for the Invoice Total form is executed when the user clicks the Exit button. This procedure closes the form, which ends the application.

Figure 3-7 The event handlers for the Invoice Total form

How to code with a readable style

When you build an application, Visual Basic makes sure that your code follows all of its rules. If it doesn't, Visual Basic reports syntax errors that you have to correct before you can continue.

Besides adhering to the coding rules, though, you should try to write your code so it's easy to read, debug, and maintain. That's important for you, but it's even more important if someone else has to take over the maintenance of your code. You can create more readable code by following the four coding recommendations presented in figure 3-8. These recommendations are illustrated by the event handler in this figure.

The first coding recommendation is to use indentation and extra spaces to align related elements in your code. This is possible because you can use one or more spaces or tabs to separate the elements in a Visual Basic statement. In this example, all of the statements within the event handler are indented. In addition, the statements within each clause of the If statement are indented and aligned so you can easily identify the parts of this statement.

The second recommendation is to separate the words, values, and operators in each statement with spaces. If you don't, your code will be less readable as illustrated by the second code example in this figure. In this example, each line of code includes at least one operator. Because the operators aren't separated from the word or value on each side of the operator, though, the code is difficult to read. In contrast, the readable code includes a space on both sides of each operator.

The third recommendation is to use blank lines before and after groups of related statements to set them off from the rest of the code. This too is illustrated by the first procedure in this figure. Here, the code is separated into four groups of statements. In a short procedure like this one, this isn't too important, but it can make a long procedure much easier to follow.

The fourth recommendation is to continue long statements onto two or more lines so they're easier to read in the Code Editor window. This also makes these statements easier to read when you print them.

Throughout this chapter and book, you'll see code that illustrates the use of these recommendations. You will also receive other coding recommendations that will help you write code that is easy to read, debug, and maintain.

By default, the Code Editor automatically formats your code as you enter it. When you press the Enter key at the end of a statement, for example, the Editor will indent the next statement to the same level. In addition, it will capitalize all variable names so they match their declarations, and it will add a space before and after each operator.

A procedure written in a readable style

```
Private Sub btnCalculate_Click(sender As Object,
        e As EventArgs) Handles btnCalculate.Click

    Dim discountPercent As Decimal
    If txtSubtotal.Text >= 500 Then
        discountPercent = 0.2
    ElseIf txtSubtotal.Text >= 250 And txtSubtotal.Text < 500 Then
        discountPercent = 0.15
    ElseIf txtSubtotal.Text >= 100 And txtSubtotal.Text < 250 Then
        discountPercent = 0.1
    Else
        discountPercent = 0
    End If

    Dim discountAmount As Decimal = txtSubtotal.Text * discountPercent
    Dim invoiceTotal As Decimal = txtSubtotal.Text - discountAmount

    txtDiscountPercent.Text = FormatPercent(discountPercent, 1)
    txtDiscountAmount.Text = FormatCurrency(discountAmount)
    txtTotal.Text = FormatCurrency(invoiceTotal)

    txtSubtotal.Select()

End Sub
```

Statements written in a less readable style

```
dim discountAmount as Decimal=txtsubtotal.Text*discountpercent
dim invoiceTotal as Decimal=txtsubtotal.Text-discountamount
txtdiscountpercent.Text=formatpercent(discountpercent,1)
txtdiscountamount.Text=formatcurrency(discountamount)
txttotal.Text=formatcurrency(invoicetotal)
```

Coding recommendations

- Use indentation and extra spaces to align statements and clauses within statements so they reflect the structure of the program.
- Use spaces to separate the words, operators, and values in each statement.
- Use blank lines before and after groups of related statements.
- Continue long lines of code onto additional lines so they're easier to read in the Code Editor window.

Notes

- As you enter code in the Code Editor, Visual Studio may adjust the indentation, spacing, and capitalization so it's easier to read. This has no effect on the operation of the code.
- If Visual Basic doesn't adjust the code, check the Pretty Listing option in the Options dialog box. To find this option, expand the Text Editor group and the Basic group and then select the VB Specific group.

Figure 3-8 How to code with a readable style

How to code comments

Comments can be used to document what the program does and what specific blocks or lines of code do. Since the Visual Basic compiler ignores comments, you can include them anywhere in a program without affecting your code. Figure 3-9 shows you how to code comments.

The basic idea is that you start a comment with an apostrophe. Then, anything after the apostrophe is ignored by the compiler. As a result, you can code whatever comments you want.

In this figure, you can see four lines of comments at the start of the procedure that describe what the procedure does. You can see one-line comments at the start of blocks of code that describe what the statements in those blocks do. And you can see one example of a comment that follows a statement on the same line.

Although some programmers sprinkle their code with comments, that shouldn't be necessary if you write your code so it's easy to read and understand. Instead, you should use comments only to clarify code that's difficult to understand. The trick, of course, is to provide comments for the code that needs explanation without cluttering the code with unnecessary comments. For example, an experienced Visual Basic programmer wouldn't need any of the comments shown in this figure.

One problem with comments is that they may not accurately represent what the code does. This often happens when a programmer changes the code, but doesn't change the comments that go along with it. Then, it's even harder to understand the code, because the comments are misleading. So if you change code that has comments, be sure to change the comments too.

Incidentally, all comments are displayed in the Code Editor in green by default, which is different from the color of the words in the Visual Basic statements. That makes it easy to identify the comments.

A procedure with comments

```
Private Sub btnCalculate_Click(sender As Object,
        e As EventArgs) Handles btnCalculate.Click

' ===================================================================
' This procedure calculates the discount and total for an invoice.
' The discount depends on the invoice subtotal.
' ===================================================================

' Determine the discount percent
    Dim discountPercent As Decimal
    If txtSubtotal.Text >= 500 Then
        discountPercent = 0.2
    ElseIf txtSubtotal.Text >= 250 And txtSubtotal.Text < 500 Then
        discountPercent = 0.15
    ElseIf txtSubtotal.Text >= 100 And txtSubtotal.Text < 250 Then
        discountPercent = 0.1
    Else
        discountPercent = 0
    End If

' Calculate the discount amount and invoice total
    Dim discountAmount As Decimal = txtSubtotal.Text * discountPercent
    Dim invoiceTotal As Decimal = txtSubtotal.Text - discountAmount

' Format the discount percent, discount amount, and invoice total
' and move these values to their respective text boxes
    txtDiscountPercent.Text = FormatPercent(discountPercent, 1)
    txtDiscountAmount.Text = FormatCurrency(discountAmount)
    txtTotal.Text = FormatCurrency(invoiceTotal)

    txtSubtotal.Select()        ' Move the focus to the Subtotal text box

End Sub
```

Coding recommendations

- Use comments only for portions of code that are difficult to understand.
- Make sure that your comments are correct and up-to-date.

Description

- *Comments* are used to help document what a program does and what the code within it does.
- To code a comment, type an apostrophe followed by the comment. You can use this technique to add a comment on its own line or to add a comment after the code on a line.
- During testing, you can comment out lines of code by coding an apostrophe before them. This is useful for testing new statements without deleting the old statements. Another way to comment out one or more lines of code is to select the lines and click on the Comment Out button in the Standard toolbar (see figure 3-11).

Figure 3-9 How to code comments

How to detect and correct syntax errors

As you enter code, Visual Studio checks the syntax of each statement. If a *syntax error*, or *build error*, is detected, Visual Studio displays a wavy line under the code in the Code Editor. In the Code Editor in figure 3-10, for example, you can see wavy lines under three different portions of code. Then, if you place the mouse pointer over one of the errors, Visual Basic will display a description of the error.

If the Error List window is open as shown in this figure, any errors that Visual Studio detects are also displayed in that window. Then, you can double-click on an error message to jump to the related code in the Code Editor. After you correct a coding problem, its message is removed from the Error List window.

If the Error List window isn't open, you can display it by selecting the Error List command from the View menu. When you're learning Visual Basic, you're going to make a lot of coding errors, so it makes sense to keep this window open. But after you get used to Visual Basic, you can conserve screen space by using the Auto Hide button so this window is only displayed when you click the Error List tab.

By the way, Visual Studio isn't able to detect all syntax errors as you enter code. So some syntax errors aren't detected until the project is built. You'll learn more about building projects later in this chapter.

The Code Editor and Error List windows with syntax errors displayed

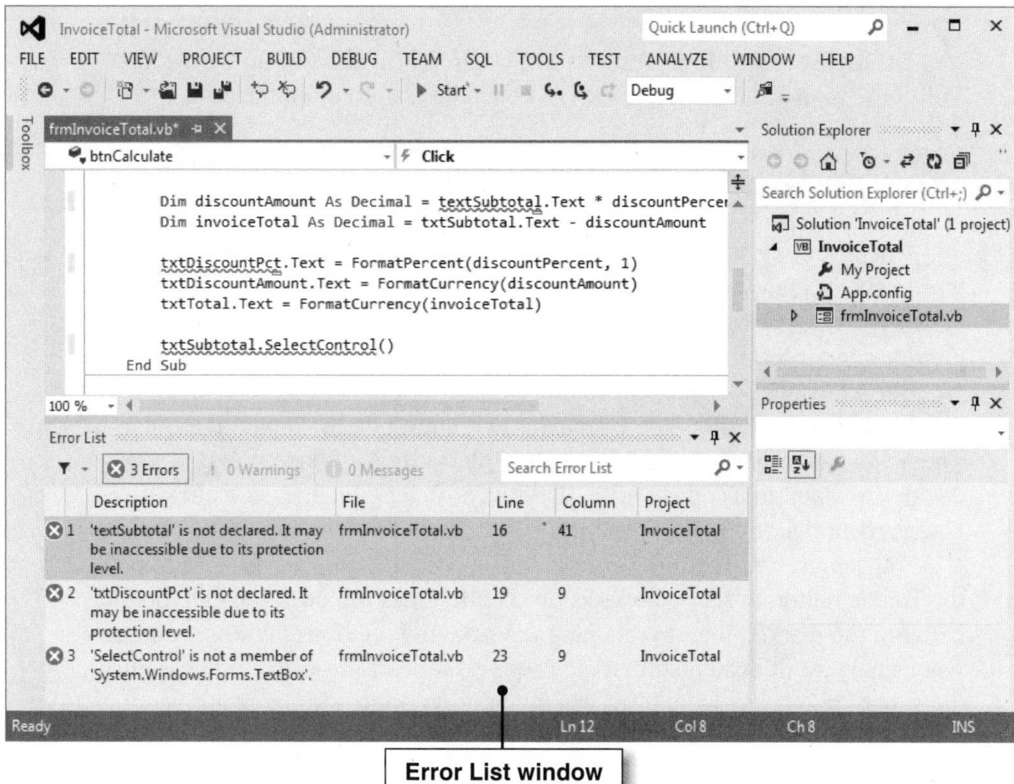

Description

- Visual Studio checks the syntax of your Visual Basic code as you enter it. If a *syntax error* (or *build error*) is detected, it's highlighted with a wavy underline in the Code Editor, and you can place the mouse pointer over it to display a description of the error.
- If the Error List window is open, all of the build errors are listed in that window. Then, you can double-click on any error in the list to take you to its location in the Code Editor. When you correct the error, it's removed from the error list.
- If the Error List window isn't open, you can display it by selecting the Error List command from the View menu.
- Visual Studio doesn't detect some syntax errors until the project is built. As a result, you may encounter more syntax errors when you build and run the project.

Figure 3-10 How to detect and correct syntax errors

Other skills for working with code

The topics that follow present some other skills for working with code. You'll use many of these skills as you code and test your applications.

How to use the toolbar buttons

Whenever you work with a Windows application like Visual Studio, it's worth taking a few minutes to see what's available from the toolbar buttons. When you're entering or editing code, both the Standard and Text Editor toolbars provide some useful functions, and they are summarized in figure 3-11.

During testing, you can *comment out* several lines of code by selecting the lines of code and clicking the Comment Out button in the Standard toolbar. Then, you can test the application without those lines of code. Later, if you decide you want to use them after all, you can select the lines and click the Uncomment button to restore them.

You can use the Text Editor toolbar to work with *bookmarks*. After you use the Toggle button to set bookmarks on specific lines of code, you can move between the marked lines by clicking the next and previous buttons. Although you usually don't need bookmarks when you're working with simple applications, bookmarks can be helpful when you're working with large applications.

How to collapse or expand code

As you write the code for an application, you may want to *collapse* or *expand* some of the code. To do that, you can use the techniques described in figure 3-11. When you collapse the procedures that are already tested, it's easier to find what you're looking for in the rest of the code.

You may also want to collapse or expand code before you print it. Then, in the dialog box for the File→Print command, you can check or uncheck the Hide Collapsed Regions box. If this box is checked, Visual Studio will only print the code that's displayed in the Code Editor.

The Code Editor and the Text Editor toolbar

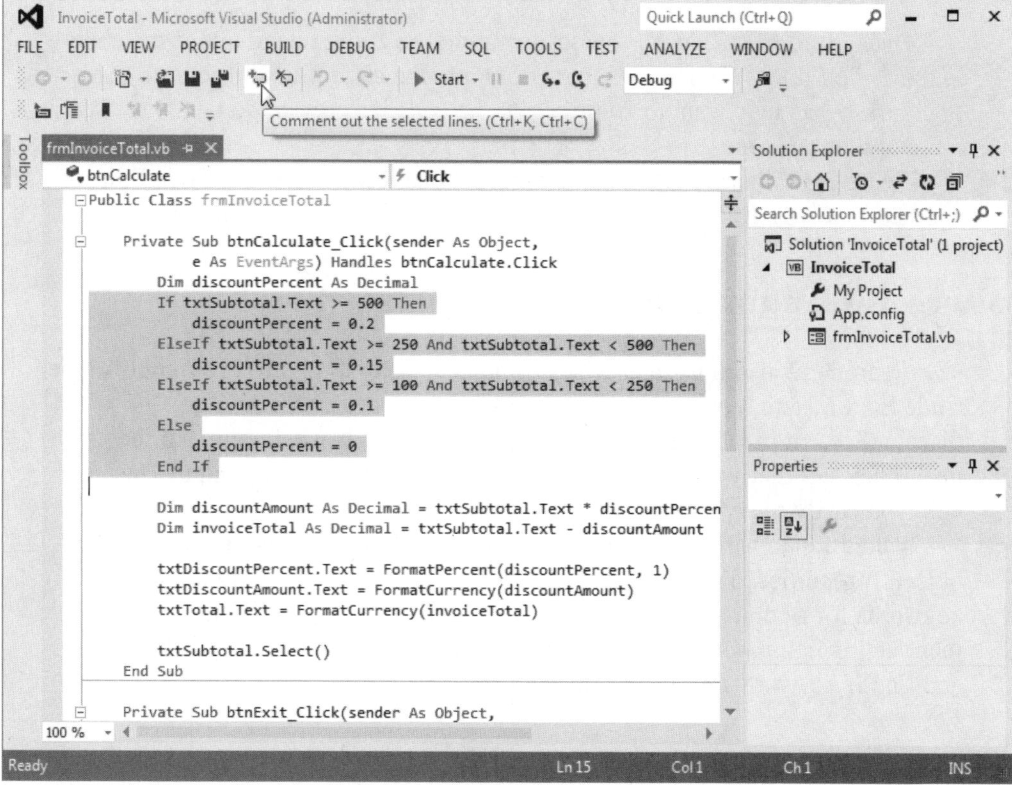

How to use the Standard toolbar to comment or uncomment lines

- Select the lines and click the Comment Out or Uncomment button. When you *comment out* coding lines during testing, you can test new statements without deleting the old ones.

How to use the Text Editor toolbar

- To display or hide the Text Editor toolbar, right-click in the toolbar area and choose Text Editor from the shortcut menu.
- To move quickly between lines of code, you can use the last four buttons on the Text Editor toolbar to set, move between, and clear *bookmarks*.

How to collapse or expand regions of code

- If a region of code appears in the Code Editor with a minus sign (-) next to it, you can click the minus sign to *collapse* the region so just the first line is displayed.
- If a region of code appears in the Code Editor with a plus sign (+) next to it, you can click the plus sign to *expand* the region so all of it is displayed.

Figure 3-11 How to use the toolbars and collapse or expand code

How to zoom in and out

Visual Studio 2012 also provides the ability to zoom in and out of the code in the Code Editor. You may want to zoom into the code if it's difficult to read. In contrast, you may want to zoom out of the code if you want to be able to see more of it at one time.

Figure 3-12 illustrates how the zoom feature works. Here, the Code Editor is zoomed in to 121% as indicated in the lower left corner of the window.

How to highlight symbols

Figure 3-12 also illustrates Visual Studio's ability to highlight symbols in the Code Editor. Here, you can see that I clicked on the variable named discountPercent in the declaration for that variable. When I did that, all the occurrences of that variable in the code for the form were highlighted. This can help you easily see where and how a symbol is used.

In addition to variable names, you can highlight the names of classes, objects, properties, methods, and procedures. You can also highlight the keywords for a control structure. If I clicked on the If keyword in the If statement in this figure, for example, that keyword, along with the Then, ElseIf, Else, and End If keywords, would be highlighted.

How to print the source code

Sometimes, it helps to print the code for the class that you're working on in the Code Editor window. To do that, you use the Print command in the File menu. Then, if you don't want to print the collapsed code, you check the Hide Collapsed Regions box. When the code is printed, any lines that extend beyond the width of the printed page are automatically wrapped to the next line.

The Code Editor with enlarged text and a highlighted variable

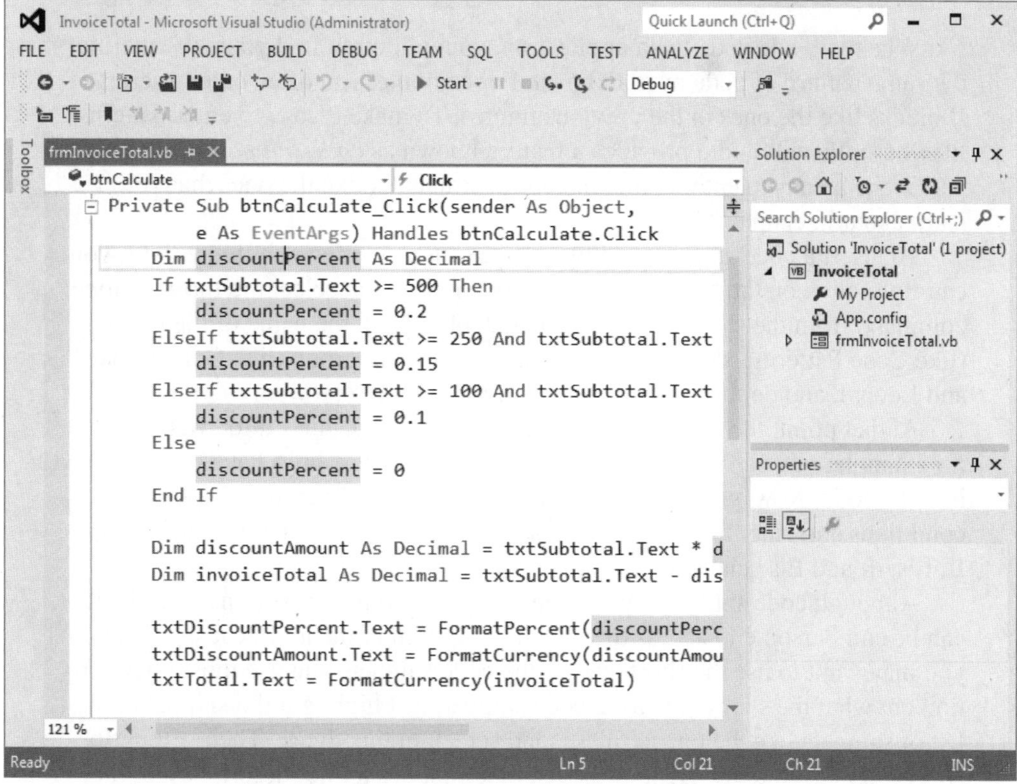

How to zoom in and out of the Code Editor

- If you have a mouse with a scroll wheel, you can zoom in and out of the Code Editor by holding down the Ctrl key as you move the wheel forward and backward.
- Before you can zoom in or out, you must click in the Code Editor to move the focus to that window.
- The current zoom percent is displayed in the lower left corner of the window.

How to highlight symbols

- If you click on a symbol in your code, all the occurrences of that symbol are highlighted.
- Symbols include the names of variables, classes, objects, properties, methods, and procedures and the keywords for control structures like the If statement.
- To move to the next highlighted symbol, press Ctrl+Shift+Down arrow. To move to the previous highlighted symbol, press Ctrl+Shift+Up arrow.
- To turn the highlighting feature off, use the Tools→Options command to display the Options dialog box. Then, expand the Text Editor node and the Basic node, click on the VB Specific category, and deselect the Enable Highlighting of References and Keywords option.

Figure 3-12 How to zoom in and out and highlight symbols

How to use code snippets

When you add code to an application, you will often find yourself entering the same pattern of code over and over. For example, you often enter a series of If blocks like the ones in the previous figures. To make it easy to enter patterns like these, Visual Studio provides a feature known as *code snippets*. Code snippets make it easy to enter common control structures like the ones that you'll learn about in chapter 5.

To insert a code snippet on a blank line of text as shown in figure 3-13, you can right-click on the blank line in the Code Editor and select the Insert Snippet command from the shortcut menu. Then, double-click the name of the group (like Code Patterns), double-click the name of the subgroup (like Conditionals and Loops), and double-click the name of the snippet you want to insert.

At that point, the code snippet is inserted into the Code Editor. In this figure, for example, you can see that If, ElseIf, Else, and End If lines have been inserted into the code. Now, you just need to replace the words True and False with conditions and enter the Visual Basic statements that you want executed for the If, ElseIf, and Else clauses.

Although code snippets make it easy to enter common patterns of code, it can be cumbersome to access them using the shortcut menu. Because of that, you may want to use the shortcuts for the code snippets you use most often. To find out what the shortcut is for a code snippet, just highlight the snippet in the list of snippets like the one in the second screen in this figure. Then, a tool tip will be displayed to the right of the list that includes a brief description of the snippet along with its shortcut. To insert a code snippet using its shortcut, you just enter the shortcut and press the Tab key.

If you find that you like using code snippets, you should be aware that it's possible to add or remove snippets from the default list. To do that, you can choose the Code Snippets Manager command from the Tools menu. Then, you can use the resulting dialog box to remove code snippets that you don't use or to add new code snippets. Be aware, however, that writing a new code snippet requires creating an XML file that defines the code snippet. To learn how to do that, you can consult the documentation for Visual Studio.

Incidentally, if you're new to programming and don't understand the If statements in this chapter, don't worry about that. Just focus on the mechanics of using code snippets. In chapter 5, you'll learn everything you need to know about coding If statements.

The list that's displayed for the Code Patterns group

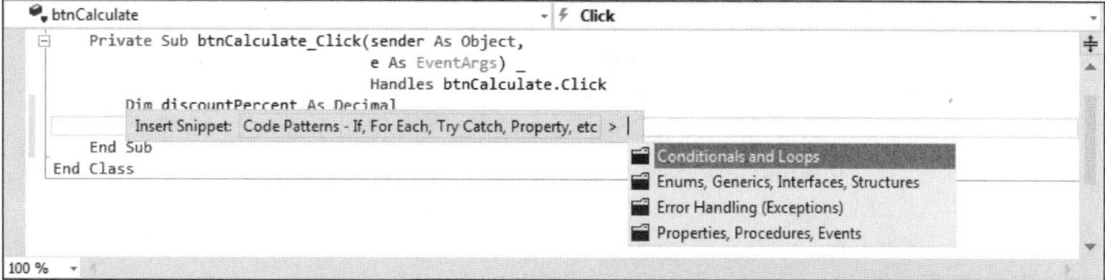

The default list of code snippets for the Conditionals and Loops group

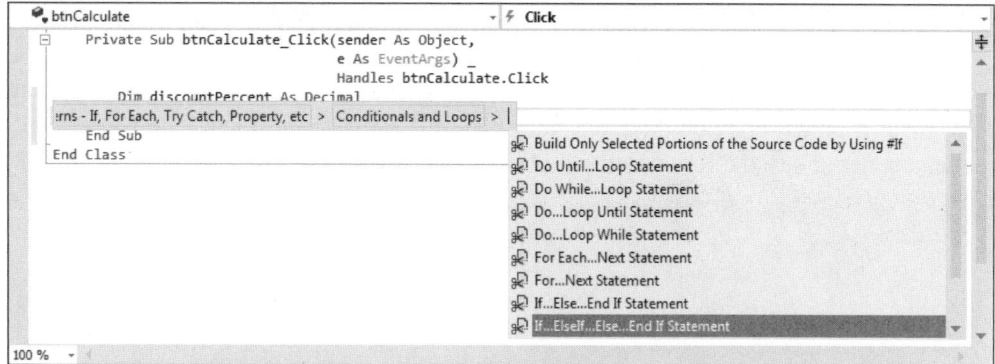

The If...ElseIf...Else...End If code snippet after it has been inserted

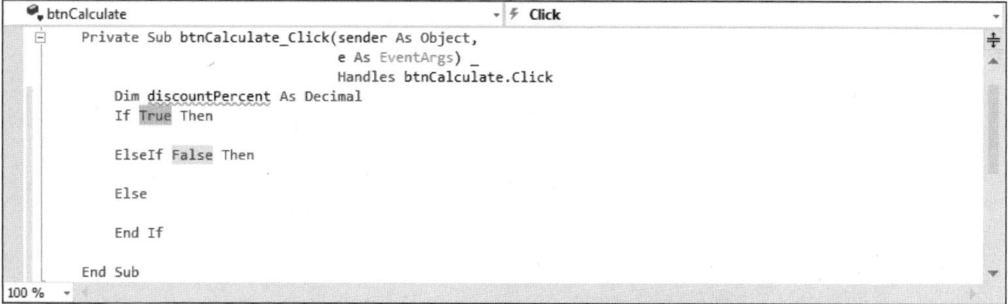

Description

- To insert a *code snippet*, right-click in the Code Editor and select the Insert Snippet command from the resulting menu. Then, go to the group that the snippet is in and double-click the snippet to insert it. You can also insert a snippet by entering its shortcut and pressing the Tab key.
- Once a snippet has been inserted into your code, you can replace the highlighted portions with your own code and add any other required code. To move from one highlighted portion of code to the next, you can press the Tab key.
- You can use the Tools→Code Snippets Manager command to display a dialog box that you can use to edit the list of available code snippets and to add custom code snippets.

Figure 3-13 How to use code snippets

How to rename identifiers

As you work on the code for an application, you may decide to change the name of a variable, procedure, class, or other *identifier*. When you do that, you'll want to be sure that you change all occurrences of the identifier. Figure 3-14 shows you two techniques you can use to rename an identifier.

The first technique shown in this figure is to rename the identifier from its declaration. Here, the name of the discountPercent variable is being changed to discountPct. When you change an identifier like this, a bar appears under the last character of the name as shown in the first screen. Then, you can move the mouse pointer over the bar and click the drop-down arrow that appears to display a *smart tag menu*. This menu shows a Rename command that you can use to change all occurrences of the identifier in your project.

You can also rename an identifier from any occurrence of that identifier. To do that, just right-click on the identifier, select the Rename command, and enter the new name into the Rename dialog box that's displayed.

How to rename an identifier from its declaration

The bar that appears under a renamed identifier

```
Dim discountPct As Decimal
```

The menu that's available from the bar

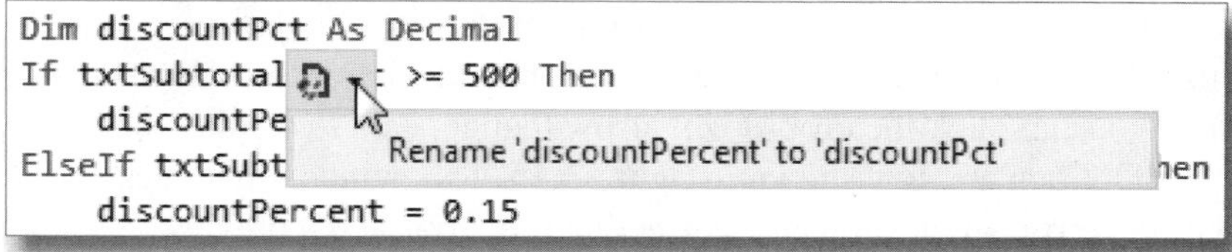

How to rename an identifier from any occurrence

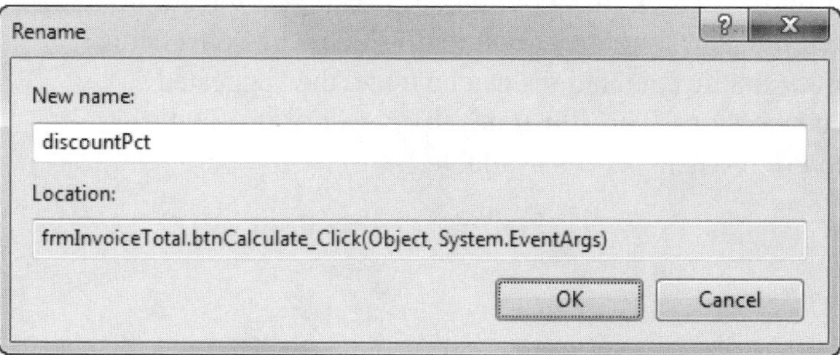

Description

- Visual Studio lets you rename *identifiers* in your code, such as variable, procedure, and class names. This works better than using search-and-replace because when you use rename, Visual Studio is aware of how the identifier is used in your project.
- When you change the declaration for an identifier in your code, Visual Studio displays a bar beneath the last character of the identifier. Then, you can move the mouse pointer over the bar, click the drop-down arrow that's displayed, and select the Rename command from the *smart tag menu*.
- You can also rename an identifier from anywhere it's used in your project. To do that, right-click the identifier and select the Rename command from the shortcut menu to display the Rename dialog box. Then, enter the new name for the identifier.

Figure 3-14 How to rename identifiers

How to use the Smart Compile Auto Correction feature

As you learned in figure 3-10, Visual Studio puts a wavy line under any syntax errors that it detects while you're entering code. In some cases, though, Visual Studio takes that one step further with its Smart Compile Auto Correction feature. In those cases, a bar appears at the right end of the wavy underline.

To use this feature, you place the mouse pointer over this bar to display a smart tag. Then, you can click the drop-down arrow that appears to display the Error Correction Options window shown in figure 3-15. This window includes a description of the error, suggestions for correcting the error, and a preview of how the code will look if you apply the corrections. If you like one of the suggested corrections, you just click on the suggestion to apply it.

For this example, I set the Option Strict option on, which you'll learn how to do in the next chapter. Because that forces you to do some data conversion before comparisons or arithmetic calculations can be done, the suggested changes do those data conversions. This illustrates the power of this feature, so you're going to want to use it whenever it's available.

The Code Editor with the Error Correction Options window displayed

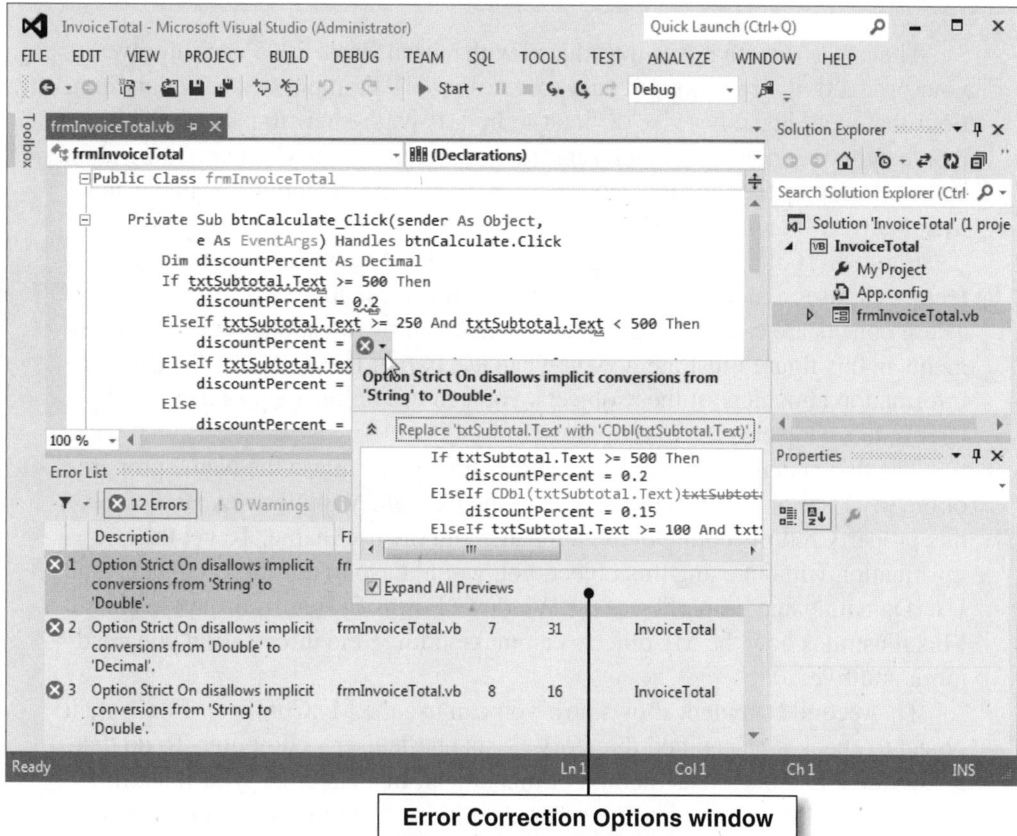

Description

- When Visual Studio detects a syntax error, it highlights the error with a wavy underline in the Code Editor.
- If a bar appears at the right end of a wavy underline, you can use the Error Correction Options window to view and apply suggested corrections.
- To display the Error Correction Options window, place the mouse pointer over the bar, then over the *smart tag* that's displayed, and click the drop-down arrow.
- To apply a correction, click the appropriate "Replace…" link.

Note

- To get the errors and the suggested corrections in the screen above, I turned the Option Strict option on. You'll learn more about that in the next chapter.

Figure 3-15 How to use the Smart Compile Auto Correction feature

How to use the My feature

The *My feature* that was introduced with Visual Basic 2005 can improve your productivity by making it easy to access .NET Framework classes and functions that would be otherwise difficult to find. If you're new to programming, this feature may not make much sense to you, but it will as you learn more about Visual Basic. So for now, it's enough to know that this feature is available and trust that you'll learn more about it later.

Figure 3-16 illustrates how this feature works. As you can see, the My feature exposes a hierarchy of objects that you can use to access information. These objects are created automatically when you run an application. The statements in this figure illustrate how you can use two of these objects. To get more information about any of these objects, you can use online help as described later in this chapter.

The first statement in this figure shows how you can use the Name property of the My.User object to get the name of the user of an application. By default, this property returns both the domain name and the user name. To get this information without using this object, you would have to use the UserName and UserDomainName properties of the Windows.Forms.SystemInformation class. This illustrates how the My objects can make finding the information you need more intuitive.

The second statement shows how you can use the My.Computer.FileSystem object to check if a specified directory exists on the user's computer. To do that, it uses the DirectoryExists method of this object. In chapter 21, you'll learn about many of the properties and methods of this object that you can use to work with drives, directories, and files.

The main My objects for Windows Forms applications

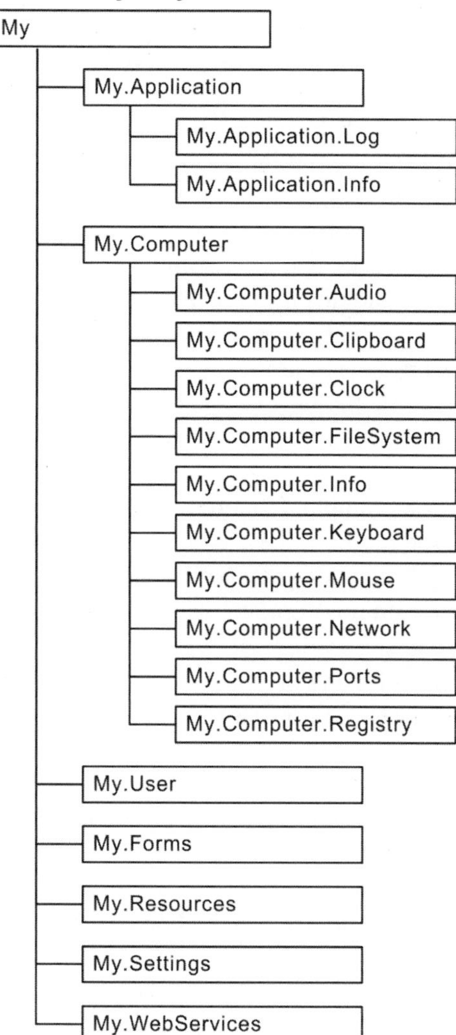

A statement that gets the name of the current user of an application

```
lblName.Text = My.User.Name
```

A statement that checks if a directory exists

```
If My.Computer.FileSystem.DirectoryExists("C:\VB 2012\Files") Then ...
```

Description

- The My feature makes it easy to access frequently used .NET Framework classes and functions using objects that are grouped by the tasks they perform. These objects are created automatically when an application is run.

Figure 3-16 How to use the My feature

How to get help information

As you develop applications in Visual Basic, it's likely that you'll need some additional information about the IDE, the Visual Basic language, an object, property, method, or event, or some other aspect of Visual Basic programming. Figure 3-17 shows how to use Microsoft's MSDN Online Library to get that information.

When you're working in the Code Editor or the Form Designer, the quickest way to get help information is to press F1 while the insertion point is in a keyword or an object is selected. Then, Visual Studio displays the available information about the selected keyword or object in your default browser. Another way to display the help information is to select the View Help command from Visual Studio's Help menu. Then, you can use the full-text search feature at the top of the window or the table of contents in the left pane of the window to locate and display the information you need.

To display the topic shown in this figure, for example, I entered "code editor" into the Search text box and then pressed the Enter key. When I did that, a list of topics that contain the search text was displayed. Then, I clicked on the link for the "Writing Code in the Code and Text Editor" topic to display the information shown here.

The table of contents that's displayed in the left pane of this window includes ancestors of the current topic and the current topic and its peers. You can click on any of these topics to display the information for that topic in the right pane.

Note that because the help information is displayed in your web browser, you can work with it just as you would any other web page. To jump to a related topic, for example, you can click on a link in the current topic. To move forward and backward through previously displayed topics, you can use the Forward and Back buttons. As a result, with a little practice, you shouldn't have much trouble using the help information.

In addition to using online help, you can install help locally. By default, some basic information about Visual Studio and the .NET Framework is installed locally when you install Visual Studio. To display this local help, you use the Help Viewer. To open the Help Viewer instead of your default browser when you display help information, you set the help preference as described in this figure.

You can also use the Help Viewer to manage your local help content. To do that, you display the Manage Content tab of the Help Viewer. This tab lists the available help documentation by category and indicates if it's installed locally. Then, you can click the Add or Remove link for a category to add or remove the documentation for that category from local help.

One advantage of using local help is that it's always available even if you don't have access to the Internet. On the other hand, local help may not always be up-to-date like online help is. Because of that, you may want to occasionally update your local help.

Online help for Visual Studio

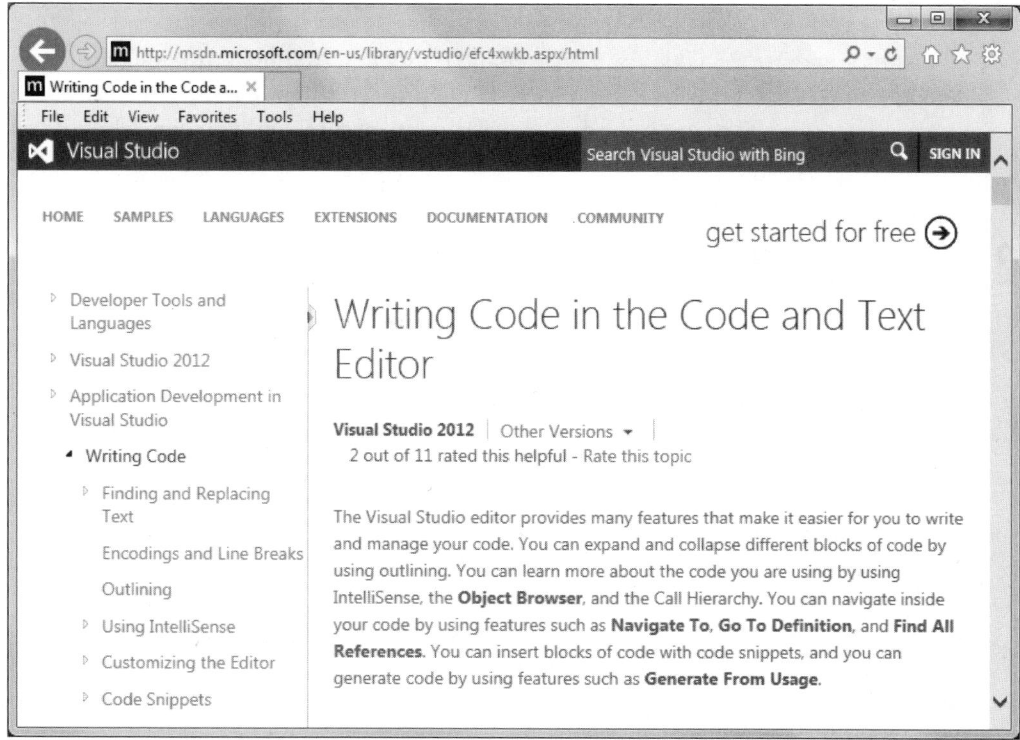

Description

- Visual Studio lets you display help content from Microsoft's MSDN Online Library in your default web browser.
- You can display context-sensitive help by selecting an object in the Form Designer or positioning the insertion point in a keyword in the Code Editor and pressing F1. You can also display Visual Studio online help by selecting the View Help command from Visual Studio's Help menu.
- Online help is divided into two panes. The left pane displays the table of contents, and the right pane displays the last help topic that you accessed.
- Controls for performing a full-text search appear in the upper right corner of the help window. To use full-text search, enter the text into the Search text box and then click on the magnifying glass or press the Enter key. A list of topics that contain the search text will be displayed, and you can click on the topic you want to display.
- To use the table of contents, click on a topic to display it in the right pane. Ancestors of the topic, the topic's peers, and peers of the topic's parent topic are displayed in the left pane.
- To display help content that resides on your local system, you use the Help Viewer. To do that, select the Set Help Preference→Launch in Help Viewer command from the Help menu.
- You can also use the Manage Content tab of the Help Viewer to add or remove content from local help.

Figure 3-17 How to get help information

How to run, test, and debug a project

After you enter the code for a project and correct any syntax errors that are detected as you enter this code, you can run the project. When the project runs, you can test it to make sure it works the way you want it to, and you can debug it to remove any programming errors you find.

How to run a project

As you learned in chapter 1, you can *run* a project by clicking the Start button in the Standard toolbar, selecting the Start Debugging command from the Debug menu, or pressing the F5 key. This *builds* the project if it hasn't been built already and causes the project's form to be displayed, as shown in figure 3-18. When you close this form, the application ends. Then, you're returned to Visual Studio where you can continue working on your program.

You can also build a project without running it as described in this figure. In most cases, though, you'll run the project so you can test and debug it.

If build errors are detected when you run a project, the errors are displayed in the Error List window, and you can use this window to identify and correct the errors as described earlier in this chapter. If it isn't already displayed, you can display this window by clicking on the Error List tab that's usually displayed at the bottom of the window or by using the View→Error List command.

The form that's displayed when you run the Invoice Total project

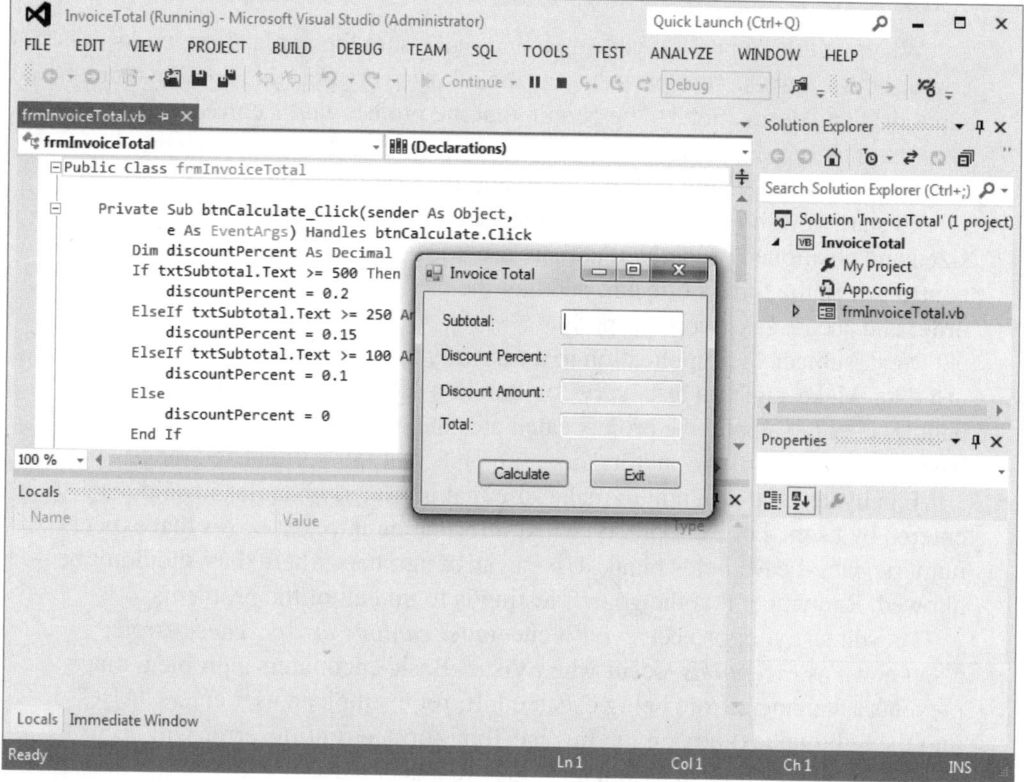

Description

- To *run* a project, click the Start button in the Standard toolbar, select the Debug→Start Debugging menu command, or press the F5 key. This causes Visual Studio to *build* the project and create an assembly. Then, if there are no build errors, the assembly is run so the project's form is displayed as shown above.
- If syntax errors are detected when a project is built, they're listed in the Error List window and the project does not run.
- You can build a project without running it by selecting the Build→Build Solution command.
- When you build a project for the first time, all of the components of the project are built. After that, only the components that have changed are rebuilt. To rebuild all components whether or not they've changed, use the Build→Rebuild Solution command.

Figure 3-18 How to run a project

How to test a project

When you *test* a project, you run it and make sure the application works correctly. As you test your project, you should try every possible combination of input data and user actions to be certain that the project works correctly in every case. In other words, your goal is to make the project fail. Figure 3-19 provides an overview of the testing process for Visual Basic applications.

To start, you should test the user interface. Make sure that each control is sized and positioned properly, that there are no spelling errors in any of the controls or in the form's title bar, and that the navigation features such as the tab order and access keys work properly.

Next, subject your application to a carefully thought-out sequence of valid test data. Make sure you test every combination of data that the project will handle. If, for example, the project calculates the discount at different values based on the value of the subtotal, use subtotals that fall within each range.

Finally, test the program to make sure that it properly handles invalid data entered by users. For example, type text information into text boxes that expect numeric data. Leave fields blank. Use negative numbers where they shouldn't be allowed. Remember that the goal of testing is to find all of the problems.

As you test your projects, you'll encounter *runtime errors*. These errors, also known as *exceptions*, occur when Visual Basic encounters a problem that prevents a statement from being executed. If, for example, a user enters "ABC" into the Subtotal text box on the Invoice Total form, a runtime error will occur when the program tries to assign that value to a decimal variable.

When a runtime error occurs, Visual Studio breaks into the debugger and displays an Exception Assistant window like the one in this figure. Then, you can use the debugging tools that you'll be introduced to in the next figure to debug the error.

Runtime errors, though, should only occur when you're testing a program. Before an application is put into production, it should be coded and tested so all runtime errors are caught by the application and appropriate messages are displayed to the user. You'll learn how to do that in chapter 7 of this book.

The Exception Assistant that's displayed when a runtime error occurs

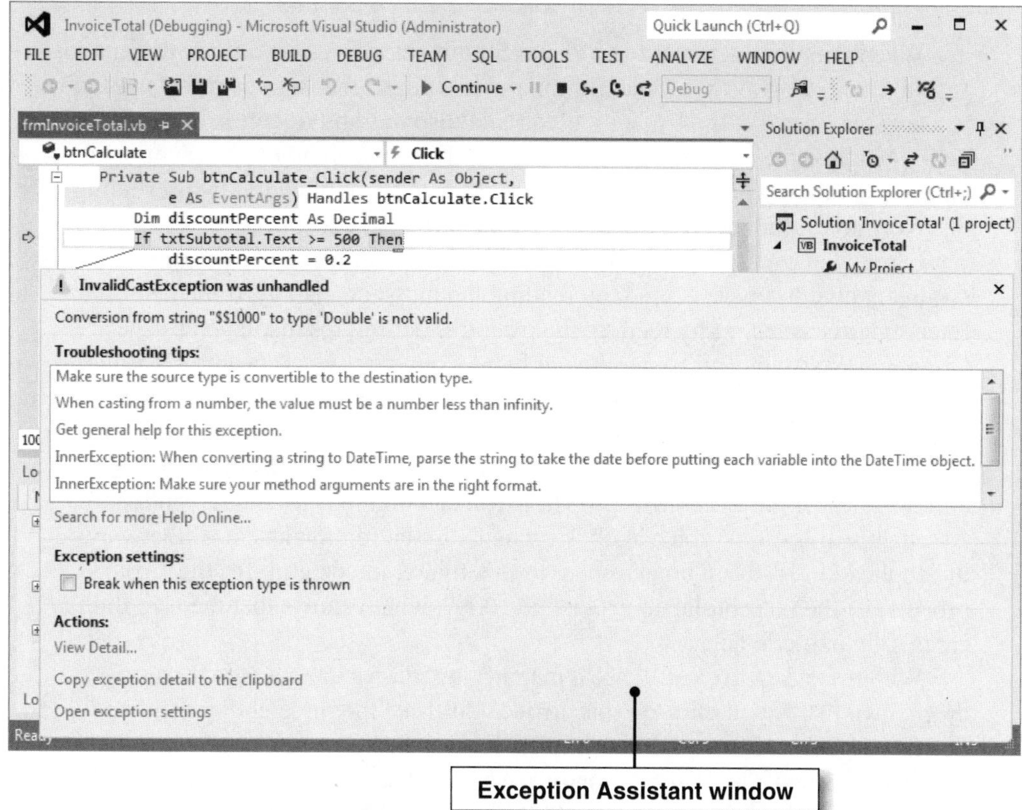

How to test a project

1. Test the user interface. Visually check all the controls to make sure they are displayed properly with the correct text. Use the Tab key to make sure the tab order is set correctly, verify that the access keys work right, and make sure that the Enter and Esc keys work properly.
2. Test valid input data. For example, enter data that you would expect a user to enter.
3. Test invalid data or unexpected user actions. For example, leave required fields blank, enter text data into numeric input fields, and use negative numbers where they are not appropriate. Try everything you can think of to make the application fail.

Description

- To *test* a project, you run the project to make sure it works properly no matter what combinations of valid or invalid data you enter or what sequence of controls you use.
- If a statement in your application can't be executed, a *runtime error*, or *exception*, occurs. Then, if the exception isn't handled by your application, the statement that caused the exception is highlighted and an Exception Assistant window like the one above is displayed. At that point, you need to debug the application.

Figure 3-19 How to test a project

How to debug runtime errors

When a runtime error occurs, Visual Studio enters *break mode*. In that mode, Visual Studio displays the Code Editor and highlights the statement that couldn't be executed, displays the Debug toolbar, and displays an Exception Assistant dialog box like the one shown in figure 3-19. This is designed to help you find the cause of the exception (the *bug*), and to *debug* the application by preventing the exception from occurring again or by handling the exception.

Often, you can figure out what caused the problem just by knowing what statement couldn't be executed, by reading the message displayed by the Exception Assistant, or by reading the troubleshooting tips displayed by the Exception Assistant. But sometimes, it helps to find out what the current values in some of the variables or properties in the program are.

To do that, you can place the mouse pointer over a variable or property in the code so a *data tip* is displayed as shown in figure 3-20. This tip displays the current value of the variable or property. You can do this with the Exception Assistant still open, or you can click on its Close button to close it. Either way, the application is still in break mode. In this figure, the data tip for the Text property of the txtSubtotal control is "$$1000", which shows that the user didn't enter valid numeric data.

Within the data tip, you'll see a magnifying glass and an arrow for a drop-down list. If you click on this arrow, you'll see the three choices shown in this figure. Then, if you click on Text Visualizer, the value in the data tip will be shown in the Text Visualizer dialog box the way it actually is. So in this simple example, the value will show as $$1000, not "$$1000". Although that isn't much different than what the data tip shows, the differences are more dramatic when the data is more complex.

Once you find the cause of a bug, you can correct it. Sometimes, you can do that in break mode and continue running the application. Often, though, you'll exit from break mode before fixing the code. To exit, you can click the Stop Debugging button in the Standard toolbar. Then, you can correct the code and test the application again.

For now, don't worry if you don't know how to correct the problem in this example. Instead, you can assume that the user will enter valid data. In chapter 7, though, you'll learn how to catch exceptions and validate all user entries for an application because that's what a professional application has to do. And in chapter 12, after you've learned the Visual Basic essentials, you'll learn a lot more about debugging.

How a project looks in break mode

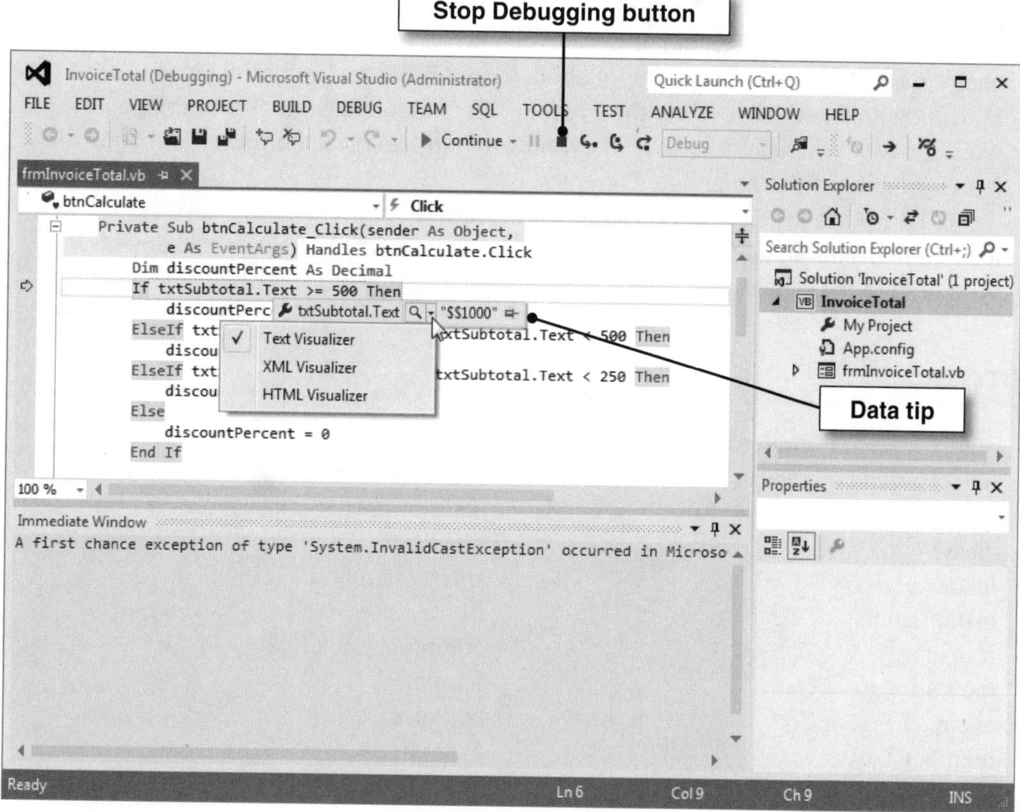

Description

- When an application encounters a runtime error, you need to fix the error. This is commonly referred to as *debugging*, and the error is commonly referred to as a *bug*.
- When an application encounters a runtime error, it enters *break mode*. In break mode, the Debug toolbar is displayed along with the Exception Assistant window.
- The information in the Exception Assistant window should give you an idea of what the error might be. You can also click on the links in the Troubleshooting Tips list to display more information in a Help window.
- If you close the Exception Assistant window, the application remains in break mode.
- To display a *data tip* for a property or variable, move the mouse pointer over it in the Visual Basic code.
- If the data tip includes a drop-down arrow to the right of a magnifying glass, you can click the error and select Text Visualizer to see exactly what the data looks like.
- To exit break mode and end the application, click the Stop Debugging button in the Standard toolbar or press Shift+F5.
- You'll learn more about debugging and the Exception Assistant window in chapter 12.

Figure 3-20 How to debug runtime errors

Perspective

If you can code and test the Invoice Total project that's presented in this chapter, you've already learned a lot about Visual Basic programming. You know how to enter the code for the event handlers that make the user interface work the way you want it to. You know how to build and test a project. And you know some simple debugging techniques.

On the other hand, you still have a lot to learn. In particular, you haven't learned much about the Visual Basic language. That's why the next six chapters present the Visual Basic essentials.

Terms

object-oriented programming
object-oriented language
object
class
instance
instantiation
property
method
event
member
dot operator
dot
argument
event-driven application
event handler
procedure declaration
procedure name
tool tip
line-continuation character
comment
syntax error
build error
code snippet
identifier
smart tag menu
My feature
comment out a line
bookmark
collapse
expand
build a project
run a project
test a project
runtime error
exception
bug
debug
break mode
data tip

Exercise 3-1 Code the Invoice Total form

In this exercise, you'll add code to the Invoice Total form that you designed in exercise 2-1. Then, you'll build and test the project to be sure it works. You'll also experiment with debugging and review some help information.

Copy and open the Invoice Total application

1. Use the Windows Explorer to copy the Invoice Total project that you created for chapter 2 from the C:\VB 2012\Chapter 02 directory to the C:\VB 2012\Chapter 03 directory.
2. Open the Invoice Total solution (InvoiceTotal.sln) that's now in the C:\VB 2012\Chapter 03\InvoiceTotal directory.

Add code to the form and correct syntax errors

3. Display the Invoice Total form in the Form Designer, and double-click on the Calculate button to open the Code Editor and generate the procedure declaration for the Click event of this object. Then, enter the code for this procedure as shown in figure 3-7. As you enter the code, be sure to take advantage of all of the Visual Studio features for coding including snippets.
4. Return to the Form Designer, and double-click the Exit button to generate the procedure declaration for the Click event of this object. Enter the statement shown in figure 3-7 for this event handler.
5. Open the Error List window as described in figure 3-10. If any syntax errors are listed in this window, double-click on each error to move to the error in the Code Editor. If the Auto Correction feature is available for an error, check to see whether its suggested correction (or one of its suggested corrections) is the one you want to make. Then, correct the error.

Test the application

6. Press F5 to build and run the project. If any syntax errors are detected, you'll need to correct the errors and press F5 again.
7. When the application runs and the Invoice Total form is displayed, enter a valid numeric value in the first text box and click the Calculate button or press the Enter key to activate this button. Assuming that the calculation works, click the Exit button or press the Esc key to end the application. If either of these procedures doesn't work right, of course, you need to debug the problems and test the application again.

Enter invalid data and display data tips in break mode

8. Start the application again. This time, enter xx for the subtotal. Then, click the Calculate button. This will cause Visual Studio to enter break mode and display the Exception Assistant.
9. Note the highlighted statement and read the message that's displayed in the Exception Assistant. Then, close the Assistant, and move the mouse pointer over the property in this statement to display its data tip. This shows that the code for this application needs to be enhanced so it checks for invalid data.
10. Click the drop-down arrow in the data tip and select Text Visualizer. This shows the data exactly as it was entered in the Text Visualizer dialog box. Then, click the Stop Debugging button in the Standard toolbar to end the application.

Experiment with the Visual Basic features

11. In the Dim statement for the discountPercent variable, change the variable name to discountPct. When you do that, a bar will appear under the last letter of the variable. Place the mouse pointer over this bar to display a drop-down arrow. Then, click on this arrow and select the Rename command. This should rename the discountPercent variable to discountPct throughout the form. But run the form to make sure it's working correctly.

12. In the If statement, right-click on any occurrence of the discountPct variable. Then, use the Rename command to rename this variable to discountPercent throughout the form. To make sure this worked, run the application.
13. Select the lines that contain the ElseIf clauses and click on the Comment Out button in the Standard toolbar. Then, run the application to see how it works when these lines are ignored. When you're done, select the lines that were commented out and click on the Uncomment button to restore them.
14. In the Code Editor, click on the minus sign in front of the btnCalculate_Click procedure to collapse it. Then, expand that procedure and collapse the btnExit_Click procedure. Print just the expanded code for this form.
15. Click on the If keyword in the btnCalculate_Click procedure, and notice that this keyword, along with the Then, ElseIf, Else, and End If keywords are highlighted. Then, click on any occurrence of txtSubtotal to see that all occurrences are highlighted.
16. If your mouse has a scroll wheel, hold down the Ctrl key and scroll the wheel forward to zoom into the code in the Code Editor window. Then, scroll it backward to zoom back out.
17. In the Solution Explorer, show all the files and double-click on the file named frmInvoiceTotal.Designer.vb to open it in the Code Editor. This is the code that determines how the form will look when it's instantiated. After you read chapter 11 and section 4, this code will make more sense to you. For now, though, just close the window with this code.

Experiment with the Help feature

18. To see how context-sensitive help works, place the insertion point in the Select method in the last statement of the first event handler and press F1. This should open online help in your default browser and display a topic that tells you more about this method.
19. Type "snippets" into the Search text box at the top of the window, and then press the Enter key to see the entries that are listed in the right pane. Scroll down and click on one of the "Code Snippets" topics to display it. Then, click on one or more topics in the table of contents to display them.
20. Return to Visual Studio and select the Help→Set Help Preference→Launch in Help Viewer command. Then, use the Help→View Help command to display the Help Viewer. Review some of the documentation that's available by expanding the nodes in the left pane and clicking on a topic to display it in the first tab of the right pane. Now, click the Manage Content tab to see that it lets you add and remove documentation. When you're done, close the Help Viewer and set the help preference back to Launch in Browser.

Exit from Visual Studio

21. Click the Close button for the Visual Studio window to exit from this application. If you did everything and got your application to work right, you've come a long way!

Section 2

The Visual Basic language essentials

In section 1, you were introduced to Visual Basic programming. In particular, you learned how to use Visual Studio to design a Windows form, to enter the code for that form, and to test that code. However, you didn't actually learn the details for coding Visual Basic statements.

Now, in this section, you'll learn the Visual Basic language essentials. In chapter 4, for example, you'll learn how to perform arithmetic operations. In chapter 5, you'll learn how to code selection and iteration statements. In chapter 6, you'll learn how to code procedures and event handlers. In chapter 7, you'll learn how to check the user's entries to make sure they're valid. In chapter 8, you'll learn how to use arrays and collections. And in chapter 9, you'll learn how to work with dates and strings. This gets you off to a great start.

After that, chapter 10 presents more skills for developing Windows Forms applications. These expand upon the skills you learned in chapter 2 and require many of the language skills that you will learn in chapters 4 through 9. Then, chapter 11 shows you how to create and use your own classes. To conclude your mastery of these essentials, chapter 12 presents more of the Visual Studio features for debugging that you were introduced to in chapter 3.

4

How to work with numeric and string data

To start your mastery of the Visual Basic language, this chapter shows you how to work with the various types of data that Visual Basic offers. In particular, you'll learn how to perform arithmetic operations on numeric data, how to work with string data, and how to convert one type of data to another.

How to work with the built-in value types

To start, this chapter shows you how to work with the *built-in data types* that the .NET Framework provides. As you will see, these consist of value types and reference types.

The built-in value types

Figure 4-1 summarizes the *value types* that the .NET Framework provides. To refer to each of these data types, Visual Basic provides a keyword. You can use the first eleven data types to store numbers, and you can use the last two data types to store characters and True or False values.

The first eight data types are used to store *integers*, which are numbers that don't contain decimal places (whole numbers). When you use one of the integer types, you should select an appropriate size. Most of the time, you can use the Integer type. However, you may need to use the Long type if the value is too large for the Integer type. On the other hand, if you're working with smaller numbers and you need to save system resources, you can use the Short or Byte type. If you're working with positive numbers, you can also use the unsigned versions of these types.

You can use the next three data types to store numbers that contain decimal places. Since the Decimal type is more accurate than the Double and Single types, it's commonly used for monetary values. If you need to save system resources, however, the Double and Single types are adequate for most situations.

You can use the Char type to store a single character. Since Visual Basic supports the two-byte *Unicode character set*, it can store practically any character from any language around the world. As a result, you can use Visual Basic to create programs that read and print Greek or Chinese characters. In practice, though, you'll usually work with the characters that are stored in the older one-byte *ASCII character set*. These characters are the first 256 characters of the Unicode character set.

Last, you can use the Boolean type to store a True value or False value. This type of value is known as a *Boolean value*.

The built-in value types

VB keyword	Bytes	.NET type	Description
`Byte`	1	Byte	A positive integer value from 0 to 255
`SByte`	1	SByte	A signed integer value from -128 to 127
`Short`	2	Int16	An integer from –32,768 to +32,767
`UShort`	2	UInt16	An unsigned integer from 0 to 65,535
`Integer`	4	Int32	An integer from –2,147,483,648 to +2,147,483,647
`UInteger`	4	UInt32	An unsigned integer from 0 to 4,294,967,295
`Long`	8	Int64	An integer from –9,223,372,036,854,775,808 to +9,223,372,036,854,775,807
`ULong`	8	UInt64	An unsigned integer from 0 to +18,446,744,073,709,551,615
`Single`	4	Single	A non-integer number with approximately 7 significant digits
`Double`	8	Double	A non-integer number with approximately 14 significant digits
`Decimal`	16	Decimal	A non-integer number with up to 28 significant digits (integer and fraction) that can represent values up to 7.9228×10^{28}
`Char`	2	Char	A single Unicode character
`Boolean`	1	Boolean	A True or False value

Description

- The *built-in data types* are actually aliases for the data types defined by the Common Type System of the .NET Framework.
- All of the data types shown in this figure are *value types*, which means that they store their own data. In contrast, *reference types* store a reference to the area of memory where the data is stored. See figure 4-10 for more information on value types and reference types.
- A *bit* is a binary digit that can have a value of one or zero. A *byte* is a group of eight bits. As a result, the number of bits for each data type is the number of bytes multiplied by 8.
- *Integers* are whole numbers, and the first eight data types above provide for signed and unsigned integers of various sizes.
- Since the Decimal type is the most accurate non-integer data type, it's typically used to store monetary values.
- The *Unicode character set* provides for over 65,000 characters, with two bytes used for each character. Each character maps to an integer value.
- The older *ASCII character set* that's used by most operating systems provides for 256 characters with one byte used for each character. In the Unicode character set, the first 256 characters correspond to the 256 ASCII characters.
- A Boolean data type stores a *Boolean value* that's either True or False.

Figure 4-1 The built-in value types

How to declare and initialize variables

A *variable* stores a value that can change as the program executes. Before you can use a variable, you must *declare* it. You can also *initialize* a variable by assigning a value to it when you declare it. Figure 4-2 shows how to declare and initialize variables.

The syntax summary at the start of this figure shows how you declare a variable. In case you aren't familiar with this syntax, the boldfaced words and symbols must be coded just as they are. The words that aren't boldfaced are created by the programmer. And the brackets [ ] indicate an optional element.

To declare a variable, then, you code the word Dim and a name that you create for the variable. In addition, you typically code the word As and the data type. If you want to initialize the variable, you code an equals sign and an expression that supplies a value. If you don't assign an initial value, the variable is assigned a default value depending on its data type.

The examples in this figure show various ways of declaring and initializing variables. For instance, the first example shows how to declare an Integer variable. Because an initial value isn't specified in this statement, the variable will be initialized with a value of 0. In contrast, the second example declares a Long variable with an initial value of 20000.

When you work with variables, you can use a *literal value*, or *literal*, as the expression that gets assigned to the variable. For example, you can assign a literal value of 1 to an integer variable. When you code a number that has a decimal point, such as 8.125, the Visual Basic compiler assumes that you want that literal value to be a Double value. If you want the literal to be interpreted as a Decimal value instead, you need to code the letter *D* after the value. Similarly, to identify a literal value as a Char value, you enclose the value in quotes and code the letter C after the closing quote. To assign a literal value to a variable with the Boolean type, you can use the True and False keywords.

You can also declare a variable without specifying its type. Then, its type is inferred from the value that's assigned to it. This is most useful when you're working with LINQ, as you'll see in chapter 23. In most other cases, we recommend that you declare variable types for clarity.

The last two examples show how you can declare two variables with a single statement. Although it's not shown here, you can also assign an initial value to each variable that's declared within a single statement.

You should also notice in the examples in this figure that the first word of each variable name starts with a lowercase letter, and the remaining words start with an uppercase letter. This is known as *camel notation*, and it's a common coding convention in Visual Basic.

How to declare and initialize a variable

Syntax

```
Dim variableName [As type] [= expression]
```

Examples

```
Dim counter As Integer
Dim numberOfBytes As Long = 20000
Dim price As Double = 14.95
Dim total As Decimal = 24218.1928D       ' D indicates a Decimal value
Dim letter As Char = "A"C                ' C indicates a Char value
Dim valid As Boolean = True
Dim numberOfTests = 8                    ' Integer type is inferred
Dim x, y As Integer                      ' declare 2 variables with 1
                                           statement
Dim i As Integer, d As Decimal           ' declare 2 variables with
                                         ' different types
```

Description

- A *variable* stores a value that can change as a program executes. Before you can use a variable, you must *declare* it by using a Dim statement.
- When you declare a variable, you can *initialize* it by assigning a value to it. If you don't do that, a default value of 0 is assigned to all numeric types, a default value of False is assigned to a Boolean type, and a default value of binary 0 is assigned to a Char type.
- A *literal value* (or just *literal*) is a specific value like 3.5 or True.
- If Option Strict is on (see figure 4-8), you may have to include a type character to identify the type of a literal value. For example, the letter *D* identifies a literal value as a decimal value, and the letter *C* identifies a literal value as a Char value.
- If Option Infer is on (the default), you can omit the As clause and Visual Basic will determine the type of the variable from the value that's assigned to it.
- To declare more than one variable in a single statement, use commas to separate the variable names. If the variables have the same data type, you can code a single As clause for them. Otherwise, you must code an As clause for each variable.

Naming conventions

- Start the names of variables with a lowercase letter, and capitalize the first letter of each word after the first word. This is known as *camel notation.*
- Assign meaningful names that will be easy to remember as you code.

Figure 4-2 How to declare and initialize variables

How to declare and initialize constants

A *constant* stores a value that can't be changed as the program executes. Many of the skills for declaring and initializing variables also apply to declaring and initializing constants. As figure 4-3 illustrates, however, you use the Const statement to declare a constant, and you must always assign an initial value to a constant. In addition, it's a common coding convention to capitalize the first letter in each word of a constant, including the first word. This is known as *Pascal notation*.

How to declare and initialize a constant

Syntax

```
Const ConstantName [As type] = expression
```

Examples

```
Const DaysInNovember As Integer = 30
Const SalesTax = .075D
```

Description

- A *constant* stores a value that can't be changed. A value must be assigned to a constant when it's declared.
- The rules for including a type character, omitting the As clause, and declaring more than one constant are the same as the rules for variables.

Naming conventions

- Capitalize the first letter of each word of a constant name. This is known as *Pascal notation.*
- Assign meaningful names that will be easy to remember as you code.

Figure 4-3 How to declare and initialize constants

How to code arithmetic expressions

Figure 4-4 shows how to code *arithmetic expressions*. To create an arithmetic expression, you use the *arithmetic operators* to indicate what operations are to be performed on the *operands* in the expression. An operand can be a literal or a variable.

The first seven operators listed in this figure work on two operands. As a result, they're referred to as *binary operators*. For example, when you use the subtraction operator (-), you subtract one operand from the other. In contrast, the last two operators work on one operand. As a result, they're referred to as *unary operators*. For example, you can code the negative sign operator (-) in front of an operand to reverse the value of the operand. You can also code a positive sign operator (+) in front of an operand to return the value of the operand. Since that doesn't change the value of the operand, however, the positive sign is rarely used as a unary operator.

While the addition (+), subtraction (-), multiplication (*), and exponentiation (^) operators are self-explanatory, the division (/), integer division (\), and modulus (Mod) operators require some additional explanation. If you're working with integer data types, the integer division operator returns an integer value that represents the number of times the right operand goes into the left operand. Then, the modulus operator returns an integer value that represents the remainder (which is the amount that's left over after dividing the left operand by the right operand). If you're working with non-integer data types, the division operator returns a value that uses decimal places to indicate the result of the division, which is usually what you want.

Arithmetic operators

Operator	Name	Description
+	Addition	Adds two operands.
-	Subtraction	Subtracts the right operand from the left operand.
*	Multiplication	Multiplies the right operand and the left operand.
/	Division	Divides the right operand into the left operand.
\	Integer division	Divides the right operand into the left operand and returns an integer quotient.
Mod	Modulus	Returns the value that is left over after dividing the right operand into the left operand.
^	Exponentiation	Raises the left operand to the power of the right operand.
+	Positive sign	Returns the value of the operand.
-	Negative sign	Changes a positive value to negative, and vice versa.

Examples of arithmetic expressions

Integer arithmetic

```
Dim x As Integer = 14
Dim y As Integer = 8
Dim result1 As Integer = x + y          ' result1 = 22
Dim result2 As Integer = x - y          ' result2 = 6
Dim result3 As Integer = x * y          ' result3 = 112
Dim result4 As Integer = x \ y          ' result4 = 1
Dim result5 As Integer = x Mod y        ' result5 = 6
Dim result6 As Integer = -y + x         ' result6 = 6
```

Decimal arithmetic

```
Dim a As Decimal = 8.5D
Dim b As Decimal = 3.4D
Dim result11 As Decimal = a + b         ' result11 = 11.9
Dim result12 As Decimal = a - b         ' result12 = 5.1
Dim result13 As Decimal = a / b         ' result13 = 2.5
Dim result14 As Decimal = a * b         ' result14 = 28.90
Dim result15 As Decimal = a Mod b       ' result15 = 1.7
Dim result16 As Decimal = -a            ' result16 = -8.5
```

Description

- An *arithmetic expression* consists of one or more *operands* and *arithmetic operators*.
- The first seven operators above are called *binary operators* because they operate on two operands. The next two are called *unary operators* because they operate on just one operand.

Figure 4-4 How to code arithmetic expressions

How to code assignment statements

Figure 4-5 shows how you can code an *assignment statement* to assign a new value to a variable. In a simple assignment statement, you code the variable name, an equals sign, and an expression. This is illustrated by the first group of assignment statements in this figure. Notice that the expression can be a literal value, the name of another variable, or any other type of expression, such as an arithmetic expression. After the expression is evaluated, the result is assigned to the variable.

When you code assignment statements, you sometimes need to code the same variable on both sides of the equals sign as shown in the second group of statements. That way, you use the current value of the variable in an expression and then update the variable by assigning the result of the expression to it. For example, you can easily add 100 to the value of a variable and store the new value in the same variable.

Since it's common to use a variable on both sides of an assignment statement, Visual Basic provides the five shorthand *assignment operators* shown in this figure. Three of these operators are illustrated in the third group of statements. Notice that these statements perform the same functions as the second group of statements. However, the statements that use the shortcut operators are more compact.

Assignment operators

Operator	Name	Description
=	Assignment	Assigns a new value to the variable.
+=	Addition	Adds the right operand to the value stored in the variable and assigns the result to the variable.
-=	Subtraction	Subtracts the right operand from the value stored in the variable and assigns the result to the variable.
*=	Multiplication	Multiplies the variable by the right operand and assigns the result to the variable.
/=	Division	Divides the variable by the right operand and assigns the result to the variable. If the variable and the operand are both integers, then the result is an integer.
\=	Integer division	Divides the variable by the right operand and assigns the integer quotient to the variable.

The syntax for a simple assignment statement

```
variableName = expression
```

Typical assignment statements

```
counter = 7
newCounter = counter
discountAmount = subtotal * .2D
total = subtotal - discountAmount
```

Statements that use the same variable on both sides of the equals sign

```
total = total + 100
total = total - 100
price = price * .8D
```

Statements that use the shortcut assignment operators

```
total += 100
total -= 100
price *= .8D
```

Description

- A simple *assignment statement* consists of a variable, an equals sign, and an expression. When the assignment statement is executed, the expression is evaluated and the result is stored in the variable.
- Besides the equals sign, Visual Basic provides the five other *assignment operators* shown above. These operators provide a shorthand way to code common assignment operations.

Figure 4-5 How to code assignment statements

How to work with the order of precedence

Figure 4-6 gives more information for coding arithmetic expressions. Specifically, it gives the *order of precedence* of the arithmetic operations. This means that all of the exponentiation operations in an expression are done first, followed by all of the positive and negative operations, and so on. If there are two or more operations at each order of precedence, the operations are done from left to right.

Because this sequence of operations doesn't always work the way you want it to, you may need to override the sequence by using parentheses. Then, the expressions in the innermost sets of parentheses are done first, followed by the expressions in the next sets of parentheses, and so on. Within each set of parentheses, though, the operations are done from left to right in the order of precedence.

The need for parentheses is illustrated by the two examples in this figure. Because parentheses aren't used in the first example, the multiplication operation is done before the subtraction operation, which gives an incorrect result. In contrast, because the subtraction operation is enclosed in parentheses in the second example, this operation is performed before the multiplication operation, which gives a correct result.

In practice, you should use parentheses to dictate the sequence of operations whenever there's any doubt about it. That way, you don't have to worry about the order of precedence.

The order of precedence for arithmetic operations

1. Exponentiation
2. Positive and negative
3. Multiplication and division
4. Integer division
5. Modulus
6. Addition and subtraction

A calculation that uses the default order of precedence

```
Dim discountPercent As Decimal = .2D     ' 20% discount
Dim price As Decimal = 100               ' $100 price
price = price * 1 - discountPercent      ' price = $99.8
```

A calculation that uses parentheses to specify the order of precedence

```
Dim discountPercent As Decimal = .2D     ' 20% discount
Dim price As Decimal = 100               ' $100 price
price = price * (1 - discountPercent)    ' price = $80 ($100 * .8)
```

Description

- Unless parentheses are used, the operations in an expression take place from left to right in the *order of precedence*.
- To specify the sequence of operations, you can use parentheses. Then, the operations in the innermost sets of parentheses are done first, followed by the operations in the next sets, and so on.

Figure 4-6 How to work with the order of precedence

How to use casting

As you develop Visual Basic programs, you'll frequently need to convert data from one data type to another. In many cases, though, Visual Basic does this *casting* automatically. Figure 4-7 shows how this works.

This figure starts by listing the conversions that Visual Basic always does automatically. These are called *widening conversions* because the receiving variable is always wider than the original variable. Because of that, the receiving variable will always be able to hold the value assigned to it. The first statement in this figure, for example, causes an Integer value to be converted to a Double value. This is known as an *implicit cast*.

Visual Basic will also perform widening conversions on the values in an arithmetic expression if some of the values have wider data types than the others. This is illustrated by the next four statements in this figure. Here, the variable a is declared with the Double data type, while b and c are declared with the Integer data type. Because of that, both b and c will be converted to Double values when the arithmetic expression in the fourth statement is evaluated.

In contrast to a widening conversion, a conversion that's done in the opposite direction is called a *narrowing conversion*. With this type of conversion, the receiving variable may not be wide enough to hold the value of the original variable. When that happens, a casting exception is thrown. Because of that, you should use a narrowing conversion only when you're sure that the receiving variable can hold the value.

By default, Visual Basic also does narrowing conversions implicitly. This is illustrated by the next group of examples in this figure. In the first statement, a Double is cast to an Integer with the decimal places rounded. In the second statement, the value in a text box is cast to a Decimal type, which will throw an exception if the value isn't valid for that type (like a value of xx). In the third statement, the Double result of the expression (7.5) is cast to an Integer so the decimal place is rounded.

To override implicit narrowing casts, you can code *explicit casts* that use Visual Basic functions like the CInt and CDec functions that are illustrated in this figure. In figure 4-12, you'll learn more about these functions, but for now you just need to know that they convert the type of the expression in parentheses to the Integer or Decimal type. Please note, however, that using these functions doesn't stop exceptions from being thrown when a conversion can't be done. They just specify what type of conversion is to be performed.

This is illustrated by the examples of explicit casts. In the first example, a Double value of 93.75 is cast to an Integer type so the value is rounded to the nearest integer. In the second example, a value in a text box is cast to the Decimal type. But here again, if the value in the text box isn't valid for the Decimal type, an exception will be thrown. In the third example, the variable a is cast to an Integer before the arithmetic expression is evaluated, and the result of the expression is cast to an Integer before it is assigned to the average variable.

Note that the value of the expression in this last example is equal to 7 rather than 8 like the expression that doesn't use the CInt function. That's because the CInt function uses a special type of rounding called banker's rounding. You'll

How implicit casting works

Widening conversions

Byte→Short→Integer→Long→Decimal

Short→Single→Double

Integer→Double

Char→Integer

Implicit casts for widening conversions

```
Dim grade As Double = 93                     ' convert Integer to Double

Dim a As Double = 6.5
Dim b As Integer = 6
Dim c As Integer = 10
Dim average As Double = (a + b + c) / 3      ' convert b and c to Doubles
                                             ' average = 7.5 (22.5 / 3)
```

Implicit casts for narrowing conversions

```
Dim grade As Integer = 93.75                 ' grade = 94 due to rounding

Dim subtotal As Decimal = txtSubtotal.Text   ' may throw an exception

Dim average As Integer = (a + b + c) / 3     ' average = 8
```

How to code explicit casts with the CInt and CDec functions

```
Dim grade As Integer = CInt(93.75)
' CInt converts to Integer with rounding (grade = 94)

Dim subtotal As Decimal = CDec(txtSubtotal.Text)
' CDec converts to Decimal; may throw an exception

Dim average As Integer = CInt((CInt(a) + b + c) / 3)
' convert a and the calculated result to Integer values; average = 7
```

Description

- *Casting* refers to the process of converting an expression from one data type to another.
- A *widening conversion* is one that casts data from a data type with a narrower range of possible values to a data type with a wider range of possible values. Visual Basic uses *implicit casts* to do widening conversions automatically.
- When you code an arithmetic expression, Visual Basic does widening conversions implicitly so all operands have the widest data type used in the expression.
- A *narrowing conversion* is one that casts data from a wider data type to a narrower data type.
- By default, Visual Basic also does narrowing conversions through implicit casts. But if the receiving data type can't hold the original data, a casting exception is thrown.
- To override implicit narrowing casts, you can code *explicit casts* with Visual Basic functions like CInt and CDec. The CInt function converts a value to an Integer type, and the CDec function converts a value to a Decimal type.
- In arithmetic expressions, explicit casts are done before any of the other operations.

Figure 4-7 How to use casting

learn more about banker's rounding in figure 4-9. For now, just realize that the CInt function rounds the value of the variable a in this example to 6 rather than 7 as it would if standard rounding was used.

How to change the type semantics

By default, Visual Basic uses *permissive type semantics*. That means that narrowing conversions are done automatically and you don't get error messages when you compile an application that requires implicit narrowing conversions.

We recommend, however, that you change this option to *strict type semantics*. Then, you have to code explicit casts for any narrowing conversions. Otherwise, your code won't compile and you'll get error messages.

When you use strict type semantics, you still get casting exceptions when a narrowing conversion can't be done. By coding explicit casts, though, you eliminate the chance that an implicit cast won't work the way you want it to. For this reason, we used strict type semantics for all of the applications that are illustrated in the rest of this book. And we recommend that you use strict type semantics too.

Figure 4-8 shows how to change the type semantics for a project as well as for all new projects. To change the type semantics for all projects, you can use the Options dialog box as described in this figure. To change them for an existing project, you can double-click the My Project folder to display the Project Designer. Then, you can display the Compile page and select the On option from the Option Strict drop-down list.

When you turn Option Strict on for an existing project, you'll see errors for any statements that require explicit casting. Then, you can use the Smart Compile Auto Correction feature to fix those errors as shown in figure 3-15 of the last chapter. If you do exercise 4-1 for this chapter, you'll get a chance to use this feature.

The Compile properties for a project

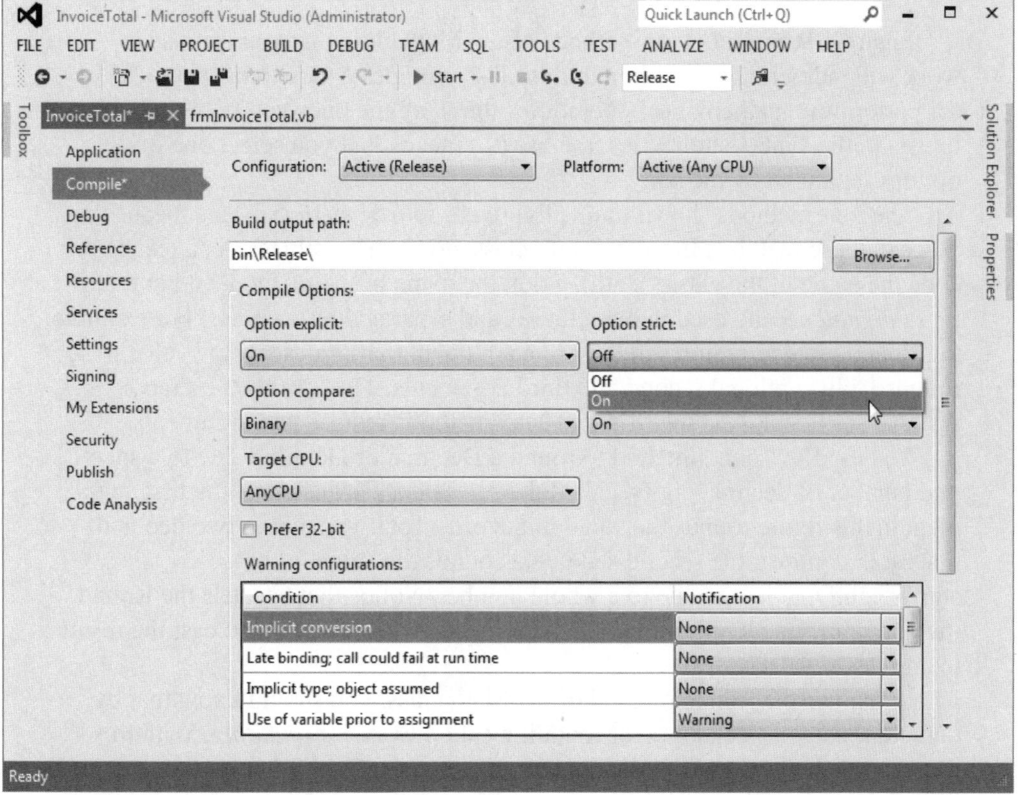

Description

- By default, Visual Basic uses *permissive type semantics*. That means that narrowing conversions can be done implicitly. If you change to *strict type semantics*, though, narrowing conversions must be done explicitly.
- We recommend that you use strict type semantics for all of your applications. That way, the compiler forces you to code explicit casts for all narrowing conversions. Note, however, that you still get casting exceptions when an explicit cast can't be done.
- To change the type semantics for all new projects, use the Tools→Options command to display the Options dialog box. Then, select the VB Defaults group within the Projects and Solutions group, and set the Option Strict option to On.
- To change the type semantics for a single project, double-click the My Project folder to display the properties for the project. Then, display the Compile tab and select On or Off for the Option Strict option.
- When you use strict type semantics, you also need to use the D character to identify Decimal literals as in 459.65D. With permissive type semantics, you don't need to do that.

Figure 4-8 How to change the type semantics that are used for casting

How to use the Math class

Figure 4-9 presents four methods of the Math class that you can use to work with numeric data. Although this class provides a variety of methods for performing mathematical operations, these are the ones you're most likely to use. In the syntax summaries, the bar (|) means that you select one of the options separated by the bar.

The four methods shown in this figure are *shared methods*. This means that you call these methods from the Math class, not from an object. As a result, you code the name of the class (Math), a dot, the name of the method, and one or more *arguments* enclosed in parentheses and separated by commas. For example, the Round method requires at least one argument that represents the value to be rounded, plus optional second and third arguments. The Sqrt method requires just one argument. And the Min and Max methods require two arguments.

You use the Round method to round a Decimal or Double value to a specified number of decimal digits, called the *precision*. For instance, the first statement in this figure rounds the value in the orderTotal variable to two decimal places. In contrast, the second statement rounds the value in the shipWeightDouble variable to a whole number. Notice that because the Round method returns a Double value, the CInt function must be used to cast the result to an Integer value.

If you use the Round method of the Math class, you should know that by default, it uses a special type of rounding called *banker's rounding*. With this type of rounding, if you round a number that ends in 5, it's always rounded to the even number. This is illustrated by the first and second statements in the second set of examples in this figure. Here, you can see that both the numbers 23.75 and 23.85 are rounded to 23.8. That can help eliminate the errors that can occur from always rounding a decimal value up to the nearest number, which is how standard rounding techniques work.

If you prefer to use standard rounding techniques, you can do that by including the mode argument as shown in the fifth statement in this set of examples. If you compare the result of this statement with the result of the fourth statement, you'll see how the mode argument works.

This figure also presents three other shared methods of the Math class: Sqrt, Min, and Max. The Sqrt method calculates the square root of a number. The Min and Max methods return the minimum or maximum of two numeric values that you specify. These three methods can be used with any of the numeric data types. However, when you use the Min or Max method, the two values you specify must be of the same type.

Four shared methods of the Math class

The syntax of the Round method

```
Math.Round(number[, precision][, mode])
```

The syntax of the Sqrt method

```
Math.Sqrt(number)
```

The syntax of the Min and Max methods

```
Math.{Min|Max}(number1, number2)
```

Statements that use shared methods of the Math class

```
Dim orderTotal As Double = Math.Round(orderTotal, 2)
Dim shipWeight As Integer = CInt(Math.Round(shipWeightDouble))
Dim sqrtX As Double = Math.Sqrt(x)
Dim maxSales As Double = Math.Max(lastYearSales, thisYearSales)
Dim minQty As Integer = Math.Min(lastYearQty, thisYearQty)
```

Results from shared methods of the Math class

Statement	Result	Statement	Result
`Math.Round(23.75, 1)`	23.8	`Math.Sqrt(20.25)`	4.5
`Math.Round(23.85, 1)`	23.8	`Math.Max(23.75, 20.25)`	23.75
`Math.Round(23.744, 2)`	23.74	`Math.Min(23.75, 20.25)`	20.25
`Math.Round(23.745, 2)`	23.74		
`Math.Round(23.745, 2, MidpointRounding.AwayFromZero)`			23.75

Description

- To use a *shared method*, you code the class name (in this case, Math), a dot, the method name, and the *arguments* in parentheses. The arguments provide the values that are used by the method, and if there are two or more, they should be separated by commas.
- The Round method rounds a number to the specified *precision*, which is the number of significant decimal digits. The number can be a decimal or a double, or a number that can be implicitly converted to one of these types, and the precision must be an integer. If the precision is omitted, the number is rounded to the nearest whole number.
- By default, if you round a decimal value that ends in 5, the number is rounded to the nearest even decimal value. This is referred to as *banker's rounding*. You can also code the mode argument with a value of MidpointRounding.AwayFromZero to round positive values up and negative values down.
- The Sqrt method returns the square root of the specified argument, which can have any numeric data type.
- The Min and Max methods return the minimum and maximum of two numeric arguments. The two arguments must have the same data type.

Figure 4-9 How to use the Math class

How to work with strings

In the topics that follow, you'll learn some basic skills for working with the String data type. These skills should be all you need for many of your applications. Then, in chapter 9, you'll learn the skills you need for advanced string operations.

How to declare and initialize a string

A *string* can consist of any letters, numbers, and characters. Figure 4-10 summarizes the techniques that you can use to declare and initialize string variables. To start, you use the String keyword to declare a string. Then, you can assign a *string literal* to a string by enclosing the characters within double quotes.

To assign an *empty string* to a variable, you can code a set of double quotes with nothing between them. You do that when you want the string to have a value, but you don't want it to contain any characters. A third alternative is to assign a *null value* to a string by using the Nothing keyword, which usually indicates that the value of the string is unknown.

How to join and append strings

Figure 4-10 also shows how to join, or *concatenate*, two or more strings into one string. To do that, you use the & operator as shown in the second example in this figure. Here, two string variables are concatenated with a string literal that consists of one space. The result is then stored in another string variable.

You can also join a string with a value data type. This is illustrated in the third example in this figure. Here, a variable that's defined with the Double data type is appended to a string. When you use this technique, Visual Basic automatically converts the value to a string.

You can also use the & and &= operators to *append* a string to the value of a string variable. This is illustrated in the last two examples in this figure. Notice that when you use the & operator, you include the string variable in the expression that you're assigning to this variable. In contrast, when you use the &= operator, you can omit the string variable from the expression. Because of that, it's common to use this operator to simplify your code.

How to declare and initialize a string

```
Dim message1 As String = "Invalid data entry"
Dim message2 As String = ""
Dim message3 As String = Nothing
```

How to join strings

```
Dim firstName As String = "Bob"                        ' firstName is "Bob"
Dim lastName As String = "Smith"                       ' lastName is "Smith"
Dim name As String = firstName & " " & lastName        ' name is "Bob Smith"
```

How to join a string and a number

```
Dim price As Double = 14.95
Dim priceString As String = "Price: " & price
' priceString is "Price: 14.95"
```

How to append one string to another string

```
Dim firstName As String = "Bob"                        ' firstName is "Bob"
Dim lastName As String = "Smith"                       ' lastName is "Smith"
Dim name As String = firstName & " "                   ' name is "Bob "
name = name & lastName                                 ' name is "Bob Smith"
```

How to append one string to another with the &= operator

```
Dim firstName As String = "Bob"                        ' firstName is "Bob"
Dim lastName As String = "Smith"                       ' lastName is "Smith"
Dim name As String = firstName & " "                   ' name is "Bob "
name &= lastName                                       ' name is "Bob Smith"
```

Description

- A *string* can consist of any characters in the character set including letters, numbers, and special characters like *, &, and #.
- To specify the value of a string, you can enclose text in double quotes. This is known as a *string literal*.
- To assign a *null value* to a string, you can use the Nothing keyword. This means that the value of the string is unknown.
- To assign an *empty string* to a string, you can code a set of double quotes with nothing between them. This usually indicates that the value of the string is known, but the string doesn't contain any characters.
- To join, or *concatenate*, a string with another string or a value data type, use an ampersand (&). If you concatenate a value data type to a string, Visual Basic will automatically convert the value to a string so it can be used as part of the string.
- When you *append* one string to another, you add one string to the end of another. To do that, you can use assignment statements.
- The &= operator is a shortcut for appending a string expression to a string variable.

Figure 4-10 Basic skills for working with strings

How to convert data types

In chapter 3, you were introduced to the use of classes, which provide properties and methods for the objects that are instantiated from the classes. Now, you'll be introduced to *structures*, which are similar to classes. Then, you'll learn how you to use structures, functions, and classes to convert data from one type to another.

The .NET structures and classes that define data types

Figure 4-11 summarizes the structures and classes that define the data types, along with the Visual Basic keywords that you can use to work with these structures and classes. To work with the Decimal structure, for example, you use the Decimal keyword. To work with the Int32 structure, you use the Integer keyword. And to work with the String class, you use the String keyword.

When you declare a variable as one of the data types that's supported by a structure, that variable is a *value type*. That means that the variable stores its own data. If, for example, you declare a variable as a Decimal type, that variable stores the decimal value. In addition, if you assign that variable to another Decimal variable, the new variable will store a separate copy of the decimal value.

In contrast, when you declare a variable as one of the data types that's supported by a class, an object is created from the class. Then, the variable stores a reference to the object, not the object itself. Because of that, object data types are called *reference types*.

In this figure, the two reference types defined by the .NET Framework are String and Object. So when you declare a variable as a string, that variable holds a reference to a String object, which contains the data for the string. As a result, it's possible for two or more variables to refer to the same String object.

In addition to the String class, the .NET Framework also provides a generic Object class. You can use a variable created from this class to hold a reference to any type of object. You'll learn more about working with the Object class in chapter 18.

Common .NET structures that define value types

Structure	VB keyword	What the value type holds
Byte	`Byte`	An 8-bit unsigned integer
Int16	`Short`	A 16-bit signed integer
Int32	`Integer`	A 32-bit signed integer
Int64	`Long`	A 64-bit signed integer
Single	`Single`	A single-precision floating-point number
Double	`Double`	A double-precision floating-point number
Decimal	`Decimal`	A 96-bit decimal value
Boolean	`Boolean`	A True or False value
Char	`Char`	A single character

Common .NET classes that define reference types

Class name	VB keyword	What the reference type holds
String	`String`	A reference to a String object
Object	`Object`	A reference to any type of object

Description

- Each built-in data type is supported by a structure or a class within the .NET Framework. When you use a Visual Basic keyword to refer to a data type, you're actually using an alias for the associated structure or class.
- A *structure* defines a *value type*, which stores its own data.
- A class defines a *reference type*. A reference type doesn't store the data itself. Instead, it stores a reference to the area of memory where the data is stored.
- All of the structures and classes shown in this figure are in the System namespace of the .NET Framework.

Note

- The .NET Framework also provides structures for the other built-in data types that were listed in figure 4-1.

Figure 4-11 The .NET structures and classes that define data types

How to use Visual Basic functions to convert data types

Unlike other .NET languages, Visual Basic provides *functions* for a variety of common tasks. One set of functions, for example, is used to convert data from one type to another. To use a Visual Basic function, you just code the function name followed by a set of parentheses that contains one or more *arguments*.

In figure 4-7, you saw how the CInt and CDec functions can be used for explicit casts that convert a data type to the Integer or Decimal data type. Now, the table in figure 4-12 summarizes those functions plus a few of the other data conversion functions. Note, however, that conversion functions are available for all of the value data types.

The first three examples in this figure are the same as three of the examples in figure 4-7, so you shouldn't have any trouble understanding them. But the fourth example shows that the CDec function allows characters like the dollar sign and comma in the value that's being converted without throwing an exception. During the conversion, the CDec function removes those characters so the resulting value can be used in arithmetic expressions.

The fifth example uses the CStr function to convert a Decimal value to a string. However, I prefer to use the ToString method of a variable for this purpose, as shown in the next figure.

The sixth example uses the CType function to get the same result as the fifth example. Although you won't normally use the CType function to do a conversion that can be done by one of the other functions, the CType function is commonly used for converting one type of object to another. As a result, you'll see this function used frequently later in this book.

Some of the Visual Basic functions for data conversion

Function	Description
`CDbl(expression)`	Converts the expression to the Double data type.
`CDec(expression)`	Converts the expression to the Decimal data type.
`CInt(expression)`	Converts the expression to the Integer data type. Any fractional portion is rounded to the nearest whole number using banker's rounding.
`CLng(expression)`	Converts the expression to the Long data type.
`CStr(expression)`	Converts the expression to the String type.
`CType(expression, Typename)`	Converts the expression to the specified type, which can be any type of object.

Examples

```
Dim grade As Integer = CInt(93.75)                          ' grade = 94

Dim subtotal As Decimal = CDec(txtSubtotal.Text)
' may throw an exception

Dim a As Double = 6.5
Dim b As Integer = 6
Dim c As Integer = 10
Dim average As Integer = CInt((CInt(a) + b + c) / 3)   ' average = 7

Dim salesString As String = "$2,574.98"
Dim salesDecimal As Decimal = CDec(salesString)
' CDec accepts $ , and .

Dim salesString = CStr(salesDecimal)              ' salesString value = 2574.98

Dim salesString = CType(salesDecimal, String)           ' same result as CStr
```

Description

- Visual Basic provides *functions* for doing a variety of tasks including the conversion of data types.
- When you code a function, you code the function name followed by one or more *arguments* within a set of parentheses. If two or more arguments are required, you separate them with commas.
- When you use these functions for explicit casts within arithmetic expressions, the casts are done before any of the arithmetic operations.
- To convert a variable to a string, you can use the CStr function or the ToString method that's shown in the next figure.
- The CType function is commonly used to convert one type of object to another type of object, but not for converting value types.

Figure 4-12 How to use Visual Basic functions to convert data types

How to use methods of the .NET data structures to convert data types

In addition to using the Visual Basic functions to convert data types, you can use the ToString, Parse, and TryParse methods presented in figure 4-13. These methods are available from any of the data structures defined by the .NET Framework.

The ToString method lets you convert any value to a string. In the first group of statements in this figure, for example, the ToString method is used to convert a Decimal value to a string value. Notice in this example that no arguments are provided on the ToString method. In figure 4-16, though, you'll learn how to code an argument that formats the resulting string.

Before I go on, you should realize that Visual Basic calls the ToString method implicitly in certain situations. You learned about one of those situations earlier in this chapter, and that example is repeated here. In this case, a Double value is automatically converted to a string when it's joined with another string.

The Parse method is a shared method that performs the reverse operation of the ToString method. In other words, it converts a string value to another data type. In the third statement in the first group of statements, for example, the Parse method of the Decimal structure is used to convert the value of a string variable to a Decimal value. However, this method only recognizes standard numeric characters. As a result, an exception will occur if you try to convert a string that includes non-numeric characters.

One way to avoid this is to use the TryParse method instead of the Parse method. This method also converts a string value to another data type as illustrated by the last statement in the first group of statements. Notice here that you don't assign the result of the TryParse method to a variable like you do when you use Parse. Instead, you name the variable on the second argument of the method. Then, if the conversion can't be performed, the TryParse method stores a value of zero in the variable and returns a False value instead of throwing an exception. To determine if the conversion was successful, you can test the return value. You'll see an example of that in chapter 7.

Common methods of the .NET data structures for data conversion

Method	Description
ToString([format]**)**	A method that converts the value to its equivalent string representation using the specified format. If the format is omitted, the value isn't formatted.
Parse(string**)**	A shared method that converts the specified string to an equivalent data value. If the string can't be converted, an exception occurs.
TryParse(string, result**)**	A static method that converts the specified string to an equivalent data value and stores it in the result variable. Returns a True value if the string is converted. Otherwise, returns a False value.

Conversion statements that use ToString, Parse, and TryParse

```
Dim sales As Decimal = 2574.98D
Dim salesString As String = sales.ToString          ' decimal to string
sales = Decimal.Parse(salesString)                  ' string to decimal
Decimal.TryParse(salesString, sales)                ' string to decimal
```

An implicit call of the ToString method

```
Dim price As Decimal = 49.5D
Dim priceString As String = "Price: $" & price      ' automatic ToString call
```

A TryParse method that handles invalid data

```
Dim salesString As String = "$2574.98"
Dim sales As Decimal = 0
Decimal.TryParse(salesString, sales)                ' sales is 0
```

Description

- The ToString, Parse, and TryParse methods are included in all of the data structures.
- In some situations where a string is expected, the compiler will automatically call the ToString method.

How to use methods of the Convert class to convert data types

A third way to convert data types is to use the shared methods of the Convert class as described in figure 4-14. These methods let you convert a value with any data type to any other data type. This is illustrated by the statements in this figure. Here, the second statement uses the ToDecimal method to convert a string that's entered in a text box to a Decimal value. The third statement uses the ToInt32 method to convert a string that's entered in a text box to an Integer value. The fourth statement uses the ToString method to convert a Decimal value to a string. And the fifth statement uses the ToInt32 method to convert a Decimal value to an Integer value.

When you use the Convert class, you should realize that the results of the conversion will vary depending on the type of conversion that you perform. If, for example, you convert a Decimal to an Integer as illustrated in the last statement in this figure, the conversion will round the decimal digits using banker's rounding. In other cases, Visual Basic won't be able to perform the conversion, and an exception will occur.

Some of the shared methods of the Convert class

Method	Description
ToDecimal(value)	Converts the value to the Decimal data type.
ToDouble(value)	Converts the value to the Double data type.
ToInt32(value)	Converts the value to the Integer data type.
ToChar(value)	Converts the value to the Char data type.
ToBool(value)	Converts the value to the Boolean data type.
ToString(value)	Converts the value to a String object.

Examples

```
Dim subtotal As Decimal
subtotal = Convert.ToDecimal(txtSubtotal.Text)       ' string to decimal

Dim years As Integer = Convert.ToInt32(txtYears.Text)
                                                     ' string to integer

txtSubtotal.Text = Convert.ToString(subtotal)        ' decimal to string

Dim subtotalInt As Integer = Convert.ToInt32(subtotal)
                                                     ' decimal to integer
```

Description

- The Convert class contains shared methods for converting all of the built-in types. To see all of the methods of this class, you can use Visual Studio's online help to look up the Convert class.

Figure 4-14 How to use methods of the Convert class to convert data types

How to use three of the formatting functions

Figure 4-15 shows how to use three of the formatting functions that Visual Basic provides. These functions let you convert a numeric value to a formatted string. Like all functions, you code these by entering the function name followed by any arguments in parentheses. If the function requires two or more arguments, they must be separated by commas.

The FormatNumber function formats a numeric value without a dollar sign. The FormatCurrency function formats a value with a dollar sign. And the FormatPercent function formats a value with a percent sign. All three functions also let you control the number of decimal positions in the result.

Although you can code up to five arguments for each of these functions, you usually code only one or two. The only argument that's required is the first one, which is an expression for the number to be formatted. Then, the second argument indicates the number of decimal digits to be used. The default is determined by your computer's regional setting, which is typically 2, so you can often omit this argument.

The basic syntax of three of the formatting functions

```
FormatNumber(expression [, numdigitsafterdecimal])
FormatCurrency(expression [, numdigitsafterdecimal])
FormatPercent(expression [, numdigitsafterdecimal])
```

Statements that use the formatting functions

```
txtDiscountAmount.Text = FormatNumber(discountAmount, 2)
txtTotal.Text = FormatNumber(invoiceTotal)
txtTotal.Text = FormatCurrency(invoiceTotal)
txtDiscountPercent.Text = FormatPercent(discountPct)
```

Results of the three formatting functions

Expression	Result
FormatNumber(-.888)	-0.89
FormatNumber(-.888, 2)	-0.89
FormatNumber(-.888, 1)	-0.9
FormatNumber(3000)	3,000.00
FormatCurrency(3000)	$3,000.00
FormatPercent(-.888)	-88.80%
FormatPercent(-.888, 1)	-88.8%

Description

- These three formatting functions are used to format a number for display or printing in number, currency, or percent format. If necessary, these functions round the values to the specified number of decimal places using standard rounding.
- Although you can code up to five arguments for these functions, you usually just code the two arguments shown above: the expression to be formatted, which can be as simple as a variable name, and the number of decimal digits to be displayed.
- If you omit the number of decimal digits, your computer's default regional setting is used.

Figure 4-15 How to use three of the formatting functions

How to use methods to convert numbers to formatted strings

Figure 4-16 shows how to use methods to convert numbers to formatted strings. Although I prefer to use the formatting functions in the previous figure, you should at least be aware that these methods are available.

The table at the start of this figure summarizes the standard codes that you can use to format a number when you use its ToString method. To use these codes, you code them as arguments, as illustrated in the first group of statements in this figure. Notice that the formatting code must be enclosed in double quotes.

You can also include an integer after any of the numeric formatting codes. In most cases, this integer indicates the number of decimal places in the resulting string. For example, if you specify the code "c0" for the value 19.95, that number will be converted to $20. Note that if you don't specify the number of decimal places, two decimal places are assumed.

If you specify a number on the D or d formatting code, it indicates the minimum number of digits in the result. Since these formatting codes are used with integers, that means that the value is padded on the left with zeros if the number you specify is greater than the number of digits in the integer. If, for example, you specify the code "d3" for the number 28, it will be converted to 028.

Another way to format numbers is to use the Format method of the String class. Since this is a shared method, you access it directly from the String class rather than from an instance of this class. You must also provide two arguments.

The first argument is a string literal that contains the format specification for the value to be formatted, and the second argument is the value to be formatted. The syntax for the format specification is shown in this figure. Here, the index indicates the value to be formatted, and the format code specifies how the value is to be formatted. Although you can format multiple values using the Format method, you'll typically use it to format a single value. In that case, the index value will be 0. In chapter 9, you'll learn how to use this method to format two or more values.

The second group of statements in this figure shows how to use the Format method. As you can see, these statements perform the same functions as the statements that use the ToString method. In this case, though, these statements use literal values so you can see what the values look like before they're formatted. Notice in these statements that the format specification is enclosed in braces. In addition, the entire argument is enclosed in double quotes.

Standard numeric formatting codes

Code	Format	Description
C or c	Currency	Formats the number as currency with the specified number of decimal places.
P or p	Percent	Formats the number as a percent with the specified number of decimal places.
N or n	Number	Formats the number with thousands separators and the specified number of decimal places.
F or f	Float	Formats the number as a decimal with the specified number of decimal places.
D or d	Digits	Formats an integer with the specified number of digits.
E or e	Exponential	Formats the number in scientific (exponential) notation with the specified number of decimal places.
G or g	General	Formats the number as a decimal or in scientific notation depending on which is more compact.

How to use the ToString method to format a number

Statement	Example
`Dim monthlyAmount As String = amount.ToString("c")`	`$1,547.20`
`Dim interestRate As String = interest.ToString("p1")`	`2.3%`
`Dim quantityString As String = quantity.ToString("n0")`	`15,000`
`Dim paymentString As String = payment.ToString("f3")`	`432.818`

How to use the Format method of the String class to format a number

Statement	Result
`Dim monthlyAmount As String = String.Format("{0:c}", 1547.2)`	`$1,547.20`
`Dim interestRate As String = String.Format("{0:p1}", 0.023)`	`2.3%`
`Dim quantityString As String = String.Format("{0:n0}", 15000)`	`15,000`
`Dim paymentString As String = String.Format("{0:f3}", 432.8175)`	`432.818`

The syntax of the format specification used by the Format method

```
{index:formatcode}
```

Description

- You can include a number after some of the numeric formatting codes to specify the number of decimal places in the result. If the numeric value contains more decimal places than are specified, the result will be rounded using standard rounding. If you don't specify the number of decimal places, the default is 2.
- You can include a number after the D or d formatting code to specify the minimum number of digits in the result. If the integer has fewer digits than are specified, zeros are added to the beginning of the integer.
- You can use the Format method of the String class to format two or more values. For more information, see chapter 9.

Figure 4-16 How to use methods to convert numbers to formatted strings

Three other skills for working with data

To complete the subject of working with data, the next three figures present three more useful skills: how to work with scope, how to work with enumerations, and how to allow value types to store null values.

How to work with scope

When you work with Visual Basic, the *scope* of a variable is determined by where you declare it, and the scope determines what code can access the variable. If, for example, you declare a variable within an event handler, the variable has *procedure scope* because an event handler is a procedure. In that case, the variable can only be referred to by statements within that procedure. This type of variable is called a *procedure-level variable*.

Often, though, you want all of the procedures of a form to have access to a variable. Then, you must declare the variable within the class for the form, but outside all of the procedures. In that case, the variable has *module scope* and can be called a *module-level variable*.

This is illustrated and summarized in figure 4-17. Here, you can see that two variables are declared at the beginning of the form class, before the first event handler for the form. As a result, these variables have module scope. In contrast, the four variables that are declared at the start of the first event handler have procedure scope. Note that the variables with module scope are used by both of the event handlers in this example, which is one reason for using module scope.

The other reason for using variables with module scope is to retain data after a procedure finishes executing. This has to do with the *lifetime* of a variable. In particular, a procedure-level variable is available only while the procedure is executing. When the event handler finishes, the variable is no longer available and the data is lost. Then, when the event handler is executed the next time, the procedure-level variables are declared and initialized again.

In contrast, a module-level variable lasts until the instance of the class is terminated. For a form, that happens when you exit the form and the form is closed. As a result, module-level variables can be used for accumulating values like invoice totals. You'll see this illustrated by the last application in this chapter.

Code that declares and uses variables with class scope

```
Public Class frmInvoiceTotal

    Dim numberOfInvoices As Integer    ] Module
    Dim totalOfInvoices As Decimal     ] scope

    Private Sub btnCalculate_Click(sender As Object,
            e As EventArgs) Handles btnCalculate.Click

        Dim subtotal As Decimal = CDec(txtEnterSubtotal.Text)          ]
        Dim discountPercent As Decimal = 0.25D                         ] Procedure
        Dim discountAmount As Decimal = subtotal * discountPercent     ] scope
        Dim invoiceTotal As Decimal = subtotal - discountAmount        ]

        numberOfInvoices += 1
        totalOfInvoices += invoiceTotal

        ' the rest of the code for the method

    End Sub

    Private Sub btnClearTotals_Click(sender As Object,
            e As EventArgs) Handles btnClearTotals.Click

        numberOfInvoices = 0
        totalOfInvoices = 0

    End Sub

    ' the rest of the code for the class

End Class
```

Description

- The *scope* of a variable determines what code has access to it. If you try to refer to a variable outside of its scope, it will cause a build error.
- The scope of a variable is determined by where you declare it. If you declare a variable within a procedure such as an event handler, it has *procedure scope*. If you declare a variable within a class but not within a procedure, it has *module scope*.
- A variable with procedure scope can only be referred to by statements within that procedure. A variable with module scope can be referred to by all of the procedures in the class.
- The *lifetime* of a variable is the period of time that it's available for use. A variable with procedure scope is only available while the procedure is executing. A variable with module scope is available while the class is instantiated.

Figure 4-17 How to work with scope

How to declare and use enumerations

An *enumeration* is a set of related constants that define a value type where each constant is known as a *member* of the enumeration. The enumerations provided by the .NET Framework are generally used to set object properties and to specify the values that are passed to methods. For example, the FormBorderStyle enumeration includes a group of constants that you can use to specify the settings for the FormBorderStyle property of a form.

The table in figure 4-18 summarizes three of the constants within the FormBorderStyle enumeration, and the first example shows how you can use code to set this form property. Normally, though, you'll use the Properties window to choose the constant from the enumeration for this form property.

When writing code, you often need to select one option from a group of related options. For example, you may need to let a user choose the payment terms for an invoice. In that case, it often makes sense to define an enumeration that contains each option.

To define an enumeration, you use the Enum statement shown in this figure. After you provide a name for an enumeration, you code each constant name on a separate line. In the first example, the enumeration is named Terms, and the constants are named Net30Days, Net60Days, and Net90Days. In this case, because values aren't provided for these constants, the default values of 0, 1, and 2 are assigned to the constants.

If you want to assign other values to the constants, you can provide a value for each constant as shown in the second example. Here, the values 30, 60, and 90 are assigned to the constants for the TermValues enumeration. In this case, these values are stored as short data types because an As clause that specifies the data type is coded after the enumeration name. If the data type is omitted, the constant values are stored as integers.

To refer to a constant value in an enumeration, you code the name of the enumeration followed by a dot and the name of the constant. This is illustrated by the first three statements in the third group of examples. Here, the first statement returns a value of the Terms type, the second statement returns the Integer type that corresponds with a member of the Terms enumeration, and the third statement returns the Integer type that corresponds to a member of the TermValues enumeration. If you want to refer to the name of a constant instead of its value, you can use the ToString method as in the last example in this group.

For now, when you code an enumeration, you can code it with module scope. In other words, you can code the enumeration outside the procedures of the class as shown in the previous figure. That way, it will be available to all of the procedures in the class. Later, when you learn how to add classes to a project, you can store an enumeration in its own file, so it's easily accessible from all classes in the project.

Some of the constants in the FormBorderStyle enumeration

Constant	Description
`FormBorderStyle.FixedDialog`	A fixed, thick border typically used for dialog boxes.
`FormBorder.Style.FixedSingle`	A single-line border that isn't resizable.
`FormBorderStyle.Sizable`	A resizable border.

A statement that uses the FormBorderStyle enumeration

```
Me.FormBorderStyle = FormBorderStyle.FixedSingle
```

The syntax for declaring an enumeration

```
Enum EnumerationName [As type]
    ConstantName1 [= value]
   [ConstantName2 [= value]]...
End Enum
```

An enumeration that sets the constant values to 0, 1, and 2

```
Enum Terms
    Net30Days
    Net60Days
    Net90Days
End Enum
```

An enumeration that sets the constant values to 30, 60, and 90

```
Enum TermValues As Short
    Net30Days = 30
    Net60Days = 60
    Net90Days = 90
End Enum
```

Statements that use the constants in these enumerations

```
Dim t As Terms = Terms.Net30Days
Dim i As Integer = CInt(Terms.Net30Days)                ' i is 0
Dim value As Integer = CInt(TermValues.Net60Days)       ' value is 60
Dim name As String = Terms.Net30Days.ToString           ' name is "Net30Days"
```

Description

- An *enumeration* defines a set of related constants. Each constant is known as a *member* of the enumeration.
- By default, an enumeration uses the Integer type and sets the first constant to 0, the second to 1, and so on.
- To use one of the other integer data types, you can code an As clause that specifies the data type after the enumeration name.
- To specify other values for the constants, you can code an equal sign after the constant name followed by the integer value.

Figure 4-18 How to declare and use enumerations

How to work with nullable types

By default, value types (such as the Integer, Decimal, and Boolean types) can't store null values. In contrast, reference types (such as the String type) can store null values. Most of the time, you won't need to use a value type to store null values. However, a feature of Visual Basic known as *nullable types* allows you to store a null value in a value type, and figure 4-19 shows how this feature works.

To declare a nullable type, you use one of the three syntaxes shown at the top of this figure. As you can see, you use the Dim statement just as you would for any other variable. On this statement, however, you can include a Nullable clause that specifies the type for the variable. You can also declare a nullable type by coding a question mark following the name of the variable or the data type. Although the technique you use is a matter of preference, we prefer the first technique because it makes it clear that the variable is a nullable type.

The examples in this figure illustrate how this works. For example, the first statement declares an Integer variable as a nullable type. Notice that no initial value is assigned to the variable. In that case, the variable is initialized to null, which is usually what you want. If you later assign a value to the variable, you can reset it to null using the Nothing keyword as shown in the fourth statement in this figure.

Typically, you use a null value to indicate that the value of the variable is unknown. For example, if a user didn't enter a quantity, you might want to assign a null value to the quantity variable to indicate that the user didn't enter a value. When working with value types, however, it's more common to assign a default value such as zero to indicate that the user didn't enter a value. As a result, unless you're working with a database that returns null values, you probably won't need to use nullable types.

Note that you can only use nullable types when you're working with value types. This figure, for example, shows how to declare nullable types for the Integer, Decimal, and Boolean types. In addition, it shows that you can declare the Terms enumeration shown in figure 4-18 as a nullable type, which is what you would expect since enumerations define value types. However, you can't declare a String type as a nullable type because the String type is a reference type and can store null values by default.

Once you declare a value type as nullable, you can use the HasValue property to check if the type stores a value or if it contains a null value. Then, if it stores a value, you can use the Value property to get that value. In the next chapter, you'll learn how to use If statements to execute different sets of statements depending on the value of the HasValue property.

You can also use nullable types in arithmetic expressions. When you do, Visual Basic uses *null propagation arithmetic*. That means that if the value of a variable with a nullable type is null, the null value is propagated to the result. In other words, the result is null. This is illustrated in the last example in this figure.

Three ways to declare a value type that can contain null values

Syntax

```
Dim variableName As Nullable(Of type) [= expression]
Dim variableName? As type [= expression]
Dim variableName As type? [= expression]
```

Examples

```
Dim quantity As Nullable(Of Integer)
quantity = 0
quantity = 20
quantity = Nothing

Dim salesTotal? As Decimal

Dim isValid As Boolean?

Dim paymentTerms As Nullable(Of Terms)

' Dim message As Nullable(Of String)     ' not allowed
```

Two properties for working with nullable types

Property	Description
`HasValue`	Returns a True value if the nullable type contains a value. Returns a False value if the nullable type is null.
`Value`	Returns the value of the nullable type.

Statements that work with nullable types

```
Dim hasValue As Boolean = quantity.HasValue
Dim qty As Integer = quantity.Value
```

How to use nullable types in arithmetic expressions

```
Dim a As Nullable(Of Decimal)                ' a = null
Dim b As Nullable(Of Decimal) = 9.5D
Dim result As Nullable(Of Decimal) = a + b   ' result = null
```

Description

- A *nullable type* is a value type that can store a null value. Null values are typically used to indicate that the value of the variable is unknown.
- To declare a nullable type, use one of the three techniques shown above.
- Although you can assign an initial value to a nullable type, you don't usually do that. Instead, you let its value default to null.
- To reset the value of a nullable type to null, you use the Nothing keyword.
- If you use a variable with a nullable type in an arithmetic expression and the value of the variable is null, the result of the arithmetic expression is always null. This is called *null propagation arithmetic*.
- You can only declare value types as nullable types. However, because reference types (such as strings) can store null values by default, there's no need to declare reference types as nullable, and your code won't compile if you try to do that.

Figure 4-19 How to work with nullable types

Two versions of the Invoice Total application

To give you a better idea of how you can use data, arithmetic, data conversion, and scope, this chapter concludes by presenting two illustrative applications.

The basic Invoice Total application

Figure 4-20 presents a simple version of the Invoice Total application that's similar to the one presented in chapter 3. Now that you have learned how to work with data, you should be able to understand all of the code in this application.

To start, this figure shows the user interface for this application, which is the same as it was in the last chapter. Then, this figure lists the six controls that the code refers to so you can see how the code relates to those controls.

This figure also presents the code for the two event handlers of the Invoice Total application. If you study the code for the Click event of the Calculate button, you'll see that it begins by converting the string value that's entered by the user to a Decimal value. Then, it sets the discount percent to .25, or 25%. This percent is then used to calculate the discount for the invoice, and the discount is subtracted from the subtotal to get the invoice total. Finally, the calculated values are formatted and displayed on the form.

If rounding is necessary when the values are displayed, the formatting statements in this application will do the rounding. Note, however, that the values stored in discountAmount and invoiceTotal aren't rounded. To round these values, you would need to use the Round method of the Math class. You often need to do that when you work with values that are going to be stored in a file or database.

You should also realize that this application will work only if the user enters a numeric value into the Subtotal text box. If the user enters any non-numeric characters, an exception will occur when the application tries to convert that value to a decimal value. One way to prevent this type of error is to use the TryParse method you learned about earlier in this chapter. Then, you can use the techniques presented in the next chapter to test if the value the user entered is valid, and you can use the technique presented in chapter 7 to display an error message to the user if the entry is invalid. Chapter 7 also presents some additional techniques you can use to prevent exceptions.

The Invoice Total form

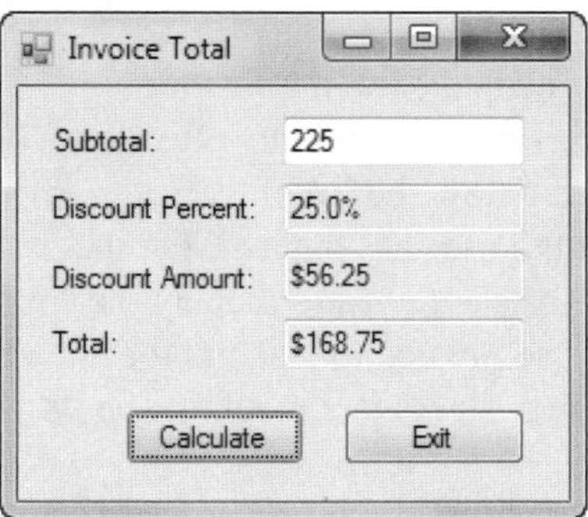

The controls that are referred to in the code

Object type	Name	Description
TextBox	**txtSubtotal**	A text box that accepts a subtotal amount
TextBox	**txtDiscountPercent**	A read-only text box that displays the discount percent
TextBox	**txtDiscountAmount**	A read-only text box that displays the discount amount
TextBox	**txtTotal**	A read-only text box that displays the invoice total
Button	**btnCalculate**	Calculates the discount amount and invoice total when clicked
Button	**btnExit**	Closes the form when clicked

The event handlers for the Invoice Total form

```
Private Sub btnCalculate_Click(sender As Object,
        e As EventArgs) Handles btnCalculate.Click

    Dim subtotal As Decimal = CDec(txtSubtotal.Text)
    Dim discountPercent As Decimal = 0.25D
    Dim discountAmount As Decimal = subtotal * discountPercent
    Dim invoiceTotal As Decimal = subtotal - discountAmount

    txtDiscountPercent.Text = FormatPercent(discountPercent, 1)
    txtDiscountAmount.Text = FormatCurrency(discountAmount)
    txtTotal.Text = FormatCurrency(invoiceTotal)

    txtSubtotal.Select()

End Sub

Private Sub btnExit_Click(sender As Object,
        e As EventArgs) Handles btnExit.Click

    Me.Close()

End Sub
```

Figure 4-20 The basic Invoice Total application

The enhanced Invoice Total application

Figure 4-21 presents an enhanced version of the Invoice Total application that illustrates some of the other skills presented in this chapter. On the left side of the form, a new label and text box have been added below the Enter Subtotal text box. These controls display the last subtotal that the user has entered. On the right side of the form, three pairs of labels and text boxes are used to display the number of invoices that have been entered, a total of the invoice totals, and the invoice average. The form also has a Clear Totals button that clears the totals on the right side of the form so the user can enter another batch of invoices.

The controls that have been added to this form are named with our standard naming conventions, which are based on the names that are used to identify text boxes and labels. In this case, txtEnterSubtotal is used for the text box that lets the user enter a subtotal, txtSubtotal is used for the text box that displays the last subtotal that the user has entered, txtNumberOfInvoices is used for the text box that displays the number of invoices, txtTotalOfInvoices is used for the text box that displays the total of the invoice totals, txtInvoiceAverage is used for the text box that displays the invoice average, and btnClearTotals is used for the Clear Totals button.

In the code for this form, the enhancements are shaded so they're easy to review. This code starts with the declarations of three module-level variables: numberOfInvoices, totalOfInvoices, and invoiceAverage. These are the variables whose values need to be retained from one execution of an event handler to another. Because the default value for each of these variables is zero, no initial value is assigned.

In the event handler for the Click event of the Calculate button, the second shaded line adds rounding to the calculation for the discount amount. That's necessary so only the exact amount of the invoice is added to the total for the invoices. Otherwise, the total for the invoices may become incorrect. Then, the next shaded statement displays the subtotal entered by the user in the Subtotal text box. That way, all of the data for the last invoice is shown in the text boxes on the left side of the form while the user enters the subtotal for the next invoice.

The next set of shaded statements shows how the module-level variables are used after each subtotal entry has been processed. The first three statements add 1 to the number of invoices, add the invoice total to the total of invoices, and calculate the invoice average. Then, the next three shaded lines assign the new values of the module-level variables to the text boxes that will display them. The last shaded line in this event handler assigns an empty string to the Enter Subtotal text box so the user can enter the subtotal for the next invoice.

In the event handler for the Click event of the Clear Totals button, the first three statements reset the module-level variables to zeros so the user can enter the subtotals for another batch of invoices. Then, the next three statements set the text boxes that display these variables to empty strings. The last statement activates the Enter Subtotal text box so the user can start the first entry of another batch of invoices.

The enhanced Invoice Total form

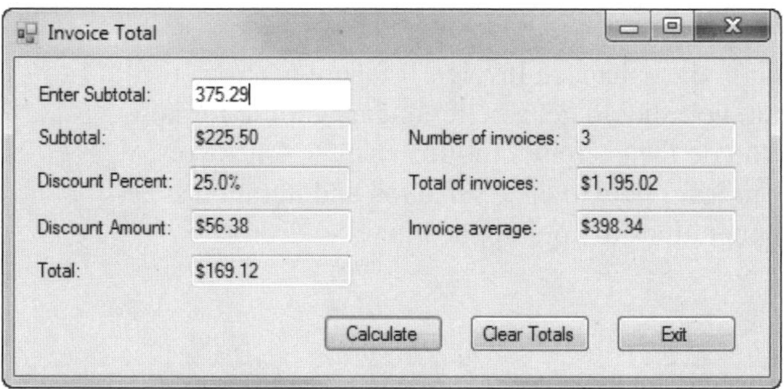

The code for the class variables and two event handlers

```
Dim numberOfInvoices As Integer
Dim totalOfInvoices As Decimal
Dim invoiceAverage As Decimal

Private Sub btnCalculate_Click(sender As Object,
        e As EventArgs) Handles btnCalculate.Click
    Dim subtotal As Decimal = CDec(txtEnterSubtotal.Text)
    Dim discountPercent As Decimal = 0.25D
    Dim discountAmount As Decimal =
        Math.Round(subtotal * discountPercent, 2)
    Dim invoiceTotal As Decimal = subtotal - discountAmount

    txtSubtotal.Text = FormatCurrency(subtotal)
    txtDiscountPercent.Text = FormatPercent(discountPercent, 1)
    txtDiscountAmount.Text = FormatCurrency(discountAmount)
    txtTotal.Text = FormatCurrency(invoiceTotal)

    numberOfInvoices += 1
    totalOfInvoices += invoiceTotal
    invoiceAverage = totalOfInvoices / numberOfInvoices

    txtNumberOfInvoices.Text = numberOfInvoices.ToString
    txtTotalOfInvoices.Text = FormatCurrency(totalOfInvoices)
    txtInvoiceAverage.Text = FormatCurrency(invoiceAverage)

    txtEnterSubtotal.Text = ""
    txtEnterSubtotal.Select()
End Sub

Private Sub btnClearTotals_Click(sender As Object,
        e As EventArgs) Handles btnClearTotals.Click
    numberOfInvoices = 0
    totalOfInvoices = 0
    invoiceAverage = 0

    txtNumberOfInvoices.Text = ""
    txtTotalOfInvoices.Text = ""
    txtInvoiceAverage.Text = ""

    txtEnterSubtotal.Select()
End Sub
```

Figure 4-21 The enhanced Invoice Total application

Perspective

If you understand the code in the enhanced Invoice Total application, you've come a long way. If not, you should get a better understanding for how this application works when you do the exercises for this chapter. Once you understand it, you'll be ready to learn how to code selection and iteration statements so you can add logical operations to your applications.

Terms

built-in data type
bit
byte
integer
Unicode character set
ASCII character set
Boolean value
variable
constant
declare
initialize
literal
camel notation
Pascal notation
arithmetic expression
arithmetic operator
operand
binary operator
unary operator
assignment statement
assignment operator
order of precedence
casting
widening conversion
implicit cast
narrowing conversion
explicit cast
permissive type semantics
strict type semantics
shared method
argument
precision
banker's rounding
string
string literal
null value
empty string
concatenate
append
structure
value type
reference type
function
scope
procedure scope
procedure-level variable
module scope
module-level variable
lifetime
enumeration
member
nullable type
null propagation arithmetic

Exercise 4-1 Modify the Invoice Total application

Open the Invoice Total application

1. Open the application in the C:\VB 2012\Chapter 04\InvoiceTotal directory. This application is almost the same as the one that's presented in figure 4-20, but it uses permissive type semantics and implicit narrowing casts.
2. Test the application with a valid subtotal to verify that the correct discount is being taken. Then, enter a valid subtotal like 225.50 that will yield a discount amount that has more than two decimal places, and make sure that only two decimal places are displayed for the discount amount and total.

Use strict type semantics

3. Stop the test run, and change the type semantics for the project to strict as shown in figure 4-8. Then, review the errors that are now underlined in the code for the Invoice Total form. Note also that both of these errors have a bar under the right character that indicates that you can use the Auto Correction feature to fix them.
4. If necessary, refer back to figure 3-15 to see how the Auto Correction feature works. Then, use it to fix the first error, which will add a CDec function to your code. Also, use this feature to see its suggestion for the second error, but don't take it. Instead, just add a D after the literal to show the compiler that this is a Decimal value. Now, compile and test to see that this code works.
5. Enter "$$1000" for the subtotal and click the Calculate button. This time, an exception should occur, Visual Studio should enter break mode, and the Exception Assistant should display a message that indicates that the input string was not in a correct format. This shows that exceptions still occur, even though you're using strict type semantics.
6. If you like using strict type semantics, turn this option on for all new applications by using the technique in figure 4-8.

Experiment with the code

7. Modify the first statement in the btnCalculate_Click procedure so it uses the Parse method of the Decimal class instead of the CDec function. Then, test the application to verify that it still works the same.
8. Round the values that are stored in the discountAmount and invoiceTotal variables to two decimal places. Then, delete the FormatCurrency functions for these variables and note the errors that this causes. To fix these errors, use the ToString method, not the suggestion from the Auto Correction feature. Then, test the application to make sure that only two decimal places are displayed for the discount amount and total.

Save and close the project

9. Save the solution and close it.

Exercise 4-2 Enhance the Invoice Total application

This exercise will guide you through the process of enhancing the Invoice Total application of exercise 4-1 so it works like the application in figure 4-21. This will give you more practice in developing forms and working with data.

Open the Invoice Total application and enhance the form

1. Open the application in the C:\VB 2012\Chapter 04\InvoiceTotalEnhanced directory.
2. Use the techniques that you learned in chapter 2 to enlarge the form and to add the new controls that are shown in figure 4-21 to the form.
3. Set the properties for each of the controls. You should be able to do this without any guidance, but try to name each control that's going to be referred to by code with the proper prefix followed by the name that identifies it in the form (like txtNumberOfInvoices).

Add the code for the enhancements

4. Switch to the Code Editor and enter the three module-level variables in figure 4-21. These are the variables that will accumulate the data for all the invoices.
5. Enhance the code for the Click event of the Calculate button so it calculates and displays the new data. Try to do this without referring to figure 4-21.
6. Use the techniques you learned in chapter 3 to start the event handler for the Click event of the Clear Totals button. Then, add the code for this event. Here again, try to do this without referring to the code in figure 4-21.
7. Test the application and fix any errors until the application works properly. Be sure that it restarts properly when you click the Clear Totals button and enter another batch of invoices.

Add more controls and code

8. Add three more labels and three more text boxes below the two columns of text boxes and labels on the right side of the form. The three labels should say "Largest invoice", "Smallest invoice", and "Mid point". The text boxes to the right of the labels should display the values for the largest invoice total, the smallest invoice total, and the value that's halfway between these totals.
9. Add the code that makes this work. If you're new to programming, this may challenge you. (Hint: To find the smallest invoice total, use the Math.Min method to compare each invoice total to a variable that contains the smallest invoice total to that point. Then, replace the variable value with the smaller of the two invoice totals. To make this work for the first invoice, you can initialize this variable to a number that will be larger than the largest invoice total, like 9999999.)
10. Test the application and fix any errors until the application works properly. Then, close the project.

5

How to code control structures

In the last chapter, you learned how to write code that works with the most common data types. Now, you'll learn how to code the three types of control structures that are common to all modern programming languages: the selection, case, and iteration structures. When you finish this chapter, you'll be able to write applications that perform a wide range of logical operations.

How to code Boolean expressions

When you code an expression that evaluates to a True or False value, that expression can be called a *Boolean expression*. Because you use Boolean expressions within the control structures you code, you need to learn how to code Boolean expressions before you learn how to code control structures.

How to use the relational operators

Figure 5-1 shows how to use eight *relational operators* to code a Boolean expression. These operators let you compare two operands, as illustrated by the examples in this figure. An operand can be any expression, including a variable, a literal, an arithmetic expression, or a keyword such as Nothing, True, or False.

The first five expressions in this figure use the equal operator (=) to test if the two operands are equal. The first two expressions compare string variables to a literal value and an empty string. The third expression compares a numeric variable to a literal value. The fourth expression compares a Boolean variable to the False value. And the fifth expression compares the value in one variable to the value in another variable.

The next expression uses the not equal operator (<>) to test if a variable is not equal to a string literal. The two expressions after that use the greater than operator (>) to test if a variable is greater than a numeric literal and the less than operator (<) to test if one variable is less than another. The next two expressions are similar, except they use the greater than or equal operator (>=) and less than or equal operator (<=) to compare operands.

As you know, you can assign a null value to a string using the Nothing keyword. You can also use the Nothing keyword to test a string for a null value as shown in the last two examples. Notice here that you can't use the = and <> operators with Nothing. Instead, you have to use the Is and IsNot operators.

If you want to include a Boolean variable in an expression, you often don't need to include the = or <> operator. That's because a Boolean variable evaluates to a Boolean value by definition. So you could code the fourth example like this:

```
isValid
```

When comparing numeric values, you usually compare values with the same data type. However, if you compare different types of numeric values, Visual Basic automatically casts the value with the less precise type to the more precise type. For example, if you compare an Integer value to a Decimal value, the Integer value will be cast to a Decimal value before the comparison is performed.

If you're coming from another programming language such as Java, you may be surprised to find that you can use relational operators on strings, which are actually String objects. This is possible because Visual Basic allows classes and structures to define operators. In this case, since the String class defines the relational operators, you can use these operators on strings.

You can also use relational operators with nullable types. In that case, the result of the Boolean expression can be True, False, or null. The result is null anytime the value of one of the operands is null.

Relational operators

Operator	Name	Description
`=`	Equal to	Returns a True value if the left and right operands are equal.
`<>`	Not equal to	Returns a True value if the left and right operands are not equal.
`>`	Greater than	Returns a True value if the left operand is greater than the right operand.
`<`	Less than	Returns a True value if the left operand is less than the right operand.
`>=`	Greater than or equal to	Returns a True value if the left operand is greater than or equal to the right operand.
`<=`	Less than or equal to	Returns a True value if the left operand is less than or equal to the right operand.
`Is`	Is	Returns a True value if the left operand refers to the same object as the right operand.
`IsNot`	IsNot	Returns a True value if the left operand does not refer to the same object as the right operand.

Examples

```
firstName = "Frank"          ' equal to a string literal
txtYears.Text = ""           ' equal to an empty string

discountPercent = 2.3        ' equal to a numeric literal
isValid = False              ' equal to the False value
code = productCode           ' equal to another variable

lastName <> "Jones"          ' not equal to a string literal

years > 0                    ' greater than a numeric literal
i < months                   ' less than a variable

subtotal >= 500              ' greater than or equal to a numeric literal
quantity <= reorderPoint     ' less than or equal to a variable

message Is Nothing           ' equal to a null value
address IsNot Nothing        ' not equal to a null value
```

Description

- You can use the *relational operators* to create a *Boolean expression* that compares two operands and returns a Boolean value.
- If you compare two numeric operands with different data types, Visual Basic will cast the less precise operand to the type of the more precise operand.
- You can also use the relational operators with nullable types. If the value of a nullable type is null, the result of the Boolean expression is always null rather than True or False.

Figure 5-1 How to use the relational operators

How to use the logical operators

Figure 5-2 shows how to use the *logical operators* to code a compound Boolean expression that consists of two or more Boolean expressions. For example, the first compound expression in this figure uses the And operator. As a result, it evaluates to True if both the expression before the And operator *and* the expression after the And operator evaluate to True. Conversely, the second compound expression uses the Or operator. As a result, it evaluates to True if either the expression before the Or operator *or* the expression after the Or operator evaluates to True.

When you use the And and Or operators, the second expression is evaluated regardless of whether the first expression is True or False. If the first expression in an And operation is False, however, there's usually no need to check the second expression. Similarly, there's usually no need to check the second expression in an Or operation if the first expression is True. To prevent the second expression in an And or Or operation from being evaluated unnecessarily, you can use the AndAlso and OrElse operators. The third and fourth examples illustrate how this works.

For the third example, suppose that the value of subtotal is less than 250. Then, the first expression evaluates to False. That means that the entire expression evaluates to False regardless of the value of the second expression. As a result, the second expression isn't evaluated. Since this is more efficient than always evaluating both expressions, you'll want to use these operators, called *short-circuit operators*, most of the time.

You can also use two or more logical operators in the same expression, as illustrated by the fifth and sixth examples. When you do, you should know that And operations are performed before Or operations. In addition, both arithmetic and relational operations are performed before logical operations. If you need to change this sequence or if there's any doubt about how an expression will be evaluated, you can use parentheses to control or clarify the sequence as shown in the sixth example.

If necessary, you can use the Not operator to reverse the value of an expression as illustrated by the last example. Because this can create code that's difficult to read, however, you should avoid using this operator whenever possible. For example, instead of coding the expression shown in this example, you can code

```
counter + 1 < years
```

This expression returns the same result, but is easier to read.

Like the relational operators, you can also use the logical operators with nullable Boolean variables. When you do that, the result can be True, False, or null as explained in this figure.

Logical operators

Operator	Description
`And`	Returns a True value if both expressions are True. This operator always evaluates both expressions.
`Or`	Returns a True value if either expression is True. This operator always evaluates both expressions.
`AndAlso`	Returns a True value if both expressions are True. This operator only evaluates the second expression if necessary.
`OrElse`	Returns a True value if either expression is True. This operator only evaluates the second expression if necessary.
`Not`	Reverses the value of the expression.

Examples

```
isValid = True And counter + 1 < years
isValid = False Or counter + 1 >= years

subtotal >= 250 AndAlso subtotal < 500
timeInService <= 4 OrElse timeInService >= 12

today > startDate AndAlso today < expirationDate OrElse isValid = True

((thisYTD > lastYTD) OrElse empType = "Part time") AndAlso
    startYear < currentYear

Not (counter + 1 >= years)
```

Description

- You can use the *logical operators* to create Boolean expressions that combine two or more Boolean expressions.
- Since the AndAlso and OrElse operators only evaluate the second expression if necessary, they're sometimes referred to as *short-circuit operators*. These operators are slightly more efficient than the And and Or operators.
- You can also use the logical operators with nullable Boolean variables.
- If a nullable Boolean variable with a value of null is used with the And operator, the result is null unless the value of the other expression in False. In that case the result is False.
- If a nullable Boolean variable with a value of null is used with the Or operator, the result is null unless the value of the other expression in True. In that case, the result is True.
- By default, Not operations are performed first, followed by And operations, and then Or operations. These operations are performed after arithmetic operations and relational operations.
- You can use parentheses to change the sequence in which the operations will be performed or to clarify the sequence of operations.

Figure 5-2 How to use the logical operators

How to code conditional statements

Now that you know how to code Boolean expressions, you're ready to learn how to code conditional statements. These statements include the If statement and the Select Case statement.

How to code If statements

Figure 5-3 shows how to use the *If statement* to control the logic of your programs. This type of statement is the primary logical statement of all programming languages. It is the Visual Basic implementation of a control structure known as the *selection structure* because it lets you select different actions based on the results of Boolean expressions.

In the syntax summary in this figure, the brackets [ ] indicate that a clause is optional, and the ellipsis (...) indicates that the preceding element can be repeated as many times as needed. In other words, this syntax shows that you can code an If clause with or without ElseIf clauses or an Else clause. It also shows that you can code as many ElseIf clauses as you need.

When an If statement is executed, Visual Basic begins by evaluating the Boolean expression in the If clause. If it's True, the statements within this clause are executed and the rest of the clauses in the If statement are skipped. If it's False, Visual Basic evaluates the first ElseIf clause (if there is one). If its Boolean expression is True, the statements within this ElseIf clause are executed and the rest of the If statement is skipped. Otherwise, Visual Basic evaluates the next ElseIf clause. This continues with any remaining ElseIf clauses. Finally, if none of the clauses contains a Boolean expression that evaluates to True, Visual Basic executes the statements in the Else clause. If the statement doesn't include an Else clause, Visual Basic doesn't execute any statements.

When coding If statements, it's a common practice to code one If statement within another If statement. This is known as *nested If statements*. When you code nested If statements, it's a good practice to indent the nested statements and their clauses. This clearly identifies where the nested statement begins and ends. In the last example in this figure, you can see that Visual Basic will execute the nested If statement only if the customer type is "R". Otherwise, it executes the statement in the outer Else clause.

When you code an If statement in Visual Basic, you need to realize that all of the code up to the End If statement is considered a single *block*. If you declare a variable within that block, the variable is available only to the other statements in the block. This is referred to as *block scope*. As a result, if you need to access a variable outside of the If statement, you need to declare it outside the If statement.

The syntax of the If statement

```
If condition Then
    statements
[ElseIf condition Then
    statements] ...
[Else
    statements]
End If
```

An If statement without an ElseIf or Else clause

```
If subtotal >= 100 Then
    discountPercent = .2D
End If
```

An If statement with an Else clause

```
If subtotal >= 100 Then
    discountPercent = .2D
Else
    discountPercent = .1D
End If
```

An If statement with ElseIf clauses

```
If subtotal >= 100 And subtotal < 200 Then
    discountPercent = .2D
ElseIf subtotal >= 200 And subtotal < 300 Then
    discountPercent = .3D
ElseIf subtotal >= 300 Then
    discountPercent = .4D
Else
    discountPercent = .1D
End If
```

Nested If statements

```
If customerType = "R" Then
    If subtotal >= 100 Then         ' start of nested if
        discountPercent = .2D
    Else
        discountPercent = .1D
    End If                          ' end of nested if
Else                                ' customerType isn't "R"
    discountPercent = .4D
End If
```

Description

- An If statement always contains an If clause. In addition, it can contain one or more ElseIf clauses and a final Else clause.
- If you type the If keyword and the condition and press the Enter key, Visual Basic adds the Then and End If keywords. You can also use code snippets to start If statements.
- If you declare a variable within an If statement, the variable has *block scope,* which means that it can only be referred to within the If statement.

Figure 5-3 How to code If statements

How to code Select Case statements

Figure 5-4 shows how to use the *Select Case statement*. This is the Visual Basic implementation of a control structure known as the *case structure*, which lets you code different actions for different cases. The Select Case statement can sometimes be used in place of an If statement with ElseIf clauses.

To code a Select Case statement, you start by coding the Select Case keyword followed by a test expression. After this expression, you code one or more Case clauses that represent the cases that are handled by the Select Case statement. Then, when the expression matches the value specified by a Case clause, the statements in that clause are executed. A Select Case statement can also contain a Case Else clause that identifies the statements that are executed if none of the values specified by the Case clauses matches the test expression.

The first example in this figure shows how to code a Select Case statement that sets the discount percent based on the values in a string variable named customerType. In other words, the test expression is just the variable name. Then, if the customer type is "R", the discount percent is set to .1. If the customer type is "C", the discount percent is set to .2. Otherwise, the discount percent is set to 0.

In the second example, the test expression is an Integer variable named orderQuantity. Then, if orderQuantity has a value of 1 or 2, discountPercent is set to zero. If the quantity is from 3 to 9, the discount is .1. If the quantity is from 10 to 24, the discount is .2. If the quantity is greater than or equal to 25, the discount is .3. And if none of these conditions is True (Else), the discount is zero. Note the variety of ways that these values can be specified in a Select Case statement using the To and Is keywords. This example also illustrates the use of a comment to describe the condition under which the Else clause is executed.

When you use a Select Case statement, you can code If statements within the cases of the statement. You can also code Select Case statements within the cases of another Select Case statement. In general, when you use Select Case statements, your goal is to make your code easier to read and understand.

Like If statements, all of the variables that are declared within a Select Case statement have block scope. So if you need to access any of these variables outside of the Select Case statement, you need to declare them outside of the statement.

The syntax of the Select Case statement

```
Select Case testexpression
    [Case expressionlist
        statements] ...
    [Case Else
        statements]
End Select
```

A Select Case statement based on customer type codes

```
Select Case customerType
    Case "R"
        discountPercent = .1D
    Case "C"
        discountPercent = .2D
    Case Else
        discountPercent = 0
End Select
```

A Select Case statement based on order quantities

```
Select Case orderQuantity
    Case 1, 2
        discountPercent = 0D
    Case 3 To 9
        discountPercent = .1D
    Case 10 To 24
        discountPercent = .2D
    Case Is >= 25
        discountPercent = .3D
    Case Else                           ' orderQuantity < 1
        discountPercent = 0
End Select
```

Keywords that you can use in the expression list

Keyword	Meaning
`To`	Specifies a range of values.
`Is`	Precedes a conditional expression.

Description

- The Select Case statement is the Visual Basic implementation of the *case structure*.
- After evaluating the test expression, the Select Case statement transfers control to the case that matches the value in the expression. If none of the cases matches, the Case Else clause is executed.
- If you type the Select Case keywords and the test expression and press the Enter key, Visual Basic adds the End Select keywords. You can also use code snippets to start Select Case statements.
- If you declare a variable within a Select Case statement, the variable has block scope so you can only refer to it within that statement.
- You can code If statements within the cases of a Select Case statement. You can also code Select Case statements within the cases of a Select Case statement.

Figure 5-4 How to code Select Case statements

An enhanced version of the Invoice Total application

To give you a better idea of how If statements can be used, figure 5-5 presents an enhanced version of the Invoice Total application that was presented in chapter 4. This time, the form for the application provides for two user entries: customer type and subtotal.

If you look at the event handler in this figure, you can see that the discount percent is determined by nested If statements. If, for example, the customer type is “R” and the subtotal is greater than or equal to 250, the discount percent is .25. Or, if the customer type is “C” and the subtotal is less than 250, the discount percent is .2.

When you code If statements like this, it’s a good practice to code the conditions in a logical order. For instance, the expressions in the nested If statement for customer type “R” go from a subtotal that’s less than 100, to a subtotal that’s greater than or equal to 100 and less than 250, to a subtotal that’s greater than or equal to 250. That covers all of the possible subtotals from the smallest to the largest. Although you could code these conditions in other sequences, that would make it harder to tell whether all possibilities have been covered.

For efficiency, it’s also good to code the conditions from the one that occurs the most to the one that occurs the least. If, for example, most customers are type “R”, that condition should be treated first so it will be processed first. In some cases, though, the most efficient sequence isn’t logical so you have to decide whether it’s worth sacrificing the readability of the code for efficiency. Typically, the performance gain isn’t significant, so you may as well code the statements in the most logical sequence.

If you prefer, you can use a Select Case statement that contains If statements to get the same result as the nested If statements in this figure. That might even make the code easier to read. On the other hand, if you use indentation properly, an extensive series of nested If statements should be easy to read and understand.

When you enter If and Select Case statements into the Code Editor, remember that you can use code snippets to enter the basic structures that you need. Then, you just need to replace the highlighted portions of code with your own code, and you can press the Tab key to move from one highlight to another. To refresh your memory about using code snippets, you can refer back to figure 3-13.

Incidentally, the Option Strict option is set to On for this project and all of the remaining projects that are presented in this book. That means that these projects use strict type semantics. That’s why the value in the subtotal text box has to be cast to the subtotal variable (in this case, by using the CDec function). And that’s why the numeric literals with decimal values that are assigned to Decimal variables have to be followed by the letter D.

The enhanced Invoice Total form

The event handler for the Click event of the Calculate button

```
Private Sub btnCalculate_Click(sender As Object,
        e As EventArgs) Handles btnCalculate.Click

    Dim subtotal As Decimal = CDec(txtSubtotal.Text)
    Dim discountPercent As Decimal

    If txtCustomerType.Text = "R" Then
        If subtotal < 100 Then
            discountPercent = 0
        ElseIf subtotal >= 100 AndAlso subtotal < 250 Then
            discountPercent = 0.1D
        ElseIf subtotal >= 250 Then
            discountPercent = 0.25D
        End If
    ElseIf txtCustomerType.Text = "C" Then
        If subtotal < 250 Then
            discountPercent = 0.2D
        Else
            discountPercent = 0.3D
        End If
    Else
        discountPercent = 0.4D
    End If

    Dim discountAmount As Decimal = subtotal * discountPercent
    Dim invoiceTotal As Decimal = subtotal - discountAmount

    txtDiscountPercent.Text = FormatPercent(discountPercent, 1)
    txtDiscountAmount.Text = FormatCurrency(discountAmount)
    txtTotal.Text = FormatCurrency(invoiceTotal)

    txtCustomerType.Select()

End Sub
```

Figure 5-5 An enhanced version of the Invoice Total application

How to code loops

Visual Basic provides several statements for controlling the execution of loops. These statements provide the Visual Basic implementations of the *iteration structure*, which is a structure that repeatedly executes the same series of statements.

How to code For loops

Figure 5-6 presents the syntax of the *For...Next statement* (or just *For statement*), which is used to implement a *For loop*. This statement lets you repeat a series of statements for each value of a variable that's called a *counter*. By default, the value of the counter is incremented by one each time the loop is completed. But if you want to increment the variable by a value other than one, you can include the Step clause in this statement.

The first example in this figure shows a For loop that adds the numbers zero through four to a sum variable. Here, the counter is declared outside the For loop. Then, the For loop says to increase the counter by one each time the loop is executed starting with a value of 0 and continuing until the counter is equal to 4. Then, the loop ends, and the program continues with the first statement after the loop.

The second and third examples show how the counter can be declared by the For statement and also how the Step clause can be used. In the second example, a positive step value causes the counter to be increased by 2 each time through the loop. In the third example, a negative step value causes the counter to be decreased by 10 each time through the loop.

Note that the Next clause in the first three examples doesn't include the name of the counter. That's because the counter name is optional. In the fourth example, though, the counter name is coded in the Next clause. In some cases, such as when you nest For loops, you may want to include the counter name on the Next clause for clarity. Incidentally, all of these examples use i as the counter name, which is a common coding practice, because counters are also commonly referred to as *indexes*.

The last example in this figure shows how you can use a For statement to calculate the future value of an investment based on the monthly investment amount, the monthly interest rate, and the number of months that the investments will be made. For each iteration of the loop, the monthly investment amount is added to the future value variable, which is then multiplied by one plus the monthly interest rate. If the math within this loop isn't clear to you right now, it will be explained later in this chapter when the Future Value application is presented.

The syntax of the For...Next statement

```
For counter [As type] = start To end [Step step]
    statements
Next [counter]
```

A For loop that adds the numbers 0 through 4

```
Dim sum As Integer                  ' the default starting value is zero
Dim i As Integer
For i = 0 To 4
    sum += i
Next
```

A For loop that adds the numbers 2, 4, 6, 8, 10, and 12

```
Dim sum As Integer                  ' the default starting value is zero
For i As Integer = 2 To 12 Step 2
    sum += i
Next
```

A For loop that adds the squares of 25, 15, 5, -5, and -15

```
Dim sum As Integer                  ' The default starting value is zero
Dim iSquared As Integer
For i As Integer = 25 To -15 Step -10
    iSquared = i ^ 2
    sum += iSquared
Next
```

A For loop that calculates a future value

```
Dim monthlyInvestment As Decimal = 100
Dim monthlyInterestRate As Decimal = .01D
Dim months As Integer = 120
Dim futureValue As Decimal          ' the default starting value is zero
For i As Integer = 1 To months
    futureValue = (futureValue + monthlyInvestment) *
                  (1 + monthlyInterestRate)
Next i                              ' the i is optional
```

Description

- The For...Next statement is used to implement a *For loop*. You typically use a For loop to repeat a series of statements for each value of a *counter* until the counter reaches a specific value.
- At the start of the For statement, you name the counter, declare the counter if necessary, assign a starting value to the counter, specify the last counter value that the loop should use, and optionally specify the value that the counter should be incremented by. Then, you code the statements that should be executed each time through the loop and end the loop with a Next clause.
- If necessary, you can nest For loops. This is often done when you're working with arrays, which you'll learn more about in chapter 8.
- If you declare a variable within a For loop, the variable has block scope so you can only refer to it within the loop.

Figure 5-6 How to code For loops

How to code Do loops

Figure 5-7 shows how you can use *Do statements* to create *Do loops* that perform the same types of repetitive processing as For loops. However, if you compare the Do loops in this figure with the For loop in the last example of figure 5-6, you'll see that a For loop generally leads to code that's easier to understand. On the other hand, Do loops give you more coding flexibility.

To start, this figure shows that there are two versions of the Do statement. In the first version, the condition is tested *before* the series of statements is executed. In the second version, the condition is tested *after* the series of statements is executed. Testing last means that the loop will always be executed at least one time.

In the examples, you can see how you can use both versions of this statement to calculate a future value like the last example in the previous figure. With Do loops, though, you must declare the i variable before the Do statement because the Do statement doesn't provide for that. You must also assign a value to the variable unless you want the default value of 0 to be used. And within the loop, you must include a statement that increments the variable like this:

```
i += 1
```

Here, a value of 1 is added to the current value of the variable each time through the loop. Then, when the value of this variable becomes greater than the value of the months variable, the Do loop ends.

When you code For loops and Do loops, you should realize that it's possible to code an *infinite loop*, which is a loop that never ends. That can happen, for example, if you forget to code a statement that increments the counter variable for a Do Until loop so the condition never becomes True. Then, you can use the Break All command in the Standard toolbar to enter break mode and debug the program as shown later in this chapter. Or, you can use the Stop Debugging command to end the application.

The syntax of the Do loop with the test first

```
Do [{While|Until} condition]
    statements
Loop
```

A Do loop with the test first that calculates future value

```
Dim monthlyInvestment As Decimal = 100
Dim monthlyInterestRate As Decimal = .01D
Dim months As Integer = 120
Dim futureValue As Decimal
Dim i As Integer = 1
Do Until i > months
    futureValue = (futureValue + monthlyInvestment) *
                  (1 + monthlyInterestRate)
    i += 1
Loop
```

The syntax of the Do loop with the test last

```
Do
    statements
Loop [{While|Until} condition]
```

A Do loop with the test last that calculates future value

```
Dim monthlyInvestment As Decimal = 100
Dim monthlyInterestRate As Decimal = .01D
Dim months As Integer = 120
Dim futureValue As Decimal
Dim i As Integer = 1
Do
    futureValue = (futureValue + monthlyInvestment) *
                  (1 + monthlyInterestRate)
    i += 1
Loop While i <= months
```

Description

- The Do statement is used to implement a *Do loop*. A Do loop lets you repeat a series of statements as long as a condition is True (While) or until a condition becomes True (Until). You can test the condition either before or after the statements are performed.
- You can use Do loops to perform the same types of repetitive processing that you do with For loops. Although For loops typically lead to simpler code, Do loops give you more coding flexibility.
- If you declare a variable within a Do loop, it has block scope so you can only refer to it within that loop.

Note

- You can also code a While...End While statement to do this type of processing. This statement isn't presented in this book, though, because the Do While statement is easier to use.

Figure 5-7 How to code Do loops

How to use Exit and Continue statements

In most applications, the statements within a loop are executed in the order that they're coded, and the loop ends when the counter reaches a specific value. Occasionally, though, you may need to use the Exit statement to exit from a loop prematurely or the Continue statement to go to the start of a loop before all of the statements in the loop have been executed. The use of these statements is illustrated in figure 5-8.

The first example in this figure shows how the Exit statement works. Here, a For loop calculates a future value as described in figure 5-6. But if the future value becomes greater than 1,000,000, this loop assigns a string literal to the message variable, and it executes an Exit statement to end the loop.

The second example shows how to use the Continue statement to return to the start of a loop before all of the statements in the loop have been executed. Then, when control is transferred to the start of the loop, the expressions that control the loop's operation are executed again. As a result, this causes the counter variable to be incremented.

Note that the keywords Exit and Continue must be followed by keywords that indicate what type of loop they're being used in. For instance, you use the Exit For and Continue For statements within For loops, and you use the Exit Do and Continue Do statements within Do loops. The Exit statement can also be used to exit from other types of structures like Sub procedures and Function procedures, in which case you use the Exit Sub and Exit Function statements.

A loop with an Exit statement

```
Dim message As String = Nothing
Dim monthlyInvestment As Decimal = 100
Dim monthlyInterestRate As Decimal = .01D
Dim months As Integer = 120
Dim futureValue As Decimal
For i As Integer = 1 To months
    futureValue = (futureValue + monthlyInvestment) *
                  (1 + monthlyInterestRate)
    If futureValue > 1000000 Then
        message = "Future value is too large."
        Exit For                                    ' the For loop ends
    End If
Next
```

A loop with a Continue statement

```
Dim sumNumbers as Integer
Dim sumBigNumbers As Integer
For i as Integer = 1 To 6 <-----------+
    sumNumbers += i                   |
    If i < 4 Then                     |
        Continue For -----------------+
    End If
    sumBigNumbers += i
Next
```

Description

- You can code an Exit For or Exit Do statement to exit from a For loop or a Do loop.
- You can code a Continue For or Continue Do statement to jump to the start of a For or Do loop.
- You can use other forms of Exit statements to exit from other types of structures. For instance, you can use the Exit Sub statement to exit from a Sub procedure.

Figure 5-8 How to use Exit and Continue statements

Debugging techniques for programs with loops

When you code programs that use loops, debugging often becomes more difficult because it's sometimes hard to tell how the loop is operating. As a result, you may want to use the debugging techniques that are summarized in figure 5-9. These techniques let you stop the execution of a program and enter break mode when a loop starts. Then, you can observe the operation of the loop one statement at a time.

To stop the execution of a program and enter break mode, you set a *breakpoint*. To do that, you can click the *margin indicator bar* at the left side of the Code Editor window. The breakpoint is then marked by a red dot. Later, when the application is run, execution will stop just prior to the statement at the breakpoint.

Once in break mode, a yellow arrow marks the next statement that will be executed, which is called the *execution point*. At this point, you can use the debugging windows to display the current values of the variables used by the loop and to watch how these variables change each time through the loop. For example, you can use the Locals window to display the current values of the variables within the scope of the current procedure. If this window isn't displayed by default, you can display it by selecting the Locals item from the Windows submenu of the Debug menu.

While in break mode, you can also *step through* the statements in the loop one statement at a time. To do that, you repeatedly press the F11 key or click the Step Into button on the Standard toolbar. This lets you observe exactly how and when the variable values change as the loop executes. Once you understand how the loop works, you can remove the breakpoint and press the F5 key to continue normal execution.

Of course, these techniques are also useful for debugging problems that don't involve loops. If, for example, you can't figure out what's wrong with a complex set of nested If statements, you can set a breakpoint at the start of the statement. Then, when the program enters break mode, you can step through the clauses in the statement to see exactly how the expressions are being evaluated.

A For loop with a breakpoint and an execution point

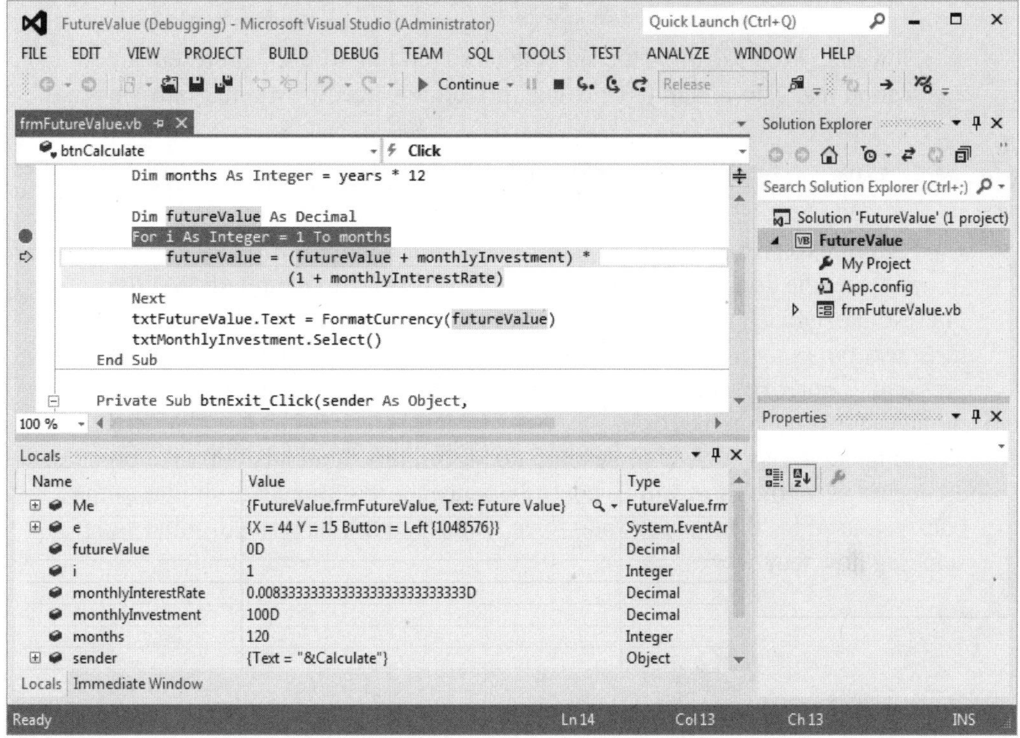

How to set and clear breakpoints

- To set a breakpoint, click in the *margin indicator bar* to the left of a statement. Or, press the F9 key to set a breakpoint at the cursor insertion point. Then, a red dot will mark the breakpoint.
- To remove a breakpoint, use either technique for setting a breakpoint. To remove all breakpoints at once, use the Delete All Breakpoints command in the Debug menu.

How to work in break mode

- In break mode, a yellow arrowhead marks the current *execution point*, which points to the next statement that will be executed.
- To *step through* your code one statement at a time, click the Step Into button on the Standard toolbar, or press the F11 key.
- To continue normal processing until the next breakpoint is reached, press the F5 key.

Description

- When you set a *breakpoint* at a specific statement, the program stops before executing that statement and enters break mode. Then, you can step through the execution of the program one statement at a time.
- In break mode, the Locals window displays the current values of the variables in the scope of the current procedure. If this window isn't displayed, you can display it by selecting the Locals item from the Windows submenu of the Debug menu.

Figure 5-9 Debugging techniques for programs with loops

The Future Value application

Now that you've learned the statements for coding loops, I'll present a new application that uses a loop to calculate the future value of a monthly investment.

The design and property settings for the form

Figure 5-10 presents the design for the Future Value form. To calculate a future value, the user must enter the monthly investment amount, the yearly interest rate, and the number of years the investment will be made into the three text boxes on the form. Then, when the user clicks the Calculate button or presses the Enter key, the application calculates the future value and displays it in the last text box on the form.

To make it easy for you to develop this form, this figure also lists the property settings for the form and its controls. Since these settings are similar to the ones you used for the Invoice Total form, you shouldn't have any trouble understanding how they work.

The Future Value form

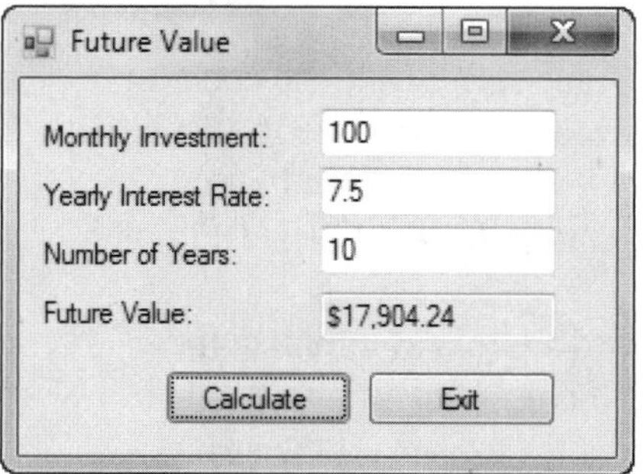

The property settings for the form

Default name	Property	Setting
Form1	Text	Future Value
	AcceptButton	btnCalculate
	CancelButton	btnExit

The property settings for the controls

Default name	Property	Setting
Label1	Text	Monthly Investment:
Label2	Text	Yearly Interest Rate:
Label3	Text	Number of Years:
Label4	Text	Future Value:
TextBox1	Name	txtMonthlyInvestment
TextBox2	Name	txtInterestRate
TextBox3	Name	txtYears
TextBox4	Name ReadOnly TabStop	txtFutureValue True False
Button1	Name Text	btnCalculate &Calculate
Button2	Name Text	btnExit E&xit

Additional property settings

- The TextAlign property of each of the labels is set to MiddleLeft.
- The TabIndex properties of the controls are set so the focus moves from top to bottom and left to right.

Figure 5-10 The form design and property settings for the Future Value application

The code for the form

Figure 5-11 presents the code for the Future Value form. Like the code for the Invoice Total form, this code consists of two event handlers: one for the Click event of the Calculate button and one for the Click event of the Exit button. Here, most of the processing occurs in the event handler for the Click event of the Calculate button.

The first three statements in this event handler declare and initialize the variables that will be used to store the values that the user enters into the three text boxes. Here, the CDec and CInt functions are used to convert the string values that are returned from the Text property of the text boxes to the appropriate numeric data types.

The next two statements perform calculations that convert the yearly values entered by the user to monthly values. That way, all of the variables used in the future value calculation will be in terms of months. The first statement divides the yearly interest rate by 12 to get a monthly interest rate, and then divides that result by 100 to convert the number to a percentage. The second statement converts the number of years to months by multiplying the years by 12.

The next group of statements uses a For loop to calculate a new future value for each month of the investment. Here, the variable that stores the future value is declared before the loop so it can be used after the loop finishes its processing. Then, within the loop, the single assignment statement that calculates the future value is executed once for each month.

Within the loop, the arithmetic expression adds the monthly investment amount to the future value, which has an initial value of zero. Then, the expression multiplies that sum by 1 plus the monthly interest rate. If, for example, the monthly investment amount is $100 and the monthly interest rate is 1% (or .01), the future value is $101 after the expression is executed the first time through the loop:

```
(0 + 100) * (1 + .01) = 100 * 1.01 = 101
```

And the future value is $203.01 after the expression is executed the second time:

```
(101 + 100) * (1 + .01) = 201 * 1.01 = 203.01
```

Continue this process for as many months as the user indicates, and the future value will contain the correct result for a series of equal monthly investments.

After the loop ends, the FormatCurrency function is used to format the future value and the formatted value is assigned to the future value text box so it will be displayed on the form. The last statement uses the Select method to move the focus to the monthly investment text box in preparation for the next series of calculations.

To keep this program simple, it doesn't validate the data that's entered by the user. As a result, an exception will occur if the user enters nonnumeric data in one of the text boxes. In chapter 7, you'll learn how to add data validation to this program to prevent exceptions like this.

The code for the event handlers in the Future Value application

```
Private Sub btnCalculate_Click(sender As Object,
        e As EventArgs) Handles btnCalculate.Click

    Dim monthlyInvestment As Decimal = CDec(txtMonthlyInvestment.Text)
    Dim yearlyInterestRate As Decimal = CDec(txtInterestRate.Text)
    Dim years As Integer = CInt(txtYears.Text)

    Dim monthlyInterestRate As Decimal = yearlyInterestRate / 12 / 100
    Dim months As Integer = years * 12

    Dim futureValue As Decimal
    For i As Integer = 1 To months
        futureValue = (futureValue + monthlyInvestment) *
                      (1 + monthlyInterestRate)
    Next

    txtFutureValue.Text = FormatCurrency(futureValue)
    txtMonthlyInvestment.Select()

End Sub

Private Sub btnExit_Click(sender As Object,
        e As EventArgs) Handles btnExit.Click

    Me.Close()

End Sub
```

Description

- This application uses a For loop to calculate the future value of a monthly investment amount. For this calculation to work correctly, all of the variables that it uses must be converted to the same time period. In this code, that time period is months.
- Each time through the For loop, the assignment statement adds the monthly investment amount to the future value, which starts at zero. Then, this sum is multiplied by 1 plus the monthly interest rate. The result is stored in the futureValue variable so it can be used the next time through the loop.
- Since this application doesn't provide data validation, the user will be able to enter invalid data, which will cause an exception to occur.

Figure 5-11 The code for the Future Value application

Perspective

Now that you've finished this chapter, you should know how to code If statements, Select Case statements, For statements, and Do statements. These are the Visual Basic statements that implement the selection, case, and iteration structures, and they provide the logic of an application. Once you master them, you'll be able to develop significant Visual Basic applications.

Terms

Boolean expression
relational operator
logical operator
short-circuit operator
If statement
selection structure
block scope
nested If statement
Select Case statement
case structure
iteration structure
For...Next statement
For statement
For loop
counter
index
Do statement
Do loop
infinite loop
breakpoint
margin indicator bar
execution point
step through

Exercise 5-1 Enhance the Invoice Total application

In this exercise, you'll use If and Select Case statements to determine the discount percent for the Invoice Total application that's in figure 5-5.

Open the application and change the If statement

1. Open the application that's in the C:\VB 2012\Chapter 05\InvoiceTotal directory. This is the application that's in figure 5-5.
2. Change the If statement so customers of type "R" with a subtotal that is greater than or equal to $250 but less than $500 get a 25% discount and those with a subtotal of $500 or more get a 30% discount. Next, change the If statement so customers of type "C" always get a 20% discount. Then, test the application to make sure this works.
3. Add another customer type to the If statement so customers of type "T" get a 40% discount for subtotals of less than $500, and a 50% discount for subtotals of $500 or more. Try using a code snippet to add an If...Else structure within the ElseIf clause for the customers of type "T". Also, make sure that customer types that aren't "R", "C", or "T" get a 10% discount. Then, test the application.

4. Test the application again, but use lowercase letters for the customer types. Note that these letters aren't evaluated as capital letters. Now, modify the code so the users can enter either capital or lowercase letters for the customer types. Then, test the application to make sure this works correctly.

Use a Select Case statement with If statements to get the same results

5. Use a code snippet to enter the start of a Select Case statement right after the If statement. Next, enhance this code so the Select Case statement provides the structure for handling the three cases for customer types: R, C, and T (as well as r, c, and t). Then, within each of these cases, copy the related code from the If statement above to provide for the discounts that are based on subtotal variations. In other words, the If statements will be nested within the cases.
6. Comment out the entire If statement above the Select Case statement. Then, test to make sure that this works correctly. Is this code easier to read and understand?
7. When you're through experimenting, close the application.

Exercise 5-2 Develop the Future Value application

In this exercise, you'll develop and test the Future Value application that was presented in this chapter. You'll also step through its loop.

Develop the form, write the code, and test the application

1. Open the New Project dialog box by selecting the File→New Project command. Then, enter "FutureValue" for the name of the project, enter "C:\VB 2012\Chapter 05" for the location, and click the OK button.
2. Add the controls to the form and set the properties of the form and its controls as shown in figure 5-10. Then, generate the event handlers for the two Click events, and add the code for these handlers. If necessary, you can refer to the code in figure 5-11, but try to write the code without doing that. Also, use a code snippet to start the For loop for the future value calculation.
3. Test the application by entering valid data in each of the three text boxes. To start, enter simple values like $100 for the monthly investment, 12% for the yearly interest rate (which is 1% per month), and 1 for the number of years. (The result should be $1,280.93).
4. After you're sure that the application works for valid data, test it with nonnumeric entries and with large values like 100 for the interest rate and 1000 for the number of years. In either case, the application will end with a runtime error, which you'll learn how to prevent in chapter 7. Then, stop the debugging.

Set breakpoints and step through the loop

5. In the Code Editor, set a breakpoint at the For statement by clicking in the Margin Indicator Bar to the left of the statement as shown in figure 5-9. A red dot will indicate that you have set the breakpoint.
6. Run the application, and enter 100 as the monthly investment, 12 as the yearly interest rate, and 1 as the number of years. Then, click the Calculate button. This will cause the program to enter break mode. If the Locals window isn't displayed, use the Debug menu to display it.
7. Press F11 to step through the loop. As you do this, the Locals window will display the values for i, futureValue, monthlyInvestment, and monthlyInterestRate. That way, you'll be able to see exactly how these values change as the loop is executed.
8. Press F11 to continue stepping through the application or press F5 to run the application until another breakpoint is reached.
9. Remove the old breakpoint and set a new breakpoint on the statement within the For loop. Then, run the application and note that the new breakpoint causes the application to enter break mode for each iteration of the loop. As a result, you can press F5 to move from one iteration to the next.
10. When you're through experimenting, remove the breakpoint.

Change the For loop to a Do loop and continue experimenting

11. Right below the For loop, use a code snippet to start a Do loop that will replace the For loop. Then, finish the Do loop, add any other statements that are required outside of the Do loop, comment out the For loop, and test this change.
12. Add an If statement and an Exit statement to the Do loop that exits from the loop when future value is greater than $1000. Then, test this change.
13. Change the Exit statement to a Continue statement so the loop will continue even though future value is greater than $1000. In other words, the loop will run to completion because the If statement doesn't do anything. Then, test this change. Note, however, that if the If statement precedes the statement that increments the counter, you'll be caught in an infinite loop.
14. When you're through experimenting, close the project.

6

How to code procedures and event handlers

So far, you've been writing procedures called event handlers for the Click events of button controls. Now, in this chapter, you'll learn how to code procedures that can be called from other procedures. That will help you logically divide the code for an application into manageable parts. You'll also learn how to code event handlers for events other than the Click event.

How to code and call procedures

In chapter 3, you learned how to code procedures that are executed automatically when a Click event occurs. Now, you'll learn how to code procedures that you call explicitly from other procedures in the application.

How to code Sub procedures

Figure 6-1 shows how to code a *Sub procedure*. To start, you code an *access modifier* that indicates whether the procedure can be called from other classes. If you use the Private access modifier, the procedure can only be called from within the class where it's coded. But if you need to call the procedure from another class, you can use the Public access modifier.

After the Sub keyword, you code the name of the procedure. In general, this name should indicate the action that the procedure performs, and a common coding convention is to start each procedure name with a verb. You can see how this convention is used in the procedure names in this figure: DisableButtons, GetDiscountPercent, and CalculateFutureValue.

After the procedure name, you code a set of parentheses. Within the parentheses, you declare the *parameters* that are required by the procedure. This is known as the *parameter list*. Later, when you call the procedure, you pass arguments that correspond to these parameters. You'll learn more about that in the next figure.

If a procedure doesn't require any parameters, you can code an empty set of parentheses as shown in the first example in this figure. Here, a procedure named DisableButtons simply assigns a False value to the Enabled properties of two buttons.

In contrast, if a procedure requires parameters, you code them within the parentheses as shown in the second and third examples. Here, the second procedure requires subtotal and discount percent parameters. And the third procedure requires monthly investment, monthly interest rate, months, and future value parameters.

When you code the name and parameter list of a procedure, you form the *signature* of the procedure, which must be unique for that class. Later in this book, you'll learn how to code two or more procedures with the same name but with different parameters, which means they don't have the same signature.

For each parameter in the list, you can code ByVal or ByRef to indicate whether the parameter will be passed by value or by reference. You'll learn more about that in figure 6-3. For now, just realize that ByVal is the default.

You also need to code an As clause for each parameter that indicates the data type for the parameter. For instance, both parameters in the second example in this figure are passed with the Decimal type. Note, however, that the first parameter is passed by value but the second parameter is passed by reference. The first three parameters in the third example are also passed by value, but the ByVal keyword has been omitted from these parameters.

Within the body of the Sub procedure, you code the statements that use the arguments that are passed to it and do the processing that's required. As you

The basic syntax for a Sub procedure

```
[Private|Public] Sub ProcedureName[(parameterlist)]
    statements
   [Exit Sub]
   [statements]
End Sub
```

The basic syntax for each parameter in a parameter list

```
[ByVal|ByRef] variableName As type
```

A procedure with no parameters

```
Private Sub DisableButtons()
    btnCalculate.Enabled = False
    btnExit.Enabled = False
End Sub
```

A procedure with two parameters that uses ByVal and ByRef

```
Private Sub GetDiscountPercent(ByVal subtotal As Decimal,
        ByRef discountPercent As Decimal)
    If subtotal >= 500 Then
        discountPercent = .2D
    Else
        discountPercent = .1D
    End If
End Sub
```

A procedure with four parameters that omits ByVal

```
Private Sub CalculateFutureValue(monthlyInvestment As Decimal,
        monthlyInterestRate As Decimal, months As Integer,
        ByRef futureValue As Decimal)
    For i As Integer = 1 To months
        futureValue = (futureValue + monthlyInvestment) *
                      (1 + monthlyInterestRate)
    Next
End Sub
```

Description

- A *Sub procedure* can be *called* by another procedure. A Sub procedure executes one or more statements, but doesn't return any data to the *calling procedure*.
- To allow other classes to access a *procedure*, use the Public *access modifier*. To prevent other classes from accessing a procedure, use the Private modifier.
- Within the parentheses of a procedure declaration, you can code a *parameter list* that contains one or more *parameters*, with the parameters separated by commas. For each parameter, you must provide a name and a data type.
- The procedure name plus the parameter list form the *signature* of the procedure, which must be unique.

Naming recommendations for procedures

- Each procedure name should start with a verb and indicate what the procedure does.
- Each word in a procedure name should start with a capital letter.

Figure 6-1 How to code Sub procedures

will see, when you change the value of an argument that has been passed by reference, you also change the data in the *calling procedure*. Then, when the last statement in the *called procedure* is executed, control is returned to the calling procedure. However, if you need to exit from the procedure before the last statement, you can code the Exit Sub statement.

Incidentally, Visual Studio doesn't provide an easy way to start the code for a new procedure. So you just start the procedure by typing the code into the class and using the IntelliSense feature whenever it's available.

How to call Sub procedures

To *call* a Sub procedure, you use the Call statement as shown in figure 6-2. Here, the syntax shows that the statement starts with an optional Call keyword, followed by the procedure name. In general, we recommend that you omit the Call keyword. Also, if the procedure that you're calling is in the same class as the Call statement, we recommend that you prefix the procedure name with Me to indicate that the called procedure is in the same class.

If the procedure requires *arguments*, you code the *argument list* within parentheses right after the procedure name. Otherwise, you code an empty set of parentheses.

Before I go on, you should realize that the terms *parameter* and *argument* are often used interchangeably. In this book, however, we'll use the term *parameter* to refer to the variables of a procedure declaration, and we'll use the term *argument* to refer to the values that are passed to a procedure.

When you code a Call statement, you typically code the arguments in the same sequence that's used by the parameter list in the called procedure. This is called *passing arguments by position*. You can also pass arguments by name, as you'll learn later in this chapter.

When you pass arguments, the data types of those arguments must be compatible with the data types of the corresponding parameters in the called procedure. In fact, it's a good coding practice to pass arguments that have the *same* data types as the parameters in the called procedure. Note, however, that the argument names don't have to be the same as the parameter names. But this is a common practice that makes code easier to read and write.

The three examples in this figure show how you would call the three procedures in figure 6-1. The first example calls the DisableButtons procedure with no arguments. The second example calls the GetDiscountPercent procedure and passes it two arguments. And the third example calls the CalculateFutureValue procedure and passes it four arguments. In all of these examples, the arguments have the same names and data types as the corresponding parameters presented in figure 6-1.

When you call a procedure in Visual Studio, IntelliSense helps you enter the name and arguments, as shown in this figure. Here, the CalculateFutureValue procedure has already been entered, so it appears in the drop-down list of procedures that are available from the current form (Me). Then, when you select the CalculateFutureValue procedure, its signature is shown. That makes it easy for you to enter the arguments in the right sequence with the right type.

The syntax for calling a Sub procedure

```
[Call] [Me.]ProcedureName([argumentlist])
```

A statement that calls a Sub procedure that has no parameters

```
Me.DisableButtons()
```

A statement that passes two arguments

```
Me.GetDiscountPercent(subtotal, discountPercent)
```

A statement that passes four arguments

```
Me.CalculateFutureValue(monthlyInvestment, monthlyInterestRate,
                        months, futureValue)
```

The IntelliSense feature for calling a procedure

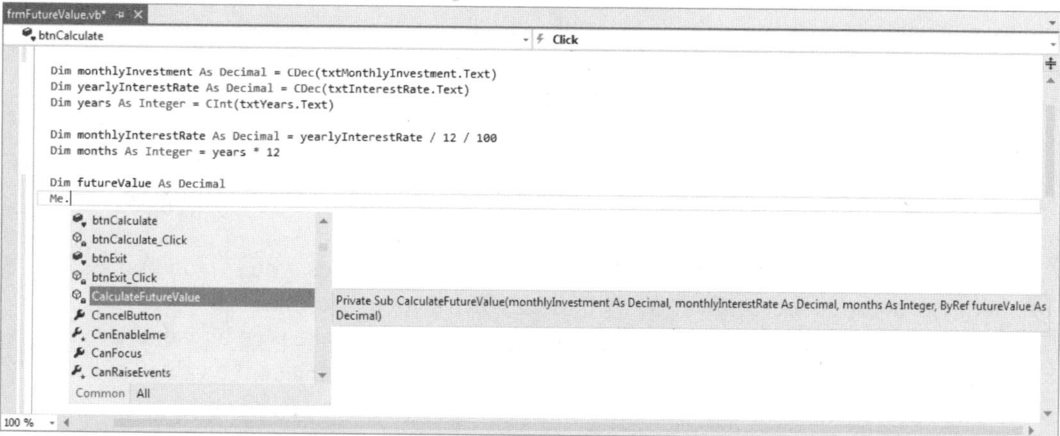

Description

- When you *call* a procedure, you code an *argument list* with the *arguments* that are passed to the procedure. You can pass arguments by position or by name. See figure 6-5 for more information on passing arguments by name.
- When you *pass arguments by position*, the arguments must be in the same order as the parameters in the parameter list defined by the procedure.
- The arguments you pass to a procedure must have data types that are compatible with their corresponding parameters. However, the names of the arguments don't need to match the names of the parameters.
- When you call a procedure, Visual Studio's IntelliSense feature helps you enter the name of the procedure and the arguments of the procedure.
- When the procedure is in the same class or module as the Call statement, we recommend that you omit the Call keyword and use the Me keyword.

When and how to pass arguments by reference and by value

By default, the arguments that are passed to a procedure are passed *by value*. That means that the value of each passed variable is assigned to the corresponding parameter in the procedure. Because of that, the procedure can change the value of the parameter without affecting the value of the variable in the calling procedure.

In some cases, though, you'll want to be able to change the value of the variable in the calling procedure from the called procedure. To do that, you can pass the argument *by reference* as shown in figure 6-3. Here, the ByRef keyword is coded before the fourth parameter in the parameter list.

Then, when you call the procedure, a reference to that variable is passed to the procedure. As a result, if the called procedure changes the value of the parameter, it also changes the value of the variable in the calling procedure. In this example, when the called procedure changes the value of the fourth parameter, which is passed by reference, the variable in the calling procedure is changed.

In general, though, it's better to use a Function procedure than a Sub procedure when you need to return a value to the calling program. In the next figure, you'll learn how to do that.

Before I show you how to work with Function procedures, you should know about an additional complication that arises when you pass a reference type rather than a value type as an argument. If you pass a reference type by value, you still can't change its value (the reference), but you can change the values of members of the object it refers to. In contrast, if you pass a reference type by reference, you can change both its value and the values of its members. This will make more sense after you learn about creating and using your own classes in chapter 11.

The basic syntax for each parameter in a parameter list

```
[ByVal|ByRef] variableName As type
```

The CalculateFutureValue procedure

```
Private Sub CalculateFutureValue(monthlyInvestment As Decimal,
        monthlyInterestRate As Decimal, months As Integer,
        ByRef futureValue As Decimal)
    For i As Integer = 1 To months
        futureValue = (futureValue + monthlyInvestment) *
                      (1 + monthlyInterestRate)
    Next
End Sub
```

Three statements that work with the CalculateFutureValue procedure

```
Dim futureValue As Decimal
Me.CalculateFutureValue(monthlyInvestment, monthlyInterestRate,
        months, futureValue)
txtFutureValue.Text = FormatCurrency(futureValue)
```

Description

- When you call a procedure, each argument can be passed to the procedure *by value* or *by reference*.
- If you pass an argument by value, the value of the variable in the calling procedure can't be changed by the called procedure. That's because the value of the variable is passed, not the variable itself.
- If you pass an argument by reference and the called procedure changes the value of the argument, the value of the variable in the calling procedure is changed. That's because the passed argument provides a reference that points to the variable in the calling procedure.
- If you pass a reference type by value, you can't change the reference itself, but you can change the members of the object that it refers to. If you pass a reference type by reference, you can change both the reference and the members of the object that it refers to.
- If you omit the ByVal and ByRef keywords from a parameter declaration, the value that's passed to the procedure will be passed by value.

Figure 6-3 When and how to pass arguments by reference and by value

How to code and call Function procedures

Figure 6-4 presents the syntax for coding and calling a *Function procedure*, or just *function*. The main difference between a Sub procedure and a function is that a function always returns a value to the calling procedure. To specify the type of data to be returned, you include the As clause in the Function statement after the parameter list. The only time you can omit this clause is if the Option Strict option is off, which we don't recommend.

The function shown in this figure requires three arguments and returns the future value of a series of monthly investments. In this case, all of the arguments are passed to the function by value. Then, the Return statement is used to return the Decimal value that the function has calculated.

In this example, though, the Return statement isn't really necessary. That's because the function has already assigned the future value that has been calculated to the function name (FutureValue). In contrast, if a variable like newFutureValue were used to calculate the future value in the For loop, a Return statement like this would be required:

```
Return newFutureValue
```

One benefit of using the Return statement is that it also ends the function. If necessary, you can also code more than one Return statement in a function. Another way to end a function is to code an Exit Function statement, but that shouldn't be necessary if you use Return statements. Since a function should always return a value, you shouldn't exit from a function without returning a value, even if it's a null value.

When you code a function like the one shown here, you should be aware that a warning message may be displayed indicating that the FutureValue variable is used before it has been assigned a value. That's because this variable, which is used on the right side of the assignment statement within the For...Next statement, isn't declared explicitly. And that means it isn't given a default value.

If you code this function without the Return statement, another warning message may be displayed indicating that the FutureValue function doesn't return a value on all code paths. That's because it's possible for the assignment statement that calculates the future value to never be executed, since it's coded within a For...Next statement. In that case, a value will never be assigned to the FutureValue function.

To avoid warning messages like these, you can use the Compile page of the Project Designer to change the warning configurations for various conditions. You can look back to figure 4-8 of chapter 4 to see this page.

Like the arguments you pass to a Sub procedure, the arguments you pass to a Function procedure must have data types that are compatible with the parameters. Those arguments can be passed by position as shown in this figure, or by name as shown in the next figure. In addition, the returned value should be compatible with the assignment statement in which it's used.

If you look at the two examples of assignment statements that call the FutureValue function in this figure, you can see how this works. In the first example, the value returned by the function is assigned to the futureValue

The basic syntax of a function

```
[Private|Public] Function FunctionName[(parameterlist)] [As type]
     statements
    [Exit Function]
    [Return expression]
    [statements]
End Function
```

A function named FutureValue with three parameters

```
Private Function FutureValue(monthlyInvestment As Decimal,
        monthlyInterestRate As Decimal, months As Integer) _
        As Decimal
    For i As Integer = 1 To months
        FutureValue = (FutureValue + monthlyInvestment) *
                      (1 + monthlyInterestRate)
    Next
    Return FutureValue          ' This statement could be omitted
End Function
```

The syntax for calling a function

```
variable = [Me.]FunctionName[(argumentlist)]
```

An assignment statement that contains a call to the FutureValue function

```
Dim futureValue As Decimal = Me.FutureValue(monthlyInvestment,
                                 monthlyInterestRate, months)
```

Another assignment statement that uses the FutureValue function

```
txtFutureValue.Text = FormatCurrency(Me.FutureValue(monthlyInvestment,
                      monthlyInterestRate, months)
```

Description

- A *Function procedure*, or just *function*, is a procedure that returns a value.
- The As clause after the argument list in the Function statement specifies the data type of the value that's returned by the function.
- To return a value to the calling procedure from a function, you can assign a value to the function name or you can code the Return statement.
- To call a function, you can code the name of the function as part of an expression in an assignment statement.
- Like a Sub procedure, you can pass arguments to a function either by value or by reference. The default is by value.

Naming recommendations for functions

- Each function name should indicate what data the function returns.
- Each word within the function name should start with a capital letter.

Figure 6-4 How to code and call Function procedures

variable that's declared in the calling procedure. In the second example, the function is called from within a FormatCurrency function, so the value is formatted and assigned to a text box without ever being declared in the calling procedure.

What if you want the procedure to return two or more values instead of just one? The best way to do that is to return one object that contains those values, and you'll learn how to do that in chapter 11.

How to use optional parameters

When you code a Sub or Function procedure, you may occasionally want to provide default values for one or more parameters in case the user doesn't provide values for them. To do that, you can use *optional parameters* as shown in figure 6-5.

To declare an optional parameter, you code the Optional keyword before the parameter name. In addition, you must assign a default value to the parameter. Then, if a value isn't passed to this parameter, the default value is used.

The examples in this figure illustrate how this works. Here, the first example is another version of the FutureValue function. In this version, the monthly investment parameter is required, but the interest rate and months parameters are optional.

The statement in the second example shows how you would pass arguments for all three parameters to this function. This works just like it would if all of the parameters were required. The statement in the third example, however, shows how you can omit the argument for the second parameter. To do that, you code a comma to indicate the location of the missing argument. Note that both of these statements pass the arguments by position.

In contrast, the statement in the fourth example passes these arguments by name. To *pass an argument by name*, you code the name of the parameter, followed by a colon, an equal sign, and the name of the argument. This technique is particularly useful for working with optional parameters because you don't have to indicate the position of arguments you omit. In addition, you can code the arguments in any sequence.

You can also pass some arguments by position and some by name as illustrated in the last example. Here, the first argument passes a value to the first parameter by position, and the second argument passes a value to the third parameter by name. Notice that when you use this technique, you don't have to code a comma to indicate that a value isn't passed to the second parameter.

The syntax for an optional parameter

```
Optional [ByVal|ByRef] variableName As type = defaultvalue
```

The FutureValue function with two optional parameters

```
Private Function FutureValue(monthlyInvestment As Decimal,
        Optional monthlyInterestRate As Decimal = 0.05D,
        Optional months As Integer = 12) As Decimal
    For i As Integer = 1 To months
        FutureValue = (FutureValue + monthlyInvestment) *
                      (1 + monthlyInterestRate)
    Next
    Return FutureValue
End Function
```

A statement that passes arguments for all three parameters

```
Dim futureValue As Decimal =
    Me.FutureValue(monthlyInvestment, monthlyInterestRate, months)
```

A statement that omits the argument for the second parameter

```
Dim futureValue As Decimal =
    Me.FutureValue(monthlyInvestment, , months)
```

A statement that passes the arguments for two parameters by name

```
Dim futureValue As Decimal =
    Me.FutureValue(months:=months, monthlyInvestment:=monthlyInvestment)
```

Another way to pass the two arguments

```
Dim futureValue As Decimal =
    Me.FutureValue(monthlyInvestment, months:=months)
```

Description

- The parameter list for a Sub or Function procedure can include one or more *optional parameters*. Then, you don't have to supply a value for those parameters when you call the procedure.
- An optional parameter must be assigned a constant value as its default. Then, if a value isn't supplied for that parameter, the default value is used.
- If you define a parameter as optional, every parameter after that parameter in the parameter list must be defined as optional.
- If you pass arguments by position, you must include a comma to indicate where the argument for an optional parameter has been omitted.
- When you use optional parameters, you may also want to *pass arguments by name*. To do that, you code the parameter name, followed by a colon and an equal sign, followed by the argument name.
- When you pass arguments by name, you can code the arguments in any sequence, and you don't have to indicate if an argument for an optional parameter is omitted.
- You can also combine the two techniques for passing arguments and pass some by position and others by name.

Figure 6-5 How to use optional parameters

How to work with events

In chapter 3, you learned how to generate the event handler for the default event of a control by double-clicking on the control in the Form Designer. Now, you'll learn how to create an event handler for any form or control event. In addition, you'll learn how to handle two or more events with the same event handler.

How to start an event handler for any event

Figure 6-6 shows how to generate an event handler for any event of a form or control. To do that, you select the form or control in the Form Designer and click the Events button in the Properties window, which displays a list of events for the form or control. In this figure, for example, you can see a list of the events for the first text box on the Future Value form. Below the list of events, you can see a short description of the highlighted event.

To generate a handler for any of these events, you can double-click on the event in this list. Then, Visual Studio will generate the procedure declaration for the event handler including a Handles clause that *wires* the event to the event handler. When you use this technique, Visual Studio will give the event handler a name that combines the name of the control and the name of the event. For example, if you double-click the Validating event for the Monthly Investment text box, Visual Studio will generate an event handler with this name:

```
txtMonthlyInvestment_Validating
```

If you want to generate an event handler with a name other than the default, you can do that by entering the name next to the event in the Properties window. In this figure, for example, the name ClearFutureValue has been assigned to the TextChanged event. Then, when you press the Enter key, Visual Studio will create an event handler with that name. In most cases, you'll use this technique only when you generate an event handler that will be used to handle more than one event, which you'll learn more about in the next figure.

If you look through the list of events for a form or a control, you'll see that there are many events for each one. For instance, there are more than 60 events for a text box and more than 70 events for a form. In practice, though, you'll use just a few events for each form or control. As you go through this book, you'll be introduced to the ones that are commonly used.

The Events list for a text box control

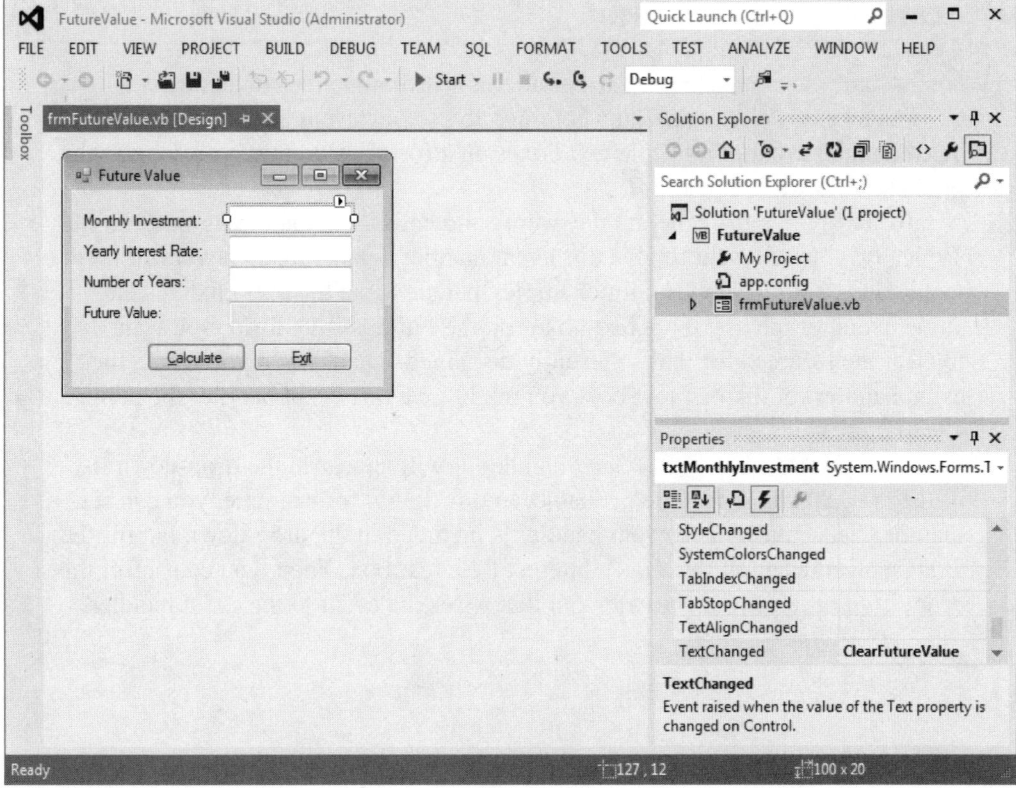

Description

- To generate the event handler for the default event of a form or control, you can double-click the form or control in the Form Designer.
- To view a list of all the events for a form or control, you can select the form or control and click the Events button in the Properties window to display the Events list. Then, you can double-click on any event to generate an event handler for that event.
- By default, an event handler is given a name that consists of the form or control name, an underscore, and the event name. To generate an event handler with a custom name, you can type the name of the event handler to the right of the event in the Events list and then press Enter to generate the start of the event handler.
- When you generate an event handler for a control, Visual Studio uses the Handles clause of the event handler to *wire* the event to the handler.

How to handle multiple events with one event handler

In some cases, you'll want to use the same event handler to handle two or more events. For example, it's common to use one event handler for the TextChanged event of multiple text boxes on a form. To do that, you can use the procedure shown in figure 6-7.

To start, you must generate the event handler as described in figure 6-6. Typically, you will want to give this event handler a name that's not specific to any one control. Suppose, for example, that any time the user changes the value in one of the first three text boxes on the Future Value form, you want to clear the future value that's currently displayed. Then, when you create the event handler for the first text box, you might give this event handler the name ClearFutureValue.

Once you've created this event handler, it will appear in the drop-down list of the event handlers that are available. In this figure, for example, you can see that the ClearFutureValue event handler is included in the drop-down list for the TextChanged event of the Yearly Interest Rate text box. Then, you can select this event handler to generate a statement that wires the event to the event handler.

How to select an existing event handler for an event

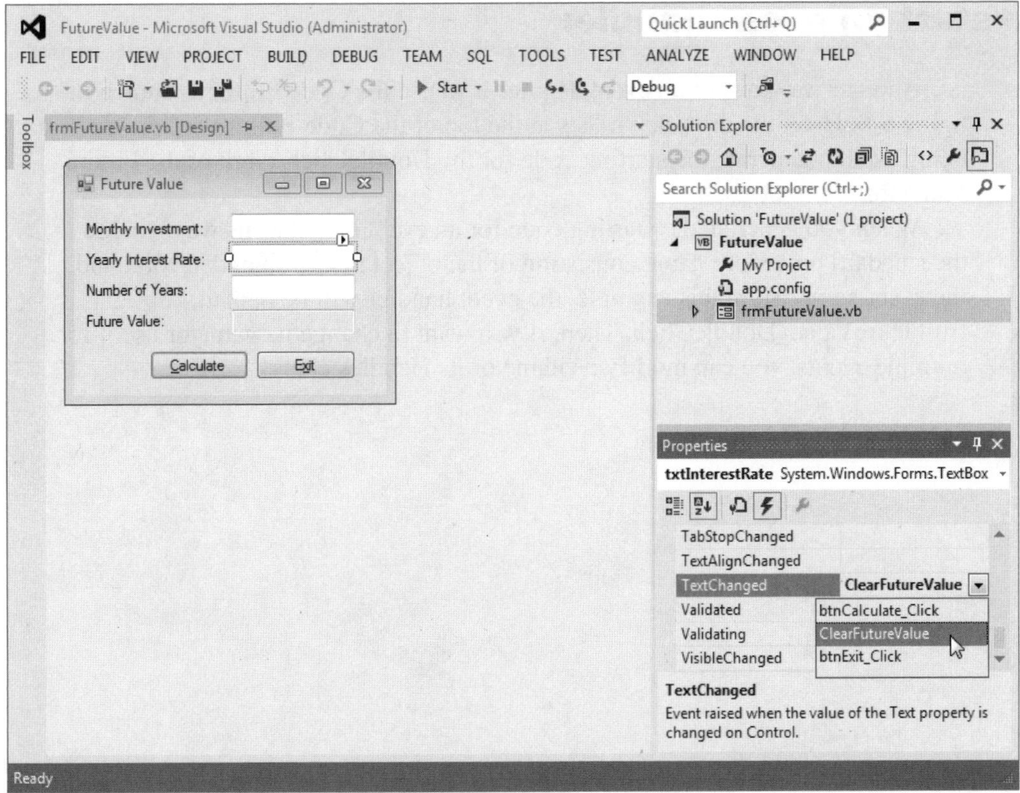

How to wire an event to an existing event handler

1. Select the control in the Form Designer.
2. If necessary, click the Events button in the Properties window to display a list of the events for the control.
3. Click to the right of the event you want to handle and display the drop-down list.
4. Select the event handler you want to use for that event.

Description

- The drop-down list that's available for each event includes all of the existing event handlers for the current form.
- When you select an event handler from the drop-down list, Visual Studio adds an event to the Handles clause of the event handler.

Figure 6-7 How to handle multiple events with one event handler

How to use the Code Editor to start an event handler

Another way to start an event handler is to use the Code Editor as shown in figure 6-8. Here, the drop-down lists at the top of the Code Editor window are being used to generate the starting code for the DoubleClick event of the Future Value form.

When you generate the starting code for an event handler this way, you get the standard procedure name consisting of the object name, an underscore, and the event name. So in this example, the event handler will be named frmFutureValue_DoubleClick. Then, if you want to change its name or use it for multiple events, you can modify its name or its Handles clause.

The events list in the Code Editor for the Future Value form

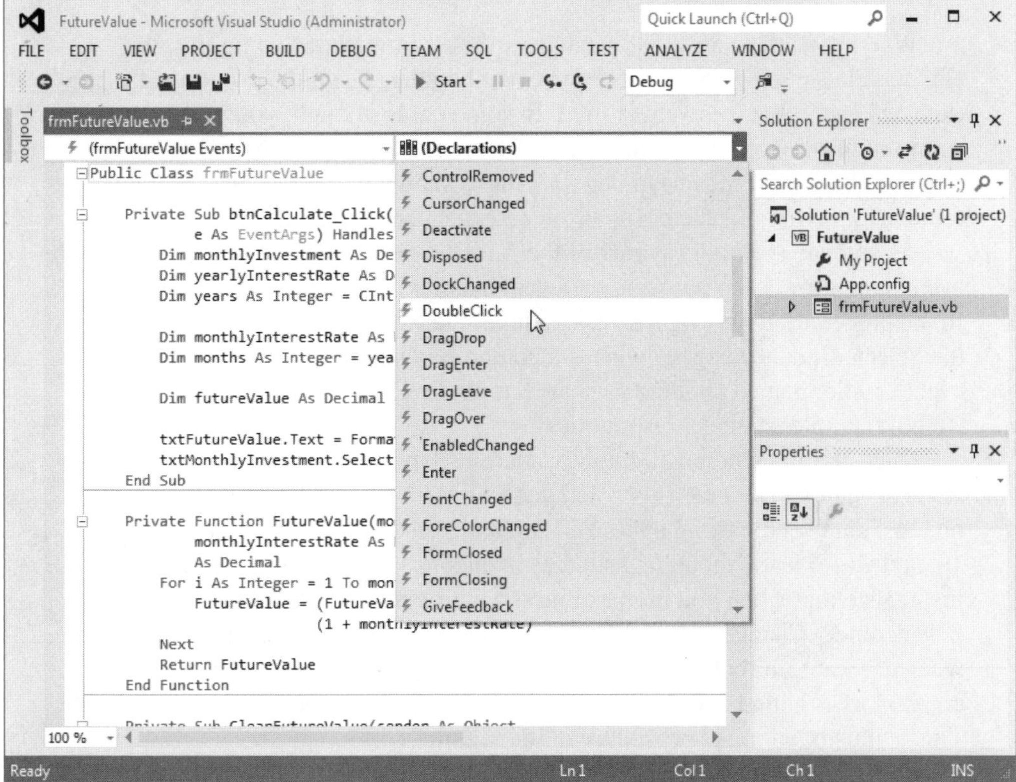

Procedure

- From the drop-down list at the upper left of the Code Editor window, select the object that you want to start an event handler for.
- From the drop-down list at the upper right of the Code Editor window, select the event that you want to start an event handler for.

Description

- To start an event handler from the Code Editor, use the drop-down lists at the top of its window. When you select the event, the Sub and End Sub statements are generated automatically.
- If you want to give the event handler a custom name or if you want to have the event handler handle multiple events, you have to adjust the code for the event handler after its starting code has been generated.
- You can also use the drop-down lists in the Code Editor window to move the cursor to the existing event handler that handles an event.

Figure 6-8 How to use the Code Editor to start an event handler

How to add and remove event wiring

When you create an event handler as shown in the last two figures, the Handles clause wires the event to the event handler. Then, the event handler is executed each time the event is fired. In some cases, though, you won't want the event handler to be executed when the event fires. Then, you can use the AddHandler and RemoveHandler statements shown in figure 6-9 to add and remove the wiring for the event as the program executes.

As you can see in the syntax of the AddHandler statement, it names the event that you want to wire and the event handler that you want to wire it to. In the procedure in this figure, for example, the AddHandler statement wires the SelectedIndexChanged event of a combo box named cboProducts to an event handler named cboProducts_SelectedIndexChanged. The syntax of the RemoveHandler statement is identical.

One situation where you might want to use the AddHandler and RemoveHandler statements is when you're binding a control such as a combo box to a data source using code. You'll learn about combo boxes in chapter 10, and you'll learn about data sources in chapters 14 through 16. For now, just realize that when you bind a combo box to a data source, it causes the SelectedIndexChanged event of the combo box to be fired, which isn't usually what you want. In that case, you can remove the wiring for this event before the combo box is bound and then add the wiring back when the binding is complete. This is illustrated in the procedure in this figure.

This figure also shows the starting code for the event handler for the SelectedIndexChanged event. Notice that this event handler doesn't include a Handles clause. Because the AddHandler statement takes care of the wiring, the Handles clause isn't needed. So when you use AddHandler to wire an event to an event handler, you can remove the Handles clause from the generated event handler, although that isn't necessary.

Although it isn't illustrated in this figure, you should know that you can also use the AddHandler statement to wire more than one event to the same event handler. To do that, you just code an AddHandler statement for each event you want to wire.

The syntax for wiring an event to an event handler

```
AddHandler eventname, AddressOf eventhandler
```

The syntax for removing the wiring for an event

```
RemoveHandler eventname, AddressOf eventhandler
```

A procedure that wires the SelectedIndexChanged event of a combo box

```
Private Sub BindProductsComboBox()

    ' Remove the wiring for the SelectedIndexChanged event.
    RemoveHandler cboProducts.SelectedIndexChanged,
        AddressOf cboProducts_SelectedIndexChanged

    ' Place code for binding the combo box here.

    ' Add the wiring for the SelectedIndexChanged event.
    AddHandler cboProducts.SelectedIndexChanged,
        AddressOf cboProducts_SelectedIndexChanged

End Sub
```

The code for the event handler

```
Private Sub cboProducts_SelectedIndexChanged(
        sender As Object, e As EventArgs)
    .
    .
    .
End Sub
```

Description

- The AddHandler and RemoveHandler statements provide for adding and removing wiring for an event at runtime. They are particularly useful when you're working with controls that are bound to a data source.
- The AddHandler statement is also useful for wiring an event that isn't available until runtime. In that case, you typically code the statement in the event handler for the Load event of the form.
- When you use the AddHandler statement to wire an event to an event handler, the event handler doesn't need to include a Handles clause. So if you want to, you can remove the Handles clause that's included when you generate an event handler.
- If you need to wire more than one event to an event handler, you can code an AddHandler statement for each event.

Figure 6-9 How to add and remove event wiring

Another version of the Future Value application

Now that you know how to code Sub and Function procedures and how to work with event handlers, you're ready to see an enhanced version of the Future Value application. This version uses a Function procedure to calculate the future value, and it uses a single event handler to clear the Future Value text box whenever the user changes the text in any of the other text boxes on the form. The code for all four procedures is shown in figure 6-10.

The Function procedure

The FutureValue procedure contains the code that calculates the future value. It's called by the shaded code in the event handler for the Click event of the Calculate button. This separates the calculation from the other code for the event. In a lengthy event handler, calling procedures like this can make it easier to code, test, and debug an application. You'll see more of this in the next chapter.

The event handlers

With one exception, the event handlers for the Click events of the Calculate button and Exit button are the same as they were in the Future Value application of chapter 5. The one exception is that the btnCalculate_Click procedure calls the FutureValue procedure instead of doing the calculation itself. That simplifies this procedure.

In addition, this version of the application has a custom event handler named ClearFutureValue. If you look at its Handles clause, you can see how the three events that it handles are coded. This clause is generated automatically when you use the techniques in figures 6-6 and 6-7 to specify custom event handling.

After the Sub statement, this procedure contains a single statement that sets the Text property of the Future Value text box to an empty string. In other words, it clears the future value that's displayed on the form whenever the data in one of the three text boxes is changed. Then, the future value isn't displayed again until the user clicks the Calculate button. This prevents the Future Value text box from displaying a value that isn't accurate for the values that are displayed in the other text boxes.

The procedures and functions of the Future Value application

```
Private Sub btnCalculate_Click(sender As Object,
        e As EventArgs) Handles btnCalculate.Click

    Dim monthlyInvestment As Decimal = CDec(txtMonthlyInvestment.Text)
    Dim yearlyInterestRate As Decimal = CDec(txtInterestRate.Text)
    Dim years As Integer = CInt(txtYears.Text)

    Dim monthlyInterestRate As Decimal = yearlyInterestRate / 12 / 100
    Dim months As Integer = years * 12

    Dim futureValue As Decimal = Me.FutureValue(monthlyInvestment,
                                 monthlyInterestRate, months)

    txtFutureValue.Text = FormatCurrency(futureValue)
    txtMonthlyInvestment.Select()
End Sub

Private Function FutureValue(monthlyInvestment As Decimal,
        monthlyInterestRate As Decimal, months As Integer) _
        As Decimal

    For i As Integer = 1 To months
        FutureValue = (FutureValue + monthlyInvestment) *
                      (1 + monthlyInterestRate)
    Next
    Return FutureValue
End Function

Private Sub ClearFutureValue(sender As Object,
        e As EventArgs) Handles txtMonthlyInvestment.TextChanged,
        txtYears.TextChanged, txtInterestRate.TextChanged

    txtFutureValue.Text = ""
End Sub

Private Sub btnExit_Click(sender As Object,
        e As EventArgs) Handles btnExit.Click
    Me.Close()
End Sub
```

Description

- The FutureValue function separates the calculation from the rest of the code for the event handler for the Click event of the Calculate button.
- The TextChanged event of the Monthly Investment, Yearly Interest Rate, and Number of Years text boxes is wired to the ClearFutureValue event handler. As a result, the Future Value text box is cleared every time the user changes the data in one of those text boxes.

Figure 6-10 The procedures for the Future Value application

Perspective

Now that you have finished this chapter, you should be able to code and call both Sub and Function procedures. You should also be able to code event handlers for any event of a form or control. With those skills, you should be able to logically divide your code into smaller procedures so it is easier to read, test, and debug.

Terms

Sub procedure
calling procedure
access modifier
parameter
parameter list
signature
called procedure
call a procedure
argument
argument list
pass by position
pass by value
pass by reference
Function procedure
function
Return statement
optional parameter
pass by name
event wiring

Exercise 6-1 Enhance the Invoice Total application

In this exercise, you'll enhance the Invoice Total application of chapter 5 by adding a procedure that determines the discount percent to it. You'll also add another event handler to the application.

1. Open the application that's in the C:\VB 2012\Chapter 06\InvoiceTotal directory.
2. Start a Sub procedure with three parameters (customer type, subtotal, and discount percent) that will set the discount percent based on the customer type and subtotal. Then, copy the code for doing that from the event handler of the btnCalculate_Click procedure to the new Sub procedure, and modify this code so it works correctly.
3. Modify the code in the btnCalculate_Click procedure so it calls the Sub procedure to get the discount percent. As you enter the call, notice how the IntelliSense feature helps you enter the arguments. Then, test these changes to make sure they work.
4. Add a Function procedure with two parameters (customer type and subtotal) that returns the discount percent. Then, modify the calling statement and any other code in the btnCalculate_Click procedure so it uses the Function procedure to get the discount percent. Now, test this change.

5. Add one event handler named ClearAllBoxes that handles the TextChanged event for both the Customer Type and Subtotal text boxes. This event handler should clear the values in the text boxes that display the results. After you test this change, close this project.

Exercise 6-2 Enhance the Future Value application

In this exercise, you'll experiment with and enhance the Future Value application that was presented in this chapter.

Experiment with the FutureValue procedure

1. Open the application that's in the C:\VB 2012\Chapter 06\FutureValue directory. This is the book application that's presented in figure 6-10. Start by testing this application.
2. Comment out the Return statement in the FutureValue function, and test the application again to see that the function still works.
3. Instead of using FutureValue within the For loop in the function, declare and use a variable named newFutureValue. Then, use the Return statement to return the value in that variable. Now, test this to make sure it works.

Code an event handler for a form event

4. Use the drop-down lists at the top of the Code Editor to start an event handler for the DoubleClick event of the form. Next, change the name of the event handler to ClearAllBoxes, and write the code for this handler so it sets the Text property for all four text boxes to an empty string. Then, test the application to make sure this works. (Be sure to double-click on the form, not on the form's title bar, because that will maximize the form.)

Code event handlers for other control events

5. In the Form Designer, select the Future Value text box. Next, select the MouseHover event, read its description, drop down its list, and select the ClearAllBoxes event handler so it will be executed whenever the user lets the mouse hover over this text box. Then, test the application to make sure this works.
6. In the Form Designer, select the Yearly Interest Rate text box, and double-click on the DoubleClick event to generate its event handler. Next, write the code for this handler so it sets the value in the Yearly Interest Rate text box to 12. Then, test this enhancement.
7. Use your own imagination to work with other events. When you're through experimenting with events, close the application.

7

How to handle exceptions and validate data

In the last two chapters, you learned how to code a Future Value application that calculates the future value of a series of monthly payments. However, if the user enters data that can't be handled by this application, an exception will occur and the application will crash. In this chapter, you'll learn how to prevent that from happening by handling any exceptions that occur and by validating data to prevent exceptions.

An introduction to data validation and exception handling

This chapter starts with a quick introduction to data validation and exception handling. As part of that introduction, you'll learn how to use the IsNumeric function and how to display a dialog box that contains an error message.

How to use the IsNumeric function for data validation

The term *data validation* (or *validity checking*) refers to the process of checking user entries to make sure they're valid. If they're valid, processing continues. Otherwise, an error message is displayed so the user can correct the entries.

One type of data validation is checking that an entry is numeric so it can be converted to a numeric data type and used in calculations. This type of checking can be done with Visual Basic's IsNumeric function as shown in figure 7-1. To use this function, you code an expression as the argument that represents the value to be tested. Often, you just code the Text property of a text box as the argument so the value in the text box is tested for numeric validity.

In the example in this figure, the IsNumeric function is coded within an If statement to test whether the subtotal that has been entered in a text box is numeric. If it isn't (Not IsNumeric), the Show method of the MessageBox class is used to display an error message. Then, the Exit Sub statement is issued to exit from the event handler. However, if the subtotal is numeric, the rest of the code in the event handler is executed.

For simple applications, the IsNumeric function may be adequate for numeric validity testing. But often, it is inadequate because it treats both positive and negative values as valid and it treats values with and without decimal places as valid. Because most applications require validity checking that is more precise than that, the rest of this chapter shows you other ways to test for numeric validity.

Incidentally, the Boolean expression in this example could also be coded as:

```
Not IsNumeric(txtSubtotal.Text) = True
```

This isn't necessary, though, because Visual Basic assumes the True value if it isn't coded. Throughout this book, then, you'll see Boolean expressions coded without the = True.

The syntax of the IsNumeric function

```
IsNumeric(expression)
```

An IsNumeric function used for data validation

```
Private Sub btnCalculate_Click(sender As Object,
        e As EventArgs) Handles btnCalculate.Click

    If Not IsNumeric(txtSubtotal.Text) Then
        MessageBox.Show(
            "Please enter a valid number for the Subtotal field.",
            "Entry Error")
        Exit Sub
    End If

    ' The code that does the processing if the entry is valid

End Sub
```

Description

- *Data validation*, or *validity checking*, is the process of verifying that all user entries are valid. One goal of this verification is to prevent runtime errors.
- The IsNumeric function tests whether the value of an expression is numeric. This function returns a Boolean value, which you can test in a conditional expression. If the Boolean value is True, the value of the expression is numeric.
- The IsNumeric function treats both positive and negative numbers as valid, as well as numbers with and without decimal places. As a result, additional validation testing is often required.
- The IsDate function can be used to verify that a user entry has a valid date format.

Figure 7-1 How to use the IsNumeric function for data validation

How to display a dialog box for error messages

One way an application can communicate with its users is by displaying a dialog box that contains a message. In this chapter, dialog boxes are used to display messages about validation errors and exceptions that have occurred. Keep in mind, however, that dialog boxes can also be used for many other purposes.

To display a simple dialog box, you use the Show method of the MessageBox class as shown in figure 7-2. The syntax shown here lets you display a dialog box that contains a message, a title, and an OK button. For now, this is adequate.

In chapter 10, however, you'll learn how to use the MessageBox class to display dialog boxes that include Yes, No, Cancel, Abort, Retry, and Ignore buttons, and you'll learn how to write code that checks which button the user selected. That way, you can handle an exception differently depending on how the user responds to the dialog box.

If you want to start a new line or skip to the next tab within the message for a dialog box, you can use either the members of the ControlChars class or the Visual Basic constants. The first alternative is illustrated by the second example in this figure. Here, ControlChars.CrLf means to do a carriage return (Cr) and a line feed (Lf). That's antiquated terminology for starting a new line. The second alternative is to code the constant vbCrLf to get the same result.

If you want to use modern terms, you can code ControlChars.NewLine or vbNewLine to get the same result. And you can code ControlChars.Tab or vbTab to skip to the next tab in the message box. From this point on in this book, vbCrLf and vbTab are used whenever control characters are needed just because they're shorter.

The syntax for displaying a dialog box with an OK button

```
MessageBox.Show(text[, caption])
```

A statement that displays a dialog box

```
MessageBox.Show(
    "Please enter a valid number for the Subtotal field.",
    "Entry Error")
```

The dialog box for the statement above

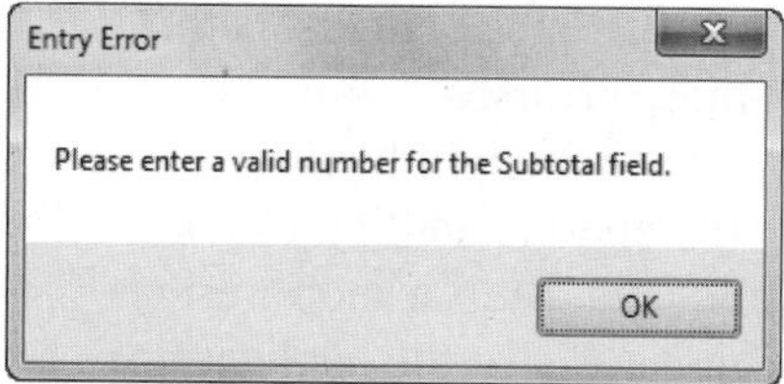

Another statement that displays a dialog box

```
MessageBox.Show(
    "An exception has occurred. " & ControlChars.CrLf &
    "The program will be cancelled.",
    "Program Error")
```

The dialog box for the statement above

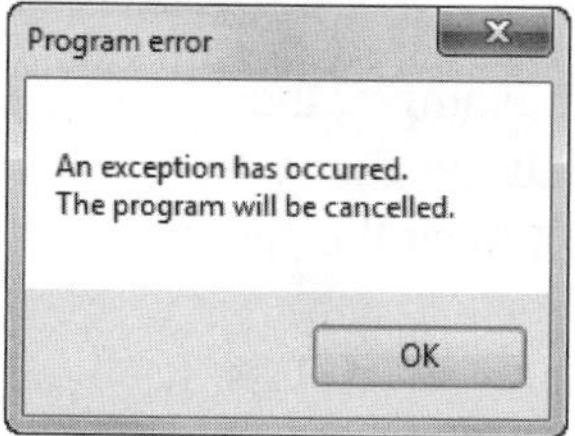

Constants that you can use for new lines and tabs

Description	ControlChars member	Visual Basic constant
Carriage-return/line-feed character	ControlChars.CrLf	vbCrLf
New line character	ControlChars.NewLine	vbNewLine
Tab character	ControlChars.Tab	vbTab

Description

- You can use the shared Show method of the MessageBox class to display a dialog box. Dialog boxes are commonly used to display validation messages.
- If you omit the caption argument, the dialog box will be displayed without a caption in its title bar.

Note

- In chapter 10, you'll learn how to use the MessageBox class to display dialog boxes that contain other buttons and accept a response from the user.

Figure 7-2 How to display a dialog box for error messages

How exception handling works

It's inevitable that your applications will encounter *exceptions*. For example, that can happen when a user enters non-numeric data when numeric data is required. Then, if the application doesn't check to be sure that the data is valid, the .NET runtime environment will *throw* an *exception* when it tries to work with that data.

As figure 7-3 shows, an exception is an object that's created from the Exception class or one of its subclasses. Exception objects represent errors that have occurred, and they contain information about those errors.

A well-coded application will *catch* any exceptions that might be thrown and handle them. This is known as *exception handling*. Exception handling can be as simple as notifying users that they must enter valid data. But for more serious exceptions, exception handling may involve notifying users that the application is being shut down, saving as much data as possible, cleaning up resources, and exiting the application as smoothly as possible.

When you're testing an application, it's common to encounter exceptions that haven't been handled. In that case, Visual Studio will enter break mode and display an Exception Assistant dialog box like the one shown in this figure. This dialog box includes the name of the class for the exception, a brief message that describes the cause of the exception, and some troubleshooting tips to help you fix the problem that caused the exception to be thrown.

All exceptions are *subclasses* of the Exception class. For example, the FormatException class is a subclass of the Exception class that represents an exception that occurs when the format of an argument doesn't meet the parameter specifications of the invoked method.

The ArithmeticException class is also a subclass of the Exception class. It represents an exception that occurs during an arithmetic, casting, or conversion operation. It contains other subclasses, including the OverflowException and DivideByZeroException classes. An *overflow exception* occurs when the result of an arithmetic operation is too large for the receiving variable. A *divide-by-zero exception* occurs if an application attempts to divide a number by zero.

The InvalidCastException class is another subclass of the Exception class. It represents an exception that occurs during explicit casts with Visual Basic functions like CDec.

For now, that's all you need to know about the Exception hierarchy. As you progress through this book, though, you'll learn about other types of exceptions. In section 3, for example, you'll learn how to work with the exceptions that can occur when you're working with databases. You'll also learn more about subclasses and how they work in chapter 18.

The dialog box for an unhandled exception

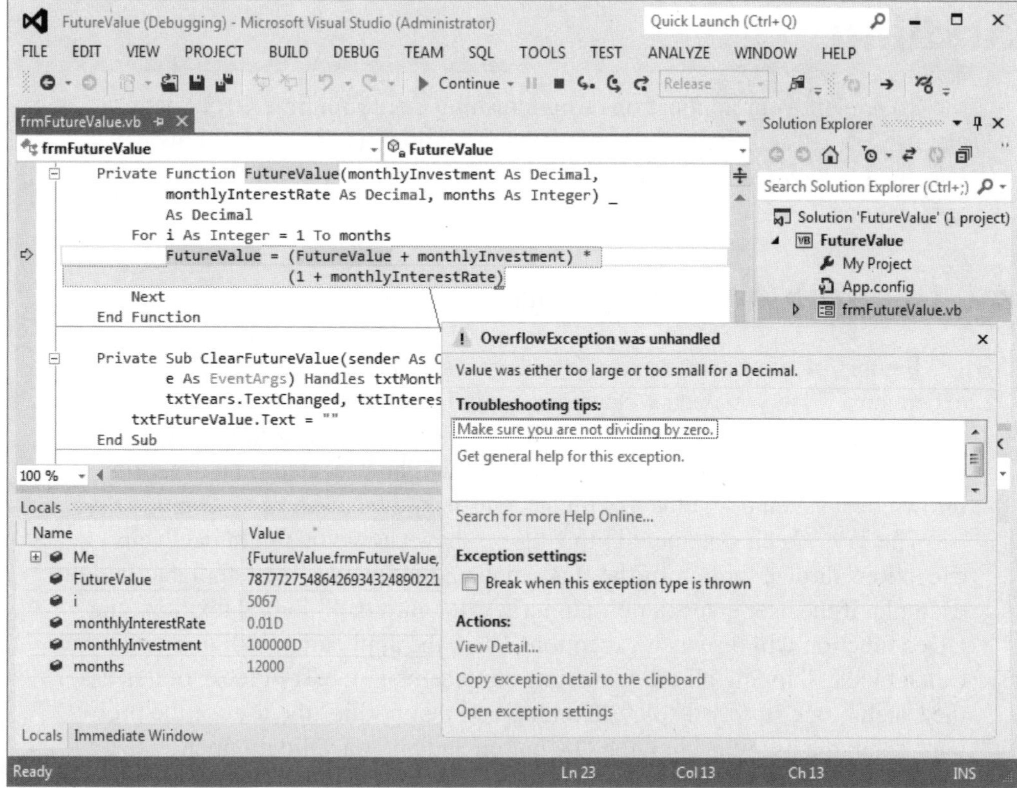

The Exception hierarchy for five common exceptions

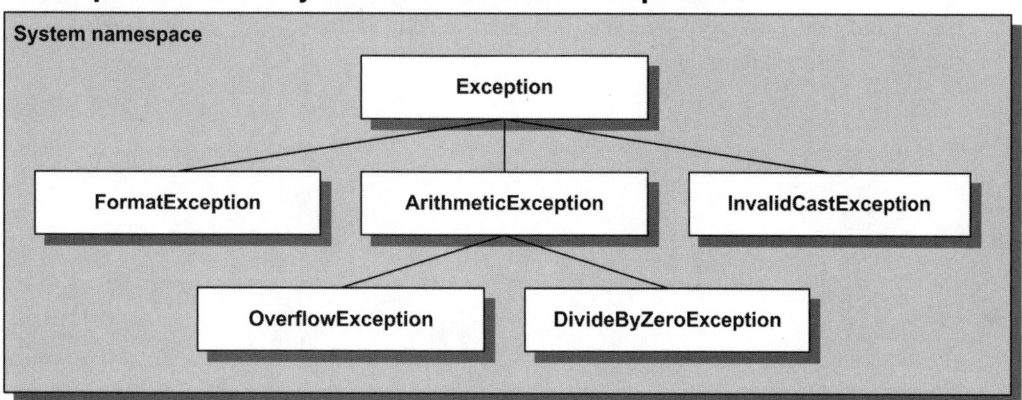

Description

- An *exception* is *thrown* when an application can't execute a statement.
- A production application should *catch* and *handle* all exceptions so the application won't end unexpectedly.
- All exceptions are subclasses of the Exception class.

Figure 7-3 How exception handling works

How to use structured exception handling

To prevent your applications from crashing due to runtime errors, you can use Try…Catch statements to handle exceptions as they occur. This is known as *structured exception handling*, and it plays an important role in most applications.

How to catch an exception

Figure 7-4 shows how to use *Try...Catch statements* to catch and handle exceptions. First, you code a *Try block* around the statement or statements that may throw an exception. Then, immediately after the Try block, you code a *Catch block* that contains the statements that will be executed if an exception is thrown by a statement in the Try block. This is known as an *exception handler*.

The Try...Catch statement in this figure shows how you might catch any exceptions thrown by four of the statements in the Invoice Total application. For example, if the user enters a non-numeric value into the Subtotal text box, the CDec function will throw an exception. Then, the application will jump into the Catch block, skipping all the remaining statements in the Try block. In this case, the Catch block simply displays a dialog box that notifies the user of the problem. Then, the user can click the OK button and enter a valid number.

Please note that all of the variables that are declared within a Try…Catch statement have *block scope*. As a result, they can't be referred to from outside the statement. That's why the four statements in the Try block in the example in this figure don't declare any variables. Instead, the four variables are declared before the Try…Catch statement.

The syntax for a simple Try...Catch statement

```
Try
    statements
Catch
    statements
End Try
```

A Try...Catch statement

```
Try
    subtotal = CDec(txtSubtotal.Text)
    discountPercent = .2D
    discountAmount = subtotal * discountPercent
    invoiceTotal = subtotal - discountAmount
Catch
    MessageBox.Show(
        "Please enter a valid number for the Subtotal field.",
        "Entry Error")
End Try
```

The dialog box that's displayed if an exception occurs

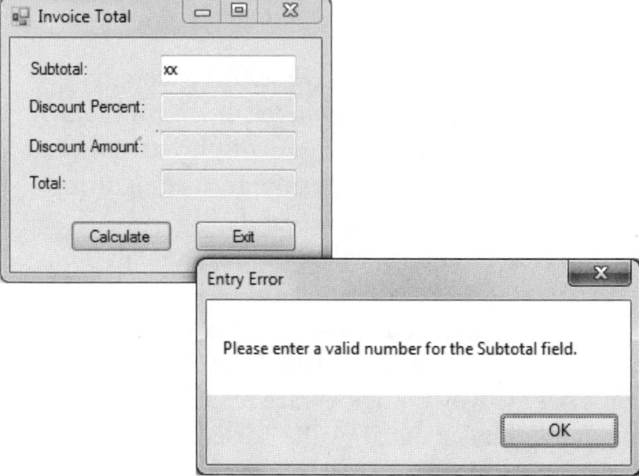

Description

- You can use a *Try...Catch statement* to code an *exception handler* that catches and handles any exceptions that are thrown.
- The *Try block* contains the code that is to be tested for exceptions, and the *Catch block* contains the code that handles the exceptions.
- If the Try block contains calls to other procedures, the Catch blocks catch any exceptions that aren't handled by the called procedures.
- All variables that are declared within a Try...Catch statement have *block scope*. As a result, you can't refer to any of those variables from outside of the Try...Catch statement.
- When you use Try...Catch statements to handle exceptions, it can be referred to as *structured exception handling*.

Figure 7-4 How to catch an exception

How to use the properties and methods of an exception

Since an exception is an object, it has properties and methods. If you want to use the properties or methods of an exception in the Catch block that catches the exception, you must supply a name for the exception as shown in figure 7-5. To do that, you code the name for the exception, the As keyword, and the name of the exception class after the Catch keyword.

If you're coding the Try...Catch statement within an event handler, you can't use e as the name of the exception. That's because, by default, the event handler already uses this name for its EventArgs parameter. As a result, you must specify another name such as x or ex. Or, you must change the name of the EventArgs parameter from e to another name.

Once you specify a name for an exception, you can use the Message property to get a brief description of the error. You can also use the GetType method to get the type of class that was used to create the exception object. Then, to get the name of that type, you can use the ToString method as shown in the example in this figure. Finally, you can use the StackTrace property to get a string that represents the *stack trace*.

A stack trace is a list of the methods that were called before the exception occurred. These methods are listed in the reverse order from the order in which they were called. As a result, the method that was called last is displayed first, and the method that was called first is displayed last. For example, reading from bottom to top, the dialog box in this figure shows that line 6 of the btnCalculate_Click method of the Invoice Total form called the ToDecimal method of the Conversions class, and so on.

Often, the stack trace refers to methods that you didn't even know were called. In this case, for example, the code in the btnCalculate_Click method called the CDec function, but that's not the way the stack trace reads. This just shows that the CDec function is actually implemented by the ToDecimal method.

When you use the properties and methods of an exception to get information about the exception, you can display that information in a dialog box. That way, if an exception is thrown, your users will be able to give you information about the exception so you can fix the problem. Or, if a serious exception occurs that prevents the application from continuing, you can write information about the exception to a log file so you can monitor and review these exceptions. You'll learn how to write data to files in chapter 21.

The syntax for a Try...Catch statement that accesses the exception

```
Try
    statements
Catch exceptionName As Exceptionclass
    statements
End Try
```

Two common properties for all exceptions

Property	Description
`Message`	Gets a message that briefly describes the current exception.
`StackTrace`	Gets a string that lists the procedures that were called before the exception occurred.

A common method for all exceptions

Method	Description
`GetType()`	Gets the type of the current exception.

A Try...Catch statement that accesses the exception

```
Dim subtotal As Decimal
Try
    subtotal = CDec(txtSubtotal.Text)
Catch ex As Exception
    MessageBox.Show(ex.Message & vbCrLf & vbCrLf & ex.StackTrace,
                    ex.GetType.ToString)
End Try
```

The dialog box that's displayed if an exception occurs

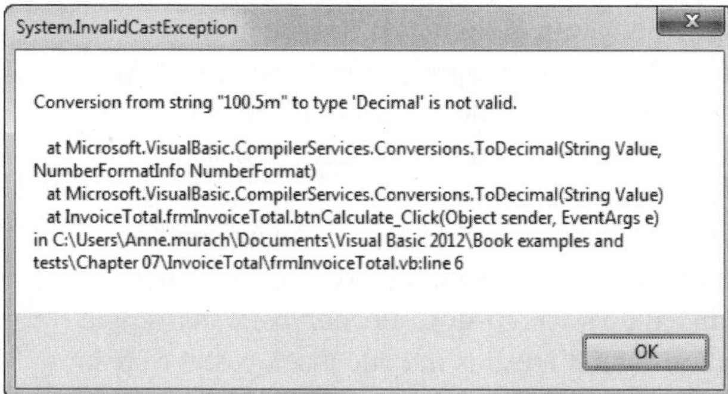
System.InvalidCastException
Conversion from string "100.5m" to type 'Decimal' is not valid.
at Microsoft.VisualBasic.CompilerServices.Conversions.ToDecimal(String Value, NumberFormatInfo NumberFormat)
at Microsoft.VisualBasic.CompilerServices.Conversions.ToDecimal(String Value)
at InvoiceTotal.frmInvoiceTotal.btnCalculate_Click(Object sender, EventArgs e) in C:\Users\Anne.murach\Documents\Visual Basic 2012\Book examples and tests\Chapter 07\InvoiceTotal\frmInvoiceTotal.vb:line 6
OK

Description

- If you want to use the properties or methods of the exception in the Catch block, you must supply a name for the exception.
- The *stack trace* is a list of the methods that were called before the exception occurred. The list appears in reverse order, from the last method called to the first method called.
- If you're coding a Try…Catch statement within an event handler, you can't use e for the name of the exception because it's used as the name of a parameter for the handler.

Figure 7-5 How to use the properties and methods of an exception

How to catch specific types of exceptions

In some cases, the statements in the Try block of a Try...Catch statement can throw more than one type of exception. Then, you may want to handle each exception differently. To do that, you can code Catch blocks like the ones shown in figure 7-6. Here, the first Catch block catches a FormatException, the second one catches an OverflowException, and the third one catches any other exceptions.

When you catch specific exceptions, you should realize that you must code the Catch blocks for the most specific exceptions in a class hierarchy first, and you must code the Catch blocks for the least specific exception last. In this figure, for example, the FormatException type and the OverflowException type are both more specific than the Exception type. As a result, their Catch blocks must be coded before the Catch block for the Exception type. If they were coded after the Exception type, you would get a build error when you tried to compile the project. That's because the Catch blocks are evaluated in sequence, which means that the Catch block for the Exception type would catch any exception that occurred. In other words, the other Catch blocks would never be executed.

Although you have to code the Catch blocks for the FormatException and OverflowException types before the Catch block for the Exception type, you don't have to code the Catch block for the FormatException type before the OverflowException type. That's because the OverflowException class is a subclass of the ArithmeticException class, not the FormatException class. In other words, the least specific exception to most specific exception rule applies only within subclasses that are based on the same class.

When you code Try...Catch statements, you may find that you have some code that should run regardless of whether an exception is thrown or what type of exception is thrown. For example, if your application is using system resources such as database connections, it's common to perform some cleanup code that releases those resources when they're no longer needed. Instead of including this code in the Try block and each Catch block, you can code it in a *Finally block*. Then, this code is executed after all of the statements in the Try block are executed. Or, if an exception is thrown, it's executed after the statements in the Catch block. This allows you to store cleanup code in a single location instead of multiple locations, which results in code that's easier to read and maintain.

Please note in the example that the shared ToInt32 method of the Convert class is used instead of the CInt function. Although both the method and the function do the conversions, the function will round strings without throwing exceptions, which can be misleading. If the user entered a value of 10.5 for the number of years on the Future Value form, for example, the CInt function would round that value to 10 and display the result using that value rather than the value the user entered. In contrast, the Convert.ToInt32 method won't perform rounding on strings. Instead, it will throw a FormatException, which is usually what you want. If you decide to use the CInt function, be aware that it throws an InvalidCastException rather than a FormatException if the conversion can't be performed.

The complete syntax for the Try...Catch statement

```
Try
    statements
Catch exceptionName As mostspecificexception
    statements
[Catch exceptionName As nextmostspecificexception
    statements] ...
[Catch exceptionName As leastspecificexception
    statements]
[Finally
    statements]
End Try
```

A Try...Catch statement that catches specific exceptions

```
Try
    monthlyInvestment = Convert.ToDecimal(txtMonthlyInvestment.Text)
    yearlyInterestRate = Convert.ToDecimal(txtInterestRate.Text)
    years = Convert.ToInt32(txtYears.Text)
Catch ex As FormatException      ' a specific exception
    MessageBox.Show(
        "A format exception has occurred. Please check all entries.",
        "Entry Error")
Catch ex As OverflowException    ' another specific exception
    MessageBox.Show(
        "An overflow exception has occurred. " &
        "Please enter smaller values.", "Entry Error")
Catch ex As Exception            ' all other exceptions
    MessageBox.Show(ex.Message, ex.GetType.ToString)
Finally                  ' this code runs whether or not an exception occurs
    PerformCleanup()
End Try
```

Description

- You can code one Catch block for each type of exception that may occur in the Try block. If you code more than one Catch block, you must code the Catch blocks for the most specific types of exceptions first.
- Since all exceptions are subclasses of the Exception class, a Catch block for the Exception class will catch all types of exceptions.
- You can code a *Finally block* after all the Catch blocks. The code in this block is executed whether or not an exception occurs. It's often used to free any system resources.

Figure 7-6 How to catch specific types of exceptions

How to throw an exception

Now that you've learned how to catch exceptions, you're ready to learn how to throw exceptions from the procedures that you code. To do that, you can use the *Throw statement* as shown in figure 7-7. As you can see, you can use this statement either to throw a new exception or to throw an existing exception.

To throw a new exception, you code the Throw keyword followed by the New keyword and the name of the exception class you want to create the exception from. (As you'll see later in this book, the New keyword is the keyword that's used to create an object from a class.) You can also supply a string argument that provides a brief description of the exception. This argument is assigned to the Message property of the exception. Then, when you handle the exception, you can use the Message property to get this string.

This use of the Throw statement is illustrated in the first example in this figure. Here, before performing its calculation, the FutureValue procedure checks if the values used in the calculation are less than or equal to zero. If so, an exception that's created from the FormatException class is thrown. Both of the Throw statements shown here include a string that briefly describes the cause of the exception.

In general, a procedure should throw an exception only when an exceptional condition occurs. In the first example, the FutureValue procedure can't perform the calculation when it receives a negative number. As a result, this is an exceptional condition, and it makes sense to throw an exception. Another way to handle this situation would be to return a negative Decimal value (such as -1.0D) to indicate that the calculation can't be performed. However, throwing an exception lets you provide a description of the exceptional condition, which is often helpful to other programmers who might want to use this procedure.

You can also use the Throw statement to test an exception handling routine as shown in the second example. Here, the Throw statement is coded within the Try block of a Try...Catch statement. Then, when this statement is executed, the code within the Catch block is executed so you can be sure that it works properly.

The third example shows how to throw an existing exception. This technique is useful if you need to catch an exception, perform some processing that partially handles the exception, and then throw the exception so another exception handler can finish handling the exception. In this case, the ToDecimal method is used within a Try block to convert the value the user enters into a text box to a Decimal type. If the user enters a value that's not a valid Decimal type, a FormatException is thrown. Then, the Catch block catches this exception, moves the focus to the text box, and rethrows the exception. That way, the calling procedure can also catch the exception and perform some additional processing.

The syntax for throwing a new exception

```
Throw New Exceptionclass([message])
```

The syntax for throwing an existing exception

```
Throw exceptionName
```

A Function procedure that throws a FormatException

```
Private Function FutureValue(monthlyInvestment As Decimal,
    monthlyInterestRate As Decimal, months As Integer) As Decimal
    If monthlyInvestment <= 0 Then
       Throw New FormatException(
           "Monthly Investment must be greater than 0.")
    End If
    If monthlyInterestRate <= 0 Then
       Throw New FormatException(
           "Interest Rate must be greater than 0.")
    End If
    .
    .
```

Code that throws an Exception for testing purposes

```
Try
    subtotal = Convert.ToDecimal(txtSubtotal.Text)
    Throw New OverflowException
Catch ex As Exception
    MessageBox.Show(ex.Message & vbCrLf & vbCrLf &
        ex.GetType.ToString & vbCrLf & vbCrLf &
        ex.StackTrace, "Exception")
End Try
```

Code that rethrows an exception

```
Try
    Convert.ToDecimal(txtSubtotal.Text)
Catch ex As FormatException
    txtSubtotal.Select()
    Throw ex
End Try
```

When to throw an exception

- When a procedure encounters a situation where it isn't able to complete its task
- When you want to generate an exception to test an exception handler
- When you want to catch the exception, perform some processing, and then throw the exception again

Description

- You can use the *Throw statement* to throw a new or existing exception. When you create a new exception, you can specify a string that's assigned to the Message property.

Figure 7-7 How to throw an exception

The Future Value application with exception handling

Figure 7-8 presents an improved version of the Future Value application you saw in the last chapter. This version uses structured exception handling to catch any exceptions that might be thrown when the user clicks the Calculate button on the form.

In the btnCalculate_Click procedure, all of the processing statements are coded within a Try block. Then, the first Catch block handles any format exceptions. And the second Catch block handles any overflow exceptions. In either case, the code in the Catch block displays a dialog box that describes the exception and indicates a corrective action that the user can take.

While the first two Catch blocks catch specific exceptions, the third Catch block catches all other exceptions. Since the cause of these exceptions isn't known, the application uses the properties and methods of the exception to display information about the exception in a dialog box. In this case, the name of the exception class is displayed in the title bar of the dialog box, and a brief description of the exception is displayed in the body of the dialog box. That way, the user will be able to provide some information about the exception to the person who is going to fix this bug.

Note that this third Catch block can't use e as the name of the exception because e is used for the System.EventArgs parameter. Instead, this Catch block uses ex as the name of the Exception object.

Note also that if an exception occurs in the FutureValue procedure, the exception isn't caught by that procedure. As a result, the exception is passed back to the calling procedure, btnCalculate_Click. Then, the appropriate Catch block in that procedure handles the exception.

The code for the Future Value application with exception handling

```
Private Sub btnCalculate_Click(sender As Object,
        e As EventArgs) Handles btnCalculate.Click
    Try
        Dim monthlyInvestment As Decimal =
            Convert.ToDecimal(txtMonthlyInvestment.Text)
        Dim yearlyInterestRate As Decimal =
            Convert.ToDecimal(txtInterestRate.Text)
        Dim years As Integer = Convert.ToInt32(txtYears.Text)

        Dim monthlyInterestRate As Decimal = yearlyInterestRate / 12 / 100
        Dim months As Integer = years * 12
        Dim futureValue As Decimal = Me.FutureValue(
            monthlyInvestment, monthlyInterestRate, months)

        txtFutureValue.Text = FormatCurrency(futureValue)
    Catch ex As FormatException
        MessageBox.Show(
            "Invalid numeric format. Please check all entries.",
            "Entry Error")
    Catch ex As OverflowException
        MessageBox.Show(
            "Overflow error. Please enter smaller values.",
            "Entry Error")
    Catch ex As Exception
        MessageBox.Show(ex.Message, ex.GetType.ToString)
    Finally
        txtMonthlyInvestment.Select()
    End Try
End Sub

Private Function FutureValue(monthlyInvestment As Decimal,
        monthlyInterestRate As Decimal, months As Integer) _
        As Decimal
    For i As Integer = 1 To months
        FutureValue = (FutureValue + monthlyInvestment) *
                      (1 + monthlyInterestRate)
    Next
End Function
```

Figure 7-8 The Future Value application with exception handling

How to validate data

Whenever a user enters data, it needs to be checked to make sure that it's valid. This is known as *data validation*. When an entry is invalid, the application needs to display an error message and give the user another chance to enter valid data. This needs to be repeated until all the entries on the form are valid.

How to validate a single entry

When a user enters text into a text box, you may want to perform several types of data validation. In particular, it's common to perform the three types of data validation shown in figure 7-9.

First, if the application requires that the user enters a value into a text box, you can check its Text property to make sure it contains one or more characters. Second, if the application requires that the user enters a number in the text box, you can use the TryParse method of the appropriate class within an If statement to check that the entry can be converted to the appropriate numeric data type. Third, if the application requires that the user enters a number within a specified range, you can use If statements to check that the number falls within that range. This is known as *range checking*.

If the data doesn't pass a validation test, you typically move the focus to the control that contains the invalid data. To do that, you call the Select method of the control as shown in all three examples in this figure. In addition, if the control contains data, you can select that data by calling the SelectAll method of the control as shown in the last two examples. That makes it easier for the user to enter a new value.

Although this figure only shows how to check data that the user has entered into a text box, the same principles apply to other types of controls, which you'll learn more about in chapter 10. You should also check strings and dates to make sure that they're valid, which you'll learn more about in chapter 9.

Often, the code that performs the data validation prevents exceptions from being thrown. For example, if the user doesn't enter a value in the Monthly Investment text box, the code in this figure displays a dialog box and moves the focus to that text box. If you didn't include this code, an exception would occur when the application tried to convert the empty string to a numeric data type.

Code that checks that an entry has been made

```
If txtMonthlyInvestment.Text = "" Then
    MessageBox.Show(
        "Monthly Investment is a required field.", "Entry Error")
    txtMonthlyInvestment.Select()
End If
```

Code that checks an entry for a valid decimal value

```
Dim number As Decimal = 0
If Not Decimal.TryParse(txtMonthlyInvestment.Text, number) Then
    MessageBox.Show("Monthly Investment must be a numeric value.",
        "Entry Error")
    txtMonthlyInvestment.Select()
    txtMonthlyInvestment.SelectAll()
End If
```

Code that checks an entry for a valid range

```
Dim monthlyInvestment As Decimal =
    Convert.ToDecimal(txtMonthlyInvestment.Text)
If monthlyInvestment <= 0 Then
    MessageBox.Show(
        "Monthly Investment must be greater than 0.", "Entry Error")
    txtMonthlyInvestment.Select()
    txtMonthlyInvestment.SelectAll()
ElseIf monthlyInvestment >= 1000 Then
    MessageBox.Show(
        "Monthly Investment must be less than 1,000.", "Entry Error")
    txtMonthlyInvestment.Select()
    txtMonthlyInvestment.SelectAll()
End If
```

Description

- When a user enters data, that data usually needs to be checked to make sure that it is valid. This is known as *data validation*.
- When an entry is invalid, the program needs to display an error message and give the user another chance to enter valid data.
- Three common types of validity checking are (1) to make sure that a required entry has been made, (2) to make sure that an entry has a valid numeric format, and (3) to make sure that an entry is within a valid range (known as *range checking*).
- To test whether a value has been entered into a text box, you can check whether the Text property of the box is equal to an empty string.
- To test whether a text box contains valid numeric data, you can code an if statement with a condition that tests if a TryParse statement that converts the data is successful.
- To test whether a value is within an acceptable range, you can use If statements.
- To move the focus to a text box, call the Select method of the text box. Then, to select all of the characters in the text box, call the SelectAll method.

Figure 7-9 How to validate a single entry

How to use generic procedures to validate an entry

Since it's common to check text boxes for valid data, it often makes sense to create generic procedures for data validation like the ones in figure 7-10. These Function procedures perform the same types of validation described in the previous figure, but they work for any text box instead of a specific text box. All of these procedures return Boolean values that indicate whether the data was valid (True) or invalid (False).

In this figure, the IsPresent procedure checks to make sure the user has entered data in a text box. Its first parameter is a variable that refers to the text box, and its second parameter is a string that contains a name for the text box. If the user hasn't entered any characters into the text box, this procedure displays a dialog box with a message that includes the name parameter, moves the focus to the text box, and returns a False value. Otherwise, the procedure returns a True value.

The IsDecimal procedure accepts the same parameters as the IsPresent procedure, but it uses an If statement that calls the TryParse method of the Decimal class to check if the value entered by the user is a Decimal value. If it isn't, the TryParse method will return a False value and the statements in the Else block will be executed. These statements display a dialog box with an appropriate message, move the focus to the text box with all characters selected, and return a False value.

Once you understand how the IsDecimal procedure works, you can code procedures for other numeric types. For example, you can code an IsInt32 procedure that uses the TryParse method of the Int32 class to check if the user has entered a valid Integer value.

The IsWithinRange procedure begins with the same two parameters as the IsPresent and IsDecimal procedures, but it includes two additional parameters: min and max. These parameters contain the minimum and maximum values that can be entered into the text box.

The IsWithinRange procedure begins by converting the value the user entered into the text box to a Decimal value. Then, it uses an If statement to check if the Decimal value is within the range specified by the min and max parameters. If not, this procedure displays a dialog box with an appropriate message, moves the focus to the text box with all characters selected, and returns a False value.

Since the IsWithinRange procedure uses the Decimal type, which is the widest numeric data type, this procedure works with all numeric types. That's because all numeric types can be automatically cast to the Decimal type. If, for example, you pass arguments of the Integer type to the min and max parameters, they will be cast to the Decimal type.

The code at the bottom of this figure shows how to call these three procedures to make sure a valid Decimal value has been entered in the Monthly Investment text box. First, this code calls the IsPresent procedure to make sure the user has entered one or more characters. Then, it calls the IsDecimal proce-

A Function procedure that checks for a required field

```
Private Function IsPresent(textBox As TextBox, name As String) _
        As Boolean
    If textBox.Text = "" Then
        MessageBox.Show(name & " is a required field.", "Entry Error")
        textBox.Select()
        Return False
    Else
        Return True
    End If
End Function
```

A Function procedure that checks for a valid Decimal format

```
Private Function IsDecimal(textBox As TextBox, name As String) _
        As Boolean
    Dim number As Decimal = 0
    If Decimal.TryParse(textBox.Text, number) Then
        Return True
    Else
        MessageBox.Show(name & " must be a decimal value.",
            "Entry Error")
        textBox.Select()
        textBox.SelectAll()
        Return False
    End If
End Function
```

A Function procedure that checks for a valid numeric range

```
Private Function IsWithinRange(textBox As TextBox,
        name As String, min As Decimal,
        max As Decimal) As Boolean
    Dim number As Decimal = CDec(textBox.Text)
    If number < min OrElse number > max Then
        MessageBox.Show(name & " must be between " & min &
            "and " & max & ".", "Entry Error")
        textBox.Select()
        textBox.SelectAll()
        Return False
    Else
        Return True
    End If
End Function
```

Code that uses the three procedures to check the validity of one entry

```
If IsPresent(txtMonthlyInvestment, "Monthly Investment") AndAlso
    IsDecimal(txtMonthlyInvestment, "Monthly Investment") AndAlso
    IsWithinRange(txtMonthlyInvestment, "Monthly Investment", 1, 1000)
Then
    MessageBox.Show("Monthly Investment is valid.", "Test")
End If
```

Description

- Since it's common to need to check text boxes for valid data, it often makes sense to create generic procedures like these for data validation.

Figure 7-10 How to use generic procedures to validate an entry

dure to make sure the user has entered a string that can be successfully converted to a Decimal value. Finally, it calls the IsWithinRange procedure to make sure that this Decimal value is greater than or equal to 1 and less than 1000. If all three procedures return a True value, this code displays a dialog box that indicates that the entry is valid.

How to validate multiple entries

Figure 7-11 shows two ways to code a procedure named IsValidData that validates multiple entries on a form. These IsValidData procedures validate the user entries in the three text boxes on the Future Value form. That way, all the data validation for the form is coded in one location, which makes the code easy to read and maintain.

The first IsValidData procedure in this figure uses a series of If statements to perform three validation tests on each user entry. Within each If statement, the Not operator is used to reverse the Boolean value that's returned by the called procedure. If, for example, an entry for the Monthly Investment text box is *not* present, the IsPresent procedure displays a dialog box and returns a False value. As a result, the rest of the If statements in the procedure aren't executed.

The second IsValidData procedure uses a single Return statement to check all the validation conditions. To do this, it returns the result of all the validation conditions, connected by the AndAlso operator. Since this operator is a short-circuit operator, the next condition is evaluated only if the previous condition returns a True value. As a result, the validation procedures will only be called until the first one returns a False value. Then, that procedure will display the appropriate dialog box, and the entire IsValidData procedure will return a False value.

Note that both of these procedures call the IsPresent procedure first, followed by the IsDecimal procedure, followed by the IsWithinRange procedure. In this case, IsDecimal must be called before IsWithinRange because IsWithinRange assumes that the text box that's being passed to it contains a valid numeric value. So if you pass it a text box that contains an invalid numeric value, the IsWithinRange procedure will throw an InvalidCastException. However, if you use the IsDecimal procedure to check the text box for a Decimal value first, the IsWithinRange procedure should never throw an InvalidCastException.

Code that uses a series of simple if statements

```
Private Function IsValidData() As Boolean
    ' Validate the Monthly Investment text box
    If Not IsPresent(txtMonthlyInvestment, "Monthly Investment") Then
        Return False
    End If
    If Not IsDecimal(txtMonthlyInvestment, "Monthly Investment") Then
        Return False
    End If
    If Not IsWithinRange(txtMonthlyInvestment, "Monthly Investment",
            1, 1000) Then
        Return False
    End If

    ' Validate the Interest Rate text box
    If Not IsPresent(txtInterestRate, "Yearly Interest Rate") Then
        Return False
    End If
    If Not IsDecimal(txtInterestRate, "Yearly Interest Rate") Then
        Return False
    End If
    If Not IsWithinRange(txtInterestRate, "Yearly Interest Rate", 1, 15) Then
        Return False
    End If

    ' Validate the Years text box
    If Not IsPresent(txtYears, "Number of Years") Then Return False
    If Not IsInt32(txtYears, "Number of Years") Then Return False
    If Not IsWithinRange(txtYears, "Number of Years", 1, 50) Then Return False

    Return True          ' If all conditions were False
End Function
```

Code that uses compound conditions in a single return statement

```
Private Function IsValidData() As Boolean
   Return _
      IsPresent(txtMonthlyInvestment, "Monthly Investment") AndAlso
      IsDecimal(txtMonthlyInvestment, "Monthly Investment") AndAlso
      IsWithinRange(txtMonthlyInvestment, "Monthly Investment", 1, 1000) AndAlso
      IsPresent(txtInterestRate, "Yearly Interest Rate") AndAlso
      IsDecimal(txtInterestRate, "Yearly Interest Rate") AndAlso
      IsWithinRange(txtInterestRate, "Yearly Interest Rate", 1, 15) AndAlso
      IsPresent(txtYears, "Number of Years") AndAlso
      IsInt32(txtYears, "Number of Years") AndAlso
      IsWithinRange(txtYears, "Number of Years", 1, 50)
End Function
```

Description

- Both of these IsValidData procedures use the procedures in the previous figure, plus an IsInt32 procedure that's similar to the IsDecimal procedure. Using procedures like these let you code all of the data validation for an entire form in one location.

Figure 7-11 How to validate multiple entries

The Future Value application with data validation

In figure 7-8, you saw a version of the Future Value application that used structured exception handling to catch all exceptions that might be thrown. Now, you'll see an improved version of this application with data validation code that prevents casting and overflow exceptions from being thrown.

The dialog boxes

Figure 7-12 shows the dialog boxes that are displayed when the user enters invalid data. For example, the first dialog box is displayed if the user doesn't enter a value for the Yearly Interest Rate text box. In contrast, the last dialog box is displayed if an exception that hasn't been anticipated is thrown. To test this dialog box, you can code a Throw statement within the code for the Future Value application as shown in figure 7-7.

The code

Figure 7-13 shows the code for this version of the Future Value application. To start, the btnCalculate_Click procedure contains an exception handler that catches and handles any unanticipated exceptions. Within the Try block, an If statement checks whether the IsValidData procedure returns a True value. If so, the future value is calculated and displayed. Otherwise, none of the statements within the If block are executed. However, the data validation procedure that detected the error will display a dialog box with an appropriate message and move the focus to the appropriate text box.

The IsValidData procedure checks all three of the text boxes on the form to make sure that they contain valid numeric entries. Within this procedure, a procedure named IsInt32 is called to check that the user entered a valid Integer value into the Number of Years text box. This procedure works much like the IsDecimal procedure.

Each procedure in this application performs a specific task. For example, the btnCalculate_Click procedure contains the code that gets the values from the form and displays values on the form. The IsValidData, IsPresent, IsDecimal, IsInt32, and IsWithinRange procedures contain the code that validates the data that's entered by the user. And the FutureValue procedure contains the code that performs the calculation. This is a good design because it leads to code that's reusable and easy to maintain.

However, this code could be more efficient. If, for example, the user enters a valid Decimal value in the Monthly Investment text box, the value is converted to a decimal three times: once by the IsDecimal procedure, once by the IsWithinRange procedure, and once by the btnCalculate_Click procedure. For most applications, however, the benefits that result from being able to reuse and maintain this code far outweigh any performance issues.

The Future Value form with a dialog box for required fields

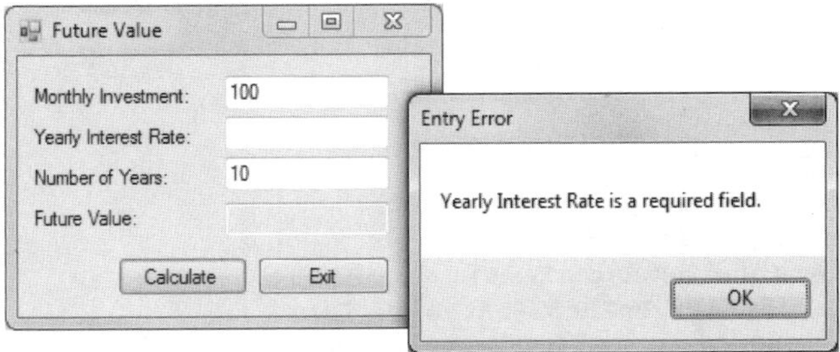

The dialog box for invalid decimals

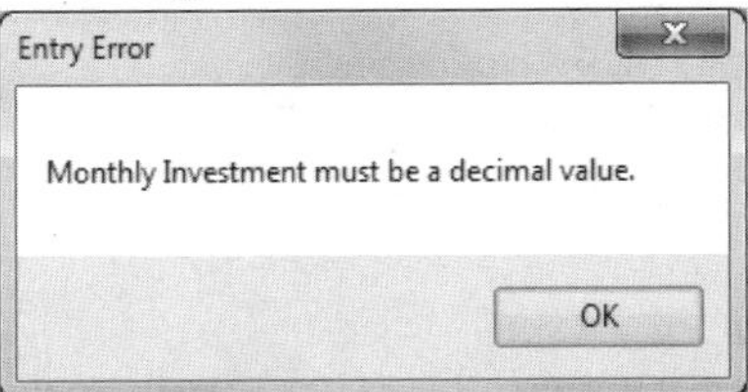

The dialog box for invalid ranges

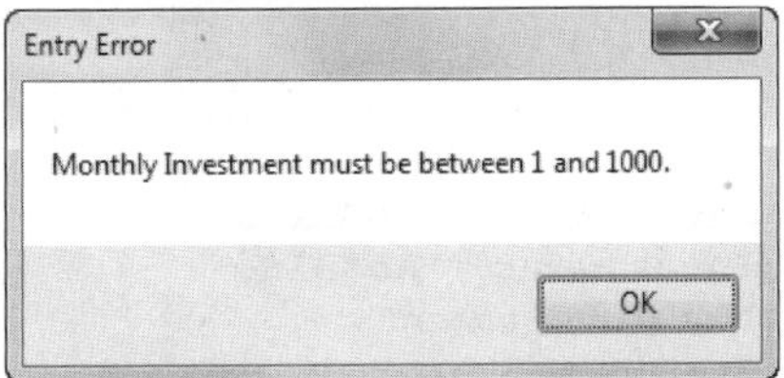

The dialog box for an unanticipated exception

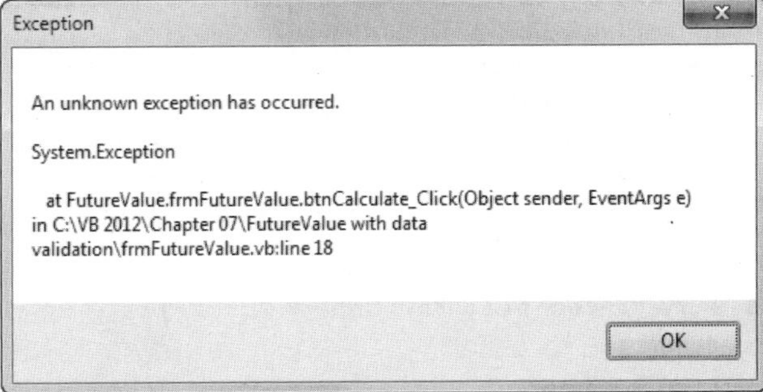

Description

- The first dialog box is displayed if the user doesn't enter a required field.
- The second dialog box is displayed if the user enters a value for the monthly investment or yearly interest rate that isn't in a valid decimal format.
- The third dialog box is displayed if the user enters a number that isn't within the range specified by the application.
- The fourth dialog box is displayed if an unanticipated exception occurs.

Figure 7-12 The dialog boxes of the Future Value application

The code for the Future Value application

Page 1

```
Private Sub btnCalculate_Click(sender As Object,
      e As EventArgs) Handles btnCalculate.Click
   Try
      If IsValidData() Then
         Dim monthlyInvestment As Decimal =
            Convert.ToDecimal(txtMonthlyInvestment.Text)
         Dim yearlyInterestRate As Decimal =
            Convert.ToDecimal(txtInterestRate.Text)
         Dim years As Integer = Convert.ToInt32(txtYears.Text)

         Dim monthlyInterestRate As Decimal = yearlyInterestRate / 12 / 100
         Dim months As Integer = years * 12
         Dim futureValue As Decimal = Me.FutureValue(
            monthlyInvestment, monthlyInterestRate, months)
         txtFutureValue.Text = FormatCurrency(futureValue)
         txtMonthlyInvestment.Select()
      End If
   Catch ex As Exception
      MessageBox.Show(ex.Message & vbCrLf & vbCrLf &
         ex.GetType.ToString & vbCrLf & vbCrLf &
         ex.StackTrace, "Exception")
   End Try
End Sub

Private Function IsValidData() As Boolean
   Return _
      IsPresent(txtMonthlyInvestment, "Monthly Investment") AndAlso
      IsDecimal(txtMonthlyInvestment, "Monthly Investment") AndAlso
      IsWithinRange(txtMonthlyInvestment, "Monthly Investment",
          1, 1000) AndAlso
      IsPresent(txtInterestRate, "Yearly Interest Rate") AndAlso
      IsDecimal(txtInterestRate, "Yearly Interest Rate") AndAlso
      IsWithinRange(txtInterestRate, "Yearly Interest Rate", 1, 15) AndAlso
      IsPresent(txtYears, "Number of Years") AndAlso
      IsInt32(txtYears, "Number of Years") AndAlso
      IsWithinRange(txtYears, "Number of Years", 1, 50)
End Function

Private Function IsPresent(textBox As TextBox, name As String) _
      As Boolean
   If textBox.Text = "" Then
      MessageBox.Show(name & " is a required field.", "Entry Error")
      textBox.Select()
      Return False
   Else
      Return True
   End If
End Function
```

Figure 7-13 The code for the Future Value application (part 1 of 2)

The code for the Future Value application Page 2

```
Private Function IsDecimal(textBox As TextBox, name As String) _
        As Boolean
    Dim number As Decimal = 0
    If Decimal.TryParse(textBox.Text, number) Then
        Return True
    Else
        MessageBox.Show(name & " must be a decimal value.", "Entry Error")
        textBox.Select()
        textBox.SelectAll()
        Return False
    End If
End Function

Private Function IsInt32(textBox As TextBox, name As String) _
        As Boolean
    Dim number As Integer = 0
    If Int32.TryParse(textBox.Text, number) Then
        Return True
    Else
        MessageBox.Show(name & " must be an integer.", "Entry Error")
        textBox.Select()
        textBox.SelectAll()
        Return False
    End If
End Function

Private Function IsWithinRange(textBox As TextBox,
      name As String, min As Decimal,
      max As Decimal) As Boolean
   Dim number As Decimal = CDec(textBox.Text)
   If number < min OrElse number > max Then
      MessageBox.Show(name & " must be between " & min &
         " and " & max & ".", "Entry Error")
      textBox.Select()
      textBox.SelectAll()
      Return False
   Else
      Return True
   End If
End Function

Private Function FutureValue(monthlyInvestment As Decimal,
      monthlyInterestRate As Decimal, months As Integer) _
      As Decimal
   For i As Integer = 1 To months
      FutureValue = (FutureValue + monthlyInvestment) *
                    (1 + monthlyInterestRate)
   Next
End Function

Private Sub btnExit_Click(sender As Object,
      e As EventArgs) Handles btnExit.Click
   Me.Close()
End Sub
```

Figure 7-13 The code for the Future Value application (part 2 of 2)

Two other ways to validate data

In general, we recommend that you use the techniques you've just learned to validate the data in your applications. However, there are two other validation techniques that you should be aware of.

How to use the Validating event

Figure 7-14 shows how you can use an event handler for the Validating event of a control to validate the data that's been entered into the control. This event occurs when the focus leaves the control. At that time, the data that has been entered into the control can be validated.

In the example, the Validating event handler for the Monthly Investment text box uses the IsPresent, IsDecimal, and IsWithinRange procedures of figure 7-10 to validate the text box entry. If the entry passes all three validity tests, nothing is done and the application continues. But if one of the tests fails, the Cancel property of the e argument is set to True, which cancels all of the events that would normally follow the Validating event. This returns the focus to the text box so the user can fix the data.

Although this technique works okay for some applications, it has a couple of weaknesses. First, it only works if the user moves the focus to the control that's being validated. So if the user clicks on a button without ever entering the control, its data is never validated.

Second, if the user clicks the Close button in the form's title bar, each Validating event handler is executed before the form is closed. That means that the data in the controls with Validating event handlers must be valid before the form can be closed. To avoid this problem, you can remove the Close button from the form—and all the other controls in the title bar—by setting the form's ControlBox property to False. Then, you can set the CausesValidation property of the Exit button on the form to False so the form can be closed without the validation being performed.

Because of these two problems, we don't typically use this validation technique. But it occasionally works okay for an application.

An event procedure for validating the Monthly Investment text box

```
Private Sub txtMonthlyInvestment_Validating(sender As Object,
        e As System.ComponentModel.CancelEventArgs) _
        Handles txtMonthlyInvestment.Validating
    If Not IsPresent(txtMonthlyInvestment, "Monthly Investment") Then
        e.Cancel = True
    ElseIf Not IsDecimal(txtMonthlyInvestment,
            "Monthly Investment") Then
        e.Cancel = True
    ElseIf Not IsWithinRange(txtMonthlyInvestment,
            "Monthly Investment", 1, 1000) Then
        e.Cancel = True
    End If
End Sub
```

Description

- The Validating event for a control occurs when the focus leaves the control either by using keystrokes like the Tab key or by using the mouse.
- An event handler for the Validating event for a control can check the validity of the entry in that control.
- If you set the Cancel property of the CancelEventArgs object (e) to True, the events that would otherwise follow the Validating event are cancelled so the focus is returned to the control that started the event.
- To prevent validation from being done when the user clicks a button like the Exit button, you can set the CausesValidation property of that button to False.

Two problems with using event handlers for Validating events

- Validating event handlers are only triggered if the user moves the focus to the control.
- Validating event handlers are triggered if the user clicks the Close button in the form's title bar.

Figure 7-14 How to use the Validating event for data validation

How to use the masked text box

Figure 7-15 shows how you can use the *masked text box* control. In effect, this control is an enhanced version of a normal text box control that helps you control the data the user can enter.

One of the key properties of this control is the Mask property. It uses mask characters that determine what data the user can enter into the control. If, for example, the Mask property is set to L, the user is forced to enter just one letter in the box. Or, if the Mask is set to ####.##, the user is forced to enter four digits before the decimal point and two after. This by itself is a type of data validation because the user can't leave the control until the requirements of the mask have been satisfied.

Beyond that, though, you can set the ValidatingType property to a data type like Decimal or DateTime to force the user to enter a value that can be converted to that type. This is done automatically by the code that's generated for the control. Note, however, that you have to set this property through code, not by using the Properties window.

By coding these two properties, you can limit the range of the entry and make sure the entry is the right data type. But often, you need to do more validity testing, and you can do that by coding an event handler for the control's TypeValidationCompleted event. If, for example, the entry can't be negative or zero, you can code an event handler like the one in this figure.

In this event handler, you can use the IsValidInput property of the TypeValidationEventArgs object (e) to determine whether the entry passed the type validation test. If it has, you can do other validation tests by using the ReturnValue property of the e parameter to get an object that contains the value the user entered. Then, if the entry doesn't pass those tests, you can display an appropriate message and set the Cancel property of the e parameter to True. At that point, the user can fix the entry in the masked text box.

If you experiment with the masked text box, you'll probably conclude that using this control is more trouble than it's worth, especially for numeric fields that require additional validity testing. Please note, however, that the masks work better for entries like dates, phone numbers, and zip codes. So for some entries, you can set just the Mask property, and that by itself will force the user to enter valid data.

When you use the Properties window to set the Mask property for a masked text box, you can select a standard mask for common entries like dates, phone numbers, and zip codes. And if you check the Help information for this control, you can learn more about the properties that you can use with it.

The Invoice Total form with two masked text boxes

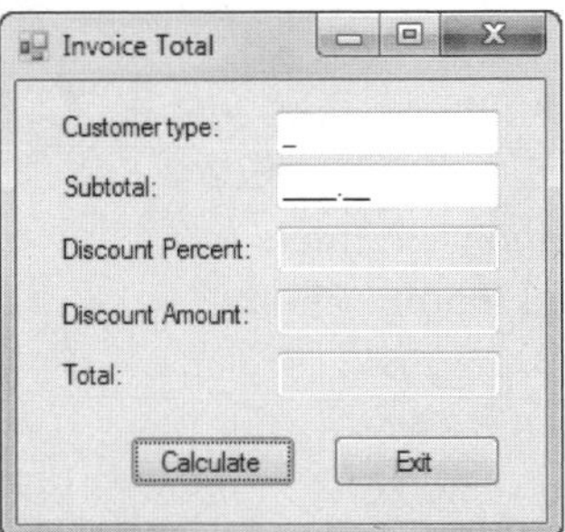

Typical masks used in the Mask property of a masked text box

Mask property	Mask when run	Typical entry	Entry requirements
L	_	C	One letter
####.##	____.__	0450.50	Six digits with two decimal places
00/00/0000	__/__/____	06/08/2007	Eight digits in date format
(999) 000-0000	(___) ___-____	(555) 432-3291	Ten digits in phone number format

Code that sets the ValidatingType property for a masked text box

```
mskSubtotal.ValidatingType = GetType(Decimal)
```

An event handler for the control's TypeValidationCompleted event

```
Private Sub mskSubtotal_TypeValidationCompleted(
        sender As Object,
        e As Windows.Forms.TypeValidationEventArgs) _
        Handles mskSubtotal.TypeValidationCompleted
    If e.IsValidInput Then
        If CDec(e.ReturnValue) <= 0 Then
            MessageBox.Show(
                "Please enter a subtotal that's greater than zero.",
                "Entry Error")
            e.Cancel = True
        End If
    Else
        e.Cancel = True
    End If
End Sub
```

Description

- The mask that you use for the Mask property of the control determines what characters the user must enter into the text box, and the user can't leave the control without entering those characters.
- If you set the ValidatingType property for the control, the entry is tested to see whether it's valid for that type. Then, you can use the TypeValidationCompleted event for further testing.

Figure 7-15 How to use a masked text box for data validation

Perspective

In this chapter, you learned how to handle exceptions and validate data so you can code applications that are "bulletproof." This means that your applications won't throw unhandled exceptions no matter what data the user enters or how the user works with the user interface. This is an essential feature of any professional application.

But there's still a lot more for you to learn about the Visual Basic language. So in chapter 8, you'll learn how to work with arrays and collections. In chapter 9, you'll learn how to work with dates, and you'll learn more about working with strings. In chapter 10, you'll learn how to develop forms that use other types of controls. And in chapter 11, you'll learn how to create and use your own classes and objects. When you finish those chapters, you'll be able to develop applications of considerable complexity.

Terms

data validation
validity checking
exception
throw an exception
catch an exception
exception handling
subclass
overflow exception
divide-by-zero exception
structured exception handling
Try...Catch statement
exception handler
Try block
Catch block
block scope
stack trace
Finally block
Throw statement
range checking

Exercise 7-1 Enhance the Future Value application

This exercise guides you through the process of enhancing the Future Value application of chapter 6 so it does data validation and exception handling.

1. Open the application that's in the C:\VB 2012\Chapter 07\FutureValue directory. This is the application from chapter 6, plus the four Function procedures for validation that are in figure 7-10.
2. Add a Try...Catch statement to the btnCalculate_Click procedure that catches and handles any InvalidCastException or OverflowException that might occur. These Catch blocks should display dialog boxes with appropriate error messages that also indicate what type of exception occurred. Then, test these enhancements.

3. Add another Catch block to the Try...Catch statement that will catch any other exception that might occur. This Catch block should display a dialog box that displays the message contained in the exception object, along with the exception type and the stack trace.
4. Add a Throw statement to the FutureValue procedure that throws an exception of the Exception class regardless of the result of the calculation. This statement will be used to test the enhancements of step 3, and it should specify a generic message that indicates an unexpected error. Then, test the application by entering valid values in the three text boxes and clicking the Calculate button. If the exception is thrown and the last Catch block works correctly, end the application and comment out the Throw statement.
5. Code an IsValidData procedure that calls the four generic procedures that this application includes. You can use either of the two techniques presented in figure 7-11 to do this.
6. Modify the code in the event handler for the Calculate button so it uses the IsValidData procedure to validate the data before it processes it. Then, test the application to be sure it works correctly.
7. Comment out the Catch blocks for the specific exceptions since these exceptions are now prevented by the data validation. Then, test this application one more time.

Exercise 7-2 Enhance the Invoice Total application

If you did exercise 6-1 in the last chapter, this chapter asks you to add data validation and exception handling to it.

1. Copy the Invoice Total application from your C:\VB 2012\Chapter 06 directory to your Chapter 07 directory. This should be your solution to exercise 6-1 of the last chapter.
2. If your application has both a Sub procedure and a Function procedure for setting the discount percent, delete the Sub procedure.
3. Go to the Function procedure for setting the discount percent and comment out the Else clause. That means that a discount percent is only set for customer type codes of R and C, so assume that these are the only valid customer type codes.
4. Add data validation for the customer type entry so it has to be either R or C. To do that, write a Function procedure named IsValidCustomerType that validates the entry, displays an error message if the entry is invalid, and returns a Boolean value that indicates whether the type is valid.

5. Call the IsValidCustomerType function at the start of the btnCalculate_Click procedure, and exit from the procedure if the customer type is invalid. Then, test this change.
6. Add data validation for the subtotal entry so it has to be a positive numeric value that is greater than zero and not greater than 1000. To do that, write a Function procedure named IsValidSubtotal that validates the entry, displays an appropriate error message if the entry is invalid, and returns a Boolean value that indicates whether the entry is valid. This should illustrate the value of generic procedures like the ones you used in the Future Value application.
7. Call the IsValidSubtotal function at the start of the btnCalculate_Click procedure, and exit from the procedure if the subtotal is invalid. Then, test this change.
8. Modify the application so T is a valid customer type that gets a standard 40% discount. Then, test this change. This illustrates how the use of Function procedures can make applications easier to modify.
9. When you're through experimenting, close the project.

8

How to use arrays and collections

Arrays and collections are objects that act as containers. As you develop Visual Basic applications, you'll find many uses for arrays and collections. For example, you can use a sales array or a sales collection to hold the sales amounts for each of the 12 months of the year. Then, you can use that array or collection to perform calculations on those amounts. In this chapter, you'll learn the basic concepts and techniques for working with arrays and collections.

How to work with one-dimensional arrays

You can use an *array* to store a set of related data. Since a one-dimensional array is the simplest type of array, you'll start by learning how to create and use one-dimensional arrays.

How to create an array

To declare a *one-dimensional array*, you use the first syntax shown in figure 8-1. This is similar to the way you declare any variables, except that you code parentheses after the variable name to indicate that the variable refers to an array. Within the parentheses, you can code a number that indicates the *upper bound* of the array. This upper bound is the index value of the last element in the array.

As you will see in the next figure, the index values for an array always start with zero. As a result, an array can hold one more element than the upper bound of the array. If, for example, you use 49 as the upper bound, the array can hold 50 elements, which is referred to as the *length*, or *size*, of the array.

If you code an upper bound when you declare an array, the *elements* in the array are initialized to the default values shown in this figure. In contrast, if you don't code an upper bound, as shown by the second syntax in this figure, the elements in the array aren't initialized. Then, you can use the third syntax and the New keyword to create an instance of the array and initialize the elements in the array.

When you use the New keyword to create an instance of an array, you are actually calling the constructor of the Array class that's provided by the .NET Framework. But whether or not you use the New keyword, an array is instantiated from the Array class. After you read chapter 11, you'll have a better understanding of how that works.

In the first example in this figure, you can see the most common way that an array is declared and initialized. Here, the upper bound is 99, so an array of 100 Integer values is declared and initialized.

In the second example, the first statement gets the upper bound from a text box and converts it to an Integer variable. Then, that variable is used to supply the upper bound for an array of Decimal values. This shows that you can get the upper bound for an array from a user entry.

The third example gets the same result as the second example. However, it uses one statement to declare but not initialize an array. Then, it uses the New keyword to call the constructor for the Array class so an instance of the array is created and initialized.

The fourth example shows another way that you can declare and initialize an array. The difference is that both the lower bound and the upper bound are specified in the parentheses after the name of the array. However, because the lower bound is always zero, coding the lower bound is unnecessary. It serves only to document the fact that the lower bound is zero. As a result, we won't code the lower bound in any other examples in this book.

The syntax for declaring and initializing a one-dimensional array

Declaring and initializing a one-dimensional array

```
Dim arrayName(upperbound) As type
```

Declaring but not initializing a one-dimensional array

```
Dim arrayName() As type
```

Initializing an array that has only been declared

```
arrayName = New type(upperbound) {}
```

How to declare and initialize an array

Declaring and initializing an array

```
Dim numbers(99) As Integer                    ' provides for 100 numbers
```

Getting the upper bound from a variable

```
Dim maxTotals As Integer = CInt(txtUpperBound.Text)
Dim totals(maxTotals) As Decimal
```

Using the New keyword to initialize an array

```
Dim maxTotals As Integer = CInt(txtUpperBound.Text)
Dim totals() As Decimal
totals = New Decimal(maxTotals) {}
```

How to document the lower bound when you declare an array

```
Dim titles(0 To 49) As String                 ' provides for 50 titles
```

Default values for array elements

Data type	Default value
All numeric types	0 (zero)
Char	Null (binary 0)
Boolean	False
Date	01/01/0001 00:00:00
All reference types	Null reference

Description

- An *array* can store one or more *elements*. The *length*, or *size*, of an array is the number of elements in the array.
- The *upper bound* of an array is one less than the length of an array. It represents the index of the last element in the array.
- When you create an array, each element of the array is set to a default value. If the array contains value types, each element is set to the value shown above. If the array contains reference types, each element is set to a null reference.
- The lower bound of an array is always zero. To document that, you can code 0 followed by the To keyword and the upper bound when you declare an array.

Figure 8-1 How to create an array

How to assign values to the elements of an array

Figure 8-2 shows how to assign values to the elements of an array. As the syntax at the top of this figure indicates, you refer to an element in an array by coding the array name followed by its *index* in parentheses. The index that you specify must be from 0, which refers to the first element in the array, to the upper bound of the array, which is one less than the length of the array.

To understand how this works, look at the first example in this figure. This example declares an array of decimals that contains four elements. Then, it uses indexes 0 through 3 to assign values to those four elements. Here, the length of the array is 4, and the upper bound is 3. Note that if you use an index that's greater than the upper bound, an IndexOutOfRangeException will be thrown.

The syntax and examples at the bottom of this figure show how to declare an array and assign values to its elements in a single statement. To assign the values, you just code a list of values in braces. Then, Visual Basic automatically sets the length of the array to the number of elements within the braces. However, if you code the New keyword followed by the type name and an upper bound, the number of values in the braces must be equal to the upper bound plus one. Otherwise, the code won't compile.

You can also create an array and assign values to it without declaring a data type for the array. This is illustrated in the last example in this figure. Here, the data type of the array is set to String because the values are all strings. You can also assign values with different types to the same array. Then, the type of the array is set to Object. Notice that when you use this technique, you omit the parentheses following the array name.

The syntax for referring to an element of an array

```
arrayName(index)
```

Examples that assign values by accessing each element

Code that assigns values to an array of Decimal types

```
Dim totals(3) As Decimal     ' this provides for 4 elements
totals(0) = 14.95D
totals(1) = 12.95D
totals(2) = 11.95D
totals(3) = 9.95D
'totals(4) = 8.95D           ' this would throw an IndexOutOfRangeException
```

Code that assigns objects to an array of strings

```
Dim names(2) As String
names(0) = "Ted Lewis"
names(1) = "Sue Jones"
names(2) = "Ray Thomas"
```

The syntax for creating an array and assigning values in one statement

```
Dim arrayName() As type =
    [New type(upperbound)] {value1[, value2][, value3]...}
```

Examples that create an array and assign values in one statement

```
Dim totals() As Decimal = {14.95D, 12.95D, 11.95D, 9.95D}
Dim names() As String = {"Ted Lewis", "Sue Jones", "Ray Thomas"}
Dim totals() As Decimal = New Decimal(3) {14.95D, 12.95D, 11.95D, 9.95D}
Dim names = {"Ted Lewis", "Sue Jones", "Ray Thomas"}
```

Description

- To refer to the elements in an array, you use an *index* where 0 is the first element, 1 is the second element, 2 is the third element, and so on. The index of the last element in an array is the upper bound.
- If you list the values to be assigned to an array without using the New keyword, an array is created with a length equal to the number of values in the list. If you use the New keyword and specify an upper bound, the number of values in the list must equal the upper bound plus one.
- If the Option Infer option is turned on, you can create an array and assign values to it in one statement without specifying a data type. Then, the data type is determined by the values you specify.
- If you specify an index that's less than zero or greater than the upper bound of an array, an IndexOutOfRangeException will be thrown when the statement is executed.

Figure 8-2 How to assign values to the elements of an array

How to use For loops to work with arrays

Now that you understand how to declare an array and assign values to its elements, you're ready to learn how to work with the values in an array. Figure 8-3 presents some of the basic techniques for doing that.

This figure starts by presenting the Length property of an array, which gets the number of elements in the array. You'll use this property frequently as you work with arrays.

The first example in this figure uses a For loop to put the numbers 0 through 9 into an array. Here, the first statement declares an array named numbers that contains ten Integer values. Then, the For loop assigns the value of the loop's counter to each of the elements in the array.

The second example uses a For loop to display the elements of the numbers array in a message box. Here, the first statement declares a string variable. Then, the For loop accesses each element of the numbers array, converts it to a string, and appends the string and two spaces to the string variable. When the For loop finishes, the next statement displays the string that contains the numbers in a message box.

The third example shows how to use a For loop to calculate the average value of the elements in the totals array. Here, the For loop gets the value of each element of the array and adds that value to the current value of the sum variable. After the loop, the next statement uses the sum variable and the Length property of the array to calculate the average.

The last example shows how to display the elements of the totals array in a message box, along with the sum and average for the array. Like the second example, this one uses a For loop to convert the values in the array to strings. Then, it appends each string and a new line character to a string variable. Finally, it displays the string and the sum and average values in a message box.

Note in all four of these examples that the counter that's used for the For loop ranges from 0 to the length of the array minus 1. That way, the index ranges from 0 to the upper bound as the statements within the loops are executed, so all elements are processed. If you don't subtract one from the length, an IndexOutOfRangeException will be thrown.

The syntax for using the Length property of an array

```
arrayName.Length
```

A For loop that puts the numbers 0 through 9 into an array

```
Dim numbers(9) As Integer
For i As Integer = 0 To numbers.Length - 1
    numbers(i) = i
Next
```

Code that displays the numbers array in a message box

```
Dim numbersString As String = ""
For i As Integer = 0 To numbers.Length - 1
    numbersString &= numbers(i).ToString & "  "
Next
MessageBox.Show(numbersString, "Numbers Test")
```

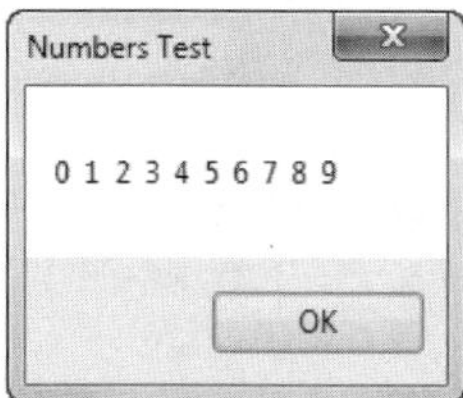

Code that uses a For loop to compute the average of a totals array

```
Dim totals() As Decimal = {14.95D, 12.95D, 11.95D, 9.95D}
Dim sum As Decimal = 0
For i As Integer = 0 To totals.Length - 1
    sum += totals(i)
Next
Dim average As Decimal = sum / totals.Length
```

Code that displays the totals array in a message box

```
Dim totalsString As String = ""
For i As Integer = 0 To totals.Length - 1
    totalsString &= totals(i).ToString & vbCrLf
Next
MessageBox.Show("The totals are:" & vbCrLf & totalsString & vbCrLf &
    "Sum: " & sum & vbCrLf & "Average: " & average, "Totals Test")
```

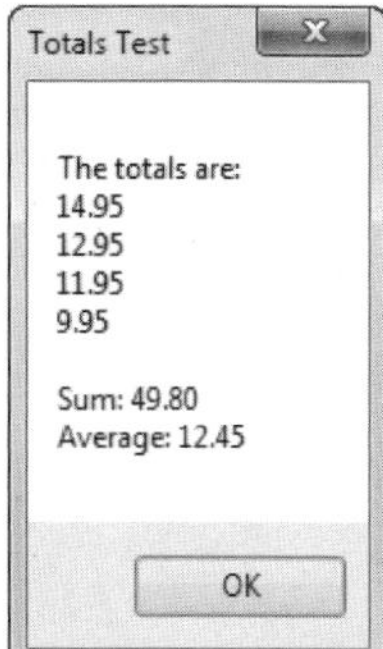

Figure 8-3 How to use For loops to work with arrays

How to use For Each loops to work with arrays

Although you can use For loops to work with the elements of an array, it's often easier to use a *For Each statement* to code a *For Each loop*. Figure 8-4 shows how to do that.

Within a For Each loop, you use a variable that represents one element in the array. As a result, the variable must have the same type as those elements. You can declare this variable outside of the For Each loop, in which case you just name the variable following the For Each keywords. You can also declare the variable following the For Each keywords. If you do that, you can omit the type and the variable will be given the same type as the elements in the array. After the variable name or declaration, you code the In keyword and the name of the array. Then, you can code one or more statements that use the variable name to work with each element in the array.

To illustrate, the first example in this figure shows how you can use a For Each loop to display the elements in the numbers array that you saw in the previous figure. Similarly, the second example computes the average of the totals array, and the third example displays the elements in the totals array. Notice that the third example doesn't declare the type of the variable that's used within the For Each loop. Because of that, the variable is given the Decimal type since the elements in the array are decimal values.

If you compare these examples to the For loop examples in the previous figure, you'll see that For Each loops are less complicated. In particular, when you use a For Each loop, you don't need to use a counter variable, and you don't need to use an index to get an element from the array. As a result, it's usually easier to use a For Each loop than a For loop.

You should realize, however, that there are times when you'll need to use a For loop to work with an array. If, for example, you only want to access some of the elements in an array, you'll need to use a For loop. You'll also need to use a For loop if you want to use a counter variable to assign values to the elements of the array as shown in the first example in figure 8-3.

The syntax of a For Each loop

```
For Each elementName [As type] In arrayName
    statements
Next
```

Code that displays the numbers array in a message box

```
Dim numbersString As String = ""
For Each number As Integer In numbers
    numbersString &= number.ToString & "  "
Next
MessageBox.Show(numbersString, "Numbers Test")
```

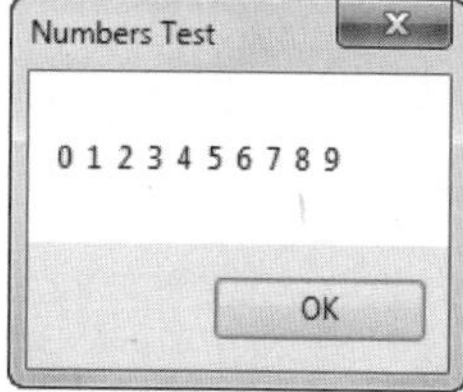

Code that computes the average of the totals array

```
Dim sum As Decimal = 0
For Each total As Decimal In totals
    sum += total
Next
Dim average As Decimal = sum / totals.Length
```

Code that displays the totals array in a message box

```
Dim totalsString As String = ""
For Each total In totals
    totalsString &= total.ToString & vbCrLf
Next
MessageBox.Show("The totals are:" & vbCrLf & totalsString & vbCrLf &
    "Sum: " & sum & vbCrLf & "Average: " & average, "Totals Test")
```

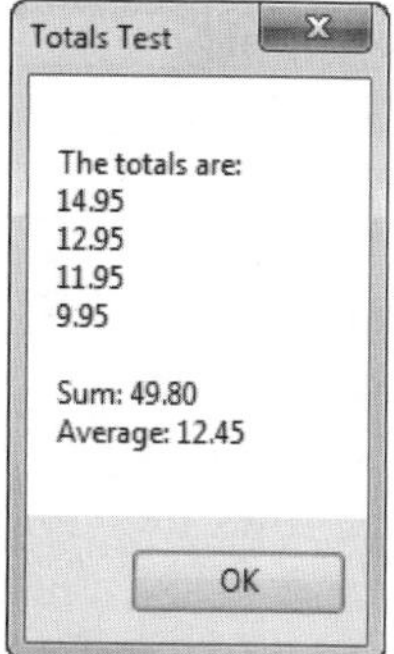

Description

- You can use a *For Each loop* to access each element of an array. You can also use For Each loops to work with collections like the ones you'll learn about later in this chapter.

Figure 8-4 How to use For Each loops to work with arrays

How to work with rectangular arrays

So far, this chapter has shown how to use an array that uses one index to store elements in a one-dimensional array. Now, you'll learn how to work with rectangular arrays that use two indexes. You can think of a *rectangular array* as a table that has rows and columns. Since rectangular arrays store data in two dimensions, they're also known as *two-dimensional arrays*.

If you need to use an array that has three or more dimensions, you can extend the two-dimensional techniques. In fact, Visual Basic provides for arrays that have up to 32 dimensions. In practice, though, you'll rarely need to go beyond three dimensions.

How to create a rectangular array

Figure 8-5 shows how to create a rectangular array. After the array name, you code a set of parentheses that contains an upper bound for the first dimension, a comma, and the upper bound for the second dimension.

For instance, the first example in this figure creates a rectangular array of Integer values. In this case, the array has three rows and two columns. After this statement is executed, each element in the array will be assigned the default value of 0 as described in figure 8-1.

How to assign values to a rectangular array

After you create an array, you can assign values to it. To do that, you refer to each element of the array using its row and column index. This is illustrated by the table of index values shown in figure 8-5. Because this array consists of three rows and two columns, the index values range from 0, 0 to 2, 1.

To assign values to the elements of a rectangular array, you can code one statement for each element as shown in the first example. These statements assign values to the elements of the numbers array that was created by the first statement in this figure.

You can also assign values to a rectangular array when you declare it as illustrated by the second, third, and fourth examples. Here, the second example creates the numbers array and assigns values to it by coding three sets of braces within an outer set of braces. The three inner braces represent the three rows in the array, and the values in these braces are assigned to the two columns in each row. The third example works the same except that it uses String values instead of Integer values, and it uses the New keyword. The fourth example also creates a String array, but it infers the data type from the specified values.

How to create a rectangular array

The syntax for declaring a rectangular array

```
Dim arrayName(firstupperbound, secondupperbound) As type
```

A statement that creates a 3x2 array

```
Dim numbers(2, 1) As Integer
```

How to assign values to a rectangular array

The syntax for referring to an element of a rectangular array

```
arrayName(rowindex, columnindex)
```

The index values for the elements of a 3x2 rectangular array

```
0, 0    0, 1
1, 0    1, 1
2, 0    2, 1
```

Code that assigns values to the numbers array

```
numbers(0, 0) = 1
numbers(0, 1) = 2
numbers(1, 0) = 3
numbers(1, 1) = 4
numbers(2, 0) = 5
numbers(2, 1) = 6
```

Code that creates a 3x2 array and assigns values with one statement

```
Dim numbers(,) As Integer = { {1, 2}, {3, 4}, {5, 6} }
```

Code that creates and assigns values to a 3x2 array of strings

```
Dim products(,) As String = New String(2, 1) _
    {{"VB2012", "Murach's Visual Basic 2012"},
     {"JAVAPRG", "Murach's Java Programming"},
     {"ASP45VB", "Murach's ASP.NET 4.5 with VB 2012"}}
```

Another way to create the array of strings

```
Dim products =
    {{"VB2012", "Murach's Visual Basic 2012"},
     {"JAVAPRG", "Murach's Java Programming"},
     {"ASP45VB", "Murach's ASP.NET 4.5 with VB 2012"}}
```

Description

- A *rectangular array* uses two indexes to store data. You can think of this type of array as a table that has rows and columns. Rectangular arrays are also referred to as *two-dimensional arrays*.
- If necessary, you can extend this two-dimensional syntax to work with arrays that have up to 32 dimensions, but using more than three dimensions is rare.

Figure 8-5 How to create a rectangular array and assign values to its elements

How to work with rectangular arrays

Figure 8-6 presents some examples that show how to work with rectangular arrays. The first example shows how to use the GetLength method to get the number of elements in a dimension of an array. Here, the first statement creates the numbers array you saw in figure 8-5. Next, the second statement gets the number of rows in the numbers array by calling the GetLength method and specifying 0 to get the length of the first dimension. Then, the third statement gets the number of columns in the array by calling the GetLength method and specifying 1 to get the length of the second dimension. Finally, the fourth statement uses indexes to get the values from both of the elements in the first row of the array and add them together.

The second example shows how to use nested For loops to display the elements of a rectangular array in a message box. In this case, the elements of the numbers array are displayed. As you can see, the outer For loop uses the counter variable to cycle through the index values for the rows in the array. Here, the indexes range from 0 to the value returned by the GetLength method minus one. Then, the inner For loop uses another counter variable to cycle through the index values for the columns in each row in the array. Just like the outer For loop, the inner For loop uses the GetLength method minus 1 to determine the highest index value.

To display the value of each element, the statement within the inner For loop uses both counter variables to get the value of the element and append it to a string. Each element is also separated from the next element by two spaces. Then, after each row is processed by the inner loop, a carriage-return/line-feed character is appended to the string so the elements in each row will appear on a separate line. When the outer loop ends, the string is displayed in a message box as shown in this figure.

The third example is similar, except that it displays the array of products you saw in figure 8-5. If you compare this code with the code in the second example, you'll see the only difference is that the elements in the two columns are separated by tab characters so they're aligned as shown here.

The syntax for using the GetLength method of a rectangular array

```
arrayName.GetLength(dimensionindex)
```

Code that works with the numbers array

```
Dim numbers(,) As Integer = { {1, 2}, {3, 4}, {5, 6} }
Dim numberOfRows As Integer = numbers.GetLength(0)
Dim numberOfColumns As Integer = numbers.GetLength(1)
Dim sumOfFirstRow As Integer = numbers(0, 0) + numbers(0, 1)
```

Code that displays the numbers array in a message box

```
Dim numbersString As String = ""
For i As Integer = 0 To numbers.GetLength(0) - 1
    For j As Integer = 0 To numbers.GetLength(1) - 1
        numbersString &= numbers(i, j) & "  "
    Next
    numbersString &= vbCrLf
Next
MessageBox.Show(numbersString, "Numbers Test")
```

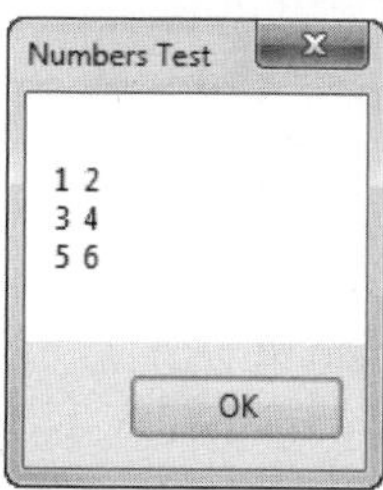

Code that displays the products array in a message box

```
Dim productsString As String = ""
For i As Integer = 0 To products.GetLength(0) - 1
    For j As Integer = 0 To products.GetLength(1) - 1
        productsString &= products(i, j) & vbTab
    Next j
    productsString &= vbCrLf
Next i
MessageBox.Show(productsString, "Products Test")
```

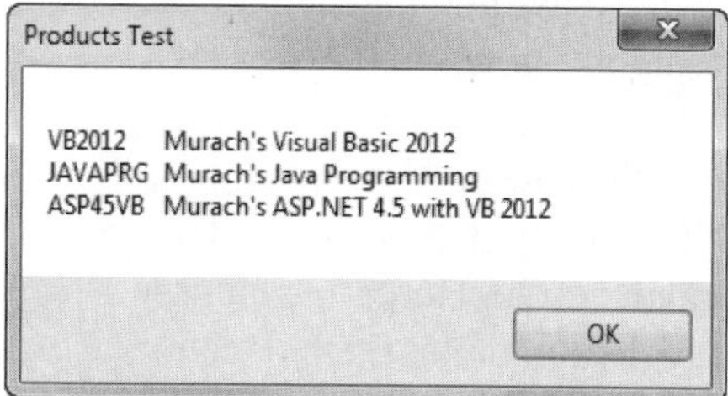

Description

- You use the GetLength method to get the number of rows or columns in a rectangular array. To get the number of rows, specify 0 for the dimension index argument. To get the number of columns, specify 1 for this argument.
- You can use nested For loops to move through the rows and columns of a rectangular array.

How to work with jagged arrays

Jagged arrays let you store data in a table that can have rows of unequal lengths. Since each row in a jagged array is stored as a separate array, a jagged array is also known as an *array of arrays*.

Although jagged arrays aren't used much, they do fill a need. One example of a jagged array is an array of 12 rows that represent the 12 months of the year. Then, the array in each row represents the number of days in the corresponding month. So the array for the first row has 31 elements, the array for the second row has 28 or 29 elements, and so on.

How to create a jagged array

Figure 8-7 shows how to create a jagged array. To declare a jagged array, you code two sets of parentheses after the array name. This indicates that each row of the first array will contain another array. Within the first set of parentheses, you also code the upper bound of the first array.

After you declare the jagged array, you declare an array for each row of the jagged array. Here, you use the New keyword followed by the data type, the upper bound, and a set of braces.

To illustrate, the first statement in the example shows how to declare a jagged array named numbers that contains three rows. Then, the next three statements declare and initialize three arrays with upper bounds of 2, 3, and 1. As a result, the first row of the numbers array has three columns, the second row has four columns, and the third row has two columns.

How to assign values to a jagged array

After you create a jagged array, you use the row and column indexes to refer to the elements in the array, just as you do for a rectangular array. When you refer to an element in a jagged array, however, you code each index within a separate set of parentheses as shown in figure 8-7. To assign values to the numbers array, for example, you can use the statements shown in the second example in this figure.

You can also create a jagged array and assign values to its elements in one statement. The third, fourth, and fifth examples illustrate how this works. The third example creates the same array as the second example. Here, you can see that a set of braces is used to enclose a list of array declarations. Each declaration in this list defines an array for one row in the jagged array. Notice in this example that the declarations don't specify the number of columns in each row. Instead, the number of columns is determined by the number of values that are specified for that row. Similarly, the number of rows in the jagged array is determined by the number of arrays in the list of arrays.

The fourth example is similar, except that each array declaration specifies the upper bound. Then, the number of values in each list must be equal to the upper bound plus one.

How to declare a jagged array

The syntax for declaring a jagged array

```
Dim arrayName(numberofrows)() As type
```

Code that declares a jagged array with three rows

```
Dim numbers (2)() As Integer            ' 3 rows are declared
numbers(0) = New Integer(2) {}          ' 3 columns for 1st row
numbers(1) = New Integer(3) {}          ' 4 columns for 2nd row
numbers(2) = New Integer(1) {}          ' 2 columns for 3rd row
```

How to refer to the elements of a jagged array

The syntax for referring to an element of a jagged array

```
arrayName(rowindex)(columnindex)
```

Statements that assign values to the numbers array

```
numbers(0)(0) = 1    numbers(1)(0) = 4    numbers(2)(0) = 8
numbers(0)(1) = 2    numbers(1)(1) = 5    numbers(2)(1) = 9
numbers(0)(2) = 3    numbers(1)(2) = 6
                     numbers(1)(3) = 7
```

Code that creates the numbers array with one statement

```
Dim numbers()() As Integer = {New Integer() {1, 2, 3},
                              New Integer() {4, 5, 6, 7},
                              New Integer() {8, 9}}
```

Code that creates a jagged array of strings

```
Dim titles()() As String =
    {New String(2) {"War and Peace", "Wuthering Heights", "1984"},
     New String(3) {"Casablanca", "Wizard of Oz", "Star Wars", "Birdy"},
     New String(1) {"Blue Suede Shoes", "Yellow Submarine"}}
```

Another way to create a jagged array of strings

```
Dim titles =
    {({"War and Peace", "Wuthering Heights", "1984"}),
     ({"Casablanca", "Wizard of Oz", "Star Wars", "Birdy"}),
     ({"Blue Suede Shoes", "Yellow Submarine"})}
```

Description

- You can use a *jagged array* to store data in a table that has rows of unequal lengths. Each row in a jagged array is stored as a separate array. Because of that, a jagged array is also known as an *array of arrays*.
- If you don't assign values to the elements of a jagged array when you declare the array, the declaration statement must specify the number of rows in the array. Then, you must declare the number of columns in each row before you assign values to the elements in that row.
- To assign values to the elements of a jagged array when you declare the array, you create a list of arrays that defines one array for each row. Then, the jagged array is created with one row for each array in that list.

Figure 8-7 How to create a jagged array and assign values to its elements

The fifth example also creates a jagged array of strings, but it infers the data type from the specified values. Notice that when you use this technique, you must enclose each array in the jagged array in parentheses.

How to work with jagged arrays

Figure 8-8 shows how to work with jagged arrays. Since the examples in this figure are similar to the examples for working with rectangular arrays shown in figure 8-6, you shouldn't have much trouble understanding how they work. However, you should notice two differences.

First, two sets of parentheses are used within the inner For loop to refer to each element in the array. Second, the inner loop uses the Length property minus one to get the highest index value for each row. That makes sense if you remember that each row in a jagged array is an array. Because each row can have a different length, you can't use the GetLength method to return the number of columns in each row as you do with rectangular arrays.

Code that displays the numbers array in a message box

```
Dim numbersString As String = ""
For i As Integer = 0 To numbers.GetLength(0) - 1
    For j As Integer = 0 To numbers(i).Length - 1
        numbersString &= numbers(i)(j) & "  "
    Next
    numbersString &= vbCrLf
Next
MessageBox.Show(numbersString, "Jagged Numbers Test")
```

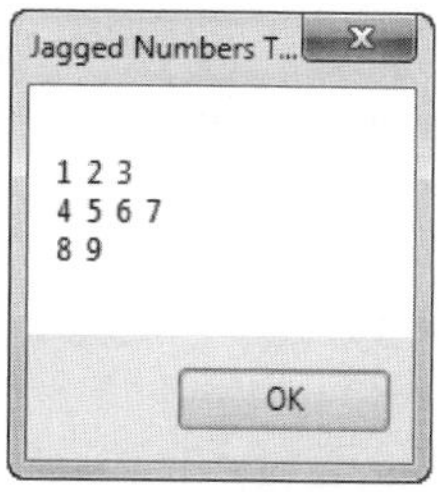

Jagged Numbers T...

1 2 3
4 5 6 7
8 9

OK

Code that displays the titles array in a message box

```
Dim titlesString As String = ""
For i As Integer = 0 To titles.GetLength(0) - 1
    For j As Integer = 0 To titles(i).Length - 1
        titlesString &= titles(i)(j) & "    "
    Next j
    titlesString &= vbCrLf
Next i
MessageBox.Show(titlesString, "Jagged Titles Test")
```

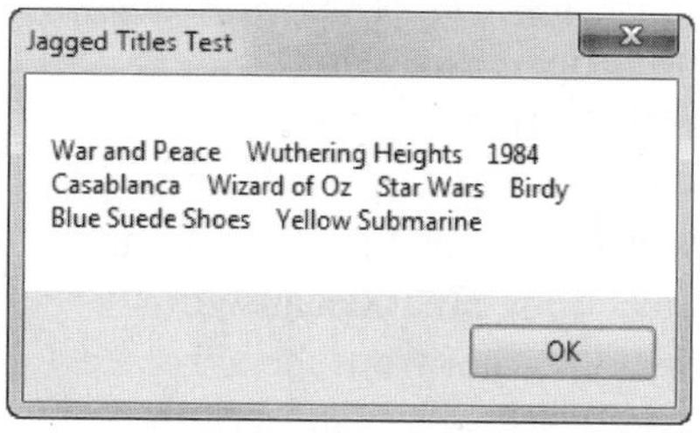

Jagged Titles Test

War and Peace Wuthering Heights 1984
Casablanca Wizard of Oz Star Wars Birdy
Blue Suede Shoes Yellow Submarine

OK

Description

- Since the number of columns in each row of a jagged array varies, you can't use the GetLength method to get the length of a row. Instead, you have to use the Length property of the array for that row.

Figure 8-8 How to work with jagged arrays

More skills for working with arrays

Now that you know how to work with one-dimensional, rectangular, and jagged arrays, you're ready to learn some additional skills for working with arrays.

How to use the Array class

Because an array is actually an instance of the Array class, you can use the properties and methods of this class to work with your arrays. Figure 8-9 presents the properties and methods you're most likely to use.

You've already seen how to use the Length property and the GetLength method. Another property you may want to use is the GetUpperBound method, which returns the index of the last element in a given dimension of an array. The first example in this figure illustrates the difference between the GetLength and GetUpperBound methods. Here, you can see that the GetLength method returns a value of 4 for a one-dimensional array that contains four elements. In contrast, the GetUpperBound method returns a value of 3 because the four elements are referred to by the index values 0 through 3.

Although values have been assigned to the elements of the array that's used in this example, you should realize that the GetLength and GetUpperBound methods return the same values whether or not values have been assigned to the array. In other words, these methods depend only on the number of elements that were declared for the array. That's true of the Length property as well.

The Sort method of the Array class lets you sort the elements in a one-dimensional array. This is illustrated by the second example in this figure. Here, the first statement declares an array that consists of four last names. Then, the Sort method is used to sort the names in that array. Notice that because this method is a shared method, it's called from the Array class, not from the array itself. After the array is sorted, a string is created that contains the values of the elements in ascending order. Then, the string is displayed in a message box.

The third example shows how you can use the BinarySearch method to locate a value in a one-dimensional array. This code uses the BinarySearch method to get the index of the specified employee in an employees array. Then, this index is used to get the corresponding sales amount from a salesAmounts array.

For the BinarySearch method to work properly, the array must be sorted in ascending sequence. If it's not, this method usually won't be able to find the specified value, even if it exists in the array. When the BinarySearch method can't find the specified value, it returns a value of -1. Then, if you try to use this value to access an element of an array, an IndexOutOfRangeException will be thrown.

Common properties and methods of the Array class

Property	Description
Length	Gets the number of elements in all of the dimensions of an array.
Instance method	**Description**
GetLength(dimension)	Gets the number of elements in the specified dimension of an array.
GetUpperBound(dimension)	Gets the index of the last element in the specified dimension of an array.
Static method	**Description**
Copy(array1, array2, length)	Copies some or all of the values in one array to another array. For more information, see figure 8-10.
BinarySearch(array, value)	Searches a one-dimensional array that's in ascending order for an element with a specified value and returns the index for that element.
Sort(array)	Sorts the elements in a one-dimensional array into ascending order.

Code that uses the GetLength and GetUpperBound methods

```
Dim numbers() As Integer = {1, 2, 3, 4}
Dim length As Integer = numbers.GetLength(0)              ' length = 4
Dim upperBound As Integer = numbers.GetUpperBound(0)      ' upperBound = 3
```

Code that uses the Sort method

```
Dim lastNames() As String = {"Boehm", "Taylor", "Murach", "Vasquez"}
Array.Sort(lastNames)
Dim message As String = ""
For Each lastName As String In lastNames
    message &= lastName & vbCrLf
Next
MessageBox.Show(message, "Sorted Last Names")
```

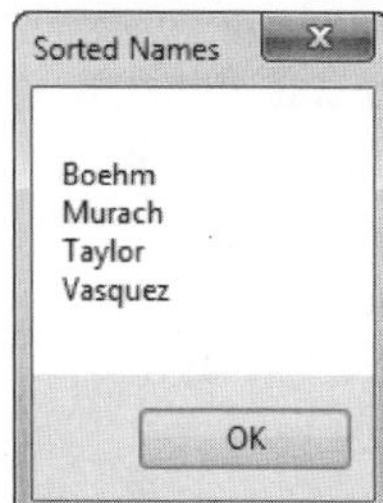

Code that uses the BinarySearch method

```
Dim employees() As String = {"Adams", "Finkle", "Lewis", "Potter"}
Dim salesAmounts() As Decimal = {3275.68D, 4298.55D, 5289.57D, 1933.98D}
Dim index As Integer = Array.BinarySearch(employees, "Finkle")
Dim salesAmount As Decimal = salesAmounts(index)   ' salesAmount = 4298.55
```

Note

- Since the BinarySearch method only works on arrays whose elements are in ascending order, you may first need to use the Sort method to sort the array.

Figure 8-9 How to use the Array class

How to refer to, copy, and resize arrays

Because arrays are created from a class, they are reference types. That means that an array variable contains a reference to an array object and not the actual values in the array. Because of that, you can use two or more variables to refer to the same array. This is illustrated by the first example in figure 8-10.

The first statement in this example declares an array variable named inches1, creates an array with three elements, and assigns values to those elements. Then, the second statement declares another array variable named inches2 and assigns the value of the inches1 variable to it. Because the inches1 variable contains a reference to the array, the inches2 variable now contains a reference to the same array. As a result, if you use the inches2 variable to change any of the elements in the array as shown in the third statement, those changes will be reflected if you use the inches1 variable to refer to the array.

If you want to create a copy of an array, you can use the Copy method of the Array class as shown in this figure. Then, each array variable will point to its own copy of the elements of the array, and any changes that are made to one array won't affect the other array.

You can use two techniques to copy the elements of an array. First, you can copy one or more elements of the array starting with the first element by specifying the source array, the target array, and the number of elements to be copied. This is illustrated by the second example in this figure. Here, all of the elements of an array named inches are copied to an array named centimeters. Notice that the Length property of the inches array is used to specify the number of elements to be copied.

You can also copy one or more elements of an array starting with an element other than the first. To do that, you specify the index of the first element you want to copy. You also specify the index of the element in the target array where you want to store the first element from the source array.

This is illustrated in the third example in this figure. Here, the first statement creates an array that contains three string values, and the second statement creates an array that can hold two string values. Then, the third statement copies the second and third strings from the first array into the second array. To do that, the first two arguments specify the source array and a starting index of 1 (the second element). Then, the next two arguments specify the target array and a starting index of 0 (the first element). The last argument specifies that two elements should be copied.

In some cases, you may need to change the size of an array so it can store more or fewer elements. One way to do that is to create a new array with the size you need and assign it to the existing array variable. If you do that, though, you'll lose the data that's stored in the existing array unless another variable refers to the array. In that case, you could copy the data from the existing array to the new array.

An easier way to change the size of an array is to use the ReDim statement as shown in this figure. When you use this statement, a new array is created with the specified size, and it's assigned to the existing array variable. To maintain the

Code that creates a reference to another array

```
Dim inches1() As Double = {1, 2, 3}
Dim inches2() As Double = inches1
inches2(2) = 4                          ' inches1(2) also = 4
```

How to copy elements of one array to another array

The syntax for copying elements of an array

```
Array.Copy(fromarray, toarray, length)
```

Another way to copy elements from one array to another

```
Array.Copy(fromarray, fromindex, toarray, toindex, length)
```

Code that copies all the elements of an array

```
Dim inches() As Double = {1, 2, 3, 4}
Dim centimeters(3) As Double
Array.Copy(inches, centimeters, inches.Length)
For i As Integer = 0 To centimeters.Length - 1
    centimeters(i) *= 2.54              ' set new values for the new array
Next
```

Code that copies some of the elements of an array

```
Dim names() As String = {"Boehm", "Murach", "Vasquez"}
Dim lastTwoNames(1) As String
Array.Copy(names, 1, lastTwoNames, 0, 2)
```

How to resize an array

The syntax for resizing an array

```
ReDim [Preserve] arrayName(firstupperbound[, secondupperbound]...)
```

A statement that resizes an array

```
ReDim Preserve inches1(19)
```

Description

- An array is a reference type, which means that an array variable contains a reference to an array object. To create another reference to an existing array, you assign the array to another array variable. Then, both array variables point to the same array.
- To copy the elements of one array to another array, you use the Copy method of the Array class. You can copy a specified number of elements from the beginning of one array to the beginning of another array. Or, you can copy a specified number of elements from the specified index in one array to a specified index of another array.
- When you copy an array, the target array must be the same type as the sending array and it must be large enough to receive all of the elements that are copied to it.
- You can use the ReDim statement to resize an array. The Preserve keyword lets you preserve the data in the array if you only change the size of the last dimension. You can only use the ReDim statement with an array variable that's declared at the procedure level.

Figure 8-10 How to refer to, copy, and resize arrays

elements in the array, you code the Preserve keyword. Then, the elements in the existing array are copied to the new array. Note that you can only change the size of the last dimension of an array if you use the Preserve keyword.

How to code procedures that work with arrays

Figure 8-11 presents the techniques you can use to code procedures that return and accept arrays. To return an array from a procedure, you follow the return type for the procedure with parentheses as shown in the first example. Then, you define an array within the code for the procedure and use the Return statement to return that array.

To call a procedure that returns an array, you use the same techniques that you use for calling any other procedure. In this figure, the statement that calls the RateArray procedure declares an array variable and assigns the return value of the procedure to this variable. In this case, the called procedure requires an argument that supplies the number of elements that the array should contain.

The second example shows how to code a procedure that accepts an array as an argument. To do that, you follow the name of the parameter that accepts the argument with parentheses to indicate that it's an array. Then, within the procedure, you can use all the techniques that you've learned for working with arrays to work with this parameter. In this case, the Sub procedure named ConvertToCentimeters converts the measurements in the array that was passed to it from inches to centimeters. Because the measurements array is passed by reference, not by value, these changes actually take place in the array that's in the calling procedure.

To call a procedure that accepts an array parameter, you just pass an array argument as shown here. In this case, because the measurements array is passed by reference, the values in that array are updated by the ConvertToCentimeters procedure. As a result, nothing has to be passed back to the calling procedure.

How to return an array from a procedure

A Function procedure that returns an array

```
Private Function RateArray(elementCount As Integer) As Decimal()
    Dim rates(elementCount - 1) As Decimal
    For i As Integer = 0 To rates.Length - 1
        rates(i) = (i + 1) / 100D
    Next
    Return rates
End Function
```

A statement that calls the procedure

```
Dim rates() As Decimal = Me.RateArray(4)
```

How to code a procedure that accepts an array argument

A Sub procedure that converts an array of inches to an array of centimeters

```
Private Sub ConvertToCentimeters(ByRef measurements() As Double)
    For i As Integer = 0 To measurements.Length - 1
        measurements(i) *= 2.54
    Next
End Sub
```

Statements that declare an array and call the procedure

```
Dim measurements() As Double = {1, 2, 3}
Me.ConvertToCentimeters(measurements)
```

Description

- To return an array from a Function procedure, you code a set of parentheses after the return type in the declaration to indicate that the return type is an array.
- To accept an array as a parameter of a procedure, you code a set of parentheses after the parameter name in the declaration to indicate that the parameter is an array.

Figure 8-11 How to code procedures that work with arrays

How to work with collections

Like an array, a *collection* can hold one or more elements. Unlike arrays, collections don't have a fixed size. Instead, the size of a collection is increased automatically when elements are added to it. In addition, most types of collections provide methods that you can use to change the capacity of a collection. As a result, collections usually work better than arrays when you need to work with a varying number of elements.

In the topics that follow, you'll learn how to use five types of collections: lists, sorted lists, queues, stacks, and array lists. Although the .NET Framework provides for other collections, these are the ones you'll use most often.

Commonly used collection classes

Prior to .NET 2.0, the collection classes in the .NET Framework could store any type of object. As a result, the collections created from these classes are sometimes referred to as *untyped collections*. In fact, you can store different types of objects in the same untyped collection, even though that's usually not a good idea. If, for example, you write code that adds the wrong type of object to an untyped collection, it will result in an error that won't be discovered until you run the application.

That's why the collection classes in the .NET Framework starting with .NET 2.0 use a new feature known as *generics* that lets you create *typed collections*. With a typed collection, you specify the type in parentheses after the name of the collection class. Then, you can only store objects of the specified type in that collection, and any errors will be discovered when you attempt to compile the application.

Figure 8-12 summarizes four of the most commonly used typed collections that were introduced with .NET 2.0. The classes for these collections are stored in the System.Collections.Generic namespace.

This figure also shows the corresponding untyped collections that were commonly used prior to .NET 2.0. The classes for these collections are stored in the System.Collections namespace and are included in the .NET 4.5 Framework. As a result, they're still available to Visual Basic 2012 applications

Because typed collections have several advantages over untyped collections, you typically use typed collections for most new development. However, you may need to use untyped collections when working with legacy applications.

How arrays and collections are similar

- Both can store multiple elements, which can be value types or reference types.

How arrays and collections are different

- An array is a feature of the Visual Basic language that inherits the Array class. Collections are other classes in the .NET Framework.
- Collection classes provide methods to perform operations that arrays don't provide.
- Arrays are fixed in size. Collections are variable in size.

Commonly used collection classes

.NET 2.0 to 4.5	.NET 1.x	Description
`List()`	`ArrayList`	Uses an index to access each element. This class is efficient for accessing elements sequentially, but inefficient for inserting elements into a list.
`SortedList()`	`SortedList`	Uses a key to access a value, which can be any type of object. This class can be inefficient for accessing elements sequentially, but it is efficient for inserting elements into a list.
`Queue()`	`Queue`	Uses special methods to add and remove elements.
`Stack()`	`Stack`	Uses special methods to add and remove elements.

Description

- A *collection* is an object that can hold one or more *elements*.
- The collection classes in the System.Collections.Generic namespace use a feature known as *generics* to allow you to create *typed collections* that can only store the specified type.
- The collection classes in the System.Collections namespace allow you to create *untyped collections*. With an untyped collection, you can store any type of object in the collection.
- The set of parentheses after a class name indicates that it is a typed collection.

Figure 8-12 Commonly used collection classes

Typed vs. untyped collections

Figure 8-13 shows the differences between typed and untyped collections. In particular, it shows that typed collections have two advantages over untyped collections. First, they check the type of each element at compile-time and thus prevent runtime errors from occurring. Second, they reduce the amount of casting that's needed when retrieving objects.

The first example shows how to use the ArrayList class to create an untyped collection. To start, the statement that creates the ArrayList object doesn't specify a data type. As a result, the Add method can be used to add elements of any type to the collection. In this figure, for example, the code adds two Integer types and a String type to the collection. This is possible because each element in the array is stored as an Object type.

Once the elements have been added to the untyped list, a For loop is used to calculate the sum of the elements. To accomplish this, the first statement in the loop casts each element to the Integer type. This is necessary because each element is an Object type. However, since a String type has been added to the collection, this will cause a runtime error when the loop tries to convert the String type to an Integer.

The second example shows how to use the List() class to create a typed collection. To start, the statement that creates the list uses parentheses to specify the Integer type. As a result, the Add method can only be used to add Integer types to the collection. In this figure, for example, the code adds two Integer types to the collection. If you tried to add another type such as a String type to the collection, you would get a compile-time error.

Once the elements have been added to the typed list, a For loop is used to calculate the sum of the elements. To accomplish this, the first statement in the loop retrieves each element and stores it in an Integer variable. Since this is a typed collection, no casting is necessary.

An example that uses an untyped collection

```
Dim numbers As New ArrayList
numbers.Add(3)
numbers.Add(70)
numbers.Add("Test")                  ' will compile, but causes an exception
Dim sum As Integer = 0
Dim number As Integer
For i As Integer = 0 To numbers.Count - 1
    number = CInt(numbers(i))        ' cast is required
    sum += number
Next
```

An example that uses a typed collection

```
Dim numbers As New List(Of Integer)
numbers.Add(3)
numbers.Add(70)
'numbers.Add("Test")                 ' won't compile - prevents runtime error
Dim sum As Integer = 0
Dim number As Integer
For i As Integer = 0 To numbers.Count - 1
    number = numbers(i)              ' no cast is required
    sum += number
Next
```

Description

- Typed collections have two advantages over untyped collections. First, they check the type of each element at compile-time and prevent runtime errors from occurring. Second, they reduce the amount of casting that's needed when retrieving objects.
- Untyped collections are part of the System.Collections namespace, while typed collections are part of the System.Collections.Generic namespace.

Figure 8-13 Typed vs. untyped collections

How to work with a list

Now that you understand the difference between typed and untyped collections, you're ready to learn how to use the List() class to create and work with a *list*. To create a list, you use the New keyword to create an object from the List() class as shown in part 1 of figure 8-14. Within the parentheses, you code the Of keyword followed by the type for the elements in the list.

To illustrate, the first example specifies the String type, and the second example specifies the Decimal type. However, you could also specify any other data types from the .NET framework (such as the DateTime type) or custom data types (such as a Product type like the one you'll learn about in chapter 11).

When you create a list, you can specify its initial capacity by coding it within parentheses after the class name. In this figure, for example, the third statement sets the initial capacity to 3. If you omit the initial capacity, though, it's set to 0 by default.

Part 1 of this figure also lists some common properties and methods of the List() class. You'll see how you can use some of these properties and methods in part 2 of this figure. For now, you should notice that some of these properties and methods provide operations that aren't available with arrays. For example, you can use the Insert method to insert an element into the middle of a list, and you can use the RemoveAt method to remove an element from a list.

You should also realize that when you use the Add or Insert method to add elements to a list, the capacity of the list is doubled each time its capacity is exceeded. This is illustrated by the last seven statements in part 1 of this figure. Each of these statements adds another element to the lastNames array that is created with an initial capacity of three elements by the first statement. Then, when the fourth element is added, the capacity is increased to six elements. Similarly, when you add the seventh element, the capacity is doubled again to 12 elements.

A statement that creates a list of String elements

```
Dim titles As New List(Of String)
```

A statement that creates a list of Decimal elements

```
Dim prices As New List(Of Decimal)
```

A statement that creates a list of strings with a capacity of 3

```
Dim lastNames As New List(Of String)(3)
```

Common properties and methods of the List() class

Property	Description
`Item(index)`	Gets or sets the element at the specified index. The index for the first item in a list is 0. Since Item is the default property, its name can be omitted.
`Capacity`	Gets or sets the number of elements the list can hold.
`Count`	Gets the number of elements in the list.
Method	**Description**
`Add(object)`	Adds an element to the end of the list and returns the element's index.
`Clear()`	Removes all elements from the list and sets its Count property to zero.
`Contains(object)`	Returns a Boolean value that indicates if the list contains the specified object.
`Insert(index, object)`	Inserts an element into the list at the specified index.
`Remove(object)`	Removes the first occurrence of the specified object from the list.
`RemoveAt(index)`	Removes the element at the specified index of the list.
`BinarySearch(object)`	Searches the list for a specified object and returns the index for that object.
`Sort()`	Sorts the elements in the list into ascending order.

Code that causes the size of a list of names to be increased

```
Dim lastNames As New List(Of String)(3)    ' capacity is 3 elements
lastNames.Add("Boehm")
lastNames.Add("Prince")
lastNames.Add("Murach")
lastNames.Add("Taylor")          ' capacity is doubled to 6 elements
lastNames.Add("Vasquez")
lastNames.Add("Steelman")
lastNames.Add("Slivkoff")        ' capacity is doubled to 12 elements
```

Description

- A *list* is a collection that automatically adjusts its capacity to accommodate new elements.
- The default capacity of a list is 0 elements, but you can specify a different capacity when you create a list. When the number of elements in a list exceeds its capacity, the capacity is automatically doubled.

Figure 8-14 How to work with a list (part 1 of 2)

Part 2 of figure 8-14 shows how to use some of the methods of the List() class to work with the elements in a list. Here, the first example creates a list of decimal values. Unlike the statements you saw in part 1 of this figure, this example uses a *collection initializer* to assign values to the list. When you use a collection initializer, you don't have to use the Add method to add elements to the list. Instead, you code the From keyword followed by the elements within braces as shown here.

The second example shows how to use an index to refer to an element in a list. The syntax for doing that is the same as the syntax for referring to an element in an array. You just specify the index in parentheses after the name of the list and the element is returned.

The third example shows how to insert and remove elements from a list. Here, a new element with a decimal value of 2745.73 is inserted at the beginning of the list named salesTotals. As a result, the other four values in the list are pushed up one index. Then, the second element of the list is removed, and the other three values are moved back down one index. The result is that the second element is replaced with a new element.

The fourth example uses a For Each loop to display the elements in the salesTotals list in a message box. As you can see, this works the same as it does for an array.

The fifth example shows how to use the Contains method to check if the salesTotals list contains an element with a specified value. If it does, the Remove method is used to remove the element from the list. In this case, the element with the value of 2745.73 is removed.

The sixth example shows how you can sort and search the elements in a list. Here, the first statement uses the Sort method to sort the elements in the salesTotals list. Then, the second statement uses the BinarySearch method to search for an element that contains the value that's stored in the variable named sales2, which is 4398.55. If that value is found, the index of its element is stored in the variable named sales2index.

Unlike the Sort method of the Array class, the Sort method of the List() class is an instance method. Because of that, you call it from the list object. That's true for the BinarySearch method too.

The syntax for retrieving a value from a list

```
listName[.Item](index)
```

Code that creates a list that holds Decimal values

```
Dim salesTotals As New List(Of Decimal) From
    {3275.68D, 4398.55D, 5289.75D, 1933.98D}
```

Code that retrieves the first value from the list

```
Dim sales1 As Decimal = salesTotals(0)       ' sales1 = 3275.68
```

Code that inserts and removes an element from the list

```
salesTotals.Insert(0, 2745.73D)              ' insert a new 1st element
sales1 = salesTotals(0)                      ' sales1 = 2745.73
Dim sales2 As Decimal = salesTotals(1)       ' sales2 = 3275.68
salesTotals.RemoveAt(1)                      ' remove the 2nd element
sales2 = salesTotals(1)                      ' sales2 = 4398.55
```

Code that displays the list in a message box

```
Dim salesTotalsString As String = ""
For Each d As Decimal In salesTotals
    salesTotalsString &= d.ToString & vbCrLf
Next
MessageBox.Show(salesTotalsString, "Sales Totals")
```

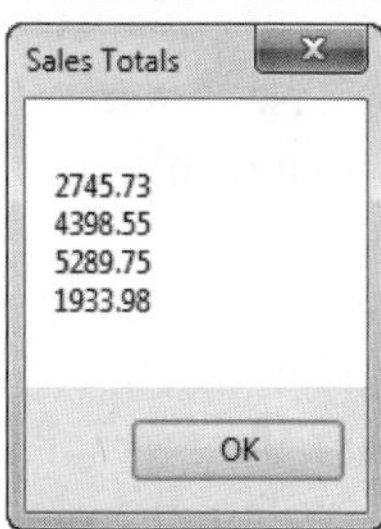

Code that checks for an element in the list and removes it if it exists

```
Dim x As Decimal = 2745.73D
If salesTotals.Contains(x) Then
    salesTotals.Remove(x)
End If
```

Code that sorts and searches the list

```
salesTotals.Sort()
Dim sales2Index As Integer = salesTotals.BinarySearch(sales2)
```

Figure 8-14 How to work with a list (part 2 of 2)

How to work with a sorted list

You can also implement a collection by using the SortedList() class that's described in figure 8-15. A *sorted list* is useful when you need to look up values in the list based on a key value. If, for example, a sorted list consists of item numbers and unit prices, the keys are the item numbers. Then, the list can be used to look up the unit price for any item number.

Each item in a sorted list is actually a KeyValuePair structure that consists of two properties: Key and Value. Here, the Value property can store value types or reference types.

Like a list, you can set the initial capacity of a sorted list by specifying the number of elements in parentheses when the list is created. Then, if the number of elements in the list exceeds the capacity as the program executes, the capacity is doubled.

The first example in this figure shows how to create and load a sorted list. Here, the first statement specifies a sorted list with keys of the String type and values of the Decimal type. Then, when you add an element to a sorted list, you specify the key along with the value associated with that key. In this example, the keys are the names of employees, and the values are the sales totals for those employees. Note that although the keys in this list are added in alphabetical order, a sorted list automatically sorts itself by key values regardless of the order in which the elements are added.

The second example shows how to look up a value in a sorted list based on a key. Here, a value of "Lewis" is specified as the key for the element. As a result, this key returns a Decimal value of 5289.75.

The third example creates a string that contains the keys and values in a sorted list. To start, it declares and initializes the string. Then, it uses a For Each loop to retrieve each KeyValuePair in the sorted list. Like the sorted list, the key/value pair is declared with String keys and Decimal values. Then, within the For Each loop, the Key and Value properties of the key/value pair are used to access each element's key and value.

Since using a sorted list makes it easy to look up a key and return its corresponding value, this is the right type of collection to use when you need to do that type of lookup. A sorted list is also the right choice when you need to keep the elements in sequence by key.

Common properties and methods of the SortedList() class

Property	Description
`Item(key)`	Gets or sets the value of the element with the specified key. Since Item is the default property, its name can be omitted.
`Keys`	Gets a collection that contains the keys in the list.
`Values`	Gets a collection that contains the values in the list.
`Capacity`	Gets or sets the number of elements the list can hold.
`Count`	Gets the number of elements in the list.
Method	**Description**
`Add(key, value)`	Adds an element with the specified key and value to the sorted list.
`Clear()`	Removes all elements from the sorted list.
`ContainsKey(key)`	Returns a Boolean value that indicates whether or not the sorted list contains the specified key.
`ContainsValue(value)`	Returns a Boolean value that indicates whether or not the sorted list contains the specified value.
`Remove(key)`	Removes the element with the specified key from the sorted list.
`RemoveAt(index)`	Removes the element at the specified index from the sorted list.

Properties of the KeyValuePair structure

Property	Description
`Key`	The key for the SortedList item.
`Value`	The value associated with the key.

Code that creates and loads a sorted list

```
Dim salesList As New SortedList(Of String, Decimal)
salesList.Add("Adams", 3274.68D)
salesList.Add("Finkle", 4398.55D)
salesList.Add("Lewis", 5289.75D)
salesList.Add("Potter", 1933.97D)
```

Code that looks up a value in the sorted list based on a key

```
Dim employeeKey As String = "Lewis"
Dim salesTotal As Decimal = salesList(employeeKey)
```

Code that converts the sorted list to a tab-delimited string

```
Dim salesTableString As String = ""
For Each employeeSalesEntry As KeyValuePair(Of String, Decimal) In
        salesList
    salesTableString &= employeeSalesEntry.Key & vbTab &
        employeeSalesEntry.Value & vbCrLf
Next
MessageBox.Show(salesTableString, "Sorted List Totals")
```

Figure 8-15 How to work with a sorted list

How to work with queues and stacks

Figure 8-16 shows the properties and methods of the Queue() and Stack() classes that you can use to create queues and stacks. Like the SortedList class, both of these classes come in typed and untyped varieties.

Unlike other collections, queues and stacks do not use the Add method to add items or an index to retrieve items. Instead, queues use the Enqueue and Dequeue methods to add and retrieve items, and stacks use the Push and Pop methods.

You can think of a *queue* (pronounced cue) as a line of items waiting to be processed. When you use the Enqueue method to add an item to the queue, the item is placed at the end of the queue. When you use the Dequeue method to retrieve an item from the queue, the item is taken from the front of the queue. Because items are retrieved from a queue in the same order in which they were added, a queue can be referred to as a *first-in, first-out* (*FIFO*) collection.

In contrast, a *stack* is a *last-in, first-out* (*LIFO*) collection. When you use the Push method to place an item on a stack, that item is placed on the top of the stack. If you then push another item onto the stack, the new item is placed on the top of the stack and the item that was previously on the top of the stack moves to second from the top. In contrast, the Pop method retrieves the top item and removes it, so the item that was second from the top moves to the top position. If it helps you, you can think of a stack as a stack of dishes. The last dish that you put on the stack is also the first dish that you take off the stack.

The two examples in this figure illustrate the differences between queues and stacks. Each example begins by defining a new queue or stack, and then adding three names. Next, a while loop is used to build a string that contains the names in the order that they are retrieved from the queue or stack, and the resulting list is displayed in a message box. If you compare the message boxes for these examples, you can see that the queue names are displayed in the same order that they were added to the queue. But in the stack example, the names are retrieved in the opposite order.

In both examples, the Do loop repeats as long as the Count property is greater than zero. This works because the Dequeue and Pop methods remove the item from the queue or stack, so the Count property is automatically decreased by one each time through the loop. When all of the items have been read from the queue or stack, the Count property reaches zero and the Do loop ends.

Compared to lists, queues and stacks don't provide as many properties and methods. However, if you need to implement a FIFO or LIFO collection, you won't need any of those extra properties and methods. In that case, it makes sense to use a queue or stack.

Properties and methods of the Queue() class

Property	Description
`Count`	Gets the number of items in the queue.
Method	**Description.**
`Enqueue(object)`	Adds the specified object to the end of the queue.
`Dequeue()`	Gets the object at the front of the queue and removes it from the queue.
`Clear()`	Removes all items from the queue.
`Peek()`	Retrieves the next item in the queue without deleting it.

Code that uses a queue

```
Dim nameQueue As New Queue(Of String)
nameQueue.Enqueue("Boehm")
nameQueue.Enqueue("Murach")
nameQueue.Enqueue("Vasquez")
Dim nameQueueString As String = ""
Do While nameQueue.Count > 0
    nameQueueString &= nameQueue.Dequeue & vbCrLf
Loop
MessageBox.Show(nameQueueString, "Queue")
```

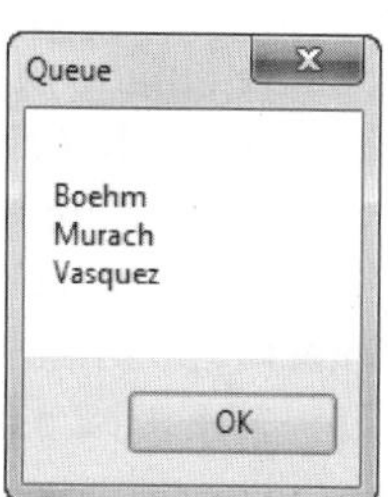

Properties and methods of the Stack() class

Property	Description
`Count`	Gets the number of items in the stack.
Method	**Description**
`Push(object)`	Adds the specified object to the top of the stack.
`Pop()`	Gets the object at the top of the stack and removes it from the stack.
`Clear()`	Removes all items from the stack.
`Peek()`	Retrieves the next item in the stack without deleting it.

Code that uses a stack

```
Dim nameStack As New Stack(Of String)
nameStack.Push("Boehm")
nameStack.Push("Murach")
nameStack.Push("Vasquez")
Dim nameStackString As String = ""
Do While nameStack.Count > 0
    nameStackString &= nameStack.Pop & vbCrLf
Loop
MessageBox.Show(nameStackString, "Stack")
```

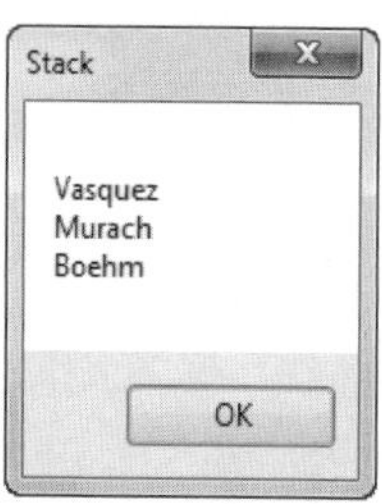

Description

- A *queue* is sometimes called a *first-in, first-out* (*FIFO*) collection because its items are retrieved in the same order in which they were added.
- A *stack* is sometimes called a *last-in, first-out* (*LIFO*) collection because its items are retrieved in the reverse order from the order in which they were added.

How to work with an array list

Although you'll probably want to use typed lists whenever possible, figure 8-17 shows how to work with an *array list*, the most common untyped collection. This should illustrate both the similarities and differences between typed and untyped lists. For the most part, an array list works like a list. However, since an array list defines an untyped collection, there are a few differences.

First, when you declare an ArrayList class, you don't define the type within parentheses. Instead, each element in the array list is stored as an Object type. As a result, any value type that you store in the array list must be converted to a reference type. To do that, an object is created and the value is stored in that object. The process of putting a value in an object is known as *boxing*, and it's done automatically whenever a value type needs to be converted to a reference type. In the first example, the Decimal value type is converted to an Object reference type before it is stored in the array list named salesTotals.

Second, when you retrieve an element from an array, you must cast the Object type to the appropriate data type. In the second example, the first element in the array list named salesTotal is cast from the Object type to the Decimal type. The process of getting a value out of the object is known as *unboxing*, and you must write code like this whenever you need to unbox a value.

The rest of the examples work the same as the examples for the List() class shown in figure 8-14. The only difference is that you must cast an object to the appropriate data type when you retrieve it from an array list. As a result, it's easy to convert code that uses the ArrayList class to code that uses the List() class. Once you understand how to do that, you should be able convert code from any untyped collection to any typed collection.

Code that creates an array list that holds decimal values

```
Dim salesTotals As New ArrayList From
    {3275.68D, 4398.55D, 5289.75D, 1933.98D}
```

Code that retrieves the first value from the array list

```
Dim sales1 As Decimal = CDec(salesTotals(0))    ' sales1 = 3275.68
```

Code that inserts and removes an element from the array list

```
salesTotals.Insert(0, 2745.73D)                 ' insert a new 1st element
sales1 = CDec(salesTotals(0))                   ' sales1 = 2745.73
Dim sales2 As Decimal = CDec(salesTotals(1))    ' sales2 = 3275.68
salesTotals.RemoveAt(1)                         ' remove the 2nd element
sales2 = CDec(salesTotals(1))                   ' sales2 = 4398.55
```

Code that displays the array list in a message box

```
Dim salesTotalsString As String = ""
For Each d As Decimal In salesTotals
    salesTotalsString &= d.ToString & vbCrLf
Next
MessageBox.Show(salesTotalsString, "Sales Totals")
```

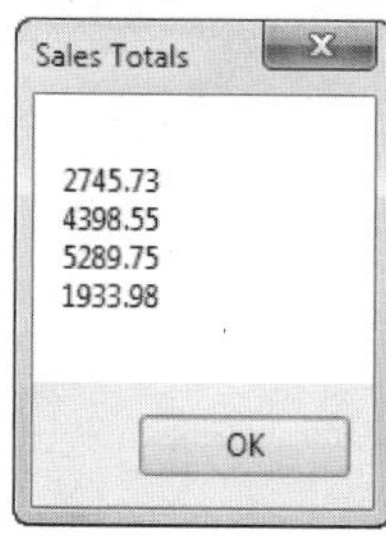

Code that checks for an element in the array list and removes it if it exists

```
Dim x As Decimal = 2745.73D
If salesTotals.Contains(x) Then
    salesTotals.Remove(x)
End If
```

Code that sorts and searches the array list

```
salesTotals.Sort()
Dim sales2Index As Integer = salesTotals.BinarySearch(sales2)
```

Description

- The ArrayList class has the same properties and methods as the List() class. As a result, it's easy to convert code that uses the ArrayList class to code that uses the List() class and vice versa.

Figure 8-17 How to work with an array list

Perspective

In this chapter, you've learned how to use both arrays and collections for working with groups of related data. You've also learned that the .NET Framework provides typed classes that offer useful properties and methods for working with collections. These include the List(), SortedList(), Queue(), and Stack() classes.

As you develop your own applications, you often need to decide between the use of an array or collection. Then, if you decide to use a collection, you need to choose the most appropriate type of collection. If you make the right decisions, your code will be easier to write, debug, and maintain.

Terms

array
one-dimensional array
element
upper bound
length
size
index
For Each statement
For Each loop
rectangular array
two-dimensional array
jagged array
array of arrays
collection
typed collection
generics
untyped collection
list
collection initializer
sorted list
queue
stack
first-in, first-out (FIFO)
last-in, first-out (LIFO)
array list
boxing
unboxing

Exercise 8-1 Use an array and a list

This exercise will guide you through the process of adding an array and a list to the Invoice Total application that you saw in chapter 5.

Open the Invoice Total application

1. Open the application that's in the C:\VB 2012\Chapter 08\InvoiceTotal directory.

Use an array to store invoice totals

2. Declare two module-level variables: (1) an array that can hold up to five invoice totals and (2) an index that you can use to work with that array.
3. Add code that adds the invoice total to the next element in the array each time the user clicks the Calculate button.

4. Add code that displays all the invoice totals in the array in a message box when the user clicks the Exit button. To do that, use a For Each loop to loop through the totals and format the message for the message box.
5. Test the program by entering three invoices and then clicking the Exit button. This should display a dialog box like the one that follows. But note that the fourth and fifth elements in the array are also displayed because they were initialized with zero values.

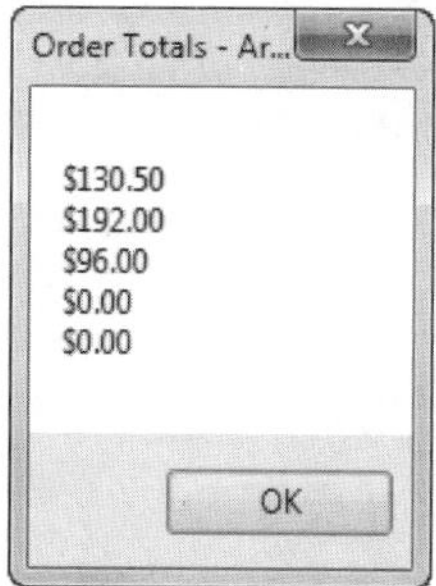

6. Fix this problem by adding an If statement to the For Each loop that ignores any array elements that are equal to zero. Then, test the program to make sure that it works.
7. Test the program by entering more than five invoices. When you do, an IndexOutOfRangeException should be thrown.

Sort the invoice totals

8. Add code to sort the invoice totals in the array.
9. Test the program again to be sure that the message box displays the invoice totals in the correct sequence.

Modify the program so it uses a list

10. Without changing any of the current code, add code that uses the List() class to hold the invoice totals. Then, when the user clicks the Exit button, sort the list elements and add a second For Each loop to format and display the totals stored in the list in a second message box. In other words, display two message boxes: one for the array and one for the list.
11. When you've got this working right, close the solution.

Exercise 8-2 Use a rectangular array

This exercise will guide you through the process of adding a rectangular array to the Future Value application that you saw in chapter 7. This array will store the values for each calculation that's performed.

Open the Future Value application

1. Open the application that's in the C:\VB 2012\Chapter 08\FutureValue directory.

Use a rectangular array to store future value calculations

2. Declare module-level variables for a row index and a rectangular array of strings that provides for 10 rows and 4 columns.
3. Add code that stores the values for each calculation in the next row of the array when the user clicks the Calculate button. Store the monthly investment and future value in currency format, and store the interest rate in percent format.
4. Add code to display the elements in the array in a message box when the user clicks the Exit button. Use tab characters to format the message box so it looks like this:

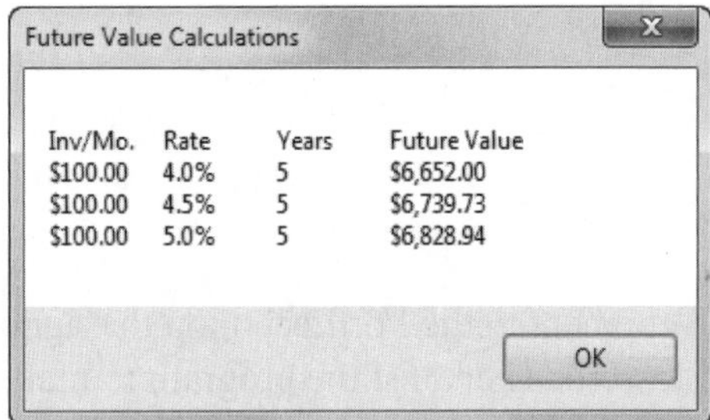

5. Test the program by making up to 10 future value calculations. When you've got this working right, close the solution.

9

How to work with dates and strings

In chapter 4, you learned some basic skills for working with strings. In this chapter, you'll learn more about working with strings, and you'll learn how to work with dates. Because you'll use dates and strings in many of the applications that you develop, these are essential programming skills.

How to work with dates and times

To work with dates and times in Visual Basic, you use the DateTime structure. As you'll see, this structure provides a variety of properties and methods for getting information about dates and times, formatting DateTime values, and performing operations on dates and times.

How to create a DateTime value

Figure 9-1 presents three ways that you can create a DateTime value. First, you can use the Date or DateTime keyword to declare a DateTime value and then assign a date literal to it. A date literal in Visual Basic is coded by enclosing the date within # symbols. This is illustrated by the first two statements in this figure. Since Date is a Visual Basic keyword that represents the DateTime structure, you can use either Date or DateTime as the type in these statements. But since Date is shorter, it is used in the examples in this chapter.

You can also create a DateTime value using the shared Parse method of the DateTime structure. When you use the Parse method, you specify the date and time as a string as illustrated by the third and fourth statements in this figure. Here, the third statement specifies just a date. Because of that, the time portion of the DateTime value is set to 12:00 AM. The fourth statement specifies both a date and time. In these statements, I used DateTime instead of Date for the type, but they are equivalent.

The third way to create a DateTime value is to use the New keyword to call the constructor of the DateTime structure and supply the required arguments. When you create a DateTime value this way, you must always specify the year, month, and day. If necessary, you can also specify the time in hours, minutes, seconds, and milliseconds. If you don't specify the time, it's set to 12:00 AM. This is illustrated by the next two statements in this figure.

The last two statements illustrate that you can create DateTime values from properties or variables that contain a date/time string. In these examples, a DateTime value is created from the Text property of a text box. Note in the last example that the value in the Text property has to be cast to a Date type before it can be assigned to the Date (or DateTime) variable.

When you use the Parse method or a date literal to create a DateTime value, the date and time you specify must be in a valid format. Some of the most common formats are listed in this figure. When you enter a date or time in a text box, you also need to use one of these valid formats.

Although the statements in this figure indicate the DateTime values that are created, you should realize that these aren't the actual values that are stored in the variables. Instead, they show what happens when a DateTime value is converted to a string. The date and time are actually stored as the number of *ticks* (100 nanosecond units) that have elapsed since 12:00:00 AM, January 1, 0001. That makes it easy to perform arithmetic operations on dates and times, as you'll see later in this chapter.

Three ways to create DateTime values

```
Dim variableName As {Date|DateTime} = #dateliteral#
Dim variableName As {Date|DateTime} = DateTime.Parse(datestring)
Dim variableName As New DateTime(
    year, month, day[, hour, minute, second[, millisecond]])
```

Statements that create DateTime values

```
Dim startDate As Date = #1/30/2013#                 ' 1/30/2013 12:00 AM
Dim startDateTime As Date = #1/30/2013 2:15:00 PM#  ' 1/30/2013 2:15 PM
Dim startDate As DateTime =
    DateTime.Parse("01/30/13")                      ' 1/30/2013 12:00 AM
Dim startDateTime As DateTime =
    DateTime.Parse("Jan 30, 2013 2:15 PM")          ' 1/30/2013 2:15 PM
Dim startDate As New DateTime(2013, 01, 30)         ' 1/30/2013 12:00 AM
Dim startDateTime As
    New DateTime(2013, 1, 30, 14, 15, 0)            ' 1/30/2013 2:15 PM
Dim invoiceDate As Date = DateTime.Parse(txtInvoiceDate.Text)
Dim invoiceDate As Date = CDate(txtInvoiceDate.Text)
```

Valid date formats

```
01/30/2013
1/30/13
01-01-2013
1-1-13
2013-01-01
Jan 30 2013
January 30, 2013
```

Valid time formats

```
2:15 PM
14:15
02:15:30 AM
```

Description

- You can use the DateTime structure of the .NET Framework to create and work with dates and times.
- Visual Basic provides the Date keyword for declaring DateTime structures. You can also code a date literal in Visual Basic by coding the date between # symbols.
- You can use the shared Parse method of the DateTime structure to create a DateTime value from a string.
- If you omit the time specification when you create a DateTime value, the time is set to 12:00 AM. You can also omit the date specification when you create a DateTime value using the Parse method. Then, the date is set to the current date.
- A date is stored as a 64-bit signed integer that represents the number of *ticks* (100 nanosecond units) that have elapsed since 12:00 AM, January 1, 0001.

Figure 9-1 How to create a DateTime value

How to get the current date and time

Figure 9-2 presents two shared properties of the DateTime structure that you can use to get the current date and time. If you use the Now property, both the date and time are returned. If you use the Today property, only the date is returned, and the time is set to 12:00:00 AM. The first two statements in this figure illustrate how this works.

How to format DateTime values

To format dates and times, you can use the four methods of the DateTime structure that are shown in figure 9-2. Note, however, that these formats may vary somewhat from the formats that are used on your system. The exact formats depend on your computer's regional settings. If these methods don't provide the format you need, you can use the formatting techniques you'll learn about later in this chapter to format the date and time the way you want them.

DateTime properties for getting the current date and time

Property	Description
`Now`	Returns the current date and time.
`Today`	Returns the current date.

Statements that get the current date and time

```
Dim currentDateTime As Date = DateTime.Now     ' 1/30/2013 4:24:59 AM
Dim currentDate As Date = DateTime.Today       ' 1/30/2013 12:00:00 AM
```

DateTime methods for formatting a date or time

Method	Description
`ToLongDateString()`	Converts the DateTime value to a string that includes the name for the day of the week, the name for the month, the day of the month, and the year.
`ToShortDateString()`	Converts the DateTime value to a string that includes the numbers for the month, day, and year.
`ToLongTimeString()`	Converts the DateTime value to a string that includes the hours, minutes, and seconds.
`ToShortTimeString()`	Converts the DateTime value to a string that includes the hours and minutes.

Statements that format dates and times

```
Dim longDate As String =
    currentDateTime.ToLongDateString          ' Wednesday, January 30, 2013
Dim shortDate As String =
    currentDateTime.ToShortDateString         ' 1/30/2013
Dim longTime As String =
    currentDateTime.ToLongTimeString          ' 4:24:59 AM
Dim shortTime As String =
    currentDateTime.ToShortTimeString         ' 4:24 AM
```

Description

- The Now and Today properties are shared properties of the DateTime structure.
- The format that's used for a date or time depends on your computer's regional settings.

Figure 9-2 How to get the current date and format DateTime values

How to get information about dates and times

The DateTime structure provides a variety of properties and methods for getting information about dates and times. These properties and methods are listed in figure 9-3, and the examples show how to work with most of them.

The first statement uses the Now property to get the current date and time. Then, the second statement uses the Month property to get the month of that date, the third statement uses the Hour property to get the hour of that time, and the fourth statement uses the DayOfYear property to get an Integer value from 1 to 366 that represents the day of the year.

The next two statements show how to use the two methods for getting information about a date. Since both of these methods are shared, they're accessed through the DateTime structure. The first method, DaysInMonth, returns the number of days in a given month and year. In this example, since 2013 isn't a leap year, there are 28 days in February. However, if you specified 2012, which is a leap year, there would be 29 days in February. The second method, IsLeapYear, returns a True or False value that indicates whether the specified year is a leap year.

The last example in this figure shows how to use the DayOfWeek property. Note that this property returns a member of the DayOfWeek enumeration. In this case, the first statement gets the day of the week for the current date. Then, an If statement checks if the current date is a Saturday or a Sunday. If so, a string variable named message is set to "Weekend". Otherwise, it's set to "Weekday".

Properties and methods for working with dates and times

Property	Description
`Date`	Returns the DateTime value with the time portion set to 12:00:00 AM.
`Month`	Returns an integer for the month portion of the DateTime value.
`Day`	Returns an integer for the day portion of the DateTime value.
`Year`	Returns an integer for the year portion of the DateTime value.
`Hour`	Returns an integer for the hour portion of the DateTime value.
`Minute`	Returns an integer for the minute portion of the DateTime value.
`Second`	Returns an integer for the second portion of the DateTime value.
`TimeOfDay`	Returns a TimeSpan value that represents the amount of time that has elapsed since 12:00:00 AM. For more information about the TimeSpan structure, see figure 9-4.
`DayOfWeek`	Returns a member of the DayOfWeek enumeration that represents the day of the week of a DateTime value.
`DayOfYear`	Returns an integer for the numeric day of the year.
Method	**Description**
`DaysInMonth(year, month)`	Returns the number of days in a specified month and year.
`IsLeapYear(year)`	Returns a Boolean value that indicates whether or not a specified year is a leap year.

Statements that get information about a date or time

```
Dim currentDateTime As Date = DateTime.Now       ' 1/30/2013 10:26:35 AM
Dim month As Integer = currentDateTime.Month                   ' 1
Dim hour As Integer = currentDateTime.Hour                     ' 10
Dim dayOfYear As Integer = currentDateTime.DayOfYear           ' 30
Dim daysInMonth As Integer = DateTime.DaysInMonth(2013, 2)     ' 28
Dim isLeapYear As Boolean = DateTime.IsLeapYear(2013)          ' False
```

Code that uses the DayOfWeek property and enumeration

```
Dim day As DayOfWeek = currentDateTime.DayOfWeek
Dim message As String = ""
If day = DayOfWeek.Saturday Or day = DayOfWeek.Sunday Then
    message = "Weekend"
Else
    message = "Weekday"
End If
```

Figure 9-3 How to get information about dates and times

How to perform operations on dates and times

Figure 9-4 presents some of the methods of the DateTime structure that you can use to perform operations on dates and times. Most of these methods let you add a specific number of intervals, like hours, days, or months, to a DateTime value. However, you can use the Add method to add a TimeSpan value to a date, and you can use the Subtract method to determine the time span between two dates, which is often required in business applications.

Like DateTime values, TimeSpan values are based on a structure defined by the .NET Framework. Also, TimeSpan values hold a number of ticks, just like DateTime values. However, a TimeSpan value represents a time interval. In contrast, a DateTime value represents a specific point in time.

The first group of statements in this figure shows how some of the Add methods work. For example, the second statement shows how to add two months to a DateTime value, and the third statement shows how to add 60 days. Similarly, the fourth statement shows how to add 30 minutes, and the fifth statement shows how to add 12 hours.

The second group of statements shows how you can use a TimeSpan variable to determine the number of days between two DateTime values. Here, the first statement retrieves the current date, and the second statement assigns a due date to another DateTime variable. Next, the third statement uses the Subtract method to subtract the current date from the due date and assign the result to a TimeSpan variable, which represents the number of days, minutes, hours, and seconds between the two dates. Then, the last statement uses the Days property of the TimeSpan structure to extract the number of days from the TimeSpan value. This is one of several properties of this structure that let you extract the data from a TimeSpan value.

In addition to the properties and methods provided by the DateTime structure, you can use some of the standard operators to work with dates. For instance, the third example in this figure shows how to use the subtraction operator to calculate the time between two dates instead of using the Subtract method. The last example shows that you can also use DateTime values in a conditional expression. Here, the conditional expression tests if one DateTime value is greater than another.

Methods for performing operations on dates and times

Method	Description
`AddDays(days)`	Adds the specified numbers of days to a DateTime value and returns another DateTime value.
`AddMonths(months)`	Adds the specified number of months to a DateTime value and returns another DateTime value.
`AddYears(years)`	Adds the specified number of years to a DateTime value and returns another DateTime value.
`AddHours(hours)`	Adds the specified number of hours to a DateTime value and returns another DateTime value.
`AddMinutes(minutes)`	Adds the specified number of minutes to a DateTime value and returns another DateTime value.
`AddSeconds(seconds)`	Adds the specified number of seconds to a DateTime value and returns another DateTime value.
`Add(timespan)`	Adds the specified TimeSpan value to a DateTime value and returns another DateTime value.
`Subtract(datetime)`	Subtracts the specified DateTime value from a DateTime value and returns a TimeSpan value.

Statements that perform operations on dates and times

```
Dim invoiceDate As Date =
    DateTime.Parse("3/1/2013 13:28")                  ' 3/1/2013 1:28:00 PM
Dim dueDate1 As DateTime = invoiceDate.AddMonths(2)     ' 5/1/2013 1:28:00 PM
Dim dueDate2 As DateTime = invoiceDate.AddDays(60)      ' 4/30/2013 1:28:00 PM
Dim runTime1 As DateTime = invoiceDate.AddMinutes(30)   ' 3/1/2013 1:58:00 PM
Dim runTime2 As DateTime = invoiceDate.AddHours(12)     ' 3/2/2013 1:28:00 AM
```

Code that results in a TimeSpan value

```
Dim currentDate As Date = DateTime.Today                   ' 1/30/2013
dueDate = DateTime.Parse("2/15/2013")                      ' 2/15/2013
Dim timeTillDue As TimeSpan = dueDate.Subtract(currentDate) ' 16:00:00:00
Dim daysTillDue As Integer = timeTillDue.Days              ' 16
```

A statement that uses the - operator to subtract two dates

```
Dim timeTillDue As TimeSpan = dueDate - currentDate        ' 16:00:00:00
```

An If statement that uses the > operator on DateTime values

```
Dim pastDue As Boolean = False
If currentDate > dueDate Then
    pastDue = True
End If
```

Description

- A TimeSpan value represents a period of time stored as ticks. The Days, Hours, Minutes, and Seconds properties of a TimeSpan value represent the time span in those units.
- In addition to the DateTime methods, you can use the +, -, =, <>, >, >=, <, and <= operators to work with DateTime values.

Figure 9-4 How to perform operations on dates and times

How to use Visual Basic properties and functions to work with dates and times

When you use the properties and methods of the DateTime structure to work with dates and times, you write code that is consistent with other .NET code. For instance, these properties and methods work the same in C# as they do in Visual Basic. In general, then, we think that it's best to use the DateTime structure to work with dates and times.

However, Visual Basic also provides its own properties and functions for working with dates and times, some of which are summarized in figure 9-5. And a few of these properties and functions like the IsDate function make it easier to do some common date-handling tasks. In those cases, you may want to use the Visual Basic properties and functions instead of the properties and methods of the DateTime structure. Incidentally, the Visual Basic properties and functions are part of the Microsoft.VisualBasic namespace, which is always available to your projects.

If you scan the properties in this figure, you can see that the Today and Now properties get the system date and the system date and time, while the TimeOfDay property gets just the time. In contrast, the DateString and TimeString properties return the date and time as string values.

If you scan the first group of functions, you can see that the Month, Day, and Year functions get the month, day, and year components of a date. The MonthName function gets the name of a specified month, the WeekDay function returns a number between 1 and 7 that represents the day of the week, and the WeekDayName function gets the name of a specified day of the week.

And if you scan the second group of functions, you can see that there's an IsDate function that tests to see whether a string has a valid DateTime format. There's a CDate function that lets you convert a string with a valid DateTime format to a DateTime type. There's an Add function that performs the same operations as the Add methods of the DateTime structure. And there's a DateDiff function that subtracts two DateTime values.

The example in this figure shows how easy it is to use these properties and functions. Here, the Today property is used to get the current date, and the IsDate function is used to check a text box entry to see whether it contains a string with a valid DateTime format. If so, the CDate function is used to convert the string to a DateTime type, and the DateDiff function is used to determine the number of days between the date of the user entry and the current date.

If you ever use the Day function, you'll discover that you have to qualify it with Microsoft.VisualBasic as in this example:

```
iDay = Microsoft.VisualBasic.Day(dtmCurrentDate)
```

That's because Day is a word that's also defined in the System.Windows.Forms namespace.

Visual Basic properties for getting the current date and time

Property	Description
`Now`	Gets the system date and time as a DateTime value.
`Today`	Gets the system date as a DateTime value.
`TimeOfDay`	Gets the system time as a DateTime value.
`DateString`	Gets the system date as a string value with the format mm-dd-yyyy.
`TimeString`	Gets the system time as a string value with the format hh:mm:ss.

Visual Basic functions for getting information about dates and times

Function	Description
`Month(datetime)`	Returns an integer for the month portion of a DateTime value.
`Day(datetime)`	Returns an integer for the day portion of a DateTime value.
`Year(datetime)`	Returns an integer for the year portion of a DateTime value.
`MonthName(month)`	Returns the name of the month specified by an integer between 1 and 12.
`WeekDay(datetime)`	Returns an integer that represents the day of the week of a DateTime value. 1 represents Sunday, 2 represents Monday, and so on.
`WeekDayName(day)`	Returns the name of the day specified by an integer between 1 and 7.

Visual Basic functions for performing operations on dates and times

Function	Description
`IsDate(string)`	Returns a Boolean value that indicates whether the string has a valid date format.
`CDate(string)`	Converts a string value to a DateTime value.
`DateAdd(interval, number, datetime)`	Adds the number of intervals to the specified date and returns the resulting DateTime value.
`DateDiff(interval, datetime1, datetime2)`	Subtracts the value of the first date from the second date and returns the difference as a Long value that contains the number of intervals.

An example that uses one property and three functions

```
Dim currentDate As Date = Today
Dim dueDate As Date
Dim daysTillDue As Long
If IsDate(txtDueDate.Text) Then
    dueDate = CDate(txtDueDate.Text)
    daysTillDue = DateDiff(DateInterval.Day, dueDate, currentDate)
End If
```

Description

- To specify the type of interval for a function, you can use the DateInterval enumeration with constants like Month, Day, Hour, Minute, and Second.
- The Day function must be qualified with the Microsoft.VisualBasic namespace since Day is defined as an enumeration in the System.Windows.Forms namespace.

Figure 9-5 Visual Basic properties and functions for working with dates and times

How to work with strings

Many types of programs require that you work with the characters within strings. If, for example, a user enters the city, state, and zip code of an address as a single entry, your program may need to divide (or parse) that single string into city, state, and zip code variables. Or, if a user enters a telephone number that includes parentheses and hyphens, you may need to remove those characters so the number can be stored as a 10-digit integer.

When you create a string, you are actually creating a String object from the String class. Then, you can use the properties and methods of the String class to work with the String object. An alternative, though, is to create StringBuilder objects from the StringBuilder class so you can use the properties and methods of that class to work with strings. In the topics that follow, you'll learn both ways of working with strings.

The properties and methods of the String class

Figure 9-6 summarizes some of the properties and methods of the String class that you can use as you work with String objects. When you use these properties and methods, you often need to use an index to refer to a specific character within a string. To do that, you use 0 to refer to the first character, 1 to refer to the second character, and so on. When you refer to a character in a string, you code the index for a string character within braces. This is the same technique that you use to refer to an element of an array. In fact, it sometimes helps to think of a string as an array of characters.

One method that's particularly useful for parsing strings is the Split method. This method returns an array where each element contains a substring of the original string. The argument that you specify for this method identifies the character that's used to delimit each substring. You'll see examples of this method in figure 9-8.

Common properties and methods of the String class

Property	Description
Chars(index)	Gets the character at the specified position. Since Chars is the default property, its name can be omitted.
Length	Gets the number of characters in the string.

Method	Description
StartsWith(string)	Returns a Boolean value that indicates whether or not the string starts with the specified string.
EndsWith(string)	Returns a Boolean value that indicates whether or not the string ends with the specified string.
IndexOf(string[, startindex])	Returns an integer that represents the position of the first occurrence of the specified string starting at the specified position. If the starting position isn't specified, the search starts at the beginning of the string. If the string isn't found, -1 is returned.
LastIndexOf(string[, startindex])	Returns an integer that represents the position of the last occurrence of the specified string starting at the specified position. If the starting position isn't specified, the search starts at the end of the string. If the string isn't found, -1 is returned.
Insert(startindex, string)	Returns a string with the specified string inserted beginning at the specified position.
PadLeft(totalwidth)	Returns a string that's right-aligned and padded on the left with spaces so it's the specified width.
PadRight(totalwidth)	Returns a string that's left-aligned and padded on the right with spaces so it's the specified width.
Remove(startindex, count)	Returns a string with the specified number of characters removed starting at the specified position.
Replace(oldstring, newstring)	Returns a string with all occurrences of the old string replaced with the new string.
Substring(startindex[, length])	Returns the string that starts at the specified position and has the specified length. If the length isn't specified, all of the characters to the end of the string are returned.
ToLower()	Returns a string in lowercase.
ToUpper()	Returns a string in uppercase.
Trim()	Returns a string with leading and trailing spaces removed.
Split(splitcharacters)	Returns an array of strings where each element is a substring that's delimited by the specified character or characters.

Description

- You can use an index to access each character in a string, where 0 is the index for the first character, 1 is the index for the second character, and so on.

Figure 9-6 The properties and methods of the String class

Code examples that work with strings

Figure 9-7 shows how to use most of the properties and methods summarized in the last figure. The first example shows how you can use an index to return a character from a string. Then, the second example shows how you can use an index and the Length property in a For loop to insert a space character between each character in the string. The third example performs the same operation as the second example, but it uses a For Each loop instead of a For loop.

The fourth example shows how you can use the StartsWith and EndsWith methods. Here, the first statement checks if the string named chars that was created in the first example starts with the string "abc", and the second statement checks if this string ends with "abc". As you can see, the result of the first statement is True, and the result of the second statement is False.

The fifth example shows how to use the IndexOf and LastIndexOf methods. Here, the first statement sets the value of the string. Then, the second statement uses the IndexOf method to retrieve the index of the first space in the string, and the third statement uses the same method to return the index of a string of characters. Since the characters don't exist in the string, this method returns a value of -1. The last statement uses the LastIndexOf method to return the index of the last space in the string.

The sixth example shows how to use the Remove, Insert, and Replace methods to work with the string in the fifth example. Here, the first statement removes the first five characters of the string. In this statement, the first argument specifies the starting index, and the second argument specifies the number of characters to remove. In this case, the number of characters to remove is calculated by adding 1 to the index of the first space, which is 4. Then, the second statement uses the Insert method to insert ", Inc." at the end of the string. Here, the first argument uses the Length method to set the starting index at the end of the string, and the second argument specifies the string to be inserted. Finally, the third statement uses the Replace method to replace all occurrences of "and" with "And".

The seventh example shows how to use the Substring, ToUpper, and ToLower methods to make sure a string is lowercase with an initial cap. Here, the second statement returns a substring that contains the first character in the string. To do that, the first argument specifies a starting index of 0 and the second argument specifies a length of 1. Then, to convert the returned substring to uppercase, this statement calls the ToUpper method. The third statement is similar, but it uses the ToLower method to return the remaining characters in the string and convert them to lowercase. The last statement combines the two strings into a single string.

The eighth example shows how to use the = operator to copy one string to another string. Because a string is a reference type, you might think that the second statement would copy the reference to the string object created by the first statement to the second string variable. In this case, however, a new string object is created and the value in the original string is copied to that object. Then, a new value is assigned to the new string variable.

Code that uses an index to access a character in a string

```
Dim chars As String = "abcdefg"
Dim a As Char = chars(0)                    ' a = "a"
Dim b As Char = chars(1)                    ' b = "b"
```

Code that uses a For loop to access each character in the string

```
Dim charsAndSpaces As String = ""
For i As Integer = 0 To chars.Length - 1
    charsAndSpaces &= chars(i) & " "
Next
MessageBox.Show(charsAndSpaces, "String Test")
```

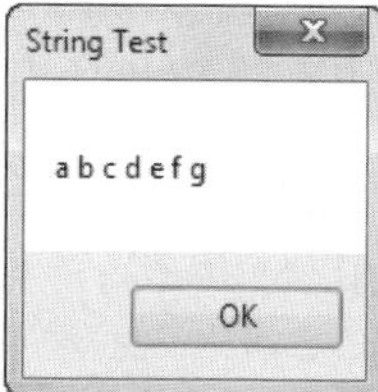

Code that uses a For Each loop to access each character in the string

```
Dim charsAndSpaces As String = ""
For Each c As Char in chars
    charsAndSpaces &= c & " "
Next
MessageBox.Show(charsAndSpaces, "String Test")
```

Code that uses the StartsWith and EndsWith methods

```
Dim startsWithABC As Boolean = chars.StartsWith("abc")    ' True
Dim endsWithABC As Boolean = chars.EndsWith("abc")        ' False
```

Code that uses the IndexOf method

```
Dim companyName As String = "Mike Murach and Associates"
Dim index1 As Integer = companyName.IndexOf(" ")          ' 4
Dim index2 As Integer = companyName.IndexOf("Inc.")       ' -1
Dim index3 As Integer = companyName.LastIndexOf(" ")      ' 15
```

Code that uses the Remove, Insert, and Replace methods

```
companyName = companyName.Remove(0, index1 + 1)
companyName = companyName.Insert(companyName.Length, ", Inc.")
companyName =
    companyName.Replace("and", "And")       ' Murach And Associates, Inc.
```

Code that uses the Substring, ToUpper, and ToLower methods

```
Dim firstName As String = "anne"
Dim firstLetter As String = firstName.Substring(0, 1).ToUpper
Dim otherLetters As String = firstName.Substring(1).ToLower
firstName = firstLetter & otherLetters                        ' Anne
```

Code that copies one string to another string

```
Dim s1 As String = "abc"
Dim s2 As String = s1    ' This creates a new string with the value "abc"
s2 = "def"               ' This doesn't change the value stored in s1
```

Figure 9-7 Code examples that work with strings

More examples that work with strings

Figure 9-8 presents some additional string-handling routines. The first four parse the data in strings. The fifth one adds characters to a string. And the sixth one replaces some of the characters in a string with other characters. If you can understand the code in these routines, you should be able to write your own routines whenever needed.

The first routine shows how to parse the first name from a string that contains a full name. Here, the full name is assigned to the fullName variable so you can visualize how the statements that follow work with that name. In practice, though, the name would be entered by a user or read from a file so you wouldn't know what it was.

To start, this routine uses the Trim method to remove any spaces from the beginning and end of the string that a user may have typed accidentally. Next, the IndexOf method is used to get the position of the first space in the string, which should be between the first name and the middle name or last name. If this method doesn't find a space in the string, though, it returns a -1. In that case, the If statement that follows assigns the entire string to the first name variable. Otherwise, it uses the Substring method to set the first name variable equal to the string that begins at the first character of the string and that has a length that's equal to the position of the first space.

The second routine in this figure shows how to parse a string that contains an address into the components of the address. In this case, a pipe character (|) separates each component of the address. In addition, the string may begin with one or more spaces followed by a pipe character, and it may end with a pipe character followed by one or more spaces.

To remove the spaces from the beginning and end of the string, this routine also uses the Trim method. Then, it uses the StartsWith and EndsWith methods to determine whether the first or last character in the string is a pipe character. If it is, the Remove method removes that character from the string.

The next three statements use the IndexOf method to determine the index values of the first character for each substring other than the first. (The first substring will start at index 0.) To do that, it determines the index of the next pipe character and then adds 1. After that, the next four statements use these index variables as arguments of the Substring method to return the street, city, state, and zip code substrings. To calculate the length of each substring, this code subtracts the starting index from the ending index and then subtracts 1 from that value. This results in the length of the substring without the pipe character.

The third and fourth routines use the Split method to perform the same operations as the first and second routines. Note that the argument for this method has to be cast to a Char type if you're using strict type semantics, but this method can simplify your code significantly.

The fifth and sixth routines show how to add hyphens to a phone number and change the hyphens in a date to slashes. To add hyphens, you simply use the Insert method to insert the hyphens at the appropriate index. And to change hyphens to slashes, you use the Replace method.

Code that parses a first name from a name string

```
Dim fullName As String = " Edward C Koop   "             ' " Edward C Koop   "
fullName = fullName.Trim                                 ' "Edward C Koop"
Dim firstSpace As Integer = fullName.IndexOf(" ")        ' 6
Dim firstName As String = ""
If firstSpace = -1 Then
    firstName = fullName
Else
    firstName = fullName.Substring(0, firstSpace)        ' "Edward"
End If
```

Code that parses a string that contains an address

```
Dim address As String = " |805 Main Street|Dallas|TX|12345| "
address = address.Trim
If address.StartsWith("|") Then
    address = address.Remove(0, 1)
End If
If address.EndsWith("|") Then
    address = address.Remove(address.Length - 1, 1)
End If
Dim cityIndex As Integer = address.IndexOf("|") + 1
Dim stateIndex As Integer = address.IndexOf("|", cityIndex) + 1
Dim zipIndex As Integer = address.IndexOf("|", stateIndex) + 1
Dim street As String = address.Substring(0, cityIndex - 1)
Dim city As String = address.Substring(
    cityIndex, stateIndex - cityIndex - 1)
Dim state As String = address.Substring(
    stateIndex, zipIndex - stateIndex - 1)
Dim zipCode As String = address.Substring(zipIndex)
```

Code that uses the Split method to parse the name string

```
fullName = fullName.Trim
Dim names() As String = fullName.Split(CChar(" "))
Dim firstName As String = names(0)                       ' "Edward"
```

Code that uses the Split method to parse the address string

```
address = address.Trim
If address.StartsWith("|") Then
    address = address.Remove(0, 1)
End If
Dim columns() As String = address.Split(CChar("|"))
Dim street As String = columns(0)                        ' 805 Main Street
Dim city As String = columns(1)                          ' Dallas
Dim state As String = columns(2)                         ' TX
Dim zipCode As String = columns(3)                       ' 12345
```

Code that adds hyphens to a phone number

```
Dim phoneNumber As String = "9775551212"
phoneNumber = phoneNumber.Insert(3, "-")
phoneNumber = phoneNumber.Insert(7, "-")                 ' 977-555-1212
```

Code that replaces the hyphens in a date with slashes

```
Dim birthDate As String = "12-27-2012"
birthDate = birthDate.Replace("-", "/")                  ' 12/27/2012
```

Figure 9-8 More examples that work with strings

Two procedures for validating user entries

In chapter 7, you learned how to code a Function procedure named IsDecimal that checked whether a user entry contained a valid decimal value. To do that, this procedure used the TryParse method to try to convert the entry string to a decimal. Then, a false value was returned if the user entered any non-numeric characters, including dollar signs, percent signs, and commas. Since these characters are often used to format numeric values, though, it makes sense to allow them in numeric entries. To do that, you can use Function procedures like the ones shown in figure 9-9.

The first procedure in this figure is another version of the IsDecimal procedure that can be used to validate decimal entries. The advantage to using this method is that it lets the user enter numeric formatting characters, including dollar signs, percentage signs, commas, and spaces. As a result, the user can enter these characters and this procedure will still recognize the entry as a valid decimal value.

This IsDecimal procedure works by using a For Each loop to check each character in the entry string to be sure it contains a number from 0 through 9, a decimal point, or a valid formatting character ($, %, comma, or space). If an invalid character is encountered, this procedure displays an error message and returns a False value. If all the characters are valid, however, the loop continues by checking if the character is a decimal point. If it is, a variable named decimalCount is incremented by 1.

The If statement that follows the For Each loop checks that the decimalCount variable is less than or equal to one. If it is, this procedure returns a True value. Otherwise, it displays an error message and returns a False value.

Because the IsDecimal procedure lets the user enter formatting characters, youl need to remove these characters before attempting to convert the string to a Decimal type. To do that, you can use the Strip procedure shown in this figure. Like the IsDecimal procedure, this procedure uses a For Each loop to check each character in the entry string. Then, if a character is one of the formatting characters, it uses the Remove method to remove that character from the string.

The code at the bottom of this figure shows how you can call these two procedures to validate the monthly investment that the user enters into the Future Value application. Here, the IsDecimal procedure is specified as the condition in an If statement. Then, if this procedure returns a True value, the Strip procedure is called to remove any formatting characters, and the resulting string is converted to a decimal.

A procedure that tests whether a string contains a decimal value

```
Public Function IsDecimal(textBox As TextBox, name As String) _
        As Boolean
    Dim s As String = textBox.Text
    Dim decimalCount As Integer = 0
    For Each c As Char In s
        If Not (c = "0" Or c = "1" Or c = "2" Or c = "3" Or c = "4" Or
               c = "5" Or c = "6" Or c = "7" Or c = "8" Or c = "9" Or
               c = "." Or c = "," Or c = "$" Or c = "%" Or c = " ") _
        Then
            MessageBox.Show(name & " must be a decimal value.",
                   "Entry Error")
            Return False
        End If
        If c = CChar(".") Then
            decimalCount += 1
        End If
    Next
    If decimalCount <= 1 Then
        Return True
    Else
        MessageBox.Show(name & " must be a decimal value.",
            "Entry Error")
        Return False
    End If
End Function
```

A procedure that strips formatting characters from a numeric string

```
Public Function Strip(s As String) As String
    Dim i As Integer
    For Each c As Char In s
        If c = "$" Or c = "%" Or c = "," Or c = " " Then
            i = s.IndexOf(c)
            s = s.Remove(i, 1)
        End If
    Next
    Return s
End Function
```

Code that calls the two procedures above

```
Dim monthlyInvestment As Decimal
If IsDecimal(txtMonthlyInvestment, "Monthly Investment") Then
    monthlyInvestment = CDec(Strip(txtMonthlyInvestment.Text))
End If
```

Description

- If you use an IsDecimal procedure like the one in this figure for validating user entries, a valid entry can include some formatting characters.
- If you allow formatting characters in a valid entry, you need to remove those characters before the value is cast to a Decimal type.

Figure 9-9 Two procedures for validating user entries

How to use the StringBuilder class

When you use the String class to create a string, the string has a fixed length and value. In other words, the String class creates strings that are *immutable*. Then, when you assign a new value to a string variable, the original String object is deleted and it's replaced with a new String object that contains the new value.

Another way to work with strings, though, is to use the StringBuilder class. Then, you create StringBuilder objects that are *mutable* so you can add, delete, or replace characters in the objects. This makes it easier to write some types of string-handling routines, and these routines run more efficiently. As a result, you should use the StringBuilder class for string-handling routines that append, insert, remove, or replace characters in strings, especially if you're working with long strings that use significant system resources.

In figure 9-10, you can see some of the most useful properties and methods for working with a string that's created from the StringBuilder class. As you can see, you can use an index to refer to a character in a StringBuilder object, and you can use the Length property to get the number of characters in a string just as you can with a String object. You can also use the Insert, Remove, and Replace methods with StringBuilder objects. However, instead of returning a new string, these methods change the existing string.

When you create a StringBuilder object, you can code one or two arguments that assign an initial value, an initial capacity, or both. The statements in the second example illustrate how this works. Here, the first statement doesn't include any arguments, so the StringBuilder object is created with a default capacity of 16 characters and an initial value of an empty string. The second statement creates a StringBuilder object with an initial capacity of 10. The third and fourth statements are similar, but they specify an initial value for the object.

The last example in this figure shows how you can use five methods of the StringBuilder class. Here, the first statement creates a StringBuilder object with an initial capacity of 10, and the second statement appends a 10-character phone number to the object. The third and fourth statements insert periods into the string to format the number. The fifth statement removes the area code and the period that follows it. The sixth statement replaces the remaining period with a hyphen. And the last statement converts the characters stored in the StringBuilder object to a string.

This example also shows how a StringBuilder object automatically increases its capacity when necessary. Here, the StringBuilder object has a capacity of 10 when it's created, and this capacity remains at 10 until the first period is inserted. Then, to be able to store the 11 characters, the StringBuilder object automatically doubles its capacity to 20.

Please note that the System.Text namespace that contains the StringBuilder class isn't automatically included with a new project. To make it available to a class, though, you can code an Imports statement like the one shown in this figure at the start the class. Or, if you want to make this namespace available to all of the classes in a project, you can double-click on My Projects in the Solution Explorer, click on the References tab, and check the box for System.Text in the Imported Namespaces list.

The syntax for creating a StringBuilder object

```
Dim variableName As New StringBuilder([value][,][capacity])
```

Common properties and methods of the StringBuilder class

Property	Description
`Chars(index)`	Gets the character at the specified position. Since Chars is the default property, you can omit its name.
`Length`	Gets the number of characters in the string.
`Capacity`	Gets or sets the number of characters the string can hold.
Method	**Description**
`Append(string)`	Adds the specified string to the end of the string.
`Insert(index, string)`	Inserts the specified string at the specified index in the string.
`Remove(startindex, count)`	Removes the specified number of characters from the string starting at the specified index.
`Replace(oldstring, newstring)`	Replaces all occurrences of the old string with the new string.
`ToString()`	Converts the StringBuilder object to a string.

A statement that simplifies references to the StringBuilder class

```
Imports System.Text
```

Statements that create and initialize StringBuilder objects

```
Dim address1 As New StringBuilder()                   ' Capacity is 16
Dim address2 As New StringBuilder(10)                 ' Capacity is 10
Dim phoneNumber1 As StringBuilder =
    New StringBuilder("9775551212")                   ' Capacity is 16
Dim phoneNumber2 As StringBuilder =
    New StringBuilder("9775551212", 10)               ' Capacity is 10
```

Code that creates a phone number and inserts dashes

```
Dim phoneNumber As New StringBuilder(10)              ' Capacity is 10
phoneNumber.Append("9775551212")                      ' Capacity is 10
phoneNumber.Insert(3, ".")                            ' Capacity is 20
phoneNumber.Insert(7, ".")                            ' 977.555.1212
phoneNumber.Remove(0, 4)                              ' 555.1212
phoneNumber.Replace(".", "-")                         ' 555-1212
lblPhoneNumber.Text = phoneNumber.ToString            ' 555-1212
```

Description

- Unlike string objects, StringBuilder objects are *mutable*, which means that they can be changed.
- To refer to the StringBuilder class, you must either qualify it with System.Text or include an Imports statement for this namespace at the start of the class that uses it.
- The capacity of a StringBuilder object is the amount of memory that's allocated to it. That capacity is increased automatically whenever necessary. If you don't set an initial capacity when you create a StringBuilder object, the default is 16 characters.

Figure 9-10 How to use the StringBuilder class

How to use Visual Basic functions to work with strings

Although the String and StringBuilder classes provide all the properties and methods that you need for working with strings, Visual Basic provides a complete set of functions for working with strings. Since these functions duplicate the operations of the .NET classes, you don't need to use them. Also, we think it's better to use the classes and objects of the .NET Framework so your code is more consistent with the code in other languages.

Nevertheless, it's worth taking a minute or two to review the functions that are summarized in figure 9-11. That way, you won't be confused if you come across one of these functions in someone else's code. Curiously, an index value of 1 refers to the first character in a string when you use one of these functions, although it refers to the second character in a string if you use String or StringBuilder properties or methods.

Visual Basic functions for working with strings

Function	Description
CStr(value)	Converts the argument to a String type.
Len(string)	Returns the number of characters in the string.
InStr(startindex, string1, string2)	Returns an integer that represents the position of the first occurrence of the second string in the first string. The search starts at the specified position in the string. If the string isn't found, this function returns 0.
Left(string, length)	Returns the specified number of characters from the beginning of the string.
Mid(string, startindex[, length])	Returns the specified number of characters from the string starting at the specified position. If the length isn't specified, all of the characters to the end of the string are returned.
Right(string, length)	Returns the specified number of characters from the end of the string.
Replace(string, oldstring, newstring)	Returns a string with all occurrences of the old string in the string replaced by the new string.
Split(string[, delimiter][, limit])	Parses a string into a one-dimensional array of one or more substrings. If the delimiter isn't specified, space is used. If the limit isn't specified, all substrings are returned.
LCase(value)	Returns a string or character in lowercase.
UCase(value)	Returns a string or character in uppercase.
Trim(string)	Returns a string with leading and trailing spaces removed.
LTrim(string)	Returns a string with leading spaces removed.
RTrim(string)	Returns a string with trailing spaces removed.
Space(number)	Returns a string that contains the specified number of spaces.

Description

- When you use Visual Basic functions to work with strings, the first index position is 1.
- The Left and Right functions must be qualified with the Microsoft.VisualBasic namespace because Left and Right are properties in the Windows.Forms.Form namespace.

Figure 9-11 Visual Basic functions for working with strings

How to format numbers, dates, and times

In chapter 4, you learned how to apply standard numeric formats to numbers. Then, earlier in this chapter, you learned how to apply standard formats to dates and times. However, you can also apply custom formatting to numbers, dates, and times.

How to format numbers

Figure 9-12 shows how to use the Format method of the String class to format numbers. Because this is a shared method, you access it directly from the String class rather than from an instance of this class. The result of this method is a string that contains the formatted number.

As you can see in the syntax for this method, the first argument is a string. This string contains the format specifications for the value or values to be formatted. Following this string, you specify one or more values that you want to format. In most cases, you'll use this method to format a single value.

For each value to be formatted, you code a format specification within the string argument. This specification is divided into three parts. The first part indicates the value to be formatted. Because the values are numbered from zero, you'll usually code a zero to indicate that the first value is to be formatted. The next part indicates the width of the formatted value along with its alignment. In most cases, you'll omit this part of the specification.

The third part of the format specification contains the actual format string. This string can contain multiple formats. If only one format is specified, it's used for all numbers. If two formats are specified, the first is used for positive numbers and zero values, and the second is used for negative values. If all three formats are specified, the first is used for positive numbers, the second is used for negative numbers, and the third is used for zero values.

Each format can consist of one of the standard numeric formatting codes listed in this figure. If, for example, you want to format a number as currency, you can code a statement like the first statement in this figure. Here, the format specification, which is enclosed in braces, indicates that the first value (0) should be formatted with the currency format (c). Then, this specification is enclosed in quotes to indicate that it is a string literal. That way, it can be passed as an argument to the Format method of the String class.

If the standard numeric formatting codes don't provide the format you want, you can create your own format using the custom codes presented in this figure. For instance, the second statement uses these codes to create a custom currency format. Here, the first format string indicates that positive numbers and the value 0 should be formatted with a decimal and thousands separators (if appropriate). In addition, the first digit to the left of the decimal point and the first two digits to the right of the decimal are always included, even if they're zero. The other digits are included only if they're non-zero.

The syntax of the Format method of the String class

```
Format(string, value1[, value2]...)
```

The syntax of a format specification within the string argument

```
{N[, M][:formatstring]}
```

Explanation

N	An integer that indicates the value to be formatted.
M	An integer that indicates the width of the formatted value. If M is negative, the value will be left-justified. If it's positive, it will be right-justified.
formatstring	A string of formatting codes.

The syntax of a format string

```
positiveformat[;negativeformat[;zeroformat]]
```

Standard numeric formatting codes

C or c	Formats the number as currency with the specified number of decimal places.
D or d	Formats an integer with the specified number of digits.
E or e	Formats the number in scientific (exponential) notation with the specified number of decimal places.
F or f	Formats the number as a decimal with the specified number of decimal places.
G or g	Formats the number as a decimal or in scientific notation depending on which is more compact.
N or n	Formats the number with thousands separators and the specified number of decimal places.
P or p	Formats the number as a percent with the specified number of decimal places.

Custom numeric formatting codes

0	Zero placeholder	,	Thousands separator
#	Digit placeholder	%	Percentage placeholder
.	Decimal point	;	Section separator

Statements that format a single number

```
Dim balance As String = String.Format("{0:c}", 1234.56)      ' $1,234.56
Dim balance2 As String =
    String.Format("{0:$#,##0.00;($#,##0.00)}", -1234.56)     ' ($1,234.56)
Dim balance3 As String =
    String.Format("{0:$#,##0.00;($#,##0.00);Zero}", 0)       ' Zero
Dim quantity As String = String.Format("{0:d3}", 43)         ' 043
Dim payment As String = String.Format("{0:f2}", 432.8175)    ' 432.82
```

A statement that formats two numbers

```
Dim totalDue As String =
    String.Format("Invoice total: {0:c} Amount due: {1:c}.", 354.75, 20)
    ' Invoice total: $354.75 Amount due: $20.00.
```

Figure 9-12 How to format numbers

The format for negative numbers is similar. However, this format includes parentheses, which means that negative numbers will be displayed with parentheses around them as shown in the result for this statement. Notice that the parentheses aren't actually formatting codes. They're simply literal values that are included in the output string. The same is true of the dollar signs.

The third statement is similar to the second one, but it includes an additional format for zero values. In this case, a zero value is displayed as the literal "Zero" as you can see in the result for this statement.

The last two statements show how to use standard formatting codes for integers and decimals. In the first statement, an integer is formatted with three digits since the number 3 is included after the formatting code. In the second statement, a decimal is formatted with two decimal places. As you can see, if the number includes more decimal places than are specified, the number is rounded.

The example at the bottom of this figure shows how you can use the Format method to format two numbers. Here, the string argument includes text in addition to the format specification for each of the two values to be formatted. In this case, the first value is formatted according to the first format specification, and the second value according to the second format specification.

How to format dates and times

You can also use the Format method of the String class to format dates and times. This method works the same way that it does for numeric formatting, but you use the standard and custom formatting codes for DateTime values that are presented in figure 9-13. The examples in this figure show how this works. If you understand how to use this method to format numbers, you shouldn't have any trouble using it to format dates and times.

Standard DateTime formatting codes

d	Short date	f	Long date, short time
D	Long date	F	Long date, long time
t	Short time	g	Short date, short time
T	Long time	G	Short date, long time

Custom DateTime formatting codes

d	Day of the month without leading zeros	h	Hour without leading zeros
dd	Day of the month with leading zeros	hh	Hour with leading zeros
ddd	Abbreviated day name	H	Hour on a 24-hour clock without leading zeros
dddd	Full day name	HH	Hour on a 24-hour clock with leading zeros
M	Month without leading zeros	m	Minutes without leading zeros
MM	Month with leading zeros	mm	Minutes with leading zeros
MMM	Abbreviated month name	s	Seconds without leading zeros
MMMM	Full month name	ss	Seconds with leading zeros
y	Two-digit year without leading zero	f	Fractions of seconds (one *f* for each decimal place)
yy	Two-digit year with leading zero	T	First character of AM/PM designator
yyyy	Four-digit year	tt	Full AM/PM designator
/	Date separator	:	Time separator

Statements that format dates and times

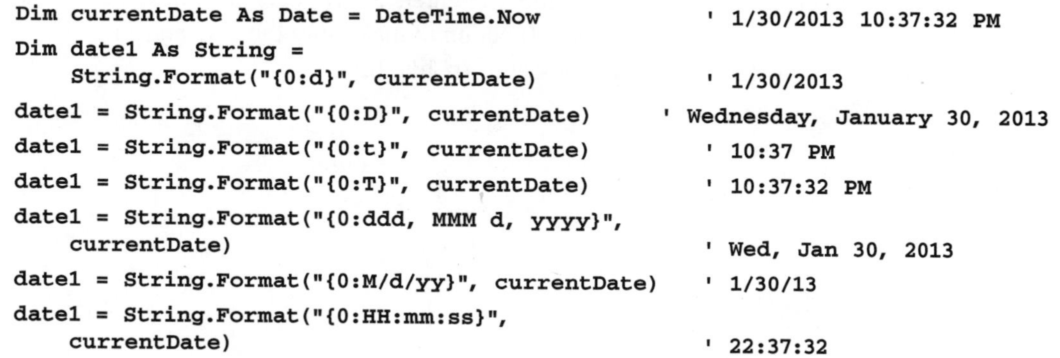

```
Dim currentDate As Date = DateTime.Now                 ' 1/30/2013 10:37:32 PM
Dim date1 As String =
    String.Format("{0:d}", currentDate)                ' 1/30/2013
date1 = String.Format("{0:D}", currentDate)          ' Wednesday, January 30, 2013
date1 = String.Format("{0:t}", currentDate)            ' 10:37 PM
date1 = String.Format("{0:T}", currentDate)            ' 10:37:32 PM
date1 = String.Format("{0:ddd, MMM d, yyyy}",
    currentDate)                                       ' Wed, Jan 30, 2013
date1 = String.Format("{0:M/d/yy}", currentDate)       ' 1/30/13
date1 = String.Format("{0:HH:mm:ss}",
    currentDate)                                       ' 22:37:32
```

Figure 9-13 How to format dates and times

Perspective

Now that you've completed this chapter, you should be able to use the DateTime structure to work with dates and times and the String and StringBuilder classes to work with strings. You should be able to use the Visual Basic properties and functions to work with dates, times, and strings. And you should be able to use the Format method of the String class to provide custom formatting for numbers, dates, and times, in case you ever need to do that.

Terms

tick
immutable
mutable

Exercise 9-1 Work with dates and times

In this exercise, you'll use the DateTime and TimeSpan structures.

1. Open the application that's in the C:\VB 2012\Chapter 09\DateHandling directory. Within this project, you'll find a form that accepts a future date and a birth date and provides buttons for calculating days due and age.
2. Add code to calculate the due days when the user enters a future date and clicks the Calculate Due Days button. Use the IsDate function to make sure the date entry is valid, and display the results in a message box like this:

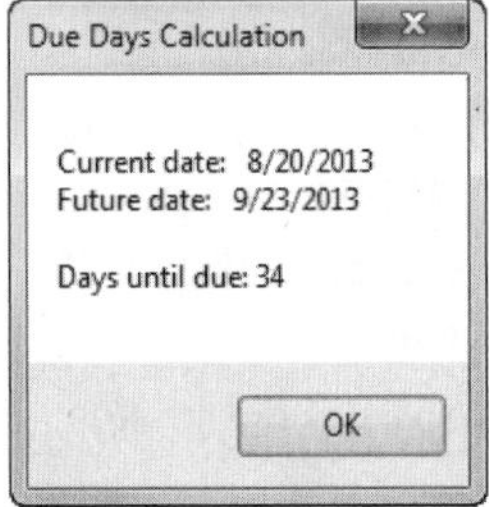

3. Test your code with a variety of date formats to see what formats can be successfully parsed. When you're done, close the form.
4. Add code to calculate the age when the user enters a birth date and clicks the Calculate Age button. Use the IsDate function to make sure the date entry is valid, and display the results in a message box like this:

5. Test your code to make sure it works for all dates. Then, close the solution.

Exercise 9-2 Work with strings

In this exercise, you'll use methods of the String class to work with strings.

Open the application and add code to parse a name

1. Open the application that's in the C:\VB 2012\Chapter 09\StringHandling directory. Within this project, you'll find a form that accepts a name and a phone number from the user and provides buttons for parsing the name and editing the phone number.
2. Add code to parse the name when the user enters a name and clicks the Parse Name button. This code should work whether the user enters a first, middle, and last name or just a first and last name. It should also convert the parsed name so the first letter of each word is uppercase but the other letters are lowercase. The results should be displayed in a message box like this:

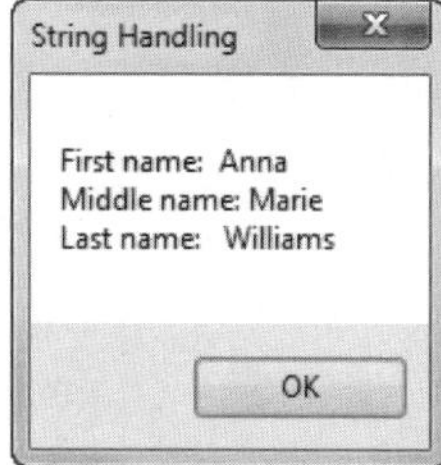

3. Test the application to see if it works. Try entering the name in all uppercase letters or all lowercase letters to make sure the parsed name is still displayed with only the first letters capitalized. When you're done, close the form.

Use the methods of the String class to edit a phone number

4. Use the methods of the String class to edit a phone number when the user enters a phone number and clicks the Edit Phone Number button. This code should remove all special characters from the user entry so the number consists of 10 digits. Then, it should format the phone number with hyphens. These results should be displayed in a message box like the one that follows. For simplicity, you can assume that the user enters ten digits.

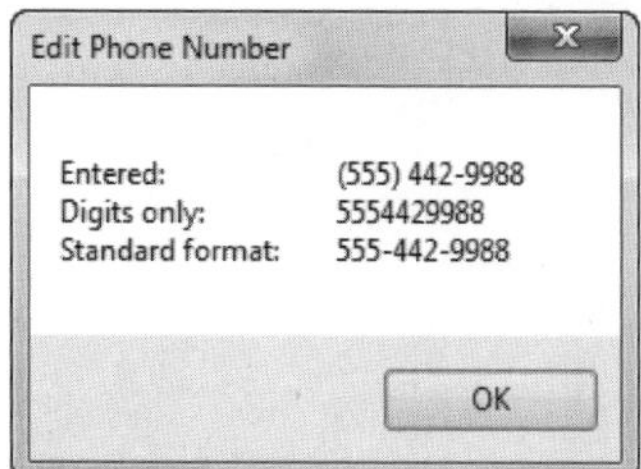

5. Test the application with a variety of entry formats to make sure it works. When you're done, close the form.

Use the methods of the StringBuilder class to edit the phone number

6. Copy all the statements that you wrote for step 4 except the MessageBox statement, and paste the statements before the MessageBox statement. Then, comment out the first set of statements. That way, you'll be able to use the MessageBox statement with the second set of statements.

7. Modify the second set of statements so they use the StringBuilder class to do what step 4 requires. When you code the word StringBuilder for the first time, you'll find that Visual Basic doesn't recognize it. That's because the form class doesn't include an Imports statement for the System.Text namespace, which contains the StringBuilder class. To fix that problem, code an Imports statement like the one in figure 9-10 at the start of the class. Then, code and test the new statements.
8. After you get the new code working right, double-click on My Project in the Solution Explorer, click on the References tab, and scroll down the Imported Namespaces list until you find the System.Text namespace. Then, check its box, which will make that namespace available to all of the classes in the project.
9. Remove the Imports statement from the start of the form class. Then, run the application again to prove that the System.Text namespace is now available to all of the classes in the project.

10

More skills for working with Windows forms and controls

In previous chapters, you learned how to work with a project that uses a single form that contains labels, text boxes, and buttons. In this chapter, you'll learn how to use some other common controls, such as combo boxes and check boxes, and you'll learn some basic skills for working with two or more forms in the same project. When you're done, you'll be able to develop a project that contains multiple forms and uses any of the controls presented in this chapter.

How to work with controls

Although you'll use label, text box, and button controls on almost every form you develop, their functionality is limited. As a result, you need to know how to use some of the other controls provided by the .NET Framework. In particular, you need to learn how to use the five controls presented in the topics that follow.

Five more types of controls

Figure 10-1 shows a form that contains two combo boxes, one list box, one group box, two radio buttons, and a check box. Although you've undoubtedly used these controls when working with Windows applications, take a moment to consider these controls from a programmer's point of view.

You can use a *combo box* to let the user select one item from a list of items. That reduces the amount of typing that's required by the user, and it reduces the chance that the user will enter invalid or inaccurate data. As you'll see in the next figure, you can also create combo boxes that let the user enter text that doesn't appear in the list.

Like a combo box, a *list box* lets the user select an item from a list of items. However, the list portion of a list box is always visible. In contrast, the list portion of a combo box is typically hidden until the user clicks the arrow at the right side of the control. The user can also select two or more items from a list box, but can only select a single item from a combo box.

Radio buttons provide a way to let the user select one item from a group of items. To create a group of radio buttons, you can place two or more radio buttons within a *group box*. Then, when the user selects one radio button, all the other radio buttons in the group are automatically deselected. Since the user can only select one radio button within each group, these buttons present mutually exclusive choices.

Check boxes provide a way to present the user with choices that are not mutually exclusive. That means that if the user checks or unchecks one check box, it doesn't affect the other check boxes on the form.

A form with five more types of controls

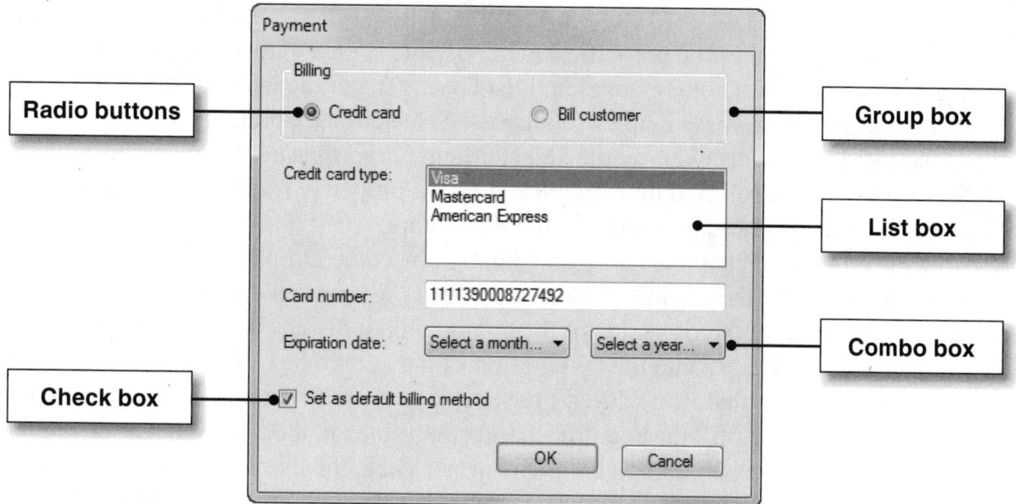

Description

- A *combo box* lets the user select one option from a drop-down list of items. A combo box can also let the user enter text into the text box portion of the combo box.
- A *list box* lets the user select one or more options from a list of items. If a list box contains more items than can be displayed at one time, a vertical scroll bar is added automatically.
- *Radio buttons* let the user select one option from a group of options.
- A *group box* can group related controls. For example, it's common to place related radio buttons within a group box. Then, the user can only select one of the radio buttons in the group.
- A *check box* lets the user select or deselect an option.

Figure 10-1 Five more types of controls

How to work with combo boxes and list boxes

Figure 10-2 shows the properties, methods, and events that you're likely to use as you work with combo boxes and list boxes. To get the index of the item that the user selects, for example, you use the SelectedIndex property. To get the selected item itself, you use the SelectedItem property. And to get a string that represents the selected item, you use the Text property. You'll see coding examples that use these properties in the next figure.

One property that applies only to a combo box is the DropDownStyle property. The default is DropDown, which means that the user can either click on the drop-down arrow at the right side of the combo box to display the drop-down list or enter a value directly into the text portion of the combo box. Note that if the user enters a value, that value doesn't have to appear in the list.

If you want to restrict user entries to just the values in the list, you can set the DropDownStyle property to DropDownList. Then, the user can only select a value from the list or enter the first character of a value that appears in the list to select it.

One property that applies only to a list box is the SelectionMode property. The default is One, which means that the user can only select one item from the list box. However, you can let the user select multiple items by setting this property to MultiSimple or MultiExtended. If you set it to MultiSimple, the user can only select multiple entries by clicking on them. If you set it to MultiExtended, the user can hold down the Ctrl and Shift keys to select nonadjacent and adjacent items. This works just as it does for any standard Windows application. By the way, you can also set this property to None, in which case the user can't select an entry. You might use this setting if you just want to display items.

If you allow the user to select multiple items from a list box, you can use the SelectedIndices property to return a collection of the selected indexes, and you can use the SelectedItems property to return a collection of selected items. Or, you can use the SelectedIndex and SelectedItem properties to return the first index or item in the collection of selected items.

When you work with the items in a list box or combo box, you should realize that you're actually working with the items in a collection. To refer to this collection, you use the Items property of the control. Then, you can use an index to refer to any item in the collection. Or, you can use properties and methods that the .NET Framework provides for working with collections. The most common properties and methods are summarized in this figure.

The most common event for working with combo boxes and list boxes is the SelectedIndexChanged event. This event occurs when the value of the SelectedIndex property changes, which happens when the user selects a different item from the list. For a combo box, you can also use the TextChanged event to detect when the user enters a value into the text portion of the control. Keep in mind, though, that this event will occur each time a single character is added, changed, or deleted.

Common members of list box and combo box controls

Property	Description
SelectedIndex	The index of the selected item. Items are numbered from 0. If no item is selected, this property has a value of -1.
SelectedItem	The object of the selected item.
Text	The text value for the selected item.
Sorted	If set to True, the items in the list are sorted alphabetically in ascending order.
Items	Provides access to the collection of items.
DropDownStyle	Determines whether the user can enter text in the text portion that's at the top of a combo box. If this property is set to DropDownList, the user must select an item from the list. If this property is set to DropDown, the user can enter data in the text portion of the combo box.
SelectionMode	Determines whether the user can select more than one item from a list box. If this property is set to One, the user can only select one item. If it's set to MultiSimple or MultiExtended, the user can select multiple items.
Event	**Description**
SelectedIndexChanged	Occurs when the user selects a different item from the list.
TextChanged	Occurs when the user enters a value into the text box portion of a combo box.

Common members of the Items collection

Property	Description
Item(index)	Gets or sets the item at the specified index in the list.
Count	Gets the number of items in the list.
Method	**Description**
Add(object)	Adds the specified item to the list.
Insert(index, object)	Inserts an item into the list at the specified index.
Remove(object)	Removes the specified item from the list.
RemoveAt(index)	Removes the item at the specified index from the list.
Clear()	Removes all items from the list.

Description

- To work with the items in a list box or combo box list, you use the Items property of the control. To refer to any item in this collection, you can use the Item property and an index.
- Since the Item property of the Items collection is the default property, you can omit it and code just the index.

Figure 10-2 Members for working with combo boxes and list boxes

After you add a combo box or list box to a form and set its properties the way you want, you can use code like that shown in figure 10-3 to work with the control. Here, the first example uses a For Each loop to load the name of each month in an array into a combo box. Each time through the loop, the Add method is used to add a month name to the Items collection for this combo box.

The first item in the array that's loaded into the list indicates that the user should select a month from the list. This is a common technique that's used to provide instructions to the user. As you'll see later in this chapter, though, you'll need to include additional code when you use this technique to be sure that the user selects an item other than the one that provides instructions.

The second example is similar, but it uses a Do loop to load eight Integer values into a combo box. The first value is the current year, and the next values are the seven years that follow. Like the combo box that contains the names of the months, the first entry in this combo box provides instructions for the user.

The third example shows how you can load a list box like the one shown in figure 10-1. To make sure that no items have already been loaded into this list box, this example begins by calling the Clear method to clear all the items. Then, it adds three items to the list box. Finally, it sets the SelectedIndex property to 0, which causes the first item in the list to be selected.

Although it's not shown here, it's common to put code that loads a combo box or list box in the event handler for the Load event of the form. That way, the control is loaded when the form is loaded. After that, the user can select an item from the combo box or list box and other procedures can get information about that item.

The statements in the fourth example show four ways that you can get information from a combo or list box. The first statement uses the SelectedIndex property to get the index of the item that's currently selected in the Years combo box. The second statement shows how to get the value that's displayed in the text portion of this combo box. The third statement shows how to get the value of the item that's currently selected in this combo box. Notice that because the SelectedItem property returns an object type, you must cast this object to the appropriate data type to get the value of the item. Finally, the fourth statement uses an index to get the second item in the Months combo box. Since the value of this item is a string type, the ToString method is used to get the value of this item. However, you could also cast the object to a string type like this:

```
Dim expMonthValue As String = CStr(cboExpirationMonth.Items(1))
```

The fifth example shows how to use the Add, Insert, and RemoveAt methods to work with the items in a combo box list. This example begins with a For Each loop that adds three names to the list. Then, the Insert method inserts a new name at the beginning of the list, and the RemoveAt method removes the last item from the list. When you use these methods, you indicate the index where you want the item inserted or removed. Finally, the last statement shows how you can initialize a combo box so that no value is selected. To do that, you set the SelectedIndex property of the control to -1.

Code that loads the Months combo box in figure 10-1

```
Dim months() As String =
    {"Select a month...",
    "January", "February", "March", "April",
    "May", "June", "July", "August",
    "September", "October", "November", "December"}
For Each month As String In months
    cboExpirationMonth.Items.Add(month)
Next
```

Code that loads the Years combo box in figure 10-1

```
Dim year As Integer = DateTime.Today.Year
Dim endYear As Integer = year + 8
cboExpirationYear.Items.Add("Select a year...")
Do While year < endYear
    cboExpirationYear.Items.Add(year)
    year += 1
Loop
```

Code that clears and loads the list box in figure 10-1

```
lstCreditCardType.Items.Clear()
lstCreditCardType.Items.Add("Visa")
lstCreditCardType.Items.Add("Mastercard")
lstCreditCardType.Items.Add("American Express")
lstCreditCardType.SelectedIndex = 0          ' Select the first item
```

Statements that get information from a combo box or list box

```
Dim expYearIndex As Integer = cboExpirationYear.SelectedIndex
Dim expYearText As String = cboExpirationYear.Text
Dim expYearValue As Integer = CInt(cboExpirationYear.SelectedItem)
Dim expMonthValue As String = cboExpirationMonth.Items(1).ToString
```

Code that works with a combo box of names

```
Dim names() As String = {"Doug Williams", "Anne Boehm", "Ed Koop"}
For Each name As String In names
    cboNames.Items.Add(name)
Next
cboNames.Items.Insert(0, "Joel Murach")
cboNames.Items.RemoveAt(3)
cboNames.SelectedIndex = -1                  ' Don't select an item
```

Notes

- You can also use the String Collection Editor to load items into a combo box or list box. To display this editor, select the control in the Form Designer and select the Edit Items command from the smart tag menu.
- In chapter 15, you'll learn techniques that can be used to load combo boxes and list boxes with data that's stored in a database.

Figure 10-3 Code examples for working with combo boxes and list boxes

How to work with check boxes and radio buttons

Figure 10-4 shows you how to work with check boxes and radio buttons. The main difference between these two types of controls is that radio buttons in a group are mutually exclusive and check boxes operate independently. In other words, if the user selects one radio button in a group, all of the other buttons are automatically turned off. In contrast, when the user selects a check box, it has no effect on the other check boxes on the form, even if they appear as a group.

To group radio buttons, you typically place them in a group box control. If you place any radio buttons outside of a group, however, all of the radio buttons on the form that aren't in a group box function as a group.

The property you're most likely to use when working with radio buttons and check boxes is the Checked property. This property can have a value of either True or False to indicate whether or not the control is checked.

The two statements in the first example set the Checked properties of a radio button and a check box to True. Then, the If statement in the second example tests the Checked property of the radio button. If the value of this property is True, a procedure named EnableControls is executed. But if the value of this property is False, it indicates that another radio button is selected. In that case, a procedure named DisableControls is executed.

Notice that the If statement in this example is coded within the event handler for the CheckedChanged event of the control. This event occurs when you select or deselect a radio button or check box, and it's the event you're most likely to use. Also note that because the Checked property contains a Boolean value, you can code the If clause without the equality operator.

The third example in this figure simply retrieves the Checked property of the check box and stores it in a Boolean variable. If the user has checked this box, this variable will be set to True. Otherwise, it will be set to False.

How to work with group boxes

Figure 10-4 also illustrates how to use a group box. For example, the group box shown at the top of this figure contains two radio buttons. That makes it clear that these controls function as a group. You specify the name of the group, which is displayed in the upper left corner of the group box, by setting the Text property of the control.

When you use a group box, you should know that all the controls it contains will move with the group box when you move it in the Form Designer. You should also know that you can't add existing controls on a form to a group box by dragging the group box over them. Instead, you have to add the group box and then drag the controls into the group box.

A group box that contains two radio buttons

Common members of radio button and check box controls

Property	Description
`Checked`	Gets or sets a Boolean value that indicates whether the control is checked.
Event	**Description**
`CheckedChanged`	Occurs when the user checks or unchecks the control.

Code that sets the value of a radio button and check box

```
rdoCreditCard.Checked = True
chkDefault.Checked = True
```

Code that checks the value of a radio button

```
Private Sub rdoCreditCard_CheckedChanged(sender As Object,
        e As EventArgs) Handles rdoCreditCard.CheckedChanged
    If rdoCreditCard.Checked Then
        Me.EnableControls()
    Else
        Me.DisableControls()
    End If
End Sub
```

Code that gets the value of a check box

```
Dim isDefaultBilling As Boolean = chkDefault.Checked
```

Description

- To determine whether a radio button or check box is checked, you test its Checked property.
- You can use a group box to group controls. Group boxes are typically used to group controls like radio buttons that function as a group.
- To add controls to a group box, drag them from the Toolbox into the group box. If you've already added the controls you want to include in the group box to the form, just drag them into the group box.
- Any radio buttons that aren't placed within a group box function as a separate group.
- If you move a group box, all of the controls it contains move with it.

Figure 10-4 How to work with radio buttons, check boxes, and group boxes

How to use Tab Order view to set the tab order

In chapter 2, you learned how to use the TabIndex property to change the *tab order* of the controls on a form. An easier way to change the tab order, though, is to use Tab Order view. This view is illustrated in figure 10-5.

When you display a form in Tab Order view, an index value is displayed at the left of each control that indicates the control's position in the tab order. Notice that the index values of the two radio button controls indicate their position in the tab order relative to the group box that contains them.

To change the tab order, you click on each control in the appropriate sequence. Then, the controls are given an index value that starts with zero and increases by one for each control you click. You can also click on the same control more than once. Then, the index value for that control is increased by one each time you click on it.

As you click on each control, the index values are displayed as shown in the second form in this figure. Here, I clicked on the list box, followed by the text box, followed by the two combo boxes, followed by the check box, followed by the two buttons and then the group box. That way, when the form is first displayed, the focus will be on the list box. Then, when the user presses the Tab key, the focus will move through the controls in sequence.

Notice that when I selected the group box control, the main indexes of the radio buttons within this control changed too so they're the same as the group box. However, the sub index of each radio button didn't change. In other words, the indexes of the radio buttons relative to each other remained the same. If you wanted to change these indexes, though, you could do that by clicking on them just like any other control.

Also notice in the second form that I didn't set the tab index for any of the labels. In most cases, it isn't necessary to change the tab order of controls that can't receive the focus. One case where you will want to include a label control explicitly in the tab order is if it defines an access key. In that case, you'll want to position it in the tab order just before the control it identifies. Then, if the user presses the access key for that control, the focus will move to the control it identifies since it's next in the tab order.

A form in Tab Order view before and after the tab order is changed

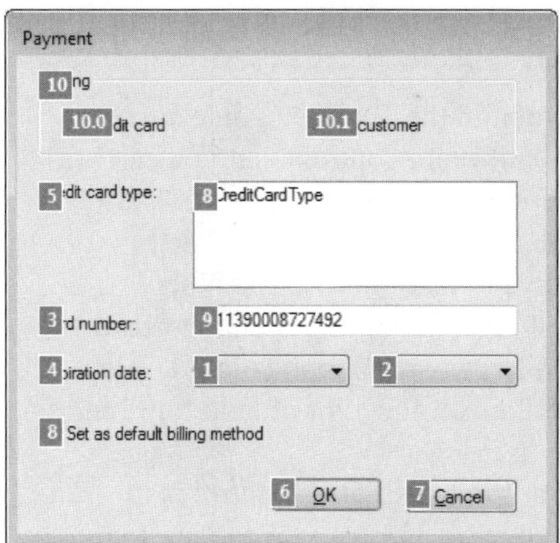

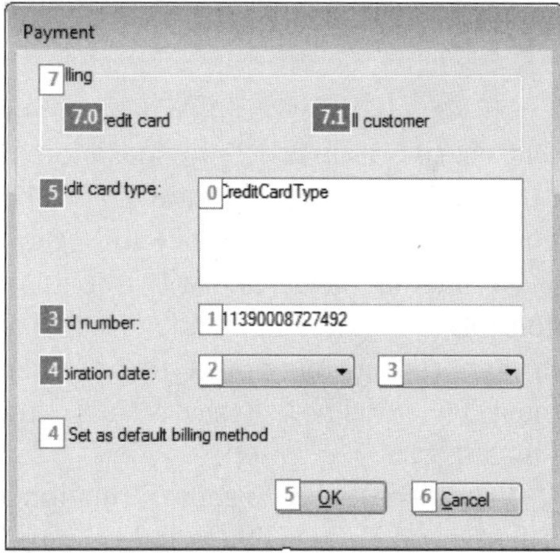

How to use Tab Order view to change the tab order

- To display a form in Tab Order view, select the form and then select the View→Tab Order command. This displays the tab index for each control as in the first form above.
- To change the tab indexes of the controls, click on the controls in the sequence you want to use. As you click, the new tab indexes appear as in the second form above.
- The first time you click on a control in Tab Order view, the tab index is set to the next number in sequence, starting with zero for the first control. If you click on the same control more than once, the tab index is increased by one each time you click.
- If a group box contains other controls, the controls in the group box are displayed with sub indexes as illustrated by the radio buttons above. Then, you can click on the group box to change its index and the main indexes of the controls it contains. To change the sub indexes of the controls in the group box, click on them individually.

Description

- The *tab order* determines the order in which controls receive the focus when the Tab key is pressed. The TabIndex property of the controls determines this order.
- By default, the value of a control's TabIndex property is determined by the sequence in which it's added to the form. The TabIndex property is set to 0 for the first control, 1 for the second control, and so on.
- A label can't receive the focus. As a result, you typically don't need to include the labels in the tab order. However, if the label defines an access key, the TabIndex property of the label should be set to one less than its related control. That way, the related control will receive the focus when the access key for the label is activated.
- When setting the tab order, you can skip controls whose TabStop, Enabled, or Visible properties have been set to False, unless those properties will change as the form runs.

Figure 10-5 How to use Tab Order view to set the tab order

How to get the information you need for using a control

If you click on the All Windows Forms group in the Toolbox, you can see that Visual Studio 2012 provides more than 60 different controls that you can use as you develop an application. In this book, though, you're only going to learn how to use the most useful controls along with their most useful members.

What that means is that you're going to have to learn how to use other controls on your own. On the job, this is a skill that every professional needs to master because doing this type of research is a large part of application development. The good news is that Visual Studio 2012 gives you a lot of help for doing this research.

The easiest way to get information about a Windows Forms control is to use Microsoft's MSDN Online Library. To access this library, you can use the View Help command in the Help menu. When you select this command, the help library is displayed in your default browser as shown in figure 10-6.

At the top of the help information that's displayed is a Search text box that you can use to enter the text you want to look for. To look for information on a control, for example, you can enter the name of the control. Then, you can select a topic from the ones that are listed in the right pane of the window.

In this figure, I entered "datetimepicker" and then selected the "DateTimePicker Control Overview (Windows Forms)" topic to display that topic in the right pane. This is usually a good place to start when you're learning how to use a control that you haven't used before.

Once you have a basic idea of how a control works, you can display other topics that describe specific features or functions of the control. You can do that by using the links that are available within a topic or by selecting topics from the table of contents.

In addition to the topics that are listed for a control, you may want to review the members of the class that defines the control. You can do that by displaying the topic for the control class. You can also display each type of member separately by selecting the appropriate topic from the table of contents. For example, you can select the "DateTimePicker Methods" topic to display all methods that are available from the DateTimePicker class.

Some of the Help documentation for the DateTimePicker control

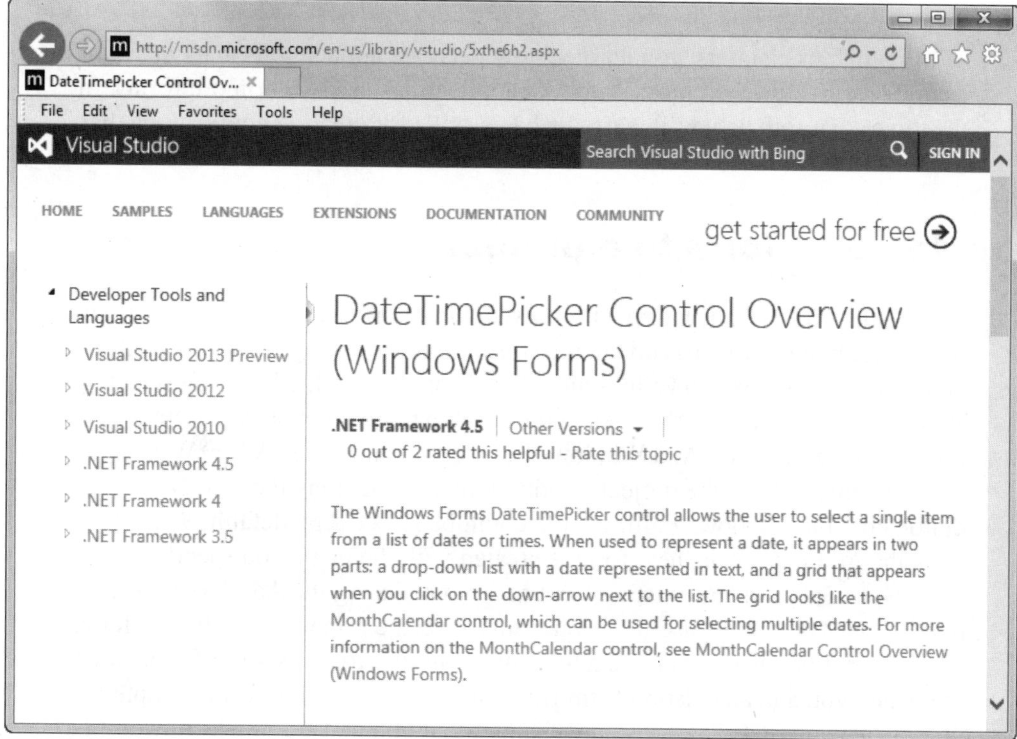

Description

- Visual Studio 2012 provides an abundance of information on the Windows Forms controls. To display this information from Microsoft's MSDN Online Library, use the Help→View Help command.
- To start, you can review the information about the basic function and usage of the control. To do that, just enter the name of the control in the Search text box and then select the appropriate topic.
- Most controls include a help topic that describes the control and a separate topic that describes the class for the control. To learn how to work with a control, you'll typically need to use both of these topics.
- The help information for most Windows Forms controls includes an "overview" topic like the one shown above that provides basic information about the control along with other related topics. Some of these topics describe specific features of the control.
- The help information for most control classes includes a summary of all members that are available from the control. You can also view a summary of the members of a specific type by selecting that type from the table of contents in the left pane.

Figure 10-6 How to get the information you need for using a control

How to work with multi-form projects

In previous chapters, you learned how to create applications that consist of a single form. However, most Windows applications use two or more forms. In the topics that follow, you'll learn the basic skills for creating applications that consist of two or more forms.

How to add a form to a project

When you start a new project for a Windows Forms application, it consists of a single blank form. To add another form to the project, you use the Add New Item dialog box shown in figure 10-7. From this dialog box, you select the Windows Form template and then enter the name of the new form. Note that if you use the Project→Add Windows Form command or the Add→Windows Form command from the project's shortcut menu to display the Add New Item dialog box, the Windows Form template will be selected by default. When you click the Add button, the new form is created with the name you specify.

You can also add an existing form to a project using the Add Existing Item dialog box. This can be useful if you want to use the same form in two different projects or if you want to create a form that's similar to an existing form. Note that when you add an existing form from another project, that form is copied into the new project. That way, any changes that you make to the form won't be applied to the original form, which is typically what you want.

How to rename a form

Figure 10-7 also describes how to rename a form. When you rename the form, Visual Studio automatically changes the name of the form anywhere it has been used in the project.

The Add New Item dialog box

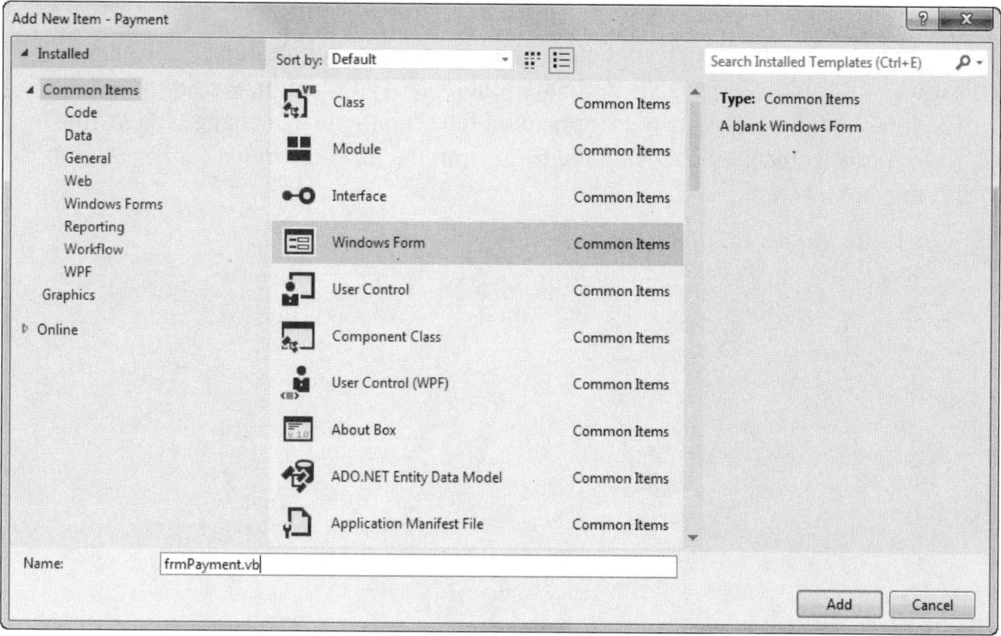

How to add a new form

- Display the Add New Item dialog box by selecting the Project→Add Windows Form or the Project→Add New Item command. Or, select the Add→Windows Form or the Add→New Item command from the shortcut menu that's displayed when you right-click on the project in the Solution Explorer.
- To add a new form, select the Windows Form template from the Add New Item dialog box, enter a name for the form, and click the Add button.

How to add an existing form

- Display the Add Existing Item dialog box by selecting the Project→Add Existing Item command. Or, select the Add→Existing Item command from the shortcut menu for the project.
- To add an existing form, select the vb file for the form from the Add Existing Item dialog box and then click the Add button.

How to rename a form

- Right-click the form in the Solution Explorer, select the Rename command, and enter the new name for the form. Or, select the form in the Solution Explorer and then change the File Name property for the form.
- When you rename a form, Visual Studio automatically changes the form name wherever it's used in the project.

Note

- When you name a form, we recommend you use the prefix *frm* so it's clear that the file contains a form.

Figure 10-7 How to add a form to a project or rename an existing form

How to change the startup form for a project

Figure 10-8 shows the Application page of the Project Designer. The easiest way to display this page is to double-click on My Project in the Solution Explorer and then click on the Application tab. Then, you can change the startup form for the project by choosing the form from the drop-down list for the Startup Form combo box.

The Application page of the Project Designer for a Payment project

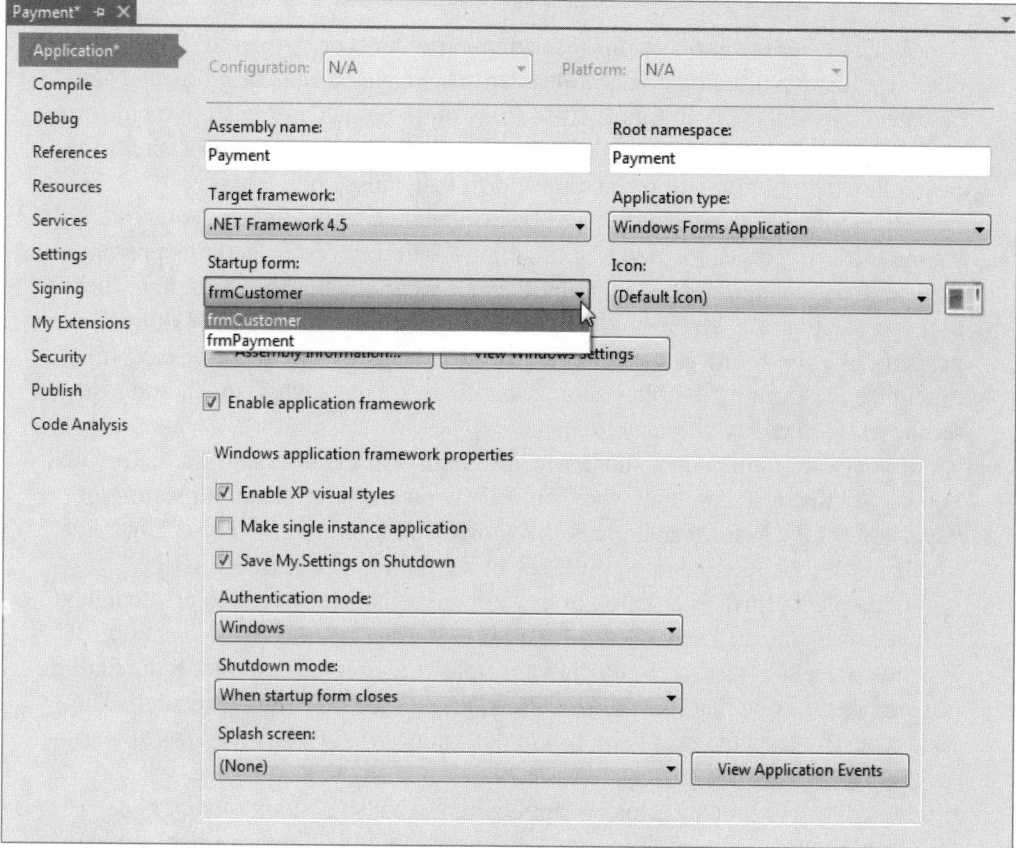

Description

- To display the Project Designer for a project, double-click on My Project in the Solution Explorer. Or, select the Properties command from the shortcut menu that's displayed when you right-click on the project in the Solution Explorer.
- To change the startup form for an application, use the Startup Form drop-down list on the Application page.

Figure 10-8 How to change the startup form for a project

How to display a form as a dialog box

When designing applications that contain two or more forms, it's common to display a form as a dialog box. A form that's displayed as a dialog box can also be called a *modal form*. In figure 10-9, for example, you can see a Payment form that's displayed as a dialog box. This form is displayed when the user clicks the Select Payment button in the Customer form that's also shown here.

When you create a form that will be displayed as a dialog box, you typically set the form properties as shown in this figure. These property settings prevent the user from changing the size of the form or from closing the form other than by using the controls you provide on the form. Although setting the ControlBox property to False removes the Maximize button from a form, the user can still maximize the form by double-clicking its title bar. That's why you should also set the MaximizeBox property to False.

If you want to include a standard Close button in the title bar of a dialog box, you can do that too. Just leave the ControlBox property at its default setting of True, and set the MaximizeBox and MinimizeBox properties to False. Then, the title bar will look like the one you'll see in the dialog box in figure 10-12.

To display a form as a dialog box, you use the New keyword to create a new instance of the form. Then, you call the ShowDialog method of the form object. When you use this method to display a form, the user must respond to the dialog box before the code that follows the ShowDialog method can be executed. This code typically tests the user response to determine what to do next. You'll learn more about getting the response from a dialog box in the next figure.

In addition to modal forms, an application can also contain *modeless forms*. When you use modeless forms, the user can typically move back and forth between the forms as necessary. In most cases, that gives the user a wider range of possible actions, which means that the program must include code that provides for all of those actions. While this type of form is appropriate for some applications, it can make an application more difficult to develop. That's why it's common to use dialog boxes to control the flow of the application and to limit possible user actions.

The Payment form displayed as a dialog box

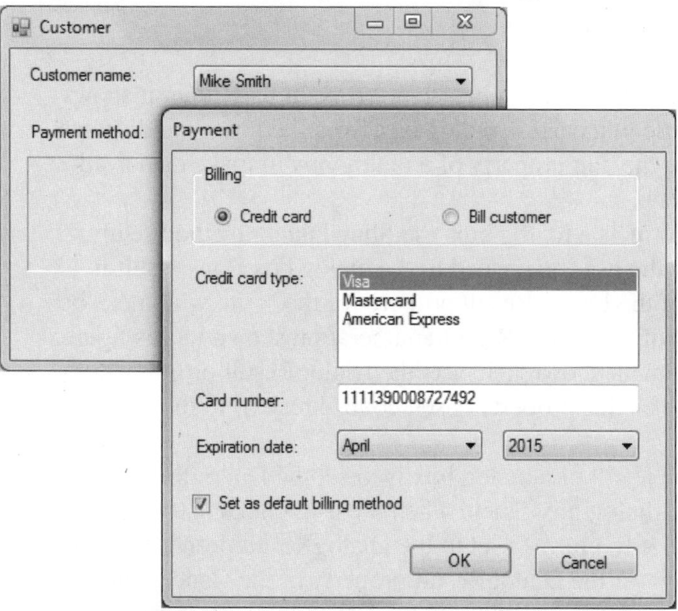

Properties for creating custom dialog boxes

Property	Description
`FormBorderStyle`	Typically set to FixedDialog to prevent the user from resizing the form by dragging its border.
`ControlBox`	Typically set to False so the control box and the Maximize, Minimize, and Close buttons don't appear in the title bar of the form.
`MaximizeBox`	Typically set to False so the user can't maximize the form by double-clicking the title bar.
`MinimizeBox`	Can be set to False to prevent the Minimize button from being displayed if the ControlBox property is set to True.

Code that creates and displays a custom dialog box

```
Dim paymentForm As New frmPayment
paymentForm.ShowDialog()
' Execution continues here after the user responds to the dialog box
```

Description

- If you display a form as a dialog box, the user must respond to the form before continuing to any other forms. A form like this is sometimes referred to as a custom dialog box or a *modal form*.
- You use the ShowDialog method of a form object to display the form as a dialog box. After the user responds to the dialog box, execution continues with the statement that follows the ShowDialog method.

Figure 10-9 How to display a form as a dialog box

How to pass data between a form and a custom dialog box

Figure 10-10 shows how to pass data between forms. In particular, it shows how to get the user response to a custom dialog box from the form that displays it, and it shows how to use the Tag property of a dialog box to make data available to the form that displays it.

When you display a form as a dialog box, the ShowDialog method returns a value that indicates how the user responded to the dialog box. This result is determined by the value of the DialogResult property of the form, which can be set to any of the members of the DialogResult enumeration shown in this figure. For instance, the first statement shown here sets the DialogResult property to DialogResult.OK. As soon as this property is set, control returns to the main form.

Another way to set the result of a dialog box is to set the DialogResult property of a button in the dialog box. Then, when the user clicks that button, the DialogResult property of the form is set to the DialogResult property of the button. If, for example, you set the DialogResult property of the Cancel button on the Payment form shown in figure 10-9 to Cancel, that value is returned when the user clicks that button and the dialog box is closed. In that case, no code is required for the Click event of that button unless some additional processing is required.

You can also set the DialogResult property of a button to Cancel by setting the CancelButton property of the form. Then, the Cancel member of the DialogResult enumeration is returned when the user clicks that button. Here again, no code is required for the Click event of the button unless some additional processing is required.

After the DialogResult property is set and control returns to the form that displayed the dialog box, that form can use the DialogResult enumeration to determine how the user responded. To see how this works, look at the third example in this figure. Here, the first statement creates an instance of the Payment form. Then, the second statement displays that form using the ShowDialog method and stores the result of that method in a DialogResult variable named selectedButton. Next, an If statement is used to test if the result is equal to DialogResult.OK.

Another way to pass data between a dialog box and another form is to use the Tag property of the dialog box. To illustrate, the second example in this figure sets the Tag property of a dialog box to a variable named message. Note that you must set this property before control returns to the main form.

Once control returns to the main form, you can get the data that was stored in the Tag property as shown in the second last statement of the third example. Here, the Text property of a label is set to the value that was stored in the Tag property of the dialog box. Notice that because the Tag property holds an Object type, the object must be converted to a String type before it can be assigned to the Text property.

An enumeration that works with dialog boxes

Enumeration	Members
`DialogResult`	OK, Cancel, Yes, No, Abort, Retry, Ignore, None

The Tag property

Property	Description
`Tag`	Gets or sets data associated with the form or a control. The Tag property holds a reference to an Object type, which means that it can hold any type of data.

A statement that sets the DialogResult property of a form

```
Me.DialogResult = DialogResult.OK
```

A statement that sets the Tag property of a form

```
Me.Tag = message
```

Code that uses the result of a dialog box and the Tag property

```
Dim paymentForm As New frmPayment
Dim selectedButton As DialogResult = paymentForm.ShowDialog
If selectedButton = DialogResult.OK Then
    lblPayment.Text = paymentForm.Tag.ToString
End If
```

How to use the DialogResult enumeration

- The DialogResult enumeration provides members that represent the values that a dialog box can return. The ShowDialog method returns a member of this enumeration.
- You can specify the result value of a custom dialog box by setting its DialogResult property. Or, you can set the DialogResult property of a button in the dialog box. Then, when the user clicks that button, the DialogResult property of the form is set accordingly.
- If you set the CancelButton property of a form to a button on that form, the DialogResult property of that button is automatically set to Cancel.
- After you set the DialogResult property of a dialog box, the form is closed and control is returned to the form that displayed it. If you close a dialog box without setting the DialogResult property, a value of Cancel is returned to the main form.

How to use the Tag property

- The Tag property provides a convenient way to pass data between forms in a multi-form application. A dialog box can set its Tag property before it returns control to the main form. Then, the main form can get the data from this property and use it as necessary.
- Because the Tag property is an Object type, you must convert it to the appropriate type to retrieve the data it contains.

Figure 10-10 How to pass data between a form and a custom dialog box

How to use the MessageBox class

Although you can create custom dialog boxes using the techniques you learned in the last two topics, it's also common to use the MessageBox class to display certain types of dialog boxes. In chapter 7, for example, you learned how to use the MessageBox class to display a simple dialog box with an error message and an OK button. Now, you'll learn how to use the MessageBox class to display more complex dialog boxes, and you'll learn how to get the user's response to these dialog boxes.

How to display a dialog box and get the user response

Figure 10-11 shows how to display a dialog box and get a response from a user. To display a dialog box, you use the Show method shown at the top of this figure. As you can see, you can specify up to five arguments for this method. The first argument is the text message that you want to display. Although this is the only argument that's required, you'll typically code the second argument too, which displays a caption in the title bar of the dialog box.

You can use the third argument to control the buttons that are displayed in the dialog box. You can use the fourth argument to control the icon that's displayed in the dialog box. And you can use the fifth argument to control the default button that's activated when the user presses the Enter key. To specify these arguments, you use the constants in the first three enumerations that are summarized in this figure.

Like the ShowDialog method, the Show method of the MessageBox class returns a value that indicates how the user responded to the dialog box. The value that's returned is one of the members of the DialogResult enumeration. These members represent the buttons that can be displayed in a dialog box, and the return value is automatically set to the appropriate member when the user clicks a button.

The first example in this figure shows how to code a Show method that specifies all five arguments. Here, the third argument indicates that only Yes and No buttons should be included in the dialog box, and the fifth argument indicates that the second button, in this case, No, should be the default button.

The second example shows how you can use the DialogResult value that's returned by the Show method to determine which button the user clicked in the dialog box. Here, an If statement tests if the DialogResult value that was returned by the Show method is equal to DialogResult.Yes. If it is, it means that the user clicked the Yes button, and the code within the If statement is executed.

The syntax for the Show method of the MessageBox class

```
MessageBox.Show(text[, caption[, buttons[, icon[, defaultbutton]]]])
```

The enumerations that work with the MessageBox class

Enumeration	Members
`MessageBoxButtons`	OK, OKCancel, YesNo, YesNoCancel, AbortRetryIgnore
`MessageBoxIcon`	None, Information, Error, Warning, Exclamation, Question, Asterisk, Hand, Stop
`MessageBoxDefaultButton`	Button1, Button2, Button3
`DialogResult`	OK, Cancel, Yes, No, Abort, Retry, Ignore

A statement that displays a dialog box and gets the user response

```
Dim button As DialogResult =
    MessageBox.Show(
        "Are you sure you want to save this data?",
        "Payment",
        MessageBoxButtons.YesNo,
        MessageBoxIcon.Question,
        MessageBoxDefaultButton.Button2)
```

The dialog box that's displayed

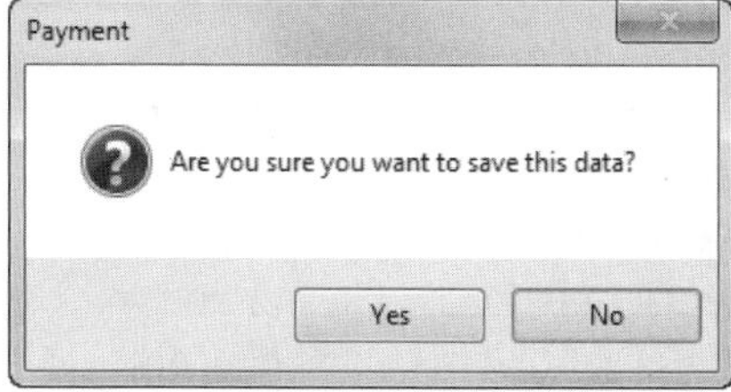

A statement that checks the user response

```
If button = DialogResult.Yes Then
    SaveData()
    isDataSaved = True
End If
```

Description

- You can use the Show method of the MessageBox class to display a message to a user and accept a response from the user.
- You use the first three enumerations listed above to specify the buttons and icon that will appear in the dialog box and the button that's treated as the default.
- If you omit the buttons argument, the OK button is displayed by default. If you omit the icon argument, no icon is displayed by default. If you omit the default button argument, the first button is the default.
- The Show method returns a DialogResult value that corresponds to one of the members of the DialogResult enumeration. You can use this value to determine which button the user clicked.

Figure 10-11 How to display a dialog box and get the user response

How to use the FormClosing event

Figure 10-12 shows how you can use a dialog box to cancel the FormClosing event of a form. This technique is often used when a user attempts to close a form that contains unsaved data.

To start, it's important to understand that the FormClosing event is executed when the user attempts to close the form but before the form is actually closed. This event occurs if the user clicks a button on the form that calls the Close method for the form. It also occurs if the user clicks the Close button in the upper right corner of the form.

This figure presents an event handler for the FormClosing event of a form. This event handler receives two parameters. You can use the Cancel property of the second parameter, which is named e, to determine whether or not the form is closed. By default, this property is set to False, which means that the FormClosing event will not be cancelled and the form will be closed. If you don't want to close the form, you can set this property to True to cancel the FormClosing event.

The event handler shown here starts by checking a class variable named isDataSaved to determine if the form contains unsaved data. If it doesn't, no additional processing is performed and the form is closed. If the form contains unsaved data, however, a dialog box is displayed that asks the user if the data should be saved. As you can see, this dialog box contains Yes, No, and Cancel buttons as well as a warning icon. Since the code for this dialog box doesn't specify a default button, the first button is the default.

After the dialog box is displayed, If statements are used to check the user's response and perform the appropriate action. If the user clicks the Cancel button, for example, the Cancel property of the e parameter is set to True. This cancels the FormClosing event and returns the user to the form. If the user clicks the Yes button, the code checks whether the form contains valid data. If it does, the SaveData procedure is called to save the data and the form is closed. If it doesn't, the Cancel property of the parameter named e is set to True and the FormClosing event is cancelled. On the other hand, if the user clicks the No button, no code is executed. As a result, the form is closed without saving the data.

The code for a dialog box that cancels the Closing event

```
Private Sub frmCustomer_FormClosing(sender As Object,
        e As Windows.Forms.FormClosingEventArgs) _
        Handles MyBase.FormClosing
    If isDataSaved = False Then
        Dim message As String =
            "This form contains unsaved data." & vbCrLf & vbCrLf &
            "Do you want to save it?"

        Dim button As DialogResult =
            MessageBox.Show(message, "Customer",
            MessageBoxButtons.YesNoCancel, MessageBoxIcon.Warning)

        If button = DialogResult.Yes Then
            If IsValidData() Then
                Me.SaveData()
            Else
                e.Cancel = True
            End If
        ElseIf button = DialogResult.Cancel Then
            e.Cancel = True
        End If
    End If
End Sub
```

The dialog box that's displayed by the code shown above

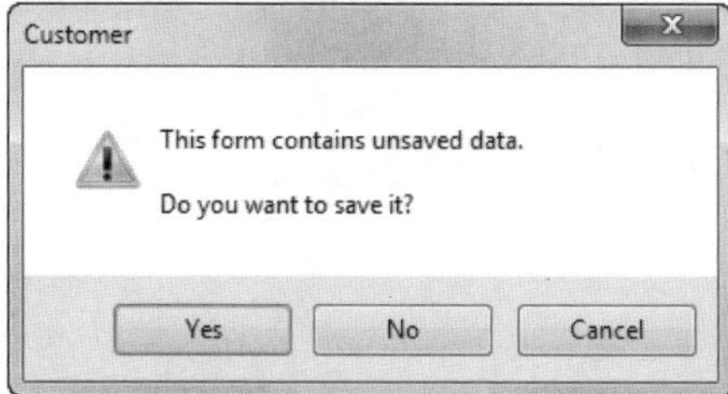

Description

- The event handler for the FormClosing event of a form receives a parameter named e that's created from the FormClosingEventArgs class. The Cancel property of this parameter lets you specify whether or not the event should be canceled. To cancel the event, set this property to True.

The Payment application

This chapter closes by presenting the operation, property settings, and code for a project that contains two forms that use the controls and coding techniques that were presented in this chapter. By studying the code for this application, you will get a better idea of how you can use these controls and techniques in your own applications.

The operation

Figure 10-13 shows how the Payment application works. To start, this application displays the Customer form. On this form, the user must select a customer from the Customer Name combo box. Then, the user must click the Select Payment button to display the Payment dialog box and specify payment information for the selected customer.

Within the Payment dialog box, the user can select to charge the customer's credit card and then enter the required information. Or, the user can select to bill the customer directly. In either case, the user can also indicate whether the selected method should be set as the default billing method.

To complete the Payment form, the user clicks the OK button. Then, control is returned to the Customer form and the payment information is displayed on that form. To save the payment information, the user clicks the Save button.

The Customer form

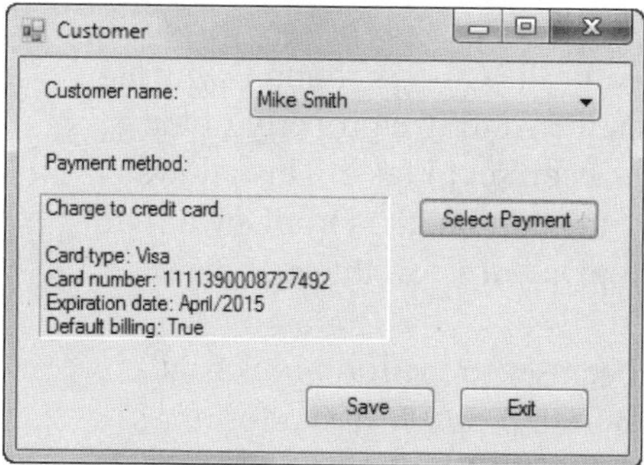

Two versions of the Payment dialog box

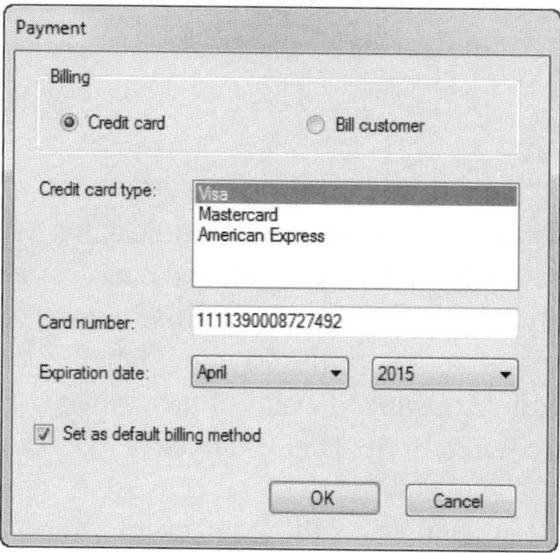

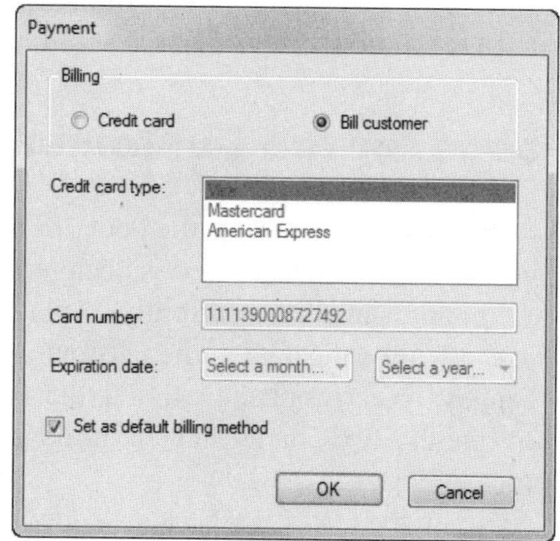

Description

- The Customer Name combo box in the Customer form lets the user select a customer.
- The Select Payment button in the Customer form displays the Payment dialog box, which lets the user specify payment information for the customer.
- If the Credit Card option is selected, the user must select a credit card type, enter a card number, and select an expiration month and year.
- If the Bill Customer option is selected, the Credit Card Type, Card Number, and Expiration Date controls are disabled.
- The user can also indicate if the billing method that's selected is the default method.
- When the user clicks the OK button on the Payment form, control returns to the Customer form and the payment information is displayed in the Payment Method label.

Note

- This application doesn't actually save the data the user enters. In a production application, however, the data would be saved to a database or file.

Figure 10-13 The operation of the Payment application

The property settings

Figure 10-14 presents the property settings for the Customer and Payment forms and their controls. In the Customer form, the AutoSize property of the label that displays the payment information has been set to false. This allows you to use the Form Designer to size the label. In addition, the DropDownStyle property for the combo box has been set to DropDownList so the user must select an item from the list.

In the Payment form, the properties have been set so the form looks and acts like a dialog box. In addition, the CancelButton property of the form has been set to the Cancel button, which causes the DialogResult property of that button to be set to Cancel. Finally, like the combo box on the Customer form, the DropDownStyle properties of the combo boxes on this form have been set to DropDownList so the user must select an item from the lists.

The code for the Customer form

Figure 10-15 presents the code for the Customer form. To start, a Boolean variable named isDataSaved is declared and set to True. This variable indicates whether the data that's currently displayed in the form has been saved. It's set to False any time the data in the Customer Name combo box or the Payment label changes. To accomplish that, both the SelectedIndexChanged event of the combo box and the TextChanged event of the label are wired to the DataChanged procedure.

When the Customer form is loaded, the event handler for the Load event adds two names to the Customer Name combo box. In a production application, of course, the combo box would include many more names, and they would be loaded from a file or database. But for the purposes of this chapter, two names are sufficient.

When the user clicks the Select Payment button, the Click event handler for that button displays the Payment form as a dialog box. Then, if the user clicks the OK button in that dialog box, the payment data is displayed in the Payment Method label on the Customer form. As you can see, this data is stored in the Tag property of the Payment form.

If the user clicks the Save button, the Click event handler for that button calls the IsValidData procedure. This procedure checks that the user has selected a customer and entered a payment. If so, the event handler for the Click event of the Save button calls the SaveData procedure. This procedure sets the SelectedIndex property of the Customer Name combo box to -1 so that no customer is selected, and it clears the Payment Method label. Then, it sets the isDataSaved variable to True and moves the focus to the combo box. In a production application, of course, this procedure would also save the data to a file or database.

The first procedure on page 2 of the listing is executed when the user tries to close the Customer form. This is the same procedure you saw in figure 10-14, so you shouldn't have any trouble understanding how it works.

The property settings for the Customer form

Default name	Property	Setting
Form1	Name Text FormBorderStyle CancelButton	frmCustomer Customer FixedSingle btnExit
ComboBox1	Name DropDownStyle	cboNames DropDownList
Label3	Name BorderStyle AutoSize Text	lblPayment Fixed3D False ""
Button1	Name	btnSave
Button2	Name	btnExit
Button3	Name	btnSelectPayment

The property settings for the Payment form

Default name	Property	Setting
Form2	Name Text AcceptButton CancelButton ControlBox MaximizeBox FormBorderStyle	frmPayment Payment btnOK btnCancel False False FixedDialog
GroupBox1	Text	Billing
RadioButton1	Name Checked	rdoCreditCard True
RadioButton2	Name	rdoBillCustomer
ListBox1	Name	lstCreditCardType
TextBox1	Name	txtCardNumber
ComboBox1	Name DropDownStyle	cboExpirationMonth DropDownList
ComboBox2	Name DropDownStyle	cboExpirationYear DropDownList
CheckBox1	Name Checked	chkDefault True
Button1	Name	btnOK
Button2	Name DialogResult	btnCancel Cancel

Description

- In addition to the properties shown above, you'll want to set the text and alignment properties so the forms look like the forms shown in figure 10-13.

Figure 10-14 The property settings for the Customer and Payment forms

The code for the Customer form **Page 1**

```
Public Class frmCustomer

    Dim isDataSaved As Boolean = True

    Private Sub frmCustomer_Load(sender As Object,
            e As EventArgs) Handles MyBase.Load
        cboNames.Items.Add("Mike Smith")
        cboNames.Items.Add("Nancy Jones")
    End Sub

    Private Sub DataChanged(sender As Object, e As EventArgs) _
            Handles cboNames.SelectedIndexChanged,
                    lblPayment.TextChanged
        isDataSaved = False
    End Sub

    Private Sub btnSelectPayment_Click(sender As Object,
            e As EventArgs) Handles btnSelectPayment.Click
        Dim paymentForm As New frmPayment
        Dim selectedButton As DialogResult = paymentForm.ShowDialog()
        If selectedButton = DialogResult.OK Then
            lblPayment.Text = paymentForm.Tag.ToString
        End If
    End Sub

    Private Sub btnSave_Click(sender As Object,
            e As EventArgs) Handles btnSave.Click
        If IsValidData() Then
            Me.SaveData()
        End If
    End Sub

    Private Function IsValidData() As Boolean
        If cboNames.SelectedIndex = -1 Then
            MessageBox.Show("You must select a customer.", "Entry Error")
            cboNames.Select()
            Return False
        End If
        If lblPayment.Text = "" Then
            MessageBox.Show("You must enter a payment.", "Entry Error")
            Return False
        End If
        Return True
    End Function

    Private Sub SaveData()
        cboNames.SelectedIndex = -1
        lblPayment.Text = ""
        isDataSaved = True
        cboNames.Select()
    End Sub
```

Figure 10-15 The code for the Customer form (part 1 of 2)

The code for the Customer form **Page 2**

```
        Private Sub frmCustomer_FormClosing(sender As Object,
                e As Windows.Forms.FormClosingEventArgs) _
                Handles MyBase.FormClosing
            If isDataSaved = False Then
                Dim message As String =
                    "This form contains unsaved data." & vbCrLf & vbCrLf &
                    "Do you want to save it?"

                Dim button As DialogResult =
                    MessageBox.Show(message, "Customer",
                    MessageBoxButtons.YesNoCancel, MessageBoxIcon.Warning)

                If button = DialogResult.Yes Then
                    If IsValidData() Then
                        Me.SaveData()
                    Else
                        e.Cancel = True
                    End If
                ElseIf button = DialogResult.Cancel Then
                    e.Cancel = True
                End If
            End If
        End Sub

        Private Sub btnExit_Click(sender As Object,
                e As EventArgs) Handles btnExit.Click
            Me.Close()
        End Sub

    End Class
```

Figure 10-15 The code for the Customer form (part 2 of 2)

The code for the Payment form

Figure 10-16 presents the code for the Payment form. To start, the event handler for the Load event adds the appropriate items to the list box and the two combo boxes on the form. In addition, this procedure sets the SelectedIndex property for these controls so the first item is selected.

When the user clicks the OK button on this form, the Click event handler starts by calling the IsValidData procedure on page 2 of this listing. If the Credit Card radio button is selected, this procedure checks that the user selected a credit card type and entered a credit card number. It also checks that the user selected an item other than the first one from the two combo boxes. That's necessary because the first item of these combo boxes contains user instructions ("Select a month…" and "Select a year…").

If the data is valid, the Click event handler for the OK button continues by calling the SaveData procedure shown on page 2 of this listing. This procedure creates a string that includes the payment information. Then, it stores that string in the Tag property of the Payment form. As you've already seen, the Customer form uses this property to display the payment information. Finally, the SaveData procedure sets the DialogResult property of the form to the OK member of the DialogResult enumeration. This is necessary to close the Payment form and allow the execution of the application to return to the Customer form.

When the user selects one of the radio buttons on this form, the CheckedChanged event occurs. For both radio buttons, this event is wired to the Billing_CheckChanged event handler that's on page 3 of the listing. If the Credit Card radio button is selected when this event handler is executed, it calls the EnableControls procedure to enable the other controls on the form so the user can enter the required information. If the Credit Card button isn't selected, however, it means that the Bill Customer button is selected. Then, this event handler calls the DisableControls procedure to disable the other controls.

The code for the Payment form

Page 1

```
Public Class frmPayment

    Private Sub frmPayment_Load(sender As Object,
            e As EventArgs) Handles MyBase.Load
        lstCreditCardType.Items.Add("Visa")
        lstCreditCardType.Items.Add("Mastercard")
        lstCreditCardType.Items.Add("American Express")
        lstCreditCardType.SelectedIndex = 0

        Dim months() As String = {"Select a month...",
            "January", "February", "March", "April",
            "May", "June", "July", "August",
            "September", "October", "November", "December"}
        For Each month As String In months
            cboExpirationMonth.Items.Add(month)
        Next
        cboExpirationMonth.SelectedIndex = 0

        Dim year As Integer = DateTime.Today.Year
        Dim endYear As Integer = year + 8
        cboExpirationYear.Items.Add("Select a year...")
        Do While year < endYear
            cboExpirationYear.Items.Add(year)
            year += 1
        Loop
        cboExpirationYear.SelectedIndex = 0

    End Sub

    Private Sub btnOK_Click(sender As Object,
            e As EventArgs) Handles btnOK.Click
        If isValidData() Then
            Me.SaveData()
        End If
    End Sub
```

Figure 10-16 The code for the Payment form (part 1 of 3)

The code for the Payment form

Page 2

```
Private Function IsValidData() As Boolean
    If rdoCreditCard.Checked Then
        If lstCreditCardType.SelectedIndex = -1 Then
            MessageBox.Show("You must select a credit card type.",
                "Entry Error")
            lstCreditCardType.Select()
            Return False
        End If
        If txtCardNumber.Text = "" Then
            MessageBox.Show("You must enter a credit card number.",
                "Entry Error")
            txtCardNumber.Select()
            Return False
        End If
        If cboExpirationMonth.SelectedIndex = 0 Then
            MessageBox.Show("You must select a month.", "Entry Error")
            cboExpirationMonth.Select()
            Return False
        End If
        If cboExpirationYear.SelectedIndex = 0 Then
            MessageBox.Show("You must select a year.", "Entry Error")
            cboExpirationYear.Select()
            Return False
        End If
    End If
    Return True
End Function

Private Sub SaveData()
    Dim message As String
    If rdoCreditCard.Checked Then
        message = "Charge to credit card." & vbCrLf & vbCrLf &
                  "Card type: " & lstCreditCardType.Text & vbCrLf &
                  "Card number: " & txtCardNumber.Text & vbCrLf &
                  "Expiration date: " & cboExpirationMonth.Text &
                  "/" & cboExpirationYear.Text & vbCrLf
    Else
        message = "Send bill to customer." & vbCrLf & vbCrLf
    End If

    Dim isDefaultBilling As Boolean = chkDefault.Checked
    message &= "Default billing: " & isDefaultBilling

    Me.Tag = message
    Me.DialogResult = DialogResult.OK
End Sub
```

Figure 10-16 The code for the Payment form (part 2 of 3)

The code for the Payment form

Page 3

```
    Private Sub BillingChecked(sender As Object, e As EventArgs) _
            Handles rdoCreditCard.CheckedChanged,
                    rdoBillCustomer.CheckedChanged
        If rdoCreditCard.Checked Then
            Me.EnableControls()
        Else
            Me.DisableControls()
        End If
    End Sub

    Private Sub EnableControls()
        lstCreditCardType.Enabled = True
        txtCardNumber.Enabled = True
        cboExpirationMonth.Enabled = True
        cboExpirationYear.Enabled = True
    End Sub

    Private Sub DisableControls()
        lstCreditCardType.Enabled = False
        txtCardNumber.Enabled = False
        cboExpirationMonth.Enabled = False
        cboExpirationYear.Enabled = False
    End Sub

End Class
```

Figure 10-16 The code for the Payment form (part 3 of 3)

Perspective

In this chapter, you learned how to use five new controls for building Windows applications. These controls are the ones you'll use most often. If you need to use any of the controls that weren't presented here, though, you should be able to figure out how to do that on your own. In most cases, it's just a matter of becoming familiar with the properties, methods, and events that are available, and you can usually do that by reviewing the documentation for the control and the class it's based on.

In addition, you learned how to work with a project that contains two or more forms. Specifically, you learned how to work with projects that use dialog boxes.

For many projects, the skills presented in this chapter are the only ones you'll need when you're working with the forms of an application. In chapter 24, though, you'll learn some additional skills for working with forms that let you enhance the user interface of an application.

Terms

combo box
list box
radio button
group box
check box
tab order
modal form
modeless form

Exercise 10-1 Create the Payment application

This exercise will guide you through the process of creating the Payment application that's described in this chapter. To make that easier for you, you'll start from a project that contains the Customer form.

Open the project and prepare the two forms

1. Open the project that's in the C:\VB 2012\Chapter 10\Payment directory. This application contains a single form named Form1.
2. Rename Form1 to frmCustomer.
3. Add a second form named frmPayment to the project.

Design the Payment form

4. Add the controls to the Payment form and set the properties for this form and its controls as described in figures 10-13 and 10-14.
5. Use Tab Order view to set the tab order for the controls on the Payment form if necessary.

Add the code for the Customer form

6. Generate the event handlers for the Load event of the Customer form, for the Closing event of the form, and for the Click event of all three buttons. Then, add the module-level isDataSaved variable, and add the code for these events.

7. Generate an event handler named DataChanged for the SelectedIndexChanged event of the Customer Name combo box. Then, wire this event handler to the TextChanged event of the Payment Method label, and add the code to this event handler so it sets the isDataSaved variable to False.
8. Add the SaveData and IsValidData procedures.
9. Test the Customer form to make sure that it works properly. At this point, you should be able to display the Payment form, but it won't work correctly since you haven't added any code to it.

Add the code for the Payment form

10. Generate the event handlers for the Load event of the Payment form and for the Click event of both buttons. Then, add the code for these events.
11. Generate an event handler named Billing_CheckChanged for the CheckChanged event of the Credit Card radio button. Then, wire this event handler to the CheckChanged event of the Bill Customer radio button, and add the code for this event handler.
12. Add the EnableControls, DisableControls, IsValidData, and SaveData procedures.
13. Test the program to be sure that it works as described in figure 10-13. When you're sure it does, close the project.

Exercise 10-2 Enhance the Future Value application

This exercise will guide you through the process of adding a combo box and a list box to the Future Value application.

Open the Future Value application and add two controls

1. Open the application that's in the C:\VB 2012\Chapter 10\FutureValue directory.
2. Delete the Number of Years text box and replace it with a Number of Years combo box. Then, delete the Future Value text box and replace it with a Future Value list box. When you're done, the form should look something like the one in step 5 below.

Add the code that works with the controls

3. Generate the event handler for the Load event of the form. Then, add code that loads the numbers 1 through 20 in the Number of Years combo box, and add code that selects 3 as the default number of years.
4. Delete the code in the IsValidData procedure that refers to the Number of Years text box since it isn't needed anymore.

5. Modify the event handler for the Click event of the Calculate button so it adds the future value for each year to the Future Value list box. For example, if you calculate the future value for three years, the Future Value form should return a result like this:

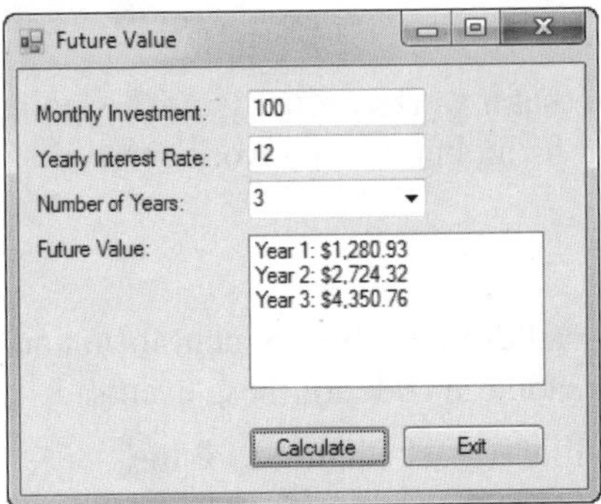

6. To get this to work correctly, you'll need to use the Clear method of the Items collection for the list box to clear the list box each time the Calculate button is clicked. In addition, you can use the Mod operator to add the future value after every twelve months of the calculation. For example:

```
If month Mod 12 = 0 Then    ' add the future value to the list box
```

7. Test this application to make sure it works correctly.

11

How to create and use classes

This chapter presents the basics of creating and using classes in Visual Basic applications. Here, you'll learn how to create classes that include properties, methods, fields, and constructors, as well as classes that contain shared members. In addition, you'll see a complete application that uses three user-defined classes, and you'll learn how to create structures, which are similar to classes.

When you complete this chapter, you'll start to see how creating your own classes can help simplify the development of an application. As a bonus, you'll have a better understanding of how the .NET classes work.

An introduction to classes

The topics that follow introduce you to the concepts you need before you create your own classes. First, you'll learn how classes are typically used in a business application to simplify the overall design of the application. Next, you'll learn about the variety of members you can add to a class. Then, you'll see a complete example of a simple class. Finally, you'll learn how classes are instantiated to create objects.

How classes can be used to structure an application

Figure 11-1 shows how you can use classes to simplify the design of a business application using a *multi-layer architecture*. In a multi-layer application, the classes that perform different functions of the application are separated into two or more layers.

A *three-layer* application architecture like the one shown in this figure consists of a presentation layer, a middle layer, and a database layer. In practice, the middle layer is sometimes eliminated and its functions split between the database and presentation layers. On the other hand, the design of some applications further develops the middle layer into additional layers.

The classes in the *presentation layer* handle the details of the application's user interface. For a Windows application, this consists of the form classes that display the user interface. One class is required for each form displayed by the application.

The classes of the *database layer* are responsible for all database access required by the application. These classes typically include methods that connect to the database and retrieve, insert, add, and delete information from the database. Then, the other layers can call these methods to access the database, leaving the details of database access to the database classes. Although we refer to this layer as the database layer, it can also contain classes that work with data that's stored in files.

The *middle layer* provides an interface between the database layer and the presentation layer. This layer often includes classes that correspond to business entities (for example, products and customers). It may also include classes that implement business rules, such as discount or credit policies. When the classes represent *business objects*, they are often called *business classes*.

One advantage of developing applications with a layered architecture is that it allows application development to be spread among members of a development team. For example, one group of developers might work on the database layer, another group on the middle layer, and still another group on the presentation layer.

Another advantage is that it allows classes to be shared among applications. In particular, the classes that make up the database and middle layers can be placed in *class libraries* that can be used by more than one project. You'll learn how to work with class libraries in chapter 20.

The architecture of a three-layer application

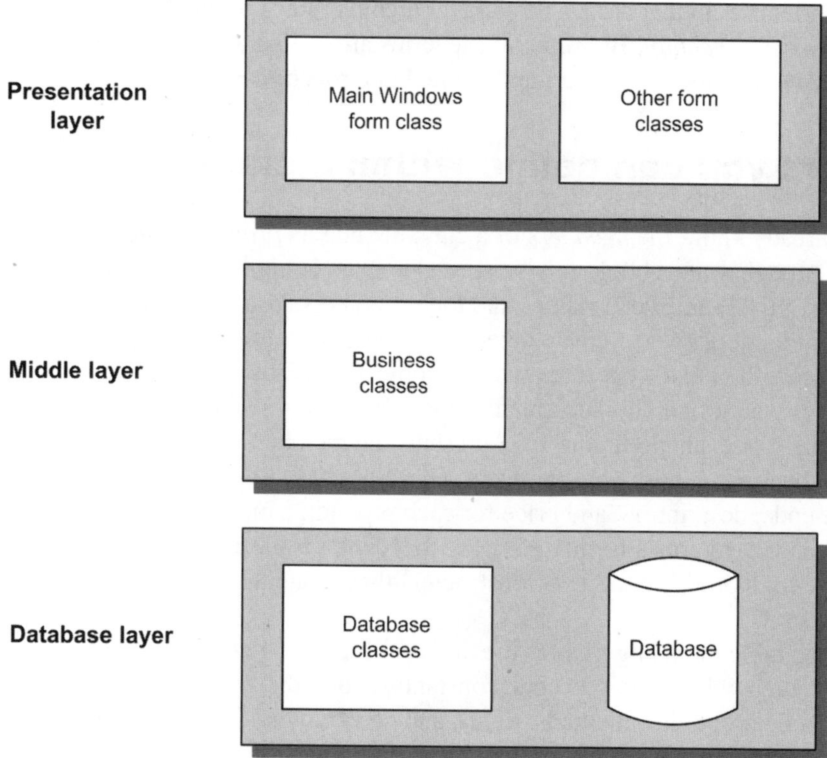

Description

- To simplify development and maintenance, many applications use a *three-layer architecture* to separate the application's user interface, business rules, and database processing. Classes are used to implement the functions performed at each layer of the architecture.
- The classes in the *presentation layer* control the application's user interface. For a Windows Forms application, the user interface consists of the various forms that make up the application.
- The classes in the *database layer* handle all of the application's data processing.
- The classes in the *middle layer*, sometimes called the *business rules layer*, act as an interface between the classes in the presentation and database layers. These classes can represent business entities, such as customers or products, or they can implement business rules, such as discount or credit policies.
- When the classes in the middle layer represent business entities, the classes can be referred to as *business classes*, and the objects that are created from these classes can be referred to as *business objects*.
- Often, the classes that make up the database layer and the middle layer are implemented in *class libraries* that can be shared among applications.

Figure 11-1 How classes can be used to structure an application

A third advantage is that you can run different layers on different servers to improve performance. In that case, a three-layer architecture is often referred to as a *three-tier architecture*. But often, these terms are used interchangeably without implying how the layers are implemented in terms of hardware.

The members you can define within a class

As you already know, the *members* of a class include its *properties*, *methods*, and *events*. Throughout this book, you've seen examples of applications that work with the .NET Framework classes and their members. You've also used the *constructors* of these classes to create objects, and these constructors are just a special type of method that's executed when an object is created.

The classes you design yourself can also have properties, methods, constructors, and events. For example, figure 11-2 presents the members of a Product class that can be used to work with products. This class has three properties that store the code, description, and price for each product; a method named GetDisplayText that returns a formatted string that contains the code, description, and price for a product; and two constructors that create instances of the class.

The second table in this figure lists the different types of members a class can have. You already know how to code constants, and in this chapter, you'll learn how to code properties, methods, fields, and constructors. Then, in chapter 17, you'll learn how to code events, default properties, and operators.

Of course, not every class you create will contain all these types of members. In fact, most classes will have just properties, methods, and constructors. But it's important to know about all possible member types so you'll be able to decide which types are appropriate for the classes you create.

This figure also reviews the basic concepts of object-oriented programming that were first introduced in chapter 3. In addition, it presents a fundamental concept of object-oriented programming that you may not be familiar with. This is the concept of *encapsulation*.

Encapsulation lets the programmer hide, or encapsulate, some of the data and operations of a class while exposing others. For example, although a property or method of a class can be called from other classes, its implementation is hidden within the class. That way, users of the class can think of it as a black box that provides useful properties and methods. This also means that you can change the code within a class without affecting the other classes that use it. This makes it easier to enhance or change an application because you only need to change the classes that need changing. You'll get a better idea of how encapsulation works when you see the code for the Product class in the next figure.

The members of a Product class

Properties	Description
Code	A String type that contains a code that identifies a product.
Description	A String type that contains a description of the product.
Price	A Decimal type that contains the product's price.
Method	**Description**
GetDisplayText(sep)	Returns a string that contains the code, description, and price in a displayable format. The *sep* parameter is a string that's used to separate the elements. It's typically set to a tab or new line character.
Constructors	**Description**
New()	Creates a Product object with default values.
New(code, description, price)	Creates a Product object using the specified code, description, and price values.

Types of class members

Class member	Description
Property	Represents a data value associated with an object instance.
Method	An operation that can be performed by an object.
Constructor	A special type of method that's executed when an object is instantiated.
Delegate	A special type of object that's used to wire an event to a method.
Event	A signal that notifies other objects that something noteworthy has occurred.
Field	A variable that's declared at the class level.
Constant	A constant.
Default property	A special type of property that is used by default if a property name isn't specified. It must include a parameter, which is typically used to access individual items within a class that represents a collection of objects.
Operator	A special type of method that's performed for a Visual Basic operator such as + or =.

Class and object concepts

- An *object* is a self-contained unit that has *properties*, *methods*, and other *members*. A *class* contains the code that defines the members of an object.
- An object is an *instance* of a class, and the process of creating an object is called *instantiation.*
- *Encapsulation* is one of the fundamental concepts of object-oriented programming. It lets you control the data and operations within a class that are exposed to other classes.
- The data of a class is typically encapsulated within a class using *data hiding*. In addition, the code that performs operations within the class is encapsulated so it can be changed without changing the way other classes use it.
- Although a class can have many different types of members, most of the classes you create will have just properties, methods, and constructors.

Figure 11-2 The members you can define within a class

The code for the Product class

Figure 11-3 shows the complete code for the Product class whose members were described in figure 11-2. As you can see, it begins with a Class statement that declares the Product class with the Public access modifier. This access modifier lets other classes access the class.

The code within the class defines the members of the Product class. In the rest of this chapter, you'll learn how to write code like the code shown here. For now, I'll just present a preview of this code so you have a general idea of how it works.

The first three statements in this class are declarations for three class variables, called *fields*. As you'll see in a minute, these fields are used to store the data for the Code, Description, and Price properties. Because these variables are defined with the Private access modifier, they can't be referred to from outside the class.

After the fields are declarations for the two constructors of the Product class. The first constructor, which accepts no arguments, creates an instance of the Product class and initializes its fields to default values. The second constructor creates an instance of the class and initializes it with values passed via the code, description, and price parameters.

Next are the declarations for the three properties of the Product class. These properties provide access to the values stored in the three fields. Within each of these property declarations are two procedures that get and set the value of the property.

Last is the declaration for the GetDisplayText method, which accepts a String parameter named sep. This method returns a String that concatenates the values of the Code, Description, and Price properties, separated by the value passed via the sep parameter.

Notice that you always use the Public access modifier to identify the properties and methods that can be accessed from other classes. In contrast, you use the Private access modifier to declare fields that you don't want to be accessed from other classes. In this case, for example, the fields can only be accessed through the properties defined by the class. You can also use the Private access modifier to code properties and methods that you don't want to be accessed from other classes.

The Product class

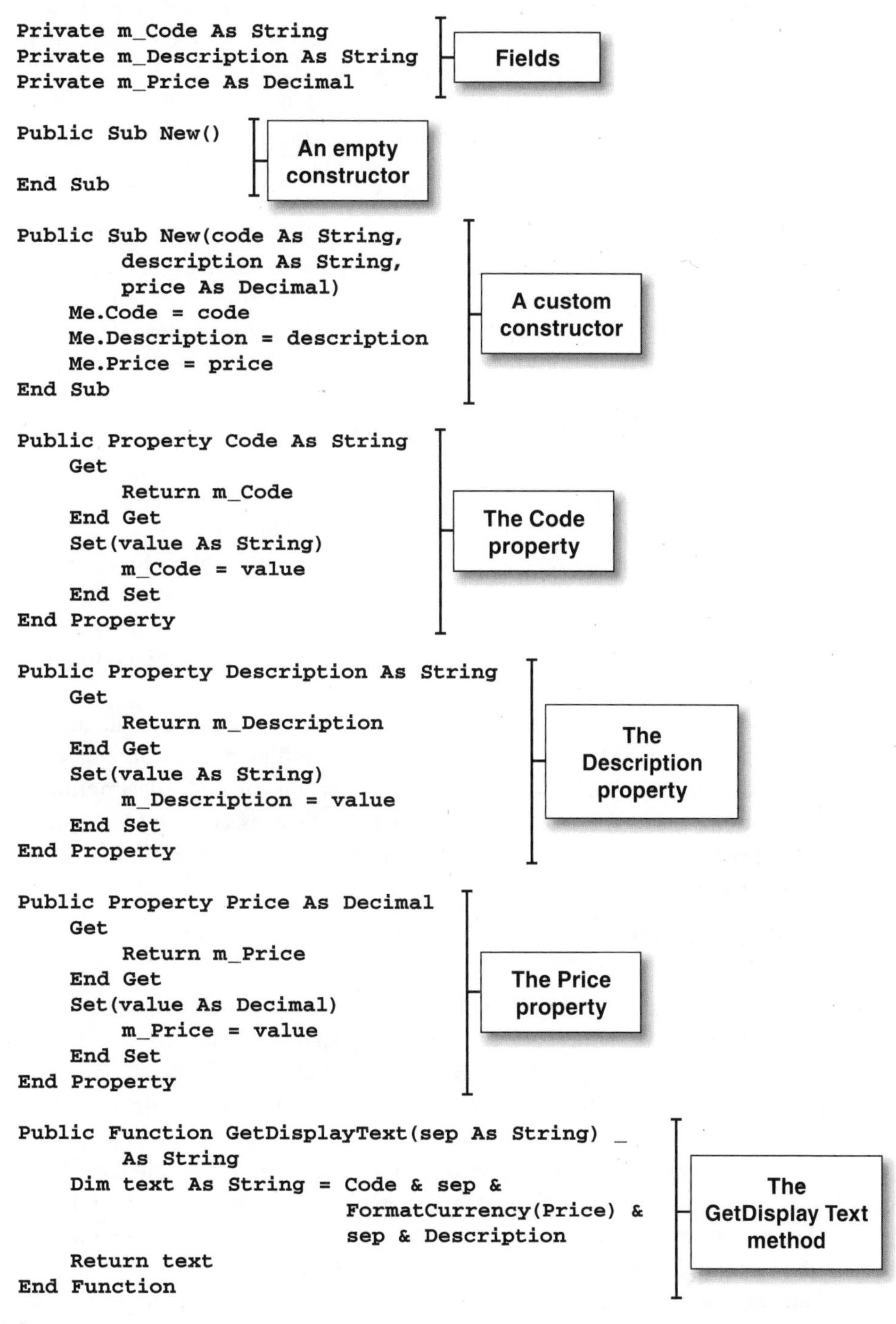


```
Public Class Product

    Private m_Code As String
    Private m_Description As String
    Private m_Price As Decimal

    Public Sub New()

    End Sub

    Public Sub New(code As String,
            description As String,
            price As Decimal)
        Me.Code = code
        Me.Description = description
        Me.Price = price
    End Sub

    Public Property Code As String
        Get
            Return m_Code
        End Get
        Set(value As String)
            m_Code = value
        End Set
    End Property

    Public Property Description As String
        Get
            Return m_Description
        End Get
        Set(value As String)
            m_Description = value
        End Set
    End Property

    Public Property Price As Decimal
        Get
            Return m_Price
        End Get
        Set(value As Decimal)
            m_Price = value
        End Set
    End Property

    Public Function GetDisplayText(sep As String) _
            As String
        Dim text As String = Code & sep &
                             FormatCurrency(Price) &
                             sep & Description
        Return text
    End Function

End Class
```

Figure 11-3 The code for the Product class

How instantiation works

The process of creating an object from a class is called *instantiation*. Figure 11-4 describes how instantiation works. Here, you can see two *instances* of the Product class. Each instance represents a different Product object. Because both instances were created from the same class, they both have the same properties. However, the instances have distinct values for each property. For example, the value of the Code property for the product1 object is CS12, but the value of the Code property for the product2 object is VB12.

The first code example in this figure shows how you can create these two object instances. Here, the first line of code declares two variables named product1 and product2 that have a type of Product. Then, the next two lines create Product objects. To do that, they use the New keyword, followed by the name of the class and the values that will be used to initialize the objects. Note that these two product instances are completely separate entities. Because of that, you can change the values that are stored in one of the objects without affecting the other object.

The second code example in this figure shows another way to create the same object instances. This code uses a feature called *object initializers*. Object initializers let you create an instance of an object and assign values to it without explicitly calling a constructor. To do that, you code the With keyword after the class name, followed by a list enclosed in braces that specifies the names of the properties or public fields to be initialized and the values to be assigned to those properties or fields.

One of the advantages of object initializers is that they let you create an object and assign values to it in a single statement. To illustrate, assume that the Product class doesn't have a constructor that accepts the code, description, and price. In that case, you would have to use the following code to create an instance of the class and assign values to it without using an object initializer:

```
product1 = New Product
product1.Code = "CS12"
product1.Description = "Murach's C# 2012"
product1.Price = 54.5D
```

At this point, it's important to realize that a class defines a *reference type*. That means that the variable that's used to access an object contains the address of the memory location where the object is stored, not the object itself. In other words, the product1 variable holds a *reference* to a Product object, not an actual Product object.

If an object variable doesn't refer to an object, it's said to contain a *null reference*. In some cases, you'll need to test an object variable for a null reference before performing an operation. To do that, you use the Is or IsNot operator with the Nothing keyword as shown in the third example in this figure.

You can also disassociate an object from the object variable that refers to it by assigning Nothing to the object variable. This is illustrated in the last example in this figure. Note that disassociating an object from an object variable doesn't destroy the object. That way, other object variables that refer to the object still have access to it.

Two Product objects that have been instantiated from the Product class

product1
Code=CS12
Description=Murach's C# 2012
Price=54.50

product2
Code=VB12
Description=Murach's Visual Basic 2012
Price=54.50

Code that creates these two object instances

```
Dim product1, product2 As Product
product1 = New Product("CS12", "Murach's C# 2012", 54.5D)
product2 = New Product("VB12", "Murach's Visual Basic 2012", 54.5D)
```

Another way to create the object instances

```
product1 = New Product With {.Code = "CS12",
    .Description = "Murach's C# 2012", .Price = 54.5D}
product2 = New Product With {.Code = "VB12",
    .Description = "Murach's Visual Basic 2012", .Price = 54.5D}
```

Code that checks if an object variable refers to an object

```
Dim product As Product
...
If Product IsNot Nothing Then...
```

Code that disassociates an object from an object variable

```
Dim product As Product
product = New Product("VB12", "Murach's Visual Basic 2012", 54.5D)
...
product = Nothing
```

Description

- When an object is instantiated, a *constructor* is executed to initialize the data that makes up the object. If a class doesn't provide a constructor, a default constructor is executed. The default constructor simply initializes all the data to default values.
- The data that makes up an object is sometimes referred to as the object's *state*. Once an object has been instantiated, you can change its state by changing the value of one of its properties or public fields or by calling a method that affects the data it contains.
- An application can create two or more instances of the same class. Then, each instance is a separate entity with its own state.
- *Object initializers* let you create an instance of an object and assign values to it in a single statement without explicitly calling a constructor.
- A class defines a *reference type*. That means that the variable that's used to access an object instantiated from a class contains the address of the object, not the actual object.
- By default, an object variable has a value of Nothing, which means that it doesn't refer to an object. An object variable with a value of Nothing is also called a *null reference*.
- To check if an object variable refers to an object, you use the Is or IsNot operator with the Nothing keyword. After you create an object and assign it to the variable, you can disassociate the object from the variable by assigning Nothing to the variable.

Figure 11-4 How instantiation works

How to create a class

Now that you've learned about the members that make up a class and you've seen the code for the Product class, you're ready to learn the basic skills for creating and using your own classes. The topics that follow present these skills.

How to add a class file to a project

To create a user-defined class, you start by adding a *class file* to your project. To do that, you use the dialog box shown in figure 11-5. When you complete this dialog box, the class file will appear in the Solution Explorer with the extension *vb*.

When you add a class to a project, Visual Studio automatically generates the class declaration. Then, you can complete the class by adding fields, constructors, properties, methods, and whatever other members the class may require.

The dialog box for adding a class

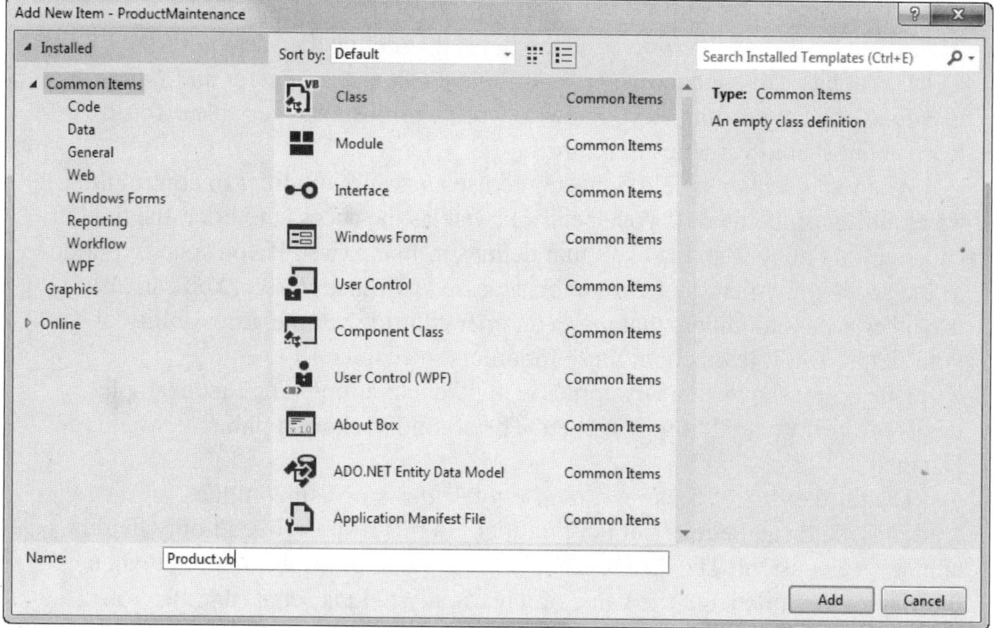

The starting code for the new class

```
Public Class Product

End Class
```

Description

- To add a new class to a project, use the Project→Add Class command, or right-click on the Project in the Solution Explorer and use the Add→Class command. Then, in the Add New Item dialog box, enter the name you want to use for the new class and click the Add button.
- When you complete the Add New Item dialog box, a *class file* is added to the project. This class file will appear in the Solution Explorer window with the extension *vb*.
- The Class and End Class statements are automatically added to the class. Then, you can enter the code for the class between those statements.

Figure 11-5 How to add a class file to a project

How to code fields

Figure 11-6 shows how to code the fields that define the variables used by a class. A class can contain two types of fields: *instance variables* and *shared variables*. This figure shows you how to work with instance variables. You'll learn about shared variables in figure 11-11.

When you declare a field, you should use an access modifier to control the accessibility of the field. If you specify Private as the access modifier, the field can be used only within the class that defines it. In contrast, if you specify Public as the access modifier, the field can be accessed by other classes. You can also use other access modifiers that give you finer control over the accessibility of your fields. You'll learn about those modifiers in chapter 18.

This figure shows three examples of field declarations. The first example declares a private field of type Integer. The second declares a public field of type Decimal.

The third example declares a *read-only field*. As its name implies, a read-only field can be read but not modified. In this respect, a read-only field is similar to a constant. The difference is that the value of a constant is set when the class is compiled, but the value of a read-only field is set at runtime. You can assign a value to a read-only field when you declare it as shown in the third example or in the code for a constructor of the class.

Note that although fields work like regular variables, they must be declared within the class body, not inside properties, methods, or constructors. That way, they're available throughout the entire class. In this book, all of the fields for a class are declared at the beginning of the class. However, when you read through code from other sources, you may find that the fields are declared at the end of the class or at other locations within the class.

This figure also presents another version of the Product class that uses public fields instead of properties. This works because the properties of the Product class that was presented in figure 11-3 didn't do anything except get and set the values of private fields. Because of that, you could just provide direct access to the fields by giving them public access as shown here. In some cases, though, a property will perform additional processing. Then, you'll need to use a property instead of a public field.

By the way, you may notice that the names of the public fields in this class and in the second and third examples at the beginning of this figure begin with a capital letter. That's because these fields are used in place of properties, and the names of properties are always capitalized. In contrast, the name of the private field in the first example is prefixed with a lowercase *m* followed by an underscore (_). Here, the letter *m* indicates that the field is a *module-level variable*. This naming convention is typically used for a field that can only be accessed within the class, particularly if it stores the value of a property.

Examples of field declarations

```
Private m_Quantity As Integer              ' A private field
Public Price As Decimal                    ' A public field
Public ReadOnly Limit As Integer = 90      ' A public read-only field
```

A version of the Product class that uses public fields instead of properties

```
Public Class Product

    Public Code As String
    Public Description As String
    Public Price As Decimal

    Public Sub New()

    End Sub

    Public Sub New(code As String, description As String,
            price As Decimal)
        Me.Code = code
        Me.Description = description
        Me.Price = price
    End Sub

    Public Function GetDisplayText(sep As String) As String
        Dim text As String = Code & sep & FormatCurrency(Price) &
                             sep & Description
        Return text
    End Function

End Class
```

Description

- A *module-level variable* that's defined within a class is called a *field*.
- A field can be a primitive data type, a class or structure from the .NET Framework, or a user-defined class or structure.
- You can use the Private access modifier to prevent other classes from accessing a field. Then, the field can be accessed only from within the class.
- An *instance variable* is a field that's defined in a class and is allocated when an object is instantiated. Each object instance has a separate copy of each instance variable.
- If you initialize an instance variable, the initialization will occur before the constructor for the class is executed. As a result, the constructor may assign a new value to the variable.
- You can create a *read-only field* by specifying the ReadOnly keyword in the field's declaration. Then, the field's value can be retrieved, but it can't be changed. You can set the value for a read-only field when you declare it or in the code for a constructor.
- A *public field* is a field that's declared with the Public access modifier. Public fields can be accessed by other classes within the application, much like properties. However, properties can have additional features that make them more useful than public fields.

Figure 11-6 How to code fields

How to code standard properties

Visual Basic provides for two types of properties: standard properties and auto-implemented properties. In this topic, you'll learn how to code standard properties, which are the type of properties that have always been available with Visual Basic. Then, in the next topic, you'll learn how to code auto-implemented properties, which were added with Visual Basic 2010.

To code a standard property, you use the Property statement as shown in figure 11-7. As you can see, this statement specifies both the name and type of the property. In addition, a property is typically declared with the Public access modifier so it can be accessed by other classes.

Within the Property statement, you can include two procedures: a get procedure and a set procedure. The *get procedure* is executed when a request to retrieve the property value is made, and the *set procedure* is executed when a request to set the property value is made. Because they provide access to the property values, the get and set procedures are sometimes called *accessors*.

A property that includes both get and set procedures is called a *read/write property*. This is illustrated in the first example in this figure. Here, the get procedure simply returns the value of an instance variable, and the set procedure assigns the value that's passed to the property to an instance variable.

You can also create a *read-only property* by including the ReadOnly keyword on the Property statement. Then, only a get procedure is included as shown in the second example. Finally, you can create a write-only property by including the WriteOnly keyword on the Property statement. This type of property, which includes only a set procedure, is uncommon.

If you include the ReadOnly keyword on the Property statement, Visual Studio automatically adds the Get, End Get, and End Property statements when you press the Enter key. Similarly, if you include the WriteOnly keyword, Visual Studio automatically adds the Set, End Set, and End Property statements. If you don't include either of these keywords, though, Visual Studio doesn't add any additional code. That's because, as you'll see in a minute, these statements aren't required for an auto-implemented property. However, if you enter the Get statement on the line following the Property statement, Visual Studio adds the End Get, Set, End Set, and End Property statements when you press the Enter key.

In most cases, each property has a corresponding private instance variable that holds the property's value. In that case, the property should be declared with the same data type as the instance variable. It's also common to use the same name for the property and the instance variable, but to add the prefix m_ to the instance variable to identify it as a module-level variable. For example, the name of the instance variable for the Code property in the first example in this figure is m_Code.

Because a get procedure returns a value, it is similar to a function. In fact, you can use the same techniques to return a property value that you use to return the result of a function. That is, you can use a Return statement or you can assign a value to the property. In most cases, you'll use a Return statement to make it clear what value is being returned. This is the technique that's used in both of the

The standard syntax for coding a public standard property

```
Public [ReadOnly|WriteOnly] Property PropertyName As type
    [Get
        [statements]
        {PropertyName = propertyvalue} | {Return propertyvalue}
     End Get]
    [Set(variableName As type)
        [statements]
         propertyvalue = newvalue
     End Set]
End Property
```

A read/write property

```
Public Property Code As String
    Get
        Return m_Code
    End Get
    Set(value As String)
        m_Code = value
    End Set
End Property
```

A read-only property

```
Public ReadOnly Property DiscountAmount As Decimal
    Get
        m_DiscountAmount = Subtotal * DiscountPercent
        Return m_DiscountAmount
    End Get
End Property
```

A statement that sets a property value

```
product.Code = txtProductCode.Text
```

A statement that gets a property value

```
Dim code As String = product.Code
```

Description

- You use a *property* to get and set data values associated with an object. Typically, each property has a corresponding private instance variable that stores the property's value.
- It's common to use the same name for the property and the related instance variable, but to prefix the instance variable with the letter m followed by an underscore (_).
- A *get procedure* is used to get the value of a property. Often, the get procedure simply returns the value of the instance variable that stores the property's value.
- A *set procedure* is used to set the value of a property. Often, the set procedure simply assigns the value passed to it via the value parameter to the instance variable that stores the property's value.
- A *read-only property* has only a get procedure; a *write-only property* has only a set procedure; and a *read/write property* has both a get and a set procedure.
- Visual Basic generates the starting code for a property depending on whether you include the ReadOnly keyword, the WriteOnly keyword, or neither keyword.

Figure 11-7 How to code standard properties

examples in figure 11-7. Notice in the second example that a get procedure can do more than just return a value. Here, the get procedure performs a calculation to determine the value that's returned.

The set procedure uses a parameter named value to access the value to be assigned to the property. This is the value that's passed to a property when it's used in an assignment statement like the first one shown in this figure. Typically, the set procedure simply assigns this value to the instance variable that stores the property's value. However, a set procedure can perform more complicated processing if necessary. For example, it could perform data validation.

How to code auto-implemented properties

In addition to standard properties, Visual Basic also provides for *auto-implemented properties*. As figure 11-8 shows, auto-implemented properties provide a shorthand for coding simple properties. Specifically, you can use them when a property simply returns the value of an instance variable and assigns the value parameter to the instance variable.

To illustrate how auto-implemented properties work, consider the version of the Product class that's presented in this figure. Here, the Code, Description, and Price properties are all coded as auto-implemented properties. As you can see, when you code an auto-implemented property, you omit the get and set procedures. Then, when you compile the class, Visual Basic generates these procedures for you.

Visual Basic also generates the private instance variables that are used to store the values of the properties. That's why no instance variables are included in this class. Notice in the GetDisplayText method, however, that you can still use the generated instance variables, called *backing fields*, within the code for the class. As you can see here, the instance variables are given the same names as the properties, preceded by an underscore.

When you use an auto-implemented property, you should realize that you can assign an initial value to it as illustrated in the second example in this figure. You should also realize that Visual Studio can help you convert an auto-implemented property to a standard property as described in this figure. Even if you know that a property will require additional code, then, you may want to start by entering just the declaration for an auto-implemented property. Then, you can add the necessary get and set procedures later.

The syntax for coding a public auto-implemented property

```
Public Property PropertyName As type
```

A version of the Product class that uses auto-implemented properties

```
Public Class Product

    Public Sub New()
    End Sub

    Public Sub New(code As String, description As String,
            price As Decimal)
        Me.Code = code
        Me.Description = description
        Me.Price = price
    End Sub

    Public Property Code As String

    Public Property Description As String

    Public Property Price As Decimal

    Public Function GetDisplayText(sep As String) As String
        Dim text As String = _Code & sep & FormatCurrency(_Price) &
                             sep & _Description
        Return text
    End Function

End Class
```

An auto-implemented property that's assigned an initial value

```
Public Property Title As String = "An error has occurred"
```

Description

- If the get and set procedures for a property simply return the value of an instance variable and assign the value parameter to the instance variable, you can use an *auto-implemented property*. Then, when you compile the class, Visual Basic creates a corresponding private instance variable called a *backing field*, along with get and set procedures.
- The backing field that's generated for an auto-implemented property is given the same name as the property, preceded by an underscore (_). This field can be accessed from code within the class just like any other private instance variable.
- You can initialize an auto-implemented property using the same techniques you use to initialize a field.
- You can't use an auto-implemented property to create a read-only or write-only property or a property that accepts parameters.
- You can generate the code for a standard property from an auto-implemented property. To generate a get procedure, place the cursor on a blank line that follows the property declaration, type the letter "G", and then press the Enter key. To generate a set procedure, enter the letter "S".

Figure 11-8 How to code auto-implemented properties

How to code methods

Figure 11-9 shows you how to code the methods for a class. Because methods are nothing more than Public Sub and Function procedures, you should already know how to code them. If you want the method to return a value, you implement it as a Function procedure. If the method doesn't need to return a value, you implement it as a Sub procedure. And if the method requires that one or more values be passed to it, you code a parameter list in parentheses.

In addition to the basic skills for coding methods, this figure illustrates the concept of overloading. When you *overload* a method, you code two or more methods with the same name, but with unique combinations of parameters. In other words, you code methods with unique *signatures*.

For a method signature to be unique, the method must have a different number of parameters than the other methods with the same name, or at least one of the parameters must have a different data type. Note that the names of the parameters aren't part of the signature, so using different names isn't enough to make the signatures unique. Also, the return type isn't part of the signature. As a result, you can't create two methods with the same name and parameters but different return types.

The purpose of overloading is to provide more than one way to invoke a given method. For example, this figure shows two versions of the GetDisplayText method. The first one is the one you saw in figure 11-3 that accepts a parameter named sep. The second one doesn't accept this parameter. Instead, it uses a comma and a space to separate the values of the Code, Price, and Description properties.

When you refer to an overloaded method, the number of arguments you specify and their types determine which version of the method is executed. The two statements in this figure that call the GetDisplayText method illustrate how this works. Because the first statement specifies an argument, it will cause the version of the GetDisplayText method that includes a parameter to be executed. In contrast, the second statement doesn't specify an argument, so it will cause the version of the GetDisplayText method that doesn't include a parameter to be executed.

In chapter 3, you learned that if you type the name of a method followed by a left parenthesis into the Code Editor, Visual Studio's IntelliSense feature displays a list of the method's parameters. You may not have realized, though, that if up and down arrows appear to the left of the argument list, it indicates that the method is overloaded. Then, you can click the up and down arrows or press the up and down arrow keys to move from one overloaded method to another.

This works with overloaded methods in user-defined classes as well. For example, the illustration in this figure shows how the IntelliSense feature displays the overloaded GetDisplayText methods. In this case, the method that accepts a parameter is displayed.

A method that accepts a parameter

```
Public Function GetDisplayText(sep As String) As String
    Dim text As String = Code & sep &
                         FormatCurrency(Price) &
                         sep & Description
    Return text
End Function
```

An overloaded version of the method that doesn't accept parameters

```
Public Function GetDisplayText() As String
    Dim text As String = Code & ", " &
                         FormatCurrency(Price) &
                         ", " & Description
    Return text
End Function
```

Two statements that call the method

```
lblProduct.Text = product.GetDisplayText(vbTab)
lblProduct.Text = product.GetDisplayText()
```

How the IntelliSense feature lists overloaded methods

```
For Each p As Product In products
    lstProducts.Items.Add(p.GetDisplayText(
Next
                    ▲ 2 of 2 ▼ GetDisplayText(sep As String) As String
```

Description

- You define a method by coding a Sub or Function procedure. To provide other classes with access to the method, you declare it using the Public access modifier. To prevent other classes from accessing a method, you declare it using the Private access modifier.
- The name of a method combined with its parameters form the method's *signature*. Although you can use the same name for more than one method, each method must have a unique signature.
- When you create two or more methods with the same name but with different parameter lists, the methods are *overloaded*. It's common to use overloaded methods to provide two or more versions of a method that work with different data types or that supply default values for omitted parameters.
- When you type a method name followed by a left parenthesis, the IntelliSense feature of Visual Studio displays the parameters expected by the method. If up and down arrows are displayed as shown above, you can click these arrows or press the up and down arrow keys to display each of the method's overloaded parameter lists.

Note

- Instead of using overloaded methods to supply default values for omitted parameters, you can use optional parameters. See chapter 6 for more information.

Figure 11-9 How to code methods

How to code constructors

By default, when you use the New keyword to create an instance of a user-defined class, Visual Basic assigns default values to all of the instance variables in the new object. If that's not what you want, you can code a special method called a *constructor* that's executed when an object is created from the class. Figure 11-10 shows you how to do that.

To create a constructor, you code a public Sub procedure named New. Within this procedure, you initialize the instance variables, and you include any additional statements you want to be executed when an object is created from the class.

The first example in this figure is a constructor that doesn't provide for any parameters, so it's called when you create an instance of the class without specifying any arguments. Because this constructor has no executable statements, it simply initializes all the instance variables to their default values (excluding read-only variables). The default values for the various data types are listed in this figure.

In some cases, a class might not be defined with any constructors. For example, you could forget to code a constructor. Or, you could code a class within another class (see chapter 20) and not declare a constructor for that class. In that case, the Visual Basic compiler generates a *default constructor* that's equivalent to the constructor shown in the first example.

The second constructor in this figure shows that you can overload constructors just like you can overload methods. Here, a constructor that accepts three arguments is defined. This constructor uses the values that are passed to it to initialize the instance variables by setting property values. Although you could initialize the instance variables directly, it's usually best to assign the values to properties in case the set procedure does something other than just set the value of the instance variable.

Notice that this constructor uses the Me keyword to refer to the properties whose values are being initialized. This is necessary because the properties have the same names as the parameters used by the constructor. In this case, then, the Me keyword distinguishes a reference to a property from a reference to a parameter.

Note also that if you code a constructor like the one in the second example, the compiler won't generate a default constructor. In that case, you'll need to code a constructor like the one in the first example, since this constructor is required.

The third constructor shows how you might provide a constructor for the Product class that accepts just a product code as an argument. This constructor calls a method named GetProduct in a database class named ProductDB to retrieve the data for the specified product. After the data is retrieved, the constructor uses it to initialize the instance variables.

This figure also presents statements that execute the three constructors shown here. The first statement executes the constructor with no parameters. The second statement executes the constructor with three parameters. And the third

A constructor with no parameters

```
Public Sub New()

End Sub
```

A constructor with three parameters

```
Public Sub New(code As String,
        description As String,
        price As Decimal)
    Me.Code = code
    Me.Description = description
    Me.Price = price
End Sub
```

A constructor with one parameter

```
Public Sub New(code As String)
    Dim p As Product = ProductDB.GetProduct(code)
    Me.Code = p.Code
    Me.Description = p.Description
    Me.Price = p.Price
End Sub
```

Statements that call these constructors

```
Dim product1 As New Product
Dim product2 As New Product("VB12", "Murach's Visual Basic 2012", 54.5D)
Dim product3 As New Product(txtCode.Text)
```

Default values for instance variables

Data type	Default value
All numeric types	0 (zero)
Boolean	False
Char	Null (binary 0)
Date	01/01/01 00:00:00
Object	Null reference

Description

- You can use a constructor to initialize instance variables and perform other initialization operations as an object is created from a class.
- A constructor is simply a public Sub procedure named New. The constructor is executed when you use the New keyword to create an instance of the class, either in the Dim statement that defines the object variable or in an assignment statement that creates an object instance and assigns it to a previously defined object variable.
- If you don't code a constructor, Visual Basic creates a default constructor that initializes all the instance variables to their default values.
- The name of a class combined with its parameter list form the signature of the constructor. Each constructor must have a unique signature.

Figure 11-10 How to code constructors

statement executes the constructor with one parameter. Although you've seen statements like these before, you should now have a better understanding of how they work.

How to code shared members

As figure 11-11 shows, *shared members* are members that can be accessed without creating an instance of a class. The idea of shared members shouldn't be new to you because you've seen them used in several chapters in this book. In chapter 4, for example, you learned how to use shared methods of the Math and Convert classes. And in chapter 9, you learned how to use shared members of the DateTime structure and the String class. This figure shows how to create shared members in your own classes.

To create a shared member, you simply include the Shared keyword on the declaration for the member. The class shown in this figure, for example, provides shared members that can be used to perform data validation. This class has a shared field named m_Title, a shared property named Title, and a shared method named IsPresent.

The IsPresent method validates the Text property of a text box control to make sure the user entered a value. If the Text property is an empty string, the IsPresent method displays an error message, activates the text box, and returns False. Otherwise, it returns True. Note that this method uses the Tag property of the text box to get the name that's displayed in the dialog box. Because of that, this property must be set for any text box that's validated by this method.

The second example in this figure shows how you might call the IsPresent method to validate three text boxes. Here, the return values from three calls to the IsPresent method are tested. If all three calls return True, a Boolean variable named isValidData is set to True. Otherwise, this variable is set to False.

Before I go on, you should realize that a class can contain both shared and non-shared members. Then, when you create an instance of that class, all of the instances share the shared members. Because of that, you can't access a shared member from the variable that refers to the instance of the class. Instead, you can access it only by coding the name of the class.

Keep in mind, too, that a shared property or method can only refer to other shared members. For example, because the Title property shown in this figure is declared as shared, the title field it refers to must be declared as shared. Similarly, if a shared property or method refers to another property or method, that property or method must be declared as shared.

A class that contains shared members

```
Public Class Validator

    Private Shared m_Title As String = "Entry Error"

    Public Shared Property Title As String
        Get
            Return m_Title
        End Get
        Set(value As String)
            m_Title = value
        End Set
    End Property

    Public Shared Function IsPresent(textBox As TextBox) As Boolean
        If textBox.Text = "" Then
            MessageBox.Show(textBox.Tag.ToString &
                " is a required field.", Title)
            textBox.Select()
            Return False
        Else
            Return True
        End If
    End Function

End Class
```

Code that uses shared members

```
If Validator.IsPresent(txtCode) AndAlso
   Validator.IsPresent(txtDescription) AndAlso
   Validator.IsPresent(txtPrice) Then
    isValidData = True
Else
    isValidData = False
End If
```

Description

- A *shared member* is a field, property, or method that belongs to the class rather than to objects created from the class.
- To define a shared member, you use the Shared keyword. Then, you can access that member through the class without creating an instance of the class.
- Shared properties and methods can refer only to other shared members or to variables declared within the property or method.
- A constant that's declared with the Public keyword is implicitly shared. You can't code the Shared keyword on a constant declaration.
- If you create an object from a class, you can't refer to a shared member of that class through the variable for the object. You can refer to a shared member only through the name of the class.

Figure 11-11 How to code shared members

How to generate code stubs

In addition to the skills you just learned for creating classes, you can use a feature of Visual Studio called *Generate From Usage* to generate code stubs for a class and its members. This feature can help you quickly generate the starting code for a class from the code that uses the class. Then, you can enhance the code for the class later as needed.

Figure 11-12 shows how the Generate From Usage feature works. In the first screen shown here, you can see that I declared a variable named product from a class named Product. Because the Product class doesn't exist, though, Visual Studio marked it as a syntax error. Then, when I displayed the Error Correction Options window for the error, I used the first link to generate the class. The second screen is similar, but in this case, I generated a stub for a method named GetDisplayText. Notice here that I could also have generated a property.

This figure also shows the code that was generated for the class and method. The code for the class simply consists of Class and End Class statements. The code for the method consists of the method declaration and a single statement. That statement throws an exception indicating that the method hasn't been implemented. Then, you can replace this statement with the code that implements the method.

Notice that because the statement that calls the GetDisplayText method assigns the return value to a string variable, the method is coded as a function that returns a string. In addition, because the statement passes a string value to the method, the method is defined with a string parameter.

Instead of automatically generating Class and End Class statements from a statement like the one in the first example, you can use the second link in the Error Correction Options window to display the Generate New Type dialog box. You can use this dialog box to specify the code you want to generate. For example, you can use it to specify an access modifier for the class since one isn't generated by default. Although this dialog box isn't shown here, you shouldn't have any trouble using it.

In most cases, you'll use IntelliSense's standard *completion mode* to enter the name of a class or member. When you use this mode, the first item in the completion list that contains the letters you type is highlighted. Then, you can insert that item into your code by entering the next character in the statement, such as a period or parenthesis, or pressing the Tab or Enter key.

When you enter the name of an undefined class or member, though, you may want to use *suggestion mode* rather than completion mode. In this mode, the completion list is still displayed, but the current item is outlined rather than highlighted. Then, to commit the name you typed, you enter the next character in the statement or press the Enter key. This helps prevent IntelliSense from inserting unwanted text. To switch between completion mode and suggestion mode, you can use either of the two techniques described in this figure.

The Error Correction Options window for generating an undefined class

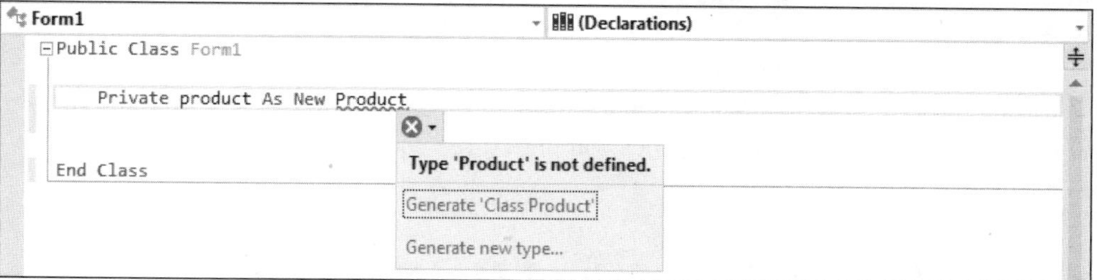

The Error Correction Options window for generating an undefined method

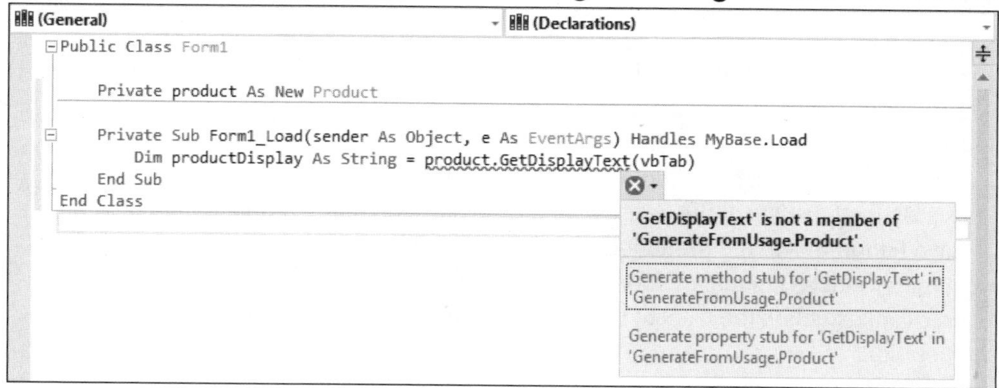

The generated code

```
Class Product
    Function GetDisplayText(vbTab As String) As String
        Throw New NotImplementedException
    End Function
End Class
```

Description

- The *Generate From Usage feature* lets you generate code stubs for any class, constructor, property, method, field, enumeration, or interface from the current location in your code.
- To generate a code stub, display the Error Correction Options window and then click the appropriate "Generate…" link.
- If your code refers to an undefined class, interface, enumeration, structure, or delegate, a "Generate new type…" link appears. You can click this link to display the Generate New Type dialog box. This dialog box lets you specify additional information about the type.
- When you enter a class or member that hasn't been defined, you should use *suggestion mode* for statement completion instead of *completion mode*. With suggestion mode, the name you type is inserted into your code rather than the highlighted entry in the completion list.
- To switch to or from suggestion mode, use the Edit→IntelliSense→Toggle Completion Mode command, or press Ctrl+Alt+Spacebar.

Figure 11-12 How to generate code stubs

The Product Maintenance application

Now that you've learned the basic skills for creating classes, the topics that follow present a Product Maintenance application that maintains a simple file of products. As you'll see, this application uses three user-defined classes in addition to the two form classes.

The operation of the Product Maintenance application

Figure 11-13 describes the operation of the Product Maintenance application. As you can see, this application uses two forms. The main form displays a list of the products that are stored in a file in a list box. The user can use this form to add or delete a product.

If the user clicks the Add Product button, the New Product form is displayed as a dialog box. Then, the user can enter the data for a new product and click the Save button to add the product to the file. After the product is saved, the list box in the Product Maintenance form is refreshed so it includes the new product. The user can also click the Cancel button on the New Product form to cancel the add operation.

To delete a product, the user selects the product in the list and clicks the Delete Product button. Then, a dialog box is displayed to confirm the operation. If the operation is confirmed, the product is deleted and the list box is refreshed so it no longer includes the deleted product.

This figure also shows how the Tag properties of the three text boxes on the New Product form are set. As you'll see in a minute, the methods of the data validation class use the Tag property of these text boxes to display meaningful error messages if the user enters incorrect data.

The Product Maintenance form

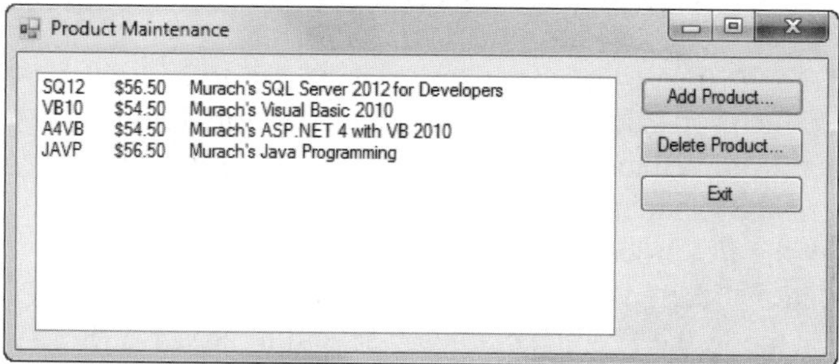

The New Product form

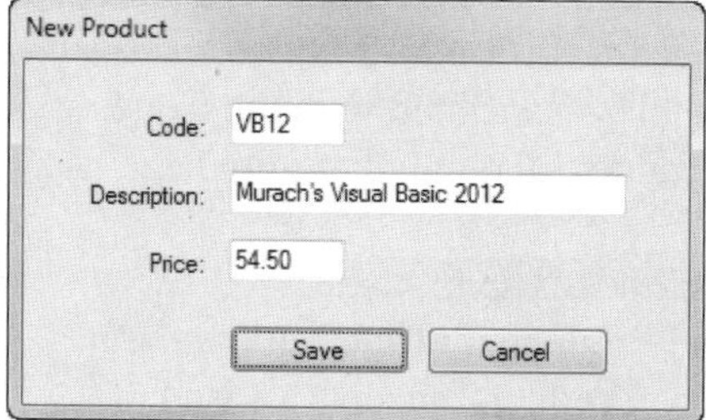

The Tag property settings for the text boxes on the New Product form

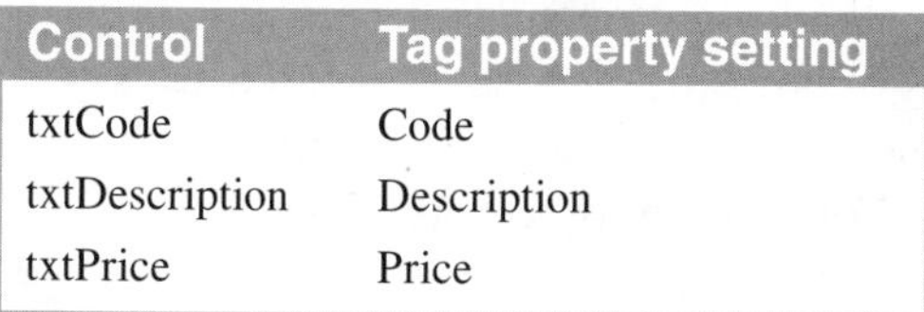

Control	Tag property setting
txtCode	Code
txtDescription	Description
txtPrice	Price

Description

- The Product Maintenance application retrieves product information from a file, displays it in a list box, and lets the user add or delete products.
- To add a product, the user clicks the Add Product button to display the New Product form. Then, the user can enter the data for the new product and click the Save button. Alternatively, the user can click the Cancel button to cancel the add operation. In either case, the user is returned to the Product Maintenance form.
- To delete a product, the user selects the product to be deleted and then clicks the Delete Product button. Before the product is deleted, the delete operation is confirmed.
- The Tag properties of the three text boxes on the New Product form are set so the Validator class can display meaningful error messages if the user enters invalid data.

Figure 11-13 The operation of the Product Maintenance application

The classes used by the Product Maintenance application

Figure 11-14 summarizes the properties, methods, and constructors for the classes used by the Product Maintenance application. As you can see, this application uses three classes. The Product class represents a single product. The ProductDB class handles the I/O processing for the Products file. And the Validator class handles the data validation for the user entries.

The Product class is the same as the Product class you saw in figure 11-3. It has three properties named Code, Description, and Price that define the values for a Product object. It has a single method named GetDisplayText that returns a string that contains the code, description, and price in a format that can be displayed in the list box of the Product Maintenance form. And it has two constructors: one that initializes the instance variables associated with the Code, Description, and Price properties to their default values, and one that initializes these variables to the specified values.

The ProductDB class contains two shared methods. The first one, GetProducts, retrieves all of the products from the Products file and returns them in a List() of Product objects. The second one, SaveProducts, accepts a List() of Product objects and writes the products in the list to the Products file, overwriting the previous contents of the file.

Note that the specifications for these methods don't indicate the format of the Products file. That's because the details of how this class saves and retrieves product information are of no concern to the Product Maintenance application. That's one of the benefits of encapsulation: You don't have to know how the class works. You just have to know what members it contains and how you refer to them.

The Validator class contains four shared methods that provide for different types of data validation. For example, the IsPresent method checks if the user entered data into a text box, and the IsDecimal method checks if the data the user entered is a valid Decimal value. If one of these methods determines that the data is invalid, it displays an error message using the Title property as the title for the dialog box, it activates the text box that's being validated, and it returns False. Otherwise, it returns True.

The Product class

Property	Description
Code	A String variable that contains a code that identifies the product.
Description	A String variable that contains a description of the product.
Price	A Decimal variable that contains the product's price.
Method	**Description**
GetDisplayText(sep)	Returns a string that contains the code, description, and price separated by the sep string.
Constructor	**Description**
New()	Creates a Product object with default values.
New(code, description, price)	Creates a Product object using the specified values.

The ProductDB class

Method	Description
GetProducts()	A shared method that returns a List() of Product objects from the Products file.
SaveProducts(list)	A shared method that writes the products in the specified List() of Product objects to the Products file.

The Validator class

Property	Description
Title	A shared string that contains the text that's displayed in the title bar of a dialog box for an error message.
Method	**Description**
IsPresent(textBox)	A shared method that returns a Boolean value that indicates if data was entered into the specified text box.
IsInt32(textBox)	A shared method that returns a Boolean value that indicates if an Integer type was entered into the specified text box.
IsDecimal(textBox)	A shared method that returns a Boolean value that indicates if a Decimal type was entered into the specified text box.
IsWithinRange(textBox, min, max)	A shared method that returns a Boolean value that indicates if the value entered into the specified text box is within the specified range.

Note: Each of these methods displays an error message in a dialog box and activates the text box if the data is invalid.

Note

- Because you don't need to know how the ProductDB class works, its code isn't shown in this chapter. Please refer to chapters 21 and 22 for three different versions of this class.

Figure 11-14 The classes used by the Product Maintenance application

The code for the Product Maintenance application

Figures 11-15 through 11-17 show the code for the Product Maintenance form, the New Product form, and the Validator class. Since you saw the code for the Product class in figure 11-3, I won't repeat it here. Also, because you don't need to know how the ProductDB class is implemented to understand how this application works, I won't present the code for that class either. If you're interested, however, you'll find three different implementations of this class in chapters 21 and 22.

The code for the Product Maintenance form, shown in figure 11-15, begins by declaring a module-level variable named products of the List() type. Next, in the Load event handler for the form, the GetProducts method of the ProductsDB class is called to fill this list with Product objects created from the data in the Products file. Then, the FillProductListBox procedure is called. This procedure uses a For Each...Next loop to add the string returned by each product's GetDisplayText method to the list box. Notice that a tab character is passed to this method so the products appear as shown in figure 11-13.

If the user clicks the Add Product button, an instance of the New Product form is created and displayed as a dialog box. Then, if the user enters a new product, the Product object for that product is stored in a public variable within the New Product form. The Product Maintenance form then checks this variable to be sure that a product was entered. If so, the product is added to the products list, the SaveProducts method of the ProductDB class is called to update the Products file, and the FillProductListBox procedure is called to refresh the list box so the new product is included.

If the user selects a product in the list and clicks the Delete Product button, a confirmation dialog box is displayed. Then, if the user confirms the deletion, the product is removed from the products list, the Products file is updated, and the list box is refreshed.

The code for the New Product form is shown in figure 11-16. It declares a public variable named Product that will hold a Product object. Then, if the user clicks the Save button on this form, the IsValidData procedure is called to validate the data. This procedure calls the IsPresent method of the Validator class for each text box on the form. In addition, it calls the IsDecimal method for the Price text box.

If all of the values are valid, a new Product object is created with the values entered by the user and the dialog box is closed. In contrast, if the user clicks the Cancel button, the dialog box is simply closed, which means that the Product variable contains its default value of Nothing.

The code for the Validator class, shown in figure 11-17, is similar to the code you saw back in figure 11-11. The only differences are that the Title property in this version of the Validator class is coded as an auto-implemented property, and this version includes an IsDecimal method as well as an IsPresent method. Note that because the Product Maintenance application doesn't use the IsInt32 or IsWithinRange methods, I omitted those methods from this figure.

The code for the Product Maintenance form

```
Public Class frmProductMaint

    Private products As List(Of Product)

    Private Sub frmProductMaint_Load(sender As Object,
            e As EventArgs) Handles MyBase.Load
        products = ProductDB.GetProducts
        Me.FillProductListBox()
    End Sub

    Private Sub FillProductListBox()
        lstProducts.Items.Clear()
        For Each p As Product In products
            lstProducts.Items.Add(p.GetDisplayText(vbTab))
        Next
    End Sub

    Private Sub btnAdd_Click(sender As Object,
            e As EventArgs) Handles btnAdd.Click
        Dim newProductForm As New frmNewProduct
        newProductForm.ShowDialog()
        If newProductForm.Product IsNot Nothing Then
            products.Add(newProductForm.Product)
            ProductDB.SaveProducts(products)
            Me.FillProductListBox()
        End If
    End Sub

    Private Sub btnDelete_Click(sender As Object,
            e As EventArgs) Handles btnDelete.Click
        Dim i As Integer = lstProducts.SelectedIndex
        If i <> -1 Then
            Dim product As Product = products(i)
            Dim message As String = "Are you sure you want to delete " &
                product.Description & "?"
            Dim button As DialogResult = MessageBox.Show(message,
                "Confirm Delete", MessageBoxButtons.YesNo)
            If button = DialogResult.Yes Then
                products.Remove(product)
                ProductDB.SaveProducts(products)
                Me.FillProductListBox()
            End If
        End If
    End Sub

    Private Sub btnExit_Click(sender As Object,
            e As EventArgs) Handles btnExit.Click
        Me.Close()
    End Sub

End Class
```

Figure 11-15 The code for the Product Maintenance form

The code for the New Product form

```
Public Class frmNewProduct

    Public Product As Product

    Private Sub btnSave_Click(sender As Object,
            e As EventArgs) Handles btnSave.Click
        If IsValidData() Then
            Product = New Product(txtCode.Text, txtDescription.Text,
                CDec(txtPrice.Text))
            Me.Close()
        End If
    End Sub

    Private Function IsValidData() As Boolean
        Return Validator.IsPresent(txtCode) AndAlso
               Validator.IsPresent(txtDescription) AndAlso
               Validator.IsPresent(txtPrice) AndAlso
               Validator.IsDecimal(txtPrice)
    End Function

    Private Sub btnCancel_Click(sender As Object,
            e As EventArgs) Handles btnCancel.Click
        Me.Close()
    End Sub

End Class
```

Figure 11-16 The code for the New Product form

The code for the Validator class

```
Public Class Validator

    Public Shared Property Title As String = "Entry Error"

    Public Shared Function IsPresent(textBox As TextBox) As Boolean
        If textBox.Text = "" Then
            MessageBox.Show(textBox.Tag.ToString &
                " is a required field.", Title)
            textBox.Select()
            Return False
        Else
            Return True
        End If
    End Function

    Public Shared Function IsDecimal(textBox As TextBox) As Boolean
        Dim number As Decimal = 0
        If Decimal.TryParse(textBox.Text, number) Then
            Return True
        Else
            MessageBox.Show(textBox.Tag.ToString &
                " must be a decimal value.", Title)
            textBox.Select()
            textBox.SelectAll()
            Return False
        End If

    End Function

End Class
```

Note

- The code for the IsInt32 and IsWithinRange methods isn't shown here because these methods aren't used by the Product Maintenance application.

Figure 11-17 The code for the Validator class

How to browse classes and use class diagrams

Now that you've seen a complete application that uses classes, you're ready to learn how to browse the classes in a solution and how to use class diagrams. Although you can create applications without using these features, they often make it easier to visualize and work with the classes of a project.

How to browse the classes in a solution

In previous versions of Visual Studio, you had to use the *Class View window* to browse the classes of a solution. The top pane of this window displayed the classes of the project, and the bottom pane displayed the members of the class selected in the top pane. Although you can still use the Class View window in Visual Studio 2012, you can also browse classes directly in the Solution Explorer. Figure 11-18 shows how you do that.

The solution in this figure is for the Product Maintenance application that was presented in figures 11-13 through 11-17. Here, I've expanded the Product.vb file in the Solution Explorer and the Product class that's subordinate to it to display the members of this class. As you can see, these members include the private fields named m_Code, m_Description, and m_Price; two constructors; the Code, Description, and Price properties; and the GetDisplayText method. Notice that the icons for the private fields include padlocks, which indicate that these fields are not accessible from outside the class.

You can also use the Solution Explorer to display the code for any member of a class in the Code Editor. To do that, just double-click on the member. In this figure, for example, you can see the code that was displayed when I double-clicked the Price property.

The Solution Explorer with the members of the Product class displayed

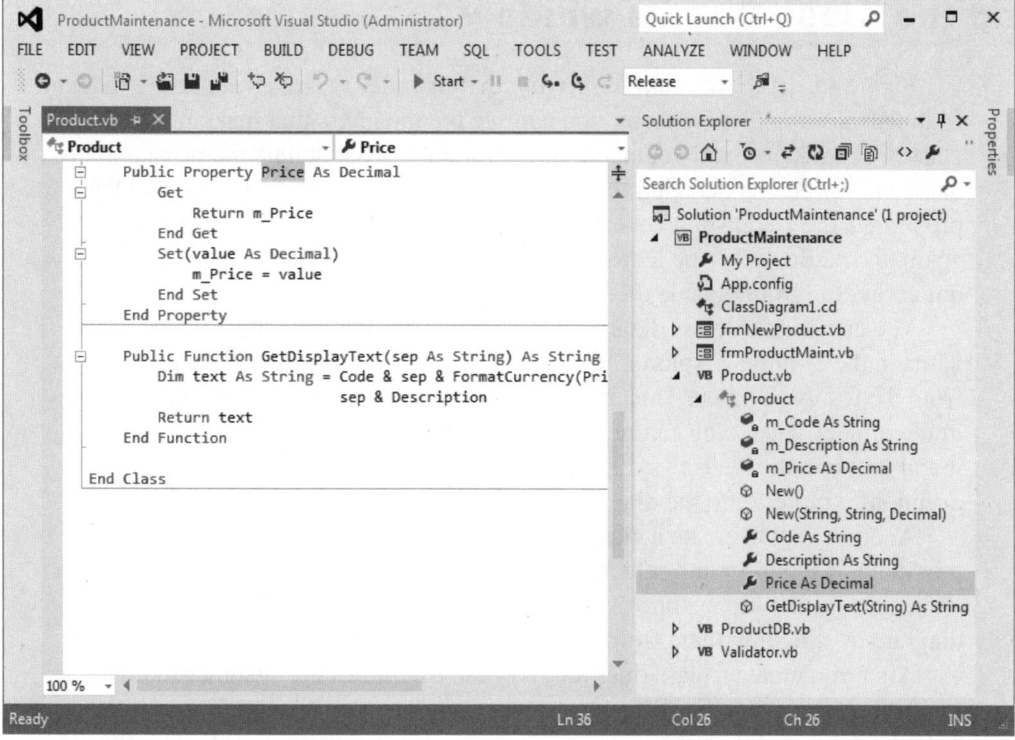

Description

- Visual Studio 2012 lets you use the Solution Explorer to browse the classes in a solution.
- To display the members of a class, including properties, methods, events, and fields, expand the Visual Basic file for the class and then expand the class.
- To display the Visual Basic code for a member in the Code Editor, double-click on the member in the Solution Explorer.
- You can also use the *Class View window* to browse the classes in a solution. This window displays the classes of a project in the top pane and the members of the selected class in the bottom pane. Then, you can double-click on a member to display its Visual Basic code.
- To display the Class View window, use the View→Class View command.

Figure 11-18 How to browse the classes in a solution

How to use class diagrams and the Class Details window

Figure 11-19 shows a *class diagram* that includes two classes in the Product Maintenance application. Here, you can see the members that make up these classes. For instance, the members of the Product class include the private fields named m_Code, m_Description, and m_Price; the Code, Description, and Price properties; the GetDisplayText method; and the overloaded constructor. Here again, the padlocks on the icons for the private fields indicate that these fields are not accessible from outside the class.

You can create a class diagram like this one by right-clicking on the project name in the Solution Explorer and selecting the View Class Diagram command from the resulting menu. This creates a class diagram that contains every class in the project. Then, you can remove any class from the diagram by clicking on it and pressing the Delete key. And you can add a class by dragging it from the Solution Explorer onto the diagram.

Another way to create a class diagram is to right-click on just one class in the Solution Explorer and select the View Class Diagram command. That creates a class diagram with just one class. Then, you can add other classes to the diagram by dragging them from the Solution Explorer.

After you create a class diagram, you can use the Class Designer toolbar to adjust the diagram. For instance, you can click on the a:T button to display both the name and type for each member of a class, and you can click on the a( ) button to display the name, type, and signature for each member.

When you select a class in a class diagram, you can use the *Class Details window* that's displayed below the diagram to view the details about the members of the class or the selected member in that class. In this figure, for example, the Code property is selected in the class diagram so it is also highlighted in the Class Details window.

To navigate to the code for any member of the selected class, you can double-click the icon for the member in either the class diagram or the Class Details window. Then, Visual Studio will open the class in the Code Editor window (if it isn't already open) and jump to the code for the selected member.

To generate the starting code for new properties, methods, fields, and events, you can click on the appropriate row or button in the Class Details window. To start a new property, for example, you can click on the <add property> row or the New Property button. Then, you can enter the name, type, and modifier in the row. To jump to the Code Editor so you can complete the code for the property, you can double-click on the icon for the row. Using the Class Details window like this is a quick way to develop the starting code for all of the members of a class.

Finally, to delete a member from a class, you can press the Delete key when the member is selected in either the class diagram or the Class Details window. This not only deletes the member from the class diagram and Class Details window, it also deletes the code from the class file.

A class diagram that shows two of the classes in the project

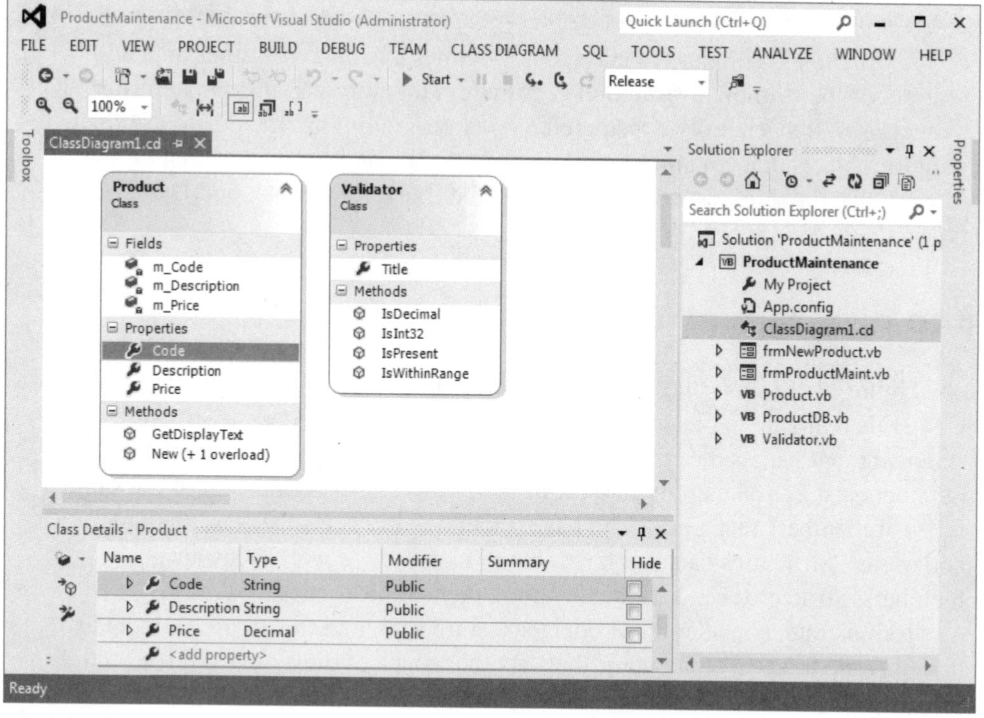

Description

- A *class diagram* is a visual representation of the methods, properties, fields, and events for one or more classes. To create a class diagram, right-click on a project or class in the Solution Explorer and select the View Class Diagram command.
- To select a class in a diagram, click on it. To expand or collapse the members of a class, click the icon in the upper right corner of the class. To delete a class, press the Delete key. To add a class, drag it from the Solution Explorer to the diagram. To adjust the way the diagram is displayed, use the buttons in the Class Designer toolbar.
- The details for the selected class or member in the class diagram are shown in the *Class Details window*. To view that window, right-click on the diagram and choose the Class Details command. Then, to jump to the code for a member in the Code Editor window, double-click on the member's icon in the class diagram or the Class Details window.
- To generate the starting code for new properties, methods, fields, and events, click on the appropriate row or button in the Class Details window and enter the required information. Then, you can switch to the Code Editor window to complete the code.
- To delete a member, select it in the class diagram or Class Details window and press the Delete key.

Express Edition limitation

- The Visual Studio Express Edition doesn't have class diagrams or the Class Details window.

Figure 11-19 How to use class diagrams and the Class Details window

How to work with structures

A *structure* is similar to a class, but it defines a *value type* rather than a reference type. Although structures require less memory and instantiate faster than classes, it's generally considered a good programming practice to use them only for objects that contain a small amount of data and for objects that you want to work like the .NET value types, such as the Integer, Decimal, and DateTime types.

How to create a structure

Figure 11-20 shows how to create a structure. To do that, you can use the Code File template to create an empty code file. Then, you code a Structure statement that names the structure. In the body of the structure, you can create members just as you can for classes. In fact, a structure can have all of the same types of members that a class can have, including fields, properties, methods, and events. Structures can also have shared members as well as instance members. Structures can't have auto-implemented properties, though.

To illustrate, consider the Product structure shown in this figure. It includes three private fields, a constructor that sets the values of those fields, three public properties that get and set the values of the fields, and a public method named GetDisplayText that formats the fields for display. This code is similar to code you would find in a class.

Note, however, that this structure doesn't contain a parameterless constructor. That's because the Visual Basic compiler always generates a default constructor, even if the structure contains other constructors. In contrast, if a class contains one or more constructors that accept parameters, a default constructor isn't generated and a parameterless constructor must be included in the class.

Another difference between structures and classes is that if a structure contains a constructor that accepts parameters, the constructor must initialize all of the structure's instance variables. That's because a structure's instance variables aren't assigned default values like the instance variables of a class are. In the structure in this figure, for example, the constructor uses the three parameter values that are passed to the constructor to assign values to the three instance variables.

Notice here that the three assignment statements refer directly to the instance variables rather than to the properties associated with them. That's because you can't refer to the properties and methods of a structure until all of its instance variables have been initialized.

The basic syntax for creating a structure

```
Public Structure StructureName
   member declarations
End Structure
```

A Product structure

```
Public Structure Product

    Private m_Code As String
    Private m_Description As String
    Private m_Price As Decimal

    Public Sub New(code As String, description As String,
            price As Decimal)
        Me.m_Code = code
        Me.m_Description = description
        Me.m_Price = price
    End Sub

    Public Property Code As String
        Get
            Return m_Code
        End Get
        Set(value As String)
            m_Code = value
        End Set
    End Property
    .
    .
    Public Function GetDisplayText(sep As String) As String
        Return Code & sep & FormatCurrency(Price) & sep & Description
    End Function

End Structure
```

Description

- A *structure* is similar to a class, but it represents a *value type*, not a reference type.
- A structure can contain the same types of members as a class, including fields, properties, methods, constructors, and events. You can't use auto-implemented properties with structures, though.
- A structure can't include a parameterless constructor because the compiler always generates one. This default constructor initializes the instance variables to default values just as the default constructor for a class does.
- A structure can contain constructors that accept parameters. A constructor that accepts parameters must initialize all the instance variables of the structure.
- To initialize an instance variable, a constructor must refer directly to that variable. It can't refer to the property associated with a variable like a constructor for a class can.
- The members of a structure are public by default. However, you typically include the Public keyword for clarity.

Figure 11-20 How to create a structure

How to use a structure

Figure 11-21 shows you how to use a structure. To start, you declare a variable with the structure type just as you would any other data type. For example, the first statement in the first code example declares a variable named p of type Product.

When you declare a variable with a structure type, an instance of that structure is created but values aren't assigned to its instance variables. Then, you must assign values to those variables before you can call any methods or get any property values of the structure. That's why the three assignment statements that follow the structure declaration in the first example set the values of the Code, Description, and Price properties before the last statement calls the GetDisplayText method.

Because an instance is automatically created when you declare a structure, you don't need to use the New keyword to create an instance. If you do use the New keyword, though, the instance variables are initialized with default values. This is illustrated by the statement in the second example. Because it uses the New keyword, the default constructor is called. Then, the m_Code and m_Description instance variables are set to null, and the m_Price instance variable is set to 0.

The third example shows how to call the constructor of the Product structure that accepts three parameters. To do that, you use the New keyword just as you would for a class.

Code that declares a variable as a structure type and assigns values to it

```
' Create an instance of the Product structure.
Dim p As Product

' Assign values to each instance variable.
p.Code = "VB12"
p.Description = "Murach's Visual Basic 2012"
p.Price = 54.5D

' Call a method.
Dim message As String = p.GetDisplayText(vbCrLf)
```

Code that uses the default constructor to initialize the instance variables

```
Dim p As New Product
```

Code that uses the constructor that accepts parameters to initialize the instance variables

```
Dim p As New Product("VB12", "Murach's Visual Basic 2012", 54.5D)
```

Description

- When you declare a variable with a structure type, an instance of that structure is created. If you don't use the New keyword to create the instance, the instance variables aren't initialized.
- To create an instance of a structure and initialize its instance variables to default values, you use the default constructor with the New keyword.
- To create an instance of a structure by calling a constructor that accepts parameters, you must use the New keyword.
- You can't call any of the properties or methods of a structure until you initialize all of its instance variables.
- Unlike classes, structures can't be inherited by other classes. For more information about how inheritance works, please see chapter 18.

Figure 11-21 How to use a structure

Perspective

At this point, you may wonder why you would go to the extra effort of dividing an application into classes. The answer is twofold. First, dividing the code into classes makes it easier to use the code in two or more applications. For example, any application that works with the data in the Products file can use the Product and ProductDB classes. Second, using classes helps you separate the business logic and database processing from the user interface. And that can make it easier to develop, maintain, and enhance the application.

To learn more about object-oriented programming, you can read the four chapters in section 4 of this book. Those chapters will give you the background you need for understanding how the .NET classes work and for creating complex classes of your own. Because you may not need the features presented in that section for typical business applications, though, I recommend you read the chapters in section 3 first. In that section, you'll learn how to develop applications that access a database, which is a common business function. In addition, you may want to read some or all of the chapters in section 5. Then, you can read the chapters in section 4 when you need the skills they present.

Terms

multi-layer architecture
three-layer architecture
presentation layer
database layer
middle layer
business rules layer
business class
business object
three-tier architecture
class library
object
property
method
event
constructor
member
class
instance
instantiation
object initializer
encapsulation
data hiding
state of an object
reference type
null reference
class file
field
instance variable
read-only field
public field
module-level variable
get procedure
set procedure
accessor
read/write property
read-only property
write-only property
auto-implemented property
signature
overloaded method
default constructor
shared member
Generate From Usage feature
suggestion mode
completion mode
Class View window
class diagram
Class Details window
structure
value type

Exercise 11-1 Create a Customer Maintenance application that uses classes

In this exercise, you'll create a Customer Maintenance application that uses three classes. To make this application easier to develop, we'll give you the starting forms, a complete Validator class, and a complete CustomerDB class that you'll use to work with the data in a file of customers. Note that the CustomerDB class assumes that the file of customers (Customers.xml) is in the C:\VB 2012\Files directory. If you placed this file in a different directory after downloading and installing the files for this book, you will need to change the path specification.

Open the project and add a Customer class

1. Open the application in the C:\VB 2012\Chapter 11\CustomerMaintenance directory. Then, review both of the forms in the Form Designer window so you get an idea of how this project should work.
2. Add a class named Customer to this project, and add the properties, method, and constructors that are shown in the table below. Implement the properties using the standard syntax.

Property	Description
`FirstName`	Gets or sets a string that contains the customer's first name.
`LastName`	Gets or sets a string that contains the customer's last name.
`Email`	Gets or sets a string that contains the customer's email address.
Method	**Description**
`GetDisplayText()`	Returns a string that contains the customer's name and email address formatted like this: Joanne Smith, jsmith@armaco.com.
Constructor	**Description**
`New()`	Creates a Customer object with default values.
`New(firstName, lastName, email)`	Creates a Customer object with the specified values.

3. When you complete the Customer class, use the Solution Explorer to review the members and jump to the code for one or more of the members. Then, review the members for the Validator class. Note that one of the methods is IsValidEmail, which you can use to validate email addresses.
4. If you're not using the Express Edition of Visual Studio, create a class diagram and use it to review the members and code of the Customer and Validator classes.

Add code to implement the Add Customer form

5. Display the code for the Add Customer form, and declare a public variable named Customer of type Customer.

6. Add an event handler for the Click event of the Save button that validates the data on the form using the methods of the Validator class (all three fields are required and the email field must be a valid email address), and then creates a new Customer object and closes the form if the data is valid.

7. Add an event handler for the Click event of the Cancel button that simply closes the form.

Add code to implement the Customer Maintenance form

8. Display the code for the Customer Maintenance form, and declare a module-level variable named customers of type List(Of Customer).

9. Add an event handler for the Load event of the form that uses the GetCustomers method of the CustomerDB class to load the customers list and then adds the customers to the Customers list box. Use the GetDisplayText method of the Customer class to format the customer data.

10. Add an event handler for the Click event of the Add button that creates a new instance of the New Customer form and displays it as a dialog box. If the Customer object that's available from the Customer variable in the New Customer form isn't equal to Nothing, this event handler should add that customer to the list, call the SaveCustomers method of the CustomerDB class to save the list, and then refresh the Customers list box.

11. Add an event handler for the Click event of the Delete button that removes the selected customer from the list, calls the SaveCustomers method of the CustomerDB class to save the list, and refreshes the Customers list box. Be sure to confirm the delete operation.

12. Add an event handler for the Click event of the Exit button that closes the form.

Run and test the application

13. Run the application and test it to be sure that it works properly. When you're done, end the application, but leave the solution open if you're going to continue with the next exercise.

Exercise 11-2 Use a structure

In this exercise, you'll modify your solution to exercise 11-1 by converting the Customer class to a structure.

1. If it isn't open already, open the project in the C:\VB 2012\Chapter 11\CustomerMaintenance directory.

2. Modify the Customer class so it defines a structure. Be sure to omit the parameterless constructor since they're not allowed in structures.

3. Run the application, and debug any errors that you encounter. Note that a Customer object can't have a value of Nothing since it's now a value type. However, the properties of a Customer object can have a value of Nothing since those properties are String types.

12

How to debug an application

In chapters 3 and 5, you learned how to work in break mode when a runtime error occurs, how to use the Exception Assistant to get information about the error, how to use data tips to find out what value a variable or property contains, how to use a breakpoint to enter break mode before a specific statement is executed, and how to step through the statements in an application from a breakpoint. These are the basic skills that you need for debugging simple applications.

As your applications get more complicated, though, debugging gets more complicated. In fact, if you've done much programming, you know that debugging is often the most difficult and time-consuming phase of programming. The good news is that Visual Studio offers many other tools for testing and debugging. In this chapter, you'll learn how to use the most useful ones, and you'll review the tools you've already been introduced to.

Basic debugging techniques

Before you begin debugging, you can set the options that control how Visual Studio handles exceptions. Then, you can use the basic debugging skills that you learned in previous chapters to find and fix most types of exceptions.

How to set the debugging options

Figure 12-1 presents the two dialog boxes you can use to set the options for debugging. The Options dialog box lets you set options like whether the Exception Assistant is displayed when an exception occurs or whether the Edit and Continue feature is enabled. In general, the default settings are satisfactory, but you may want to change one of the General options in the Debugging group. That option, which causes text that's intended for the Output window to be redirected to the Immediate window, is shown in the Options dialog box in this figure. You'll learn more about this option in figure 12-11. For now, just realize that if you want debugging output displayed in the Output window, you need to turn this option off.

In contrast to the Options dialog box, the Exceptions dialog box lets you determine which exceptions are thrown and how they're handled. These exceptions are grouped by categories (namespaces), and you can set the options for a namespace or a specific exception within a namespace. In the dialog box in this figure, for example, the User-unhandled option is set for most of the exceptions for the Common Language Runtime.

By default, the Thrown box is unchecked for all categories and exceptions, and the User-unhandled box is usually checked. As a result, the application will continue when an exception is thrown instead of breaking into the debugger. This gives any exception-handling code that you have written a chance to be executed, which is usually what you want. However, if you check the Thrown box, you can enter break mode when the exception is thrown and use the debugging features described in this chapter *before* any exception-handling code is executed.

When you use the Exceptions dialog box, the options that you set cascade down to all exceptions below the specified category. As a result, the settings for the Common Language Runtime Exceptions apply to all of the namespaces and exceptions below that entry. However, you can override any of the namespaces and exceptions below an entry by checking the boxes for each namespace or exception. For example, if you want to break any time an exception in the System namespace is thrown (even if the exception is handled), you can check the Thrown box for the System namespace.

The Options dialog box

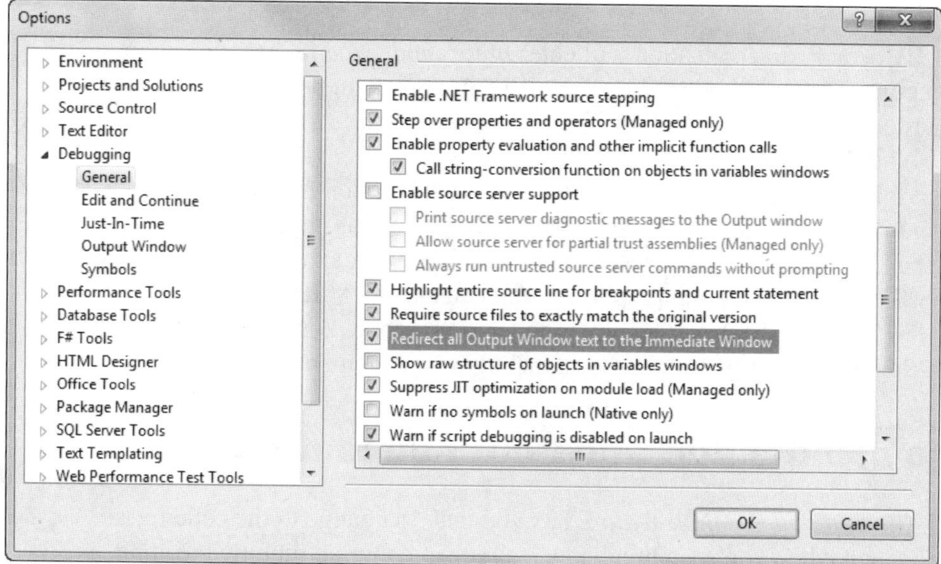

The Exceptions dialog box

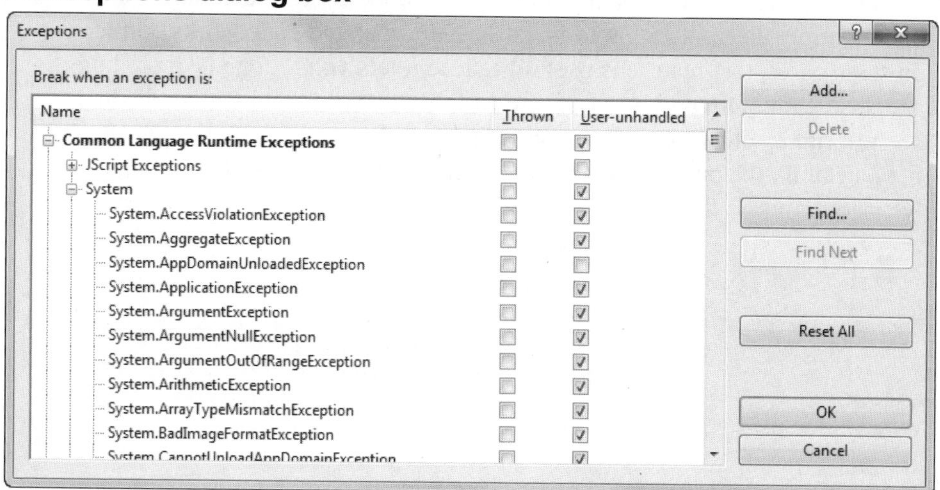

Description

- To display the Options dialog box, use the Tools→Options command.
- By default, the Edit and Continue feature is on in the Options dialog box. This feature lets you change the code while in break mode and continue running the application.
- If you don't want text such as debugging output that would typically go to the Output window to go to the Immediate window, you can remove the check mark from the appropriate option.
- To display the Exceptions dialog box, use the Debug→Exceptions command.
- By default, an application will enter break mode only when an exception is thrown and there is no exception-handling code for that exception.

Figure 12-1 How to set the debugging options

How to work in break mode

By default, an application will enter *break mode* when it encounters an exception that isn't handled. You can also enter break mode by using one of the other techniques listed in figure 12-2.

When you enter break mode after an unhandled exception occurs, the statement that was executing is highlighted and the Exception Assistant is displayed as shown in this figure. Then, you can use the Exception Assistant to try to determine the cause of the exception. In addition, you can use data tips to display the values of variables and properties. You can also look in the Locals window to see the values of the variables within the current scope. You'll learn more about working with data tips and the Locals window in a moment.

How to use the Edit and Continue feature

The *Edit and Continue feature* lets you make a change to the code for an application while you're in break mode and then continue running the application. If, for example, you realize that a calculation is wrong while you're testing an application, you can enter break mode, fix the code for the calculation, and continue running the application to make sure the changed code works correctly.

In some cases, this feature is useful because it lets you fix one or more bugs in a single test run. Often, though, it's just as easy to exit from break mode and end the test run by clicking on the Stop Debugging button in the Debug toolbar. Then, you can fix the bugs and restart the application to test the changes that you've made.

The Future Value application in break mode

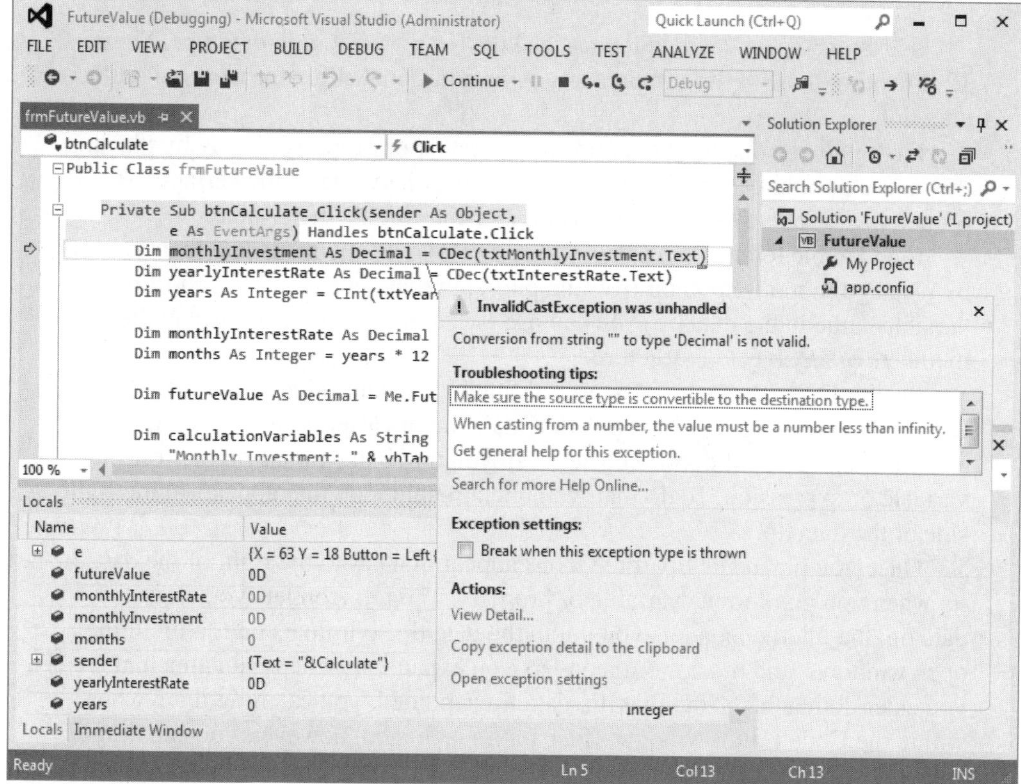

Four ways to enter break mode

- Force an unhandled exception to be thrown.
- Set a breakpoint and run the application.
- Choose the Debug→Step Into command or press F11 to begin debugging at the first line of the application.
- Choose the Debug→Break All command or press Ctrl+Alt+Break while the application is executing.

Description

- If an unhandled exception occurs, Visual Studio enters *break mode*, displays the Exception Assistant, and highlights the statement that was executing when the exception occurred. Then, you can use the Exception Assistant and the debugging windows to determine the cause of the exception.
- The *Edit and Continue feature* lets you make changes to the code while in break mode and continue running the application with the changes in force.
- To exit break mode and end the application, click on the Stop Debugging button in the Standard toolbar or use the Debug→Stop Debugging command.

Figure 12-2 How to work in break mode

How to work with data tips

In chapter 3, you learned the basic skills for working with data tips. Figure 12-3 reviews these skills and presents some additional skills for working with data tips.

First, you can display a data tip for a variable or property simply by placing the mouse pointer over it. Then, you can change the value of the variable or property by clicking on it in the data tip and entering the new value.

If a variable refers to an array, you can display its elements and their values by placing the mouse pointer over the plus sign that appears to the left of the variable name in the data tip. You can use the same technique to display the members of an object or structure.

In addition to these features, Visual Studio 2010 introduced some new features for working with data tips that make them easier to use. To start, you can pin a data tip so it doesn't close when you move the mouse pointer off the variable or expression. To do that, you click the pin icon that appears at the right side of the data tip.

Once you pin a data tip, three icons appear in a bar to the right of the data tip when you point to the variable or property. The top icon lets you close the data tip, the middle icon lets you unpin the data tip so it floats on top of all the open windows, and the bottom icon lets you expand or collapse an area that lets you enter comments. Note that if a data tip is pinned, you can drag it anywhere within the Code Editor window. If a data tip is floated, however, you can drag it over any window and you will still be able to see it on top of that window.

In this figure, I displayed a data tip for the Text property of the Monthly Investment text box. Then, I pinned the data tip so it remained displayed. Finally, I clicked the bottom icon to open a small text area where I could enter a comment.

The Future Value application with a data tip displayed

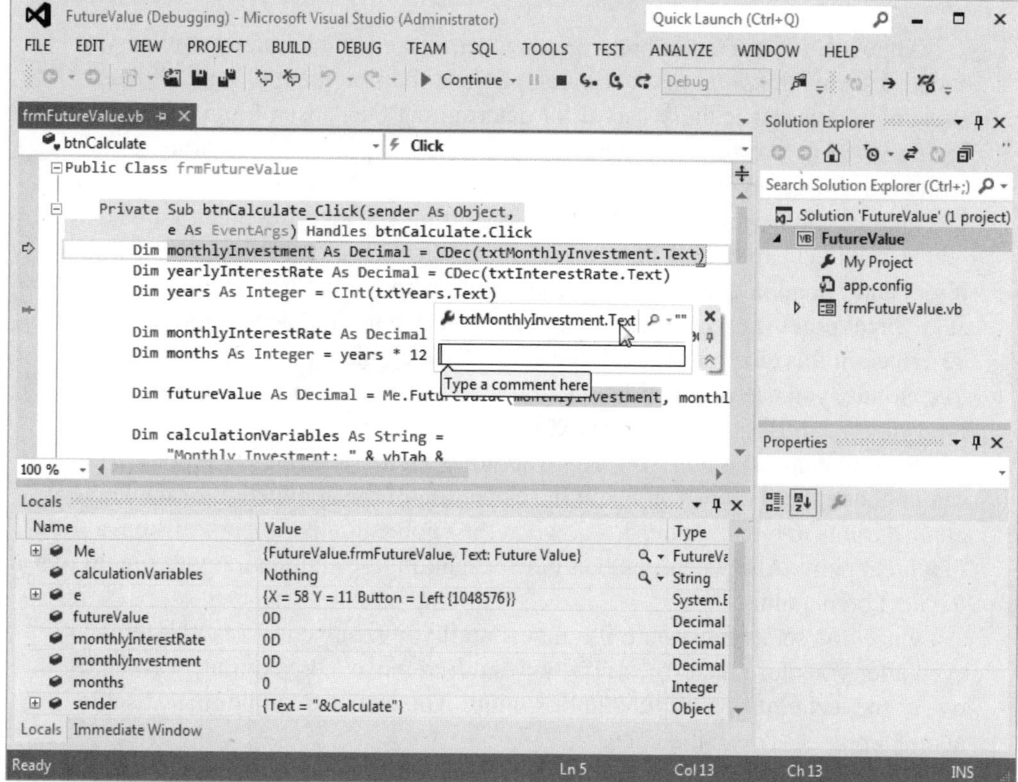

Description

- To display the value of a variable or property in a *data tip*, position the mouse pointer over it in the Code Editor.
- To change the value of a property or variable using a data tip, click on the value in the data tip and enter the new value.
- You can expand a variable that refers to an array to view its elements, and you can expand a variable that refers to an object or structure to view its members. To do that, point to the plus sign to the left of the variable name in the data tip.
- To pin a data tip so it remains displayed, click the "Pin to source" icon that appears to the right of the data tip. Then, a pin icon appears in the margin indicator bar to indicate the location of the data tip, and you can drag the data tip anywhere in the Code Editor.
- To unpin a data tip so it floats on top of all other open windows, click the "Unpin from source" icon that appears after you pin a data tip. Then, the pin icon in the margin indicator bar disappears, and you can drag the data tip onto any window.
- To add a comment to a data tip, click the "Expand to see comments" icon. Then, enter a comment in the box that appears. To hide the comments, click the "Collapse comments" icon.
- To close a data tip, click the Close icon. If you don't close a data tip, it will be displayed again the next time you enter break mode.

Figure 12-3 How to work with data tips

How to use breakpoints

Although you can enter break mode when you encounter an exception, you can also set a *breakpoint* to enter break mode at the statement of your choice. Breakpoints are particularly useful for determining the cause of logical errors. A *logical error* is an error that causes an application to produce inaccurate results without throwing an exception.

Figure 12-4 reviews the techniques for setting and clearing breakpoints that you learned in chapter 5. When you run an application after setting a breakpoint, it will enter break mode when it reaches the breakpoint but before the statement at the breakpoint is executed. At that point, you can use the debugging tools described in this chapter to check the state of the application. When you're ready to continue, you can press F5 or click on the Continue button, or you can use the Step commands described in the next figure.

For some applications, you may want to set more than one breakpoint. You can do that either before you begin the execution of the application or while the application is in break mode. Then, when the application is run, it will stop at the first breakpoint. And when you continue execution, the application will run up to the next breakpoint.

Once you set a breakpoint, it remains until you remove it. In fact, it remains even after you close the project. If you want to remove a breakpoint, you can use one of the techniques presented in this figure. You can also temporarily disable all breakpoints as described here.

You can also work with breakpoints from the Breakpoints window. For example, you can disable a breakpoint by removing the check mark in front of the breakpoint. Then, the breakpoint remains in the Breakpoints window, but it is disabled until you enable it again. To disable or enable all breakpoints, you can use the Disable All Breakpoints/Enable All Breakpoints button that's available from the Breakpoints window. Similarly, you can use the Delete All Breakpoints button to remove all breakpoints.

You can also use the Breakpoints window to label and filter breakpoints. You use labels to group related breakpoints. To assign a label to one or more breakpoints, select the breakpoints in the Breakpoints window. Then, right-click on the breakpoints and select Edit Labels to display the Edit Breakpoint Labels dialog box. From this dialog box, you can enter the label you want to use or select a label you created previously.

To filter breakpoints, select the column you want to search from the In Column drop-down list or use the default to search all columns. To search just the Labels column, for example, choose Labels from this list. Then, enter the search text in the Search box and press the Enter key. The breakpoints will be filtered so only those that contain the search text will be displayed. You can also control the columns that are displayed using the Columns drop menu, and you can remove the filtering using the Reset button.

The Future Value application with a breakpoint

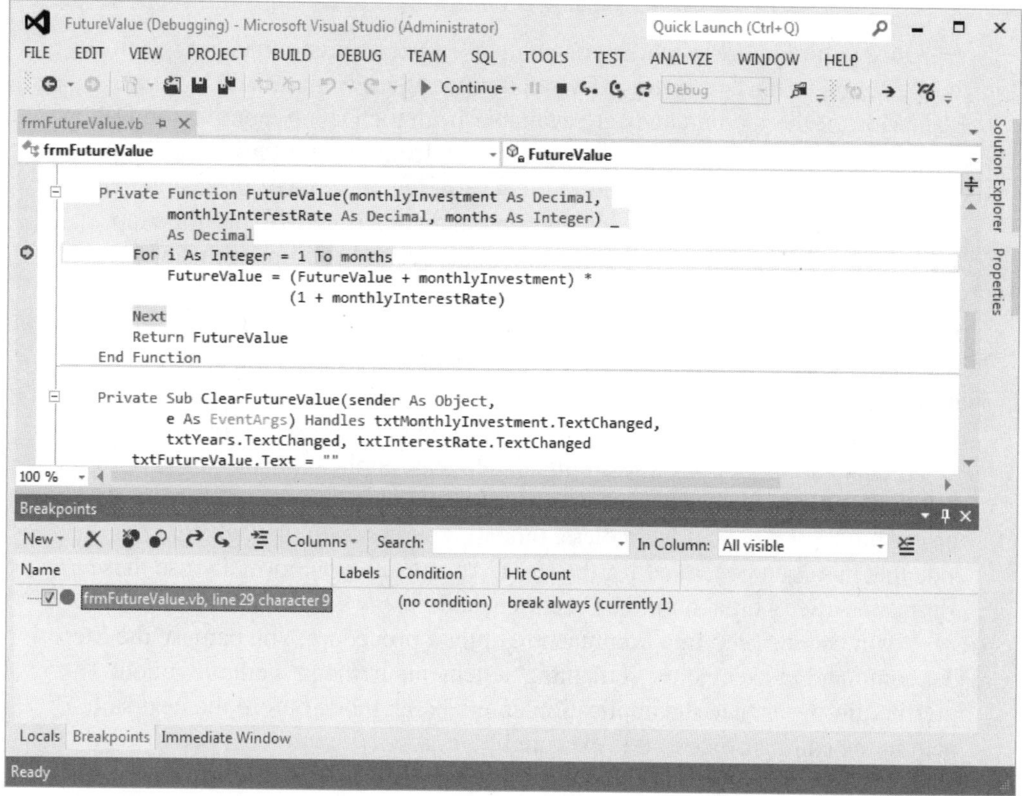

How to set and clear breakpoints

- To set a *breakpoint*, click in the margin indicator bar to the left of a statement. Or, press the F9 key to set a breakpoint at the insertion point. You can set a breakpoint before you run an application or while the application is in break mode.
- To remove a breakpoint, use either technique for setting a breakpoint. To remove all breakpoints at once, use the Debug→Delete All Breakpoints command.
- To disable all breakpoints, use the Debug→Disable All Breakpoints command. To enable all breakpoints, use the Debug→Enable All Breakpoints command.

Description

- You can set a breakpoint on any line except a blank line.
- When Visual Studio encounters a breakpoint, it enters break mode before it executes the statement that contains the breakpoint.
- The current breakpoints are displayed in the Breakpoints window. To display this window, use the Debug→Windows→Breakpoints command.
- The Breakpoints window is most useful for enabling and disabling existing breakpoints, but you can also use it to add, modify, move, delete, label, or filter breakpoints.

Figure 12-4 How to use breakpoints

How to control the execution of an application

Once you're in break mode, you can use a variety of commands to control the execution of the application. These commands are summarized in figure 12-5. Most of these commands are available from the Debug menu or the Debug toolbar, but a couple of them are available only from the shortcut menu for the Code Editor. You can also use shortcut keys to execute some of these commands.

To *step through* an application one statement at a time, you use the Step Into command. Then, the application enters break mode before each statement is executed so you can test the values of properties and variables and perform other debugging functions. If a statement calls another procedure, the Step Into command causes the application to execute each statement of the called procedure. The Step Over command works similarly except that the statements in called procedures are executed without interruption (they are "stepped over").

You can use either of these commands to start application execution or to restart execution when an application is in break mode. If you use them to start the execution of a typical form class, though, you first step through some of the code that has been generated for the form. As a result, you normally use these commands after a breakpoint has been reached.

If you use the Step Into command to enter a procedure, you can use the Step Out command to execute the remaining statements in the procedure without interruption. After that, the application enters break mode before the next statement in the calling procedure is executed.

To skip code that you know is working properly, you can use the Run To Cursor or Set Next Statement command. You can also use the Set Next Statement command to rerun lines of code that were executed before an exception occurred. And if you've been working in the Code Editor and have forgotten where the next statement to be executed is, you can use the Show Next Statement command to move to it.

Commands in the Debug menu and the Standard and Debug toolbars

Command	Toolbar	Keyboard	Description
Start/Continue	▶ Continue	F5	Start or continue execution of the application.
Break All	‖	Ctrl+Alt+Break	Suspend execution of the application.
Stop Debugging	■	Shift + F5	Stop debugging and end execution of the application.
Step Into		F11	Execute one statement at a time.
Step Over		F10	Execute one statement at a time except for called procedures.
Step Out		Shift+F11	Execute the remaining lines in the current procedure.
Show Next Statement	→		Display the next statement to be executed. Also available from the shortcut menu for the Code Editor.

Commands in the Code Editor's shortcut menu

Command	Description
Run to Cursor	Execute the application until it reaches the statement that contains the insertion point.
Set Next Statement	Set the statement that contains the insertion point as the next statement to be executed.

Description

- If you use the Step Into or Step Over command to start the execution of an application, Visual Studio will enter break mode before it executes the first statement in the application. If you use the Run to Cursor command, Visual Studio will enter break mode when it reaches the statement that contains the insertion point.
- Once the application enters break mode, you can use the Step Into, Step Over, Step Out, and Run To Cursor commands to execute one or more statements.
- To alter the normal execution sequence of the application, you can use the Set Next Statement command. Just place the insertion point in the statement you want to execute next, issue this command, and click on the Continue button.
- To enter break mode when you need to stop the execution of an application, you can use the Break All command.

Note

- By default, you can also use the Visual Basic 6 keyboard shortcuts, unless you're using the Visual Studio Express Edition.

Figure 12-5 How to control the execution of an application

How to use the debugging windows

Now that you know how to work with break mode, you're ready to learn how to use the primary debugging windows. These windows include the Locals window, the Autos window, the Watch windows, the Immediate window, the Call Stack window, the Call Hierarchy window, and the Output window.

How to use the Locals window to monitor variables

If you need to see the values of several variables used in the same area of an application, you can do that using the Locals window as shown in figure 12-6. This window displays information about the variables that are in the current scope. In this figure, for example, the Locals window shows the five variables that are in the scope of the For loop in the FutureValue procedure. In addition, it shows the Me keyword that includes information about the current form.

Whenever a variable contains other variables, the Locals window displays a plus sign (+) to the left of the variable. To drill down through this information, you can click the plus sign to expand the entry. In this figure, for example, you can click the plus sign to the left of the Me keyword to view information about the current form. That includes information about all of the properties for the form and all of the properties for each control on the form.

Besides displaying the values of variables, you can use the Locals windows to change these values. To do that, you double-click on the value you want to change and enter a new value. Then, you can continue the execution of the application.

How to use the Autos window to monitor variables

If you want to limit the number of variables that are displayed, you can use the Autos window instead of the Locals window. This window works similarly to the Locals window, except it only displays information about the variables used in the current statement and the previous statement. As a result, it doesn't display as many variables, especially if the current block of code has a large number of variables within scope. To display this window, you can select the Autos command from the Windows submenu of the Debug menu.

The Locals window

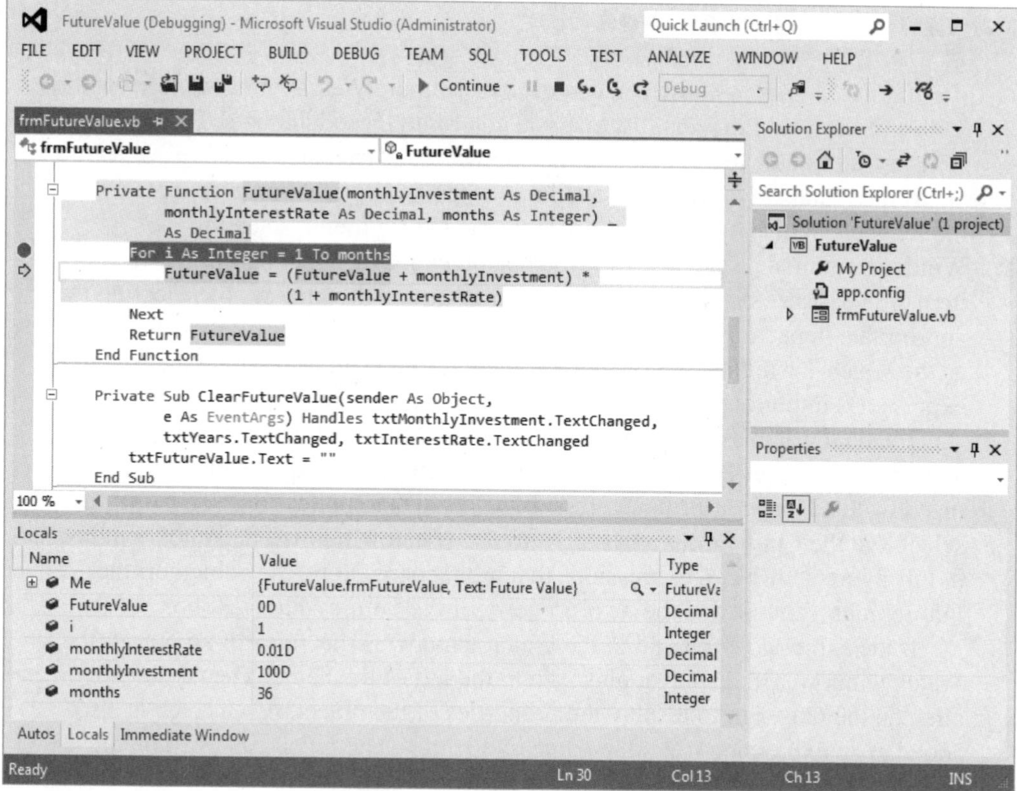

How to use the Locals window

- The Locals window displays information about the variables within the current scope.
- To display the Locals window, use the Debug→Windows→Locals command or click on the Locals tab.
- If you are debugging a form and you click on the plus sign to the left of the Me keyword, the properties and variables of the form are displayed.
- To change the value of a property or variable, double-click on the value in the Value column, then type a new value and press the Enter key.

How to use the Autos window

- The Autos window works like the Locals window, but it only displays information about variables used by the current statement and the previous statement.
- To display the Autos window, use the Debug→Windows→Autos command.

Figure 12-6 How to use the Locals and Autos windows to monitor variables

How to use Watch windows to monitor expressions

Figure 12-7 shows how you can use one or more Watch windows to view the values of the *watch expressions* that you enter into these windows. These expressions are automatically updated as the application is executed.

If the Watch 1 window isn't available when an application enters break mode, you can display it by pulling down the Debug menu, selecting the Windows submenu, selecting the Watch submenu, and selecting the Watch 1 item. You can also display any of the other three watch windows by selecting the appropriate item from this submenu. These windows provide the same features as the Watch 1 window, so you can use them if you want to separate the watch expressions into groups.

To add a watch expression, you click in the Name column of an empty row and enter the expression. A watch expression can be any expression that's recognized by the debugger. If the expression exists in the application, you can also select it in the Code Editor and drag it to the Watch window. The Watch window in this figure shows two expressions that are recognized by the debugger: the FutureValue variable and the Text property of the Future Value text box.

If the expression you add to the Watch window is the name of an object, the Watch window will display a plus sign to the left of the name. Then, you can click on the plus sign to display the properties of the object. A plus sign is also added to an expression if it's the name of an array. Then, you can click on the plus sign to display the elements in the array.

You can change the value of a watch expression by double-clicking on the value in the Value column and entering the new value. To delete a watch expression, you can use the Delete Watch command on the shortcut menu that's displayed when you right-click on an expression. To delete all watch expressions, you can use the Select All command on the shortcut menu followed by the Delete Watch command.

A Watch window

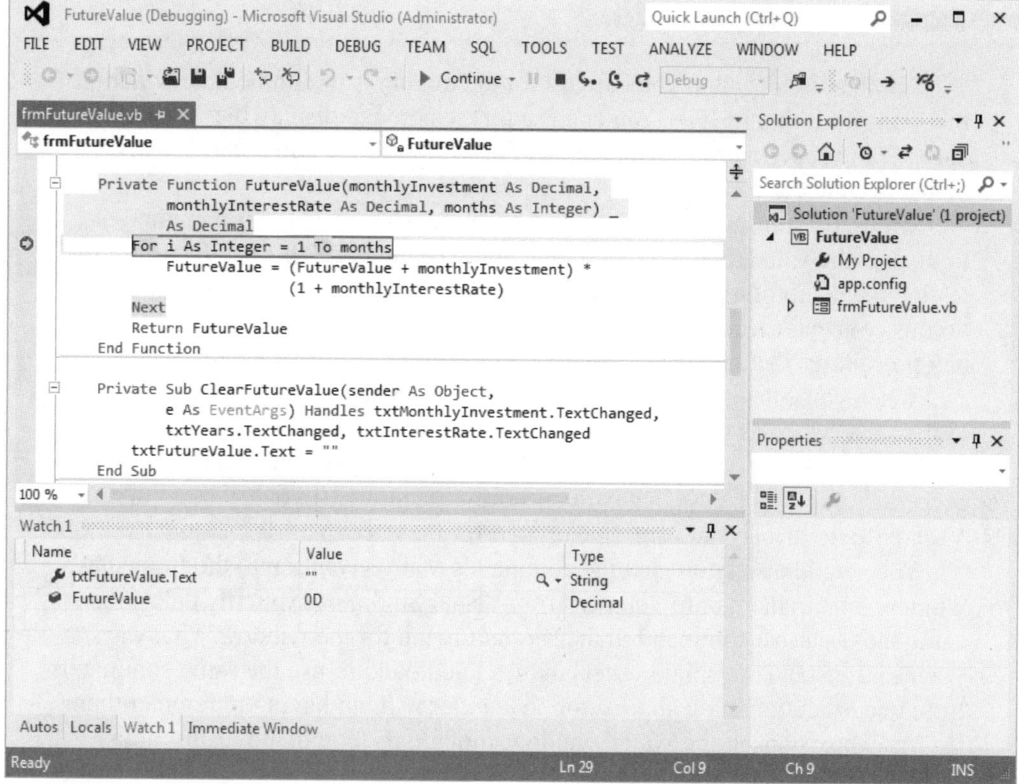

Description

- The Watch windows let you view the values of *watch expressions* while an application is in break mode. To display a Watch window, click on its Watch tab. Or, select Debug→Windows→Watch and choose Watch 1, Watch 2, Watch 3, or Watch 4.
- To add an expression to a Watch window, click on an empty row in the Name column, then type the expression. You can also highlight an expression in the Code Editor and drag it into a Watch window.
- If an expression is out of scope, it will appear dimmed in the Watch window along with a message that says the expression isn't valid in the current context.
- If you enter the name of an object, array, or collection in the Watch window, a tree control will appear next to its name. Then, you can use this control to expand or collapse this entry.
- To change the value of a watch expression, double-click on its value in the Value column, enter the new value, and press the Enter key.
- To delete a watch expression, right-click on the expression and select the Delete Watch command from the shortcut menu. To delete all watch expressions, right-click on the Watch window, select the Select All command, and select the Delete Watch command.

Figure 12-7 How to use Watch windows to monitor expressions

How to use the Immediate window to execute commands

Another window that you can use for debugging is the Immediate window that's shown in figure 12-8. You can use this window to display the value of a variable or property or to execute code. For example, you can enter an assignment statement to change the value of a variable or property.

Similarly, you can use this window to execute a procedure or a method or to display the value returned by the procedure or method. This can be useful for testing the result of a procedure or method with different arguments. When you do this, you can execute methods from classes in the .NET Framework as well as any procedures that you have coded in your project.

When you enter commands in the Immediate window, they're executed in the same scope as the application that's running. That means that you can't display the value of a variable that's out of scope and you can't execute a private procedure that's in a class that isn't currently executing. If you try to do that, Visual Studio displays a blank line or an error message.

You should also know that the commands that you enter into the Immediate window remain there until you exit from Visual Studio or explicitly delete them using the Clear All command in the shortcut menu for the window. That way, you can use standard Windows techniques to edit and re-use the same commands from one execution of an application to another without having to re-enter them. Unlike expressions in the Watch window, though, the command results aren't updated as the application executes.

To execute a command that you've already entered in the Immediate window, press the Up or Down arrow keys to locate the command. This displays the command at the bottom of the window. Then, if you want, you can edit the command. Or, you can press Enter to execute the command.

The Immediate window

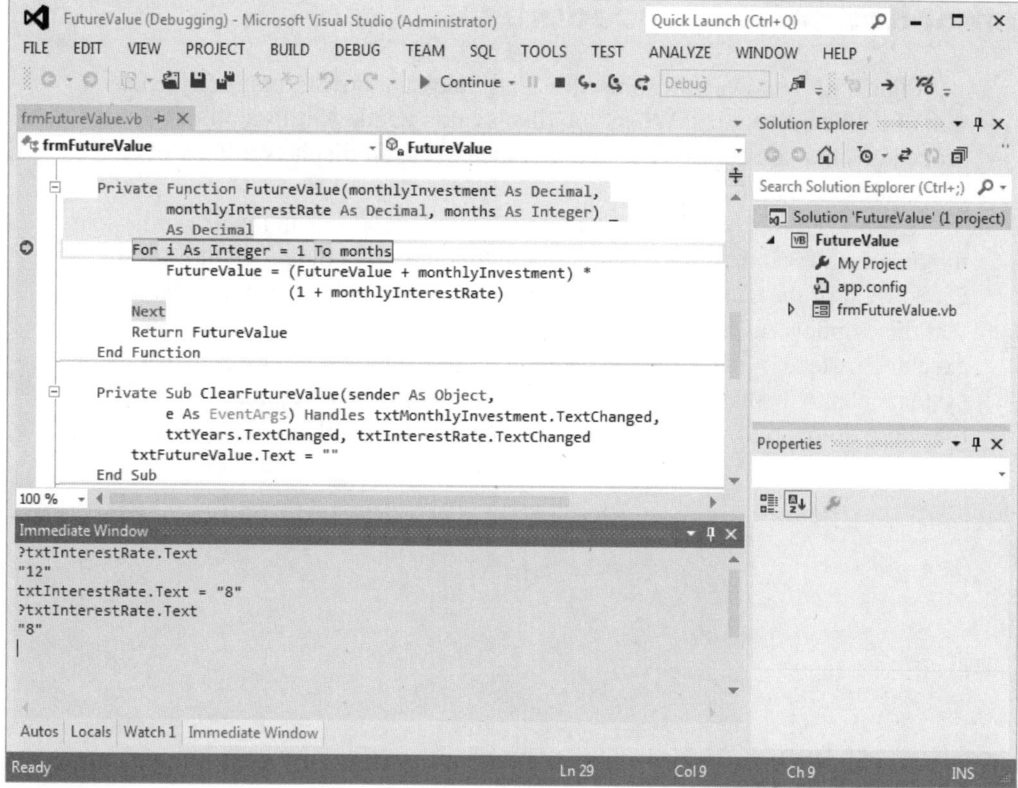

Description

- You can use the Immediate window to display and assign values from an application during execution. To display this window, click on the Immediate Window tab or use the Debug→Windows→Immediate command.
- To display a value, enter a question mark followed by the expression whose value you want to display. Then, press the Enter key.
- To assign a different value to a variable or property, enter an assignment statement. Then, press the Enter key.
- To execute a procedure or method, enter its name and any arguments it requires. Then, press the Enter key. If you want to display the results, precede the procedure or method call with a question mark.
- To reissue a command, use the Up or Down arrow keys to display the command you want. Then, you can edit the command or press the Enter key to execute it.
- To remove all commands and output from the Immediate window, use the Clear All command in the shortcut menu for the window.

Figure 12-8 How to use the Immediate window to execute commands

How to use the Call Stack window to monitor called procedures

Figure 12-9 shows how to use the Call Stack window to monitor the execution of called procedures. When you display this window, it lists all of the procedures that are currently active. In other words, it displays a stack of called procedures, or a *call stack*.

The procedures listed in the Call Stack window appear in reverse order from the order in which they were called. So in this example, the procedure for the Click event of the Calculate button called the FutureValue procedure. Notice that this window displays a single line that indicates that external code has been executed instead of displaying all of the non-user-defined procedures that the system calls to display the Future Value form. Note, however, that you can use the shortcut menu for this window to change what it displays.

The Call Stack window

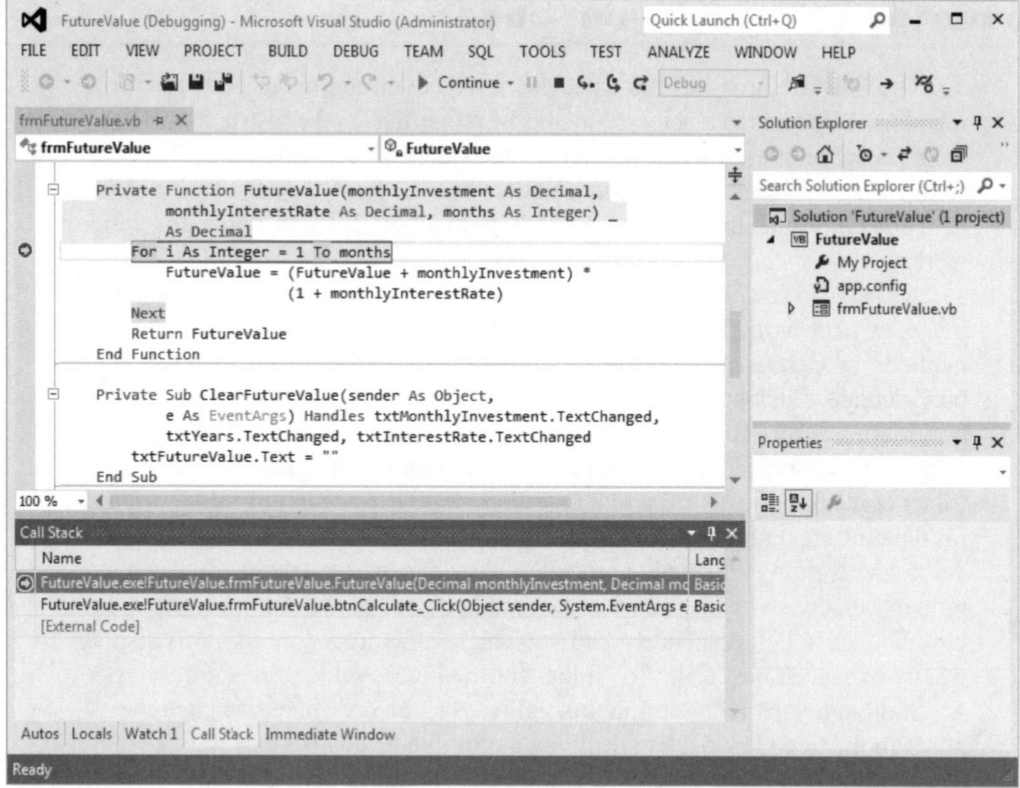

Description

- The Call Stack window lists all of the procedures that are active when an application enters break mode. To display this window, click on the Call Stack tab or use the Debug→Windows→Call Stack command.
- In the Call Stack window, the current procedure is listed at the top of the window, followed by the procedure that called it (if any), and so on. This list of procedure names is referred to as a *call stack*.
- You can use the commands in the shortcut menu for the Call Stack window to control what's displayed in this window.

Figure 12-9 How to use the Call Stack window to monitor called procedures

How to use the Call Hierarchy window to navigate through your code

The Call Hierarchy window lets you navigate through your code by displaying all calls to and from selected methods, properties, and constructors. That includes procedures you add to your forms, which are actually methods of the form class. This can help you better understand the flow of your code, which can help you determine the cause of errors. Figure 12-10 illustrates how this window works.

As you can see, the Call Hierarchy window is divided into two panes. The tree view pane at the left side of the window displays all the calls to and from the methods, properties, and constructors you select. In this example, I selected the btnCalculate_Click and FutureValue procedures. When I expanded each of these procedures, "Calls To" and "Calls From" folders were displayed. The "Calls To" folder for each procedure contains the calls to that method, and the "Calls From" folder contains the calls from that procedure. You can see both of these folders for the btnCalculate_Click procedure in this figure, and you can see the "Calls To" folder for the FutureValue procedure. You can also see the methods and property that were displayed when I expanded the "Calls From" folder for the btnCalculate_Click procedure. And you can see the procedure that was displayed when I expanded the "Calls To" folder for the FutureValue procedure.

Although you can't see it in this figure, you can continue to expand the nodes in the tree view pane to drill down multiple levels. If I expanded the FutureValue procedure subordinate to the "Calls From" folder for the btnCalculate_Click procedure, for example, two additional folders for calls to and calls from the FutureValue procedure would be displayed. Then, if I expanded the "Calls To" folder, the btnCalculate_Click procedure would be displayed. Although this information may not be very useful for a simple application like the one shown here, it should give you an idea of how you might use this window to navigate through a more complicated application.

In addition to listing the calls to and from methods, properties, and constructors, you can select a member in the tree view pane to display a list of the statements that call the member along with the locations of those statements. This information is displayed in the details pane at the right side of the Call Hierarchy window. In this figure, for example, I selected the btnCalculate_Click procedure in the "Calls To" folder for the FutureValue procedure. Then, the statement that calls the FutureValue procedure in the btnCalculate_Click procedure was listed in the details pane.

One more thing you should know about the Call Hierarchy window is that you can display it at either design-time or runtime. That way, you can check the flow of your applications before you run them or as they're executing.

The Call Hierarchy window with two procedures displayed

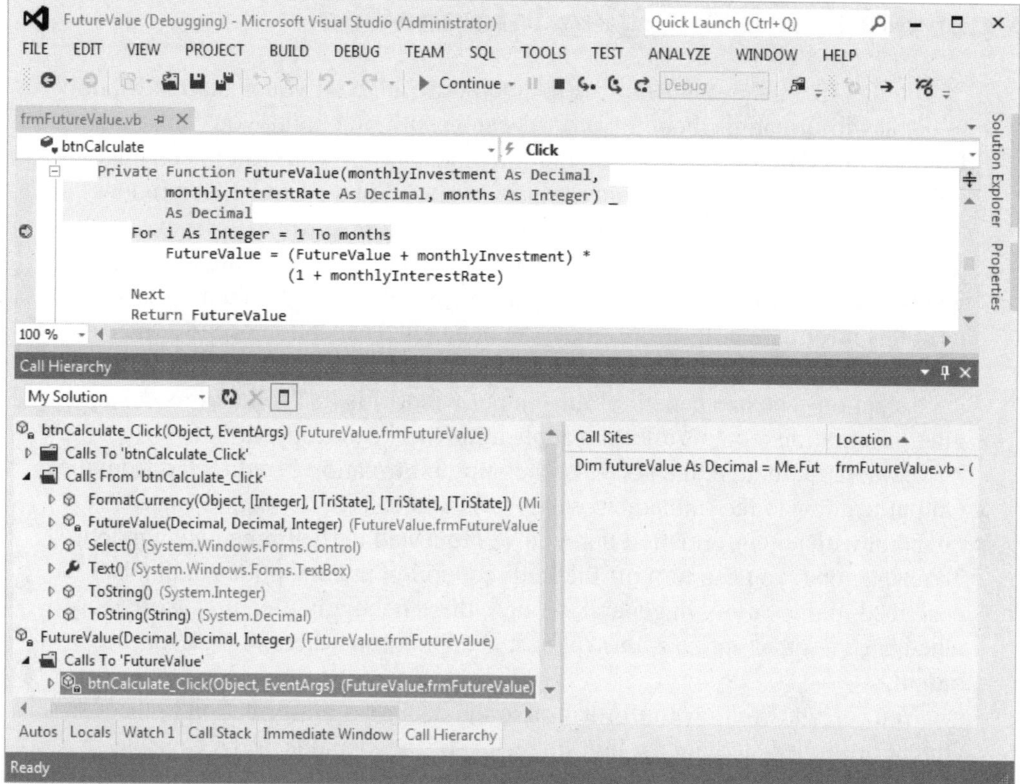

Description

- The Call Hierarchy window displays calls to and from the methods, properties, and constructors you select. To display this window, use the View→Other Windows→Call Hierarchy command. You can display this window at both design-time and at runtime.
- To add a method, property, or constructor to the Call Hierarchy window, right-click on it and then choose the View Call Hierarchy command from the menu that's displayed. This also opens the Call Hierarchy window if it isn't already open.
- To display the calls to or from a member, click the ▷ symbol in the tree view pane. To hide the calls to or from a member, click the ◢ symbol.
- To display the locations of the calls to or from a member in the details pane at the right side of the Call Hierarchy window, click the member in the tree view pane.
- To jump to the location of a member in the Code Editor window, double-click on it in the tree view pane of the Call Hierarchy window. To jump to the location of a call, double-click on it in the details pane.
- To remove a member from the Call Hierarchy window, select the root node for that member and then click the Remove Root button at the top of the window.
- You can use the drop-down list at the top of the Call Hierarchy window to select whether calls in the current document, the current project, or the solution are displayed.

Figure 12-10 How to use the Call Hierarchy window to navigate through your code

How to use the Output or Immediate window to get build or debugging information

Figure 12-11 shows how to use the Output window. If you want this window to display information about the progress and result of a build, you can select Build from its drop-down list. Most of the time, though, you won't need this information, because build errors are also displayed in the Error List window. Then, you can use that window to locate and correct the errors.

Similarly, if you want the Output window to display debugging information, you can select Debug from its drop-down list. But here again, you usually won't need this information. If, for example, an unhandled exception occurs, you can use the information in the Exception Assistant window to identify the cause of the exception. The one benefit of the Output window is that some of its debugging information remains after the application has been stopped.

By default, though, the normal debugging information is redirected from the Output window to the Immediate window. That means that this information is mixed in with any information that you've requested in the Immediate window. To change that, you can turn off the Redirect option in the Options dialog box as described in this figure. In general, though, these debugging features work okay whether or not that option is on. You just need to know where to look for the output.

You can add your own information to the debugging information in the Output or Immediate window by using some of the methods of the Console or Debug class. This is illustrated by the examples in this figure. Here, the WriteLine method of the Console class is used to write information to the Output window. This works whether or not the Redirect option is on.

The WriteLine method of the Debug class works the same way. The only difference is that it sends its output to the Immediate window if the Redirect option is on and to the Output window if the Redirect option is off.

Information like this can be useful for tracing the execution of an application or for documenting the changing value of a property or variable. The advantage of writing information to the Output or Immediate window is that it remains available even when the application is no longer in break mode. As a result, you can review this information after the application has finished running.

Sometimes, you may only want to display data in the Output or Immediate window when a certain condition is True. If, for example, you only want to display the future value every 12 months, you can use an If statement like the one in the second example. Here, the Mod operator is used to check if the month is a multiple of 12. If it is, the WriteLine method displays the future value.

An Output window that displays debugging information

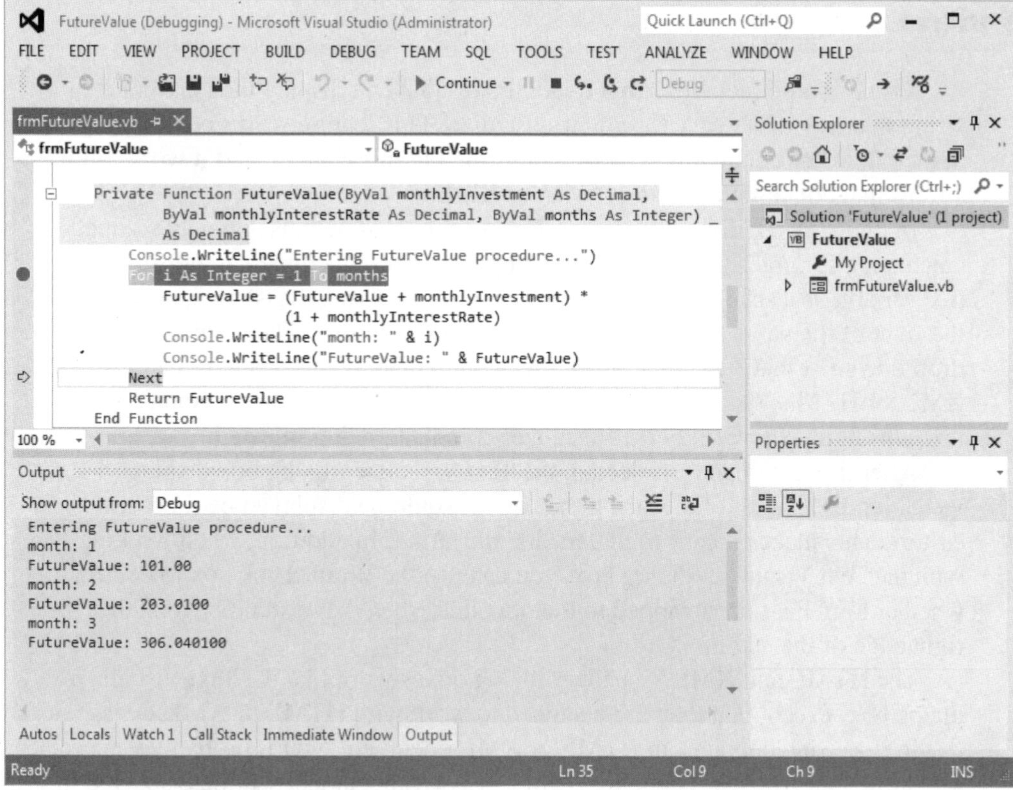

Three statements that write data to the Output window

```
Console.WriteLine("Entering FutureValue procedure...")
Console.WriteLine("month: " & index)
Console.WriteLine("FutureValue: " & FutureValue)
```

An If statement that controls when data is written to the Output window

```
If index Mod 12 = 0 Then
    Console.WriteLine("FutureValue: " & FutureValue)
End If
```

Description

- To display the Output window, use the Debug→Windows→Output command. Then, use the combo box at the top of this window to select build or debug output.
- By default, debugging output is redirected to the Immediate window. If you want to change that, use the Tools→Options command, select the General options in the Debugging group, and uncheck the box for this Redirect option.
- You can use the WriteLine method of the Console class to write data to the Output window. This can be useful for tracing application execution or for documenting changes in the values of variables.
- You can use the WriteLine method of the Debug class to write data to the Immediate window or the Output window, depending on the setting for the Redirect option.

Figure 12-11 How to use the Output or Immediate window for debugging output

How use the Visualizer dialog boxes to view strings

Visual Studio includes some dialog boxes that can display the result of a string in a way that's easy for you to visualize. This feature works consistently across all of the debugging windows described in this chapter, and it works with strings that contain plain text, HTML, or XML.

In figure 12-12, for example, the Locals window contains a variable named calculationVariables that contains a string that represents three variables. Since this variable is a string, the Visualizer icon (a magnifying glass) is displayed to the right of the value that's displayed in the Value column. Then, you can use the drop-down list that's available from this icon to display the string in the Text, XML, or HTML Visualizer dialog box. Since this particular string contains plain text, this figure shows the Text Visualizer command being selected.

After this command is selected, the Text Visualizer dialog box displays a visual representation of the string the way it would be displayed by most text editors. This makes it easy to understand the string. In addition, when working with the Text Visualizer dialog box, you can use the Wrap check box to control whether long lines are wrapped to the next line when they extend beyond the right edge of the text box.

The HTML and XML Visualizer dialog boxes work like the Text Visualizer dialog box, except that they are designed to work with HTML or XML. As a result, if a string contains an HTML or XML document, you'll probably want to use these dialog boxes. Then, the HTML or XML document will be displayed in a user-friendly format.

The Visualizer drop-down menu in the Locals window

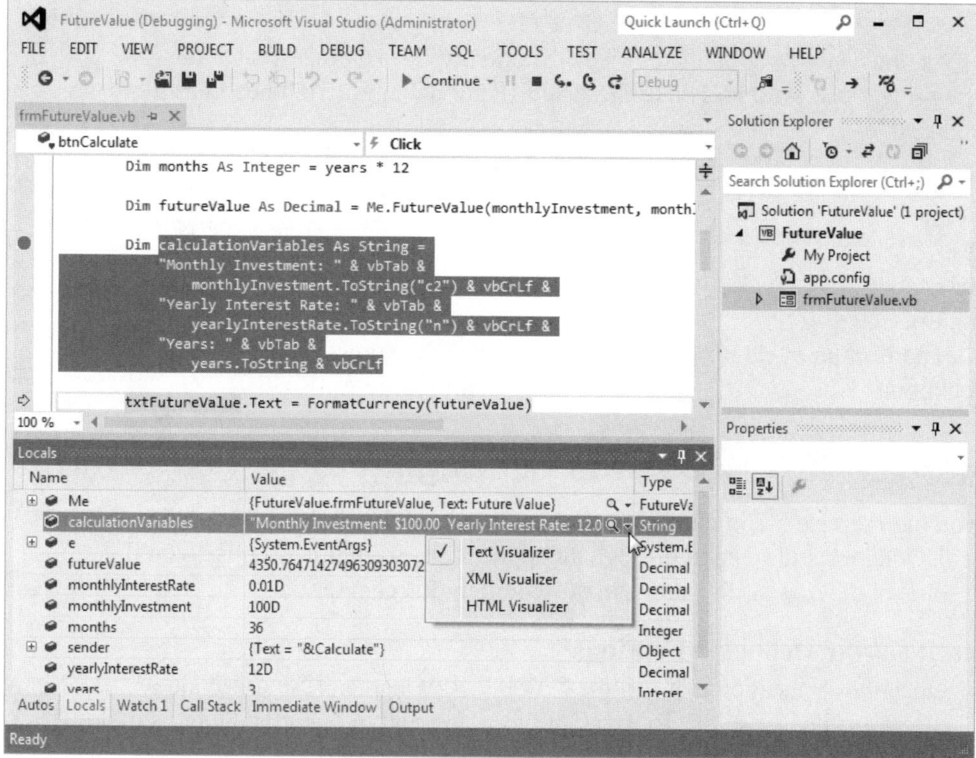

The Text Visualizer dialog box

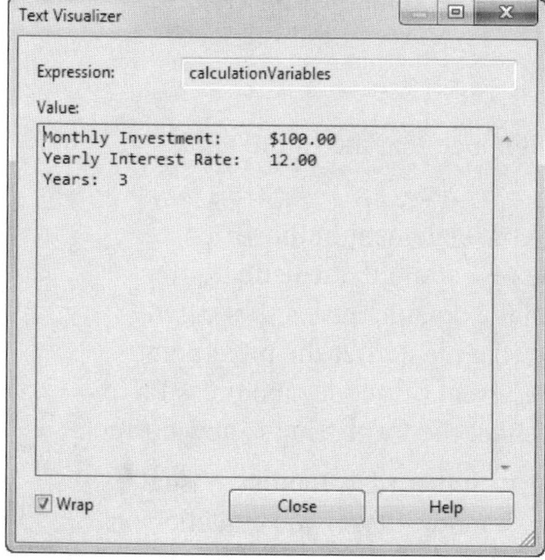

Description

- All string values that are displayed by the debugging windows have a Visualizer icon (a magnifying glass) to their right.
- To display a Visualizer dialog box for the string value, select the appropriate command from the drop-down list that's available from the Visualizer icon.

Figure 12-12 How to use the Visualizer dialog boxes to view strings

Perspective

As you can now appreciate, Visual Studio provides a powerful set of debugging tools. With tools like these, a difficult debugging job becomes more manageable.

Terms

break mode
data tip
Edit and Continue feature
breakpoint
logical error
step through an application
watch expression
call stack

Exercise 12-1 Use the debugging tools

If you did exercise 5-2 in chapter 5, you've already set breakpoints, used the Locals window, and stepped through an application. So in this exercise, you'll use some of the new skills that were presented in this chapter.

Check out the Debugging options

1. Open the application that's in the C:\VB 2012\Chapter 12\FutureValue directory. Then, use the Tools→Options command to open the Options dialog box.
2. Review the options in the Debugging group. In particular, notice that the Redirect all Output Window text to the Immediate Window option in the General options is selected by default.

Use the Edit and Continue feature

3. Run the project with the default entries, and notice that the future value amount is formatted as a percent.
4. End the application and set a breakpoint on the statement in the btnCalculate_Click procedure that calls the procedure that calculates the future value. Then, run the application with the default entries so it enters break mode. In break mode, notice that the statement after the breakpoint uses p instead of c as the formatting code. Correct this code, and press F5 to continue running the application and notice that the formatting is now correct.
5. This illustrates the Edit and Continue feature. Sometimes, though, Visual Studio won't let you change the code in break mode. Then, you can click on the Stop Debugging button, make the change, and restart the application.

Use the Locals windows

6. Click on the Calculate button to enter break mode again, display the Locals window, click on the plus sign to the left of the Me keyword, scroll down to txtMonthlyInvestment, and click on its plus sign to expand this entry. Then, scroll down to the Text property to see its string value and the Visualizer icon in the Value column.

7. Use the Visualizer icon to display the value in the Text Visualizer dialog box. Then, close this dialog box, and click on the minus sign to the left of the Me keyword to collapse this entry.
8. Press F11 to step through the statements. Notice the parameters and variables that are displayed in the Locals window at each step. Then, set a second breakpoint on the last statement in the FutureValue procedure (the Return statement), and press F5 to run the application until it enters break mode again. Now, you can see the final values for the calculation.
9. Press F5 to restart the application and display the Future Value form. Click on the Calculate button to start another calculation and enter break mode again. Next, locate the months variable in the Locals window, double-click in the Value column, enter 24, and press the Enter key to change the value. Then, press F5 to continue execution, and notice that 24 is used as the value of the months variable in the future value calculation.

Use the Breakpoints window to disable both breakpoints

10. Display the Breakpoints window and click the Disable All Breakpoints button at the top of the Breakpoints window. This disables both break points without removing them. Then, press F5 to continue execution. Since no breakpoints are enabled, this should display the Future Value form.
11. Click the Exit button to end the program. Then, click the Enable All Breakpoints button in the Breakpoints window to enable both breakpoints, and run the application until it enters break mode at the first breakpoint.

Use the Immediate window to work with a variable and a method

12. Display the Immediate window, and display the value of the months variable in this window. Then, display the percentage format of the monthly interest rate by calling the ToString method from the monthlyInterestRate variable like this:

```
? monthlyInterestRate.ToString("p")
```

13. Assign a value of 12 to the months variable by entering an assignment statement in the Immediate window. Then, continue running the application so you can see that this value is used in the calculations.

Use a Watch window to monitor expressions

14. Delete the two breakpoints that you've set, and set a new breakpoint on the assignment statement in the body of the For loop for the FutureValue procedure.
15. Run the application one more time with a value of 1 for the years entry. When the application enters break mode, display a Watch window, highlight the FutureValue variable, and drag it to that window. Next, drag the index variable to that window. Then, click in the Name column of the first blank row in the Watch window and enter this expression:

```
i < months
```

16. Press F11 to step through the For loop and check the values in the Watch window until the value of i < months becomes False.

Use the Output window

17. Use the Console.WriteLine method in the FutureValue procedure to display the values of the i and FutureValue variables each time through the loop. Then, run the application and check the Output window to see how these values are displayed.
18. Change the Console.WriteLine methods to Debug.WriteLine methods, run the application again, and check the Immediate window to see how the output is displayed.
19. When you're through experimenting, close the project.

Exercise 12-2 Step through the Product Maintenance application

In this exercise, you'll see how stepping through a project that contains multiple forms and classes can help you understand how it works.

1. Open the application that's in the C:\VB 2012\Chapter 12\ProductMaintenance directory. This is the application that you studied in chapter 11. It consists of two form classes and three other classes.
2. Set a breakpoint on the first statement in the Load event handler for the Product Maintenance form. Then, start the application, which will enter break mode when it reaches that breakpoint.
3. Use the F11 key to step through the statements in this application. As you step, notice that Visual Studio opens whichever class has the next statement to be executed in the Code Editor window. This lets you see how the flow of the application moves from one procedure and class to another. Whenever necessary, use the Step Out button to execute the remaining statements in a procedure.
4. Display one or more data tips, and experiment with pinning, unpinning, and adding comments to them. When you're through experimenting, end the application and close the project.

Section 3

Database programming

Most real-world applications store their data in databases. As a result, this section is devoted to teaching you the essentials of database programming in Visual Basic. When you complete the four chapters in this section, you should be able to develop substantial database applications. You should also have a solid foundation for learning other ADO.NET techniques on your own.

To start, chapter 13 introduces you to the concepts and terms you need to know when you develop database applications with ADO.NET. Then, chapters 14 and 15 show you how to use Visual Studio's data sources feature to develop database applications quickly and easily. Finally, chapter 16 shows you how to write your own ADO.NET code that uses commands to access the underlying database. When you're done with these chapters, you'll have the basic skills you need to develop database applications of your own.

Remember, though, that you don't have to read the sections in this book in sequence. So if you prefer, you can skip to section 4 or 5 before returning to this section. In particular, you may want to read chapter 24 to learn some skills for enhancing the user interface of your applications. Then, when you have more coding experience, you can return to this section and learn the database programming skills that you're going to need.

13

An introduction to database programming

Before you can develop a database application, you need to be familiar with the concepts and terms that apply to database applications. In particular, you need to understand what a relational database is and how you work with it using SQL and ADO.NET. In this chapter, I'll illustrate these concepts and terms using the *Microsoft SQL Server 2012* database server.

An introduction to client/server systems

In case you aren't familiar with client/server systems, this topic introduces you to their essential hardware and software components. Then, the rest of this chapter presents additional information on these components and on how you can use them in database applications.

The hardware components of a client/server system

Figure 13-1 presents the three hardware components of a *client/server system*: the clients, the network, and the server. The *clients* are usually the PCs that are already available on the desktops throughout a company. And the *network* is made up of the cabling, communication lines, network interface cards, hubs, routers, and other components that connect the clients and the server.

The *server*, commonly referred to as a *database server*, is a computer that has enough processor speed, internal memory (RAM), and disk storage to store the files and databases of the system and provide services to the clients of the system. This computer is usually a high-powered PC, but it can also be a midrange system like an IBM Power System or a Unix system, or even a mainframe system. When a system consists of networks, midrange systems, and mainframe systems, often spread throughout the country or world, it is commonly referred to as an *enterprise system*.

To back up the files of a client/server system, a server usually has a tape drive or some other form of offline storage. It often has one or more printers or specialized devices that can be shared by the users of the system. And it can provide programs or services like email that can be accessed by all the users of the system. In larger networks, however, features such as backup, printing, and email are provided by separate servers. That way, the database server can be dedicated to the task of handling database requests.

In a simple client/server system, the clients and the server are part of a *local area network* (*LAN*). However, two or more LANs that reside at separate geographical locations can be connected as part of a larger network such as a *wide area network* (*WAN*). In addition, individual systems or networks can be connected over the Internet.

A simple client/server system

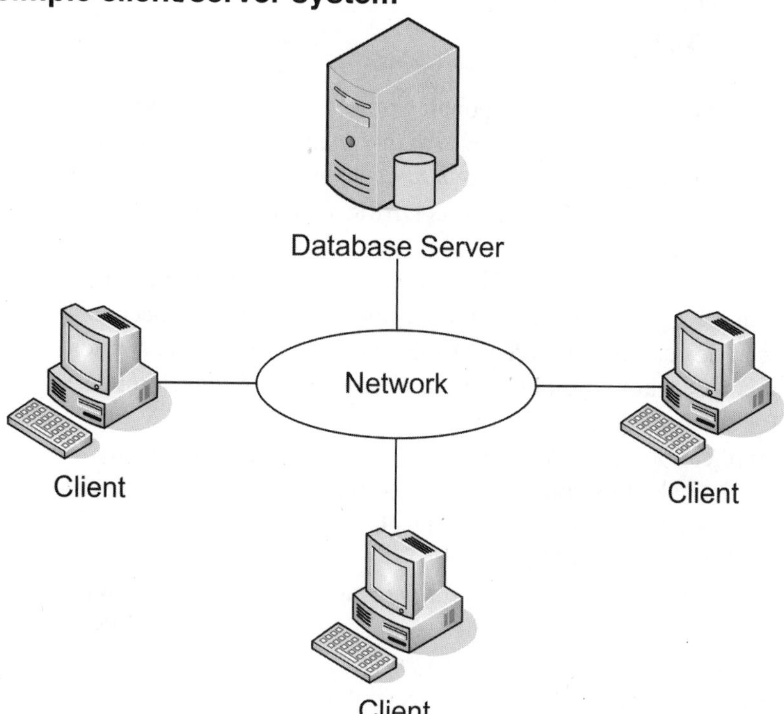

The three hardware components of a client/server system

- The *clients* are the PCs, Macintoshes, or workstations of the system.
- The *server* is a computer that stores the files and databases of the system and provides services to the clients. When it stores databases, it's often referred to as a *database server*.
- The *network* consists of the cabling, communication lines, and other components that connect the clients and the servers of the system.

Client/server system implementations

- In a simple *client/server system* like the one shown above, the server is typically a high-powered PC that communicates with the clients over a *local area network* (*LAN*).
- The server can also be a midrange system, like an IBM Power System or a Unix system, or it can be a mainframe system. Then, special hardware and software components are required to make it possible for the clients to communicate with the midrange and mainframe systems.
- A client/server system can also consist of one or more PC-based systems, one or more midrange systems, and a mainframe system in dispersed geographical locations. This type of system is commonly referred to as an *enterprise system*.
- Individual systems and LANs can be connected and share data over larger private networks, such as a *wide area network* (*WAN*) or a public network like the Internet.

Figure 13-1 The hardware components of a client/server system

The software components of a client/server system

Figure 13-2 presents the software components of a typical client/server system. In addition to a *network operating system* that manages the functions of the network, the server requires a *database management system* (*DBMS*) like Microsoft SQL Server, Oracle, or MySQL. This DBMS manages the databases that are stored on the server.

In contrast to a server, each client requires *application software* to perform useful work. This can be a purchased software package like a financial accounting package, or it can be custom software that's developed for a specific application. This book, of course, shows you how to use Visual Basic for developing custom software for database applications.

Although the application software is run on the client, it uses data that's stored on the server. To make this communication between the client and the data source possible for a Visual Basic application, the client accesses the database via a *data access API* such as ADO.NET 4.5.

Once the software for both client and server is installed, the client communicates with the server by passing *SQL queries* (or just *queries*) to the DBMS through the data access API. These queries are written in a standard language called *Structured Query Language* (*SQL*). SQL lets any application communicate with any DBMS. After the client sends a query to the DBMS, the DBMS interprets the query and sends the results back to the client. (In conversation, SQL is pronounced as either *S-Q-L* or *sequel*.)

As you can see in this figure, the processing done by a client/server system is divided between the clients and the server. In this case, the DBMS on the server is processing requests made by the application running on the client. Theoretically, at least, this balances the workload between the clients and the server so the system works more efficiently. In contrast, in a file-handling system, the clients do all of the work because the server is used only to store the files that are used by the clients.

Client software, server software, and the SQL interface

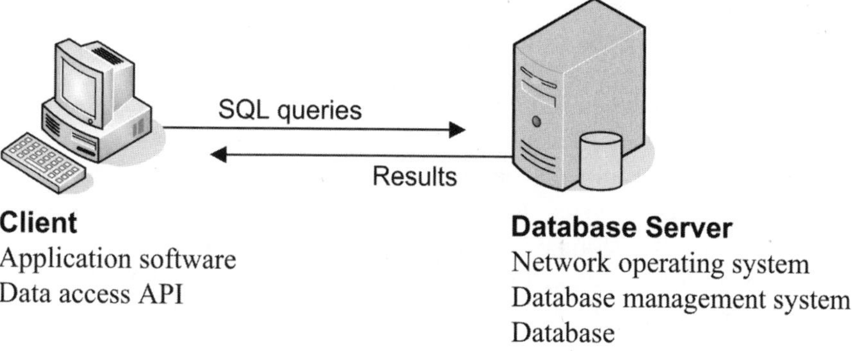

Client
Application software
Data access API

Database Server
Network operating system
Database management system
Database

Server software

- To manage the network, the server runs a *network operating system* such as Windows Server 2012.
- To store and manage the databases of the client/server system, each server requires a *database management system* (*DBMS*) such as Microsoft SQL Server.
- The processing that's done by the DBMS is typically referred to as *back-end processing*, and the database server is referred to as the *back end*.

Client software

- The *application software* does the work that the user wants to do. This type of software can be purchased or developed.
- The *data access API* (*application programming interface*) provides the interface between the application and the DBMS. The newest data access API is ADO.NET 4.5, which is a part of Microsoft's .NET Framework.
- The processing that's done by the client software is typically referred to as *front-end processing*, and the client is typically referred to as the *front end*.

The SQL interface

- The application software communicates with the DBMS by sending *SQL queries* through the data access API. When the DBMS receives a query, it provides a service like returning the requested data (the *query results*) to the client.
- *SQL*, which stands for *Structured Query Language*, is the standard language for working with a relational database.

Client/server versus file-handling systems

- In a client/server system, the processing done by an application is typically divided between the client and the server.
- In a file-handling system, all of the processing is done on the clients. Although the clients may access data that's stored in files on the server, none of the processing is done by the server. As a result, a file-handling system isn't a client/server system.

Figure 13-2 The software components of a client/server system

An introduction to relational databases

In 1970, Dr. E. F. Codd developed a model for what was then a new and revolutionary type of database called a *relational database*. This type of database eliminated some of the problems that were associated with standard files and other database designs. By using the relational model, you can reduce data redundancy, which saves disk storage and leads to efficient data retrieval. You can also view and manipulate data in a way that is both intuitive and efficient. Today, relational databases are the de facto standard for database applications.

How a table is organized

The model for a relational database states that data is stored in one or more *tables*. It also states that each table can be viewed as a two-dimensional matrix consisting of *rows* and *columns*. This is illustrated by the relational table in figure 13-3. Each row in this table contains information about a single product.

In practice, the rows and columns of a relational database table are sometimes referred to by the more traditional terms, *records* and *fields*. In fact, some software packages use one set of terms, some use the other, and some use a combination.

If a table contains one or more columns that uniquely identify each row in the table, you can define these columns as the *primary key* of the table. For instance, the primary key of the Products table in this figure is the ProductCode column.

In this example, the primary key consists of a single column. However, a primary key can also consist of two or more columns, in which case it's called a *composite primary key*.

In addition to primary keys, some database management systems let you define additional keys that uniquely identify each row in a table, called *non-primary keys*. In SQL Server, these keys are also called *unique keys*, and they're implemented by defining *unique key constraints* (also known simply as *unique constraints*). The only difference between a unique key and a primary key is that a unique key can be null and a primary key can't.

Indexes provide an efficient way to access the rows in a table based on the values in one or more columns. Because applications typically access the rows in a table by referring to their key values, an index is automatically created for each key you define. However, you can define indexes for other columns as well. If, for example, you frequently need to sort the rows in the Products table by the Description column, you can set up an index for that column. Like a key, an index can include one or more columns.

The Products table in the MMABooks database

Primary key | Columns | Rows

ProductCode	Description	UnitPrice	OnHandQuantity
ACS45	Murach's ASP.NET 4.5 Web Programming with C# 2012	56.5000	4637
ADC4	Murach's ADO.NET 4 with C# 2010	56.5000	3756
ADV4	Murach's ADO.NET 4 with VB 2010	56.5000	4538
AVB45	Murach's ASP.NET 4.5 Web Programming with VB 2012	56.5000	3974
CRFC	Murach's CICS Desk Reference	50.0000	1865
CS12	Murach's C# 2012	56.5000	5136
DB1R	DB2 for the COBOL Programmer, Part 1 (2nd Edition)	42.0000	4825
DB2R	DB2 for the COBOL Programmer, Part 2 (2nd Edition)	45.0000	621
JAVP	Murach's Java Programming	56.5000	3455
JSP2	Murach's JAVA Servlets and JSP (2nd Edition)	52.5000	4999
MCBL	Murach's Structured COBOL	62.5000	2386
MCCP	Murach's CICS for the COBOL Programmer	54.0000	2368
MDOM	Murach's JavaScript and DOM Scripting	54.5000	6937
SQ12	Murach's SQL Server 2012	57.5000	2465
VB10	Murach's Visual Basic 2010	56.5000	2193
ZJLR	Murach's OS/390 and z/os JCL	62.5000	677

Concepts

- A *relational database* uses *tables* to store and manipulate data. Each table consists of one or more *records*, or *rows*, that contain the data for a single entry. Each row contains one or more *fields*, or *columns*, with each column representing a single item of data.
- Most tables contain a *primary key* that uniquely identifies each row in the table. The primary key often consists of a single column, but it can also consist of two or more columns. If a primary key uses two or more columns, it's called a *composite primary key*.
- In addition to primary keys, some database management systems let you define one or more *non-primary keys*. In SQL Server, these keys are called *unique keys*, and they're implemented using *unique key constraints*. Like a primary key, a non-primary key uniquely identifies each row in the table.
- A table can also be defined with one or more *indexes*. An index provides an efficient way to access data from a table based on the values in specific columns. An index is automatically created for a table's primary and non-primary keys.

Figure 13-3 How a table is organized

How the tables in a database are related

The tables in a relational database can be related to other tables by values in specific columns. The two tables shown in figure 13-4 illustrate this concept. Here, each row in an Invoices table is related to one or more rows in an InvoiceLineItems table. This is called a *one-to-many relationship*.

Typically, relationships exist between the primary key in one table and the *foreign key* in another table. The foreign key is simply one or more columns in a table that refer to a primary key in another table. In SQL Server, relationships can also exist between a unique key in one table and a foreign key in another table. For simplicity, though, I'll assume relationships are based on primary keys.

Although it isn't apparent in this figure, the InvoiceLineItems table has a composite primary key that consists of two columns: InvoiceID and ProductCode. As a result, any row in the InvoiceLineItems table can be uniquely identified by a combination of its invoice ID and product code. However, the InvoiceLineItems table can have more than one row for a given invoice ID and more than one row for a given product code.

One-to-many relationships are the most common type of database relationship. However, two tables can also have a one-to-one or many-to-many relationship. If a table has a *one-to-one relationship* with another table, the data in the two tables could be stored in a single table. Because of that, one-to-one relationships are used infrequently.

In contrast, a *many-to-many relationship* is usually implemented by using an intermediate table, called a *linking table*, that has a one-to-many relationship with the two tables in the many-to-many relationship. In other words, a many-to-many relationship can usually be broken down into two one-to-many relationships.

The relationship between the Invoices and InvoiceLineItems tables

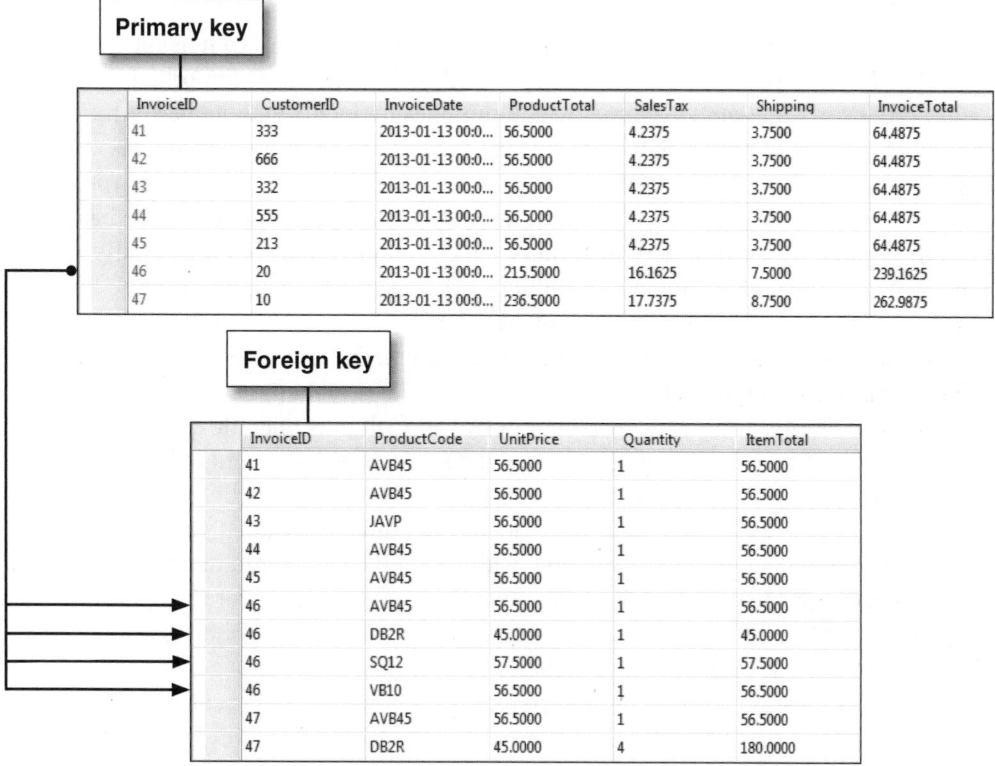

InvoiceID	CustomerID	InvoiceDate	ProductTotal	SalesTax	Shipping	InvoiceTotal
41	333	2013-01-13 00:0...	56.5000	4.2375	3.7500	64.4875
42	666	2013-01-13 00:0...	56.5000	4.2375	3.7500	64.4875
43	332	2013-01-13 00:0...	56.5000	4.2375	3.7500	64.4875
44	555	2013-01-13 00:0...	56.5000	4.2375	3.7500	64.4875
45	213	2013-01-13 00:0...	56.5000	4.2375	3.7500	64.4875
46	20	2013-01-13 00:0...	215.5000	16.1625	7.5000	239.1625
47	10	2013-01-13 00:0...	236.5000	17.7375	8.7500	262.9875

InvoiceID	ProductCode	UnitPrice	Quantity	ItemTotal
41	AVB45	56.5000	1	56.5000
42	AVB45	56.5000	1	56.5000
43	JAVP	56.5000	1	56.5000
44	AVB45	56.5000	1	56.5000
45	AVB45	56.5000	1	56.5000
46	AVB45	56.5000	1	56.5000
46	DB2R	45.0000	1	45.0000
46	SQ12	57.5000	1	57.5000
46	VB10	56.5000	1	56.5000
47	AVB45	56.5000	1	56.5000
47	DB2R	45.0000	4	180.0000

Concepts

- The tables in a relational database are related to each other through their key columns. For example, the InvoiceID column is used to relate the Invoices and InvoiceLineItems tables above. The InvoiceID column in the InvoiceLineItems table is called a *foreign key* because it identifies a related row in the Invoices table.
- Usually, a foreign key corresponds to the primary key in the related table. In SQL Server, however, a foreign key can also correspond to a unique key in the related table.
- When two tables are related via a foreign key, the table with the foreign key is referred to as the *foreign key table* and the table with the primary key is referred to as the *primary key table*.
- The relationships between the tables in a database correspond to the relationships between the entities they represent. The most common type of relationship is a *one-to-many relationship* as illustrated by the Invoices and InvoiceLineItems tables. A table can also have a *one-to-one relationship* or a *many-to-many relationship* with another table.

Figure 13-4 How the tables in a database are related

How the columns in a table are defined

When you define a column in a table, you assign properties to it as indicated by the design of the Products table in figure 13-5. The two most important properties for a column are Name, which provides an identifying name for the column, and Data Type, which specifies the type of information that can be stored in the column. With SQL Server, you can choose from *system data types* like the ones in this figure, and you can define your own data types that are based on the system data types. As you define each column in a table, you generally try to assign the data type that will minimize the use of disk storage because that will improve the performance of the queries later.

In addition to a data type, you must indicate whether the column can be *null*. Null represents a value that's unknown, unavailable, or not applicable. It isn't the same as an empty string or a zero numeric value. Columns that allow nulls often require additional programming, so many database designers avoid columns that allow nulls unless they're absolutely necessary.

You can also assign a *default value* to each column. Then, that value is assigned to the column if another value isn't provided. If a column doesn't allow nulls and doesn't have a default value, you must supply a value for the column when you add a new row to the table. Otherwise, an error will occur.

Each table can also contain a numeric column whose value is generated automatically by the DBMS. In SQL Server, a column like this is called an *identity column*. Identity columns are often used as the primary key for a table.

A *check constraint* defines the acceptable values for a column. For example, you can define a check constraint for the Invoices table in this figure to make sure that the ProductTotal column is greater than zero. A check constraint like this can be defined at the column level because it refers only to the column it constrains. If the check constraint for a column needs to refer to other columns in the table, however, it can be defined at the table level.

After you define the constraints for a database, they're managed by the DBMS. If, for example, a user tries to add a row with data that violates a constraint, the DBMS sends an appropriate error code back to the application without adding the row to the database. The application can then respond to the error code.

An alternative to constraints is to validate the data that is going to be added to a database before the program tries to add it. That way, the constraints shouldn't be needed and the program should run more efficiently. In many cases, both data validation and constraints are used. That way, the programs run more efficiently if the data validation routines work, but the constraints are there in case the data validation routines don't work or aren't coded.

The Server Explorer design view window for the Invoices table

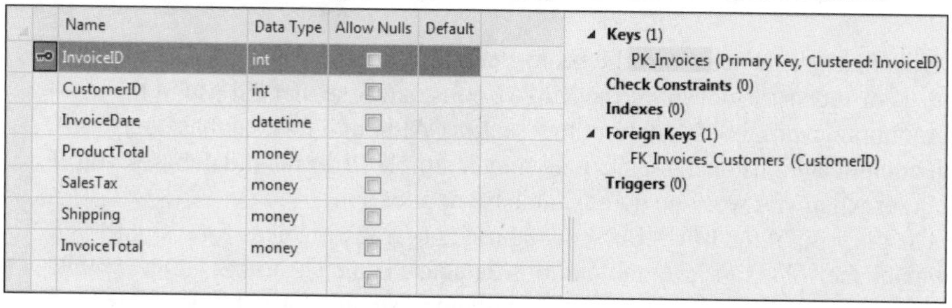

Name	Data Type	Allow Nulls	Default
InvoiceID	int	☐	
CustomerID	int	☐	
InvoiceDate	datetime	☐	
ProductTotal	money	☐	
SalesTax	money	☐	
Shipping	money	☐	
InvoiceTotal	money	☐	
		☐	

- **Keys** (1)
  - PK_Invoices (Primary Key, Clustered: InvoiceID)
- **Check Constraints** (0)
- **Indexes** (0)
- **Foreign Keys** (1)
  - FK_Invoices_Customers (CustomerID)
- **Triggers** (0)

Common SQL Server data types

Type	Description
bit	A value of 1 or 0 that represents a True or False value.
char, varchar, text	Any combination of letters, symbols, and numbers.
datetime, smalldatetime	Alphanumeric data that represents a date and time. Various formats are acceptable.
decimal, numeric	Numeric data that is accurate to the least significant digit. The data can contain an integer and a fractional portion.
float, real	Floating-point values that contain an approximation of a decimal value.
bigint, int, smallint, tinyint	Numeric data that contains only an integer portion.
money, smallmoney	Monetary values that are accurate to four decimal places.

Description

- The *data type* that's assigned to a column determines the type of information that can be stored in the column. Depending on the data type, the column definition can also include its length, precision, and scale.
- Each column definition also indicates whether or not the column can contain *null values*. A null value indicates that the value of the column is not known.
- A column can be defined with a *default value*. Then, that value is used for the column if another value isn't provided when a row is added to the table.
- A column can also be defined as an *identity column*. An identity column is a numeric column whose value is generated automatically when a row is added to the table.
- To restrict the values that a column can hold, you define *check constraints*. Check constraints can be defined at either the column level or the table level.

Note

- When you select a column in design view, its properties are displayed in the Properties window. Then, you can use this window to change any of the properties of the column, including those that aren't displayed in design view.

Figure 13-5 How the columns in a table are defined

The design of the MMABooks database

Now that you've seen how the basic elements of a relational database work, figure 13-6 shows the design of the MMABooks database that I'll use in the programming examples throughout this section. Although this database may seem complicated, its design is actually much simpler than most databases you'll encounter when you work on actual database applications.

The purpose of the MMABooks database is to track invoices for a small book publisher. The top-level table in this database is the Customers table, which contains one row for each of the customers who have purchased books. This table records the name and address for each customer. The primary key for the Customers table is the CustomerID column. This column is an identity column, so SQL Server automatically generates its value whenever a new customer is created.

Information for each invoice is stored in the Invoices table. Like the Customers table, the primary key for this table, InvoiceID, is an identity column. To relate each invoice to a customer, the Invoices table includes a CustomerID column. A *foreign key constraint* is used to enforce this relationship and maintain *referential integrity*. That way, an invoice can't be added for a customer that doesn't exist. The foreign key constraint also causes deletes to be cascaded from the Customers table to the Invoices table.

The InvoiceLineItems table contains the line item details for each invoice. The primary key for this table is a combination of the InvoiceID and ProductCode columns. The InvoiceID column relates each line item to an invoice, and a foreign key constraint that cascades updates and deletes from the Invoices table is defined to enforce this relationship. The ProductCode column relates each line item to a product in the Products table and gives each line item a unique primary key value.

The Products table records information about the company's products. The primary key for this table is the ProductCode column, which can contain a 10-character code. In addition to the product code, each product row contains a description of the product, the unit price, and the number of units currently on hand.

The Customers table is also related to the States table through its State column. The States table contains the state name and the 2-letter state code for each state. Its primary key is the StateCode column.

The final table in the MMABooks database, OrderOptions, contains information that's used to calculate the sales tax and shipping charges that are applied to each invoice. Because this table consists of a single row, it doesn't have a primary key.

The tables that make up the MMABooks database

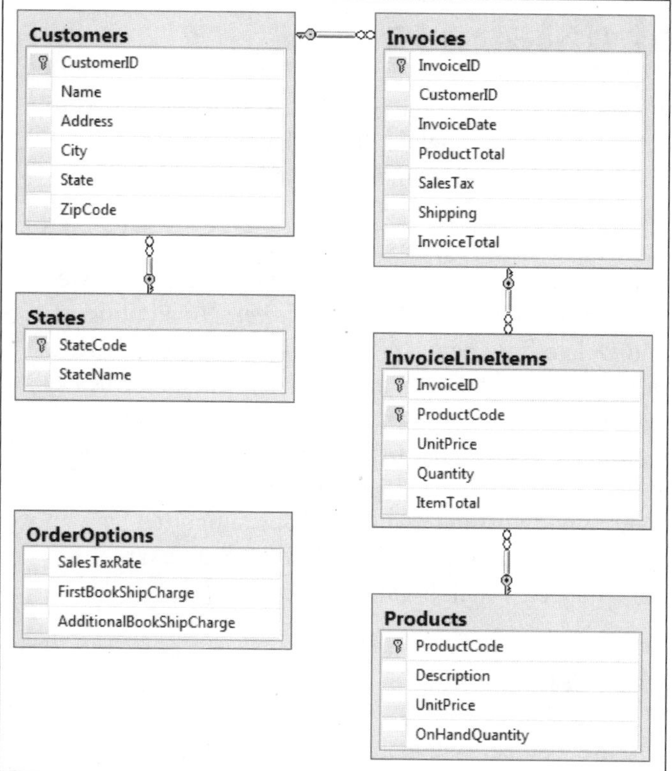

Description

- The Customers table contains a row for each customer. Its primary key is CustomerID, an identity column that's generated automatically when a new customer is created. State is a foreign key that relates each customer to a row in the States table.
- The Invoices table contains a row for each invoice. Its primary key is InvoiceID, an identity column that's generated automatically when a new invoice is created. CustomerID is a foreign key that relates each invoice to a customer.
- The InvoiceLineItems table contains one row for each line item of each invoice. Its primary key is a combination of InvoiceID and ProductCode. InvoiceID is a foreign key that relates each line item to an invoice, and ProductCode is a foreign key that relates each line item to a product.
- The Products table contains a row for each product. Its primary key is ProductCode, a 10-character code that identifies each product.
- The States table contains a row for each state. Its primary key is StateCode.
- The OrderOptions table contains a single row that stores the sales tax and shipping charges used by the application.
- The relationships between the tables in this diagram appear as links, where the endpoints indicate the type of relationship. A key indicates the "one" side of a relationship, and the infinity symbol (∞) indicates the "many" side.

Figure 13-6 The design of the MMABooks database

How to use SQL to work with a relational database

In the topics that follow, you'll learn about the four SQL statements that you can use to manipulate the data in a database: Select, Insert, Update, and Delete. To master the material in this book, you need to understand what these statements do and how they're coded.

Although you'll learn the basics of coding these statements in the topics that follow, you may want to know more than what's presented here. In that case, we recommend our book, *Murach's SQL Server 2012 for Developers*. In addition to the Select, Insert, Update, and Delete statements, this book teaches you how to code the statements that you use to define the data in a database, and it teaches you how to use other features of SQL Server that the top professionals use.

Although SQL is a standard language, each DBMS is likely to have its own *SQL dialect*, which includes extensions to the standard language. So when you use SQL, you need to make sure you're using the dialect that's supported by your DBMS. In this chapter and throughout this book, all of the SQL examples are for Microsoft SQL Server's dialect, which is called *Transact-SQL*.

How to query a single table

Figure 13-7 shows how to use a Select statement to query a single table in a database. In the syntax summary at the top of this figure, you can see that the Select clause names the columns to be retrieved and the From clause names the table that contains the columns. You can also code a Where clause that gives criteria for the rows to be selected. And you can code an Order By clause that names one or more columns that the results should be sorted by and indicates whether each column should be sorted in ascending or descending sequence.

If you study the Select statement below the syntax summary, you can see how this works. Here, the Select statement retrieves two columns from the Customers table for all customers who live in the state of Washington. It sorts the returned rows by the Name column.

This figure also shows the *result table*, or *result set*, that's returned by the Select statement. A result set is a logical table that's created temporarily within the database. When an application requests data from a database, it receives a result set.

Simplified syntax of the Select statement

```
 Select column-1 [, column-2]...
 From table-1
[Where selection-criteria]
[Order By column-1 [Asc|Desc][, column-2 [Asc|Desc]]...]
```

A Select statement that retrieves and sorts selected columns and rows from the Customers table

```
Select Name, City
From Customers
Where State = 'WA'
Order By Name
```

The result set defined by the Select statement

	Name	City
1	Allen, Craig	Pullman
2	Antalocy, S.	Seattle
3	Cassara, Glenn	Van
4	Giraka, Eric	Seatle
5	Hester, Maurice	Kennewickm
6	Howell, Kim	Renton
7	Mcmillen, G	Kirkland
8	Millard, Dwayne	Seattle
9	Oneil, Ri	Olympia
10	Seaver, Glenda	Mountlake Terrace
11	Smith, Lloyd	Pullman
12	Sundaram, Kelly	Oregon

Concepts

- The result of a Select statement is a *result table*, or *result set*, like the one shown above. A result set is a logical set of rows that consists of all of the columns and rows requested by the Select statement.
- The Select clause lists the columns to be included in the result set. This list can include *calculated columns* that are calculated from other columns.
- The From clause names the table the data will be retrieved from.
- The Where clause provides a condition that specifies which rows should be retrieved. To retrieve all rows from a table, omit the Where clause.
- The Order By clause lists the columns that the results are sorted by and indicates whether each column is sorted in ascending or descending sequence.
- To select all of the columns in a table, you can code an asterisk (*) in place of the column names. For example, this statement will select all of the columns from the Customers table:

  ```
  Select * From Customers
  ```

  However, this technique is typically not used in production applications because it can retrieve more data than is needed or introduce errors if the table changes.

Figure 13-7 How to query a single table

How to join data from two or more tables

Figure 13-8 presents the syntax of the Select statement for retrieving data from two tables. This type of operation is called a *join* because the data from the two tables is joined together into a single result set. For example, the Select statement in this figure joins data from the InvoiceLineItems and Products tables into a single result set.

An *inner join* is the most common type of join. When you use an inner join, rows from the two tables in the join are included in the result set only if their related columns match. These matching columns are specified in the From clause of the Select statement. In the Select statement in this figure, for example, rows from the InvoiceLineItems and Products tables are included only if the value of the ProductCode column in the Products table matches the value of the ProductCode column in one or more rows in the InvoiceLineItems table.

Notice that each column in the Select clause is qualified to indicate which table the column is to be retrieved from. For example, the InvoiceID, ProductCode, UnitPrice, and Quantity columns are retrieved from the InvoiceLineItems table, but the Description column comes from the Products table. Qualification is only required for columns that exist in both tables. In this case, only the ProductCode column requires qualification because both the InvoiceLineItems and the Products tables have a column named ProductCode. However, I recommend that you qualify all of the columns just to make it clear which table each column is being retrieved from.

Although this figure shows how to join data from two tables, you should know that you can extend this syntax to join data from additional tables. If, for example, you want to include data from the Invoices table along with the InvoiceLineItems and Products data, you could code a From clause like this:

```
From Invoices
    Inner Join InvoiceLineItems
        On Invoices.InvoiceID = InvoiceLineItems.InvoiceID
    Inner Join Products
        On InvoiceLineItems.ProductCode = Products.ProductCode
```

Then, in the column list of the Select statement, you can include any of the columns in the Invoices, InvoiceLineItems, and Products tables.

The syntax of the Select statement for joining two tables

```
Select column-list
From table-1
    [Inner] Join table-2
    On table-1.column-1 {=|<|>|<=|>=|<>} table-2.column-2
[Where selection-criteria]
[Order By column-list]
```

A Select statement that joins data from the InvoiceLineItems and Products tables

```
Select InvoiceLineItems.InvoiceID, InvoiceLineItems.ProductCode,
       Products.Description, InvoiceLineItems.UnitPrice,
       InvoiceLineItems.Quantity
From InvoiceLineItems
    Inner Join Products
        On Products.ProductCode = InvoiceLineItems.ProductCode
Where InvoiceID = 46
```

The result set defined by the Select statement

	InvoiceID	ProductCode	Description	UnitPrice	Quantity
1	46	AVB45	Murach's ASP.NET 4.5 Web Programming with VB 2012	56.50	1
2	46	DB2R	DB2 for the COBOL Programmer, Part 2 (2nd Edition)	45.00	1
3	46	SQ12	Murach's SQL Server 2012	57.50	1
4	46	VB10	Murach's Visual Basic 2010	56.50	1

Concepts

- A *join* lets you combine data from two or more tables into a single result set.
- The most common type of join is an *inner join*. This type of join returns rows from both tables only if their related columns match.

How to add, update, and delete data in a table

Figure 13-9 presents the basic syntax of the SQL Insert, Update, and Delete statements. You use these statements to add new rows to a table, to update the data in existing rows, and to delete existing rows.

To add a single row to a table, you specify the name of the table you want to add the row to, the names of the columns you're supplying data for, and the values for those columns. The statement in this figure, for example, adds a row to the Products table. If you're going to supply values for all the columns in a table, you can omit the column names. If you do that, though, you must be sure to specify the values in the same order as the columns appear in the table. To avoid errors, I recommend you always code the column list.

Note that if a table includes an identity column, you shouldn't provide a value for that column in an Insert statement. Instead, SQL Server will generate a value for the identity column when it inserts the row.

Also note that you can use single quotes to identify strings. For example, the string for the ProductCode column is enclosed in single quotes. However, if a string value contains a single quote, you can code two single quotes. For example, the string for the Description column uses two single quotes to identify the single quote in *Murach's*.

To change the values of one or more columns in a table, you use the Update statement. On this statement, you specify the name of the table you want to update, expressions that indicate the columns you want to change and how you want to change them, and a condition that identifies the rows you want to change. In the example in this figure, the Update statement changes the UnitPrice column for the product identified by product code MCCP to 54.00.

To delete rows from a table, you use the Delete statement. On this statement, you specify the table you want to delete rows from and a condition that indicates the rows you want to delete. The Delete statement in this figure deletes the row for customer 558 from the Customers table.

How to add a single row

The syntax of the Insert statement for adding a single row

```
Insert [Into] table-name [(column-list)]
    Values (value-list)
```

A statement that adds a single row to the Products table

```
Insert Into Products
    (ProductCode, Description, UnitPrice, OnHandQuantity)
    Values ('VB12', 'Murach''s Visual Basic 2012', 58.50, 3000)
```

How to update rows

The syntax of the Update statement

```
Update table-name
    Set expression-1[, expression-2]...
    [Where selection-criteria]
```

A statement that updates the UnitPrice column for a specified product

```
Update Products
    Set UnitPrice = 54.00
    Where ProductCode = 'MCCP'
```

How to delete rows

The syntax of the Delete statement

```
Delete [From] table-name
    [Where selection-criteria]
```

A statement that deletes a specified customer

```
Delete From Customers
    Where CustomerID = 558
```

Description

- You use the Insert, Update, and Delete statements to maintain the data in a database table.
- The Insert statement can be used to add one or more rows to a table. Although the syntax shown above is for adding just one row, there is another syntax for adding more than one row.
- The Update and Delete statements can be used to update or delete one or more rows in a table using the syntax shown above.

An introduction to ADO.NET

ADO.NET (*ActiveX Data Objects .NET*) is the primary data access API for the .NET Framework. It provides the classes that you use as you develop database applications with Visual Basic as well as other .NET languages. These classes can be divided into two categories: the .NET data providers, which provide the classes that you use to access the data in a database, and datasets, which provide the classes that you use to store and work with data in your applications.

The .NET data providers

A *.NET data provider* is a set of classes that enable you to access data that's managed by a particular database server. All .NET data providers must include core classes for creating the four types of objects listed in the first table in figure 13-10. You'll learn more about how these objects work in the topics that follow.

The second table in this figure lists the four data providers that come with the .NET Framework. The SQL Server data provider is designed to provide efficient access to a Microsoft SQL Server database. The OLE DB data provider is a generic data provider that can access any database that supports the industry standard OLE DB interface. Although you can use the OLE DB data provider to access a SQL Server database, you shouldn't do that unless you plan on migrating the data to another database since the SQL Server data provider is optimized for accessing SQL Server data. The ODBC provider lets you access any database that can work with ODBC, another industry standard database interface. The Oracle provider lets you access data stored in Oracle databases.

Note that the Oracle provider has been deprecated and will be dropped from a future release of the .NET Framework. Because of that, you'll want to avoid using this provider for new application development. Instead, you can use the .NET data provider that is available from Oracle.

In addition to the .NET data provider developed by Oracle, several other database vendors have developed .NET data providers that are optimized for use with their databases. For example, .NET data providers are available for the popular MySQL database and for SQL Anywhere. Before you develop an application using the OLE DB or ODBC providers, then, you should check with your database vendor to see if a specialized .NET data provider is available.

The third table in this figure lists the names of the classes you use to create objects using the SQL Server, OLE DB, ODBC, or Oracle providers. Notice that these classes use prefixes ("Sql," "OleDb," "Odbc," and "Oracle") to indicate which provider each class belongs to.

When you develop a Visual Basic application that uses ADO.NET, you'll want to add an Imports statement for the namespace that contains the data provider classes at the beginning of each source file that uses those classes. That way, you won't have to qualify the references to these classes. These namespaces are listed in the second table in this figure.

.NET data provider core objects

Object	Description
Connection	Establishes a connection to a database.
Command	Represents an individual SQL statement that can be executed against the database.
Data reader	Provides read-only, forward-only access to the data in a database.
Data adapter	Provides the link between the command and connection objects and a dataset object.

Data providers included with the .NET Framework

Provider	Namespace	Description
SQL Server	`System.Data.SqlClient`	Lets you access SQL Server databases.
OLE DB	`System.Data.OleDb`	Lets you access any database that supports OLE DB.
ODBC	`System.Data.Odbc`	Lets you access any database that supports ODBC.
Oracle	`System.Data.OracleClient`	Lets you access Oracle databases.

Class names for the data providers

Object	SQL Server	OLE DB	ODBC	Oracle
Connection	SqlConnection	OleDbConnection	OdbcConnection	OracleConnection
Command	SqlCommand	OleDbCommand	OdbcCommand	OracleCommand
Data reader	SqlDataReader	OleDbDataReader	OdbcDataReader	OracleDataReader
Data adapter	SqlDataAdapter	OleDbDataAdapter	OdbcDataAdapter	OracleDataAdapter

An Imports statement for the SQL Server data provider namespace

```
Imports System.Data.SqlClient
```

Description

- The *.NET data providers* provide the ADO.NET classes that are responsible for working directly with a database. In addition to the core classes shown above, classes are provided for other functions such as passing parameters to commands or working with transactions.
- To use a .NET data provider in a program, you should add an Imports statement for the appropriate namespace at the beginning of the source file. Otherwise, you'll have to qualify each class you refer to with the SqlClient, OleDb, Odbc, or OracleClient namespace since these namespaces aren't included as references by default.
- Other .NET data providers are available to provide efficient access to non-Microsoft databases, such as MySQL and SQL Anywhere.

Note

- The Oracle data provider has been deprecated and will be dropped from a future release of the .NET Framework.

Figure 13-10 The .NET data providers

How the basic ADO.NET components work

Figure 13-11 shows the primary ADO.NET components you use to work with data in a Windows application. To start, the data used by an application is stored in a *dataset* that contains one or more *data tables*. To retrieve data from the database and load it into a data table, you use a *data adapter*.

The main function of the data adapter is to manage the flow of data between a dataset and a database. To do that, it uses *commands* that define the SQL statements to be issued. The command for retrieving data, for example, typically defines a Select statement. Then, the command connects to the database using a *connection* and passes the Select statement to the database. After the Select statement is executed, the result set it produces is sent back to the data adapter, which stores the results in the data table.

To update the data in a database, the data adapter determines which rows in the data table have been inserted, updated, or deleted. Then, it uses commands that define Insert, Update, and Delete statements for the data table to update the associated rows in the database. Like the command that retrieves data from the database, the commands that update the database use a connection to connect to the database and perform the requested operation.

Although it's not apparent in this figure, the data in a dataset is independent of the database that the data was retrieved from. In fact, the connection to the database is typically closed after the data is retrieved from the database. Then, the connection is opened again when it's needed. Because of that, the application must work with the copy of the data that's stored in the dataset. The architecture that's used to implement this type of data processing is referred to as the *disconnected data architecture*.

Although this approach is more complicated than a connected architecture, it has several advantages. One advantage is that using the disconnected architecture can improve system performance due to the use of fewer system resources for maintaining connections. Another advantage is that it makes ADO.NET compatible with ASP.NET web applications, which are inherently disconnected.

Basic ADO.NET components

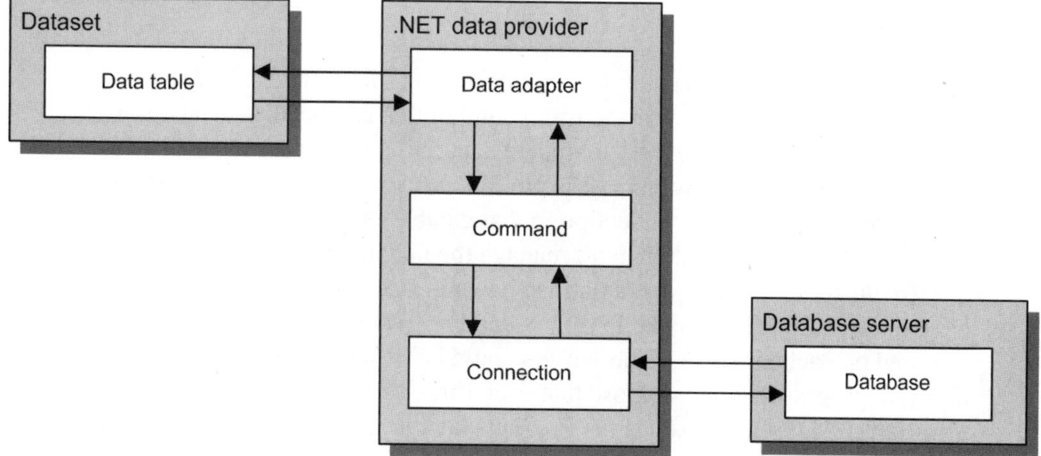

Description

- When you use the .NET data provider objects to retrieve data from a database, you can store the data in an object called a *dataset.*
- A dataset contains one or more *data tables* that store the data from the database. Then, the application can retrieve and work with the data in the data tables, and it can insert, update, and delete rows in the data tables.
- To retrieve data from a database and store it in a data table, a *data adapter* object issues a Select statement that's stored in a *command* object. Next, the command object uses a *connection* object to connect to the database and retrieve the data. Then, the data is passed back to the data adapter, which stores the data in a table within the dataset.
- To update the data in a database based on the data in a data table, the data adapter object issues an Insert, Update, or Delete statement that's stored in a command object. Then, the command object uses a connection to connect to the database and update the data.
- The data provider remains connected to the database only long enough to retrieve or update the specified data. Then, it disconnects from the database and the application works with the data via the dataset object. This is referred to as a *disconnected data architecture.*
- The disconnected data architecture offers improved system performance due to the use of fewer system resources for maintaining connections.

Figure 13-11 How the basic ADO.NET components work

Concurrency and the disconnected data architecture

Although the disconnected data architecture has advantages, it also has some disadvantages. One of those is the conflict that can occur when two or more users retrieve and then try to update data in the same row of a table. This is called a *concurrency* problem. It is possible because once a program retrieves data from a database, the connection to that database is dropped. As a result, the database management system can't manage the update process.

To illustrate, consider the situation shown in figure 13-12. Here, two users have retrieved the Products table from a database, so a copy of the Products table is stored on each user's PC. These users could be using the same program or two different programs. Now, suppose that user 1 modifies the unit price in the row for product ADV4 and updates the Products table in the database. And suppose that user 2 modifies the description in the row for the same product, then tries to update the Products table in the database. What will happen? That depends on the *concurrency control* that's used by the programs.

When you use ADO.NET, you have two choices for concurrency control. By default, a program uses *optimistic concurrency*, which checks whether a row has been changed since it was retrieved. If it has, the update or deletion will be refused and a *concurrency exception* will be thrown. Then, the program should handle the error. For example, it could display an error message that tells the user that the row could not be updated and then retrieve the updated row so the user can make the change again.

In contrast, the "*last in wins*" technique works the way its name implies. Since no checking is done with this technique, the row that's updated by the last user overwrites any changes made to the row by a previous user. For the example above, the row updated by user 2 will overwrite changes made by user 1, which means that the description will be right but the unit price will be wrong. Since errors like this corrupt the data in a database, optimistic concurrency is used by most programs, which means that your programs have to handle the concurrency exceptions that are thrown.

If you know that concurrency will be a problem, you can use a couple of programming techniques to limit concurrency exceptions. If a program uses a dataset, one technique is to update the database frequently so other users can retrieve the current data. The program should also refresh its dataset frequently so it contains the recent changes made by other users.

Another way to avoid concurrency exceptions is to retrieve and work with just one row at a time. That way, it's less likely that two users will update the same row at the same time. In contrast, if two users retrieve the same table, they will of course retrieve the same rows. Then, if they both update the same row in the table, even though it may not be at the same time, a concurrency exception will occur when they try to update the database.

Of course, you will understand and appreciate this more as you learn how to develop your own database applications. As you develop them, though, keep in mind that most applications are multi-user applications. That's why you have to be aware of concurrency problems.

Two users who are working with copies of the same data

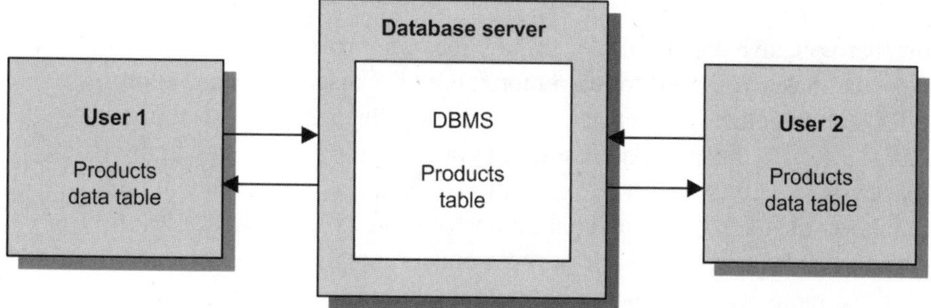

What happens when two users try to update the same row

- When two or more users retrieve the data in the same row of a database table at the same time, it is called *concurrency*. Because ADO.NET uses a disconnected data architecture, the database management system can't prevent this from happening.
- If two users try to update the same row in a database table at the same time, the second user's changes could overwrite the changes made by the first user. Whether or not that happens, though, depends on the *concurrency control* that the programs use.
- By default, ADO.NET uses *optimistic concurrency*. This means that the program checks to see whether the database row that's going to be updated or deleted has been changed since it was retrieved. If it has, a *concurrency exception* occurs and the update or deletion is refused. Then, the program should handle the exception.
- If optimistic concurrency isn't in effect, the program doesn't check to see whether a row has been changed before an update or deletion takes place. Instead, the operation proceeds without throwing an exception. This is referred to as "*last in wins*" because the last update overwrites any previous update. And this can lead to errors in the database.

How to avoid concurrency errors

- For many applications, concurrency errors rarely occur. As a result, optimistic concurrency is adequate because the users will rarely have to resubmit an update or deletion that is refused.
- If concurrency is likely to be a problem, a program that uses a dataset can be designed so it updates the database and refreshes the dataset frequently. That way, concurrency errors are less likely to occur.
- Another way to avoid concurrency errors is to design a program so it retrieves and updates just one row at a time. That way, there's less chance that two users will retrieve and update the same row at the same time.

Figure 13-12 Concurrency and the disconnected data architecture

How a dataset is organized

Now that you have a general idea of how the data provider classes provide access to a database, you need to learn more about the disconnected part of ADO.NET's architecture: the dataset. Figure 13-13 illustrates the basic organization of an ADO.NET dataset. The first thing you should notice in this figure is that a dataset is structured much like a relational database. It can contain one or more tables, and each table can contain one or more columns and rows. In addition, each table can contain one or more constraints that can define a unique key within the table or a foreign key of another table in the dataset. If a dataset contains two or more tables, the dataset can also define the relationships between those tables.

Although a dataset is structured much like a relational database, it's important to realize that each table in a dataset corresponds to the result set that's returned from a Select statement, not necessarily to an actual table in a database. For example, a Select statement may join data from several tables in a database to produce a single result set. In this case, the table in the dataset would represent data from each of the tables involved in the join.

You should also know that each group of objects in the diagram in this figure is stored in a collection. All of the columns in a table, for example, are stored in a collection of columns, and all of the rows are stored in a collection of rows.

The basic dataset object hierarchy

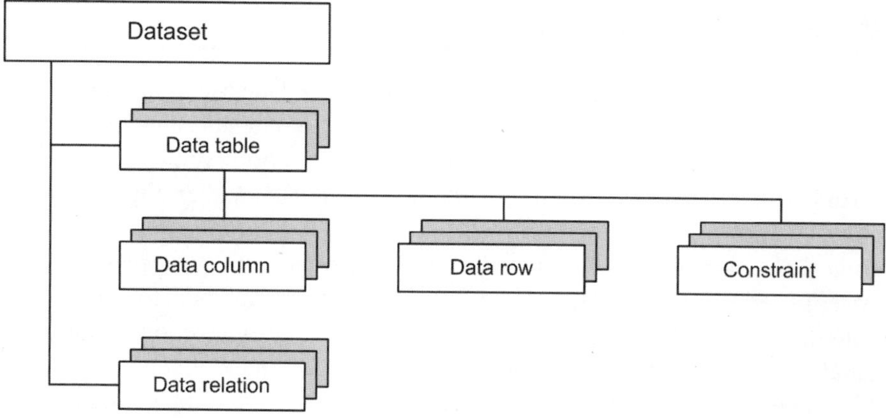

Description

- A dataset object consists of a hierarchy of one or more data table and data relation objects.
- A data table object consists of one or more *data column* objects and one or more *data row* objects. The data column objects define the data in each column of the table, including its name, data type, and so on, and the data row objects contain the data for each row in the table.
- A data table can also contain one or more *constraint* objects that are used to maintain the integrity of the data in the table. A unique key constraint ensures that the values in a column, such as the primary key column, are unique. And a foreign key constraint determines how the rows in one table are affected when corresponding rows in a related table are updated or deleted.
- The data relation objects define how the tables in the dataset are related. They are used to manage constraints and to simplify the navigation between related tables.
- All of the objects in a dataset are stored in collections. For example, the data table objects are stored in a data table collection, and the data row objects are stored in a data row collection. You can refer to these collections through properties of the containing objects.

Figure 13-13 How a dataset is organized

How to work with data without using a data adapter

When you want to work with two or more rows from a database at the same time, you typically use a data adapter to retrieve those rows and store them in a dataset as described earlier in this chapter. You should know, however, that you can also work with the data in a database without using a data adapter. Figure 13-14 shows you how.

As you can see, you still use command and connection objects to access the database. Instead of using a data adapter to execute the commands, though, you execute the commands directly. When you do that, you also have to provide code to handle the result of the command. If you issue a command that contains an Insert, Update, or Delete statement, for example, the result is an integer that indicates the number of rows that were affected by the operation. You can use that information to determine if the operation was successful.

If you execute a command that contains a Select statement, the result is a result set that contains the rows you requested. To read through the rows in the result set, you use a *data reader* object. Although a data reader provides an efficient way of reading the rows in a result set, you can't use it to modify those rows. In addition, it only lets you read rows in a forward direction. Once you read the next row, the previous row is unavailable. Because of that, you typically use a data reader to retrieve and work with a single database row at a time.

ADO.NET components for accessing a database directly

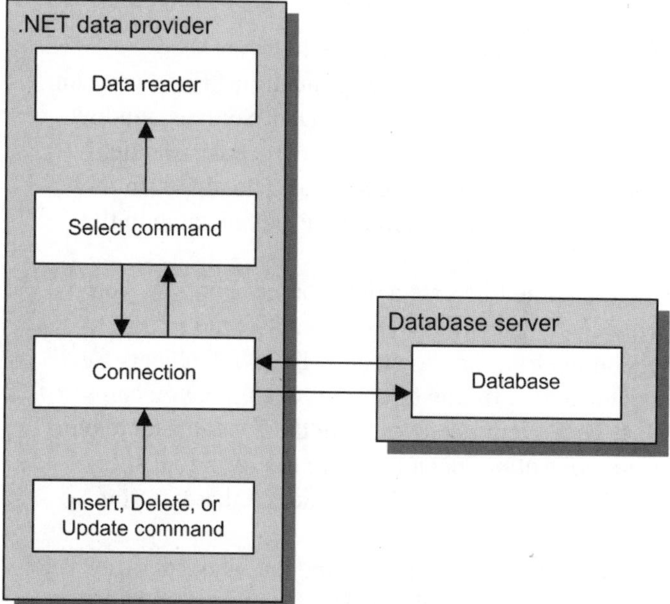

Description

- Instead of using a data adapter to execute commands to retrieve, insert, update, and delete data from a database, you can execute those commands directly.
- To retrieve data from a database, you execute a command object that contains a Select statement. Then, the command object uses a connection to connect to the database and retrieve the data. You can then read the results one row at a time using a *data reader* object.
- To insert, update, or delete data in a database, you execute a command object that contains an Insert, Update, or Delete statement. Then, the command object uses a connection to connect to the database and update the data. You can then check the value that's returned to determine if the operation was successful.
- If you use this technique in an application that maintains the data in a database, you typically work with a single row at a time. Because of that, the chance of a concurrency error is reduced.

Figure 13-14 How to work with data without using a data adapter

Two ways to create ADO.NET objects

Figure 13-15 shows two basic techniques you can use to create the ADO.NET objects you need as you develop database applications. First, you can create ADO.NET objects from a *data source* listed in the Data Sources window. Data sources became available with .NET 2.0, and they make it easy to quickly create forms that work with the data in a data source such as a database. In this example, the data source corresponds with the data in the Products table in the MMABooks database.

In the next chapter, you'll learn how to create a data source. For now, you should know that once you create a data source, you can drag it onto a form to automatically display controls on the form and to create ADO.NET objects for working with the data in the data source. In this figure, for example, you can see the controls and objects that are generated when you drag the Products table onto the form. Here, a DataGridView control has been added to the form to display the products in the Products table, and a toolbar has been added that lets you work with this data.

In addition, five objects have been added to the Component Designer tray below the form. three of these are ADO.NET objects. The first one, named MMABooksDataSet, defines the dataset for the form. Then, an object named ProductsTableAdapter defines the table adapter for the Products table. A *table adapter* is similar to a data adapter, but it can only be generated by the designer. You'll learn more about table adapters in the next chapter. Finally, an object named TableAdapterManager makes sure that if two or more related tables are updated by the form, referential integrity is maintained.

The other two objects in the Component Designer tray are used to bind the controls on the form to the data source. The first object, named ProductsBindingSource, identifies the Products table as the data source for the controls. The second object, named ProductsBindingNavigator, defines the toolbar that's displayed across the top of the form.

Although you don't usually need to change the properties of the objects in the Component Designer tray, you should know that you can do that using the same technique you use to change the properties of a control on a form. That is, you just select an object to display its properties in the Properties window and then work with them from there.

The second technique for creating ADO.NET objects is to write the code yourself. The code shown in this figure, for example, creates four objects: a connection, a command named selectCommand that contains a Select statement, a data adapter named productsDataAdapter, and a dataset named productsDataSet.

Although creating ADO.NET objects through code is more time-consuming than using data sources, it can result in more compact and efficient code. In addition, creating ADO.NET objects through code lets you encapsulate an application's database processing in specialized database classes. You'll learn how this works in chapter 16.

ADO.NET objects created using the Data Sources window

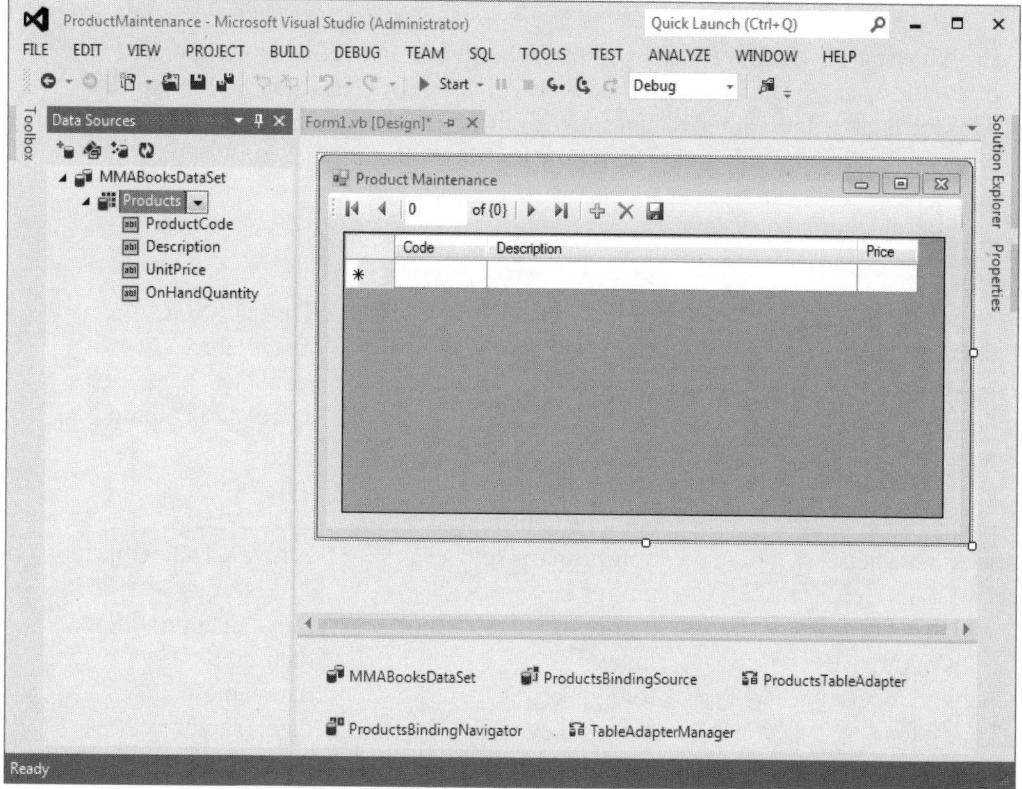

ADO.NET objects created using code

```
Dim connectionString As String =
    "Data Source=localhost\SqlExpress;Initial Catalog=MMABooks;" &
    "Integrated Security=True"
Dim connection As New SqlConnection(connectionString)

Dim selectStatement As String =
    "SELECT * FROM Products ORDER BY ProductCode"
Dim selectCommand As New SqlCommand(selectStatement, connection)

Dim productsDataAdapter As New SqlDataAdapter(selectCommand)

Dim productsDataSet As DataSet = New DataSet
```

Description

- You can use the Data Sources window to create a *data source*. Then, you can drag the data source onto the form to automatically generate a table adapter object and a dataset. A *table adapter* is similar to a data adapter, but it can only be generated by the designer, it has a built-in connection object, and it can contain more than one query. You'll learn how to work with data sources and table adapters in chapter 14.
- To create ADO.NET objects in code, you write a declaration that identifies the class each object is created from. You'll learn how to write code like this in chapter 16.

Figure 13-15 Two ways to work with ADO.NET objects

Perspective

This chapter has introduced you to the hardware and software components of a multi-user system and described how you use ADO.NET and SQL to work with the data in a relational database. With that as background, you're now ready to develop a database application with Visual Basic 2012.

Terms

Microsoft SQL Server
client
server
database server
network
client/server system
enterprise system
local area network (LAN)
wide area network (WAN)
network operating system
database management system (DBMS)
back-end processing
application software
data source
data access API
application programming interface
front-end processing
SQL query
query
Structured Query Language (SQL)
query results
relational database
table
record
row
field
column
primary key
composite primary key
non-primary key
unique key
unique key constraint
index
foreign key
foreign key table
primary key table
one-to-many relationship
one-to-one relationship
many-to-many relationship
linking table
data type
system data type
null value
default value
identity column
check constraint
foreign key constraint
referential integrity
SQL dialect
Transact-SQL
result table
result set
calculated column
join
inner join
ADO.NET
ActiveX Data Objects .NET
.NET data provider
dataset
data table
data adapter
command
connection
disconnected data architecture
concurrency
concurrency control
optimistic concurrency
concurrency exception
"last in wins"
data relation
data column
data row
constraint
data reader
data source
table adapter

14

How to work with data sources and datasets

In this chapter, you'll learn how to use data sources and datasets to develop database applications. This is the easiest way to generate Windows forms that work with the data in a database. And this is especially useful for developing simple applications or prototyping larger applications.

All of the applications in this chapter and the rest of the chapters in this section use the Microsoft *SQL Server 2012 Express LocalDB* database engine that comes with Visual Studio 2012. Because LocalDB is based on SQL Server 2012, the applications you develop with LocalDB are compatible with applications you develop with SQL Server 2012. The only difference is the connection string you use to connect to the database.

How to create a data source

As its name implies, a *data source* specifies the source of the data for an application. Since most applications get their data from a database, the next six figures show how to create a data source that gets data from a database.

How to use the Data Sources window

The data sources that are available to a project are listed in the Data Sources window as shown in figure 14-1. Here, the second screen shows a data source for the Products table that's available from the MMABooks database described in the previous chapter. As you can see, this data source includes three columns from the Products table named ProductCode, Description, and UnitPrice.

If no data sources are available to a project, the Data Sources window will display an Add New Data Source link as shown in the first screen. Then, you can click on this link to start the Data Source Configuration Wizard described in figures 14-2 through 14-6. This wizard lets you add a new data source to the project. When you're done, you can drag the data source onto a form to create bound controls as described later in this chapter.

An empty Data Sources window

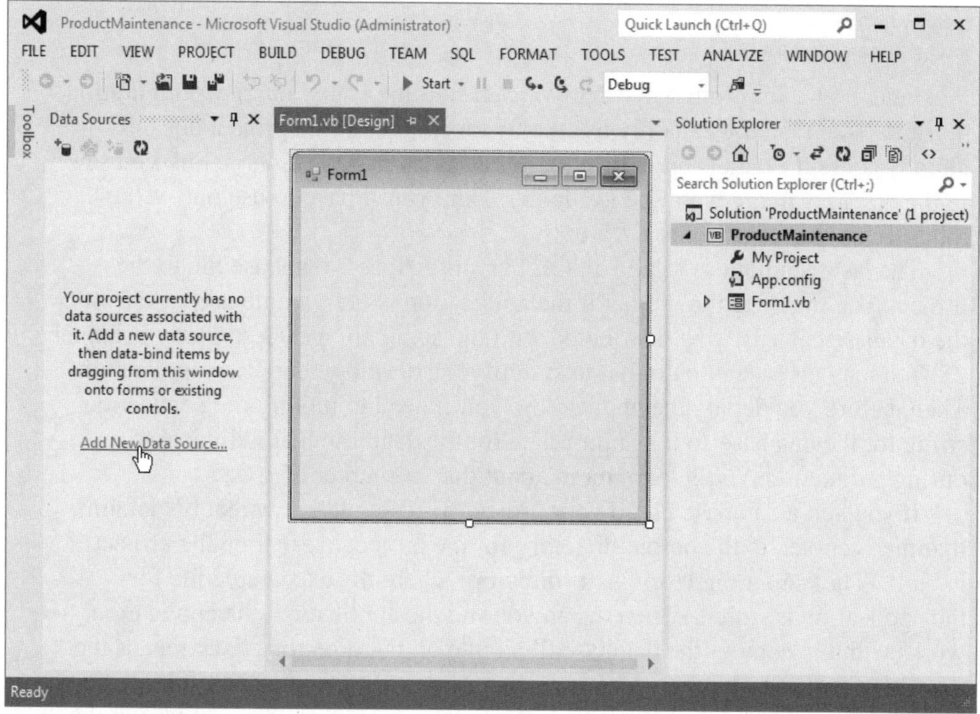

A Data Sources window after a data source has been added

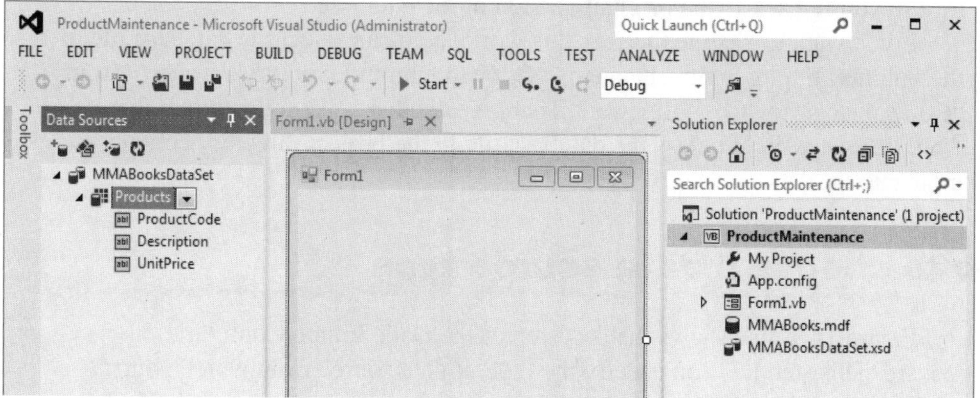

Description

- A *data source* shows all the tables and columns in the dataset that are available to your application.
- You can display the Data Sources window by clicking on the Data Sources tab that usually appears at the left edge of the Visual Studio window or by selecting the Data Sources command from the View→Other Windows menu.
- To create a data source, you can click the Add New Data Source link. Then, you can drag the data source to a form to create controls that are bound to the data source.

Figure 14-1 How to use the Data Sources window

How to start the Data Source Configuration Wizard

Figure 14-2 lists four ways that you can start the Data Source Configuration Wizard. Note that you can only use the first technique if the project doesn't already contain a data source. If it does, the Add New Data Source link you saw in the previous figure won't be available. Then, you'll have to use one of the other techniques to start the wizard.

The last technique is to add a SQL Server or Access database file to the project. You may want to do that if the application is for a single user. That way, the database can easily be distributed with the application as described in chapter 25. You may also want to do that to simplify the development of an application. Then, before you deploy the application, you'll need to modify the connection string for the database so it's appropriate for the database that will be used during production. You'll learn more about that in chapter 25 too.

If you add a database file to your project, you should know that by default, that file is copied to the output directory for the project every time the project is built. (The output directory is the directory where the executable file for the application is stored.) Then, when you run the application, the application works with the copy of the database file in the output directory. That means that any changes you make to the database aren't applied to the database file in the project directory. And each time you rebuild the application, the database in the output directory is overwritten by the unchanged database in the project directory so you're back to the original version of the database.

If you want to change the way this works, you can select the database file in the Solution Explorer and change its "Copy to Output Directory" property from "Copy always" to "Copy if newer." Then, the database file in the output directory won't be overwritten unless the database file in the project directory contains more current data.

How to choose a data source type

Figure 14-2 also shows the first step of the Data Source Configuration Wizard. This step lets you specify the type of data source from which your application will get its data. To work with data from a database as described in this chapter, you select the Database option.

You can also select the Service option to work with data from a Windows Communication Foundation (WCF) service, a data service developed using WCF Data Services, or a web service. You can select the Object option to work with data that's stored in a business object. Or you can select the SharePoint option to work with data from a SharePoint site. For more information on these options, please see Visual Studio help.

The first step of the Data Source Configuration Wizard

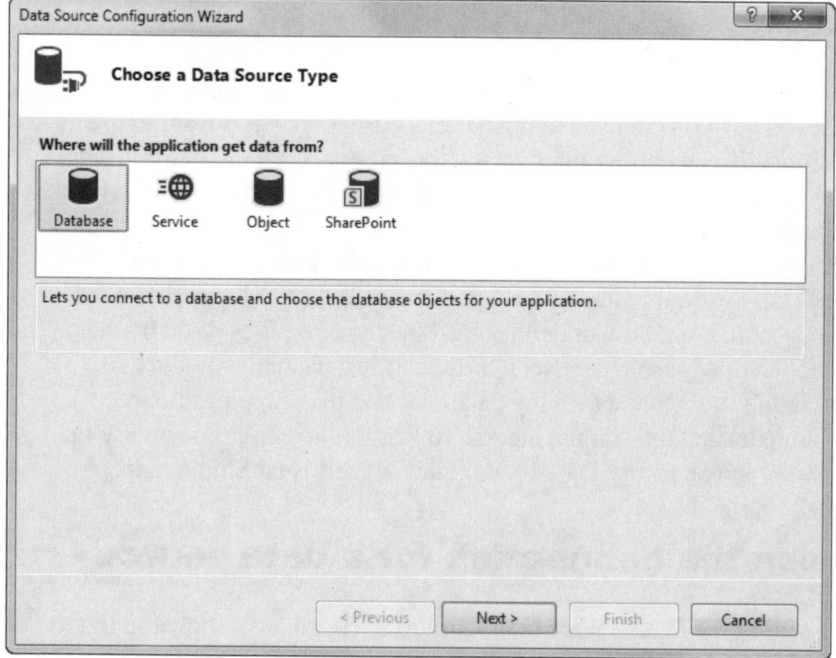

How to start the Data Source Configuration Wizard

- Click on the Add New Data Source link that's available from the Data Sources window when a project doesn't contain any data sources.
- Click on the Add New Data Source button at the top of the Data Sources window.
- Select the Add New Data Source command from Visual Studio's Project menu.
- Add a SQL Server (.mdf) or Access (.mdb) data file to the project using the Project→Add Existing Item command. Then, the wizard will display only the steps for choosing the database model and database objects as shown in figures 14-3 and 14-6.

How to choose a data source type

- To get your data from a database, select the Database option. This option lets you create applications like the ones described in this chapter.
- To get your data from a Windows Communication Foundation (WCF) service, a data service developed using WCF Data Services, or a web service, select the Service option.
- To get your data from a business object, select the Object option.
- To get data from a SharePoint site, select SharePoint.

Note

- If you will be using SQL Server Express on your own PC, you will need to install your database server software and create your database before you start this procedure. For more information, please refer to appendix A.

Figure 14-2 How to start the Data Source Configuration Wizard and choose a data source type

How to choose the database model for a data source

The second step of the Data Source Configuration Wizard, shown at the top of figure 14-3, lets you choose the type of database model you want to use for the data source. If you choose the Dataset option, Visual Studio generates a dataset as shown in this chapter. Then, the data that's retrieved from the database is stored in the dataset.

The second technique for working with the data in a database is to use the Entity Framework. To use this framework, you create an Entity Data Model that consists of a conceptual model that defines the objects, or entities, used by the application and the relationships between those entities; a storage model that defines the structure of the objects in the database; and the mappings between the conceptual model and the storage model. To learn more about how to use the Entity Framework and an Entity Data Model, please see Visual Studio help.

How to choose the connection for a data source

The third step of the Data Source Configuration Wizard, also shown in figure 14-3, lets you choose the data connection you want to use to connect to the database. If you've previously defined a data connection, you can choose that connection from the drop-down list. To be sure you use the right connection, you can click the button with the plus sign on it to display the connection string.

In this example, the connection string will attach the MMABooks.mdf file at the specified location to the LocalDB engine. If you use a connection string like this, Visual Studio will display a dialog box when you click the Next button that asks if you want to include the file in your project. If you respond by clicking the Yes button in this dialog box, Visual Studio will modify the connection string so the AttachDbFilename value looks like this:

```
AttachDbFilename=|DataDirectory|\MMABooks.mdf
```

Here, DataDirectory refers to the output directory for the project. As mentioned earlier, this is the directory where the executable file for the application is stored.

Note that when you run an application that uses LocalDB, the database engine is started if it isn't already running, and the database is attached. In addition, the first time you try to connect to the LocalDB engine, an instance of the engine has to be created before it's started. Because of that, the connection may fail with a timeout message. If that happens, you should wait a few seconds while the creation finishes and then run the application again.

If the connection you want to use hasn't already been defined, you can click the New Connection button. Then, you can use the dialog boxes shown in the next figure to create the connection.

Before I go on, you should know that once you create a connection using the Data Source Configuration Wizard, it's available to any other project you create. To see a list of the existing connections, you can open the Server Explorer window (View→Server Explorer) and then expand the Data Connections node.

The second and third steps of the Data Source Configuration Wizard

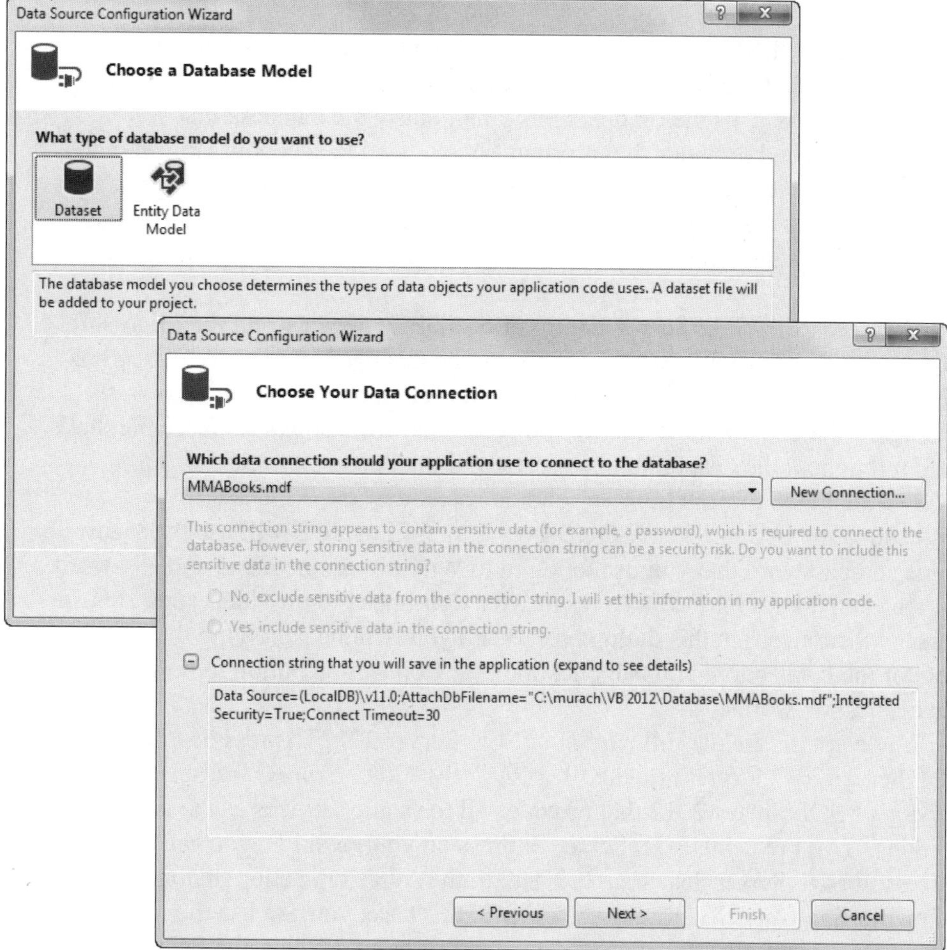

How to choose the database model

- When you click the Next button in the first step of the Data Source Configuration Wizard, the Choose a Database Model step is displayed.
- The two options let you create a dataset as shown in this book, or create an Entity Data Model. For more information on using the Entity Framework and an Entity Data Model, see Visual Studio help.

How to choose the connection

- When you click the Next button in the second step of the Data Source Configuration Wizard, the Choose Your Data Connection step shown above is displayed.
- If you've already established a connection to the database you want to use, you can choose that connection. Otherwise, you can click the New Connection button to display the Add Connection dialog box shown in the next figure.
- To see the connection string for an existing connection, click the button with the plus sign on it.

Figure 14-3 How to choose the database model and connection for a data source

How to create a connection to a database

If you click the New Connection button from the third step of the Data Source Configuration Wizard, the Add Connection dialog box shown in figure 14-4 is displayed. This dialog box helps you identify the database that you want to access and provides the information you need to access it. How you do that, though, varies depending on whether you're using SQL Server Express LocalDB, which can only run on your own PC; a SQL Server Express database server that's running on your own PC; or a database server that's running on a remote server.

If you're using SQL Server Express LocalDB, you can select the Microsoft SQL Server Database File data source from the Change Data Source dialog box. Then, you just identify the database file in the Add Connection dialog box. In this figure, for example, the connection is for the MMABooks database file that's used throughout the chapters in this section of the book.

For the logon information, you should select the Use Windows Authentication option. Then, SQL Server Express LocalDB will use the login name and password that you use to log in to Windows as the name and password for the database server too. As a result, you won't need to provide a separate user name and password in this dialog box. When you're done supplying the information for the connection, you can click the Test Connection button to be sure that the connection works.

You can also use the full edition of SQL Server 2012 Express instead of SQL Server 2012 Express LocalDB. *SQL Server 2012 Express* is a scaled-back version of SQL Server 2012 that provides all the same services as the full editions. If you're using SQL Server Express on your own PC, you can use the Microsoft SQL Server data source. Then, in the Add Connection dialog box, you will need to specify the server name. In this case, you can use the localhost keyword to specify that the database server is running on the same PC as the application. This keyword should be followed by a backslash and the name of the database server: SqlExpress.

After you enter the name of the server, you can enter or select the name of the database you want to connect to. You can also enter the required logon information. Just as you do when you use SQL Server Express LocalDB, though, you typically use Windows authentication with SQL Server Express.

If you need to connect to a SQL Server database that's running on a database server that's available through a network, you can use the Microsoft SQL Server data source just like you do for SQL Server Express. This works for SQL Server 2005, 2008, and 2012 databases. Then, you need to get the connection information from the network or database administrator. This information will include the name of the database server, logon information, and the name of the database. Once you establish a connection to the database, you can use that connection for all of the other applications that use that database.

The first time you create a connection, Visual Studio automatically displays the Change Data Source dialog box so you can select the data source and data provider you want to use. In most cases, the data provider that's selected by

The Add Connection and Change Data Source dialog boxes

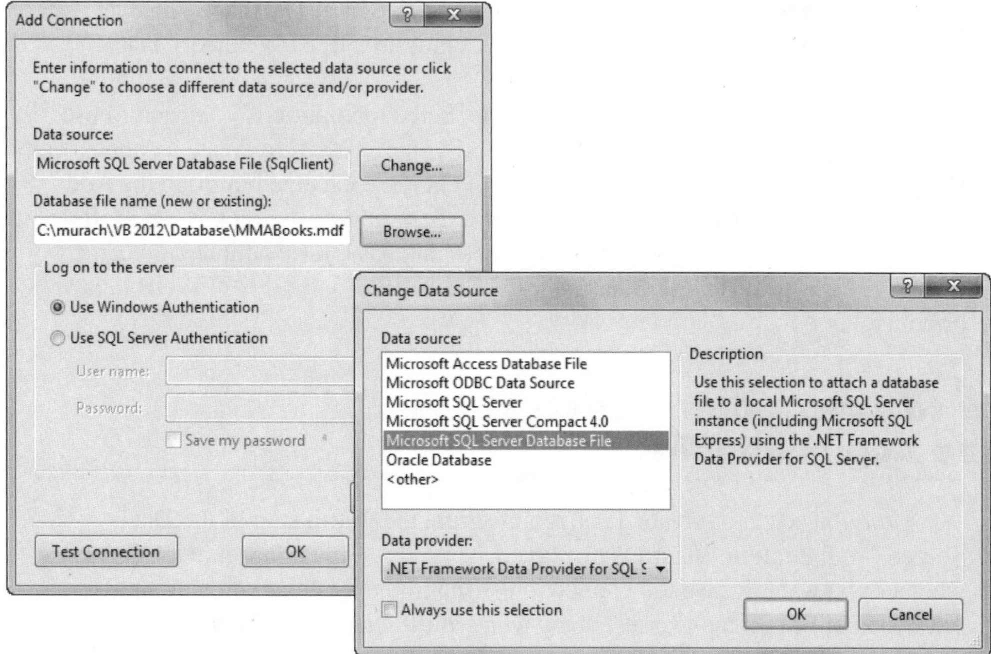

Description

- The first time you create a connection, the Change Data Source dialog box is displayed so you can select the data source and data provider you want to use. If you check the Always Use This Selection option, your selections will be used each time you create a connection. To change these options, click the Change button in the Add Connection dialog box.
- To create a connection for a database file that uses SQL Server Express LocalDB, use the Microsoft SQL Server Database File data source. Then, specify the name and path for the file and enter the information that's required to log on to the server in the Add Connection dialog box.
- To create a connection for a database on a local or remote SQL Server database server, use the Microsoft SQL Server data source. Then, specify the name of the server that contains the database, enter the information that's required to log on to the server, and specify the name of the database you want to connect to in the Add Connection dialog box.
- To be sure that the connection is configured properly, you can click the Test Connection button in the Add Connection dialog box.

Express Edition difference

- The Change Data Source dialog box doesn't include the Microsoft ODBC Data Source and Oracle Database options.

Figure 14-4 How to create a connection to a database

default when you select a data source will be the one you want to use. If you select the Microsoft SQL Server or Microsoft SQL Server Database File data source, for example, the data provider will default to .NET Framework Data Provider for SQL Server.

You can also check the Always Use This Selection option if you want to use the selected data provider by default. Then, if you ever need to create a connection for a different type of database, you can click the Change button in the Add Connection dialog box to display the Change Data Source dialog box again. If you want to create a connection for an Access database, for example, you can select the Microsoft Access Database File data source to use the OLE DB data provider.

How to save a connection string in the App.config file

After you select or create a data connection, the fourth step of the Data Source Configuration Wizard is displayed. This step, shown in figure 14-5, asks whether you want to save the connection string in the application configuration file (App.config). In most cases, that's what you'll want to do. Then, any table adapter that uses the connection can refer to the connection string by name. That way, if the connection information changes, you only need to change it in the App.config file. Otherwise, the connection string is stored in each table adapter that uses the connection, and you'll have to change each table adapter if the connection information changes.

This figure also shows how the connection string is stored in the App.config file. Although this file contains XML data, you should be able to understand it even if you don't know XML. Here, for example, you can see that the connectionStrings element contains an add element that contains three attributes. The first attribute, name, specifies the name of the connection string, in this case, MMABooksConnectionString. The second attribute, connectionString, contains the actual connection string. And the third attribute, providerName, identifies the data provider, in this case, SqlClient. Note that, in this example, the database file has been added to the project, so the connection string refers to the file in the data directory for the project.

The fourth step of the Data Source Configuration Wizard

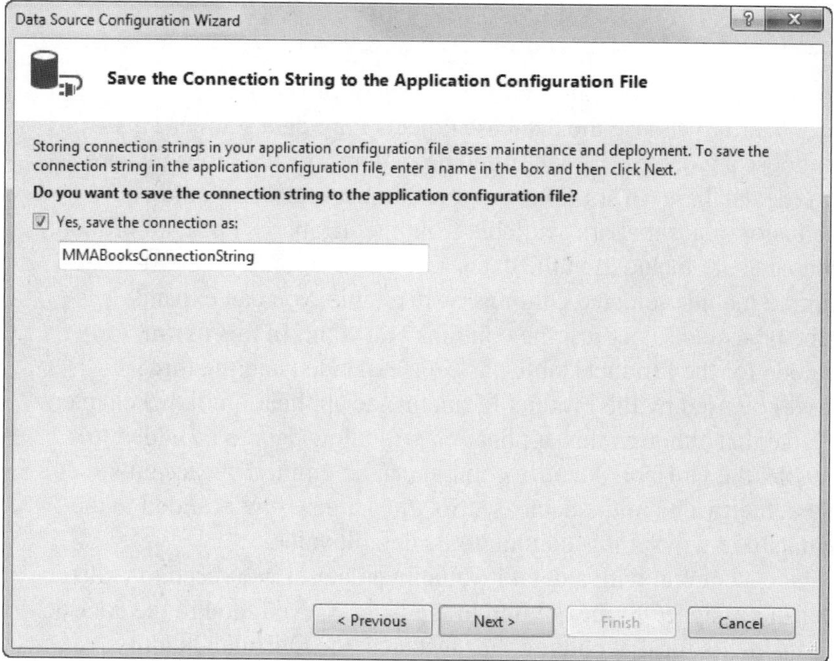

The information that's stored in the App.config file

```
<connectionStrings>
    <add name="ProductMaintenance.Properties.Settings.MMABooksConnectionString"
        connectionString="Data Source=(LocalDB)\v11.0;
                          AttachDbFilename=|DataDirectory|\MMABooks.mdf;
                          Integrated Security=True;
                          Connect Timeout=30"
        providerName="System.Data.SqlClient" />
</connectionStrings>
```

Description

- By default, the connection string is saved in the application configuration file (App.config). If that's not what you want, you can remove the check mark from the Yes option in the fourth step of the Data Source Configuration Wizard shown above.
- If you don't save the connection string in the App.config file, the string is specified for the connection of each table adapter you create from the data source. Because of that, we recommend you always save the connection string in the App.config file. Then, only the name of the connection string is stored in the connection for each table adapter.
- You can also enter the name you want to use for the connection string in this dialog box. By default, the connection string is given a name that consists of the database name appended with "ConnectionString".

Figure 14-5 How to save a connection string in the App.config file

How to choose database objects for a data source

Figure 14-6 shows how you can use the last step of the Data Source Configuration Wizard to choose the database objects for a data source. This step lets you choose any tables, views, stored procedures, or functions that are available from the database. In some cases, you can just select the table you need from the list of tables that are available from the database. Then, all of the columns in the table are included in the dataset.

If you want to include selected columns from a table, you can expand the node for the table and select just the columns you want. In this figure, for example, the node for the Products table has been expanded and the three columns that will be used by the Product Maintenance application in this chapter are selected. Note that although this application will allow data to be added to the Products table, the OnHandQuantity column can be omitted because it's defined with a default value in the database. So when a new row is added to the database, the database will set this column to its default value.

If you include a column with a default value in a dataset, you need to realize that this value isn't assigned to the column in the dataset, even though the dataset enforces the constraints for that column. For instance, the OnHandQuantity column in the MMABooks database has a default value of zero and doesn't allow nulls. But if you include this column in the dataset, its definition will have a default value of null and won't allow nulls. As a result, an exception will be thrown whenever a new row is added to the dataset with a null value for the OnHandQuantity column.

This means that the application must provide an acceptable value for the OnHandQuantity column. One way to do that is to provide a way for the user to enter a value for the column. Another way is to use the Dataset Designer to set the DefaultValue property for this column as described in this figure. You'll learn more about working with the Dataset Designer later in this chapter.

In a larger project, you might want to include several tables in the dataset. Then, the dataset will maintain the relationships between those tables whenever that's appropriate. Or, you might want to use views, stored procedures, or functions to work with the data in the database. If you have experience working with views, stored procedures, and functions, you shouldn't have any trouble understanding how this works. Otherwise, you can get another book such as *Murach's SQL Server 2012 for Developers* to learn more about working with these types of objects.

The last step of the Data Source Configuration Wizard

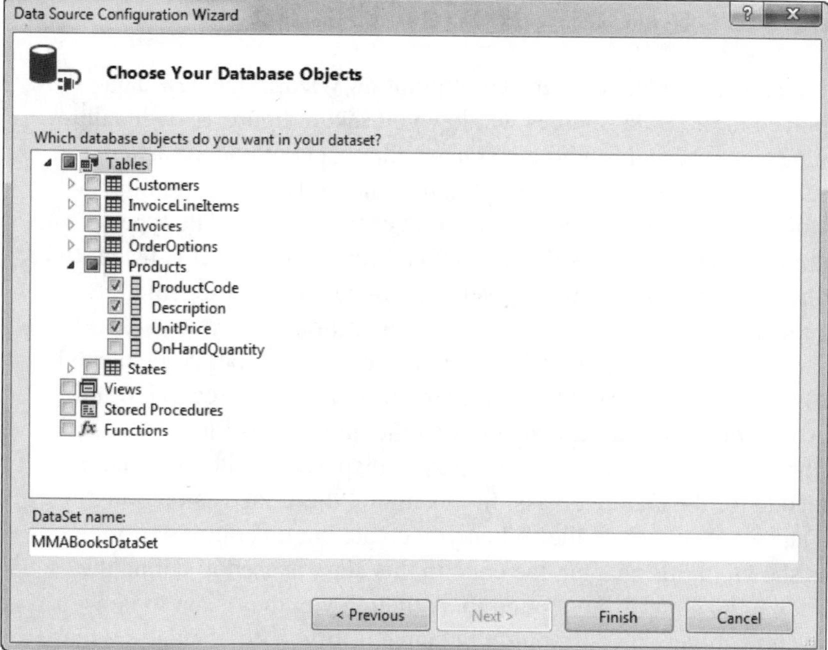

Description

- In the last step of the Data Source Configuration Wizard, you can choose the database objects that you want to include in the dataset for your project.
- In this step, you can choose from any tables, views, stored procedures, or functions that are available from the database. In addition, you can expand the node for any table, view, stored procedure, or function and choose just the columns you want to include in the data source.
- You can also enter the name you want to use for the dataset in this dialog box. By default, the name is the name of the database appended with "DataSet".

How to work with columns that have default values

- If a column in a database has a default value, that value isn't included in the column definition in the dataset. Because of that, you may want to omit columns with default values from the dataset unless they're needed by the application. Then, when a row is added to the table, the default value is taken from the database.
- If you include a column that's defined with a default value, you must provide a value for that column whenever a row is added to the dataset. One way to do that is to let the user enter a value. Another way is to display the Dataset Designer as described in figure 14-16, click on the column, and use the Properties window to set the DefaultValue property.

Figure 14-6 How to choose database objects for a data source

The schema file created by the Data Source Configuration Wizard

After you complete the Data Source Configuration Wizard, the new data source is displayed in the Data Sources window you saw in figure 14-1. In addition to this data source, Visual Studio generates a file that contains the *schema* for the DataSet class. This file defines the structure of the dataset, including the tables it contains, the columns that are included in each table, the data types of each column, and the constraints that are defined for each table. It is listed in the Solution Explorer window and is given the same name you specified for the dataset in the last step of the Data Source Configuration Wizard with a file extension of *xsd*. In figure 14-7, for example, you can see the schema file named MMABooksDataSet.xsd. As you'll learn later in this chapter, you can view a graphic representation of this schema by double-clicking on this file.

Beneath the schema file, the Solution Explorer displays the file that contains the generated code for the DataSet class. In this figure, this code is stored in the MMABooksDataSet.Designer.vb file. When you create bound controls from the data source as shown in this chapter, the code in this class is used to define the DataSet object that the controls are bound to. Although you may want to view this code to see how it works, you shouldn't change it. If you do, the dataset may not work correctly.

By the way, you should know that a dataset that's created from a dataset class like the one shown here is called a *typed dataset*. The code in the dataset class makes it possible for you to refer to the tables, rows, and columns in the typed dataset using the simplified syntax you'll see in this chapter and the next chapter. In contrast, when you use an *untyped dataset*, you have to refer to the tables, columns, and rows through the collections that contain them. In this book, you'll learn only how to create and work with typed datasets.

A project with a dataset defined by a data source

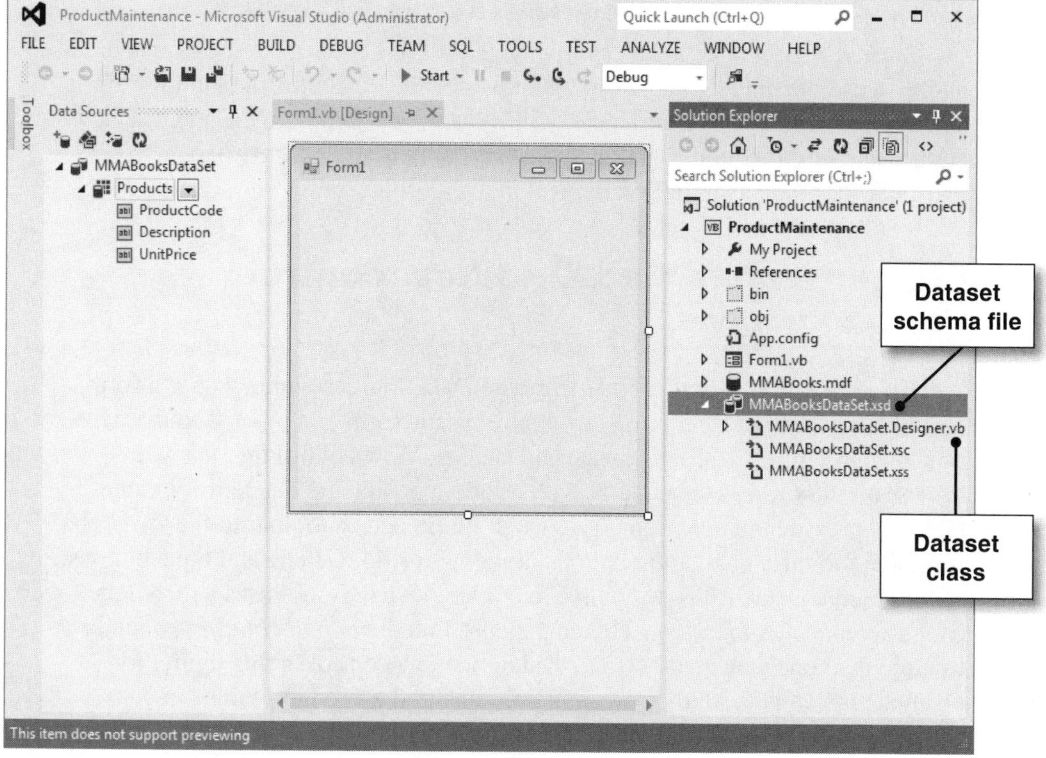

Description

- After you create a data source, it's displayed in the Data Sources window. Then, you can use it to create bound controls as shown in this chapter.
- Visual Studio also generates a file that contains the *schema* for the dataset defined by the data source. This file appears in the Solution Explorer and has a file extension of *xsd*. It defines the structure of the dataset, including the tables it contains, the columns in each table, the data types of each column, and the constraints for each table.
- Subordinate to the schema file is a file that contains the generated code for the dataset class. Visual Studio uses this class to create a dataset object when you add the data source to a form.

Note

- To see the files that are subordinate to the schema file, click the Show All Files button at the top of the Solution Explorer. Then, expand the node for the schema file.

Figure 14-7 The schema file created by the Data Source Configuration Wizard

How to use a data source

Once you've created a data source, you can bind controls to the data source and then use the bound controls to add, update, and delete the data in the data source. In this chapter, for example, you'll learn how to bind the DataGridView control and TextBox controls to a data source. Then, in the next chapter, you'll learn how to bind a ComboBox control to a data source.

How to generate a DataGridView control from a data source

By default, if you drag a table from the Data Sources window onto a form, Visual Studio adds a DataGridView control to the form and *binds* it to the table as shown in figure 14-8. This creates a DataGridView control that lets you browse all the rows in the table as well as add, update, and delete rows in the table. To provide this functionality, Visual Studio adds a toolbar to the top of the form that provides navigation buttons along with Add, Delete, and Save buttons.

To bind a DataGridView control to a table, Visual Studio uses a technique called *complex data binding*. This just means that the *bound control* is bound to more than one data element. The DataGridView control in this figure, for example, is bound to all the rows and columns in the Products table.

When you generate a DataGridView control from a data source, Visual Studio also adds five additional objects to the Component Designer tray at the bottom of the Form Designer. First, the DataSet object defines the dataset that contains the Products table. Second, the TableAdapter object provides commands that can be used to work with the Products table in the database. Third, the TableAdapterManager provides for writing the data in two or more related tables to the database so that referential integrity is maintained. Fourth, the BindingSource object specifies the data source (the Products table) that the controls are bound to, and it provides functionality for working with the data source. Finally, the BindingNavigator defines the toolbar that contains the controls for working with the data source.

Before I go on, I want to point out that the TableAdapter object is similar to the DataAdapter object you learned about in the previous chapter. However, it can only be created by a designer. In addition, it has a built-in connection and, as you'll see in the next chapter, it can contain more than one query.

I also want to mention that, in general, you shouldn't have any trouble figuring out how to use the binding navigator toolbar. However, you may want to know that if you click the Add button to add a new row and then decide you don't want to do that, you can click the Delete button to delete the new row. However, there's no way to cancel out of an edit operation. Because of that, you may want to add a button to the toolbar that provides this function. You'll learn how to do that in the next chapter.

A form after the Products table has been dragged onto it

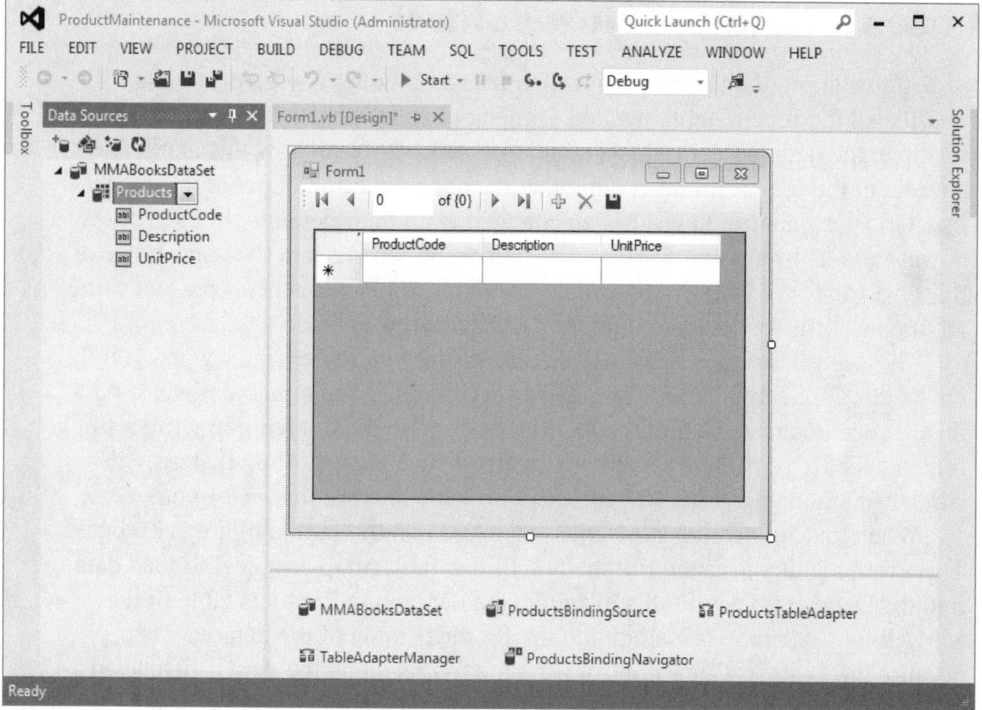

The controls and objects created when you drag a data source to a form

Control/object	Description
DataGridView control	Displays the data from the data source in a grid.
BindingNavigator control	Defines the toolbar that can be used to navigate, add, update, and delete rows in the DataGridView control.
BindingSource object	Identifies the data source that the controls on the form are bound to and provides functionality for working with the data source.
DataSet object	Provides access to all of the tables, views, stored procedures, and functions that are available to the project.
TableAdapter object	Provides the commands that are used to read and write data to and from the specified table in the database.
TableAdapterManager object	Provides for writing data in related tables to the database while maintaining referential integrity.

Description

- To *bind* a DataGridView control to a table in a dataset, just drag the table from the Data Sources window onto the form. Then, Visual Studio automatically adds a DataGridView control to the form along with the other controls and objects it needs to work properly.
- Because the DataGridView control is bound to the table, it can be referred to as a *bound control*. To bind a DataGridView control to a data table, Visual Studio uses a technique called *complex data binding*. This means that the control is bound to more than one data element, in this case, all the rows and columns in the table.

Figure 14-8 How to generate a DataGridView control from a data source

A Product Maintenance application that uses a DataGridView control

At this point, the DataGridView control and binding navigator toolbar provide all the functionality needed for an application that can be used to maintain the data in the Products table. Figure 14-9 shows how this application appears to the user at runtime. Note that the appearance and operation of the DataGridView control haven't been changed from their defaults. In most cases, however, you'll want to at least make some minor changes in the appearance of this control. You'll learn how to do that in the next chapter when I present some additional skills for working with the DataGridView control.

This figure also presents the code that Visual Studio generates when you create this application, which includes everything needed to make it work. As a result, you can create an application like this one without having to write a single line of code. If you've ever had to manually write an application that provides similar functionality, you can appreciate how much work this saves you.

When this application starts, the first event handler in this figure is executed. This event handler uses the Fill method of the TableAdapter object to load data into the DataSet object. In this example, the data in the Products table of the MMABooks database is loaded into the Products table of the dataset. Then, because the DataGridView control is bound to this table, the data is displayed in this control and the user can use it to modify the data in the table by adding, updating, or deleting rows.

When the user changes the data in the DataGridView control, those changes are saved to the dataset automatically. However, the changes aren't saved to the database until the user clicks the Save button in the toolbar. Then, the second event handler in this figure is executed. This event handler starts by calling the Validate method of the form, which causes the Validating and Validated events of the control that's losing focus to be fired. Although you probably won't use the Validated event, you may use the Validating event to validate a row that's being added or modified. However, I've found that this event doesn't work well with the binding navigator toolbar, so you won't see it used in this book.

Next, the EndEdit method of the BindingSource object applies any pending changes to the dataset. That's necessary because when you add or update a row, the new or modified row isn't saved until you move to another row.

Finally, the UpdateAll method of the TableAdapterManager object saves the data in the DataSet object to the MMABooks database. When this method is called, it checks each row in each table of the dataset to determine if it's a new row, a modified row, or a row that should be deleted. Then, it causes the appropriate SQL Insert, Update, and Delete statements to be executed for these rows. As a result, the UpdateAll method works efficiently since it only updates the rows that need to be updated. In addition, the Insert, Update, and Delete statements are executed in a sequence that maintains referential integrity.

Now that you understand this code, you should notice that it doesn't provide for any exceptions that may occur during this processing. Because of that, you need to add the appropriate exception handling code for any production applica-

The user interface for the Product Maintenance application

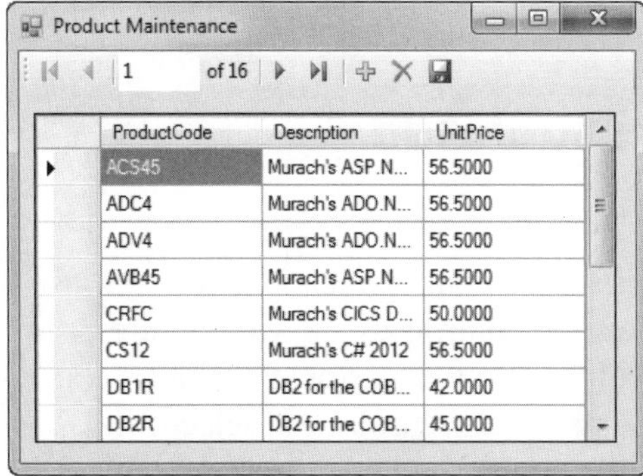

The code that's generated by Visual Studio

```
Private Sub Form1_Load(sender As Object,
        e As EventArgs) Handles MyBase.Load
    'TODO: This line of code loads data into the 'MMABooksDataSet.Products'
    'table. You can move, or remove it, as needed.
    Me.ProductsTableAdapter.Fill(Me.MMABooksDataSet.Products)
End Sub

Private Sub ProductsBindingNavigatorSaveItem_Click(
        sender As Object, e As EventArgs) _
        Handles ProductsBindingNavigatorSaveItem.Click
    Me.Validate()
    Me.ProductsBindingSource.EndEdit()
    Me.TableAdapterManager.UpdateAll(Me.MMABooksDataSet)
End Sub
```

The syntax of the Fill method

```
TableAdapter.Fill(DataSet.TableName)
```

The syntax of the UpdateAll method

```
TableAdapterManager.UpdateAll(DataSet)
```

Description

- Visual Studio automatically generates the code shown above and places it in the source code file when you drag a data source onto a form.
- The generated code uses the Fill method of the TableAdapter object that's generated for the table to read data from the database, and it uses the UpdateAll method of the TableAdapterManager object that's generated for the dataset to write data to the database. It also uses the EndEdit method of the BindingSource object to save any changes that have been made to the current row to the dataset.
- The Validate method causes the Validating and Validated events of the control that is losing the focus to be fired. You can use the Validating event to perform any required data validation for the form.
- Users of a DataGridView control can sort the rows by clicking on a column heading and can size columns by dragging the column separators to the left or right. They can also reorder the columns by dragging them if that option is enabled (see figure 15-9).

Figure 14-9 A Product Maintenance application that uses a DataGridView control

tions that you develop so they won't crash. You'll learn how to do that later in this chapter.

How to change the controls associated with a data source

If the DataGridView control isn't appropriate for your application, you can bind the columns of a data source to individual controls as shown in figure 14-10. Here, the data source consists of the columns in the Customers table.

To associate the columns in a table with individual controls, you select the Details option from the drop-down list that's available when you select the table in the Data Sources window. This is illustrated in the first screen in this figure. Then, if you drag that table from the Data Sources window onto a form, Visual Studio generates a label and a bound control for each column in the table.

For most string and numeric columns, Visual Studio generates a TextBox control. That's the case for the Customers table, as you'll see in the next figure. If you want to change the type of control that's associated with a column, though, you can select the column in the Data Sources window and then use the drop-down list that's displayed to select a different type of control. You can see the list of controls that are available in the second screen in this figure.

How to change the default control for a data table

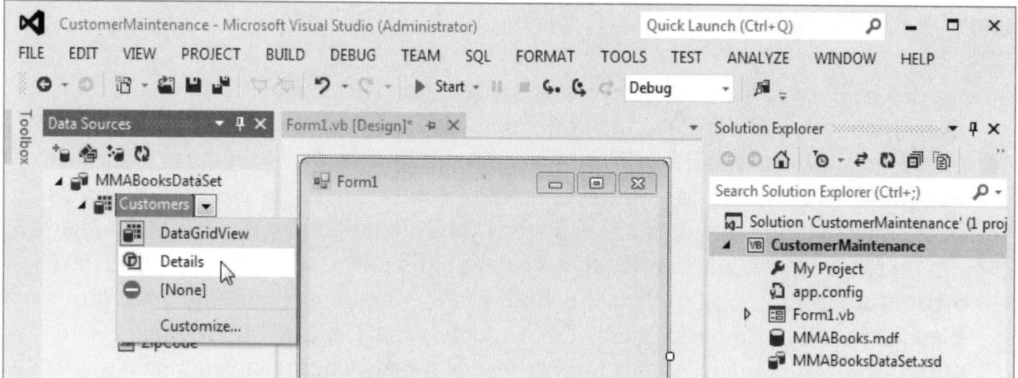

How to change the default control for a column in a data table

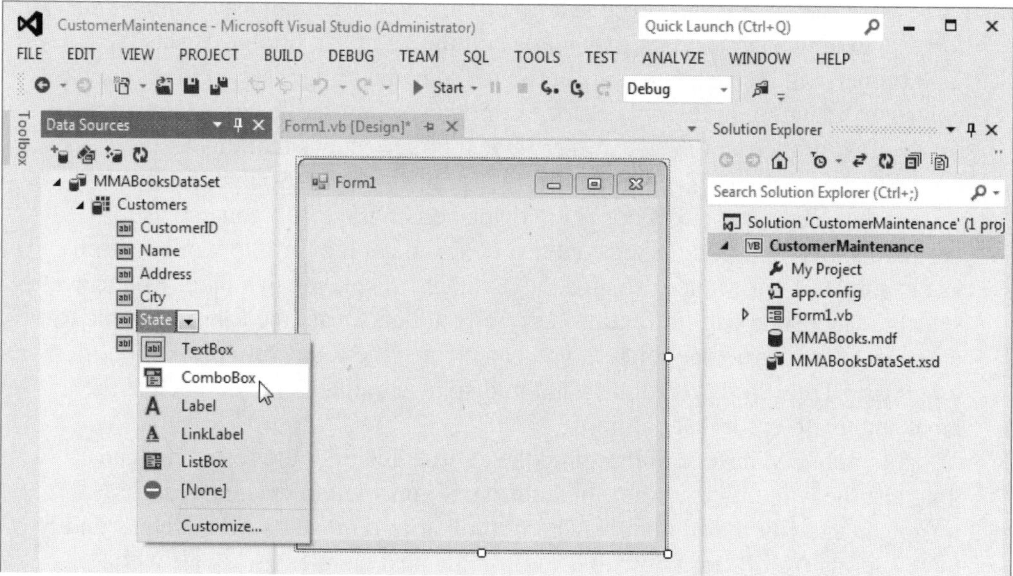

Description

- By default, a data table is associated with a DataGridView control. To change this default so that each column in the table is displayed in a separate control, select the Details option from the drop-down list for the table.
- By default, most string and numeric columns within a data table are associated with the TextBox control. To change this default, select the type of control you want to use from the drop-down list for the column.

Figure 14-10 How to change the controls associated with a data source

How to generate detail controls from a data source

If you change the control type that's associated with a table from DataGridView to Details and then drag that table from the Data Sources window onto a form, Visual Studio will add the appropriate controls to the form as shown in figure 14-11. In addition, it will bind those controls to the appropriate columns in the table, and it will add a Label control for each column to identify it. In this figure, for example, you can see that Visual Studio added a TextBox control and a Label control for each of the six columns in the Customers table. In addition, it added DataSet, BindingSource, TableAdapter, and TableAdapterManager objects and a binding navigator toolbar just as it does when you generate a DataGridView control.

Notice that when you use text boxes to work with the data in a table, only one row of the table is displayed at a time. Then Visual Studio uses *simple data binding* to bind each text box to a single column value. To do that, it sets the Text property in the DataBindings group to the name of the data column that the control is bound to. In this figure, for example, you can see the drop-down list for the Text property of the Customer ID text box. It shows that this text box is bound to the CustomerID column of the CustomersBindingSource object.

Once the labels and text boxes are displayed on the form, you can use standard skills for editing labels and text boxes to get the form to work correctly. For example, if you want to change the text that's displayed in a label, you can select the label and edit its Text property. If you don't want the user to be able to enter data for a particular column, you can change the ReadOnly property of the text box to True. Or, if you don't want to display a column, you can delete the label and text box for that column.

Alternatively, instead of dragging the entire table onto the form, you can drag just the columns you want. In addition, if you want to create a read-only form, you can edit the BindingNavigator toolbar to remove its Add, Delete, and Save buttons. You'll learn how to do that in the next chapter.

A form after the Customers table has been dragged onto it

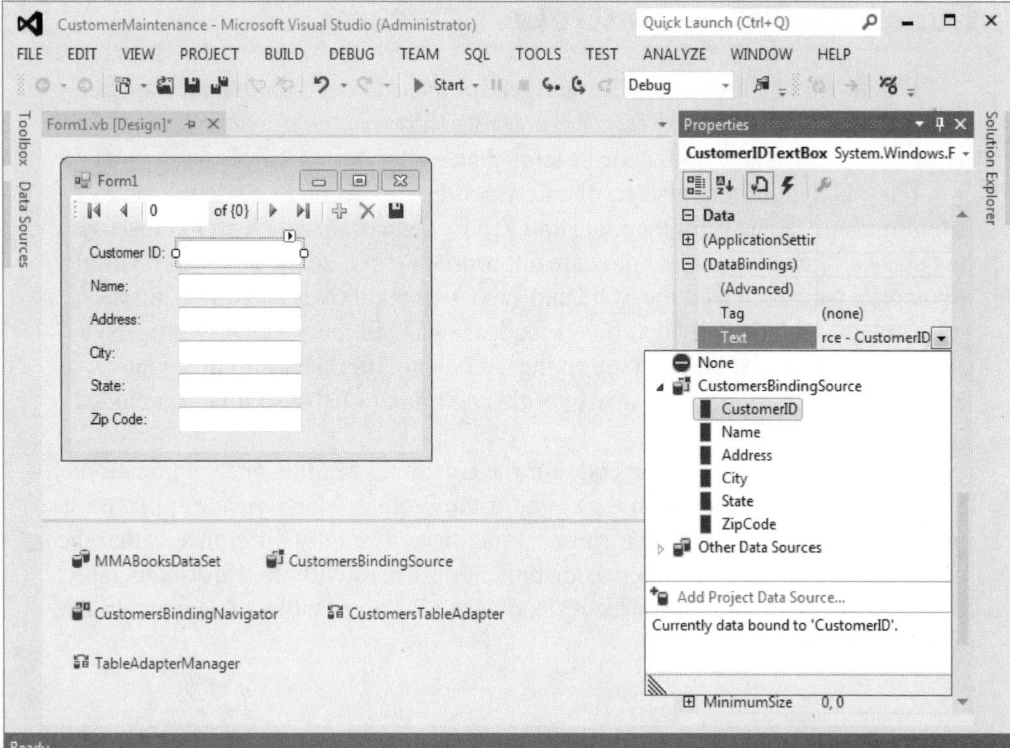

Description

- When you drag a table whose columns are associated with individual controls to a form, Visual Studio automatically adds the controls along with labels that identify the columns. It also adds a binding navigator toolbar and the objects for working with the bound data just as it does for a DataGridView control.
- To display the value of a column in a text box, Visual Studio sets the Text property in the DataBindings collection to the name of the data column. This is known as *simple data binding* because the control is bound to a single column value. To change the binding, you can use the drop-down list for the Text property as shown above.
- To disable the adding, deleting, or updating of rows when you use individual controls, you can remove those buttons from the toolbar. See chapter 15 to learn how to do that.

Note

- When you drag individual controls to a form, don't drop them at the top of the form. If you do, the toolbar will overlay the first label and text box and make them difficult to move.

Figure 14-11 How to generate detail controls from a data source

A Customer Maintenance application that uses TextBox controls

Figure 14-12 shows the user interface for a Customer Maintenance application that uses the Label and TextBox controls shown in the previous figure. However, I rearranged and made several changes to those controls.

First, I changed the label for the City text box to "City, State, Zip:", and I removed the labels from the State and Zip Code text boxes. Next, I changed the sizes of the text boxes so they are appropriate for the data they will be used to display. Next, I moved the State and Zip Code text boxes so they're aligned horizontally with the City text box. Finally, I changed the ReadOnly property of the Customer ID text box to True so the user can't enter data into this control, and I changed the TabStop property of this text box to False so it isn't included in the tab sequence.

This figure also shows the code for the Customer Maintenance application. If you compare this code with the code for the Product Maintenance application in figure 14-9, you'll see that it's almost identical. The only difference is that the code for the Customer Maintenance application works with the Customers table, table adapter, and binding source instead of the Products table, table adapter, and binding source.

The user interface for the Customer Maintenance application

The code for the application

```
Public Class Form1

    Private Sub Form1_Load(sender As Object,
            e As EventArgs) Handles MyBase.Load
        'TODO: This line of code loads data into the
        ''MMABooksDataSet.Customers' table.
        'You can move, or remove it, as needed.
        Me.CustomersTableAdapter.Fill(Me.MMABooksDataSet.Customers)
    End Sub

    Private Sub CustomersBindingNavigatorSaveItem_Click(
            sender As Object, e As EventArgs) _
            Handles CustomersBindingNavigatorSaveItem.Click
        Me.Validate()
        Me.CustomersBindingSource.EndEdit()
        Me.TableAdapterManager.UpdateAll(Me.MMABooksDataSet)
    End Sub

End Class
```

Figure 14-12 A Customer Maintenance application that uses TextBox controls

How to handle data errors

When you develop an application that uses a data source, you'll want to provide code that handles any data errors that might occur. In general, those errors fall into three categories: data provider errors, ADO.NET errors, and errors that the DataGridView control detects. You'll learn how to provide for these errors in the topics that follow.

How to handle data provider errors

When you access a database, there is always the possibility that an unrecoverable error might occur. For example, the database server might be shut down when you try to access it, or the network connection to the database server might be broken. Either way, your applications should usually anticipate such problems by catching any database exceptions that might occur.

Figure 14-13 shows the exceptions thrown by the .NET data providers when an unrecoverable error occurs. You can refer to these errors as *data provider errors*. As you can see, each data provider has its own exception class. So, if you're using the SQL Server data provider, you should catch exceptions of the SqlException class. If you're using the ODBC data provider, you should catch exceptions of the OdbcException class. And so on.

The code example in this figure shows how you can catch a SqlException that might occur when attempting to fill a dataset using a table adapter. Here, the shaded lines show the code that has been added to the generated code. This code will display an error message when a SqlException occurs, and it uses the Number and Message properties of the SqlException class to display details about the exception. It also uses the GetType method to indicate the type of exception that occurred.

Although it's uncommon, more than one server error can occur as the result of a single database operation. In that case, an error object is created for each error. These objects are stored in a collection that you can access through the Errors property of the exception object. Each error object contains a Number and Message property just like the exception object. However, because the Number and Message properties of the exception object are set to the Number and Message properties of the first error in the Errors collection, you don't usually need to work with the individual error objects.

.NET data provider exception classes

Class	Description
`SqlException`	Thrown if a server error occurs when accessing a SQL Server database.
`OracleException`	Thrown if a server error occurs when accessing an Oracle database.
`OdbcException`	Thrown if a server error occurs when accessing an ODBC database.
`OleDbException`	Thrown if a server error occurs when accessing an OLE DB database.

Common members of the .NET data provider exception classes

Property	Description
`Number`	An error number that identifies the type of error.
`Message`	A message that describes the error.
`Source`	The name of the provider that generated the error.
`Errors`	A collection of error objects that contain information about the errors that occurred during a database operation.
Method	**Description**
`GetType()`	Gets the type of the current exception.

Code that catches a SQL exception

```
Private Sub Form1_Load(sender As Object,
        e As EventArgs) Handles MyBase.Load
    Try
        Me.CustomersTableAdapter.Fill(Me.MMABooksDataSet.Customers)
    Catch ex As SqlException
        MessageBox.Show("Database error # " & ex.Number &
            ": " & ex.Message, ex.GetType.ToString)
    End Try
End Sub
```

Description

- Whenever the data provider (SQL Server, Oracle, ODBC, or OLE DB) encounters a situation it can't handle, a data provider exception is thrown. You can handle these types of exceptions by catching them and displaying appropriate error messages.
- The Number and Message properties pinpoint the specific server error that caused the data provider exception to be thrown.
- The SqlException class is stored in the System.Data.SqlClient namespace.

Figure 14-13 How to handle data provider errors

How to handle ADO.NET errors

When you work with bound controls, *ADO.NET errors* can occur when the data in those controls is saved to the dataset (not the database), or when an Insert, Update, or Delete statement can't be executed against the database. Figure 14-14 presents some of the most common of those errors.

Here, ConstraintException and NoNullAllowedException are subclasses of the DataException class, so you can catch either of these errors by catching DataException errors. In contrast, DBConcurrencyException isn't a subclass of the DataException class, so you must catch DBConcurrencyException errors separately. All of the ADO.NET exception classes are members of the System.Data namespace.

The error-handling code in this figure catches errors caused by the EndEdit method of a binding source and the UpdateAll method of a table adapter manager. The first exception, DBConcurrencyException, occurs if the number of rows that are affected by an insert, update, or delete operation is zero, which typically indicates that concurrency errors have occurred. Then, a message box is used to display an error message, and the Fill method of the table adapter is used to retrieve the current data from the database and load it into the dataset. That will help prevent further concurrency errors from occurring.

Although you might think that a concurrency error would be generated by the database rather than ADO.NET, that's not the case. To understand why, you need to realize that the Update and Delete statements that are generated for a table adapter contain code that checks that a row hasn't changed since it was retrieved. But if the row has changed, the row with the specified criteria won't be found and the SQL statement won't be executed. When the table adapter discovers that the row wasn't updated or deleted, however, it realizes there was a concurrency error and throws an exception.

Like other exception classes provided by the .NET Framework, each ADO.NET exception class has a Message property and a GetType method that you can use to display information about the error. You can see how this property and method are used in the second Catch block, which catches any other ADO.NET exceptions that may occur. This Catch block displays a dialog box that uses the Message property and the GetType method of the DataException object to describe the error. Then, it uses the CancelEdit method of the binding source to cancel the current edit operation.

Incidentally, to test your handling of concurrency exceptions, you can start two instances of Visual Studio and run the same application from both of them. Then, you can access and update the same row from both instances.

Common ADO.NET exception classes

Class	Description
DBConcurrencyException	The exception that's thrown if the number of rows affected by an insert, update, or delete operation is zero. This exception is typically caused by a concurrency violation.
DataException	The general exception that's thrown when an ADO.NET error occurs.
ConstraintException	The exception that's thrown if an operation violates a constraint. This is a subclass of the DataException class.
NoNullAllowedException	The exception that's thrown when an add or update operation attempts to save a null value in a column that doesn't allow nulls. This is a subclass of the DataException class.

Common members of the ADO.NET classes

Property	Description
Message	A message that describes the exception.
Method	**Description**
GetType()	Gets the type of the current exception.

Code that handles ADO.NET errors

```
Try
    Me.CustomersBindingSource.EndEdit()
    Me.TableAdapterManager.UpdateAll(Me.MMABooksDataSet)
Catch ex As DBConcurrencyException
    MessageBox.Show("A concurrency error occurred. " &
        "Some rows were not updated.", "Concurrency Error")
    Me.CustomersTableAdapter.Fill(Me.MMABooksDataSet.Customers)
Catch ex As DataException
    MessageBox.Show(ex.Message, ex.GetType.ToString)
    CustomersBindingSource.CancelEdit()
Catch ex As SqlException
    MessageBox.Show("Database error # " & ex.Number &
        ": " & ex.Message, ex.GetType.ToString)
End Try
```

Description

- An ADO.NET exception is an exception that occurs on any ADO.NET object. All of these exceptions are members of the System.Data namespace.
- In most cases, you'll catch specific types of exceptions if you want to perform special processing when those exceptions occur. Then, you can use the DataException class to catch other ADO.NET exceptions that are represented by its subclasses.

Figure 14-14 How to handle ADO.NET errors

How to handle data errors for a DataGridView control

Because the DataGridView control was designed to work with data sources, it can detect some types of data entry errors before the data is saved to the dataset. If, for example, a user doesn't enter a value for a column that's required by the data source, or if a user tries to add a new row with a primary key that already exists, the DataGridView control will raise the DataError event. Then, you can code an event handler for this event as shown in figure 14-15.

The second parameter that's received by this event handler has properties you can use to display information about the error. The one you'll use most often is the Exception property, which provides access to the exception object that was thrown as a result of the error. Like any other exception object, this object has a Message property that provides a description of the error. You can also use the RowIndex and ColumnIndex properties of the second parameter to identify the row and column that caused the data error.

An event of the DataGridView control

Event	Description
`DataError`	Raised when the DataGridView control detects a data error such as a value that isn't in the correct format or a null value where a null value isn't valid.

Three properties of the DataGridViewDataErrorEventArgs class

Property	Description
`Exception`	The exception that was thrown as a result of the error. You can use the Message property of this object to get additional information about the exception.
`RowIndex`	The index for the row where the error occurred.
`ColumnIndex`	The index for the column where the error occurred.

Code that handles a data error for a DataGridView control

```
Private Sub ProductsDataGridView_DataError(sender As Object,
        e As Windows.Forms.DataGridViewDataErrorEventArgs) _
        Handles ProductsDataGridView.DataError
    Dim row As Integer = e.RowIndex + 1
    Dim errorMessage As String = "A data error occurred." & vbCrLf &
        "Row: " & row & vbCrLf &
        "Error: " & e.Exception.Message
    MessageBox.Show(errorMessage, "Data Error")
End Sub
```

Description

- You can code an event handler for the DataError event of the DataGridView control to handle any data errors that occur when working with the DataGridView control.
- You can use the Exception, RowIndex, and ColumnIndex properties of the second parameter of the event handler to display a meaningful error message.

Figure 14-15 How to handle data errors for a DataGridView control

How to use the Dataset Designer

The *Dataset Designer* lets you work with a dataset schema using a graphic interface. In the topics that follow, you'll learn some basic skills for working with the Dataset Designer.

How to view the schema for a dataset

To learn more about a dataset, you can display its schema in the Dataset Designer. In figure 14-16, for example, you can see the schema for the MMABooks dataset used by the Customer Maintenance application. For this simple application, this dataset contains just the Customers table since this is the only table used by the application. The key icon in this table indicates that the CustomerID column is the primary key for the table.

For each table, the dataset schema also includes a table adapter that lists the queries that can be used with the table. Each table adapter includes at least a *main query* named Fill that determines the columns that are used when you drag the table from the Data Sources window. This query is also used to generate the Insert, Update, and Delete statements for the table. In addition, the table adapter includes any other queries you've defined for the table. You'll learn more about defining additional queries in the next chapter.

If you click on a table adapter in the Dataset Designer, you'll see that its properties in the Properties window include the ADO.NET objects that the table adapter defines. That includes a Connection object, as well as SelectCommand, InsertCommand, UpdateCommand, and DeleteCommand objects. If you expand any of these command objects, you can look at the CommandText property that defines the SQL statement it executes. In this figure, for example, you can see the beginning of the Select statement for the SelectCommand object that's used by the Fill query of the table adapter for the Customers table. If you click on the ellipsis button for this property, you can work with the query using the Query Builder as shown in the next figure.

Note that the Dataset Designer also makes it easy to set the properties for a column in a table that's in the dataset. To do that, just select a column and use the Properties window. For instance, you can use this technique to set the DefaultValue property for a column in the dataset, which is something that you often have to do.

The schema displayed in the Dataset Designer

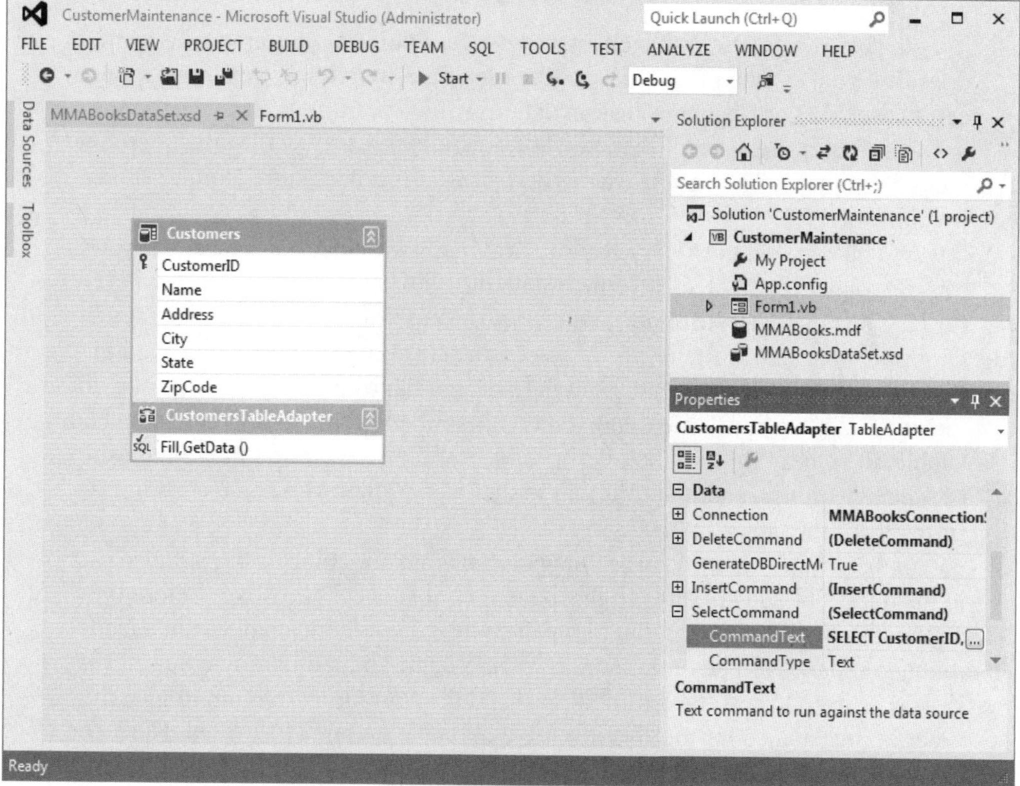

Description

- To view the schema for the dataset of a data source, double-click on the schema file for the dataset (.xsd) in the Solution Explorer, or select the schema file and then use the View→Designer command. The schema is displayed in the *Dataset Designer*.
- To view the properties for a table adapter in the Properties window, select the table adapter in the Dataset Designer. These properties include the Connection object that's used to connect to the database, and the SelectCommand, InsertCommand, UpdateCommand, and DeleteCommand objects that are used to work with the data in the database.
- To view the properties for a query, select the query in the Dataset Designer.
- For each table adapter, the query named Fill is the *main query*. This query determines the columns that are used when you drag a table from the Data Sources window onto a form. The Insert, Update, and Delete statements for the table are also based on this query.
- To work with the SQL statement in a CommandText property, you can click on the ellipsis button that appears when that property is selected. This displays the statement in the Query Builder, which you'll learn about in the next figure.
- To view and set the properties for a column in a table, select the column. This is an easy way to set the DefaultValue property for a column.

Figure 14-16 How to view the schema for a dataset

How to use the Query Builder

As you saw earlier in this chapter, the Data Source Configuration Wizard doesn't give you much flexibility for creating data sources. For example, you can't specify a sort sequence or join data from two or more tables when you use this wizard. Because of that, you'll frequently want to modify the query the wizard generates. The easiest way to do that is to use the Query Builder shown in figure 14-17.

As you can see, the Query Builder provides a graphical interface that you can use to modify a Select statement without even knowing the proper syntax for it. When the Query Builder first opens, the current table is displayed in the *diagram pane*. In this figure, for example, the Customers table is displayed in the diagram pane. If you need to include related tables in this pane, you can do that by using the Add Table dialog box as described in this figure. When you add a table, the Query Builder includes a connector icon that shows the relationship between the tables, and it adds a join to the query. Then, you can use columns from any of the tables in the query.

In the *grid pane*, you can see the columns that are going to be included in the query. To add columns to this pane, you just check the boxes before the column names listed in the diagram pane. Once the columns have been added to the grid pane, you can use the Sort Type column to identify any columns that should be used to sort the returned rows and the Sort Order column to give the order of precedence for the sort if more than one column is identified. Here, for example, the rows will be sorted in ascending sequence by the Name column.

Similarly, you can use the Filter column to establish the criteria to be used to select the rows that will be retrieved by the query. For example, to retrieve just the customer with a specific ID, you can specify @CustomerID in the Filter column for the CustomerID column. You'll learn more about coding this type of query in the next chapter.

As you create the query, the *SQL pane* shows the resulting Select statement. You can also run this query at any time to display the selected rows in the *results pane*. That way, you can be sure that the query works the way you want it to. To run the query, click the Execute Query button.

When you get the query the way you want it, you can click the OK button to save the query. When you do that, Visual Studio will display a dialog box that asks if you want to regenerate the updating commands based on the new command syntax. In other words, do you want to modify the Insert, Update, and Delete statements so they match the Select statement. Depending on the changes you made, you may or may not want to do that. If, for example, you simply changed the sort sequence, it's not necessary to update the Insert, Update, and Delete statements. On the other hand, if you added or deleted one or more columns from the original table, you'll want to update the Insert, Update, and Delete statements so they include the same columns as the Select statement.

The Query Builder

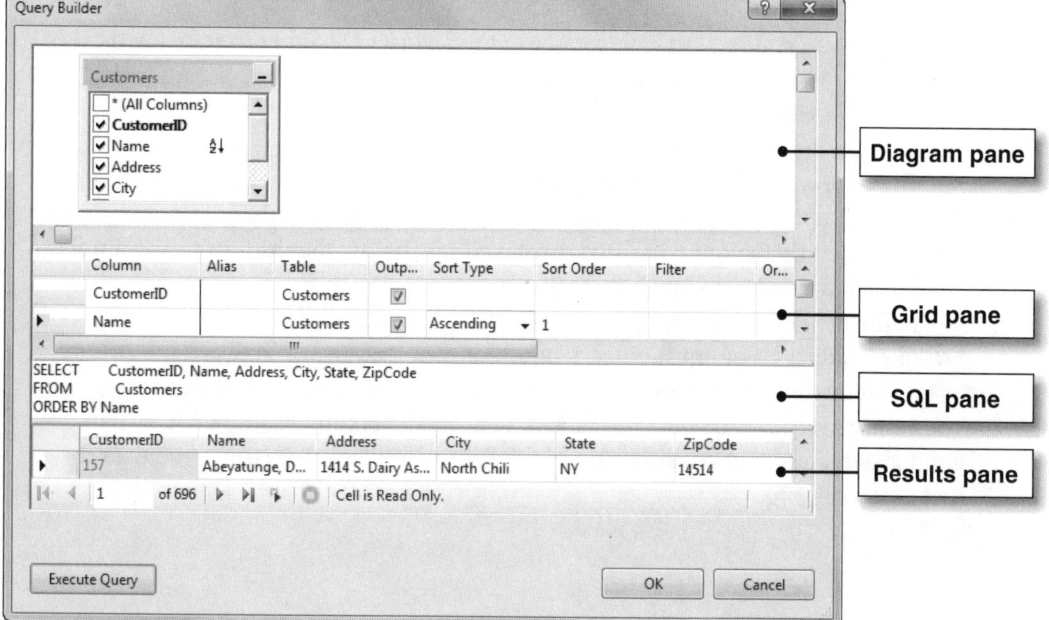

Description

- To display the Query Builder for the main query, select the table adapter that contains the query and then click on the ellipsis to the right of the CommandText property of the SelectCommand object in the Properties window.
- By default, the current table is displayed in the *diagram pane*. To add a related table to this pane, right-click in the pane, select Add Table, and select the table from the dialog box that's displayed. Then, a join is added to the query.
- To include a column in a query, click on the box to its left to add it to the *grid pane*. Or, select all the columns by checking the * (All Columns) item.
- To create a calculated column, enter an expression in the Column column and then enter the name you want to use for the column in the Alias column.
- To sort the returned rows by one or more columns, select the Ascending or Descending option from the Sort Type column for those columns in the sequence you want them sorted. You can also use the Sort Order column to set the sort sequence.
- To specify selection criteria (like a specific value that the column must contain to be selected), enter the criteria in the Filter column.
- To use a column for sorting or for specifying criteria without including it in the query results, remove the check mark from the Output column.
- As you select columns and specify sort and selection criteria, the Query Builder builds the SQL statement and displays it in the *SQL pane*.
- To display the results of a query in the *results pane*, click the Execute Query button.
- When you accept the query, a dialog box will be displayed that asks if you want to update the Insert, Update, and Delete queries that are generated from the main query.

Figure 14-17 How to use the Query Builder

How to preview the data for a query

After you create a query, you can use the Dataset Designer to preview the data it retrieves. To do that, you use the Preview Data dialog box as shown in figure 14-18. Here, the data returned by the Fill query for the Customers table adapter is being previewed.

To preview the data for a query, you just click the Preview button. When you do, the data will be displayed in the Results grid, and the number of columns and rows returned by the query will be displayed just below the grid. In this example, the query retrieved 6 columns and 696 rows.

In the next chapter, you'll learn how to create queries that use parameters. For those queries, you must enter a value for each parameter in the Value column of the Parameters grid before you can preview its data. For example, suppose you want to retrieve the data for a customer with a specific customer ID. Then, you have to enter that customer ID in the Parameters grid to retrieve the data for that customer.

The Preview Data dialog box

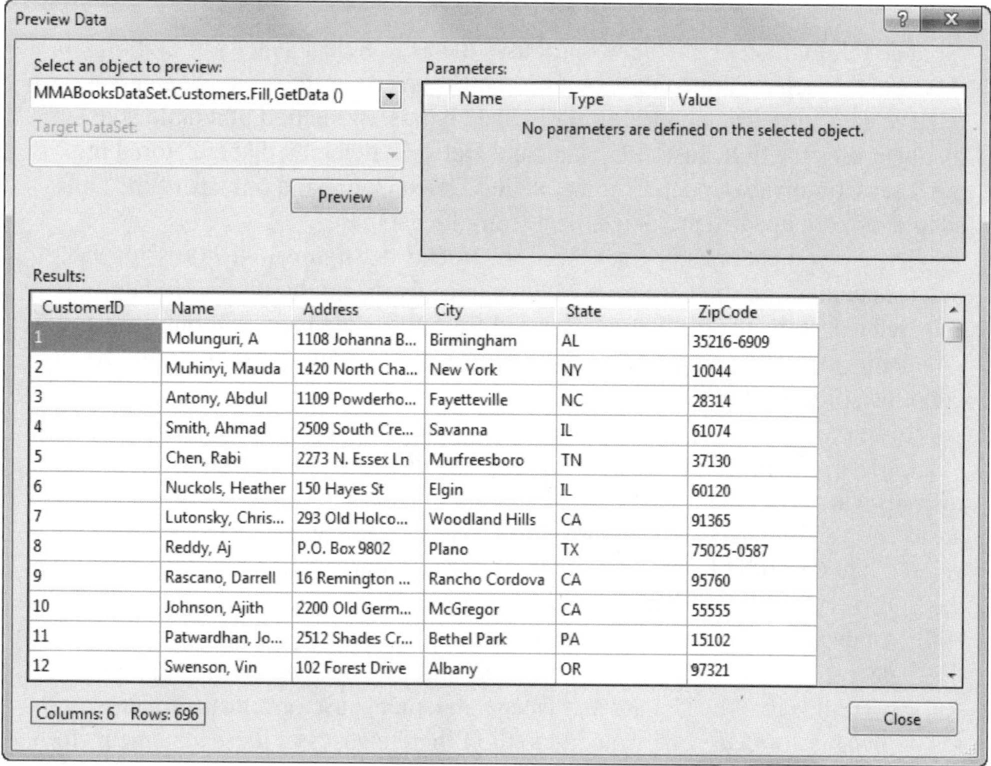

Description

- To display the Preview Data dialog box for a query, right-click on the query in the Dataset Designer and select the Preview Data command, or select the query and then use the Data→Preview Data command.
- To preview the data, click the Preview button. When you do, the data will be displayed in the Results grid, and the number of columns and rows returned by the query will be displayed just below the Results grid.
- If a query requires parameters, you must enter a value for each parameter in the Value column of the Parameters grid. See chapter 15 for more information on query parameters.

Figure 14-18 How to preview the data for a query

How to interpret the generated SQL statements

The Fill method of a table adapter uses the SQL Select statement that's stored in the SelectCommand object for the Fill query of the table adapter to retrieve data from a database. Similarly, the UpdateAll method of a table adapter manager uses the SQL Insert, Update, and Delete statements that are stored in the InsertCommand, UpdateCommand, and DeleteCommand objects of the table adapter to add, update, and delete data from the database.

To help you understand what these statements do, figure 14-19 presents the Select statement for the Customer Maintenance form and the Insert, Update, and Delete statements that were generated from this statement. Although these statements may look complicated, the information presented here will give you a good idea of how they work.

To start, notice that the Insert statement is followed by a Select statement that retrieves the row that was just added to the database. That may be necessary in cases where the database generates some of the data for the new row. When a customer row is added to the database, for example, the database generates the value of the CustomerID column. Then, the Select statement in this figure uses the SQL Server SCOPE_IDENTITY function to retrieve the row with this ID. If the database doesn't generate or calculate any of the column values, however, this Select statement, as well as the one after the Update statement, isn't needed.

Also notice that the Update and Delete statements use optimistic concurrency. Because of that, code is added to the Where clauses of these statements to check whether any of the column values have changed since they were retrieved from the database. This code compares the current value of each column in the database against the original value of the column, which is stored in the dataset. If none of the values have changed, the operation is performed. Otherwise, it's not.

Finally, notice that most of the statements in this figure use one or more parameters. For example, parameters are used in the Values clause of the Insert statement and the Set clause of the Update statement to refer to the current values of the columns in the dataset. Parameters are also used in the Where clauses of the Update and Delete statements to refer to the original values of the columns in the dataset. And one is used in the Where clause of the Select statement after the Update statement to refer to the current row. The wizard inserts these parameters when it creates the command objects for a table adapter. Then, before each statement is executed, Visual Studio substitutes the appropriate value for each parameter.

This should give you more perspective on how the dataset is refreshed and how optimistic concurrency is provided when you use ADO.NET. Because of the disconnected data architecture, these features can't be provided by the database management system or by ADO.NET. Instead, they are provided by the SQL statements that are generated by the Data Source Configuration Wizard.

SQL that retrieves customer rows

```
SELECT   CustomerID, Name, Address, City, State, ZipCode
FROM     Customers
```

SQL that inserts a customer row and refreshes the dataset

```
INSERT INTO Customers
        (Name, Address, City, State, ZipCode)
VALUES  (@Name, @Address, @City, @State, @ZipCode);

SELECT   CustomerID, Name, Address, City, State, ZipCode
FROM     Customers
WHERE   (CustomerID = SCOPE_IDENTITY())
```

SQL that updates a customer row and refreshes the dataset

```
UPDATE   Customers
SET      Name = @Name,
         Address = @Address,
         City = @City,
         State = @State,
         ZipCode = @ZipCode
WHERE   ((CustomerID = @Original_CustomerID) AND
        (Name = @Original_Name) AND
        (Address = @Original_Address) AND
        (City = @Original_City) AND
        (State = @Original_State) AND
        (ZipCode = @Original_ZipCode));

SELECT    CustomerID, Name, Address, City, State, ZipCode
FROM      Customers
WHERE     (CustomerID = @CustomerID)
```

SQL that deletes a customer row

```
DELETE FROM Customers
WHERE   (CustomerID = @Original_CustomerID) AND
        (Name = @Original_Name) AND
        (Address = @Original_Address) AND
        (City = @Original_City) AND
        (State = @Original_State) AND
        (ZipCode = @Original_ZipCode)
```

Description

- By default, the Data Source Configuration Wizard adds code to the Where clause of the Update and Delete statements that checks that the data hasn't changed since it was retrieved.
- By default, the Data Source Configuration Wizard adds a Select statement after the Insert and Update statements to refresh the new or modified row in the dataset.
- The SQL statements use parameters to identify the new values for an insert or update operation. Parameters are also used for the original column values, which are used to check that a row hasn't changed for an update or delete operation. And one is used in the Where clause of the Select statement after the Update statement to refer to the current row. The values for these parameters are stored in and retrieved from the dataset.

Figure 14-19 How to interpret the generated SQL statements

Perspective

Now that you've completed this chapter, you should be able to use a data source to create simple applications that let you view and maintain the data in one table of a database. That should give you some idea of how quickly and easily you can create applications when you use the data source feature. And in the next chapter, you'll learn how you can use data sources to build more complex applications.

Terms

SQL Server Express LocalDB
data source
SQL Server Express
schema
typed dataset
untyped dataset
binding a control
bound control
complex data binding
simple data binding
parameterized query
data provider error
ADO.NET error
Dataset Designer
main query

Exercise 14-1 Build a DataGridView application

In this exercise, you'll build the Product Maintenance application shown in figure 14-9. That will show you how to build a simple application with data sources, a dataset, and a DataGridView control.

Build the form and test it with valid data

1. Start a new application named ProductMaintenance in the C:\VB 2012\Chapter 14 directory, and use the techniques in figures 14-1 through 14-8 to create a data source by adding the MMABooks.mdf file that's in the C:\VB 2012\Database directory to the project. Then, change the "Copy to output Directory" property of the database file to "Copy if newer".
2. Drag the data source onto the form and adjust the size of the form and the DataGridView control as needed, but don't change anything else.
3. Test the application with valid data in three phases. First, sort the rows by clicking on a column header, and size one of the columns by dragging its column separator. Second, change the data in one column of a row, and move to another row to see that the data is changed in the dataset. Third, add a new row with valid data in all columns, and move to another row to see that the row has been added. At this point, the changes have been made to the dataset only, not the database. Now, click the Save button in the toolbar to save the changes to the database.

Test the form with invalid data and provide exception handling

4. Test the application with invalid data by deleting the data in the Description column of a row and moving to another row. This should cause a NoNullAllowedException that's automatically handled by the DataGridView control so the application doesn't crash.
5. Add an exception handler for the DataError event of the DataGridView control as shown in figure 14-15. To start the code for that handler, click on the control, click on the Events button in the Properties window, and double-click on the DataError event. Then, write the code for the event, and redo the testing of step 3 to see how your code works.
6. When you're through experimenting, end the application, and close the project.

Exercise 14-2 Build an application with text boxes

In this exercise, you'll build the Customer Maintenance application shown in figure 14-12. That will show you how to use data sources with controls like text boxes.

Build the form and test it with valid data

1. Start a new application named CustomerMaintenance in the C:\VB 2012\Chapter 14 directory, and create a data source for the Customers table by adding the MMABooks.mdf file in the C:\VB 2012\Database directory to the project. Then, change the "Copy to output Directory" property of the database file to "Copy if newer".
2. Use the techniques in figures 14-10 and 14-11 to add the data source fields to the form as text boxes. At this point, the form should look like the one in figure 14-11.
3. Test the application with valid data in three phases. First, use the toolbar to navigate through the rows. Second, change the data in one column of a row (other than the CustomerID column), move to another row, and return to the first row to see that the data has been changed in the dataset. Third, add a new row with valid data in all columns (leave the customer ID at -1), move to another row, and return to the added row to see that the row has been added to the dataset. Now, click the Save button in the toolbar to save the dataset to the database. Notice that the customer ID that was generated by the database is now displayed.

Test the form with invalid data and provide exception handling

4. Add a new row to the dataset, but don't enter anything into the City field. Then, click on the Save button. This should cause a NoNullAllowedException, since City is a required field.

5. Add exception handling code for an ADO.NET DataException as shown in figure 14-14 to catch this type of error. Then, run the application and redo the testing of step 4 to see how this error is handled now.
6. Delete the data in the Name column of a row, which means that the column contains an empty string. Next, move to another row, and return to the first row to see that the row has been accepted into the dataset. Then, click on the Save button and discover that this doesn't throw an exception because an empty string isn't the same as a null value. This indicates that data validation is required because an empty string isn't an acceptable value in the database. In the next chapter, you'll see an enhanced version of the Customer Maintenance application that provides data validation.
7. Adjust the controls on the form and any related properties so the form looks like the one in figure 14-12. This should take just a minute or two.

Use the Dataset Designer

8. Use one of the techniques in figure 14-16 to view the schema for the dataset in the Dataset Designer.
9. Click on the table adapter in the Dataset Designer and review its properties in the Properties window. Then, look at the Select statement that's used for getting the data into the dataset. To do that, click on the plus sign in front of SelectCommand, and click on the ellipsis button for the CommandText property to open up the Query Builder.
10. Use the Query Builder to modify the Select statement so the rows are sorted in ascending sequence by the Name column as shown in figure 14-17. When you're done, close the Query Builder and click the No button in the dialog box that's displayed.
11. Right-click on the query in the Dataset Designer, and preview the data that will be retrieved by that query as shown in figure 14-18. Note that since you changed the sort sequence, the rows will be displayed in order by the Name column rather than by the CustomerID column.
12. When you're through experimenting, close the Dataset Designer, and close the project.

15

How to work with bound controls and parameterized queries

In the last chapter, you learned the basic skills for developing applications by using data sources and datasets. Now, you'll learn some additional skills for building database applications that way. Specifically, you'll learn how to work with bound controls, how to use parameterized queries, how to customize the generated toolbars, and how to work with a DataGridView control.

How to work with bound text boxes and combo boxes

The topics that follow show you how to work with bound text boxes and combo boxes. First, you'll learn how to format the data that's displayed in text boxes. Second, you'll learn how to bind data to a combo box. And third, you'll learn how to work with the BindingSource object to make sure that the data and controls are synchronized.

How to format the data displayed in a text box

In the last chapter, you learned how to use bound text boxes to work with the data in a Customers table. However, because the columns of that table contain string data, it wasn't necessary to format the data when it was displayed. In many cases, though, you'll want to format the data so it's displayed properly.

Figure 15-1 shows how you can apply standard formatting to the data that's displayed in a bound text box. To do that, you use the Formatting and Advanced Binding dialog box. From this dialog box, you can select the format you want to apply from the Format Type list. Then, you can enter appropriate values for the options that are displayed to the right of this list. In this figure, for example, a currency format is being applied to the text box that's bound to the UnitPrice column of the Products table.

The dialog box that you can use to apply formatting to a column

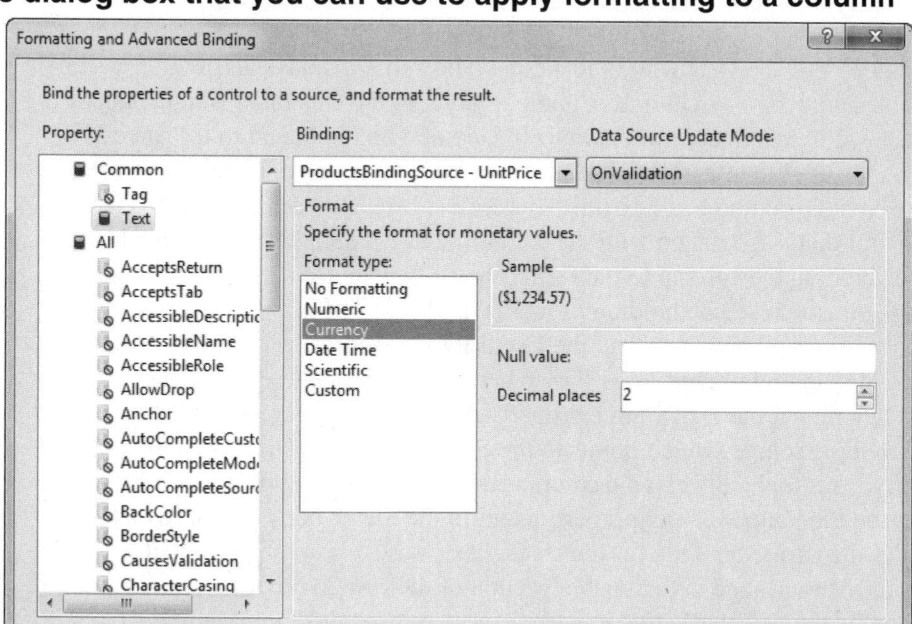

Description

- To display the Formatting and Advanced Binding dialog box, select the text box whose data you want to format, expand the DataBindings group in the Properties window, and then click the ellipsis button that appears when you select the Advanced option.
- To apply a format, select the format you want to use from the Format Type list and enter any additional options that appear to the right of the list. Numeric, Currency, and Scientific let you enter the number of decimal places to be displayed. Date Time lets you select from a number of date and time formats. And Custom lets you enter a custom format.
- Each format also lets you enter the value you want to display in place of a null value. The default is an empty string.
- If you select the Custom format, a note is displayed indicating that the format may not be applied and that you should use the Format or Parse event of the Binding object to apply it instead. See Visual Studio help for more information.

Figure 15-1 How to format the data displayed in a text box

How to bind a combo box to a data source

Figure 15-2 shows how to bind a combo box so it displays all of the rows in one table and updates a column in another table. In the Customer Maintenance form shown in this figure, for example, the combo box is bound to the States table and is used to update the State column in the Customers table. The easiest way to create a combo box like this is to use the Data Sources window to change the control that's associated with the column in the main table to a combo box before you drag the column to the form. Then, you can use the combo box's smart tag menu to set the binding properties.

To start, you'll need to select the Use Data Bound Items check box to display the binding properties as shown here. Then, you can set these properties.

In this figure, the DataSource property of the State combo box is set to StatesBindingSource (which points to the States table), the DisplayMember property is set to the StateName column (which provides the full name of the state), and the ValueMember property is set to the StateCode column (which provides the two-letter code for the state). That way, this combo box will list the full name of each state in the visible portion of the combo box.

Finally, the SelectedValue property is used to bind the ValueMember property to a column in another data source. In this case, the SelectedValue property is set to the State column of the CustomersBindingSource. That way, the StateCode column of the States table is bound to the State column of the Customers table. Then, when the data for a customer is displayed, the state that's selected in the combo box is determined by the State column of the Customers table. Also, if the user selects a different item from the combo box list, the State column in the Customers table is changed to the value selected by the user.

In addition to the four properties in the smart tag menu, you may also need to set a couple of other properties when you bind a combo box. In particular, you can set the DropDownStyle property to DropDownList to prevent the user from entering text into the text portion of the combo box. Then, you can set the Text property in the DataBindings group to None so the application doesn't bind the value stored in this property to the data source. *If this property isn't set correctly, the combo box won't work properly.*

Although you've learned only how to bind combo boxes in this topic, you should realize that you can use similar skills to work with other types of controls. In particular, you can use most of these skills to work with list boxes. If you experiment with this on your own, you shouldn't have any trouble figuring out how it works.

A combo box that's bound to a data source

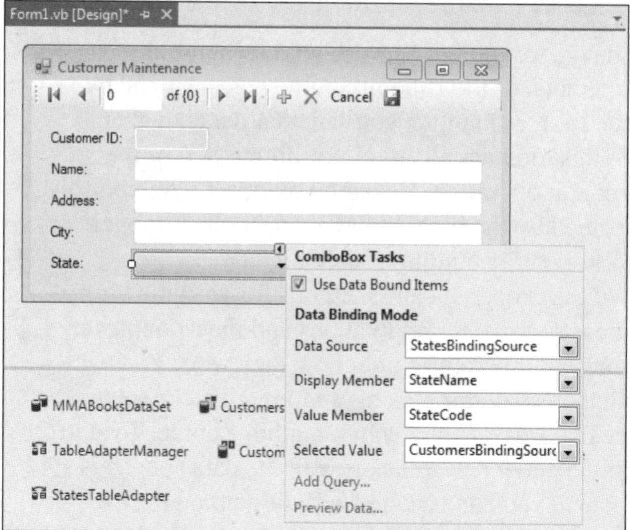

Combo box properties for binding

Property	Description
`DataSource`	The name of the binding source that points to the data table that contains the data displayed in the list.
`DisplayMember`	The name of the data column whose data is displayed in the list.
`ValueMember`	The name of the data column whose value is stored in the list. This value is returned by the SelectedValue property of the control.
`SelectedValue`	Gets the value of the currently selected item. You can use this property to bind the ValueMember property to a column in another data source.

Description

- To access the most common properties for binding a combo box, you can display the smart tag menu for the combo box and select the Use Data Bound Items check box. This will display the properties shown above.
- To set the DataSource property, display the drop-down list; expand the Other Data Sources node, the Project Data Sources node, and the node for the dataset; and select the table you want to use as the data source. This adds BindingSource and TableAdapter objects for the table to the form. Then, you can set the DisplayMember and ValueMember properties to columns in this table.
- The SelectedValue property is typically bound to a column in the main table. That way, if you select a different item from the combo box, the value of this column is set to the value of the ValueMember property for the selected item.
- When you bind a combo box to a data source, you'll typically set the DropDownStyle property of the combo box to DropDownList so the user can only select a value from the list. You'll also want to change the (DataBindings) - Text property to None to remove the binding from the text portion of the combo box.

Figure 15-2 How to bind a combo box to a data source

How to use code to work with a binding source

When you use the binding navigator toolbar to work with a data source, it works by using properties and methods of the BindingSource object. In the two applications presented in chapter 14, for example, you saw that the code that's generated for the Save button of this toolbar calls the EndEdit method of the binding source to end the current edit operation. Because you don't have control over most of the code that's executed by the binding navigator toolbar, though, you may sometimes want to work with the binding source directly.

Figure 15-3 presents some of the properties and methods for working with a binding source. If you review these properties and methods and the examples in this figure, you shouldn't have any trouble figuring out how they work.

You can use the first four methods listed in this figure to modify the rows that are stored in the data source that's associated with a binding source. To start, you can use the AddNew method to add a new, blank row to the data source as illustrated in the first example. Then, you can use the EndEdit method to save the data you enter into the new row as illustrated in the second example. You can also use this method to save changes you make to an existing row.

If an error occurs when you try to save changes to a row, or if the user decides to cancel an edit operation, you can use the CancelEdit method to cancel the changes as illustrated in the third example. Note, however, that you don't have to explicitly start an edit operation. The binding source takes care of that automatically when you make changes to a row. Finally, you can use the RemoveCurrent method to remove the current row from the data source as illustrated in the fourth example.

You can use the last four methods in this figure to move to the first, previous, next, or last row in a data source. You can also use the Position property to get or set the index of the current row. And you can use the Count property to get the number of rows in the data source.

To illustrate how you might use these properties and methods, the last example in this figure presents an event handler that responds to the Click event of a button. This event handler uses the MoveNext method to move to the next row in the data source. Then, it uses the Position property to get the index of the current row, and it adds one to the result since the index is zero-based. Finally, it uses the Count property to get the total number of rows in the data source, and it displays the position and count in a text box. This is similar to the display that's included in the binding navigator toolbar.

Common properties and methods of the BindingSource class

Property	Description
`Position`	The index of the current row in the data source.
`Count`	The number of rows in the data source.
Method	**Description**
`AddNew()`	Adds a new, blank row to the data source.
`EndEdit()`	Saves changes to the current row.
`CancelEdit()`	Cancels changes to the current row.
`RemoveCurrent()`	Removes the current row from the data source.
`MoveFirst()`	Moves to the first row in the data source.
`MovePrevious()`	Moves to the previous row in the data source, if there is one.
`MoveNext()`	Moves to the next row in the data source, if there is one.
`MoveLast()`	Moves to the last row in the data source.

A statement that adds a new row to a data source

```
Me.CustomersBindingSource.AddNew()
```

A statement that saves the changes to the current row and ends the edit

```
Me.CustomersBindingSource.EndEdit()
```

A statement that cancels the changes to the current row

```
Me.CustomersBindingSource.CancelEdit()
```

A statement that removes the current row from a data source

```
Me.CustomersBindingSource.RemoveCurrent()
```

Code that moves to the next row and displays the position and count

```
Private Sub btnNext_Click(sender As Object,
        e As EventArgs) Handles btnNext.Click
    Me.CustomersBindingSource.MoveNext()
    Dim position As Integer = CustomersBindingSource.Position + 1
    txtPosition.Text = position & " of " & CustomersBindingSource.Count
End Sub
```

Description

- The binding source ensures that all controls that are bound to the same data table are synchronized. That way, when you move to another row, the data-bound controls will display the values in that row.
- If a form provides for updating the rows in a data table, moving from one row to another causes any changes made to the current row to be saved to the data table.
- When you add a new row using the AddNew method, the Position property of the binding source is set to one more than the position of the last row in the data table.
- You can use the EndEdit and CancelEdit methods to save or cancel the changes to an existing row or a new row that was added using the AddNew method.

Figure 15-3 How to use code to work with a binding source

How to work with parameterized queries

In the last chapter, you learned how the Data Source Configuration Wizard uses parameters in the SQL statements it generates. A query like this that contains parameters is called a *parameterized query*. In the topics that follow, you'll learn one way to create parameterized queries for your forms.

How to create a parameterized query

For some applications, such as the Product Maintenance application presented in the previous chapter, it's acceptable (or even preferable) to fill the table in the dataset with every row in the database table. However, if a database table contains many columns and rows, this can have a negative impact on the performance of your application. In addition, for some types of applications, you will only want to allow the user to retrieve certain rows from a table. In either case, the solution is to use a parameterized query.

Fortunately, Visual Studio provides an easy way to create a parameterized query, as shown in figure 15-4. When you use this technique, Visual Studio generates a toolbar that lets the user enter the parameters for the query. It also generates the code that fills the table in the dataset with the results of the query.

To create a parameterized query, you can begin by displaying the smart tag menu for any control that's bound to the data source. Then, you can select the Add Query command from this menu. When you do, Visual Studio will display a Search Criteria Builder dialog box like the one shown here. This dialog box lets you enter the name and parameters for the query.

By default, a query is named FillBy, but you can change it to anything you want. I recommend that you name a query based on the function it performs. In this figure, for example, the query has been named FillByCustomerID because it will be used to retrieve a customer row based on the customer ID.

After you enter the query name, you can modify the Where clause of the query so it includes one or more parameters. In SQL Server, you specify a parameter by coding an @ sign in front of the parameter name. In this figure, for example, the query will return all rows where the value in the CustomerID column equals the value of the @CustomerID parameter.

When you finish specifying the query in the Search Criteria Builder dialog box, Visual Studio automatically adds a toolbar to your form. This toolbar contains one or more text boxes that let the user enter the parameters that are needed by the query and a button that lets the user execute the query. You can see this toolbar in the Customer Maintenance form shown in this figure.

Using this toolbar, the user can retrieve a single row that contains the customer's data by entering the ID for the customer and then clicking the FillByCustomerID button. In this figure, for example, the user has displayed the row for the customer with an ID of 35. That's why the binding navigator toolbar shows that only one row exists in the Customers data table.

The dialog box for creating a parameterized query

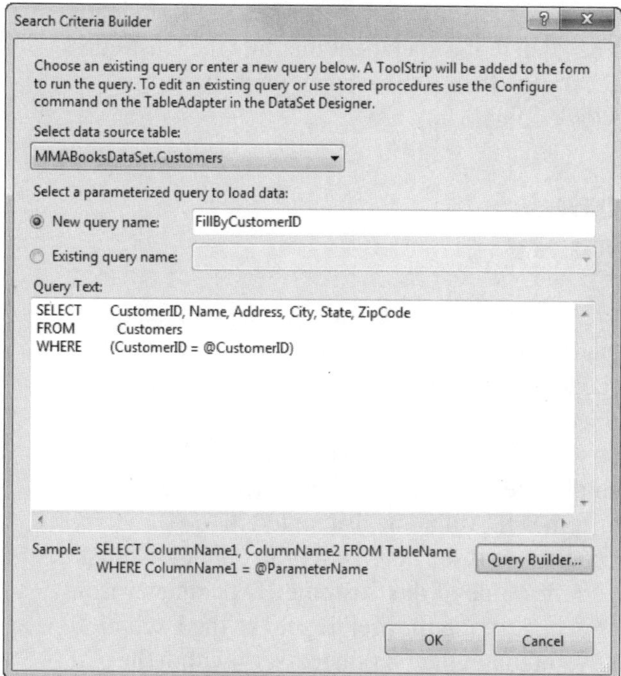

The Customer Maintenance form with a toolbar for the query

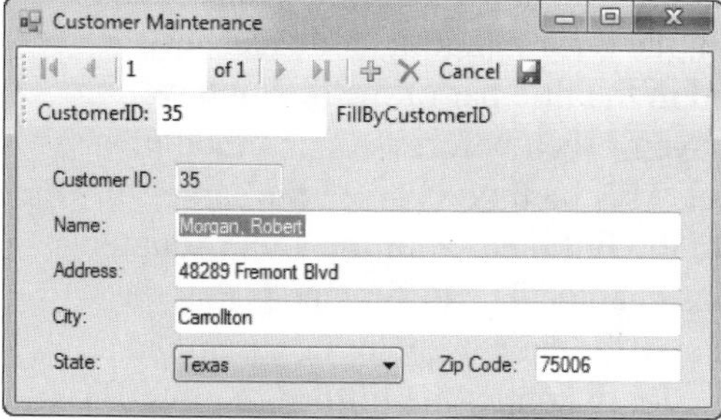

Description

- You can add a *parameterized query* to a data table using the Search Criteria Builder dialog box. To display this dialog box, display the smart tag menu for a control that's bound to the data table and then select the Add Query command.
- When you finish specifying the query in the Search Criteria Builder dialog box, Visual Studio automatically adds a toolbar to your form. This toolbar contains the text boxes that let the user enter the parameters that are needed by the query, and it contains a button that lets the user execute the query.
- You can add more than one parameterized query to a data table using the Search Criteria Builder. Each query you add is displayed in its own toolbar. Because of that, you may want to modify one of the toolbars so it provides for all the queries.

Figure 15-4 How to create a parameterized query

Although the parameterized query in this example retrieves a single row from the Customers table, all of the rows are still retrieved when the form loads. If that's not what you want, you can delete the statement that fills the Customers table from the Load event handler for the form. Then, when the form is first displayed, the Customers table won't contain any rows.

How to use code to work with a parameterized query

As I mentioned, when you create a parameterized query using the Search Criteria Builder dialog box, Visual Studio automatically generates code to fill the data table using the query. This code is shown at the top of figure 15-5. It calls a method of the TableAdapter object to fill the appropriate table in the dataset based on the values the user enters for the parameters when the user clicks the button in the toolbar. In this example, the code fills the Customers table with the row for the customer with the customer ID value the user entered.

If you review the generated code, you'll see that it's a little unwieldy. First, it uses the CType function to convert the value of the CustomerID parameter from a String type to an Integer type. Second, it qualifies references to the Exception class and the MessageBox class even though that isn't necessary within the context of this form. To make this code easier to read, you can clean it up as shown in the second example in this figure. Here, the CType function has been replaced with the more concise Convert.ToInt32 method and all the unnecessary qualification has been removed. In addition, the error handling code has been enhanced so the exception type is displayed in the title bar of the dialog box.

The only piece of code here that you haven't seen before is the method of the TableAdapter object that fills the dataset. This method is given the same name as the query, and it works similarly to the Fill method of the TableAdapter object that you learned about in the previous chapter. The difference is that the method for a parameterized query lets you specify the parameter or parameters that are required by the query. In this figure, for example, the FillByCustomerID method of the CustomersTableAdapter object requires a single parameter of the Integer type. To get this parameter, the code gets the string that's entered by the user into the text box on the toolbar, and it converts this string to an Integer type.

Note that the FillByCustomerID method of the table adapter fills the Customers table of the dataset with only one row. Then, if the user makes any changes to that row, he or she must click the Save button to save those changes to the database. If the user retrieves another row instead, that row fills the dataset and the changes are lost. Similarly, the user must click the Save button to save a deletion before moving to another row. Although this user interface works, it isn't very intuitive. As a result, you'll typically want to modify interfaces like this one.

The generated code for a parameterized query

```
Private Sub FillByCustomerIDToolStripButton_Click(
        sender As Object, e As EventArgs) _
        Handles FillByCustomerIDToolStripButton.Click

    Try
        Me.CustomersTableAdapter.FillByCustomerID(
            Me.MMABooksDataSet.Customers,
            CType(CustomerIDToolStripTextBox.Text, Integer))
    Catch ex As System.Exception
        System.Windows.Forms.MessageBox.Show(ex.Message)
    End Try

End Sub
```

The same code after it has been cleaned up and enhanced

```
Private Sub FillByCustomerIDToolStripButton_Click(
        sender As Object, e As EventArgs) _
        Handles FillByCustomerIDToolStripButton.Click

    Try
        Dim customerID As Integer =
            Convert.ToInt32(CustomerIDToolStripTextBox.Text)
        Me.CustomersTableAdapter.FillByCustomerID(
            Me.MMABooksDataSet.Customers, customerID)
    Catch ex As Exception
        MessageBox.Show(ex.Message, ex.GetType.ToString)
    End Try

End Sub
```

The syntax of the method for filling a table using a parameterized query

```
TableAdapter.QueryName(DataSet.TableName, param1[, param2]...)
```

Description

- When you finish specifying a query in the Search Criteria Builder dialog box, Visual Studio automatically generates the code that uses the appropriate method to fill the table in the dataset when the user clicks the button in the toolbar.
- If necessary, you can modify the generated code to make it easier to read or to change the way it works.

Figure 15-5 How to use code to work with a parameterized query

How to work with the ToolStrip control

Although the toolbar that Visual Studio generates for a parameterized query works well for simple applications, you may want to modify it as your applications become more complex. For example, you may want to change the text on the button that executes the query. Or, you may want to add additional text boxes and buttons that work with other queries. To do that, you work with the ToolStrip control that defines the toolbar.

Before I go on, you should know that the binding navigator toolbar that gets generated when you drag a data source onto a form is a customized ToolStrip control. As a result, you can work with this toolbar just as you would any other ToolStrip control. If, for example, a form won't provide for inserts, updates, and deletes, you can remove the Add, Delete, and Save buttons from this toolbar. You can also add controls that perform customized functions.

How to use the Items Collection Editor

To work with the items on a ToolStrip control, you use the Items Collection Editor shown in figure 15-6. To start, you can add an item by selecting the type of control you want to add from the combo box in the upper left corner and clicking the Add button. This adds the item to the bottom of the Members list. Then, if necessary, you can move the item using the up and down arrow buttons to the right of the Members list.

You can also use the Items Collection Editor to set the properties for a new or existing item. To do that, just select the item in the Members list and use the Properties list at the right side of the dialog box to set the properties. The table in this figure lists the four properties you're most likely to change. Note that when you add a new Button control, the DisplayStyle property is set to Image by default. If you want to display the text that you specify for the Text property instead of an image, then, you need to change the DisplayStyle property to Text.

Finally, you can use the Items Collection Editor to delete an existing item. To do that, just select the item and click the Delete button to the right of the Members list.

The Items Collection Editor for an enhanced ToolStrip control

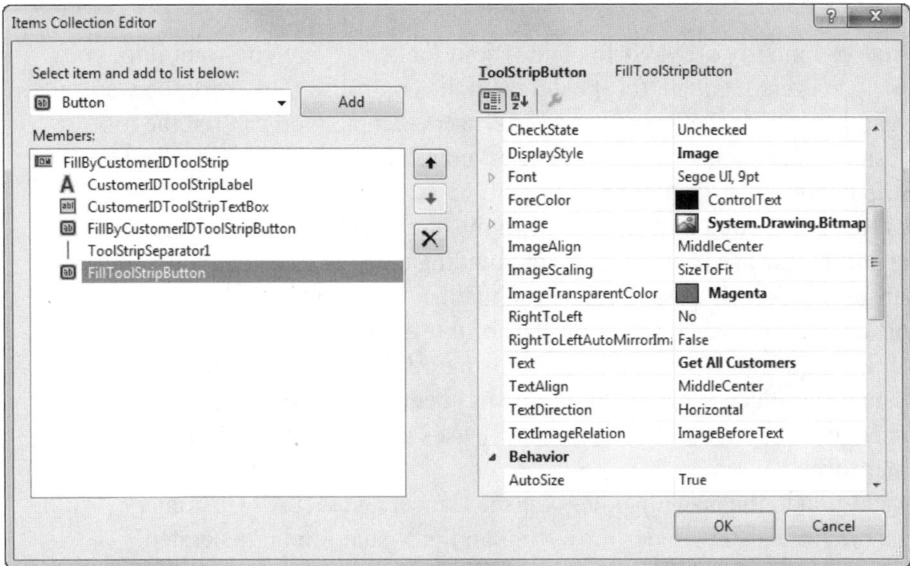

Common properties of ToolStrip items

Property	Description
`DisplayStyle`	Indicates whether a button displays an image, text, or both an image and text.
`Image`	The image that's displayed on a button if you select Image or ImageAndText for the DisplayStyle property.
`Text`	The text that's displayed on a button if you select Text or ImageAndText for the DisplayStyle property.
`Width`	The width of the item.

Description

- To display the Items Collection Editor dialog box, display the smart tag menu for the ToolStrip and select the Edit Items command.
- To add an item, select the type of control you want to add from the combo box and click the Add button. To add a separator bar, choose Separator. You can also add an item by using the drop-down list that's displayed when the ToolStrip is selected in the Form Designer.
- To move an item, select the item in the Members list and click the up and down arrows to the right of the list.
- To delete an item, select it in the members list and click the Delete button to the right of the list.
- To set the properties for an item, select the item in the Members list and use the Properties list on the right side of the dialog box. You can also set the properties of an item by selecting it in the Form Designer and then using the Properties window.

Figure 15-6 How to use the Items Collection Editor

How to code an event handler for a ToolStrip item

After you modify a ToolStrip control so it looks the way you want it to, you need to code event handlers for the items on the control so they work the way you want them to. At the top of figure 15-7, for example, you can see the top of a Customer Maintenance form that uses a binding navigator toolbar and the ToolStrip control that was defined in figure 15-6.

For this application to work, the form must include an event handler for the Cancel button that has been added to the binding navigator toolbar and an event handler for the Get All Customers button that has been added to the ToolStrip control. To generate the code for the start of those event handlers, you can use the technique that's summarized in this figure. For the Cancel button, the event handler just cancels the editing that has been started. And for the Get All Customers button, the event handler simply uses the Fill query to retrieve all the customer rows.

In addition to the event handlers for the Cancel and Get All Customers buttons, the form also includes the event handler Visual Studio generated when the FillByCustomerID parameterized query was created. You can see an enhanced version of that event handler in this figure. Here, code has been added so that if the customer with the customer ID the user enters isn't found, an error message is displayed. In addition, the single Catch block that Visual Studio generated to catch any exception has been replaced by two Catch blocks that catch specific exceptions. The first one catches a FormatException, which will occur if the customer ID isn't an integer, and the second one catches a SqlException.

Customized toolbars for a Customer Maintenance application

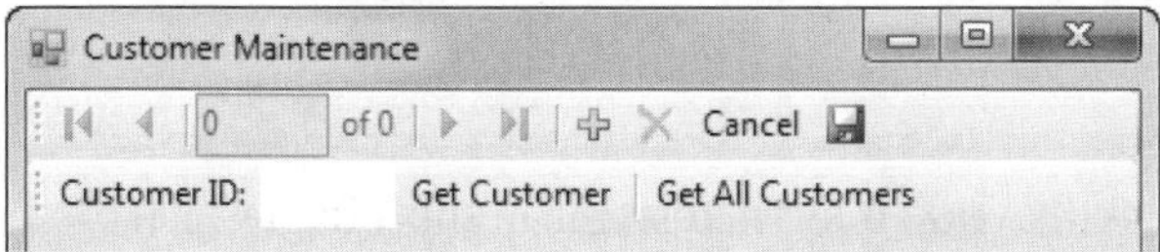

The event handler for the Cancel ToolStrip button

```
Private Sub BindingNavigatorCancelItem_Click(
        sender As Object, e As EventArgs) _
        Handles BindingNavigatorCancelItem.Click
    CustomersBindingSource.CancelEdit()
End Sub
```

The event handler for the Get All Customers ToolStrip button

```
Private Sub FillToolStripButton_Click(sender As Object,
        e As EventArgs) Handles FillToolStripButton.Click
    Try
        Me.CustomersTableAdapter.Fill(Me.MMABooksDataSet.Customers)
    Catch ex As SqlException
        MessageBox.Show("SQL Server error # " & ex.Number &
            ": " & ex.Message, ex.GetType.ToString)
    End Try
End Sub
```

The event handler for the Get Customer ToolStrip button

```
Private Sub FillByCustomerIDToolStripButton_Click(
        sender As Object, e As EventArgs) _
        Handles FillByCustomerIDToolStripButton.Click
    Try
        Dim customerID As Integer =
            Convert.ToInt32(CustomerIDToolStripTextBox.Text)
        Me.CustomersTableAdapter.FillByCustomerID(
            Me.MMABooksDataSet.Customers, customerID)
        If CustomersBindingSource.Count = 0 Then
            MessageBox.Show("No customer found with this ID. " &
                "Please try again.", "Customer Not Found")
        End If
    Catch ex As FormatException
        MessageBox.Show("Customer ID must be an integer.",
            "Entry Error")
    Catch ex As SqlException
        MessageBox.Show("SQL Server error # " & ex.Number &
            ": " & ex.Message, ex.GetType.ToString)
    End Try
End Sub
```

Description

- To code an event handler for a ToolStrip item, display the form in the Form Designer, click on the item to select it, and click on the Events button of the Properties window to display the list of events for the item. Then, you can use standard techniques to generate or select an event handler for a specified event.

Figure 15-7 How to code an event handler for a ToolStrip item

An enhanced Customer Maintenance application

To illustrate some of the new skills you've learned so far in this chapter, I'll now present an enhanced version of the Customer Maintenance application that you saw in the last chapter.

The user interface

Figure 15-8 presents the user interface for the Customer Maintenance application. This time, the application uses two queries. The first one retrieves a row from the Customers table based on its customer ID, and the second one retrieves all the rows from the Customers table. In addition, the form uses a combo box that lets the user select a state, and its generated toolbars have been modified.

The code

Figure 15-8 also presents the code for the Customer Maintenance application. Since you've already seen most of this code, you shouldn't have any trouble understanding how it works. So I'll just point out some highlights.

First, the event handler for the Load event of the form doesn't load all the customers into the Customers table. That's because the second toolbar on the form provides a way for the user to do that if necessary. This is more efficient than retrieving all the customers when the form is loaded because the customers are retrieved only if requested.

Second, the event handler for the Click event of the Cancel button contains a single statement that cancels the current edit operation. Since this operation can't cause any exceptions, you don't have to use a Try...Catch statement with it.

Third, the event handler for the Click event of the Save button starts by checking if the data source contains at least one row. If not, it indicates that the row that was retrieved has been deleted. In that case, the data shouldn't be validated. Instead, the database should just be updated.

If the data source contains at least one row, a function named IsValidData is called. You saw procedures like this in chapter 7. It checks that the user has entered a value into each control on the form by calling another function named IsPresent for each of those controls. Unlike the IsPresent function you saw in chapter 7, this function checks for values in both text boxes and combo boxes. To do that, it uses the GetType method of the control that's passed to the function to get the control type, and it uses the ToString method of that type to get the name of the type. Then, it compares that name with type names that are specified as strings, and it processes the data in the control accordingly.

The user interface for the Customer Maintenance application

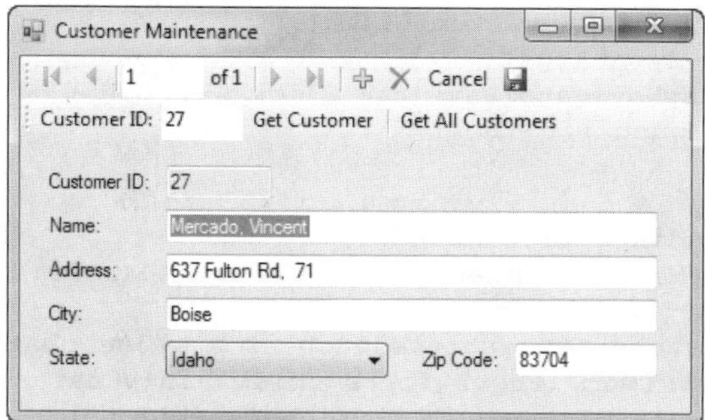

The code for the application

Page 1

```
Imports System.Data.SqlClient

Public Class Form1

    Private Sub Form1_Load(sender As Object,
            e As EventArgs) Handles MyBase.Load
        Try
            Me.StatesTableAdapter.Fill(Me.MMABooksDataSet.States)
            StateComboBox.SelectedIndex = -1
        Catch ex As SqlException
            MessageBox.Show("SQL Server error # " & ex.Number &
                ": " & ex.Message, ex.GetType.ToString)
        End Try
    End Sub

    Private Sub FillByCustomerIDToolStripButton_Click(
            sender As Object, e As EventArgs) _
            Handles FillByCustomerIDToolStripButton.Click
        Try
            Dim customerID As Integer =
                Convert.ToInt32(CustomerIDToolStripTextBox.Text)
            Me.CustomersTableAdapter.FillByCustomerID(
                Me.MMABooksDataSet.Customers, customerID)
            If CustomersBindingSource.Count = 0 Then
                MessageBox.Show("No customer found with this ID. " &
                    "Please try again.", "Customer Not Found")
            End If
        Catch ex As FormatException
            MessageBox.Show("Customer ID must be an integer.",
                "Entry Error")
        Catch ex As SqlException
            MessageBox.Show("SQL Server error # " & ex.Number &
                ": " & ex.Message, ex.GetType.ToString)
        End Try
    End Sub

    Private Sub BindingNavigatorCancelItem_Click(
            sender As Object, e As EventArgs) _
            Handles BindingNavigatorCancelItem.Click
        CustomersBindingSource.CancelEdit()
    End Sub
```

Figure 15-8 An enhanced Customer Maintenance application (part 1 of 3)

The code for the application **Page 2**

```
Private Sub CustomersBindingNavigatorSaveItem_Click(
        sender As Object, e As EventArgs) _
        Handles CustomersBindingNavigatorSaveItem.Click
    If CustomersBindingSource.Count > 0 Then
        If IsValidData() Then
            Try
                Me.CustomersBindingSource.EndEdit()
                Me.TableAdapterManager.UpdateAll(Me.MMABooksDataSet)
            Catch ex As ArgumentException
                ' This block catches exceptions such as a value that's
                ' beyond the maximum length for a column in a dataset.
                MessageBox.Show(ex.Message, "Argument Exception")
                CustomersBindingSource.CancelEdit()
            Catch ex As DBConcurrencyException
                MessageBox.Show("A concurrency error occurred. " &
                    "The row was not updated.",
                    "Concurrency Exception")
                Me.CustomersTableAdapter.Fill(
                    Me.MMABooksDataSet.Customers)
            Catch ex As DataException
                MessageBox.Show(ex.Message, ex.GetType.ToString)
                CustomersBindingSource.CancelEdit()
            Catch ex As SqlException
                MessageBox.Show("SQL Server error # " & ex.Number &
                    ": " & ex.Message, ex.GetType.ToString)
            End Try
        End If
    Else
        Try
            Me.TableAdapterManager.UpdateAll(Me.MMABooksDataSet)
        Catch ex As DBConcurrencyException
            MessageBox.Show("A concurrency error occurred. " &
                "The row was not updated.", "Concurrency Exception")
            Me.CustomersTableAdapter.Fill(
                Me.MMABooksDataSet.Customers)
        Catch ex As SqlException
            MessageBox.Show("SQL Server error # " & ex.Number &
                ": " & ex.Message, ex.GetType.ToString)
        End Try
    End If
End Sub

Private Function IsValidData() As Boolean
    Return _
        IsPresent(NameTextBox, "Name") AndAlso
        IsPresent(AddressTextBox, "Address") AndAlso
        IsPresent(CityTextBox, "City") AndAlso
        IsPresent(StateComboBox, "State") AndAlso
        IsPresent(ZipCodeTextBox, "Zip code")
End Function
```

Figure 15-8 An enhanced Customer Maintenance application (part 2 of 3)

The code for the application Page 3

```
Private Function IsPresent(control As Control,
        name As String) As Boolean
    If control.GetType.ToString = "System.Windows.Forms.TextBox" Then
        Dim textBox As TextBox = CType(control, TextBox)
        If textBox.Text = "" Then
            MessageBox.Show(name & " is a required field.",
                "Entry Error")
            textBox.Select()
            Return False
        Else
            Return True
        End If
    ElseIf control.GetType.ToString =
            "System.Windows.Forms.ComboBox" Then
        Dim comboBox As ComboBox = CType(control, ComboBox)
        If comboBox.SelectedIndex = -1 Then
            MessageBox.Show(name & " is a required field.",
                "Entry Error")
            comboBox.Select()
            Return False
        Else
            Return True
        End If
    End If
End Function

Private Sub FillToolStripButton_Click(sender As Object,
        e As EventArgs) Handles FillToolStripButton.Click
    Try
        Me.CustomersTableAdapter.Fill(Me.MMABooksDataSet.Customers)
    Catch ex As SqlException
        MessageBox.Show("SQL Server error # " & ex.Number &
            ": " & ex.Message, ex.GetType.ToString)
    End Try
End Sub

End Class
```

Figure 15-8 An enhanced Customer Maintenance application (part 3 of 3)

How to work with a DataGridView control

In chapter 14, you saw how easy it is to use a DataGridView control to work with the data in a table of a dataset. Now, you'll learn how to modify a DataGridView control so it looks and functions the way you want. In addition, you'll learn how to use a DataGridView control to create a Master/Detail form.

How to modify the properties of a DataGridView control

When you generate a DataGridView control from a data source, Visual Studio usually sets the properties of this control and the other objects it creates the way you want them. However, if you want to modify any of these properties, you can do that just as you would for any other type of object. In particular, you'll probably want to edit the properties of the DataGridView control to change its appearance and function.

To change the most common properties of a DataGridView control, you can use its smart tag menu as shown in figure 15-9. From this menu, you can create a read-only data grid by removing the check marks from the Enable Adding, Enable Editing, and Enable Deleting check boxes as shown here. Or, you can let a user reorder the columns by checking the Enable Column Reordering check box.

In addition to editing the properties for the grid, you may want to edit the properties for the columns of the grid. For example, you may want to apply currency formatting to a column, or you may want to change the column headings or widths. To do that, you can select the Edit Columns command to display the Edit Columns dialog box shown in the next figure.

By default, when you run an application that uses a DataGridView control, you can sort the rows in a column by clicking in the header at the top of the column. The first time you do this, the rows are sorted in ascending sequence by the values in the column; the next time, in descending sequence. Similarly, you can drag the column separators to change the widths of the columns. Last, if the Enable Column Reordering option is checked, you can reorder the columns by dragging them. These features let the user customize the presentation of the data.

The smart tag menu for a DataGridView control

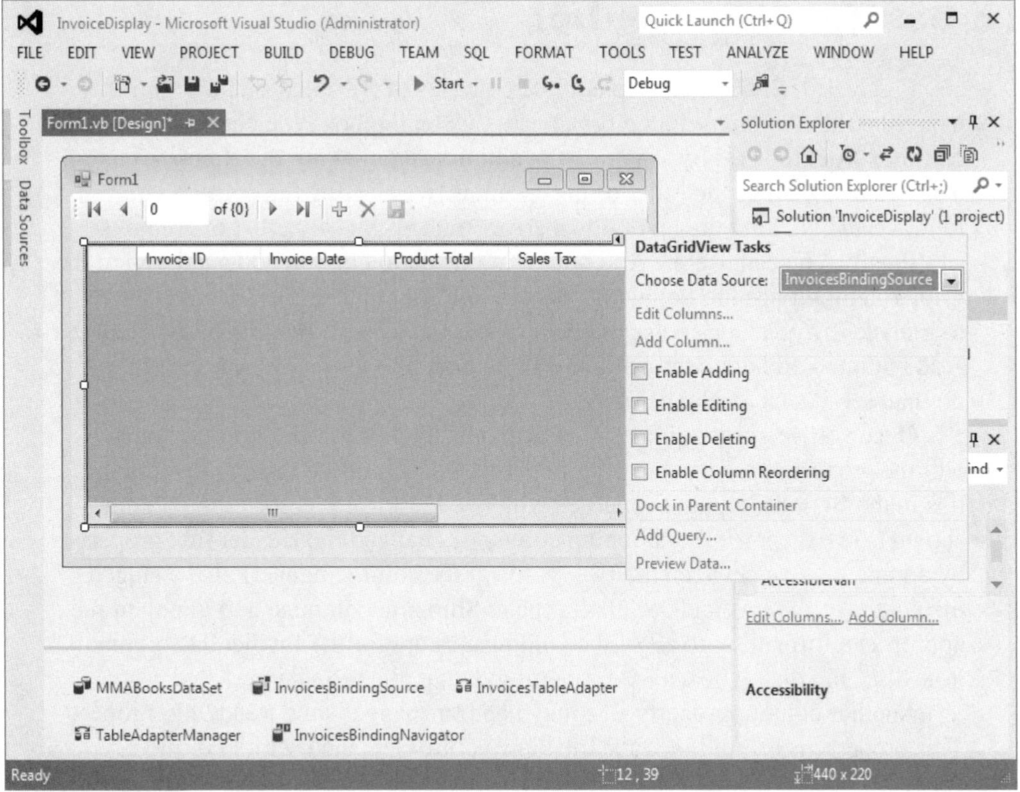

Description

- You can use the smart tag menu of a DataGridView control to edit its most commonly used properties.
- To edit the columns, select the Edit Columns command to display the Edit Columns dialog box. Then, you can edit the columns as described in the next figure.
- To prevent a user from adding, updating, or deleting data that's displayed in the DataGridView control, uncheck the Enable Adding, Enable Editing, or Enable Deleting check boxes.
- To allow a user to reorder the columns in a DataGridView control by dragging them, check the Enable Column Reordering check box.
- You can edit other properties of a DataGridView control by using the Properties window for the control.

Figure 15-9 How to modify the properties of a DataGridView control

How to edit the columns of a DataGridView control

Figure 15-10 shows how to edit the columns of a DataGridView control using the Edit Columns dialog box. From this dialog box, you can remove columns from the grid by selecting the column and clicking the Remove button. You can also change the order of the columns by selecting the column you want to move and clicking the up or down arrow to the right of the list of columns.

Finally, you can use the Add button in this dialog box to add a column to the grid. You might need to do that if you delete a column and then decide you want to include it. You can also use the dialog box that's displayed when you click the Add button to add unbound columns to the grid. For more information on how to do that, see Visual Studio help.

Once you've got the right columns displayed in the correct order, you can edit the properties for a column by selecting the column to display its properties in the Bound Column Properties window. For example, for each column shown here except for the Shipping column, I changed the HeaderText property by adding a space between the two words in the column name. I also changed the widths of the InvoiceID, SalesTax, and Shipping columns, and I applied the appropriate formatting to all of the columns except for the InvoiceID column. You'll see the dialog boxes for formatting data in the next figure.

Another column property you may need to change is the ReadOnly property. This property is useful if a DataGridView control lets the user add or modify rows, but you only want the user to be able to enter data in selected columns. Then, you can set the ReadOnly property of the other columns to True so the user can't enter data into those columns.

The dialog box for editing the columns of a DataGridView control

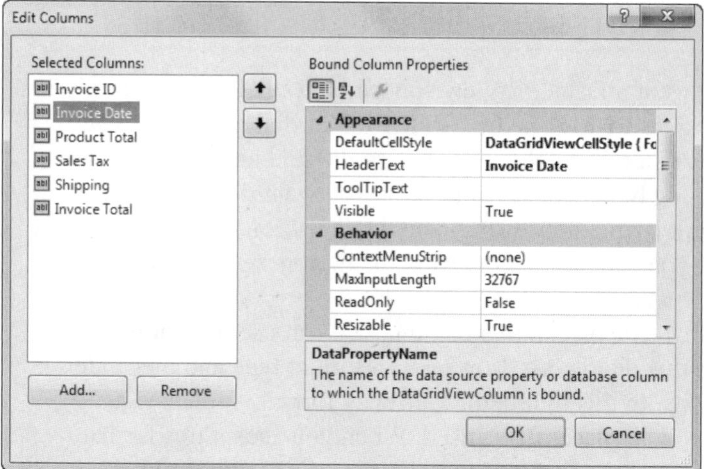

Common properties of a column

Property	Description
`HeaderText`	The text that's displayed in the column header.
`Width`	The number of pixels that are used for the width of the column.
`DefaultCellStyle`	The style that's applied to the cell. You can use dialog boxes to set style elements such as color, format, and alignment.
`ReadOnly`	Determines if the data in the column can be modified.
`SortMode`	Determines if the data in the grid can be sorted by the values in the column and how the sorting is performed. The default option is Automatic, which uses the built-in sorting mechanism. To provide for custom sorting, select the Programmatic option. To turn off sorting, select the NotSortable option.

Description

- You can use the Edit Columns dialog box to control which columns are displayed in the grid and to edit the properties of those columns. To display this dialog box, choose the Edit Columns command from the smart tag menu for the control.
- To remove columns from the grid, select the column and click the Remove button.
- To add a column to the grid, click the Add button and then complete the dialog box that's displayed. This dialog box lets you add both bound and unbound columns.
- To change the order of the columns, select the column you want to move and click the up or down arrow to the right of the list of columns.
- To edit the properties for a column, select the column and use the Bound Column Properties window to edit the properties.

Figure 15-10 How to edit the columns of a DataGridView control

How to format the data in the columns of a DataGridView control

To format the columns of a DataGridView control, you can use the two dialog boxes shown in figure 15-11. The CellStyle Builder dialog box lets you specify the general appearance of a column including the font and colors it uses. You can also use this dialog box to specify the value you want displayed in place of a null value (the default is an empty string) and the layout of the column. In this figure, for example, you can see that the Alignment property has been set to MiddleRight.

To format the data that's displayed in a column, you can use the Format String dialog box. From this dialog box, you select a format type and then enter any other available options. In this figure, the Currency format is selected and the default number of decimal places (2) is used. When you accept this format, the format code is assigned to the Format property in the CellStyle Builder dialog box as shown here. Of course, if you already know the format code you want to use, you can enter it directly into the CellStyle Builder dialog box.

The dialog boxes for formatting the columns of a DataGridView control

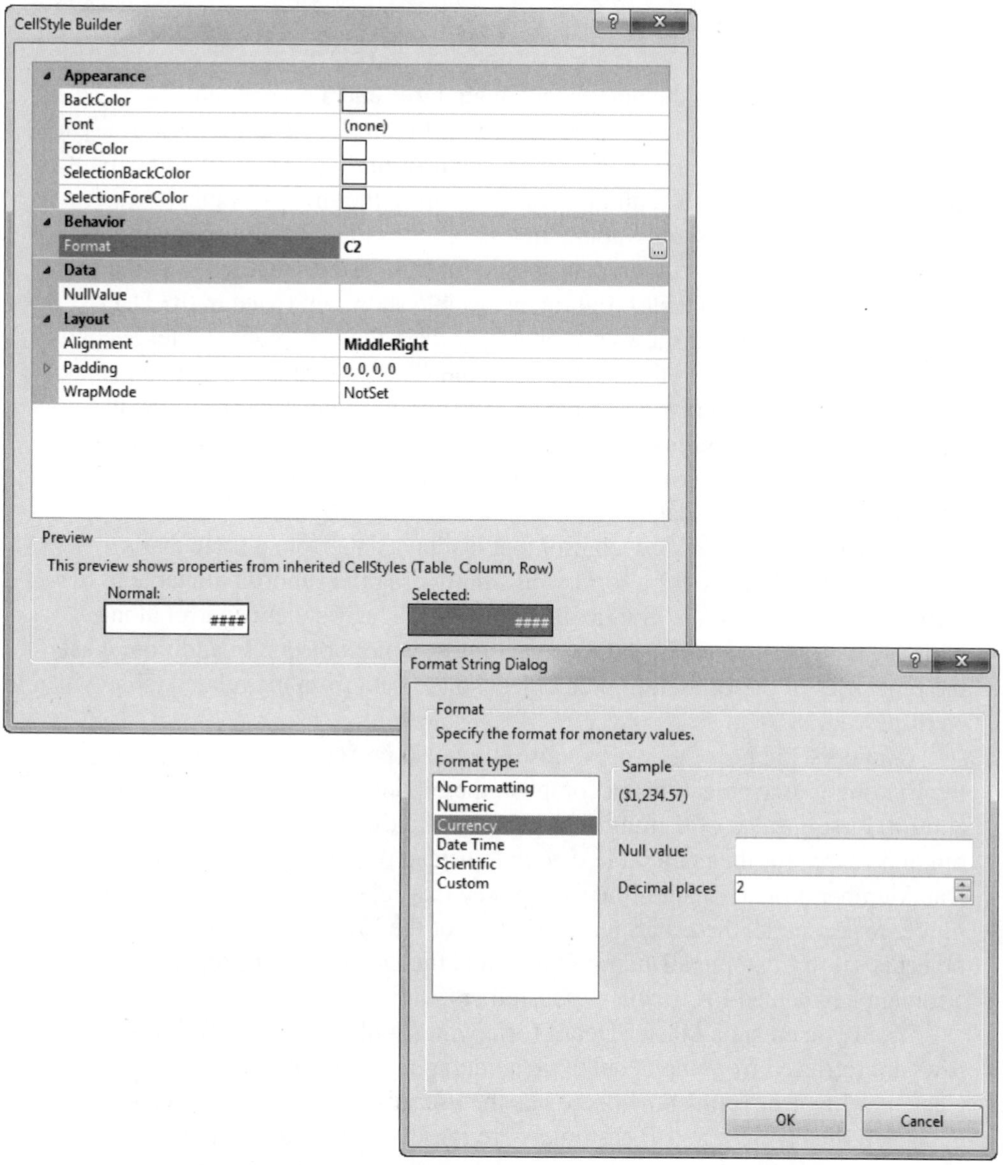

Description

- To display the CellStyle Builder dialog box, click the ellipsis button that appears when you select the DefaultCellStyle property in the Edit Columns dialog box.
- To apply a format to a column, select the Format property and then click the ellipsis button to display the Format String dialog box. Select the format you want to use from the Format Type list and enter any options that appear to the right of the list.

Figure 15-11 How to format the data in the columns of a DataGridView control

How to use a DataGridView control to create a Master/Detail form

A form that displays the data from a main table and a related table is commonly referred to as a *Master/Detail form*. Figure 15-12 shows how to use a DataGridView control to create a Master/Detail form. In this example, the main table is the Customers table, and the related table is the Invoices table.

The first thing you should notice in this figure is the Data Sources window. Although you would expect the data source for this form to include both the Customers and Invoices tables, the Invoices table shows up twice in the Data Sources window. First, it shows up separately from the Customers table. Second, it shows up subordinate to the Customers table. This subordinate entry indicates that the Customers and Invoices tables have a one-to-many relationship with each other. It's this relationship, which is based on the CustomerID column in each table, that Visual Studio uses to generate a DataGridView control that displays the appropriate data.

To create a DataGridView control that displays data from a table that's related to the main table for a form, you simply drag the subordinate table to the form. When you do, Visual Studio generates the DataGridView control along with the appropriate BindingSource and TableAdapter objects. In addition, it sets the properties of the BindingSource object so the data from the related table will be displayed.

To understand how this works, this figure also presents the properties of the BindingSource object that accomplish the binding for the DataGridView control. First, instead of naming a dataset, the DataSource property names the binding source for the main table. Second, instead of naming a data table, the DataMember property names the foreign key that relates the two tables. In this figure, for example, the DataSource property of the InvoicesBindingSource object is set to CustomersBindingSource, and the DataMember property is set to a foreign key named FK_Invoices_Customers.

When you create a Master/Detail form, you should realize that all of the rows are retrieved from the detail table by default. For example, because the Customer Invoices form shown here lets the user display all the invoices for any customer, the invoices for all customers are retrieved when the form is loaded. If the Invoices table contains a large number of rows, that may not be what you want. In that case, you can create a parameterized query to retrieve the invoices just for the customer the user selects. You'll see an example of that in the Customer Invoice Display application that's presented next.

A form that uses a DataGridView control to display data from a related table

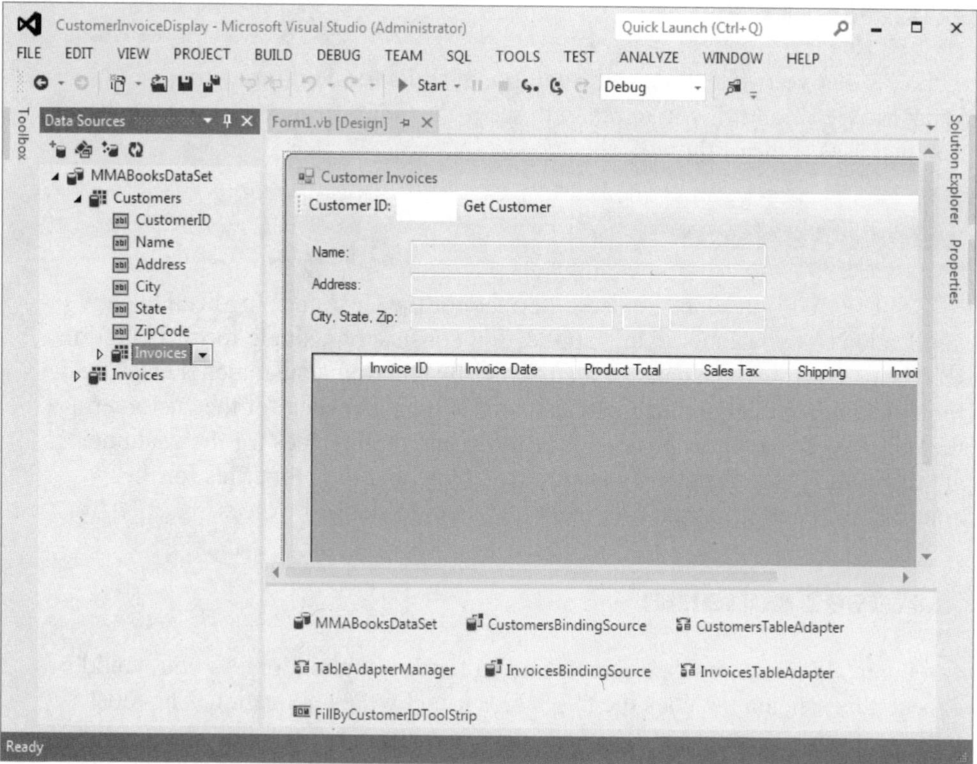

Two BindingSource properties for displaying data from a related table

Property	Description
DataSource	The source of the data for the BindingSource object. To display data from a table that's related to the main table for the form, this property should be set to the BindingSource object for the main table.
DataMember	A sub-list of the data source for the BindingSource object. To display data from a table that's related to the main table for the form, this property should be set to the foreign key that relates the two tables.

The property settings for the InvoicesBindingSource object

Property	Setting
DataSource	CustomersBindingSource
DataMember	FK_Invoices_Customers

Description

- If a table has a one-to-many relationship with another table, that table will appear subordinate to the main table in the Data Sources window. Then, you can drag the subordinate table to a form to create a DataGridView control that displays the rows in the subordinate table that are related to the current row in the main table.

Figure 15-12 How to use a DataGridView control to create a Master/Detail form

A Customer Invoice Display application

Now that you've learned some additional skills for working with a DataGridView control, you're ready to see a Customer Invoice Display application that uses some of those skills.

The user interface

Figure 15-13 presents the user interface for the Customer Invoice Display application. As you can see, this application consists of a single form. This form lets the user retrieve the data for a customer by entering a customer ID into the toolbar and then clicking the Get Customer button. The data for the customer is then displayed in the text boxes on the form, and the invoices for the customer are displayed in the DataGridView control. Note that the properties for this control have been set so the user can't add, edit, or delete invoices.

The dataset schema

Figure 15-14 shows the dataset schema for this application. As you would expect, this schema includes the two tables used by the application. The most important thing to notice here is the FillByCustomerID query that's been created for each table adapter. These queries are used to retrieve the appropriate data based on the customer ID the user enters.

Please note, however, that you don't need the FillByCustomerID query for the Invoices table when you use a Master/Detail form that relates the Customers and Invoices tables. For this application, this FillByCustomerID query will be used just to make the application more efficient. You'll see how this query is used in the code that follows. And you can get some hands-on experience with this by doing exercise 15-2 at the end of this chapter.

The code for the Customer Invoices form

Figure 15-15 presents the code for the Customer Invoices form. The first thing you should notice here is that this form doesn't include a Load event handler. Because of that, no data is loaded into the dataset when the application starts. Instead, when a user enters a customer ID and clicks the Get Customer button, the row for that customer is loaded into the Customers table using the FillByCustomerID query of the Customers table adapter. In addition, any invoices for the customer are loaded into the Invoices table using the FillByCustomerID query of the Invoices table adapter. You can see the code that accomplishes this in the event handler in this figure.

The Customer Invoices form

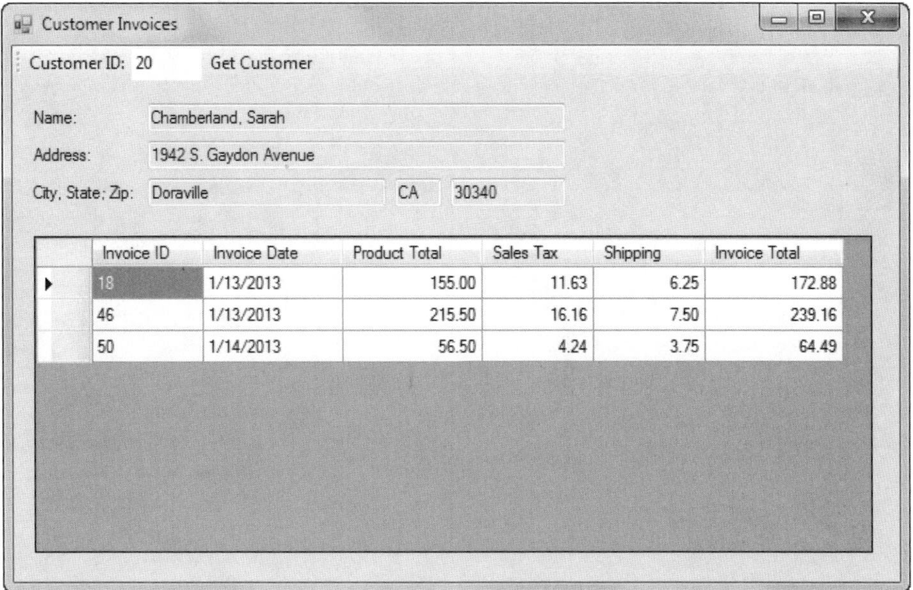

Description

- The Customer Invoices form is a Master/Detail form that displays the Invoices for a selected customer. For efficiency, this form doesn't retrieve any data when the form is loaded. Instead, when the user enters a customer number, the customer and invoice data for that customer is retrieved.
- Because this application doesn't let the user add, modify, or delete invoices, the binding navigator toolbar has been omitted from the Customer Invoices form.

Figure 15-13 The user interface for the Customer Invoice Display application

The dataset schema

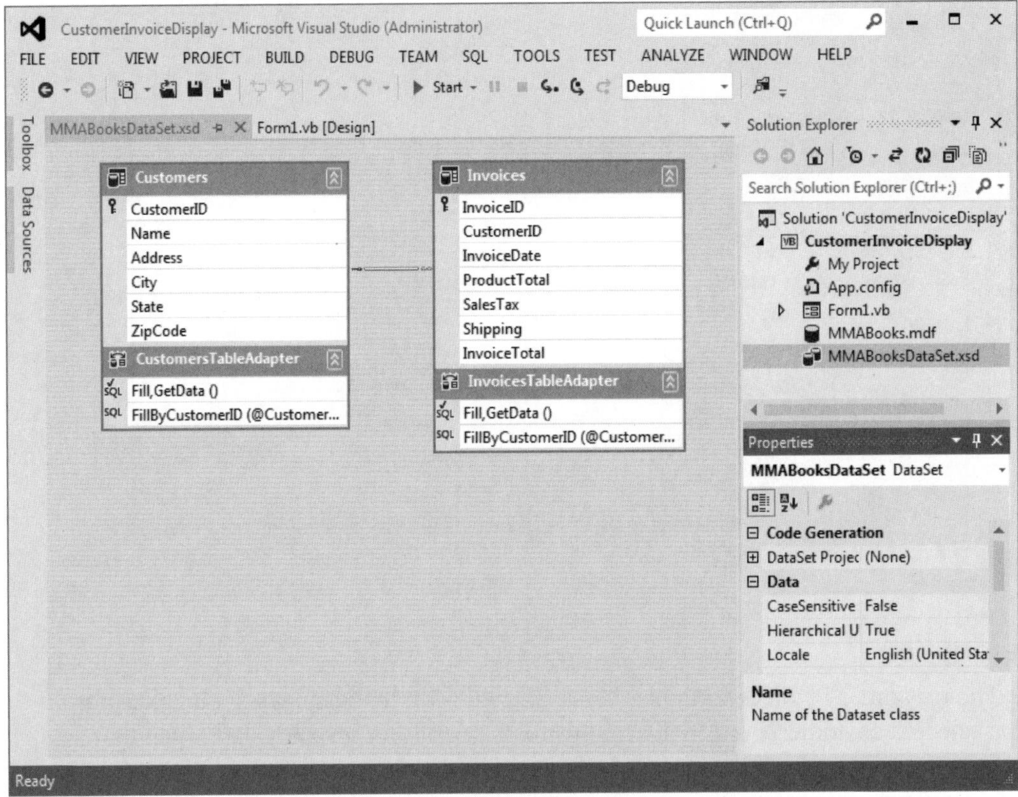

Description

- The MMABooks dataset defines the two tables used by this application: Customers and Invoices.
- The FillByCustomerID query for the Customers table adapter is used to retrieve the customer data that's displayed on the Customer Invoices form. This query is based on the customer ID the user enters into the toolbar on the form.
- The FillByCustomerID query for the Invoices table adapter is used to retrieve the invoice data that's displayed on the Customer Invoices form. This query is also based on the customer ID the user enters into the toolbar on the form.

Figure 15-14 The dataset schema for the Customer Invoice Display application

The code for the Customer Invoices form

```
Imports System.Data.SqlClient

Public Class Form1

    Private Sub FillByCustomerIDToolStripButton_Click(
            sender As Object, e As EventArgs) _
            Handles FillByCustomerIDToolStripButton.Click
        Try
            Dim customerID As Integer =
                Convert.ToInt32(CustomerIDToolStripTextBox.Text)
            Me.CustomersTableAdapter.FillByCustomerID(
                Me.MMABooksDataSet.Customers, customerID)
            Me.InvoicesTableAdapter.FillByCustomerID(
                Me.MMABooksDataSet.Invoices, customerID)
        Catch ex As FormatException
            MessageBox.Show("Customer ID must be an integer.",
                "Entry Error")
        Catch ex As SqlException
            MessageBox.Show("SQL Server error # " & ex.Number &
                ": " & ex.Message, ex.GetType.ToString)
        End Try
    End Sub

End Class
```

Description

- The only code that's required for this form is the code that retrieves the customer and invoice data. This code is executed when the user enters a customer ID and then presses the Get Customer button on the Customer Invoices form.

Figure 15-15 The code for the Customer Invoice Display application

Perspective

Now that you've completed this chapter, you should be able to use data sources and datasets to develop substantial database applications. You should also realize how quickly you can prototype these applications. But if you do the exercises that follow, which guide you through the development of the chapter applications from scratch, you should start to see that using data sources isn't quite as easy as it may at first appear. Because of that, you may want to use other techniques to develop more complex database applications. In the next chapter, for example, you'll learn the basics of developing applications by writing your own ADO.NET code.

Terms

parameterized query
Master/Detail form

Exercise 15-1 Build the Customer Maintenance application

This exercise will guide you through the development of the application in figure 15-8. You'll learn a lot by doing that.

Build the user interface

1. Start a new project named CustomerMaintenance in the C:\VB 2012\Chapter 15 directory. Then, add the MMABooks.mdf file in the C:\VB 2012\Database directory to the project, and create a data source that includes all the columns in the Customers and States tables. Be sure to change the "Copy to Output Directory" property of the database file to "Copy if newer".
2. Change the control that's associated with the State column of the Customers table to a combo box. Then, drag the Customers table onto the form so that detail controls are generated, but leave enough room at the top for two toolbars. Rearrange the controls and change any required properties so those controls look like the ones in figure 15-8.
3. Use the procedure in figure 15-2 to bind the State combo box on the form to the States table in the data source. Then, set the DropDownStyle property for the combo box to DropDownList, and set its (DataBindings) – Text property to None.
4. Test the application to see how this user interface works. If the state that's displayed for the first customer is incorrect, it's because the Customers table is loaded before the States table. That means that the first customer is displayed before the binding defined by the State combo box is applied. To correct this problem, end the application and switch the statements in the Load event handler for the form so that the States table is loaded first.

5. Run the application again to see how this works. Then, use the combo box to change one of the State entries. End the application, and review the other code that has been generated for the form.

Add a parameterized query

6. Use the procedure in figure 15-4 to add a parameterized query named FillByCustomerID that gets the Customer row for a specific customer ID. Then, note the toolbar that has been added to the form. Now, review the code that has been added to the application, and review the schema for the dataset.
7. Test the application to see how it works. First, use the binding navigator toolbar to move through the rows. Then, enter a customer ID of 9 in the second toolbar and click the FillByCustomerID button. Now, go back to the binding navigator toolbar, and you'll discover that you can't use it to go through the rows anymore because the dataset contains only one row.
8. With the application still running, use the second toolbar to go to row 13, and select a new state from the combo box, but don't click the Save button. Then, go to row 10, select a new state, and click the Save button. Now, go to row 13 to see that the state has reverted to what it was originally, and go to row 10 to see that the state has been changed. This shows that you must click the Save button after each change if you want the changes to be made to the database. That's because the dataset consists of only one row at a time.
9. Add a valid row to the dataset and click the Save button. Then, note that the binding navigator toolbar lets you navigate between the previous row and the one you just added because two rows are now in the dataset. As soon as you use the second toolbar to go to a different row, though, the first toolbar shows only one row in the dataset.
10. Delete the row that you added in step 9 by going to that row and clicking the Delete button, which makes the row disappear. Then, click the Save button to apply the deletion to the database. If you don't do that, the row won't be deleted. When you're done, end the application.

Modify the toolbars

11. Use the procedure in figure 15-6 to add a Cancel button to the binding navigator toolbar, to change the text on the FillByCustomerID button in the second toolbar to Get Customer, and to add a separator bar and a second button with the text Get All Customers on it to the second toolbar.
12. Use the procedure in figure 15-7 to start the event handler for the Click event of the Cancel button, and add the one line of code that it requires. Then, start an event handler for the Get All Customers button. This event handler should contain a statement like the one in the Load event handler that loads the Customers table.
13. Test these changes to see how they work. At this point, the application should work like the one in figure 15-8. You just need to enhance the code so that no customer rows are retrieved when the form is loaded and so it provides for data validation and error handling.

Enhance the code

14. Comment out the code for filling the Customers table in the Load event handler, and run the application. As you'll see, only the State combo box has a value when the application starts because no customer has been selected. To fix that, use this statement to set the index for the State combo box to -1:
    ```
    StateComboBox.SelectedIndex = -1
    ```
    Then, test this change.
15. At this point, you have a prototype of the application. Although you could add the data validation and error handling code that's shown in figure 15-8, that isn't always necessary for a prototype. Just experiment more if you want to, and then end the application.

Add another parameterized query to the form

16. Add a parameterized query named FillByState that gets all the customer rows for a specific state based on the state code. Next, run the application and use the third toolbar to get all of the rows for a specific state code like CA. Note that the binding navigator toolbar lets you navigate through these rows.
17. Add a separator at the right of the controls on the FillByCustomerID ToolStrip, followed by a label, text box, and button that look like the three controls on the FillByState ToolStrip. Then, delete the FillByState ToolStrip.
18. Modify the code for the form so the FillByState button in the FillByCustomerID ToolStrip gets the customer rows by state. Then, test this enhancement. When you've got it working right, close the project.

Exercise 15-2 Build the Customer Invoice Display application

This exercise will guide you through the development of the application in figure 15-13. Here again, you'll learn a lot by doing that.

Build the user interface for the Customer Invoices form

1. Start a new project named CustomerInvoiceDisplay in the C:\VB 2012\Chapter 15 directory. Then, add the MMABooks.mdf file in the C:\VB 2012\Database directory to the project, and create a data source for the tables and columns shown in the schema in figure 15-14.
2. Drag the columns in the Customers table onto the form as text boxes, and adjust them as shown in figure 15-13. Then, drag the Invoices table that's subordinate to the Customers table onto the form as a DataGridView control.
3. Run the application and use the binding navigator toolbar to scroll through the customer rows. When you come to a row that has related invoice rows, like the row for CustomerID 10, you'll see that the invoice rows are displayed. Now, close the application, and review the code that has been generated for it.

4. Delete the binding navigator toolbar, and comment out the code in the Load event handler for the form that fills the Customers table. Next, use the procedure in figure 15-4 to create a parameterized query named FillByCustomerID that gets the Customer data for a specific CustomerID. Then, run the form and use customer IDs like 10 and 20 to see how the Customer and Invoice data is displayed.
5. Use the procedures in figures 15-9 and 15-10 to disable adding, editing, and deleting rows in the DataGridView control, to delete the CustomerID column, to set the widths of the InvoiceID, SalesTax, and Shipping columns to 80, and to modify the text in the column headings. Then, set the formatting for the InvoiceDate column so it's displayed as shown in figure 15-13. Next, set the formatting for the ProductTotal, SalesTax, Shipping, and InvoiceTotal columns to Numeric with 2 decimal places, and set their Alignment properties to MiddleRight. Now, run the application to make sure that you've got everything right.

Change the way the application gets the invoice data

6. Review the code for the Load event handler for the form. There, you can see that all the rows in the Invoices table are loaded into the dataset when the form is loaded. Then, the data rows for a specific CustomerID are displayed in the DataGridView control each time the CustomerID changes. For some applications that may be okay, but if there are thousands of invoice rows in the dataset that may be inefficient.
7. To change the way that works, create a parameterized query named FillByCustomerID for the DataGridView control that gets the invoice rows for a specific CustomerID, and delete the ToolStrip and event handler that get generated. Then, modify the code in the event handler for the Click event of the FillByCustomerIDToolStripButton so it looks like the code in figure 15-15 (but don't bother with the error handling code).
8. Delete the Load event handler for this form. Then, test the application again. It should work the same as it did before, but now only the invoice rows for the selected customer are in the Invoices table in the dataset.

Complete the application

9. At this point, you have a prototype of the application, and you should have learned a lot about how building applications with data sources and datasets works. Now, if you want to finish this application, you just need to: (1) add the error handling code for the form and (2) make sure all of the properties for the form and all of the controls are set right.

16

How to use ADO.NET to write your own data access code

In the last two chapters, you learned how to use data sources to develop database applications. When you do that, Visual Studio generates the ADO.NET objects you need. That lets you develop database applications with a minimum of code.

Now, you'll learn how to create and work with ADO.NET objects through code. That lets you separate the data access code from the presentation code by placing the ADO.NET code in database classes. These classes are often reusable and can make your applications easier to read and maintain.

How to work with connections and commands

Before you can access the data in a database, you must create a connection object. Then, you must create one or more command objects that contain the SQL statements you want to execute against the database.

How to create and work with connections

Figure 16-1 shows how you create and use a connection to access a SQL Server database. As you can see from the syntax at the top of this figure, you can specify a connection string when you create the connection. If you do, this string is assigned to the ConnectionString property. That's the case in the code example shown in this figure. If you don't specify a connection string when you create the connection, you have to assign a value to the ConnectionString property after you create the connection object.

Before you can use a command to access a database, you need to open the database connection. And when you're done working with a database, you should close the connection. To open and close a connection, you use the Open and Close methods shown in this figure.

This figure also shows some of the common values that you specify in a connection string for a SQL Server database. Then, the first two examples show connection strings for a SQL Server Express LocalDB database and a SQL Server Express database. The connection string for the LocalDB database uses (LocalDB)\v11.0 for the server name, as you saw in chapter 14. In addition, it specifies the name and location of the .mdf file for the database and the type of security to be used.

The connection string for the SQL Server Express database specifies the name of the server where the database resides, the name of the database, and the type of security to be used. Here, the localhost keyword indicates that the SqlExpress database server is running on the same machine as the application. However, if you're accessing a SQL Server database that resides on a remote server, you'll need to modify this connection string to point to that server.

Because the requirements for each provider differ, you may need to consult the documentation for that provider to determine what values to specify. The second connection string shown in this figure, for example, is for an Access database, which uses the Jet OLE DB provider. As you can see, this connection string includes the name of the provider and the name and location of the database.

Before I go on, you should realize that the connection strings for production applications are frequently stored in configuration files outside the application. That way, they can be accessed by any application that needs them, and they can be modified without having to modify and recompile each application. How an application actually retrieves the connection string depends on how it's stored. If it's stored in a text file, for example, the application can use a text reader as shown in chapter 21; if it's stored in an XML file, the application can use an XML reader as shown in chapter 22.

Two constructors for the SqlConnection class

```
New SqlConnection()
New SqlConnection(connectionString)
```

Common properties and methods of the SqlConnection class

Property	Description
ConnectionString	Provides information for accessing a SQL Server database.
Method	**Description**
Open()	Opens the connection using the specified connection string.
Close()	Closes the connection.

Common values used in the ConnectionString property for SQL Server

Name	Description
Data source|Server	The name of the instance of SQL Server you want to connect to.
Initial catalog|Database	The name of the database you want to access.
AttachDbFilename	The path and file name for the database's .mdf file.
Integrated security	Determines whether the connection is secure. Valid values are True, False, and SSPI. SSPI uses Windows integrated security and is equivalent to True.
User ID	The user ID that's used to log in to SQL Server.
Password|Pwd	The password that's used to log in to SQL Server.

Two connection strings for the SQL Server provider

A connection string for a SQL Server Express LocalDB database

```
Data Source=(LocalDB)\v11.0;AttachDbFilename=|DataDirectory|\MMABooks.mdf;
Integrated Security=True
```

A connection string for a SQL Server Express database

```
Data Source=localhost\SqlExpress;Initial Catalog=MMABooks; Integrated
Security=True
```

A connection string for the Jet OLE DB provider

```
Provider=Microsoft.Jet.OLEDB.4.0;Data Source=C:\Databases\MMABooks.mdb
```

Code that creates, opens, and closes a SQL connection

```
Dim connectionString As String =
    "Data Source=localhost\SqlExpress;Initial Catalog=MMABooks;" &
    "Integrated Security=True"
Dim connection As New SqlConnection(connectionString)
connection.Open()
...
connection.Close()
```

Description

- You can set the ConnectionString property after you create a connection or as you create it by passing the string to the constructor of the connection class.
- The values you specify for the ConnectionString property depend on the type of database you're connecting to.

Figure 16-1 How to create and work with connections

How to create and work with commands

After you define the connection to the database, you create the command objects that contain the SQL statements you want to execute against the database. Figure 16-2 shows three constructors for the SqlCommand class. The first one doesn't require arguments. When you use this constructor, you must set the Connection property to the connection to be used by the command and the CommandText property to the text of the SQL statement before you execute the command.

The second constructor accepts the SQL command text as an argument. Then, you just have to set the Connection property before you can execute the command. The third constructor accepts both the connection and the command text as arguments. The code example in the figure uses this constructor.

Another property you may need to set is the CommandType property. This property determines how the value of the CommandText property is interpreted. The values you can specify for this property are members of the CommandType enumeration that's shown in this figure. The default value is Text, which causes the value of the CommandText property to be interpreted as a SQL statement. If the CommandText property contains the name of a stored procedure, however, you'll need to set this property to StoredProcedure. And if the CommandText property contains the name of a table, you'll need to set this property to TableDirect. Then, all the rows and columns will be retrieved from the table. Note that this setting is only available for the OLE DB data provider.

The last property that's shown in this figure, Parameters, lets you work with the collection of parameters for a command. You'll see how to use this property in the next three topics.

To execute a query that a command contains, you use the Execute methods of the command shown in this figure. To execute a command that returns a result set, you use the ExecuteReader method of the command. In contrast, you use the ExecuteScalar method to execute a query that returns a single value, and you use the ExecuteNonQuery method to execute an action query. You'll learn how to use all three of these methods later in this chapter.

Three constructors for the SqlCommand class

```
New SqlCommand()
New SqlCommand(commandText)
New SqlCommand(commandText, connection)
```

Common properties and methods of the SqlCommand class

Property	Description
`Connection`	The connection used to connect to the database.
`CommandText`	A SQL statement or the name of a stored procedure.
`CommandType`	A member of the CommandType enumeration that determines how the value in the CommandText property is interpreted.
`Parameters`	The collection of parameters for the command.
Method	**Description**
`ExecuteReader()`	Executes the query identified by the CommandText property and returns the result as a SqlDataReader object.
`ExecuteNonQuery()`	Executes the query identified by the CommandText property and returns an integer that indicates the number of rows that were affected.
`ExecuteScalar()`	Executes the query identified by the CommandText property and returns the first column of the first row of the result set.

CommandType enumeration members

Member	Description
`Text`	The CommandText property contains a SQL statement. This is the default.
`StoredProcedure`	The CommandText property contains the name of a stored procedure.
`TableDirect`	The CommandText property contains the name of a table (OLE DB only).

Code that creates a SqlCommand object that executes a Select statement

```
Dim connection As New SqlConnection(connectionString)
Dim selectStatement As String =
    "SELECT CustomerID, Name, Address, City, State, ZipCode " &
    "FROM Customers"
Dim selectCommand As New SqlCommand(selectStatement, connection)
```

Description

- The CommandText and Connection properties are set to the values you pass to the constructor of the command class. If you don't pass these values to the constructor, you must set the CommandText and Connection properties after you create the command object.
- If you set the CommandText property to the name of a stored procedure, you must set the CommandType property to StoredProcedure.

Figure 16-2 How to create and work with commands

How to create and work with parameters

In chapter 15, you learned how to generate a parameterized query from a bound control that was created using a data source. In that case, the parameters were generated for you based on the Select statement you defined. When you work with commands directly, however, you have to create the parameters yourself. You'll learn how to do that in just a minute. But first, you need to know how to use parameters in the SQL statements you code.

How to use parameters in SQL statements

A *parameter* is a variable that's used in a SQL statement. Parameters let you create statements that retrieve or update database data based on variable information. For example, an application that maintains the Customers table can use a parameter in the Where clause of a Select statement to retrieve a specific row from the Customers table based on the value of the CustomerID column. A Select statement that uses parameters in the Where clause is called a *parameterized query*. You can also use parameters in other types of SQL statements, including Insert, Update, and Delete statements.

To use parameters in a SQL statement, you use placeholders as shown in figure 16-3. These placeholders indicate where the parameters should be inserted when the statement is executed. Unfortunately, database management systems don't use a standard syntax for coding placeholders.

For example, the first Select statement in this figure is for SQL Server. As you can see, you use a *named variable* to identify a parameter. Note that the name of the variable must begin with an at sign (@) and is usually given the same name as the column it's associated with. Oracle also uses named variables, but the names must begin with a colon (:) as illustrated in the second Select statement. In contrast, the placeholder for an OLE DB or ODBC parameter is a question mark, as shown in the third Select statement.

The fourth example in this figure shows how you can use parameters in an Insert statement. Here, a row is being inserted into the Customers table. To do that, a variable is included in the Values clause for each required column in the table.

A SQL Server Select statement that uses a parameter

```
SELECT CustomerID, Name, Address, City, State, ZipCode
FROM Customers
WHERE CustomerID = @CustomerID
```

An Oracle Select statement that uses a parameter

```
SELECT CustomerID, Name, Address, City, State, ZipCode
FROM Customers
WHERE CustomerID = :CustomerID
```

An OLE DB or ODBC Select statement that uses a parameter

```
SELECT CustomerID, Name, Address, City, State, ZipCode
FROM Customers
WHERE CustomerID = ?
```

A SQL Server Insert statement that uses parameters

```
INSERT INTO Customers
(Name, Address, City, State, ZipCode)
VALUES (@Name, @Address, @City, @State, @ZipCode)
```

Description

- A *parameter* lets you place variable information into a SQL statement.
- When you use a parameter in the Where clause of a Select statement, the resulting query is often called a *parameterized query* because the results of the query depend on the values of the parameters.
- Parameters are also often used in Insert or Update statements to provide the values for the database row or rows to be inserted or updated. Likewise, you can use parameters in a Delete statement to indicate which row or rows should be deleted.
- To use parameters, you code a SQL statement with placeholders for the parameters. Then, you create a parameter object that defines each parameter, and you add it to the Parameters collection of the command object that contains the SQL statement.
- The placeholder for a parameter in a SQL Server command is a *named variable* whose name begins with an at sign (@). For Oracle, the name of a variable begins with a colon (:). In most cases, you'll give the variable the same name as the column it's associated with.
- If you're using the OLE DB or ODBC provider, you code the placeholder for a parameter as a question mark. The question mark simply indicates the position of the parameter.

Figure 16-3 How to use parameters in SQL statements

How to create parameters

After you define a SQL statement that contains parameters, you create the parameter objects. Figure 16-4 shows you how to do that. Here, you can see four constructors for the SqlParameter class. Although there are others, these are the ones you're most likely to use. You can create a parameter for an OLE DB, ODBC, or Oracle command using similar techniques.

Before you can use a parameter, you must assign a name and value to it. If you don't pass these values as arguments to the constructor when you create the parameter, you can do that using some of the properties shown in this figure.

Note here that you can specify the data type using either the DbType or SqlDbType property for a SQL Server parameter. Because the data type is inferred from the value of the parameter, however, you usually won't set the type. Similarly, you won't usually set the size of a parameter because it can also be inferred from the parameter's value.

The first example in this figure shows how to create a parameter object using the first constructor for the SqlParameter class. This parameter is assigned to a variable named customerIDParm. Then, this variable is used to set the parameter's properties.

The second example shows how to create a parameter using a single statement. This statement uses the second constructor for the SqlParameter class to create a parameter named @CustomerID with the value specified by the customerID variable.

When you assign a name to a SQL Server or Oracle parameter, that name must be the same as the name that's specified in the SQL statement. That's because ADO.NET associates the parameters with the placeholders by name. In contrast, ADO.NET associates OLE DB and ODBC parameters with the placeholders by position since the placeholders aren't named.

Four constructors for the SqlParameter class

```
New SqlParameter()
New SqlParameter(name, value)
New SqlParameter(name, type)
New SqlParameter(name, type, size)
```

Common properties of the SqlParameter class

Property	Description
`DbType`	A member of the DbType enumeration that determines the type of data that the parameter can hold.
`ParameterName`	The name of the parameter.
`Size`	The maximum size of the value that the parameter can hold.
`SqlDbType`	A member of the SqlDbType enumeration that determines the type of data that the parameter can hold. This property is synchronized with the DbType property.
`Value`	The value of the parameter stored as an Object type.

Code that creates a parameter

```
Dim customerIDParm As New SqlParameter()
customerIDParm.ParameterName = "@CustomerID"
customerIDParm.Value = customerID
```

Another way to create a parameter

```
Dim customerIDParm As New SqlParameter("@CustomerID", customerID)
```

Description

- When you create a parameter, you can specify the parameter name along with a value, a data type, or a data type and size. If you don't specify the appropriate values, you can set the values of the associated properties after you create the parameter.
- In addition to a name, you must set the value for a parameter before you can use it. However, the type and size can be inferred from the value.
- When you create parameters for a SQL Server or Oracle command, you must give them the same names you used in the SQL statement since ADO.NET refers to them by name.
- Because the parameters for an OLE DB or ODBC command aren't named in the SQL statement, the parameters can be given any name you want.

Figure 16-4 How to create parameters

How to work with parameters

After you create a parameter, you must add it to the Parameters collection of the command that will use the parameter. Because ADO.NET refers to SQL Server and Oracle parameters by name, you can add them to the Parameters collection in any sequence. In contrast, you must add OLE DB and ODBC parameters in the same order that they appear in the SQL statement since ADO.NET refers to them by position.

The first example in figure 16-5 shows how to use the Add method to add a parameter object to the Parameters collection. Here, the Parameters property of the command is used to refer to the Parameters collection. Then, the Add method of that collection is used to add the customerIDParm parameter that was created in the previous figure.

You can also use one of the overloaded Add methods to create a parameter and add it to the Parameters collection in a single statement. These methods let you specify a name and type or a name, type, and size, and they return the parameter that's created. That way, you can store the parameter in a variable so you can refer to it later if you need to.

Another way to create a parameter and add it to the Parameters collection is to use the AddWithValue method. This is illustrated in the second example in this figure, and this is the easiest way to create a parameter if you're not going to change its value. Like the Add methods, the AddWithValue method returns the parameter that's created in case you want to refer to it later.

If you don't create a variable to hold a parameter, you can refer to it through the Parameters collection as illustrated in the third example. Here, the value of the @CustomerID parameter is set to the value of a variable named customerID.

Common properties and methods of the Parameters collection

Property	Description
Item(index)	Gets the parameter with the specified name or position from the collection.
Method	**Description**
Add(parameter)	Adds the specified parameter to the collection.
Add(name, type)	Creates a parameter with the specified name and type and adds it to the collection.
Add(name, type, size)	Creates a parameter with the specified name, type, and size and adds it to the collection.
AddWithValue(name, value)	Creates a parameter with the specified name and value and adds it to the collection.

A statement that adds a parameter to the Parameters collection

```
selectCommand.Parameters.Add(customerIDParm)
```

A statement that creates a parameter and adds it to the Parameters collection

```
selectCommand.Parameters.AddWithValue("@CustomerID", customerID)
```

A statement that changes the value of an existing parameter

```
selectCommand.Parameters("@CustomerID").Value = customerID
```

Description

- To work with the parameters for a command, you use the Parameters property of the command. This property returns a SqlParameterCollection object that contains all the parameters for the command.
- To add an existing parameter to the Parameters collection, you use the Add method. You can also use the Add method to create a parameter with the specified name and type or name, type, and size, and add that parameter to the Parameters collection.
- You can use the AddWithValue method of the Parameters collection to create a parameter with the specified name and value and add that parameter to the collection.
- All the Add methods return the parameter that's created so you can assign it to a variable.
- You can add SQL Server and Oracle parameters to the Parameters collection in any order you want since ADO.NET refers to the parameters by name. However, you must add OLE DB and ODBC parameters in the same order that they appear in the SQL statement since ADO.NET refers to them by position.

How to execute commands

The method you use to execute the SQL statement associated with a command object depends on the operation the SQL statement performs. The three methods you're most likely to use are ExecuteReader, which lets you retrieve and work with a result set created by a Select statement; ExecuteScalar, which lets you retrieve a single value using a Select statement; and ExecuteNonQuery, which lets you execute an Insert, Update, or Delete statement.

How to create and work with a data reader

To execute a command that contains a Select statement that returns a result set, you use the ExecuteReader method as shown in figure 16-6. This method executes the Select statement and creates a data reader object. Then, you can use the properties and methods of the data reader to work with the result set.

When you execute the ExecuteReader method, you can use the CommandBehavior enumeration to specify a behavior. The most commonly used members of this enumeration are listed in this figure. You can use these members to simplify your code or to improve the efficiency of your application.

After you create a data reader, you use the Read method to retrieve the next row of data in the result set. Note that you must also execute the Read method to retrieve the first row of data. It's not retrieved automatically when the data reader is created.

To access a column from the most recently retrieved row, you can use the Item property with either the column name or index. Since the Item property is the default property of a data reader, it can be omitted.

The code example in this figure illustrates how you use a data reader. First, the connection that's used by the SqlCommand object is opened. Although it's not shown here, this command contains a Select statement that retrieves all the data from the States table. Then, the ExecuteReader method is used to retrieve that data and create a data reader that can process the state rows. Because the CloseConnection behavior is included on this method, the connection will be closed automatically when the data reader is closed. The ExecuteReader method also opens the data reader and positions it before the first row in the result set.

Next, a List() object that can hold State objects is created, and a Do While statement is used to loop through the rows in the result set. The condition on the Do While statement executes the Read method of the data reader. This works because the Read method returns a Boolean value that indicates whether the result set contains additional rows. As long as this condition is True, the program processes the row that was retrieved. In this case, the program creates a State object for each row in the States table and adds it to the List() object. After all of the rows have been processed, the data reader is closed.

Two ways to create a SqlDataReader object

```
sqlCommand.ExecuteReader()
sqlCommand.ExecuteReader(behavior)
```

Common CommandBehavior enumeration members

Member	Description
`CloseConnection`	Closes the connection when the data reader is closed.
`Default`	Equivalent to specifying no command behavior.
`SingleRow`	Only a single row is returned.

Common properties and methods of the SqlDataReader class

Property	Description
`IsClosed`	Gets a value that indicates if the data reader is closed.
`Item(index)`	Gets the value of the column with the specified name or position.
Method	**Description**
`Close()`	Closes the data reader.
`Read()`	Retrieves the next row and returns a Boolean value that indicates whether there are additional rows.

Code that uses a data reader to read a list of State objects

```
connection.Open()
Dim reader As SqlDataReader =
    selectCommand.ExecuteReader(CommandBehavior.CloseConnection)
Dim stateList As New List(Of State)
Do While reader.Read()
    Dim state As New State
    state.StateCode = reader("StateCode").ToString
    state.StateName = reader("StateName").ToString
    stateList.Add(state)
Loop
reader.Close()
```

Description

- You must open the connection that's used by the data reader before you execute the ExecuteReader method of the command object.
- The data reader is opened automatically when it's created. While it's open, no other data readers can be opened on the same connection. The exception is if you're using an Oracle data reader, in which case other Oracle data readers can be open at the same time.
- When you first create a data reader, it's positioned before the first row in the result set. To retrieve the first row, you have to execute the Read method.
- You can combine two or more command behavior members using the & operator.

Figure 16-6 How to create and work with a data reader

How to execute queries that return a single value

The first example in figure 16-7 shows you how to execute a command that returns a single value, called a *scalar value*. To do that, you execute the ExecuteScalar method of the command. In this case, the command contains a Select statement that retrieves a sum of the invoice totals in the Invoices table. This type of summary value is often called an *aggregate value*. A scalar value can also be the value of a single column, a calculated value, or any other value that can be retrieved from the database.

Since the ExecuteScalar method returns an Object type, you must cast that object to a appropriate data type to get its value. In this example, the object is cast to a Decimal value.

Before I go on, you should realize that you can use the ExecuteScalar method with a Select statement that retrieves more than one value. In that case, though, the ExecuteScalar method returns only the first value and the others are discarded.

How to execute action queries

As you know, you can use an Insert, Update, or Delete statement to perform actions against a database. These statements are sometimes referred to as *action queries*. To execute an action query, you use the ExecuteNonQuery method of a command as shown in the second example in figure 16-7.

This example executes a command that contains an Insert statement that adds a row to the Products table. Notice that the ExecuteNonQuery method returns an integer that indicates the number of rows in the database that were affected by the operation. You can use this value to check that the operation was successful. You'll see an example of that in the Customer Maintenance application that follows.

Code that creates and executes a command that returns an aggregate value

```
Dim selectStatement As String =
    "SELECT SUM(InvoiceTotal) FROM Invoices"
Dim selectCommand As New SqlCommand(selectStatement, connection)
connection.Open()
Dim invoiceTotal As Decimal = CDec(selectCommand.ExecuteScalar)
connection.Close()
```

Code that creates and executes a command that inserts a row

```
Dim insertStatement As String =
    "INSERT Products " &
    "(ProductCode, Description, UnitPrice) " &
    "VALUES (@ProductCode, @Description, @UnitPrice)"
Dim insertCommand As New SqlCommand(insertStatement, connection)
insertCommand.Parameters.AddWithValue("@ProductCode", product.Code)
insertCommand.Parameters.AddWithValue("@Description", product.Description)
insertCommand.Parameters.AddWithValue("@UnitPrice", product.Price)
Try
    connection.Open()
    Dim insertCount As Integer = insertCommand.ExecuteNonQuery
Catch ex As SqlException
    MessageBox.Show("SQL Server error # " & ex.Number &
        ": " & ex.Message, ex.GetType.ToString)
Finally
    connection.Close()
End Try
```

How to execute queries that return a single value

- You use the ExecuteScalar method of a command object to retrieve a single value, called a *scalar value*.
- The value that's returned can be the value of a single column and row in the database, a calculated value, an *aggregate value* that summarizes data in the database, or any other value that can be retrieved from the database.
- If the Select statement returns more than one column or row, only the value in the first column and row is retrieved by the ExecuteScalar method.

How to execute action queries

- You use the ExecuteNonQuery method of a command object to execute an Insert, Update, or Delete statement, called an *action query*.
- The ExecuteNonQuery method returns an integer that indicates the number of rows that were affected by the query.
- You can also use the ExecuteNonQuery method to execute statements that affect the structure of a database object. For more information, see the documentation for your database management system.

Figure 16-7 How to execute queries that don't return a result set

A Customer Maintenance application that uses commands

In the topics that follow, you'll see another version of the Customer Maintenance application that was first presented in chapter 14. Unlike the application shown in that chapter, this version doesn't use a dataset and a table adapter. Instead, it uses commands to retrieve, insert, update, and delete rows from the Customers table. Although this presentation is lengthy, it's worth taking the time to go through it because it will give you a thorough understanding of how you build applications with commands.

The user interface

Figure 16-8 presents the user interface for the Customer Maintenance application. As you can see, this application consists of two forms. The Customer Maintenance form lets the user select an existing customer and then displays the information for that customer on the form. Then, the user can click the Modify button to modify the information for the customer or the Delete button to delete the customer. The user can also click the Add button to add a new customer.

If the user clicks the Add or Modify button, the Add/Modify Customer form is displayed. Note that the title of this form changes depending on whether a customer is being added or modified. In this case, the user that was selected in the Customer Maintenance form is being modified.

After entering the appropriate values on the Add/Modify Customer form, the user can click the Accept button or press the Enter key to accept the new or modified customer. Alternatively, the user can click the Cancel button or press the Esc key to cancel the operation.

If the user clicks the Delete button, a dialog box like the one shown in this figure is displayed to confirm the delete operation. Then, if the user confirms the operation, the customer is deleted and the form is cleared.

At this point, you may be wondering why I used two forms to implement the Customer Maintenance application. The answer is that, in the real world, most maintenance applications aren't this simple. In many cases, in fact, the maintenance of a table will be combined with other functions. Even if the table maintenance is provided by a separate application, however, it can be easier to implement the application using two forms because it simplifies the program logic.

The Customer Maintenance form

The Add/Modify Customer form

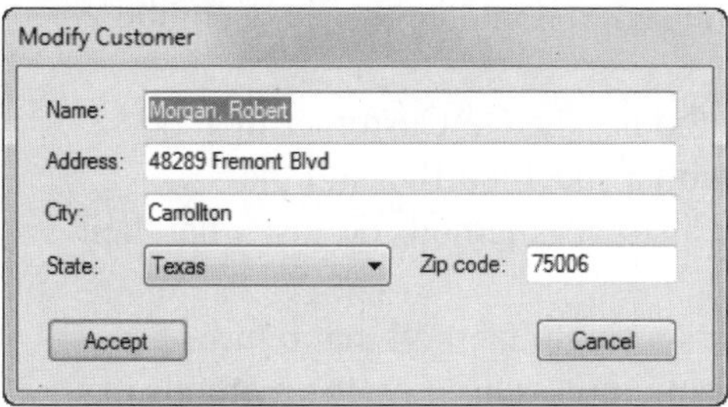

The dialog box that's displayed to confirm a delete operation

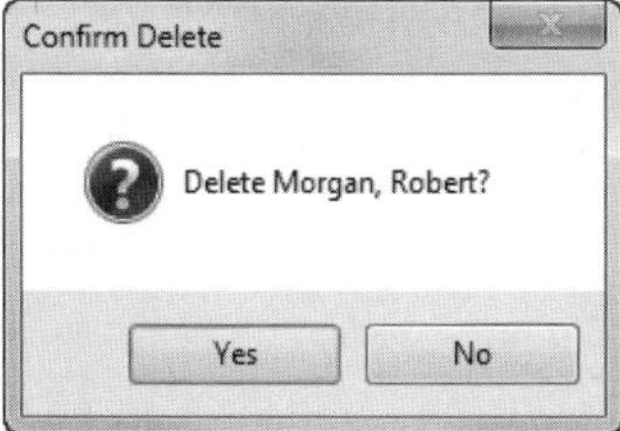

Description

- To add a customer, the user clicks the Add button on the Customer Maintenance form to display a blank Add Customer form. Then, the user enters the data for the new customer and clicks the Accept button to return to the Customer Maintenance form.
- To modify the data for an existing customer, the user enters the customer ID and clicks the Get Customer button to display the information for that customer. Then, the user clicks the Modify button to display the Modify Customer form, makes the appropriate modifications, and clicks the Accept button to return to the Customer Maintenance form.
- To delete a customer, the user enters the customer ID and clicks the Get Customer button to display the information for that customer. Then, the user clicks the Delete button and responds to the dialog box that's displayed to confirm the delete operation.

Figure 16-8 The user interface for the Customer Maintenance application

The class diagram for the business and database classes

Figure 16-9 presents a class diagram for the Customer Maintenance project. This diagram shows the business and database classes that are used by the Customer Maintenance application.

The Customer and State classes define the business objects that are used by this application. Each of these classes contains auto-implemented properties that can be used to store the values of the columns in the associated table. In addition, each class is defined with a parameterless constructor.

The CustomerDB and StateDB classes provide methods for working with the tables in the MMABooks database. The StateDB class contains a method for getting a list of State objects. This list is then used to populate the State combo box.

The CustomerDB class contains four methods. The GetCustomer method returns a Customer object for the customer with a specified ID. And the AddCustomer, UpdateCustomer, and DeleteCustomer methods do just what their names imply.

Finally, the MMABooksDB class contains a single method that returns a connection to the MMABooks database. This method is used by the methods in the CustomerDB and StateDB classes.

The class diagram

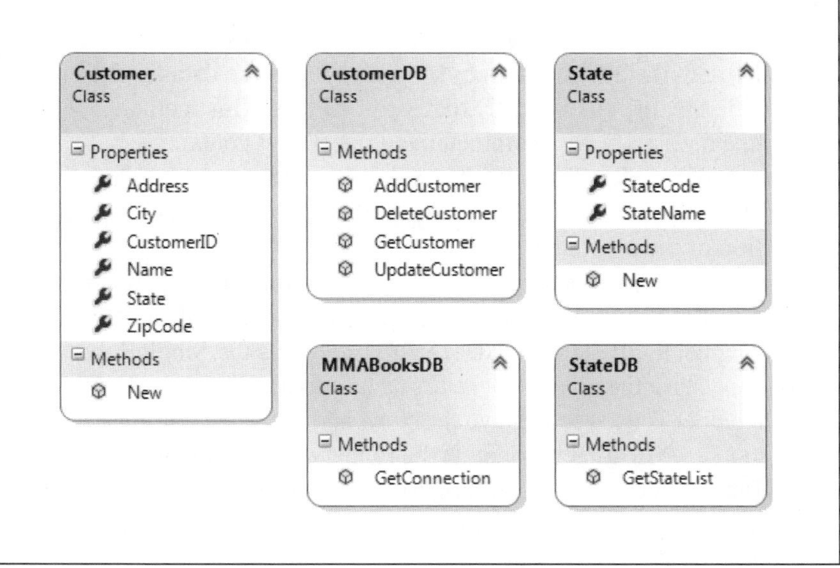

Description

- The Customer Maintenance project contains the classes that define the business objects used by the Customer Maintenance application and the database classes that are used to work with the MMABooks database.
- The business objects are defined by the Customer and State classes. These objects will hold data from the associated tables in the MMABooks database.
- The classes that end with DB, including CustomerDB, StateDB, and MMABooksDB, are the database classes. These classes provide shared methods for working with the MMABooks database.
- The StateDB class provides a public method for getting a list of states from the States table. The CustomerDB class provides public methods for getting the data for a customer and for adding, updating, and deleting a customer. And the MMABooksDB class provides a public method for getting a connection to the MMABooks database.

Figure 16-9 The class diagram for the business and database classes

The code for the CustomerDB class

Figure 16-10 shows the code for the CustomerDB class. To start, the GetCustomer method returns a Customer object that contains the data for the customer row specified by the customer ID that's passed to it. This method creates a SqlCommand object with a parameterized query that contains a placeholder for the customer ID. Then, it creates the parameter, sets its value to the customerID that was passed to the method, and adds the parameter to the Parameters collection of the command.

After the command and parameter are created, the connection is opened and the ExecuteReader method is used to execute the command and create a data reader object. Notice that the ExecuteReader method specifies the SingleRow command behavior because the query will return just one row. Then, the Read method of the data reader is used to retrieve that row, and the values of that row are assigned to a new Customer object. If the reader doesn't contain a row, however, the Customer object is set to Nothing to indicate that the customer wasn't found. Then, the reader and connection are closed and the Customer object is returned to the calling procedure.

Notice that the statements that open the connection and data reader and process the rows in the data reader are coded within a Try...Catch...Finally statement. Then, if a SqlException occurs, the Catch block throws the exception to the calling procedure. Because of that, the procedure that calls this method should catch this exception. Whether or not an exception occurs, the statement that closes the connection is coded within the Finally block. That way, if the statement that opens the connection is successful but the statement that executes the command isn't, the connection is still closed.

The AddCustomer method adds a new row to the Customers table. This method receives a Customer object that contains the data for the new row. Then, a command object that contains an Insert statement with a parameter for each column in the row is created. After the command is created, the parameters are created and added to the Parameters collection of the command.

The code for the CustomerDB class — Page 1

```
Imports System.Data.SqlClient

Public Class CustomerDB

    Public Shared Function GetCustomer(customerID As Integer) _
            As Customer
        Dim customer As New Customer
        Dim connection As SqlConnection = MMABooksDB.GetConnection
        Dim selectStatement As String =
            "SELECT CustomerID, Name, Address, City, State, ZipCode " &
            "FROM Customers " &
            "WHERE CustomerID = @CustomerID"
        Dim selectCommand As New SqlCommand(selectStatement, connection)
        selectCommand.Parameters.AddWithValue("@CustomerID", customerID)
        Try
            connection.Open()
            Dim reader As SqlDataReader =
                selectCommand.ExecuteReader(CommandBehavior.SingleRow)
            If reader.Read Then
                customer.CustomerID = CInt(reader("CustomerID"))
                customer.Name = reader("Name").ToString
                customer.Address = reader("Address").ToString
                customer.City = reader("City").ToString
                customer.State = reader("State").ToString
                customer.ZipCode = reader("ZipCode").ToString
            Else
                customer = Nothing
            End If
            reader.Close()
        Catch ex As SqlException
            Throw ex
        Finally
            connection.Close()
        End Try
        Return customer
    End Function

    Public Shared Function AddCustomer(customer As Customer) As Integer
        Dim connection As SqlConnection = MMABooksDB.GetConnection
        Dim insertStatement As String =
            "INSERT Customers " &
            "(Name, Address, City, State, ZipCode) " &
            "VALUES (@Name, @Address, @City, @State, @ZipCode)"
        Dim insertCommand As New SqlCommand(insertStatement, connection)
        insertCommand.Parameters.AddWithValue("@Name", customer.Name)
        insertCommand.Parameters.AddWithValue("@Address",
            customer.Address)
        insertCommand.Parameters.AddWithValue("@City", customer.City)
        insertCommand.Parameters.AddWithValue("@State", customer.State)
        insertCommand.Parameters.AddWithValue("@ZipCode",
            customer.ZipCode)
```

Figure 16-10 The code for the CustomerDB class (part 1 of 3)

Next, the connection is opened and the ExecuteNonQuery method of the command object is executed within a Try…Catch…Finally statement that catches SQL Server exceptions. Then, if an exception occurs, this method throws the exception so it can be handled by the calling procedure. Otherwise, another command object that contains a Select statement that retrieves the ID of the customer that was just added is created, and this command is executed using the ExecuteScalar method. The customer ID that's returned by this statement is then returned to the calling procedure.

The UpdateCustomer method receives two arguments: a Customer object named oldCustomer that contains the original data for the customer row to be updated, and another Customer object named newCustomer that supplies the updated values for the customer. The properties of these objects are used to set the values of the parameters defined by the Update statement associated with the command object. Notice that the properties of the oldCustomer object are assigned to parameters in the Where clause of the Update statement. That way, the Update statement will update the row only if none of the customer columns have been changed since the customer was retrieved.

The code for the CustomerDB class

Page 2

```
        Try
            connection.Open()
            insertCommand.ExecuteNonQuery()
            Dim selectStatement As String =
                "SELECT IDENT_CURRENT('Customers') FROM Customers"
            Dim selectCommand As New SqlCommand(selectStatement,
                connection)
            Dim customerID As Integer = CInt(selectCommand.ExecuteScalar)
            Return customerID
        Catch ex As SqlException
            Throw ex
        Finally
            connection.Close()
        End Try
    End Function

    Public Shared Function UpdateCustomer(oldCustomer As Customer,
            newCustomer As Customer) As Boolean
        Dim connection As SqlConnection = MMABooksDB.GetConnection
        Dim updateStatement As String =
            "UPDATE Customers SET " &
            "Name = @NewName, " &
            "Address = @NewAddress, " &
            "City = @NewCity, " &
            "State = @NewState, " &
            "ZipCode = @NewZipCode " &
            "WHERE CustomerID = @OldCustomerID " &
            "AND Name = @OldName " &
            "AND Address = @OldAddress " &
            "AND City = @OldCity " &
            "AND State = @OldState " &
            "AND ZipCode = @OldZipCode"
        Dim updateCommand As New SqlCommand(updateStatement, connection)
        updateCommand.Parameters.AddWithValue("@NewName",
            newCustomer.Name)
        updateCommand.Parameters.AddWithValue("@NewAddress",
            newCustomer.Address)
        updateCommand.Parameters.AddWithValue("@NewCity",
            newCustomer.City)
        updateCommand.Parameters.AddWithValue("@NewState",
            newCustomer.State)
        updateCommand.Parameters.AddWithValue("@NewZipCode",
            newCustomer.ZipCode)
        updateCommand.Parameters.AddWithValue("@OldCustomerID",
            oldCustomer.CustomerID)
        updateCommand.Parameters.AddWithValue("@OldName",
            oldCustomer.Name)
        updateCommand.Parameters.AddWithValue("@OldAddress",
            oldCustomer.Address)
        updateCommand.Parameters.AddWithValue("@OldCity",
            oldCustomer.City)
        updateCommand.Parameters.AddWithValue("@OldState",
            oldCustomer.State)
        updateCommand.Parameters.AddWithValue("@OldZipCode",
            oldCustomer.ZipCode)
```

Figure 16-10 The code for the CustomerDB class (part 2 of 3)

After the parameter values are set, the UpdateCustomer method uses the ExecuteNonQuery method to execute the Update statement. If no error occurs, the value that's returned by the ExecuteNonQuery method is tested to determine whether the update was successful. If it wasn't, it probably means that the customer has been modified or deleted by another user. In that case, this method returns False to the calling procedure. Otherwise, it returns True.

The DeleteCustomer method receives a Customer object as an argument. This method implements concurrency checking using the same technique as the UpdateCustomer method. That is, it specifies the value of each of the customer columns in the Where clause of the Delete statement. Then, if the delete operation is unsuccessful due to a concurrency error, the method returns False. Otherwise, it returns True.

Like the AddCustomer and UpdateCustomer methods, the DeleteCustomer method also catches SQL Server errors. Then, if an error occurs, it's thrown to the calling procedure.

The code for the CustomerDB class

Page 3

```
        Try
            connection.Open()
            Dim count As Integer = updateCommand.ExecuteNonQuery
            If count > 0 Then
                Return True
            Else
                Return False
            End If
        Catch ex As SqlException
            Throw ex
        Finally
            connection.Close()
        End Try
    End Function

    Public Shared Function DeleteCustomer(customer As Customer) _
            As Boolean
        Dim connection As SqlConnection = MMABooksDB.GetConnection
        Dim deleteStatement As String =
            "DELETE FROM Customers " &
            "WHERE CustomerID = @CustomerID " &
            "AND Name = @Name " &
            "AND Address = @Address " &
            "AND City = @City " &
            "AND State = @State " &
            "AND ZipCode = @ZipCode"
        Dim deleteCommand As New SqlCommand(deleteStatement, connection)
        deleteCommand.Parameters.AddWithValue("@CustomerID",
            customer.CustomerID)
        deleteCommand.Parameters.AddWithValue("@Name", customer.Name)
        deleteCommand.Parameters.AddWithValue("@Address",
            customer.Address)
        deleteCommand.Parameters.AddWithValue("@City", customer.City)
        deleteCommand.Parameters.AddWithValue("@State", customer.State)
        deleteCommand.Parameters.AddWithValue("@ZipCode",
            customer.ZipCode)

        Try
            connection.Open()
            Dim count As Integer = deleteCommand.ExecuteNonQuery
            If count > 0 Then
                Return True
            Else
                Return False
            End If
        Catch ex As SqlException
            Throw ex
        Finally
            connection.Close()
        End Try
    End Function
End Class
```

Figure 16-10 The code for the CustomerDB class (part 3 of 3)

The code for the StateDB class

Figure 16-11 shows the code for the StateDB class. This class contains a single method named GetStateList that returns a generic List() object that contains one State object for each of the rows in the States table, sorted by state name.

To get this list, the GetStateList method creates a SqlCommand object with a Select statement that retrieves the appropriate data. Then, it calls the ExecuteReader method of this command to create a data reader that can be used to read each state. Once the data reader is created, this method uses this reader to read each row in the table, it creates a State object for each row, and it adds each State object to the List() object. Finally, it closes the data reader and connection and returns the list of State objects.

The code for the MMABooksDB class

The MMABooksDB class contains a single method named GetConnection that returns a connection to the MMABooks database. As you've already seen, the CustomerDB and StateDB classes call this method to get the connection that's used by the commands they execute. Note that, because a LocalDB database is being used and the database file is included in the project, the DataDirectory keyword is used to identify the location of this file. As you learned in chapter 14, the data directory is the directory where the executable file for the application is stored.

Although SQL Server Express LocalDB was designed to be used only during development, you can also use it for small production databases. In that case, you won't need to change the connection string when you put the application into production. Otherwise, if the application will use a database that's stored on a database server, you'll need to change the connection string so it points to that server.

In addition, you may want to store the connection string in an external configuration file as I explained earlier in this chapter. Then, the GetConnection method would read the connection string from this file. That way, you could change the location of the database without recompiling the application.

The code for the StateDB class

```
Imports System.Data.SqlClient

    Public Class StateDB

        Public Shared Function GetStateList() As List(Of State)
            Dim stateList As New List(Of State)
            Dim connection As SqlConnection = MMABooksDB.GetConnection
            Dim selectStatement As String =
                "SELECT StateCode, StateName " &
                "FROM States " &
                "ORDER BY StateName"
            Dim selectCommand As New SqlCommand(selectStatement, connection)
            Try
                connection.Open()
                Dim reader As SqlDataReader = selectCommand.ExecuteReader()
                Dim state As State
                Do While reader.Read
                    state = New State
                    state.StateCode = reader("StateCode").ToString
                    state.StateName = reader("StateName").ToString
                    stateList.Add(state)
                Loop
                reader.Close()
            Catch ex As SqlException
                Throw ex
            Finally
                connection.Close()
            End Try
            Return stateList
        End Function

    End Class
```

The code for the MMABooksDB class

```
    Imports System.Data.SqlClient

    Public Class MMABooksDB

        Public Shared Function GetConnection() As SqlConnection
            Dim connectionString As String =
                "Data Source=(LocalDB)\v11.0;" &
                "AttachDbFilename=|DataDirectory|\MMABooks.mdf;" &
                "Integrated Security=True"
            Return New SqlConnection(connectionString)
        End Function

    End Class
```

Figure 16-11 The code for the StateDB and MMABooksDB classes

The code for the Customer Maintenance form

Figure 16-12 shows the code for the Customer Maintenance form. Because this form doesn't contain a Load event handler, no data is displayed when the form is first displayed. Then, the user must enter a customer ID and click the Get Customer button to retrieve the data for a customer or click the Add button to add a new customer.

The event handler for the Click event of the Get Customer button starts by calling the IsPresent and IsInt32 methods in a class named Validator to check that the user entered a customer ID and that the customer ID is an integer. This class contains methods like the ones you saw in the Validator class in chapter 11.

If the customer ID is an integer, this value is passed to a procedure named GetCustomer. This procedure calls the GetCustomer method of the CustomerDB class to get the customer with the specified ID. Then, the Customer object that's returned by this method is stored in a module-level variable named customer.

Notice that the statement that calls the GetCustomer method of the CustomerDB class is coded within a Try...Catch statement. That's because, if a SQL Server error occurs during the execution of this method, the exception is thrown to the calling procedure. Then, this procedure must catch the exception. You'll see this same technique used for all the methods of the database classes that are called by this application.

After it executes the GetCustomer procedure, the event handler checks if the Customer object contains a value of Nothing. If so, a message is displayed indicating that the customer wasn't found, and a procedure named ClearControls is called. This procedure assigns empty strings to the text boxes on the form, disables the Modify and Delete buttons, and moves the focus to the Customer ID text box so the user can enter another ID.

If the Customer object doesn't contain a value of Nothing, a procedure named DisplayCustomer is called to display the properties of the Customer object in the text boxes on the form. This procedure also enables the Modify and Delete buttons so the user can modify or delete the selected customer. (These buttons are disabled when the form is first displayed, and they're disabled every time the form is cleared.)

If the user clicks the Add button, the Click event handler for this button displays the Add/Modify Customer form as a dialog box. But first, it sets the public addCustomer field of this form to True so the form will know that a new customer is being added. If the customer is added successfully, the new customer is retrieved from the Add/Modify Customer form. Then, the data for the new customer is displayed on the form and the Modify and Delete buttons are enabled.

The code for the Customer Maintenance form — Page 1

```
Public Class frmCustomerMaintenance
    Dim customer As Customer

    Private Sub btnGetCustomer_Click(sender As Object,
            e As EventArgs) Handles btnGetCustomer.Click
        If Validator.IsPresent(txtCustomerID) AndAlso
           Validator.IsInt32(txtCustomerID) Then
            Dim customerID As Integer = CInt(txtCustomerID.Text)
            Me.GetCustomer(customerID)
            If customer Is Nothing Then
                MessageBox.Show("No customer found with this ID. " &
                    "Please try again.", "Customer Not Found")
                Me.ClearControls()
            Else
                Me.DisplayCustomer()
            End If
        End If
    End Sub

    Private Sub GetCustomer(customerID As Integer)
        Try
            customer = CustomerDB.GetCustomer(customerID)
        Catch ex As Exception
            MessageBox.Show(ex.Message, ex.GetType.ToString)
        End Try
    End Sub

    Private Sub ClearControls()
        txtCustomerID.Text = ""
        txtName.Text = ""
        txtAddress.Text = ""
        txtCity.Text = ""
        txtState.Text = ""
        txtZipCode.Text = ""
        btnModify.Enabled = False
        btnDelete.Enabled = False
        txtCustomerID.Select()
    End Sub

    Private Sub DisplayCustomer()
        txtName.Text = customer.Name
        txtAddress.Text = customer.Address
        txtCity.Text = customer.City
        txtState.Text = customer.State
        txtZipCode.Text = customer.ZipCode
        btnModify.Enabled = True
        btnDelete.Enabled = True
    End Sub

    Private Sub btnAdd_Click(sender As Object,
            e As EventArgs) Handles btnAdd.Click
        Dim addCustomerForm As New frmAddModifyCustomer
        addCustomerForm.addCustomer = True
        Dim result As DialogResult = addCustomerForm.ShowDialog
        If result = DialogResult.OK Then
            customer = addCustomerForm.customer
            txtCustomerID.Text = customer.CustomerID.ToString
            Me.DisplayCustomer()
        End If
    End Sub
```

Figure 16-12 The code for the Customer Maintenance form (part 1 of 2)

The Click event handler for the Modify button is similar. However, it sets the addCustomer field of the Add/Modify Customer form to False to indicate that a customer is being modified. In addition, it sets the public customer field to the current Customer object. That way, the form can display this data without having to retrieve it from the database again.

If the customer is modified successfully, the updated customer is retrieved from the Add/Modify Customer form and the new data for the customer is displayed on the form. If a concurrency error occurs, however, the result of the Add/Modify Customer form is set to DialogResult.Retry. Then, the GetCustomer procedure is called to retrieve the customer again.

If the customer is found, it means that the concurrency error was caused by another user modifying the customer. In that case, the updated data for that customer is displayed on the form. If the customer isn't found, however, it means that another user deleted the customer. Then, the ClearControls procedure is called to clear the text boxes on the form, disable the Modify and Delete buttons, and move the focus to the Customer ID text box.

If the user clicks the Delete button, the Click event handler for that button starts by displaying a dialog box to confirm the delete operation. If the operation is confirmed, it calls the DeleteCustomer method of the CustomerDB class to delete the customer. If this method returns False, an error message is displayed indicating that the customer has been updated or deleted and the customer is retrieved again. Then, if the customer is found, the updated data for the customer is displayed. Otherwise, the form is cleared. The form is also cleared if the customer is successfully deleted.

The code for the Customer Maintenance form **Page 2**

```
    Private Sub btnModify_Click(sender As Object,
            e As EventArgs) Handles btnModify.Click
        Dim modifyCustomerForm As New frmAddModifyCustomer
        modifyCustomerForm.addCustomer = False
        modifyCustomerForm.customer = customer
        Dim result As DialogResult = modifyCustomerForm.ShowDialog
        If result = DialogResult.OK Then
            customer = modifyCustomerForm.customer
            Me.DisplayCustomer()
        ElseIf result = DialogResult.Retry Then
            Me.GetCustomer(customer.CustomerID)
            If customer IsNot Nothing Then
                Me.DisplayCustomer()
            Else
                Me.ClearControls()
            End If
        End If
    End Sub

    Private Sub btnDelete_Click(sender As Object,
            e As EventArgs) Handles btnDelete.Click
        Dim result As DialogResult =
            MessageBox.Show("Delete " & customer.Name & "?",
                "Confirm Delete", MessageBoxButtons.YesNo,
                MessageBoxIcon.Question)
        If result = DialogResult.Yes Then
            Try
                If Not CustomerDB.DeleteCustomer(customer) Then
                    MessageBox.Show("Another user has updated or deleted " &
                        "that customer.", "Database Error")
                    Me.GetCustomer(customer.CustomerID)
                    If customer IsNot Nothing Then
                        Me.DisplayCustomer()
                    Else
                        Me.ClearControls()
                    End If
                Else
                    Me.ClearControls()
                End If
            Catch ex As Exception
                MessageBox.Show(ex.Message, ex.GetType.ToString)
            End Try
        End If
    End Sub

    Private Sub btnExit_Click(sender As Object,
            e As EventArgs) Handles btnExit.Click
        Me.Close()
    End Sub
End Class
```

Figure 16-12 The code for the Customer Maintenance form (part 2 of 2)

The code for the Add/Modify Customer form

Figure 16-13 shows the code for the Add/Modify Customer form. This form starts by declaring the two public fields that are also used by the Customer Maintenance form.

When the form is first loaded, the Load event handler starts by calling the LoadStateComboBox procedure. This procedure uses the GetStateList method of the StateDB class to get a generic list that contains State objects. Then, it binds the State combo box on the form to this list.

If a new customer is being added, the Load event handler continues by setting the Text property of the form to "Add Customer" and initializing the State combo box so that no state is selected. Otherwise, it sets the Text property of the form to "Modify Customer" and calls the DisplayCustomerData procedure. This procedure displays the current data for the customer on the form. After that, the user can enter the data for a new customer or modify the data for an existing customer.

The code for the Add/Modify Customer form Page 1

```
Public Class frmAddModifyCustomer

    Public addCustomer As Boolean
    Public customer As Customer

    Private Sub frmAddModifyCustomer_Load(sender As Object,
            e As EventArgs) Handles MyBase.Load
        Me.LoadStateComboBox()
        If addCustomer Then
            Me.Text = "Add Customer"
            cboStates.SelectedIndex = -1
        Else
            Me.Text = "Modify Customer"
            Me.DisplayCustomerData()
        End If
    End Sub

    Private Sub LoadStateComboBox()
        Dim stateList As List(Of State)
        Try
            stateList = StateDB.GetStateList
            cboStates.DataSource = stateList
            cboStates.DisplayMember = "StateName"
            cboStates.ValueMember = "StateCode"
        Catch ex As Exception
            MessageBox.Show(ex.Message, ex.GetType.ToString)
        End Try
    End Sub

    Private Sub DisplayCustomerData()
        txtName.Text = customer.Name
        txtAddress.Text = customer.Address
        txtCity.Text = customer.City
        cboStates.SelectedValue = customer.State
        txtZipCode.Text = customer.ZipCode
    End Sub
```

Figure 16-13 The code for the Add/Modify Customer form (part 1 of 2)

If the user clicks the Accept button, the Click event handler for this button starts by calling the IsValidData function. This function calls the IsPresent method of the Validator class for each text box to determine if it contains data. It also calls the IsPresent method for the State combo box to be sure that a state is selected.

If the data is valid, the event handler continues by checking whether a customer is being added or modified. If a customer is being added, the customer field is set to a new Customer object and the PutCustomerData procedure is called. This procedure sets the properties of the Customer object to the values that the user entered on the form.

Next, the event handler executes the AddCustomer method of the CustomerDB class and assigns the new customer ID that's returned by this method to the CustomerID property of the Customer object. Then, if no SQL Server error occurs, the DialogResult property of the form is set to DialogResult.OK, which causes the form to be closed and control to be returned to the Customer Maintenance form. Otherwise, the exception is caught and an error message is displayed.

If a customer is being modified, this event handler starts by creating a new Customer object and storing it in the newCustomer variable. Then, it sets the CustomerID property of that object to the CustomerID property of the current Customer object since the customer ID can't be changed, and it calls the PutCustomerData procedure to set the rest of the properties. Next, it calls the UpdateCustomer method of the CustomerDB class and passes it both the old and new Customer objects. If a concurrency error occurs, a value of False is returned. In that case, an error message is displayed and the DialogResult property of the form is set to DialogResult.Retry. Otherwise, the new Customer object is assigned to the original Customer object and the DialogResult property is set to DialogResult.OK. In either case, the form is closed.

The code for the Add/Modify Customer form Page 2

```
    Private Sub btnAccept_Click(sender As Object,
            e As EventArgs) Handles btnAccept.Click
        If IsValidData() Then
            If addCustomer Then
                customer = New Customer
                Me.PutCustomerData(customer)
                Try
                    customer.CustomerID = CustomerDB.AddCustomer(customer)
                    Me.DialogResult = DialogResult.OK
                Catch ex As Exception
                    MessageBox.Show(ex.Message, ex.GetType.ToString)
                End Try
            Else
                Dim newCustomer As New Customer
                newCustomer.CustomerID = customer.CustomerID
                Me.PutCustomerData(newCustomer)
                Try
                    If Not CustomerDB.UpdateCustomer(customer,
                            newCustomer) Then
                        MessageBox.Show("Another user has updated or " &
                            "deleted that customer.", "Database Error")
                        Me.DialogResult = DialogResult.Retry
                    Else
                        customer = newCustomer
                        Me.DialogResult = DialogResult.OK
                    End If
                Catch ex As Exception
                    MessageBox.Show(ex.Message, ex.GetType.ToString)
                End Try
            End If
        End If
    End Sub

    Private Function IsValidData() As Boolean
        Return _
            Validator.IsPresent(txtName) AndAlso
            Validator.IsPresent(txtAddress) AndAlso
            Validator.IsPresent(txtCity) AndAlso
            Validator.IsPresent(cboStates) AndAlso
            Validator.IsPresent(txtZipCode)
    End Function

    Private Sub PutCustomerData(customer As Customer)
        customer.Name = txtName.Text
        customer.Address = txtAddress.Text
        customer.City = txtCity.Text
        customer.State = cboStates.SelectedValue.ToString
        customer.ZipCode = txtZipCode.Text
    End Sub

End Class
```

Figure 16-13 The code for the Add/Modify Customer form (part 2 of 2)

Perspective

In this chapter, you were introduced to another way to develop database applications. Instead of using data sources and datasets, you learned how to use code to create and work with connections, commands, and data readers. When you work this way, your code has to do all of the functions that are done by the table adapter when you use data sources and datasets. This means that you have to write more code, but it also means that you have complete control over how the data is processed.

Terms

parameter
parameterized query
named variable
scalar value
aggregate value
action query

Exercise 16-1 Build the Customer Maintenance application

For this exercise, you'll develop the Customer Maintenance application presented in figure 16-8. To make that easier for you to do, we'll give you the two forms for the project as well as the business classes and the Validator class. That way, you'll just need to create the database classes.

Review the application

1. Open the application in the C:\VB 2012\Chapter 16\CustomerMaintenance directory and review the code for the forms and classes. Notice that some of the statements in the forms have been commented out. These are the statements that call the methods of the database classes that you'll create.
2. Run the application, enter 27 in the Customer ID text box, and click the Get Customer button. When you do, an error message will be displayed indicating that the customer wasn't found. That's because the application doesn't include the code to retrieve the customer. Respond to the dialog box and then end the application.

Write the code to retrieve a customer

3. Add a class named MMABooksDB to the project. Then, add a method named GetConnection to this class, and add code like that shown in figure 16-11 to this method. For this to work, you'll also need to add an Imports statement for the System.Data.SqlClient namespace at the beginning of the class.

   Note: If you're not using SQL Server Express LocalDB and you completed any of the exercises for chapter 18 or 19, you can get the connection string you need from one of those projects. To do that, display the dataset schema for the project in the Dataset Designer, select the table adapter for a table, and expand the Connection group in the Properties windows to see the ConnectionString property that was generated.

4. Add another class named CustomerDB to the project, and add an Imports statement for the System.Data.SqlClient namespace to this class.
5. Add a method named GetCustomer to the CustomerDB class. This method should receive the customer ID of the customer to be retrieved, and it should return a Customer object for that customer. Add the code for this method as shown in part 1 of figure 16-10, but try to do that without looking at this figure.
6. Display the code for the Customer Maintenance form, and uncomment the statement in the GetCustomer procedure that calls the GetCustomer method of the CustomerDB class. Then, run the application and try to display the data for customer number 27. If this doesn't work, modify your code until it does.
7. Click the Modify button to display the Modify Customer form, and notice that no value is displayed in the State combo box. Drop-down the combo box list to see that it doesn't contain any items. That's because you haven't added the code to retrieve the list of states. Click the Cancel button to return to the Customer Maintenance form and then end the application.

Write the code to retrieve the list of states

8. Add a class named StateDB to the project, and add an Imports statement for the System.Data.SqlClient namespace to this class.
9. Add a method named GetStateList to the StateDB class. This method should return a List() of State objects. Add the code for this method as shown in figure 16-11, but again, try to do that without looking at this figure.
10. Display the code for the Add/Modify Customer form, and uncomment the statement in the LoadStateComboBox procedure that calls the GetStateList method. Then, run the application, display the data for customer number 27, and click the Modify button. This time, the correct state should be displayed for the customer and the State combo box should be populated with a list of all the states. However, you still can't modify the data for the customer because you haven't added the code to do that. Cancel out of the Modify Customer form and then end the application.

Write the code to modify a customer

11. Add a method named UpdateCustomer to the CustomerDB class. This method should receive two Customer objects. The first one should contain the original customer data and should be used to provide for optimistic concurrency. The second one should contain the new customer data and should be used to update the customer row. This method should also return a Boolean value that indicates if the update was successful. Add the code for this method using figure 16-10 as a guide if necessary.

12. Display the code for the Add/Modify Customer form, and uncomment the If...Else...End If statement in the event handler for the Click event of the Accept button. Then, run the application, retrieve customer 27, click the Modify button, and make a change to the data for the customer. Now, click the Accept button. If you coded the UpdateCustomer method correctly, the updated data should now be displayed on the Customer Maintenance form. Otherwise, you'll need to correct the code.

Write the code to add a customer

13. Add a method named AddCustomer to the CustomerDB class. This method should receive a Customer object with the data for the new customer, and it should return an integer with the ID for the new customer. Add the code for this method using figure 16-10 as a guide if necessary.
14. Display the code for the Add/Modify Customer form, and uncomment the statement that calls the AddCustomer method. Then, run the application and click the Add button to display the Add Customer form.
15. Enter the data for a new customer. Then, click the Accept button to add the customer to the database and display the customer data on the Customer Maintenance form. Note the customer ID for the new customer. When you have this working correctly, end the application.

Write the code to delete a customer

16. Add a method named DeleteCustomer to the CustomerDB class. This method should receive a Customer object with the data for the customer to be deleted, and it should return a Boolean value that indicates if the delete operation was successful. The Customer object should be used to provide for optimistic concurrency. Add the code for this method using figure 16-10 as a guide if necessary.
17. Display the code for the Customer Maintenance form, and uncomment the If...Else...End If statement in the event handler for the Click event of the Delete button. Then, run the application and retrieve the customer you added in step 15.
18. Click the Delete button to see the message that's displayed. Then, click the Yes button to delete the customer. If this worked correctly, the data should be cleared from the Customer Maintenance form and the Modify and Delete buttons should be disabled. When you have this working correctly, end the application and close the project.

Section 4

Object-oriented programming

In chapter 11, you learned the basic skills for creating and using classes. For many applications, those will be the only skills you'll need. However, Visual Basic also provides many other features for object-oriented programming, and the most useful ones are presented in this section.

In chapter 17, you'll learn how to create and use classes that define default properties, events, and overloaded operators. In chapter 18, you'll learn how to use inheritance, one of the most important features of object-oriented programming. In chapter 19, you'll learn how to use interfaces (another important feature of object-oriented programming) as well as generics. Last, in chapter 20, you'll learn how to document and organize your classes, including how to work with class libraries. When you're done with this section, you'll not only have the most important skills for creating and using your own classes, but you'll also understand how the .NET classes work.

17

How to work with default properties, events, and operators

In this chapter, I'll expand on the skills you learned in chapter 11 by presenting skills that you can use to create more complex classes. That includes creating default properties, throwing argument exceptions, raising events, and overloading operators.

An introduction to the ProductList class

As you may recall, the Product Maintenance application that was presented in chapter 11 used the List() class to store Product objects. To demonstrate the techniques that are presented in this chapter, I'll use a new class named ProductList with this application. As you'll see, this class represents a collection of Product objects.

The code for a simple ProductList class

Figure 17-1 shows a simple version of the ProductList class. This class uses only the coding techniques described in chapter 11. As a result, you shouldn't have any trouble understanding how this class works.

To start, the ProductList class defines a private List() variable named products to store the list of Product objects. Then, it provides a constructor with no parameters that instantiates a new list, followed by a Count property that returns the number of products in the product list.

Next, this class includes an overloaded Add method. The first version of this method accepts a single argument: a Product object that's added to the product list. The second version accepts three arguments: code, description, and price. The Add method uses these arguments to create a Product object, which is then added to the list.

After that, the ProductList class provides a Remove method that removes a specified product from the list, and a GetProductByIndex method that returns a Product object from the list based on the specified index. The last two methods in this class are a Fill method that fills the product list with the data from a file, and a Save method that saves the product list to a file. Both of these methods call shared methods in the ProductDB class.

Of these methods, only the Fill and Save methods provide functionality that isn't available from the List() class itself. In fact, the ProductList class actually limits the functionality of the List() class. For example, the ProductList class doesn't provide many of the properties and methods that are available from the List() class (such as the Insert method). Still, this class works for the purposes of this chapter. In the next chapter, though, you'll learn how to use inheritance to code a ProductList class that provides access to all the functionality of the List() class.

The code for a simple ProductList class

```
Public Class ProductList

    Private products As List(Of Product)

    Public Sub New()
        products = New List(Of Product)
    End Sub

    Public ReadOnly Property Count As Integer
        Get
            Return products.Count
        End Get
    End Property

    Public Sub Add(product As Product)
        products.Add(product)
    End Sub

    Public Sub Add(code As String, description As String,
            price As Decimal)
        Dim p As New Product(code, description, price)
        products.Add(p)
    End Sub

    Public Sub Remove(product As Product)
        products.Remove(product)
    End Sub

    Public Function GetProductByIndex(i As Integer) As Product
        Return products(i)
    End Function

    Public Sub Fill()
        products = ProductDB.GetProducts
    End Sub

    Public Sub Save()
        ProductDB.SaveProducts(products)
    End Sub

End Class
```

Figure 17-1 The code for a simple ProductList class

The specifications for the enhanced ProductList class

Figure 17-2 shows the specifications for an enhanced version of the ProductList class. You'll learn how to add these enhancements to the ProductList class of figure 17-1 as you move through the rest of this chapter.

First, the enhanced ProductList class provides an overloaded default property name Item. The first version of this property lets you access a product in the list based on its index, and the second version lets you access a product based on its product code. This overloaded method replaces the GetProductByIndex method you saw in the last figure.

Second, the enhanced class includes a + operator that adds a product to the list and a - operator that removes a product from the list. You can use these operators instead of the Add and Remove methods.

Finally, the enhanced class includes an event named Changed that is raised whenever the contents of the product list change due to a product being added to or removed from the list. As you'll see, the Product Maintenance application uses this event to determine when it should save the product list and refresh the list box that displays the products.

The members of the ProductList class

Property	Description
Count	An integer that indicates how many Product objects are in the list.
Item(index)	A default property that provides access to the product at the specified position.
Item(code)	A default property that provides access to the product with the specified code.
Method	**Description**
Add(product)	Adds the specified Product object to the list.
Add(code, description, price)	Creates a Product object with the specified code, description, and price values, and then adds the Product object to the list.
Remove(product)	Removes the specified Product object from the list.
Fill()	Fills the list with product data from a file.
Save()	Saves the products to a file.
Operator	**Description**
+	Adds a Product object to the list.
-	Removes a Product object from the list.
Event	**Description**
Changed	Raised whenever a Product object is added to or removed from the list.

Description

- The enhanced ProductList class improves upon the simple ProductList class by providing an overloaded default property named Item that provides access to any product in the list. It also includes overloaded + and - operators and a Changed event.

Figure 17-2 The specifications for the enhanced ProductList class

How to work with default properties

A *default property* is a property that Visual Basic will use if you refer to an object without specifying a member. You've already learned about some of the classes of the .NET Framework that provide default properties. For example, the List() and SortedList() classes you learned about in chapter 8 both have a default property named Item. Now, you'll learn how to code default properties in your own classes.

How to create a default property

Figure 17-3 shows you how to create a default property. To do that, you code a Property statement just as you do for any other property, but you include the Default keyword. In addition, a default property must be declared with at least one parameter.

Default properties are typically used with classes that represent collections of objects. This type of property can be referred to as an *indexed property* or an *indexer*. An indexer lets other classes that use the class access a specific item in the collection by specifying an index value.

The first example in this figure shows an indexer for the ProductList class. Notice that this class starts by declaring a private List() field named products. This list will be used to store products within a ProductList object. Then, an indexer with the name Item and a return type of Product is declared. This indexer uses a single parameter that identifies the index used by the indexer.

Like any other property, an indexer can provide get and set procedures. For example, the get procedure in the first example uses an integer index to return a Product object from the products list based on its position in the list. Conversely, the set procedure assigns a Product object to the products list at the specified position.

The second example shows another possible indexer for the ProductList class. This indexer varies from the first one in two ways. First, it includes the ReadOnly keyword, so it provides read-only access to the products list. Second, it uses a string index that provides for accessing the products by product code. To do that, the get procedure uses a For Each...Next loop to search the products list, and it returns the first product whose Code property matches the index value. If no match is found, Nothing is returned.

The third example shows how you can use these indexers. The first two statements create a new ProductList object and add a product to it using the Add method. Then, the next two statements use the two indexers to retrieve products from the list by index and by product code. The last statement in this group uses the set procedure of the first indexer to add a new product to the list at the index specified by the variable i.

A default property that uses an integer as a parameter

```
Private products As List(Of Product)

Default Public Property Item(index As Integer) As Product
    Get
        Return products(index)
    End Get
    Set(value As Product)
        products(index) = value
    End Set
End Property
```

A read-only default property that uses a string as a parameter

```
Default Public ReadOnly Property Item(code As String) As Product
    Get
        For Each p As Product In products
            If p.Code = code Then
                Return p
            End If
        Next
        Return Nothing
    End Get
End Property
```

Code that uses these default properties

```
Dim products As New ProductList
products.Add("VB12", "Murach's Visual Basic 2012", 54.5D)
Dim p1 As Product = products(0)
Dim p2 As Product = products("VB12")
products(i) = New Product(code, description, price)
```

Description

- A *default property* is a special type of property that you can use without specifying the property name. Default properties are almost always named Item, and they are typically used to implement an *indexed property*, also called an *indexer*.
- An indexer lets a user of the class access individual items within the class by specifying an index value. Indexers are used for classes that represent collections of objects.
- Before you add an indexer to a class, you should create an array or a collection as a private instance variable to hold the objects that will be accessed by the indexer.
- The declaration for a default property includes the Default keyword and one or more parameters. If the default property is an indexer, the parameter defines the index that will be used to access an item in the collection.
- An indexer's get procedure should return the object specified by the index value that's passed to it from the underlying collection. An indexer's set procedure should set the object in the underlying collection that's specified by the index to the object passed via the value keyword.
- Although the index used by an indexer is typically an integer, it doesn't have to be.

Figure 17-3 How to create a default property

How to throw an argument exception

When you code properties and methods, it's often a good idea to check the arguments that are passed to the properties or methods to make sure that they are valid. Then, if an argument isn't valid, an exception should be thrown to notify the user of the class that an error has occurred. For example, when you code indexers, you may want to check to make sure that the index argument falls within a valid range.

Figure 17-4 shows how argument exceptions should be handled. Here, the get procedure for the first indexer checks that the integer value that's passed to it falls within a valid range. If this value is less than zero or if it's greater than or equal to the number of products in the list, the indexer throws an exception. Otherwise, the integer is used to return the specified Product object from the product list.

The second indexer works similarly to the first indexer, but it accepts a string that specifies the product's code. To start, the get procedure checks if the string contains more than four characters. If so, the indexer throws an exception. Otherwise, it looks for a product with the product code in the list. If the product is found, the get procedure returns the Product object. Otherwise, it returns Nothing.

As you learned in chapter 7, the Throw statement specifies an exception object for the exception to be thrown. The .NET Framework defines the three exception classes in this figure as the exceptions that you should throw when validating arguments. If, for example, an argument is outside the range of acceptable values, you should throw an ArgumentOutOfRangeException. If an attempt is made to set a property to a null value when a value is required, you should throw an ArgumentNullException. For any other argument errors, you should throw an ArgumentException.

Notice that you can code both the parameter name and an error message on the constructor for these exceptions. Then, this information is included in the Message property of the exception.

When you code a statement that uses a property or method that throws an argument exception, you might think that you should enclose the statement in a Try…Catch statement so you can catch any exception when it occurs. But I don't recommend that. Instead, you should validate the data before passing it to the property or method. The If statement shown in this figure, for example, checks the length of the product code that the user enters before it passes this product code to the second indexer. That way, the exception should never occur.

So why include the validation code in the class at all? Because if you design your classes so they're reusable, you can't always count on other programmers to validate the data they pass to the class. By including this validation code, you make the class completely self-contained.

An indexer that checks the range and throws an argument exception

```
Default Public Property Item(index As Integer) As Product
    Get
        If index < 0 OrElse index >= products.Count Then
            Throw New ArgumentOutOfRangeException("index",
                "The index must be between 0 and " &
                products.Count - 1 & ".")
        Else
            Return products(index)
        End If
    End Get
    ...
End Property
```

An indexer that validates data and throws an argument exception

```
Default Public ReadOnly Property Item(code As String) As Product
    Get
        If code.Length > 4 Then
            Throw New ArgumentException(
                "Maximum length of Code is 4 characters.")
        Else
            For Each p As Product In products
                If p.Code = code Then
                    Return p
                End If
            Next
            Return Nothing
        End If
    End Get
End Property
```

Three argument exceptions

Exception	Description
`ArgumentOutOfRangeException( paramname[, message])`	Use when the value is outside the acceptable range of values.
`ArgumentNullException( paramname[, message])`	Use when the value is null and a null value is not allowed.
`ArgumentException( message[, paramname])`	Use when the value is invalid for any other reason.

An If statement that validates data before setting a property value

```
Dim p As Product
If txtCode.Text.Length <= 4 Then
    p = products(txtCode.Text)
End If
```

Description

- If a class detects an invalid argument, it should throw one of the three argument exceptions with arguments that describe the error.
- All of the argument exceptions are part of the System namespace.

Figure 17-4 How to throw an argument exception

How to work with events

In addition to fields, properties, methods, and constructors, a class can also define events. Then, when a particular condition occurs, the class can cause the event to be raised. To respond to that event, you can code an event handler for an object created from the class.

How to define events

An *event* is a signal that a particular action has occurred on an object that's created from the class. To define an event, you use an Event statement as shown at the top of figure 17-5. On this statement, you code the name of the event along with parameters for any arguments that will be passed to the event handler when the event is raised. In addition, you usually include the Public keyword to indicate that the event is available from outside the class that defines it. This keyword is optional, however, since Public is the default.

To cause an event to be raised, you code a RaiseEvent statement as shown in this figure. On this statement, you name the event you want to raise, and you code values for any arguments defined by the event. Like the arguments you code for procedures, the arguments you code on a RaiseEvent statement must match the arguments defined by the event it raises.

The first code example in this figure shows how you might code an event for the ProductList class. The first statement declares an event named Changed that accepts a ProductList object as an argument. Then, the Add method raises this event when a product is added to the list. Notice that the keyword Me is used as the argument on the RaiseEvent statement. This causes the ProductList object that raised the event to be passed to the event handler.

How to use events

To use an event defined by a class, you use code like that shown in the second example in figure 17-5. To start, when you declare the object variable that will refer to an instance of the class, you include the WithEvents keyword to indicate that the class can raise events. When you code the WithEvents keyword, the object and its events are included in the drop-down lists at the top of the Code Editor window. Then, you can generate the starting code for an event handler using these lists. In this example, you can see an event handler for the Changed event that's raised by the ProductList class.

The syntax for declaring an event

```
Public Event EventName[(parameterlist)]
```

The syntax for raising an event

```
RaiseEvent EventName[(argumentlist)]
```

Code that declares and raises an event in the ProductList class

```
Public Event Changed(products As ProductList)  ' Declare the event.

Public Sub Add(product As Product)
    products.Add(product)
    RaiseEvent Changed(Me)   ' Raise the event.
End Sub
```

Code that handles the event

```
' Declare the object as one that can raise events.
Dim WithEvents products As New ProductList

' Handle the Changed event of the object.
Private Sub Products_Changed(products As ProductList) _
        Handles products.Changed
    products.Save()
    Me.FillProductListBox()
End Sub
```

Description

- An *event* is a signal that an action has occurred on an object that was created from the class. To create an event that can be used by other classes, you code an Event statement with public access at the class level. Then, the event can be raised from any properties or methods in the class.
- To raise an event, you use the RaiseEvent statement. On this statement, you code any arguments required by the event.
- To handle an event from another class, you code the WithEvents keyword on the declaration for the object variable that will store the instance of the class that raises the event. Then, you code an event handler for the event using the drop-down lists at the top of the Code Editor window.
- When an event occurs, control is passed to the event handler for that event. If the event requires arguments, the arguments are also passed. When the event handler completes, control is returned to the statement after the RaiseEvent statement that caused the event to occur.
- You can also use the AddHandler statement to wire an event to an event handler at runtime (see chapter 6). You must use this technique for shared events or events that are defined within a structure.

Figure 17-5 How to define and use events

How to overload operators

The ProductList class in figure 17-2 uses overloaded operators. Specifically, this class overloads the + and - operators so you can add products to and remove products from the product list using these operators rather than using the Add and Remove methods. The following topics explain how you implement overloaded operators like these.

An introduction to operator overloading

Figure 17-6 presents some basic information about *operator overloading*. First, you should know that you can overload both unary and binary operators. The most common operators you can overload are listed in this figure.

Visual Basic defines the meanings of these operators for built-in types such as Decimal, Integer, String, and Date. However, for user-defined types such as the Product class presented in chapter 11 or the ProductList class presented in this chapter, these operators are either undefined or are defined in ways that may not be appropriate for the class. For example, the + operator isn't defined for user-defined types, but the = operator is. By default, if you compare two object variables using the = operator, they're considered equal if they refer to the same object.

With operator overloading, you can create your own implementations of Visual Basic operators that are appropriate for your classes. For example, a more appropriate definition of the = operator for the Product class would be to consider two Product variables equal if they refer to objects with the same Code, Description, and Price properties.

As the syntax at the top of this figure shows, you use the Operator statement to declare an operator. On this statement, you specify the operator you want to define, followed by one or two operands depending on whether the operator is a unary or a binary operator. Then, you specify the type of object that's returned by the operation.

Notice that operators are always declared as shared. That way, they can deal with operands that don't refer to object instances. That will make more sense when you see the code for the overloaded = operator.

Overloaded operators often depend on methods that are defined by the class. In figure 17-7, for example, you'll see that the + operator for the ProductList class uses the Add method of the class to add a product to the list. Then, in figure 17-8, you'll see that the = and <> operators for the Product class are implemented by overriding the Equals method of the Object class, which is inherited by all other classes.

Also note that some of the operators must be overloaded in pairs. If you overload the + operator, for example, you must also overload the – operator. And if you overload the = operator, you must also overload the <> operator.

The syntax for overloading unary operators

```
Public Shared Operator unary-operator(operand As type) As returntype
```

The syntax for overloading binary operators

```
Public Shared Operator binary-operator(
    operand-1 As type-1, operand-2 As type-2) As returntype
```

Common operators you can overload

Unary operators

```
+ - Not
```

Binary operators

```
+ - * / \ Mod ^ & = <> > >= < <= And Or
```

The Equals method of the Object class

Method	Description
`Equals(object)`	Returns a Boolean value that indicates whether the current object refers to the same instance as the specified object. If that's not what you want, you can override this method as shown in figure 17-8.
`Equals(object1, object2)`	A shared version of the Equals method that compares two objects to determine if they refer to the same instance.

The GetHashCode method of the Object class

Method	Description
`GetHashCode()`	Returns an integer value that's used to identify objects in a hash table. If you override the Equals method, you must also override the GetHashCode method.

Description

- You use the Operator keyword to *overload an operator* within a class. For example, you might overload the + and - operators in the ProductList class so they can be used to add and remove products from the list. You might also overload the = and <> operators in the Product class so you can compare two Product objects to see if they contain identical data rather than whether they refer to the same instance.
- You can overload all of the unary and binary operators shown above, as well as some others that aren't presented in this book. When you overload a binary operator, *operand-1* is the operand that appears to the left of the operator, and *operand-2* is the operand that appears to the right of the operator.
- *Overloaded operators* are always shared so they can deal with null operands properly.
- When you overload relational operators like = and <>, you need to provide your own versions of the Equals and GetHashCode methods. See figure 17-8 for details.
- Some operators must always be overloaded in pairs. That includes + and -, = and <>, and <= and >=.

Figure 17-6 An introduction to operator overloading

How to overload arithmetic operators

Figure 17-7 shows how to overload arithmetic operators such as + and -. For instance, the code at the top of this figure shows an implementation of the + operator for the ProductList class. This operator is used to add a Product object to the product list. As you can see, the declaration for the + operator specifies ProductList as the return type, which means that it will return a ProductList object. In addition, this operator accepts two parameters: a ProductList object named pl and a Product object named p. Then, the code for the + operator calls the Add method of the pl operand, passing the p object as the argument. This method adds the p object to the product list that's stored in the p1 object. Then, the + operator returns the pl object.

The second code example shows how you might use the + operator in an application to add a Product object to a product list. First, a new ProductList object named products is created. Then, a new Product object named p is created. Finally, the + operator is used in an assignment statement to add the product to the product list.

The last statement in this figure shows another way that you can use the overloaded + operator of the ProductList class to add a Product object to a product list. As you can see, this statement uses the += shortcut assignment operator. You may remember from chapter 4 that you can use shortcut operators like these in place of the assignment operator when the expression that's being assigned involves an arithmetic operation. You can use these shortcut operators with overloaded operators as well. Note that you don't need to provide any special code to use a shortcut operator. That's because when you use a shortcut operator, the compiler automatically converts it to an equivalent assignment statement that uses the assignment operator (=) and an arithmetic operator.

Part of a ProductList class that overloads the + operator

```
Public Class ProductList

    Private products As List(Of Product)

    Public Sub Add(product As Product)
        products.Add(product)
    End Sub

    Public Shared Operator +(pl As ProductList, p As Product) _
            As ProductList
        pl.Add(p)
        Return pl
    End Operator
    .
    .
End Class
```

Code that uses the + operator of the ProductList class

```
Dim products As New ProductList
Dim p As New Product("VB12", "Murach's Visual Basic 2012", 54.5D)
products = products + p
```

Another way to use the + operator

```
products += p
```

Description

- You can overload the built-in arithmetic operators so they perform customized functions on objects created from the class that defines them.
- You should overload only those arithmetic operators that make sense for a class. For example, it's reasonable to overload the + operator for the ProductList class as a way to add products to a product list. But it doesn't make sense to overload the * or / operators for this class.
- You don't overload the += or -= operators separately. Instead, these operators are handled automatically by the overloaded + and - operators.

Figure 17-7 How to overload arithmetic operators

How to overload relational operators

Figure 17-8 shows that relational operators are often more difficult to overload than arithmetic operators. Here, the first example shows how to implement the = operator for the Product class so you can compare products based on their values rather than on object references. The two objects that will be compared are passed as arguments to this operator.

The = operator starts by checking both operands to see if they're equal to Nothing. This testing is necessary to prevent the overloaded = operator from throwing an exception if one of the operands doesn't contain an object reference.

If both operands are equal to Nothing, the = operator returns True. If the first operand is equal to Nothing but the second one isn't, it returns False. Similarly, if the first operand isn't equal to Nothing but the second one is, it returns False. Finally, if neither operand is equal to Nothing, the = operator calls the Equals method of the first operand to compare it with the second operand and then returns the result of the comparison.

Notice that the declaration for the Equals method includes the Overrides keyword. That means that it overrides the Equals method defined by the Object class that every class inherits. In the next chapter, you'll learn how to work with inheritance. Then, you'll have a better understanding of how this code works.

The Equals method starts by converting the object that's passed to it to a Product object named p. Then, it compares its own Code, Description, and Price properties with the Code, Description, and Price properties of the p object. If all three properties are equal, it returns True. Otherwise, it returns False.

The code that's used to implement the <> operator in the Product class is also shown in this figure. As you can see, this operator defines itself in terms of the = operator. That way, you can be sure that these operators return consistent results.

The last method that's required when you overload the = operator is the GetHashCode method. Like the Equals method, this method overrides the GetHashCode method that's defined by the Object class. The main requirement for the GetHashCode method is that it must always return the same value for any two objects that are considered equal by the Equals method. The easiest way to do that is to (1) combine the values that are used for the comparison in the Equals method to create a string, (2) call the GetHashCode method of that string, and (3) return the Integer value that's returned by that method.

The second example in this figure shows how you can use the = operator to compare two Product objects. First, two object variables named p1 and p2 are created from the Product class with identical values. Then, the products are compared in an If statement using the = operator. Because both products have the same Code, Description, and Price values, this comparison returns True. If the Product class didn't override the = operator, however, this comparison would return False because the p1 and p2 variables refer to different instances of the Product class, even though they both have the same values.

Before I go on, you might want to consider why it's necessary for the = operator to be shared. If it weren't, you would have to call it from an instance of the Product class, for example, p1. But what if p1 was equal to Nothing? In other

Code that overloads the = operator for a Product class

```
Public Shared Operator =(p1 As Product, p2 As Product) As Boolean
    If p1 Is Nothing Then
        If p2 Is Nothing Then
            Return True
        Else
            Return False
        End If
    Else
        If p2 Is Nothing Then
            Return False
        Else
            Return p1.Equals(p2)
        End If
    End If
End Operator

Public Shared Operator <>(p1 As Product, p2 As Product) As Boolean
    Return Not (p1 = p2)
End Operator

Public Overrides Function Equals(obj As Object) As Boolean
    Dim p As Product = CType(obj, Product)
    If Me.Code = p.Code AndAlso
            Me.Description = p.Description AndAlso
            Me.Price = p.Price Then
        Return True
    Else
        Return False
    End If
End Function

Public Overrides Function GetHashCode() As Integer
    Dim hashString As String = Me.Code & Me.Description & Me.Price.ToString
    Return hashString.GetHashCode
End Function
```

Code that uses the = operator of the Product class

```
Dim p1 As New Product("VB12", "Murach's Visual Basic 2012", 54.5D)
Dim p2 As New Product("VB12", "Murach's Visual Basic 2012", 54.5D)
If p1 = p2 Then...    ' This evaluates to True. Without the overloaded
                      ' = operator, it would evaluate to False.
```

Description

- If you overload the = operator, you must also override the non-shared Equals method. Then, the = operator should use this Equals method for its equality test.
- Before it calls the Equals method, the overloaded = operator should check that the operands aren't equal to Nothing. If both operands are Nothing, they should be considered equal. If only one operand is Nothing, the operands should be considered unequal.
- When you override the Equals method, you must also override the GetHashCode method. That's because the GetHashCode method must return the same hash code for any two instances that are considered equal by the Equals method.

Figure 17-8 How to overload the = operator

words, what if p1 didn't refer to an instance of the Product class? In that case, you couldn't use the = operator. To work with operands that don't refer to object instances, then, overloaded operators must be declared as shared.

An enhanced version of the Product Maintenance application

Now that you've learned the techniques for enhancing your classes, the topics that follow present an enhanced version of the Product Maintenance application that uses those techniques. From the user's standpoint, this application operates exactly like the one that was presented in chapter 11. The only difference is that the classes in this version of the application are implemented differently. Specifically, the ProductList class includes the additional members that are shown in figure 17-2.

Because the code for the Product class is the same as the code that's presented in chapter 11, I won't repeat it here. Similarly, the code for the New Product form that's used in this version of the Product Maintenance application is identical to the code shown in chapter 11. As a result, I won't repeat that code here either. Finally, like the application in chapter 11, you should know that this application will work with any of the three versions of the ProductDB class that are presented in chapters 21 and 22.

The code for the ProductList class

Figure 17-9 shows the code for the ProductList class, which stores a collection of Product objects. To help you follow it, I've highlighted some of the critical statements.

As you can see, this class begins by declaring a List() object named products. This instance variable is used to store the list of Product objects. Next, the ProductList class declares an event named Changed that accepts a ProductList object as an argument. This event is raised whenever the contents of the product list are changed.

The two default properties for this class are indexers that let users of the class access a specific product in the list by specifying an integer value or a product code. Since these indexers are similar to the two indexers in figure 17-3, you shouldn't have any trouble understanding how they work. The differences are that the get procedure for the first indexer checks the value of the index that's passed to it and throws an ArgumentOutOfRangeException if necessary. In addition, the set procedure for this indexer raises the Changed event to indicate that the contents of the product list have changed.

The code for the ProductList class

Page 1

```
Public Class ProductList

    Private products As List(Of Product)

    Public Event Changed(products As ProductList)

    Public Sub New()
        products = New List(Of Product)
    End Sub

    Public ReadOnly Property Count As Integer
        Get
            Return products.Count
        End Get
    End Property

    Default Public Property Item(index As Integer) As Product
        Get
            If index < 0 OrElse index >= products.Count Then
                Throw New ArgumentOutOfRangeException("index",
                   "The index must be between 0 and " & products.Count - 1)
            Else
                Return products(index)
            End If
        End Get
        Set(value As Product)
            products(index) = value
            RaiseEvent Changed(Me)
        End Set
    End Property

    Default Public ReadOnly Property Item(code As String) As Product
        Get
            For Each p As Product In products
                If p.Code = code Then
                    Return p
                End If
            Next
            Return Nothing
        End Get
    End Property
```

Figure 17-9 The code for the enhanced ProductList class (part 1 of 2)

The Fill method of the ProductList class calls the GetProducts method of the ProductDB class to get the products from a file. Similarly, the Save method calls the SaveProducts method of this class to save the products to a file.

The ProductList class also provides two overloads for the Add method: one that accepts a Product object and one that accepts a code, description and price. It also includes a Remove method that removes the specified Product object. As you can see, all three of these methods raise the Changed event.

Finally, this class provides overloaded + and - operators. The overloaded + operator calls the first Add method to add the specified object to the product list and then returns the updated product list. Similarly, the - operator calls the Remove method to remove the specified product from the product list and then returns the updated product list. In effect, since the Add and Remove methods raise the Changed event, the + and - operators do too.

The code for the ProductList class

Page 2

```
    Public Sub Fill()
        products = ProductDB.GetProducts
    End Sub

    Public Sub Save()
        ProductDB.SaveProducts(products)
    End Sub

    Public Sub Add(product As Product)
        products.Add(product)
        RaiseEvent Changed(Me)
    End Sub

    Public Sub Add(code As String, description As String,
            price As Decimal)
        Dim p As New Product(code, description, price)
        products.Add(p)
        RaiseEvent Changed(Me)
    End Sub

    Public Sub Remove(product As Product)
        products.Remove(product)
        RaiseEvent Changed(Me)
    End Sub

    Public Shared Operator +(pl As ProductList, p As Product) _
            As ProductList
        pl.Add(p)
        Return pl
    End Operator

    Public Shared Operator -(pl As ProductList, p As Product) _
            As ProductList
        pl.Remove(p)
        Return pl
    End Operator

End Class
```

Figure 17-9 The code for the enhanced ProductList class (part 2 of 2)

The code for the Product Maintenance form

Figure 17-10 shows the code for the enhanced version of the Product Maintenance form. Because most of this code is the same as in chapter 11, I've highlighted the key differences here.

First, the products variable that's used by the class to store Product objects is a ProductList object, not a List() object. As a result, this version of the application can use the features of the ProductList class, such as the indexer, the Fill and Save methods, and the overloaded + and - operators. Because the products variable is declared with the WithEvents keyword, the form can also respond to the Changed event of the ProductList class.

The Load event handler for the form starts by calling the Fill method of the products object to fill the product list. Then, it calls the FillProductListBox procedure to fill the list box. Notice that this procedure uses a For...Next loop to retrieve each product in the product list by its index. Although you might think that you could use the For Each...Next statement like you could when the products were stored in a List() object, you can't. That's because the ProductList class doesn't provide all the functionality of the List() class.

The Click event handler for the Add button displays the New Product form. This form creates a new Product object and stores it in a public variable named Product. Then, if the Product object isn't equal to Nothing, the += operator is used to add the product to the product list.

The Click event handler for the Delete button uses an indexer of the ProductList class to retrieve the selected product from the product list. Then, if the user confirms that the product should be deleted, it uses the -= operator to remove the product from the list.

The last event handler handles the Changed event of the ProductList class, which occurs whenever a product is added to or removed from the product list. As a result, this event handler calls the Save method of the ProductList class to save the updated list of products. Then, it calls the FillProductListBox procedure so the updated list is displayed in the list box.

The code for the Product Maintenance form

```
Public Class frmProductMaint

    Dim WithEvents products As New ProductList

    Private Sub frmProductMaint_Load(sender As Object,
            e As EventArgs) Handles MyBase.Load
        products.Fill()
        Me.FillProductListBox()
    End Sub

    Private Sub FillProductListBox()
        Dim p As Product
        lstProducts.Items.Clear()
        For i As Integer = 0 To products.Count - 1
            p = products(i)
            lstProducts.Items.Add(p.GetDisplayText(vbTab))
        Next
    End Sub

    Private Sub btnAdd_Click(sender As Object,
            e As EventArgs) Handles btnAdd.Click
        Dim newProductForm As New frmNewProduct
        newProductForm.ShowDialog()
        If newProductForm.Product IsNot Nothing Then
            products += newProductForm.Product
        End If
    End Sub

    Private Sub btnDelete_Click(sender As Object,
            e As EventArgs) Handles btnDelete.Click
        Dim i As Integer = lstProducts.SelectedIndex
        If i <> -1 Then
            Dim product As Product = products(i)
            Dim message As String = "Are you sure you want to delete " &
                product.Description & "?"
            Dim button As DialogResult = MessageBox.Show(message,
                "Confirm Delete", MessageBoxButtons.YesNo)
            If button = DialogResult.Yes Then
                products -= product
            End If
        End If
    End Sub

    Private Sub btnExit_Click(sender As Object,
            e As EventArgs) Handles btnExit.Click
        Me.Close()
    End Sub

    Private Sub Products_Changed(products As ProductList) _
            Handles products.Changed
        products.Save()
        Me.FillProductListBox()
    End Sub

End Class
```

Figure 17-10 The code for the Product Maintenance form

Perspective

In this chapter, you've learned about a variety of features that you can include in the classes you create. You should keep in mind, however, that not all classes require these features. In fact, many classes require just the features you learned about in chapter 11. Nevertheless, it's important that you know about the features presented in this chapter so you can use them when that's appropriate.

Now that you've read this chapter, you should begin to appreciate the power and complexity of Visual Basic classes. Still, there's much more to learn about coding them. In the next chapter, then, you'll learn about one of the most important and potentially confusing aspects of object-oriented programming in Visual Basic: inheritance.

Terms

default property
indexed property
indexer
event
overload an operator
operator overloading

Exercise 17-1 Create a Customer Maintenance application that uses classes

In this exercise, you'll create a Customer Maintenance application that uses classes with the features presented in this chapter. To make this application easier to develop, we'll give you the starting forms and classes.

Open the project and add validation code to the Customer class

1. Open the application in the C:\VB 2012\Chapter 17\CustomerMaintenance directory.
2. Open the Customer class and note how the constructor for this class sets the FirstName, LastName, and Email properties to the appropriate parameters. Then, add code to the set accessors for these properties that throws an exception if the value is longer than 30 characters.
3. Test the class by trying to add a new customer with an email address that's longer than 30 characters. When you do, an exception should be thrown. Then, end the application.
4. Set the MaxLength properties of the First Name, Last Name, and Email text boxes to 30. Then, run the application again and try to add a new customer with an email address that's longer than 30 characters. This shows one way to avoid the exceptions, but your classes should still throw them in case they are used by other applications that don't avoid them.

Add a CustomerList class

5. Add a class named CustomerList to the project, and add the following members to this class:

Property	Description
`Count`	An integer that indicates how many Customer objects are in the list.
`Item(index)`	An indexer that provides access to the Customer at the specified position.
Method	**Description**
`Add(customer)`	Adds the specified Customer object to the list.
`Remove(customer)`	Removes the specified Customer object from the list.
`Fill()`	Fills the list with customer data from a file using the GetCustomers method of the CustomerDB class.
`Save()`	Saves the customers to a file using the SaveCustomers method of the CustomerDB class.
Constructor	**Description**
`New()`	Creates a CustomerList object with default values.

6. Modify the Customer Maintenance form to use this class. To do that, you'll need to use the Fill and Save methods of the CustomerList object instead of the methods of the CustomerDB class. In addition, you'll need to use a For...Next loop instead of a For Each...Next loop when you fill the list box.
7. Run the application and test it to be sure it works properly.

Add overloaded operators to the CustomerList class

8. Add overloaded + and - operators to the CustomerList class that add and remove a customer from the customer list.
9. Modify the Customer Maintenance form to use these operators instead of the Add and Remove methods. Then, run and test the application.

Add an event to the CustomerList class

10. Add an event named Changed to the CustomerList class. This event should accept a CustomerList argument and should be raised any time the customer list changes.
11. Modify the Customer Maintenance form to use the Changed event to save the customers and refresh the list box any time the list changes. To do that, you'll need to add the WithEvents keyword to the declaration for the products variable, you'll need to code an event handler for the Changed event of the products object, and you'll need to remove any unnecessary code from the event handlers for the Save and Delete buttons.
12. Run and test the application.

18

How to work with inheritance

Inheritance is one of the key concepts of object-oriented programming. It lets you create a class that's based on another class. As you'll see in this chapter, inheritance is used throughout the classes of the .NET Framework. In addition, you can use it in the classes that you create.

An introduction to inheritance

Inheritance lets you create a class that's based on another class. When used correctly, inheritance can simplify the overall design of an application. The following topics present an introduction to the basic concepts of inheritance. You need to understand these concepts before you learn how to write the code needed to implement classes that use inheritance.

How inheritance works

Figure 18-1 illustrates how inheritance works. When inheritance is used, a *derived class* inherits the properties, methods, and other members of a *base class*. Then, the objects that are created from the derived class can use these inherited members. The derived class can also provide its own members that extend the base class. In addition, the derived class can *override* properties and methods of the base class by providing replacement definitions for them.

The two classes shown in this figure illustrate how this works. Here, the base class is System.Windows.Forms.Form, the .NET Framework class that all Windows forms inherit. As this figure shows, this class has several public properties and methods, such as the Text property and the Close method. (This class has many more properties and methods. I included just a few representative ones here.)

The derived class in this figure is the class for the New Product form in the Product Maintenance application (ProductMaintenance.frmNewProduct). As you can see, two groups of members are listed for this class. The first group includes the properties and methods that the class inherits from its base class. The second group includes the members that have been added to the derived class. In this case, the derived class includes five new properties (the text box and button controls) and one new method (GetNewProduct).

Although this figure doesn't show it, a derived class can also replace an inherited property or method with its own version of the property or method. You'll learn how this works later in this chapter.

How inheritance works

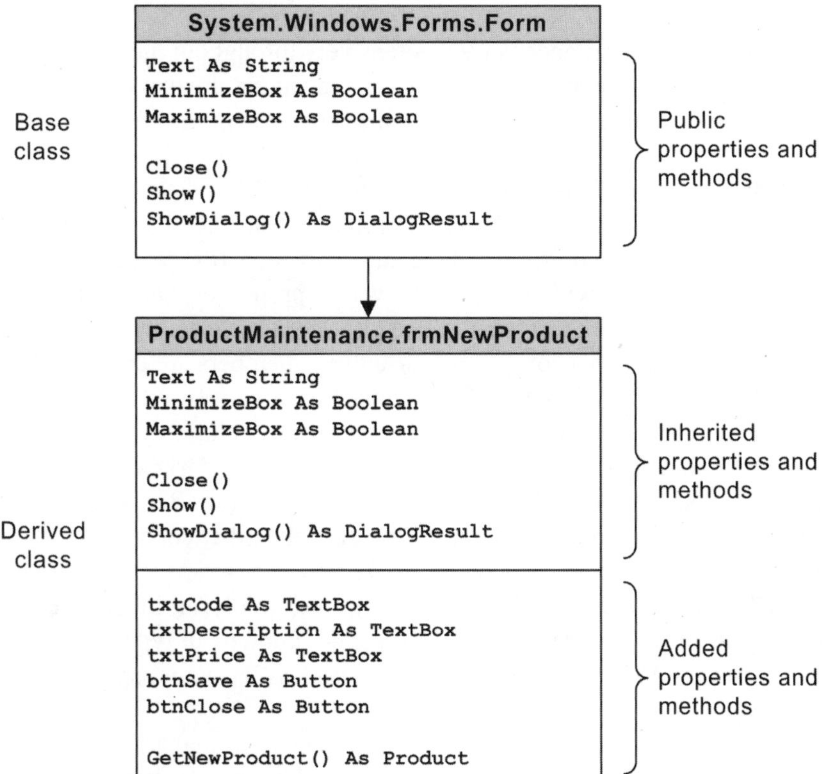

Description

- *Inheritance* lets you create a new class based on an existing class. Then, the new class *inherits* the properties, methods, and other members of the existing class.
- A class that inherits from an existing class is called a *derived class*, *child class,* or *subclass.* A class that another class inherits is called a *base class*, *parent class*, or *superclass*.
- A derived class can *extend* the base class by adding new properties, methods, or other members to the base class. It can also replace a member from the base class with its own version of the member. Depending on how that's done, this is called *hiding* or *overriding*.
- When you create a new form in Visual Basic, the form inherits the .NET Framework class named System.Windows.Forms.Form. As a result, all Visual Basic forms inherit the members defined by this base class. Then, as you add controls and code to the form, you extend the base class by creating new properties and methods.

Figure 18-1 How inheritance works

How the .NET Framework uses inheritance

Figure 18-2 shows that inheritance is used extensively throughout the .NET Framework. This figure shows a portion of the inheritance hierarchy that's used by several of the Windows form control classes in the System.Windows.Forms namespace.

The Control class provides features that are common to all Windows form controls. For example, the Control class provides properties such as Visible and Enabled that indicate whether a control is visible and enabled, a Text property that specifies the text associated with a control, as well as properties that specify a control's display location. The Control class also provides the Select method, which lets you move the focus to a control. Because these members are provided by the Control class, they are available to all Windows form controls.

The shaded classes in this figure are ten of the form control classes you've learned about so far in this book. Note that all of these classes are derived directly or indirectly from the Control class. For example, the GroupBox and Label controls inherit the Control class directly. However, the other controls inherit classes that are derived from the Control class.

The Button, CheckBox, and RadioButton classes, for example, all inherit the ButtonBase class. This class provides features that are common to all types of button controls. For example, the Image property of this class lets you display an image on a button control.

Similarly, combo boxes and list boxes have common features that are provided by the ListControl class. The most important of these are the Items property, which provides the list that's displayed by the control, and the SelectedIndex, SelectedValue, and SelectedItem properties, which let you access the item that's selected in the list.

Likewise, the TextBoxBase class provides some members that are common to text box controls such as the standard text box and the masked text box. That includes the MultiLine property that lets you display multiple lines and the ReadOnly property that lets you create read-only text boxes.

You may be surprised to learn that the Form class itself is also derived from the Control class by way of two other classes: ContainerControl and ScrollableControl. A form's ability to contain other controls is provided by the ContainerControl class. And a form's ability to display scroll bars if its controls can't all be displayed at once is provided by the ScrollableControl class.

Don't be dismayed by the amount of detail presented in this figure. In fact, the actual inheritance hierarchy for the classes in the System.Windows.Forms namespace is far more complicated than indicated here. The intent of this figure is simply to illustrate that inheritance is a feature that's used extensively within the .NET Framework.

The inheritance hierarchy for form control classes

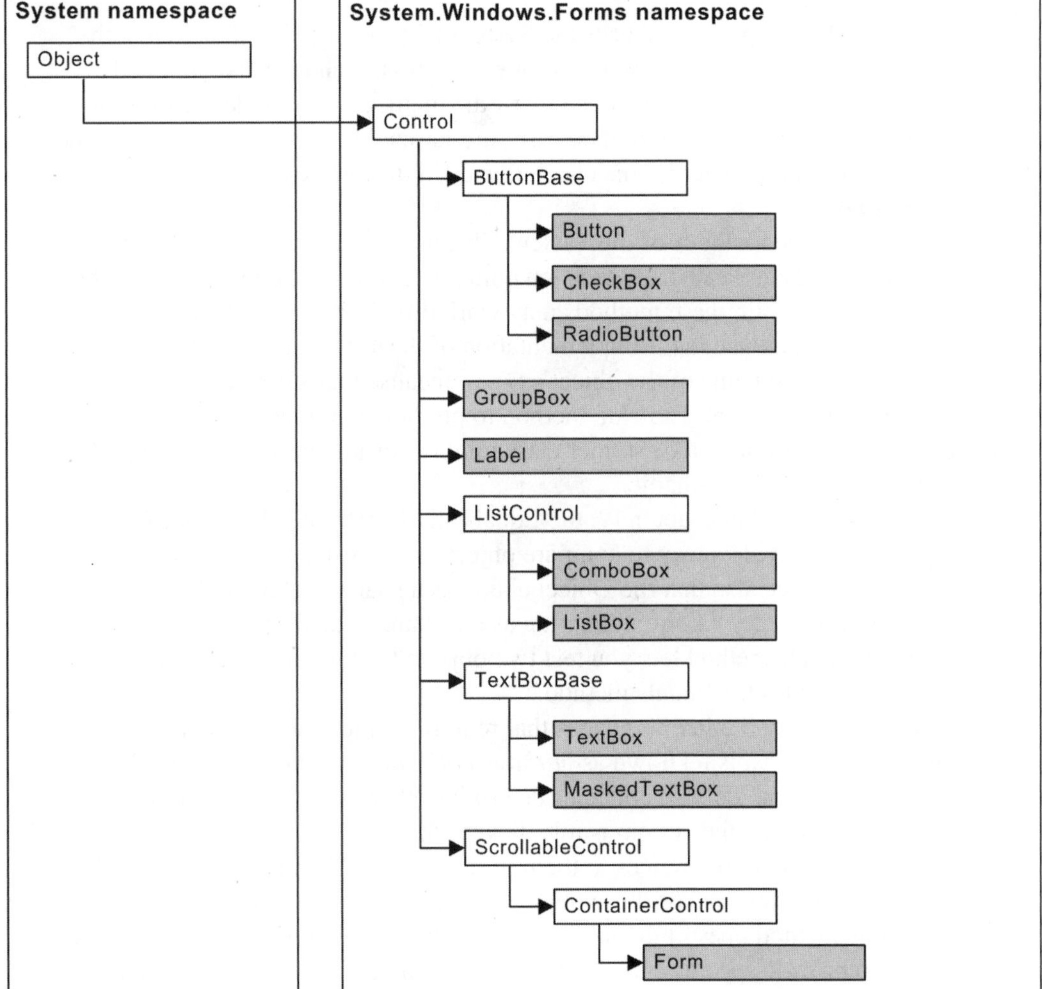

Description

- The .NET Framework uses inheritance extensively in its own classes. For example, inheritance is used throughout the System.Windows.Forms namespace.
- All of the control classes are derived from a base Control class. This class provides properties and methods that all controls have in common, such as Tag and Text. Like all classes, the Control class is ultimately derived from System.Object.
- Some controls have an additional layer of inheritance. For example, the ListControl class provides features common to ListBox and ComboBox controls, such as the SelectedValue property.
- The *fully qualified name* of a class includes the name of the namespace that the class belongs to. For example, the fully qualified name for the ComboBox control is System.Windows.Forms.ComboBox.

Figure 18-2 How the .NET Framework uses inheritance

Methods inherited from the System.Object class

Every class implicitly inherits the System.Object class. In other words, the System.Object class is the base class for every class, including user-defined classes. This means that all classes inherit the methods that are defined for the System.Object class. These methods are summarized in figure 18-3. I'll describe the GetType method later in this chapter, and I'll describe each of the other methods now.

Although the methods of the System.Object class are available to every class, a derived class can provide its own implementation of one or more of these methods. As a result, these methods may work differently from class to class.

For example, the default implementation of the ToString method returns the fully qualified name of the object's type. Because that's not very useful, it's common to override the ToString method to provide a more useful string representation. For example, a Customer class might override the ToString method so it returns the customer's name.

As you learned in chapter 17, the Equals and GetHashCode methods are often used to provide a way to compare objects using values rather than instance references. Notice also that the Object class has a shared ReferenceEquals method that provides the same function as the shared Equals method. The ReferenceEquals method lets you test two objects for reference equality even if the class overrides the Equals method.

Unlike C++ and other languages that require you to manage memory, Visual Basic uses a mechanism known as *garbage collection* to automatically manage memory. When the garbage collector determines that the system is running low on memory and that the system is idle, it frees the memory for any objects that don't have any more references to them. Before it does that, though, it calls the Finalize method for each of those objects, even though the default implementation of this method doesn't do anything. Although you can override the Finalize method to provide specific finalization code for an object, you rarely need to do that.

The last method shown in this figure is MemberwiseClone. You can use this method to create a simple copy of an object that doesn't expose other objects as properties or fields. You'll learn more about cloning objects in the next chapter.

Methods of the System.Object class

Method	Description
`ToString()`	Returns a string that contains the fully qualified name of the object's type.
`Equals(object)`	Returns True if this object refers to the same instance as the specified object. Otherwise, it returns False, even if both objects contain the same data.
`Equals(object1, object2)`	A shared version of the Equals method that compares two objects to determine if they refer to the same instance.
`ReferenceEquals(object1, object2)`	A shared method that determines whether two object references refer to the same instance. This method is typically not overridden, so it can be used to test for instance equality in classes that override the Equals method.
`GetType()`	Returns a Type object that represents the type of an object.
`GetHashCode()`	Returns the integer hash code for an object.
`Finalize()`	Frees resources used by an object. This method is called by the garbage collector when it determines that there are no more references to the object.
`MemberwiseClone()`	Creates a shallow copy of an object. For more information, refer to chapter 19.

Description

- System.Object is the root base class for all classes. In other words, every class inherits either System.Object or some other class that ultimately inherits System.Object. As a result, the methods defined by System.Object are available to all classes.
- When creating classes, it's a common practice to override the ToString and Equals methods so they work appropriately for each class. For example, the ToString method might return a value that uniquely identifies an object. And the Equals method might compare two objects to see if their values are equal.
- The *hash code* for an object is an integer that uniquely identifies the object. Object instances that are considered equal should return the same hash code. A common way to implement the GetHashCode method is to return ToString.GetHashCode. This returns the hash code of the object's ToString result.
- In general, you don't need to override the Finalize method for an object, even though its default implementation doesn't do anything. That's because the .NET *garbage collector* automatically reclaims the memory of an object whenever it needs to. Before it does that, though, it calls the Finalize method of the object.

Figure 18-3 Methods inherited from the System.Object class

How to use inheritance in your applications

Figure 18-4 describes the two main ways inheritance is used in business applications. First, it can be used to simplify the task of creating classes that represent similar types of objects. For example, the first inheritance hierarchy in this figure shows how you might use inheritance to create classes for two types of products: books and software products. As you can see, the Product class is used as the base class for the Book and Software classes. These derived classes inherit the Code, Description, and Price properties as well as the GetDisplayText method from the Product class. In addition, each class adds a property that's unique to the class: The Book class adds an Author property, and the Software class adds a Version property.

The second inheritance hierarchy in this figure shows how you can use the classes of the .NET Framework as base classes for your own classes. Here, a ProductList class inherits the System.Collections.Generic.List(Of Product) class. That way, the ProductList class has all the features of a List() of Product objects (such as an indexer and a Remove method). However, the ProductList class provides its own Add method that is used instead of the Add method that's available from the List(Of Product) class. This lets you change any members in the base class that don't work the way you want them to. You'll learn more about how this works in figure 18-6. Finally, the ProductList class provides two more methods (Fill and Save) that don't exist in the base class. These methods let you read and write the list to a data store.

An important aspect of inheritance is that you can use a derived class as an argument or return value for any method that is designed to work with the base class. For example, the Add method of the ProductList class accepts a parameter of type Product. However, because both the Book and Software classes are derived from the Product class, you can pass either a Book or a Software object to the Add method to add a book or software product to the product list. You'll learn more about how this works in figure 18-7.

Business classes for a Product Maintenance application

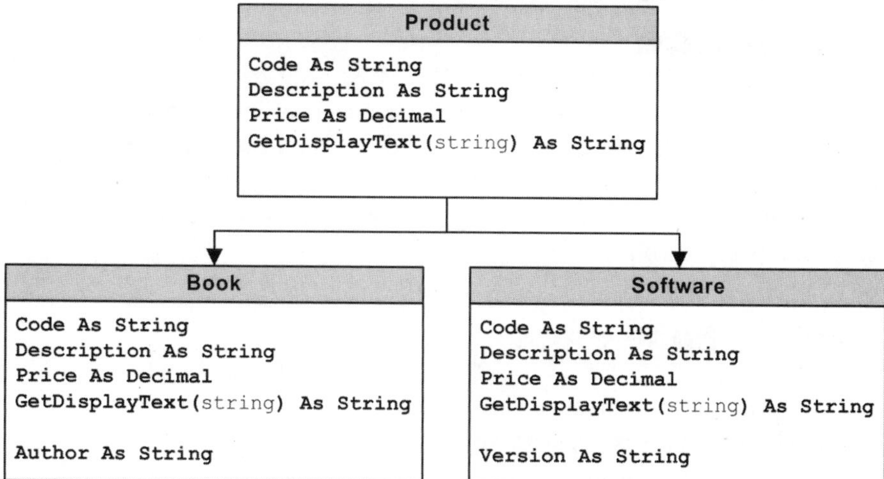

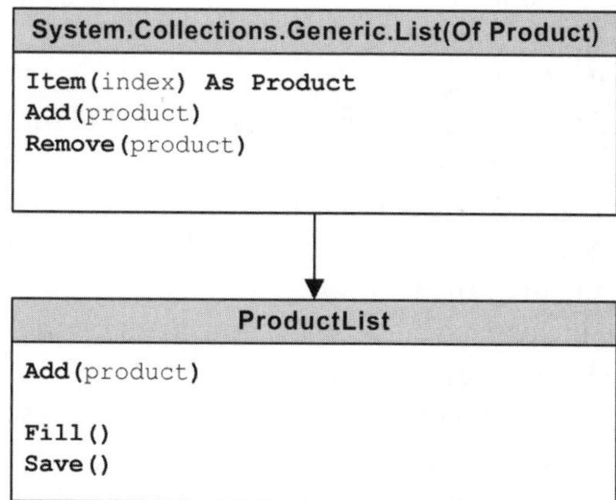

Description

- You can use inheritance in your applications to create generic base classes that implement common elements of related derived classes. For example, if you need separate classes to represent distinct types of products, you can create a Product base class and then use it to create a separate derived class for each type of product.
- It's also common to create classes that inherit from classes that are defined by the .NET Framework. For example, you might create a ProductList class that inherits the List(Of Product) class.
- When you inherit a class, you can use the derived class whenever an instance of the base class is called for. For example, a ProductList object based on a class that inherits List(Of Product) can be used whenever a List(Of Product) object is called for.

Figure 18-4 How to use inheritance in your applications

Basic skills for working with inheritance

Now that you've been introduced to the basic concepts of inheritance, you're ready to see how inheritance is implemented in Visual Basic. In the topics that follow, you'll learn how to create both base classes and derived classes. In addition, you'll learn how to take advantage of one of the major features of inheritance, called polymorphism.

How to create a base class

Figure 18-5 shows how to create a class that can be used as a base class for one or more derived classes. To start, you define the properties, methods, and other members of the class just as you would for any other class. Then, if you want a class that's derived from this class to be able to override one of the members of the base class, you include the Overridable keyword on the declaration for that member. The code shown in this figure, for example, uses the Overridable keyword on the GetDisplayText method.

Notice that the Product class provides an implementation of the GetDisplayText method that returns a string containing the values for the Code, Description, and Price properties. If a derived class doesn't override the GetDisplayText method, that class will simply inherit the version implemented by this class. As a result, creating an *overridable member* gives you the option of overriding the member in the derived class or allowing the derived class to defer to the version of the member defined by the base class.

The table in this figure lists several *access modifiers* you can use to indicate whether members of a base class are accessible to other classes. You already know how to use the Private and Public modifiers to create private and public members. When you work with inheritance, you also need to know about the Protected modifier. A *protected member* is a member that can be accessed within the defining class and within any class that's derived from the defining class, but not by any other class. Protected members let derived classes access certain parts of the base class without exposing those parts to other classes.

The Friend and Protected Friend access modifiers are sometimes useful when you work with class libraries or with solutions that have more than one project. To understand how they work, remember that when you build a project, all of the classes that make up the project are compiled into a single assembly. Members that use the Friend keyword alone are accessible to all of the classes within that assembly, but not to classes in other assemblies. Similarly, members that specify Protected Friend are accessible to derived classes that are a part of the same assembly, but not to derived classes in other assemblies.

The code for a simplified version of the Product base class

```
Public Class Product

    Public Property Code As String

    Public Property Description As String

    Public Property Price As Decimal

    Public Overridable Function GetDisplayText(sep As String) _
           As String
        Return Code & sep & FormatCurrency(Price) & sep & Description
    End Function

End Class
```

Access modifiers

Keyword	Description
`Public`	Available to all classes.
`Protected`	Available only to the current class or to derived classes.
`Friend`	Available only to classes in the current assembly.
`Protected Friend`	Available only to the current class, derived classes, or classes in the current assembly.
`Private`	Available only to the current class.

Description

- You create a base class the same way you create any other class: by defining its properties, methods, events, and other members.
- *Access modifiers* specify the accessibility of the members declared by a class. Public members are accessible to other classes, while private members are accessible only to the class in which they're declared.
- *Protected members* are accessible within the class in which they're declared. They can also be used by any class that inherits the class in which they're declared.
- A derived class can access the public and protected members of its base class, but not the private members.
- *Friend members* are accessible by other classes in the same assembly, but not by classes in other assemblies. This can sometimes be useful to control access to members declared by classes in a class library. For more information about class libraries, see chapter 20.
- If you don't code an access modifier, the default access is private.
- If you want to be able to override a member in a derived class, you must include the Overridable keyword on the member declaration.

How to create a derived class

Figure 18-6 shows how to create a derived class. First, you code an Inherits statement that names the base class right after the Class statement. For example, the code for the Book class shown in this figure specifies that the Book class inherits the Product class.

After you identify the base class, you can extend its functionality by coding additional properties, methods, or other members. In this figure, for example, the Book class adds a new constructor and a new property named Author. In addition, it overrides the GetDisplayText method defined by the Product class.

The constructor for the Book class accepts four parameters: code, description, author, and price. The first statement in this constructor uses the MyBase keyword to call the constructor of the base class that accepts code, description, and price arguments. Then, the base class constructor initializes the Code, Description, and Price properties with these values. After it calls the base class constructor, the constructor of the Book class initializes the Author field with the value passed to the author parameter.

To override the GetDisplayText method, the method declaration includes the Overrides keyword. Note that when you override a method, the override must have the same signature as the method it's overriding. In this case, the method must have a single String parameter. This parameter receives the separator that's used to format the Code, Description, Author, and Price properties.

Notice that this GetDisplayText method provides its own complete implementation. In contrast, the GetDisplayText method in the second code example adds on to the implementation of this method in the Product class. To do that, it starts by using the MyBase keyword to call the GetDisplayText method of the base class, which returns a formatted string that contains the Code, Description, and Price properties. Then, it adds the Author property to the end of this string.

This figure also introduces the concept of *hiding*. When you use the Shadows keyword on a member of a derived class, the member *hides* the corresponding base class member. As a result, the derived class doesn't inherit the original version of the member, but uses the new version instead. Hiding is similar to overriding, but can be used only with non-overridable methods or properties. Because hiding doesn't provide for polymorphism as described in the next topic, you should avoid using it if possible. Instead, you should use overridable methods and properties whenever you expect to provide a different implementation of a method or property in a derived class.

The syntax for creating a derived class

To declare a derived class

```
Public Class ClassName
    Inherits BaseClassName
```

To call a base class method or property

```
Mybase.MethodName(parameterlist)
Mybase.PropertyName
```

To override a method or property

```
Public Overrides {Sub|Function|Property} name [As type]
```

To hide a non-overridable method or property

```
Public Shadows {Sub|Function|Property} name [As type]
```

The code for a Book class

```
Public Class Book
    Inherits Product

    Public Property Author As String           ' A new property.

    Public Sub New(code As String, description As String,
            author As String, price As Decimal)
        MyBase.New(code, description, price)   ' Call the base class constructor.
        Me.Author = author                     ' Initialize the Author field.
    End Sub

    Public Overrides Function GetDisplayText(sep As String) As String
        Return Code & sep & Description & " (" & Author & ")" & sep &
            FormatCurrency(Price)
    End Function

End Class
```

Another way to override a method

```
Public Overrides Function GetDisplayText(sep As String) As String
    Return MyBase.GetDisplayText(sep) & " (" & Author & ")"
End Function
```

Description

- You use the Overrides keyword to override a member of the base class. Then, you can use the MyBase keyword to refer to a member of the base class.
- A constructor of a derived class automatically calls the default constructor of the base class before the derived class constructor executes. To call a non-default base class constructor, you use the MyBase keyword and you pass the appropriate parameters to the base class constructor. The call to the base class constructor must be the first statement in the constructor of the derived class.
- You can use the Shadows keyword to provide a new implementation for a method or property of the base class that can't be overridden. This is called *hiding*. In most cases, it's better to override the method or property so you can benefit from polymorphism.

Figure 18-6 How to create a derived class

How polymorphism works

Polymorphism is one of the most important features of object-oriented programming and inheritance. As figure 18-7 shows, polymorphism lets you treat objects of different types as if they were the same type by referring to a base class that's common to both objects. For example, consider the Book and Software classes that were presented in figure 18-4. Because both of these classes inherit the Product class, objects created from these classes can be treated as if they were Product objects.

One benefit of polymorphism is that you can write generic code that's designed to work with a base class. Then, you can use that code with instances of any class that's derived from the base class. For example, the Add method for the List(Of Product) class described in figure 18-4 accepts a Product object as a parameter. Since the ProductList class inherits the List(Of Product) class, this method is also available to the ProductList class. And since the Book and Software classes are derived from the Product class, this Add method will work with Book or Software objects.

The code examples in this figure illustrate a confusing but useful aspect of polymorphism. The first example shows an overridable method named GetDisplayText that's defined in the Product base class. This method returns a string that includes the Code, Description, and Price properties. The next two examples show overridden versions of the GetDisplayText method for the Book and Software classes. The Book version of this method calls the GetDisplayText method of the base class and then adds the author's name to the end of the string that's returned by that method. Similarly, the Software version calls the GetDisplayText method of the base class and then adds the software version to the end of the string that's returned.

The last code example in this figure shows how you can use polymorphism with these classes. This code begins by creating an instance of the Book class and assigning it to a variable named b. Then, it creates an instance of the Software class and assigns it to a variable named s.

Next, a variable named p of type Product is declared, and the Book object is assigned to it. Then, the GetDisplayText method of the Product class is called. When the .NET Framework sees that the GetDisplayText method of the Product class is an overridable method, however, it checks to see what type of object the p variable refers to. In this case, the p variable refers to a Book object, so it calls the overridden version of the GetDisplayText method that's defined by the Book class.

The example then does the same thing with the Software object. First, this object is assigned to the p variable. Then, the GetDisplayText method defined by the Product class is called. This time, .NET determines that the product is a Software object, so it calls the overridden version of the GetDisplayText method that's defined by the Software class.

Note that to use this type of polymorphism, you must code the Overridable keyword on the base class member. Otherwise, you can't override the member in the derived classes. Then, any call to the base class member executes that member regardless of the object type.

Three versions of the GetDisplayText method

An overridable GetDisplayText method in the Product base class

```
Public Overridable Function GetDisplayText(sep As String) As String
    Return Code & sep & FormatCurrency(Price) & sep & Description
End Function
```

An overridden GetDisplayText method in the Book class

```
Public Overrides Function GetDisplayText(sep As String) As String
    Return MyBase.GetDisplayText(sep) & sep & Author
End Function
```

An overridden GetDisplayText method in the Software class

```
Public Overrides Function GetDisplayText(sep As String) As String
    Return MyBase.GetDisplayText(sep) & sep & Version
End Function
```

Code that uses the overridden methods

```
Dim b As New Book("VB12", "Murach's Visual Basic 2012",
    "Anne Boehm", 54.5D)
Dim s As New Software("NPTK", ".NET Programmer's Toolkit",
    "4.5", 179.5D)
Dim p As Product
p = b
MessageBox.Show(p.GetDisplayText(vbCrLf))   ' Calls Book.GetDisplayText
p = s
MessageBox.Show(p.GetDisplayText(vbCrLf))   ' Calls Software.GetDisplayText
```

Description

- *Polymorphism* is a feature of inheritance that lets you treat objects of different classes that are derived from the same base class as if they had the type of the base class. If, for example, the Book class is derived from the Product class, you can treat a Book object as if it were a Product object.
- If you access an overridable member of a base class object and the member is overridden in the classes that are derived from that class, polymorphism determines the member that's executed based on the object's type. For example, if you call the GetDisplayText method of a Product object, the GetDisplayText method of the Book class is executed if the object is a Book object.
- Polymorphism is most useful when you have two or more derived classes that use the same base class. It lets you write generic code that targets the base class rather than having to write specific code for each object type.

Figure 18-7 How polymorphism works

An inheritance version of the Product Maintenance application

Now that you've learned how to create base classes and derived classes, the following topics present a version of the Product Maintenance application that uses inheritance. This version of the application uses the classes that were described in figure 18-4. It works with a Products file that can hold two distinct types of products: books and software.

Note that this version of the Product Maintenance application won't work with the ProductDB classes that are presented in chapters 22 and 23, since those classes are designed to work only with Product objects. Instead, this version of the application requires a ProductDB class that can save and retrieve data for both Book and Software objects. Although this class isn't presented here, you shouldn't have any trouble figuring out how to implement it after you read chapter 21 or 22.

The operation of the Product Maintenance application

Figure 18-8 shows the operation of this version of the Product Maintenance application. As you can see, the Product Maintenance form looks just like the one you saw in chapter 11. From this form, you can click the Add Product button to display the New Product form, or you can select a product in the list and then click the Delete Product button to delete the product.

The main difference between this application and the application presented in chapter 11 is that the New Product form includes two radio buttons. These buttons let the user choose whether a book or a software product is added to the file. Note that the label that's displayed for the third text box changes depending on which of these buttons is selected. If the Book button is selected, this label is set to Author. If the Software button is selected, it's set to Version.

The Product Maintenance form

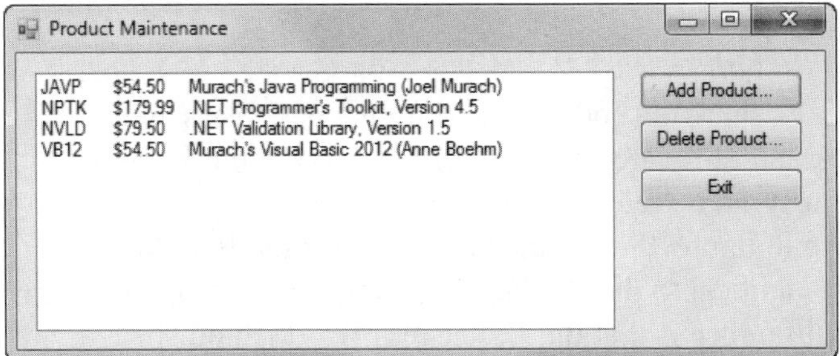

Two versions of the New Product form

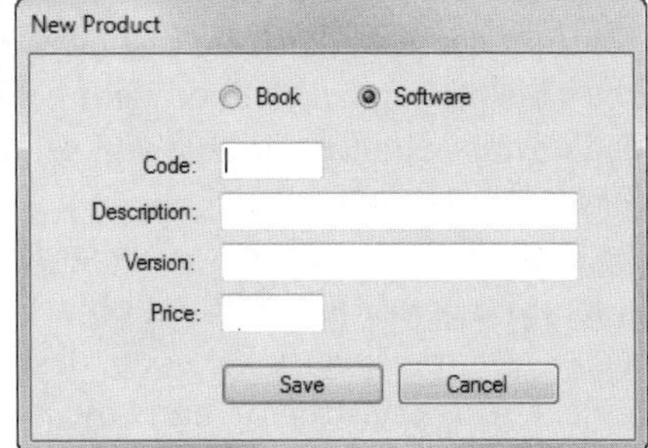

Description

- This version of the Product Maintenance application handles two types of products: books and software.
- The New Product form has a radio button that lets the user choose to create a book or a software product. The label for the third text box changes depending on which option is selected.

Figure 18-8 The operation of the Product Maintenance application

The code for the Product, Book, and Software classes

Figures 18-9 through 18-11 show the code for the Product base class and its two derived classes, Book and Software. You've seen portions of this code in previous figures, so most of it should already be familiar to you.

The Product class, shown in figure 18-9, is the base class for the Book and Software classes. It's almost identical to the Product class you saw in chapter 11. In fact, the only significant difference is that the GetDisplayText method specifies the Overridable keyword. That way, this method can be overridden by the Book and Software classes.

The Book class, shown in figure 18-10, specifies that it inherits the Product class. Then, it declares a private instance variable to hold the value of the Author property. This property is defined with get and set procedures that simply return the value of this instance variable and set the value of this variable to the value that's passed to the procedure.

The Book class provides two constructors. The first is an empty constructor that lets you create a new Book object with default values. The second constructor lets you specify the code, description, author, and price for a new Book object. This constructor starts by calling the constructor of the base class to initialize the Code, Description, and Price properties. Then, it initializes the Author property.

The overridden GetDisplayText method for the Book class calls the GetDisplayText method of the base class to get a string that includes the code, price, and description. Then, it adds the author's name in parentheses to the end of this string.

The Software class, shown in figure 18-11, is similar to the Book class, but it adds a property named Version. It too provides a constructor that calls the constructor of the base class to initialize the Code, Description, and Price properties before it initializes the Version property. It also overrides the GetDisplayText method by calling the GetDisplayText method of the base class and then adding the version information to the end of the string that's returned.

The code for the Product class

```
Public Class Product

    Private m_Code As String
    Private m_Description As String
    Private m_Price As Decimal

    Public Sub New()

    End Sub

    Public Sub New(code As String, description As String,
            price As Decimal)
        Me.Code = code
        Me.Description = description
        Me.Price = price
    End Sub

    Public Property Code As String
        Get
            Return m_Code
        End Get
        Set(value As String)
            m_Code = value
        End Set
    End Property

    Public Property Description As String
        Get
            Return m_Description
        End Get
        Set(value As String)
            m_Description = value
        End Set
    End Property

    Public Property Price As Decimal
        Get
            Return m_Price
        End Get
        Set(value As Decimal)
            m_Price = value
        End Set
    End Property

    Public Overridable Function GetDisplayText(sep As String) As String
        Return Code & sep & FormatCurrency(Price) & sep & Description
    End Function

End Class
```

Figure 18-9 The code for the Product class

The code for the Book class

```
Public Class Book
    Inherits Product

    Private m_Author As String

    Public Sub New()

    End Sub

    Public Sub New(code As String, description As String,
            author As String, price As Decimal)
        MyBase.New(code, description, price)
        Me.Author = author
    End Sub

    Public Property Author As String
        Get
            Return m_Author
        End Get
        Set(value As String)
            m_Author = value
        End Set
    End Property

    Public Overrides Function GetDisplayText(sep As String) As String
        Return MyBase.GetDisplayText(sep) & " (" & Author & ")"
    End Function

End Class
```

Description

- The Book class inherits the Product class. It adds a property named Author and overrides the GetDisplayText method.

Figure 18-10 The code for the Book class

The code for the Software class

```
Public Class Software
    Inherits Product

    Private m_Version As String

    Public Sub New()

    End Sub

    Public Sub New(code As String, description As String,
            version As String, price As Decimal)
        MyBase.New(code, description, price)
        Me.Version = version
    End Sub

    Public Property Version As String
        Get
            Return m_Version
        End Get
        Set(value As String)
            m_Version = value
        End Set
    End Property

    Public Overrides Function GetDisplayText(sep As String) As String
        Return MyBase.GetDisplayText(sep) & ", Version " & Version
    End Function

End Class
```

Description

- The Software class inherits the Product class. It adds a property named Version and overrides the GetDisplayText method.

Figure 18-11 The code for the Software class

The code for the ProductList class

Figure 18-12 shows the code for the ProductList class, which is used to hold the Book and Software objects that are maintained by the Product Maintenance application. This class inherits the List(Of Product) class. As a result, the basic functions of the ProductList class, such as its ability to hold multiple Product objects, are provided by the base class. For example, even though the ProductList class doesn't provide code for an indexer or a Remove method, both of these members are available from the ProductList class because they are available from the base class.

However, the ProductList class does provide an implementation of an Add method that hides the Add method that's available from the List(Of Product) class. To start, the declaration for this Add method uses the Shadows keyword to indicate that it hides rather than overrides the Add method from the base class. Since this method isn't declared as overridable in the base class, this is the only way to modify this method. Then, the statement within this method uses the Mybase keyword to call the Insert method of the List(Of Product) class to insert the Product object that's passed to the method at the beginning of the list. As a result, the Add method for this version of the ProductList class adds products to the beginning of the list instead of adding them to the end of the list. Although this might not be the behavior you would want for most lists, it does show how you can change the functionality of a derived class by hiding a method from the base class.

The last two methods of the ProductList class, Fill and Save, aren't available from the base class. These methods can be used to read or write the list of products to a data store. For example, the Fill method calls the GetProducts method of the ProductDB class to load the products in the Products file into a list of products. Then, it uses a For Each…Next loop to add each product in the list to the base list by calling the Add method of the base class. Conversely, the Save method calls the SaveProducts method of the ProductDB class to save the current instance of the ProductList class to the Products file.

The code for the ProductList class

```
Public Class ProductList
    Inherits List(Of Product)

    ' Modify the behavior of the Add method of the List(Of Product) class.
    Public Shadows Sub Add(product As Product)
        MyBase.Insert(0, product)
    End Sub

    ' Provide two additional methods.

    Public Sub Fill()
        Dim products As List(Of Product) = ProductDB.GetProducts
        For Each p As Product In products
            MyBase.Add(p)
        Next
    End Sub

    Public Sub Save()
        ProductDB.SaveProducts(Me)
    End Sub

End Class
```

Description

- This version of the ProductList class inherits the List() class of the .NET Framework. As a result, it doesn't need to define a List() instance variable because the class is itself a type of List() class.

Figure 18-12 The code for the ProductList class

The code for the Product Maintenance form

Figure 18-13 shows the code for this version of the Product Maintenance form. The first thing you should notice here is the code for the FillProductListBox procedure. You may remember that the code for this procedure in the Product Maintenance form in chapter 17 had to use a For...Next loop along with the indexer for the ProductList class to process the product list. In contrast, because the ProductList class in this chapter inherits the List(Of Product) class, I was able to use a For Each...Next loop to process the product list. You'll learn more about the features of the List() class that make this possible in the next chapter.

You can also see polymorphism at work in this For Each...Next loop. Here, the statement that adds the text to the Items collection of the list box calls the GetDisplayText method for each product. Because GetDisplayText is overridden by both the Book and Software classes, this code calls the GetDisplayText method of the Book class for Book objects and the GetDisplayText method of the Software class for Software objects. To confirm that's what's happening, you can look back to figures 18-10 and 18-11 to see the differences between these two methods, and you can look back to figure 18-8 to see the differences in the resulting display.

I also used a slightly different technique to display the New Product form and get the resulting Product object in the event handler for the Click event of the Add Product button. Here, I used a public method of the New Product form named GetNewProduct that returns a Product object. You'll see the code for this method in the next figure.

The code for the Product Maintenance form

```
Public Class frmProductMaint

    Dim products As New ProductList

    Private Sub frmProductMaint_Load(sender As Object,
            e As EventArgs) Handles MyBase.Load
        products.Fill()
        Me.FillProductListBox()
    End Sub

    Private Sub FillProductListBox()
        lstProducts.Items.Clear()
        For Each p As Product In products
            lstProducts.Items.Add(p.GetDisplayText(vbTab))
        Next
    End Sub

    Private Sub btnAdd_Click(sender As Object,
            e As EventArgs) Handles btnAdd.Click
        Dim newProductForm As New frmNewProduct
        Dim product As Product = newProductForm.GetNewProduct
        If product IsNot Nothing Then
            products.Add(product)
            products.Save()
            Me.FillProductListBox()
        End If
    End Sub

    Private Sub btnDelete_Click(sender As Object,
            e As EventArgs) Handles btnDelete.Click
        Dim i As Integer = lstProducts.SelectedIndex
        If i <> -1 Then
            Dim product As Product = products(i)
            Dim message As String = "Are you sure you want to delete " &
                product.Description & "?"
            Dim button As DialogResult = MessageBox.Show(message,
                "Confirm Delete", MessageBoxButtons.YesNo)
            If button = DialogResult.Yes Then
                products.Remove(product)
                products.Save()
                Me.FillProductListBox()
            End If
        End If
    End Sub

    Private Sub btnExit_Click(sender As Object,
            e As EventArgs) Handles btnExit.Click
        Me.Close()
    End Sub

End Class
```

Figure 18-13 The code for the Product Maintenance form

The code for the New Product form

Figure 18-14 shows the code for the New Product form. Here, you can see that the product variable has been declared as Private, which means it's not accessible from the Product Maintenance form. Instead, the GetNewProduct method, which returns this product variable, is declared as Public so it can be called from the Product Maintenance form. This method starts by displaying the form that contains it, in this case, the New Product form. Then, after the user enters and accepts the data for a new product, the GetNewProduct method returns the product to the Product Maintenance form.

You can also see that the event handler for the CheckedChanged events of the two radio buttons tests the Checked property of the Book radio button to determine how the Text property of the third label control and the Tag property of the third text box are set. Similarly, the event handler for the Click event of the Save button tests the Checked property of the Book radio button to determine whether it should create a Book or Software object. Last, the IsValidData method in this form uses the IsPresent method of the Validator class to validate the author or version that the user enters.

The code for the New Product form

```
Public Class frmNewProduct

    Private product As Product

    Public Function GetNewProduct() As Product
        Me.ShowDialog()
        Return product
    End Function

    Private Sub Product_CheckedChanged(sender As Object,
            e As EventArgs) Handles rdoBook.CheckedChanged,
            rdoSoftware.CheckedChanged
        If rdoBook.Checked Then
            lblAuthorOrVersion.Text = "Author: "
            txtAuthorOrVersion.Tag = "Author"
        Else
            lblAuthorOrVersion.Text = "Version: "
            txtAuthorOrVersion.Tag = "Version"
        End If
        txtCode.Select()
    End Sub

    Private Sub btnSave_Click(sender As Object,
            e As EventArgs) Handles btnSave.Click
        If IsValidData() Then
            If rdoBook.Checked Then
                Product = New Book(txtCode.Text, txtDescription.Text,
                    txtAuthorOrVersion.Text, CDec(txtPrice.Text))
            Else
                Product = New Software(txtCode.Text, txtDescription.Text,
                    txtAuthorOrVersion.Text, CDec(txtPrice.Text))
            End If
            Me.Close()
        End If
    End Sub

    Private Function IsValidData() As Boolean
        Return Validator.IsPresent(txtCode) AndAlso
               Validator.IsPresent(txtDescription) AndAlso
               Validator.IsPresent(txtAuthorOrVersion) AndAlso
               Validator.IsPresent(txtPrice) AndAlso
               Validator.IsDecimal(txtPrice)
    End Function

    Private Sub btnCancel_Click(sender As Object,
            e As EventArgs) Handles btnCancel.Click
        Me.Close()
    End Sub

End Class
```

Figure 18-14 The code for the New Product form

Object types and casting

Now that you've learned the basics of inheritance and you've seen an example of an application that uses it, you're ready to learn some additional techniques that are often required when you work with inheritance. That includes casting objects and getting information about an object's type.

How to use the Type class to get information about an object's type

As you know, the System.Object class includes a GetType method that you can use to get a Type object that represents the type of a .NET object. Figure 18-15 lists some of the members of the Type class that you can use to get information about an object. For example, you can use the Name property to get the name of a type, such as "Product" or "Book;" you can use the Namespace property to get the name of the namespace that contains a type, such as "ProductMaintenance;" and you can use the FullName property to get the fully qualified name of a type, such as "ProductMaintenance.Book." In addition, you can use the BaseType property to get a Type object that represents the type of the class that a type inherits.

The first example in this figure shows how you can use these properties to display information about an object. Here, the GetType method is used to get information about a Book object that's accessed through a variable of type Product. Notice that even though the variable has a type of Product, the Type object that's returned by the GetType method represents a Book object.

The second example shows how you can code an If statement to test an object's type. Here, I simply called the Product object's GetType method to get a Type object. Then, I compared the Name property of that object with a string to determine if the object is of type Book.

You can also test an object's type without using the Type class. To do that, you use the TypeOf keyword with the Is operator as illustrated in the third example. As you can see, the statement in this example is easier to read and code than the statement in the second example. So I recommend you use it whenever that makes sense.

The Type class

Property	Description
`Name`	Returns a string that contains the name of a type.
`FullName`	Returns a string that contains the fully qualified name of a type, which includes the namespace name and the type name.
`BaseType`	Returns a Type object that represents the class that a type inherits.
`Namespace`	Returns a string that contains the name of the namespace that contains a type.
Method	**Description**
`GetType()`	Returns a Type object that contains information about a type.

Code that uses the Type class to get information about an object

```
Dim p As Product
p = New Book("VB12", "Murach's Visual Basic 2012", "Anne Boehm", 54.5D)
Dim t As Type = p.GetType
Dim message As String = "Name: " & t.Name & vbCrLf &
                        "Namespace: " & t.Namespace & vbCrLf &
                        "Full name: " & t.FullName & vbCrLf &
                        "Base type: " & t.BaseType.Name
MessageBox.Show(message)
```

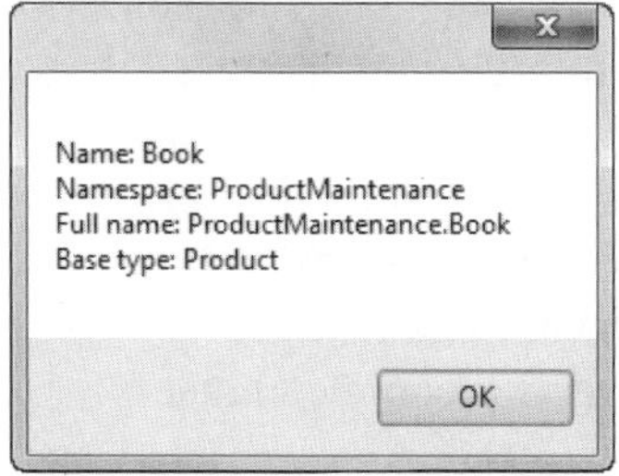

How to test an object's type

```
If p.GetType.Name = "Book" Then...
```

Another way to test an object's type

```
If TypeOf p Is Book Then...
```

Description

- Every object has a GetType method that returns a Type object that corresponds to the object's type.
- You can use the properties of the Type class to obtain information about the type of any object, such as the type's name and the name of its base class.
- The properties and methods shown above are only some of the more than 100 properties and methods of the Type class.
- Instead of using a Type object to test an object's type, you can use the TypeOf operator and the Is keyword.

Figure 18-15 How to use the Type class to get information about an object's type

How to use casting with inheritance

Another potentially confusing aspect of using inheritance is knowing when to cast inherited objects explicitly. The basic rule is that Visual Basic can implicitly cast a derived class to its base class, but you must use explicit casting if you want to treat a base class object as one of its derived classes. Figure 18-16 illustrates how this works.

The two methods at the top of this figure both call the GetDisplayText method to get data in a displayable format. The first method, named DisplayProduct, accepts a Product object and executes the GetDisplayText method of the Product class, so it can be used with either a Book or a Software object. In contrast, the second method, named DisplayBook, accepts a Book object and calls the GetDisplayText method of the Book class, so it can only be used with Book objects.

The second example shows code that doesn't require casting. Here, the first statement creates a new Book object and assigns it to a variable of type Book. Then, the DisplayProduct method is called to format the Book object that this variable refers to. Although the DisplayProduct method expects a Product object, it can cast the Book object to a Product object since the Book class is derived from the Product class.

The third example is similar, but it assigns the new Book object to a variable of type Product. Then, it calls the DisplayBook method. Because this method expects a Book object, however, the Product object must be explicitly cast to a Book object. If it isn't, the Visual Basic compiler will display a compiler error indicating that it can't convert a Product object to a Book object. The exception is if you have the Option Strict option set to off, in which case this cast will be done implicitly. As mentioned earlier in this book, however, I recommend that you set Option Strict on for all your applications.

The last example shows code that results in a casting exception. Here, a Software object is assigned to a variable of type Product. Then, the DisplayBook method is called to format the object that this variable refers to. Notice that this variable is explicitly cast to a Book object since that's what the DisplayBook method expects. Because the p variable refers to a Software object rather than a Book object, however, this cast results in a casting exception.

Two methods that display product information

```
Public Sub DisplayProduct(p As Product)
    MessageBox.Show(p.GetDisplayText(vbTab))
End Sub

Public Sub DisplayBook(b As Book)
    MessageBox.Show(b.GetDisplayText(vbTab))
End Sub
```

Code that doesn't require casting

```
Dim b As New Book("VB12", "Murach's Visual Basic 2012",
    "Anne Boehm", 54.5D)
DisplayProduct(b)
```

Code that requires casting if Option Strict is on

```
Dim p As Product = New Book("VB12", "Murach's Visual Basic 2012",
    "Anne Boehm", 54.5D)
DisplayBook(CType(p, Book))
```

Code that throws a casting exception

```
Dim p As Product = New Software("NPTK", ".NET Programmer's Toolkit",
    "4.5", 179.99)
DisplayBook(CType(p, Book))
```

Description

- Visual Basic can implicitly cast a derived class to its base class. As a result, you can use a derived class whenever a reference to its base class is called for. For example, you can specify a Book object whenever a Product object is expected because the Book class is derived from the Product class.
- If Option Strict is on, you must explicitly cast a base class object when a reference to one of its derived classes is required. For example, you must explicitly cast a Product object to Book if a Book object is expected.
- If you attempt to cast a base class object to a derived class, InvalidCastException will be thrown if the object is not of the correct type. For example, if you store a Software object in a variable of type Product and then try to cast the Product variable to a Book, a casting exception will be thrown.

Figure 18-16 How to use casting with inheritance

How to work with abstract and sealed classes

The last two topics of this chapter show how you can require or restrict the use of inheritance in the classes you create by using abstract and sealed classes.

How to work with abstract classes

An *abstract class* is a class that can't be instantiated. In other words, it can be used only as a base class that other classes can inherit. Figure 18-17 shows how to work with abstract classes.

To declare an abstract class, you include the MustInherit keyword in the class declaration as shown in the Product class at the top of this figure. Then, you can code any members you want within this class. In addition, you can code *abstract methods* and *abstract properties*. For example, the Product class shown here includes an abstract method named GetDisplayText. As you can see, the declaration for this method includes the MustOverride keyword, and no method body or End statement are coded. You code an abstract property using a similar technique, as illustrated by the second example.

When you include abstract properties and methods in an abstract class, you must override them in any class that inherits the abstract class. This is illustrated in the third example in this figure. Here, you can see that a class named Book that inherits the Product class overrides the abstract GetDisplayText method that's defined by that class. Although you must override abstract properties and methods, you should notice that they're not declared with the Overridable keyword. That's because abstract properties and methods are implicitly overridable.

At this point, you may be wondering why you would use abstract classes. To help you understand, consider the Product Maintenance application that's presented in this chapter. This application uses two types of product objects: Book objects and Software objects. However, there's nothing to stop you from creating instances of the Product class as well. As a result, the Product class hierarchy actually allows for three types of objects: Book objects, Software objects, and Product objects.

If that's not what you want, you can declare the Product class as an abstract class. Then, you can't create instances of the Product class itself. Instead, the Product class can only be used as the base class for other classes.

Note that this doesn't mean that you can't declare variables of an abstract type. It simply means that you can't use the New keyword with an abstract type to create an instance of the type. For example, if you declared the Product class as an abstract class, you could still declare a Product variable that could hold Book or Software objects like this:

```
Dim p As Product = New Book("VB12", "Murach's Visual Basic 2012",
    "Anne Boehm", 54.5D)
```

However, you wouldn't be able to use the New keyword with the Product class to create a Product object.

An abstract Product class

```
Public MustInherit Class Product

    Public Property Code As String

    Public Property Description As String

    Public Property Price As Decimal

    Public MustOverride Function GetDisplayText(sep As String) _
            As String
    ' No method body or End statement is coded.

End Class
```

An abstract read-only property

```
Public MustOverride ReadOnly Property IsValid As Boolean
```

A class that inherits the abstract Product class

```
Public Class Book
    Inherits Product

    Public Property Author As String

    Public Overrides Function GetDisplayText(sep As String) As String
        Return Code & sep & Description & " (" & Author & ")" & sep &
            FormatCurrency(Price)
    End Function

End Class
```

Description

- An *abstract class* is a class that can be inherited by other classes but that you can't use to create an object. To declare an abstract class, code the MustInherit keyword in the class declaration.
- An abstract class can contain properties, methods, and other members just like other base classes. In addition, an abstract class can contain abstract methods and properties.
- To create an *abstract property* or an *abstract method*, you code the MustOverride keyword in the property or method declaration and you code just the declaration.
- Abstract properties and methods are implicitly overridable, and you can't code the Overridable keyword on an abstract property or method.
- When a derived class inherits an abstract class, all abstract properties and methods in the abstract class must be overridden in the derived class.
- An abstract class doesn't have to contain abstract properties or methods. However, any class that contains an abstract property or method must be declared as abstract.

Figure 18-17 How to work with abstract classes

How to work with sealed classes

In contrast to an abstract class that must be inherited, a *sealed class* is a class that can't be inherited. Because Visual Basic doesn't have to generate code that provides for inheritance and polymorphism when it compiles sealed classes, using them can result in a minor performance benefit. If you know that a class won't be used as a base class, then, you should consider creating a sealed class.

Figure 18-18 shows how to create and work with sealed classes, as well as sealed properties and methods. To create a sealed class, you include the NotInheritable keyword in the class declaration as shown in the example at the top of this figure. Then, you add the members that are required by the class just as you do for any other class.

You can also seal selected properties and methods of a class by omitting the NotInheritable keyword from the class declaration and coding the NotOverridable keyword on just the properties and methods you want to seal. Then, you can use the class as a base class for other classes, but you can't override the sealed members. This is illustrated by the example in this figure.

This example uses three classes named A, B, and C. Class A is a base class that declares an overridable method named ShowMessage. Class B inherits class A and overrides the ShowMessage method. In addition, class B seals this method. Then, class C inherits class B and attempts to override the ShowMessage method. Because class B sealed the ShowMessage method, however, this results in a compiler error.

Although you can't override a sealed property or method, you should know that you can hide a sealed property or method. In the class named C in this figure, for example, you could declare the ShowMessage method like this:

```
Public Shadows Sub ShowMessage()
```

Then, you could provide a new implementation for this method.

In most cases, an entire class will be sealed rather than specific methods or properties. Because of that, you won't have to worry about whether individual properties and methods of a class are sealed. If you ever encounter sealed properties or methods, however, you should now understand how they work.

Keep in mind too that it's often hard to know when someone else might want to inherit a class that you create. So you shouldn't seal a class unless you're certain that no one else will benefit by extending it.

The class declaration for a sealed Book class

```
Public NotInheritable Class Book
    Inherits Product
```

How sealed methods work

A base class named A that declares an overridable method

```
Public Class A

    Public Overridable Sub ShowMessage()
        MessageBox.Show("Hello from class A")
    End Sub

End Class
```

A class named B that inherits class A and overrides and seals its method

```
Public Class B
    Inherits A

    Public NotOverridable Overrides Sub ShowMessage()
        MessageBox.Show("Hello from class B")
    End Sub

End Class
```

A class named C that inherits class B and tries to override its sealed method

```
Public Class C
    Inherits B

    Public Sub Overrides ShowMessage()    ' Not allowed
        MessageBox.Show("Hello from class C")
    End Sub

End Class
```

Description

- A *sealed class* is a class that can't be inherited. To create a sealed class, you code the NotInheritable keyword in the class declaration.
- Sealing a class can result in a minor performance improvement for your application because the Visual Basic compiler doesn't have to allow for inheritance and polymorphism. As a result, it can generate more efficient code.
- You can also seal individual properties and methods. To create a *sealed property* or a *sealed method*, code the NotOverridable keyword in the property or method declaration.
- You can only seal a property or method if the property or method overrides a member of the base class. This allows you to create an overridable member in a base class, and then seal it in a derived class so that any classes derived from that class can't override the member. This feature is rarely used in business applications.

Figure 18-18 How to work with sealed classes

Perspective

Conceptually, this is one of the most difficult chapters in this book. Although the basic idea of inheritance isn't that difficult to understand, the complications of overridable members, overridden members, casting, and abstract and sealed classes are enough to make inheritance a difficult topic. So if you find yourself a bit confused right now, don't be disheartened. It will become clearer as you actually use the techniques you've learned here.

The good news is that you don't have to understand every nuance of how inheritance works to use it. In fact, you've used inheritance in every Visual Basic application you've written without even knowing it. Now that you've completed this chapter, though, you should have a better understanding of how the .NET Framework works, and you should have a greater appreciation for how much the Framework does on your behalf. In addition, you should have a better idea of how you can use inheritance to improve the design of your own classes.

Terms

inheritance
derived class
child class
subclass
base class
parent class
superclass
overriding
fully qualified name
hash code
garbage collector
overridable member
access modifier
protected member
friend member
hiding
polymorphism
abstract class
abstract method
abstract property
sealed class
sealed property
sealed method

Exercise 18-1 Create a Customer Maintenance application that uses inheritance

In this exercise, you'll create a Customer Maintenance application that uses classes with the inheritance features presented in this chapter. This application works with two types of customers: retail customers and wholesale customers. Both customer types are derived from a Customer base class, both extend the Customer class by adding a property, and separate forms are used to add the two types of customers. To make this application easier to develop, we'll give you the starting forms and classes.

The design of the Customer Maintenance form

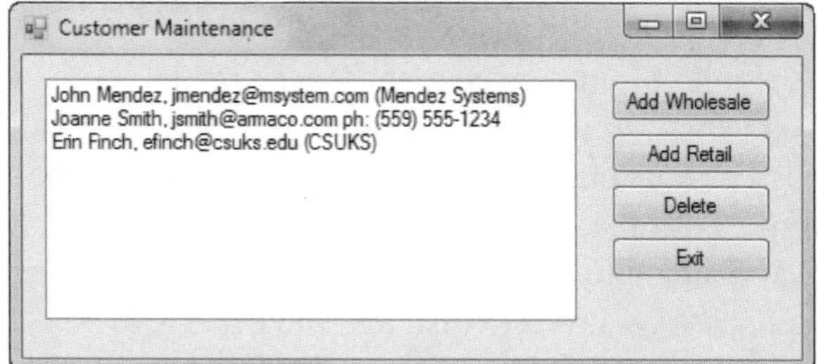

The design of the Add Customer forms

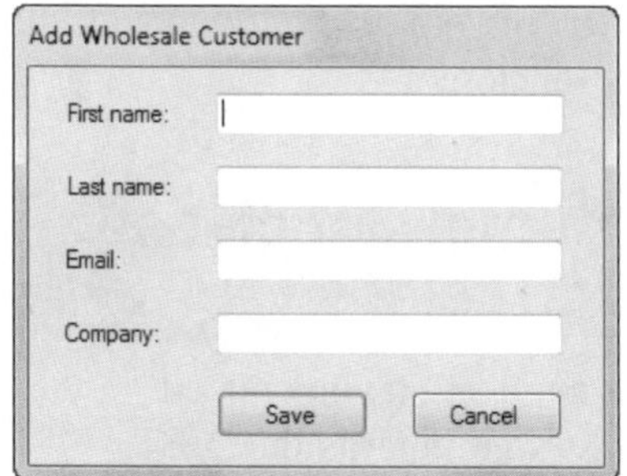

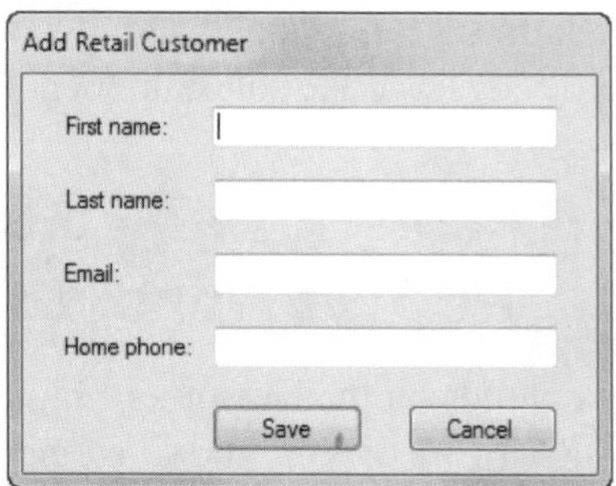

Open the project and create the derived classes

1. Open the application in the C:\VB 2012\Chapter 18\CustomerMaintenance directory.
2. Display the Customer class and modify the GetDisplayText method so it's overridable.
3. Add a class named WholesaleCustomer that inherits the Customer class. This new class should add a string property named Company. It should also provide a default constructor and a constructor that accepts four parameters (first name, last name, email, and company) to initialize the class properties. This constructor should call the base class constructor to initialize the properties defined by that class. Finally, this class should override the GetDisplayText method to add the company name in parentheses to the end of the display string, as in this example:

   John Mendez, jmendez@msystem.com (Mendez Systems)

4. Add another class named RetailCustomer that inherits the Customer class and adds a string property named HomePhone. Like the WholesaleCustomer class, the RetailCustomer class should provide a default constructor and a constructor that accepts four parameters, and it should override the GetDisplayText method so the phone number is added to the end of the string like this:

   Joanne Smith, jsmith@armaco.com ph: (559) 555-1234

Complete the code for the forms

5. Complete the event handlers for the Click events of the Save buttons on the Add Wholesale Customer and Add Retail Customer forms so they create a new customer of the appropriate type using the data entered by the user.
6. Complete the event handlers for the Click events of the Add Wholesale and Add Retail buttons on the Customer Maintenance form. These methods should create an instance of the appropriate Add Customer form and then call its GetNewCustomer method. The Customer object that's returned should be saved in a local variable of type Customer. Then, if the returned value isn't Nothing, the customer should be added to the customer list. Since this changes the list, this should cause the data to be saved to disk and the list box to be updated, but that should be done by the event handler for the Change event of the CustomerList object.
7. Run the application to make sure it works. If you're going to continue with the next exercise, leave the solution open. Otherwise, close it.

Exercise 18-2 Modify the CustomerList class to inherit the List() class

This exercise builds on the Customer Maintenance application you created in exercise 18-1 by modifying the CustomerList class so it inherits the .NET Framework's List() class.

1. If it isn't already opened, open the project in the C:\VB 2012\Chapter 18\CustomerMaintenance directory.
2. Modify the CustomerList class so it inherits the List(Of Customer) class instead of using a private List() variable to hold the customer list. To do that, you can delete the Count method because it's provided by the base class. You can use the Shadows keyword to hide the Item property and the Add and Remove methods in the base class so you can use the ones that are already in this CustomerList class. And you can use the Mybase keyword to refer to the base class whenever that's necessary. As you do this step, you may want to use figure 18-12 as a guide.
3. Modify the FillCustomerListBox method of the Customer Maintenance form so it fills the list box using a For Each…Next statement instead of a For…Next statement.
4. Run the application and test it to be sure it works properly.

19

How to work with interfaces and generics

This chapter starts by showing you how to use interfaces. Interfaces are similar to abstract classes, but they have several advantages that make them easier to create and more flexible to use. Then, this chapter shows you how to use generics so you can code your own collection classes that work like the generic collection classes of the .NET Framework that you learned about in chapter 8. Along the way, you'll learn how to work with the generic interfaces that are used with generic collections.

How to work with interfaces

In some object-oriented programming languages, such as C++ and Perl, a class can inherit more than one class. This is known as *multiple inheritance*. In Visual Basic, however, a class can inherit only one class.

Although Visual Basic doesn't support multiple inheritance, it does support a special type of coding element known as an *interface*. An interface provides many of the advantages of multiple inheritance without some of the problems that are associated with it. In the topics that follow, you'll learn how to work with interfaces.

An introduction to interfaces

In some ways, an interface is similar to an abstract class. That's why figure 19-1 compares interfaces to abstract classes. To start, abstract classes and interfaces can both include one or more members that aren't implemented. In the case of an abstract class, the implementation for these members must be provided by any class that inherits the abstract class. Similarly, the implementation for the members of an interface must be included in any class that *implements* the interface. The difference is that an interface can't include the implementation for any of its members, but an abstract class can.

An important difference between abstract classes and interfaces is that a Visual Basic class can inherit only one class (abstract or not), but it can implement more than one interface. This is how Visual Basic interfaces can be used to provide some of the features of multiple inheritance.

The examples in this figure show how a simple interface is declared and implemented by a class. The first example shows the declaration for a custom interface named IDisplayable. This interface includes a single method named GetDisplayText that lets an object return a string that can be used to display the object. Any class that implements the IDisplayable interface must provide an implementation of the GetDisplayText method.

The second example shows a simplified version of a Product class that implements the IDisplayable interface. Here, you can see that an Implements statement that names the IDisplayable interface is coded after the Class statement. Then, the class provides an implementation of the GetDisplayText method that returns a string that contains all three properties of the Product class.

The third example shows that a Product object that implements the IDisplayable interface can be stored in a variable of the IDisplayable type. In other words, an object created from a Product class that implements the IDisplayable interface is both a Product object and an IDisplayable object. As a result, you can use this object anywhere an IDisplayable object is expected.

In this figure, the interface name begins with the capital letter I. Although that's not a requirement, it's a coding convention that's followed by all the interfaces in the .NET Framework, and it helps you distinguish between interfaces and classes. So when you create your own interfaces, we recommend that you follow this coding convention.

The IDisplayable interface

```
Public Interface IDisplayable

    Function GetDisplayText(sep As String) As String

End Interface
```

A Product class that implements the IDisplayable interface

```
Public Class Product
    Implements IDisplayable

    Public Property Code As String
    Public Property Description As String
    Public Property Price As Decimal

    Public Sub New(code As String, description As String,
            price As Decimal)
        Me.Code = code
        Me.Description = description
        Me.Price = price
    End Sub

    Public Function GetDisplayText(sep As String) As String _
            Implements IDisplayable.GetDisplayText
        Return Code & sep & Description & sep & FormatCurrency(Price)
    End Function
End Class
```

Code that uses the IDisplayable interface

```
Dim product As IDisplayable = New Product("VB12",
        "Murach's Visual Basic 2012", 54.5D)
MessageBox.Show(product.GetDisplayText(vbCrLf))
```

A comparison of interfaces and abstract classes

- Both interfaces and abstract classes provide declarations for properties and methods that a class must implement.
- All of the members of an interface are abstract. In contrast, an abstract class can implement some or all of its members.
- A class can inherit only one class (including abstract classes), but a class can implement more than one interface.
- Interfaces can't declare shared members, but abstract classes can.

Description

- An *interface* consists of a set of declarations for one or more properties, methods, or events. An interface doesn't provide an implementation for any of its members. Instead, it indicates what members must be defined by any class that *implements* the interface.
- By convention, interface names begin with the letter I to distinguish them from classes.
- To implement an interface, a class must name the interface on the Implements statement, and it must provide an implementation for every member of the interface.

Figure 19-1 An introduction to interfaces

Some of the interfaces defined by the .NET Framework

The .NET Framework defines hundreds of interfaces. Fortunately, most of them are intended for use by other Framework classes. As a result, you don't need to learn them all. To give you an idea of what some of these interfaces do, however, figure 19-2 lists a few of them.

The first table in this figure lists four general purpose .NET interfaces: ICloneable, IComparable, IConvertible, and IDisposeable. Of these four, the one you're most likely to implement is ICloneable. This interface lets you create objects that can produce copies of themselves. It consists of a single method (Clone) that returns a copy of the object. You'll see an example of a Product class that implements this interface in figure 19-5.

While the other three interfaces in the first table are commonly used by .NET interfaces, you typically won't need to implement any of them for the classes that you code. For example, the IComparable interface provides a standard way for an object to compare itself with another object. However, most business classes don't have any real basis for determining whether one instance of the class is greater than, equal to, or less than another.

The second table in this figure lists several interfaces that are used by collection classes in the System.Collections namespace. The most important of these are IEnumerable and IEnumerator, which provide a standard mechanism for iterating through the items of a collection. If you implement these interfaces in a class, you can then use the class in a For Each...Next statement. In fact, this is the main benefit of implementing the IEnumerable and IEnumerator interfaces.

The other three interfaces listed in the second table provide standard ways to implement collection features. The ICollection interface defines a basic collection that maintains a count of items, can be synchronized, and can copy the collection items to an array. The IList interface adds an indexer and methods to add, clear, and remove items. And the IDictionary interface implements a dictionary, which can be used to maintain key/value pairs.

When reviewing the interfaces in this figure, keep in mind that these are the interfaces that were used by the .NET Framework prior to the introduction of generics. As a result, they aren't used by the generic collection classes in the System.Collections.Generic namespace. Instead, the generic collection classes use the generic interfaces you'll learn about later in this chapter.

Commonly used .NET interfaces

Interface	Members	Description
ICloneable	Clone() As Object	Creates a duplicate copy of an object.
IComparable	CompareTo(object) As Integer	Compares objects.
IConvertible	GetTypeCode() As TypeCode ToDecimal() As Decimal ToInt32() As Integer ...	Converts an object to one of the common language runtime types, such as Int32, Decimal, or Boolean.
IDisposeable	Dispose()	Frees unmanaged resources.

Commonly used .NET interfaces for collections

Interface	Members	Description
IEnumerable	GetEnumerator() As IEnumerator	Gets an enumerator for the collection.
IEnumerator	Current As Object MoveNext() As Boolean Reset()	Defines an enumerator that provides read-only, forward-only access to a collection.
ICollection	Count As Integer IsSynchronized As Boolean SyncRoot As Object CopyTo(array, index)	Provides basic properties and methods for an enumerable collection. This interface inherits IEnumerable.
IList	Item(index) As Object Add(object) As Integer Clear() Remove(object) RemoveAt(index)	Manages a basic list of objects. This interface inherits ICollection and IEnumerable.
IDictionary	Item(key) As Object Keys As ICollection Values As ICollection Add(key, value) Clear()	Manages a collection of key/value pairs. This interface inherits ICollection and IEnumerable.

Description

- The .NET Framework defines many interfaces that you can implement in your classes. However, many of these interfaces have been updated by the generic interfaces that are presented later in this chapter.
- The ICollection interface inherits the IEnumerable interface, which means that any class that implements ICollection must also implement IEnumerable. Similarly, the IList and IDictionary interfaces inherit ICollection and IEnumerable.
- This table lists only the most important members of each interface. For a complete description of these interfaces and a list of their members, see Visual Studio help.
- The interfaces for working with Collections are stored in the System.Collections namespace.

Figure 19-2 Some of the interfaces defined by the .NET Framework

How to create an interface

Figure 19-3 shows how to create an interface. As you can see in the syntax diagram at the top of this figure, you declare an interface using the Interface keyword. This keyword is followed by the interface name.

Within the body of an interface, you can declare one or more methods, properties, and events. Although these declarations are similar to the declarations for a class, there are three important differences. First, because an interface doesn't provide the implementation for its members, properties and methods consist of just their declarations. Second, you can't code access modifiers on a member declaration for an interface. Instead, all members are considered to be public and abstract. If you inadvertently code the Public or Abstract keyword on a member declaration, the compiler will generate an error message. Third, interfaces can't define shared members, so you can't use the Shared keyword.

To create an interface, you can select the Project→Add New Item command and then select the Interface template and enter a name for the interface from the resulting dialog box. This will generate the Interface and End Interface statements. Then, you can enter the member declarations between these two statements.

Note that the Interface template isn't available with the Visual Studio Express Edition. You can still create an interface with that edition, though. To do that, you can use the Code File template to create an empty code file and then enter the interface declaration yourself.

In the first example in this figure, the IDisplayable interface has been declared as Public, so it's available to all classes in the current namespace. In addition, a GetDisplayText method has been declared. The signature for this method specifies that the method accepts a separator string as a parameter and returns a string that contains the display text for the object.

In the second example, the IPersistable interface defines two methods and a property. Here, the Read and Save methods can be used to read and write the object, and the HasChanges property can be used to determine if the object contains any unsaved changes.

If an interface inherits other interfaces, the Interface statement is followed by an Inherits statement that lists the inherited interfaces. In the last example, for instance, the IDataAccessObject interface inherits the IDisplayable and IPersistable interfaces. As a result, any class that implements IDataAccessObject must implement all three of the methods and the one property defined by IDisplayable and IPersistable. Although it isn't shown in this figure, IDataAccessObject could also add additional members.

The syntax for creating an interface

```
Public Interface InterfaceName

    {Sub|Function} MethodName(parameterlist) [As type]  ' Method

    Property PropertyName As type                       ' Property
    .
    .
End Interface
```

An interface that defines one method

```
Public Interface IDisplayable

    Function GetDisplayText(sep As String) As String

End Interface
```

An interface that defines two methods and a property

```
Public Interface IPersistable

    Function Read(id As String) As Object

    Function Save(o As Object) As Boolean

    Property HasChanges As Boolean

End Interface
```

The syntax for creating an interface that inherits other interfaces

```
Public Interface InterfaceName
    Inherits InterfaceName1[, InterfaceName2]...

    interface members...

End Interface
```

An interface that inherits two interfaces

```
Public Interface IDataAccessObject
    Inherits IDisplayable, IPersistable

    ' Add additional members here.

End Interface
```

Description

- The declaration for an interface is similar to the declaration for a class. The only difference is that you use the Interface keyword instead of the Class keyword.
- Methods and properties that are declared within an interface can't include implementation.
- You shouldn't include any access modifiers on interface members. All members are considered to be public and abstract, and shared members aren't allowed.

Figure 19-3 How to create an interface

How to implement an interface

Figure 19-4 shows how to code a class that implements one or more interfaces. To do that, you code an Implements statement that lists the interfaces following the Class statement. Note that if the class also inherits another class, you must code the Inherits statement before the Implements statement.

The three class declarations in this figure illustrate how this works. The first class declaration is for a Product class that implements the ICloneable interface. The second class declaration is for a Product class that implements two interfaces: ICloneable and IDisplayable. And the third class declaration is for a Book class that inherits the Product class and implements the ICloneable and IDisplayable interfaces.

When you code an Implements statement, you can automatically generate starting code for each member of each interface. To do that, press the Enter key at the end of the statement. Then, code that's similar to the code in the last example in this figure is inserted into the class. Here, starting code for the Clone method of the ICloneable interface is shown. At this point, you can enter the code that's needed to implement this method.

Notice in this example that the Clone method includes the Implements keyword followed by the name of the interface that declares the method. That makes it clear that the method is an implementation of a method that's declared by an interface. If a class implements more than one interface, it also makes it clear which interface declares the method.

The syntax for implementing an interface

```
Public Class ClassName
    Inherits BaseClassName
    Implements InterfaceName1[, InterfaceName2]...
```

A Product class that implements ICloneable

```
Public Class Product
    Implements ICloneable
```

A Product class that implements two interfaces

```
Public Class Product
    Implements ICloneable, IDisplayable
```

A class that inherits a class and implements two interfaces

```
Public Class Book
    Inherits Product
    Implements ICloneable, IDisplayable
```

The code that's generated for implementing the ICloneable interface

```
Public Function Clone() As Object Implements ICloneable.Clone

End Function
```

Description

- To declare a class that implements one or more interfaces, code an Implements statement that lists the interfaces following the Class statement.
- If a class inherits another class, you must code the Inherits statement before the Implements statement.
- When you code an Implements statement and press Enter, Visual Studio generates the starting code for the members that must be implemented for each interface. Then, you can add the code to implement each member.

Figure 19-4 How to implement an interface

A Product class that implements the ICloneable interface

Now that you've seen the basic skills for creating and implementing interfaces, figure 19-5 presents an example of a Product class that implements the IDisplayable and ICloneable interfaces. This example is similar to the example that was shown in figure 19-1.

The Product class begins by declaring three properties named Code, Description, and Price. Then, after the constructors for the class, the GetDisplayText method provides the implementation for the GetDisplayText method that's declared by the IDisplayable interface, and the Clone method provides the implementation for the Clone method that's declared by the ICloneable interface. This method creates a new product, copies the Code, Description, and Price values from the current product to the new product, and returns the new product.

The second example in this figure illustrates how you can use the Clone and GetDisplayText methods of the Product class. First, a Product variable named p1 is declared and a new product is created and assigned to it. Then, a second Product variable named p2 is declared, and the Clone method of the p1 product is used to create a copy that's assigned to this variable. Notice that because the Clone method returns an Object type, the return value must be converted to the Product type so it can be assigned to the p2 variable. Next, the Code and Description fields of the second object are modified. Finally, the GetDisplayText method is used to construct a string that contains the values from both products, and the string is displayed in a dialog box. As you can see, the products contain different data, which proves that the clone worked.

In this example, the data for a Product object is stored in three fields with built-in value types. But what if you wanted to clone a more complicated object with fields that represent other objects? For example, consider an Invoice class with a Customer property that returns a Customer object that's stored in a private field. In that case, you can clone the Invoice object using either a shallow copy or a deep copy.

If you use a *shallow copy*, the Customer field of the cloned Invoice object would refer to the same Customer object as the original Invoice object. In contrast, if you use a *deep copy*, the Customer field of the cloned Invoice object would refer to a clone of the Customer object. The easiest way to accomplish that would be to implement the ICloneable interface in the Customer class and then call the Clone method of this class from the Clone method of the Invoice class.

As defined by the ICloneable interface, the Clone method doesn't specify whether the returned value should be a deep copy or a shallow copy. So you can implement whichever type of copy you think is most appropriate for a class. Just be sure to specify whether the Clone method returns a deep copy or a shallow copy in the class documentation so users of the class will know what to expect when they use the Clone method.

The code for the cloneable Product class

```
Public Class Product
    Implements IDisplayable, ICloneable

    Public Property Code As String
    Public Property Description As String
    Public Property Price As Decimal

    Public Sub New()

    End Sub

    Public Sub New(code As String, description As String,
            price As Decimal)
        Me.Code = code
        Me.Description = description
        Me.Price = price
    End Sub

    Public Function GetDisplayText(sep As String) As String _
            Implements IDisplayable.GetDisplayText
        Return Code & sep & Description & sep & FormatCurrency(Price)
    End Function

    Public Function Clone() As Object Implements ICloneable.Clone
        Dim p As New Product
        p.Code = Me.Code
        p.Description = Me.Description
        p.Price = Me.Price
        Return p
    End Function
End Class
```

Code that creates and clones a Product object

```
Dim p1 As New Product("JSE6", "Murach's Java SE 6", 54.5D)
Dim p2 As Product = CType(p1.Clone, Product)
p2.Code = "JAVP"
p2.Description = "Murach's Java Programming"
Dim displayText As String =
    p1.GetDisplayText(vbCrLf) & vbCrLf & vbCrLf &
    p2.GetDisplayText(vbCrLf)
MessageBox.Show(displayText, "Cloned Product")
```

The resulting dialog box

Figure 19-5 A Product class that implements the ICloneable interface

How to use an interface as a parameter

Figure 19-6 shows how to use an interface as a parameter of a method. To do that, you code the name of the interface as the parameter type as shown in the first example. Here, a method named CreateList is declared with two parameters: an object that implements ICloneable and an integer. This method returns a list that's filled with copies of the object specified by the first parameter. The number of copies to be included in the list is specified by the second parameter. To generate the copies, the CreateList method uses the Clone method of the object that's passed to it.

The second example shows how to code a method named GetDisplayableText that accepts an object that implements the IDisplayable interface. This method uses the GetDisplayText method of the IDisplayable interface to return the display text for the object.

When you declare a method that accepts an interface as an argument, you can pass any object that implements that interface to the method. This is illustrated in the third code example in this figure. Here, a new Product object is created and stored in a variable named product. Then, the CreateList method is used to create three copies of this object. Next, the GetDisplayableText method is used within a For Each loop to get the display text for each Product and add it to a string variable. Finally, the text is displayed in a dialog box.

The key point here is that the CreateList method doesn't know what type of object it's cloning. All it knows is that the object implements the ICloneable interface, which means that it has a Clone method. Similarly, the GetDisplayableText method doesn't know what type of object it's getting display text for. All it knows is that the object implements the IDisplayable interface, which means that it has a GetDisplayText method. Both of these methods work for a Product object because the Product class implements ICloneable and IDisplayable.

This example also illustrates a larger point. In short, a Product object can be thought of as an ICloneable or IDisplayable object. As a result, you can supply a Product object anywhere an ICloneable or IDisplayable object is expected. In this figure, interfaces are used to specify the type for a parameter of a method. However, interfaces can be used to specify a type in other places too. For example, an interface can be used as a return type for a method or to specify the type of a property. And anywhere an interface is used to specify a type, you can supply any object that implements that interface.

A CreateList method that uses an interface as a parameter

```
Public Function CreateList(obj As ICloneable,
        count As Integer) As List(Of Object)
    Dim objects As New List(Of Object)
    For i As Integer = 0 To count - 1
        Dim o As Object = obj.Clone
        objects.Add(o)
    Next
    Return objects
End Function
```

A GetDisplayableText method that uses an interface as a parameter

```
Public Function GetDisplayableText(obj As IDisplayable) As String
    Return obj.GetDisplayText(vbTab) & vbCrLf & vbCrLf
End Function
```

Code that uses these methods

```
Dim product As New Product("VB12", "Murach's Visual Basic 2012", 54.5D)
Dim products As List(Of Object) = CreateList(product, 3)
Dim displayText As String = ""
For Each p As Product In products
    displayText &= GetDisplayableText(p)
Next
MessageBox.Show(displayText, "Cloned Objects")
```

The resulting dialog box

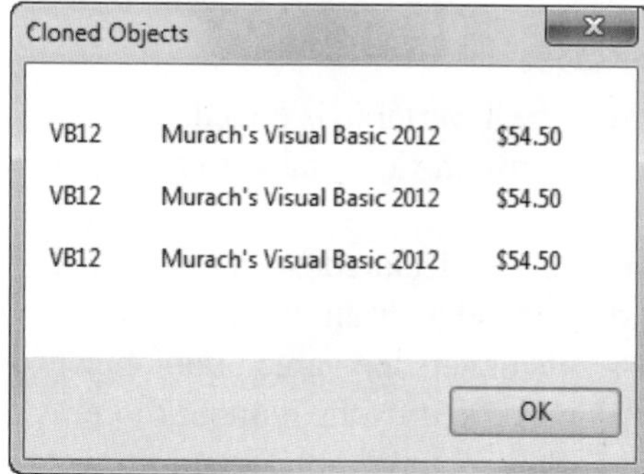

Description

- You can declare a parameter that's used by a method as an interface type. Then, you can pass any object that implements the interface to the parameter.
- Since the Product class implements both the ICloneable and IDisplayable interfaces, it can be passed as an argument to a method that accepts an object of the ICloneable or IDisplayable type.

How to work with generics

In chapter 8, you learned how to work with generic collections such as the ones defined by the List(), SortedList(), Stack(), and Queue() classes. Most of the time, you can use these or other collections from the .NET Framework whenever you need to work with a collection of objects. However, there may be times when you need to use *generics* to define your own generic collection to add some functionality that isn't provided by the .NET Framework generic collections. If so, the topics that follow show you how to do that. In addition, they shed some light on the inner workings of the generic collections available from the .NET Framework.

How to code a class that defines a generic collection

Part 1 of figure 19-7 shows a class named CustomList() that defines a generic collection. Although this class is simple and doesn't provide any additional functionality that improves upon the List() class, it illustrates all of the basic principles that are needed to define a generic collection.

To start, the Of keyword and a data type variable named T are coded within the parentheses that immediately follow the class name. The T variable represents the data type that's specified for the class when an object is created from the class. For example, if you create a custom list class like this:

```
Dim products As New CustomList(Of Product)
```

the compiler substitutes the Product type wherever the T variable is coded. As a result, when you code the CustomList class, you can use the T variable to represent the data type that's specified for the class.

Within the class, a private List() variable of type T is declared. As a result, this private list can store any data type. Then, the Add method adds an object of type T to the private list. Next, the indexer for this class gets or sets the value of an object of type T at the specified index, and the Count property returns the number of items in the list. Finally, this class declares a standard ToString method that returns a string that represents the objects of type T that are stored in the list.

Although this CustomList class uses T as the name of the type parameter for the class, you can use any parameter name you want. For example, you could use a longer name such as DocumentType. However, most generic classes use T as the name of the type parameter. The main exception to this rule is the generic collections that work with dictionaries that contain keys and values. These generic collections typically use K for the key type and V for the value type like this:

```
Public Class CustomDictionary(Of K, V)
```

Incidentally, this shows how to define a generic class that accepts two type parameters, which is possible but rare.

A CustomList() class that uses generics

```
Public Class CustomList(Of T)

    Private list As New List(Of T)

    ' An Add method
    Public Sub Add(item As T)
        list.Add(item)
    End Sub

    ' An indexer
    Default Public Property Item(index As Integer) As T
        Get
            Return list(index)
        End Get
        Set(value As T)
            list(index) = value
        End Set
    End Property

    ' A read-only property
    Public ReadOnly Property Count As Integer
        Get
            Return list.Count
        End Get
    End Property

    ' The ToString method
    Public Overrides Function ToString() As String
        Dim listString As String = ""
        For i As Integer = 0 To list.Count - 1
            listString &= list(i).ToString & vbCrLf
        Next
        Return listString
    End Function

End Class
```

Description

- You can use *generics* to define a type-safe collection that can accept elements of any type.
- To define a class for a generic collection, you code parentheses after the name of the class, and you code the Of keyword followed by the type parameter within these parentheses. Then, within the class, you can use the type parameter anywhere that a data type might be used. For example, you can use it as a return type or a parameter type for a method.
- By convention, most programmers use the letter T as the type parameter for most classes. However, you can use any parameter name you like.

Part 2 of figure 19-7 shows two examples that use the CustomList() class defined in part 1. The first example creates a CustomList() class that can store Integer types, adds two Integer values to the list, and displays these values in a dialog box. Then, the second example creates a CustomList() class that can store Product types, adds two Product objects to the list, and displays these objects in a dialog box. Note that this example assumes that the Product class contains a ToString method that returns a string that includes the product's code, description, and price separated by tabs.

This example shows that the CustomList() class can store value types (such as Integer types) or reference types (such as Product types). More importantly, it shows that the CustomList() class works like the other generic classes defined by the .NET Framework, although it doesn't yet provide as much functionality as any of those classes.

Code that uses the CustomList() class to store integers

```
Dim list As New CustomList(Of Integer)
Dim i1 As Integer = 11
Dim i2 As Integer = 7
list.Add(i1)
list.Add(i2)
MessageBox.Show(list.ToString, "List of Integers")
```

The resulting dialog box

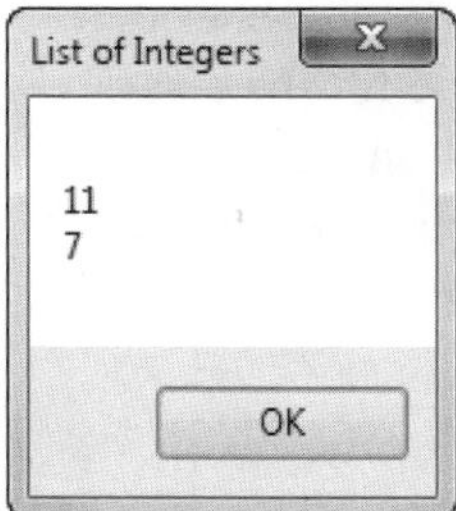

Code that uses the CustomList() class to store products

```
Dim list As New CustomList(Of Product)
Dim p1 As New Product("CS12", "Murach's C# 2012", 54.5D)
Dim p2 As New Product("VB12", "Murach's Visual Basic 2012", 54.5D)
list.Add(p1)
list.Add(p2)
MessageBox.Show(list.ToString, "List of Products")
```

The resulting dialog box

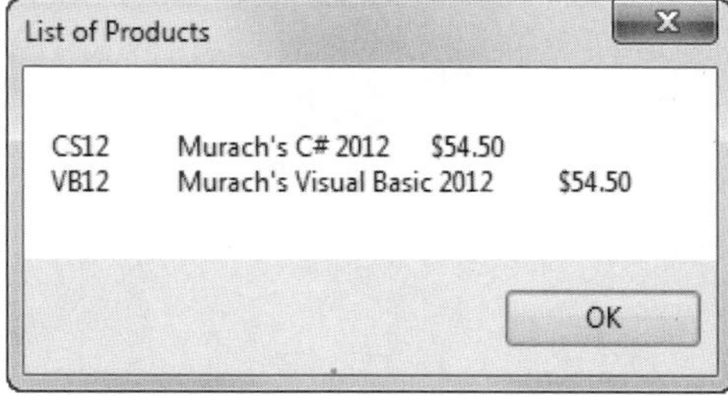

Description

- The generic CustomList() class works like the generic collection classes of the .NET Framework described in chapter 8.
- The resulting output shown above assumes that the Product class includes a ToString method that displays the product code, description, and price separated by tabs.

Some of the generic interfaces defined by the .NET Framework

The generic collections of the .NET Framework work with the generic interfaces described in figure 19-8. If you compare these with the interfaces presented in figure 19-2, you'll see that most of these generic interfaces have corresponding regular interfaces. However, the generic interfaces use parentheses and the Of keyword to specify the data type for the interface, just as generic classes use parentheses and the Of keyword to specify the data type for the class. In addition, the generic interfaces are stored in the System.Collections.Generic namespace and are designed to work with the generic collection classes stored in that namespace.

Commonly used generic .NET interface

Interface	Member	Description
`IComparable()`	`CompareTo(T) As Integer`	Compares objects of type T.

Commonly used .NET interfaces for generic collections

Interface	Members	Description
`IEnumerable()`	`GetEnumerator() As IEnumerator(Of T)`	Gets an enumerator of type T for the collection.

`ICollection()`	`Count As Integer`
	`IsReadOnly As Boolean`
	`Add(T)`
	`Clear()`
	`Contains(T) As Boolean`
	`CopyTo(array, index)`
	`Remove(T) As Boolean`
		Provides basic properties and methods for an enumerable collection. This interface inherits IEnumerable().

`IList()`	`Item(index) As T`
	`IndexOf(T) As Integer`
	`Insert(index, T)`
	`RemoveAt(index)`
		Manages a basic list of objects. This interface inherits ICollection() and IEnumerable().

`IDictionary()`	`Item(K) As V`
	`Keys As ICollection(Of K)`
	`Values As ICollection(Of V)`
	`Add(K, V)`
	`ContainsKey(K) As Boolean`
	`Remove(K) As Boolean`
	`TryGetValue(K, V) As Boolean`
		Manages a collection of key/value pairs. This interface inherits ICollection() and IEnumerable().

Description

- The .NET Framework defines many generic interfaces. These interfaces are particularly useful for working with classes that define generic collections, and they correspond to most of the regular interfaces described in figure 19-2.
- The ICollection() interface inherits the IEnumerable() interface, which means that any class that implements ICollection() must also implement IEnumerable(). Similarly, the IList() and IDictionary() interfaces inherit ICollection() and IEnumerable().
- The interfaces for working with generic collections are stored in the System.Collections.Generic namespace.
- This table only lists the most important members of each interface. For a complete description of these interfaces and a list of their members, see Visual Studio help.

Figure 19-8 Some of the generic interfaces defined by the .NET Framework

How to implement the IComparable() interface

To illustrate how you implement a generic interface, figure 19-9 shows a Product class that implements the IComparable() interface. To start, the Implements statement indicates that this class implements the IComparable() interface for the Product type. Since you would typically want to compare one Product object to another Product object, this makes sense.

Then, this class implements the IComparable() interface's only member, the CompareTo method. Since the class specifies an IComparable() interface for a Product type, this method compares a parameter of the Product type against the current Product object and returns an integer. For this method to work properly, this integer should be greater than zero if the current product is greater than the compared product, less than zero if the current product is less than the compared product, and zero if the two products are equal.

To accomplish this task, this method uses the CompareTo method of the String class to compare the Code field for the two Product objects. The CompareTo method of the String class compares the two strings alphabetically and returns a 1 when the current string comes later in the alphabet than the compared string or when the compared string has a null value. Conversely, this method returns -1 when the current string comes earlier in the alphabet than the compared element. And it returns 0 when the two strings are the same. As a result, the CompareTo method of the Product class lets you define a generic collection of Product objects that are sorted alphabetically by their Code fields. You'll see an example of this in the next figure.

The second example shows some code that uses the CompareTo method of the Product class. To start, this code creates two Product objects. The first has a Code field of "CS12", and the second has a Code field of "VB12". Then, this example uses the CompareTo method to compare these two objects. Since the Code field for the first object comes earlier in the alphabet, the CompareTo method returns an value of -1. As a result, the If statement in this example displays a dialog box that indicates that the first Product object is less than the second one.

A class that implements the IComparable() interface

```
Public Class Product
    Implements IComparable(Of Product)

    Public Property Code As String
    Public Property Description As String
    Public Property Price As Decimal

    ' Other methods

    Public Function CompareTo(other As Product) As Integer _
            Implements IComparable(Of Product).CompareTo
        Return Me.Code.CompareTo(other.Code)
    End Function

End Class
```

Code that uses the class

```
Dim p1 As New Product("CS12", "Murach's C# 2012", 54.5D)
Dim p2 As New Product("VB12", "Murach's Visual Basic 2012", 54.5D)
Dim compareValue As Integer = p1.CompareTo(p2)
If compareValue > 0 Then
    MessageBox.Show("p1 is greater than p2", "Compare Products")
ElseIf compareValue < 0 Then
    MessageBox.Show("p1 is less than p2", "Compare Products")
ElseIf compareValue = 0 Then
    MessageBox.Show("p1 is equal to p2", "Compare Products")
End If
```

Values that can be returned by the CompareTo method

Value	Meaning
-1	The current element is less than the compare element.
0	The current element is equal to the compare element.
1	The current element is greater than the compare element.

Description

- Since the IComparable() interface is a generic interface, you can identify the type of objects you want to compare in the parentheses that follow the interface name.
- To implement the IComparable() interface, you must implement the CompareTo method. This method returns an integer that determines if the current object is less than, equal to, or greater than the object that's passed as an argument to the method.

Figure 19-9 How to implement the IComparable() interface

How to use constraints

As you work with generic classes, you may occasionally encounter situations where you need to restrict the possible data types that the generic class can accept. For example, you may need to make sure that the generic class only accepts reference types, not value types. Or, you may need to make sure that the generic class inherits another class or implements an interface. To do that, you can code a *constraint* as shown in figure 19-10.

The example at the top of this figure shows the beginning of a CustomList() class that uses the CompareTo method of an object to insert the object at a point in the list so the list is always sorted. In other words, it implements a sorted list. To accomplish this task, this class restricts the types it can accept to classes (which define reference types) that implement the IComparable() interface.

Since any T variable in this class must be a reference type, the Add method can assign Nothing to a variable of type T. Then, later in the method, the code can check if that variable is still equal to Nothing. This wouldn't be possible without the constraint since you can't assign a null value to a structure (which defines a value type).

Similarly, since the T variable must implement the IComparable() interface, the Add method can call the CompareTo method from that variable. Without the constraint, this wouldn't be possible, as there would be no guarantee that the T variable would implement the IComparable() interface.

To declare a constraint, you begin by coding the As keyword after the type parameter. Then, you code a list of the constraints, separating each constraint with a comma and enclosing the list in braces. Note that if you specify a single constraint, you can omit the braces.

If you want to constrain a generic type to a class or structure, you can code the Class or Structure keyword in the constraint list. Similarly, if you want to constrain a generic type to a specific class or a class that's derived from that class, you code the name of the class in the constraint list. Note that if you code the name of a specific class, you can't use the Class or Structure keywords. If you want to constrain a generic type to types that implement one or more interfaces, you code the names of the interfaces in the constraint list. Finally, if you want to constrain a generic type to a class that has a parameterless constructor, you code the New keyword in the constraint list.

If you study the code in the Add method of the CustomList() class, you can see that this figure doesn't present all of the code for this method. That's because this code is too long to fit here, and because there are many ways that this method could be implemented. However, the code shown here does illustrate the main point, which is that the constraints for this class make it possible to use the CompareTo method to compare two T items.

A class that uses a constraint

```
Public Class CustomList(Of T As {Class, IComparable(Of T)})

    Private list As New List(Of T)

    ' An Add method that keeps the list sorted.
    Public Sub Add(item As T)
        If list.Count = 0 Then
            list.Add(item)
        Else
            For i As Integer = 0 To list.Count - 1
                Dim currentItem As T = list(i)
                Dim nextItem As T = Nothing
                If i < list.Count - 1 Then
                    nextItem = list(i + 1)
                End If
                Dim currentCompare As Integer = currentItem.CompareTo(item)
                If nextItem Is Nothing Then
                    If currentCompare >= 0 Then
                        list.Insert(i, item)   ' Insert before current item.
                        Exit For
                    End If
                End If
            Next
        End If
    ...
    End Sub
...
End Class
```

Keywords that can be used to define constraints

Keyword	Description
`Class`	The type argument must be a class.
`Structure`	The type argument must be a structure.
`New`	The type argument must have a parameterless constructor. You can't use this keyword when the type argument must be a structure.

A class that's constrained to value types

```
Public Class StructureList(Of T As Structure)
```

A class that's constrained to Product types that have a parameterless constructor

```
Public Class ProductList(Of T As {Product, New})
```

Description

- When you define a generic class, you can use *constraints* to restrict the data types that the class accepts.
- To add constraints to a generic class, code the As keyword after the type parameter on the Class statement, followed by the list of constraints enclosed in braces. If you code a single constraint, you can omit the braces.

Figure 19-10 How to use constraints

How to code an interface that uses generics

Figure 19-11 shows how to define a generic interface. In particular, it shows how to define a generic interface named IGenericPersistable(). The code for this interface provides a standard way for a business object to read itself from or write itself to a data source such as a database.

To give you an idea of how the IGenericPersistable() interface might be used, this figure also shows part of a Customer class that implements this interface. Here, you can see the starting code that has been generated for the members of the interface. As a result, the Read method must return a Customer object based on the id that's passed to it. The Save method must accept a Customer object as a parameter and return a Boolean value that indicates whether the save was successful. And the HasChanges property must have procedures that get and set the property to indicate whether the Customer object has been changed since the last time it was saved.

An interface named IGenericPersistable() that uses generics

```
Interface IGenericPersistable(Of T)

    Function Read(id As String) As T

    Function Save(obj As T) As Boolean

    Property HasChanges As Boolean

End Interface
```

A class that implements the IGenericPersistable() interface

```
Public Class Customer
    Implements IGenericPersistable(Of Customer)

    ' Other members

    Public Function Read(id As String) As Customer _
            Implements IGenericPersistable(Of Customer).Read

    End Function

    Public Function Save(obj As Customer) As Boolean _
            Implements IGenericPersistable(Of Customer).Save

    End Function

    Public Property HasChanges As Boolean _
            Implements IGenericPersistable(Of Customer).HasChanges
        Get

        End Get
        Set(value As Boolean)

        End Set
    End Property

End Class
```

Description

- When defining an interface, you can use generics just as you do when defining a class that uses generics.
- When implementing a generic interface that you defined, you can specify the type argument just as you do when implementing generic interfaces from the .NET Framework.

Figure 19-11 How to code an interface that uses generics

Perspective

In this chapter, you learned how to work with interfaces. Depending on the type of programming you're doing, you may or may not need to define your own interfaces. However, understanding interfaces is critical to working with the .NET Framework and to using an object-oriented language like Visual Basic.

You also learned how to define classes and interfaces that use generics. This lets you create collection classes and interfaces that can accept any data type and still be type-safe. Again, depending on the type of programming you're doing, you may never need to create these types of custom collection classes. However, understanding generics helps you understand the inner workings of the generic collection classes of the .NET Framework.

Now that you've completed this chapter, you have all the critical skills you need for developing object-oriented programs. In the next chapter, though, you'll learn some skills for documenting and organizing these classes. This will make it easier for you to share the classes that you develop with other programmers.

Terms

multiple inheritance
interface
implement an interface
shallow copy
deep copy
generics
constraint

Exercise 19-1 Implement the ICloneable interface

In this exercise, you'll create an application that includes a Customer class that implements the ICloneable interface. This application creates a List() that contains clones of a pre-defined Customer object and displays the cloned customers in a list box as shown below. To make this application easier to develop, we'll give you the starting form and classes.

The design of the Clone Customer form

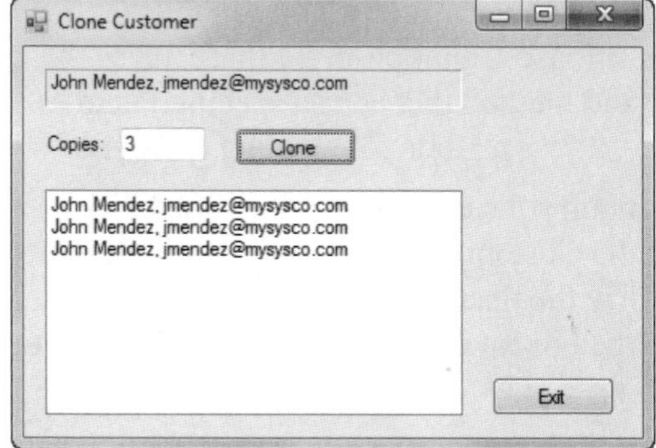

Development procedure

1. Open the application in the C:\VB 2012\Chapter 19\CloneCustomer directory.
2. Display the code for the form, and notice that the Load event handler creates a Customer object, stores it in a variable named customer, and displays the customer in the label at the top of the form.
3. Modify the Customer class so it implements the ICloneable interface.
4. Add an event handler for the Click event of the Clone button. This event handler should use the methods in the Validator class to check the value in the Copies text box to be sure it's present and also an integer. Then, it should create a List() object that contains the required number of clones of the Customer object. Finally, it should display the cloned customers in the list box.
5. Run the application and test it to make sure it works properly. If you're going to continue with the next exercise, leave the solution open. Otherwise, close it.

Exercise 19-2 Create a generic collection class

In this exercise, you'll modify the Clone Customer application you worked on in the last exercise so it uses a generic collection class.

1. If it isn't already open, open the application in the C:\VB 2012\Chapter 19\CloneCustomer directory.
2. Add a class named CustomList to the project that defines a generic list of elements. This class should consist of a private variable that holds the list, a parameterless constructor that initializes the private variable, an indexer that returns the element at a specified position, a Count property that returns the number of items in the list, and an Add method that adds a specified item to the list. You can use part 1 of figure 19-7 as a guide for creating this class.
3. Display the code for the form, and modify the event handler for the Click event of the Clone button so it uses the CustomList() class instead of the List() class. To do that, you'll need to modify the declaration for the customers variable, and you'll need to replace the For Each statement that loads the list box with a For statement.
4. Run the application and test it to be sure it works properly. Then, close the solution.

20

How to organize and document your classes

In the last three chapters, you learned how to develop object-oriented programs that use classes. Now, you'll learn how to organize and document your classes, and you'll learn how to store your classes in class libraries. This makes it easier for other programmers to use your classes.

How to organize your classes

In the next three topics, you'll learn how to organize applications that use multiple classes by coding more than one class per file, by splitting a single class across multiple files, and by working with namespaces.

How to code multiple classes in a single file

In most cases, you'll code each class that's required by an application in a separate file. If two or more classes are closely related, however, you might want to consider storing them in the same file. Figure 20-1 shows two ways you can do that.

First, you can simply code the class declarations one after the other as shown in the first example. The advantage of doing that is that it makes it easier to manage the files that make up the application. If the classes are large, however, you should place them in separate files even if they are closely related. Otherwise, it may be difficult to locate the code for a specific class.

You can also code two or more classes in a single file by nesting one class within another class. *Nested classes* are useful when one class only makes sense within the context of the other class. The second example in this figure illustrates how to nest two classes. Here, the class named InnerClass is nested within a class named OuterClass.

If you want to refer to the inner class from a class other than the outer class, you have to qualify it with the name of the outer class like this:

```
Dim ic As New OuterClass.InnerClass
```

However, you typically only need to refer to the inner class from the outer class, and you can do that without qualifying the name of the inner class.

A file with two classes coded one after the other

```
Public Class Class1

    ' Body of Class1

End Class

Public Class Class2

    ' Body of Class2

End Class
```

A file with nested classes

```
Public Class OuterClass

    ' Body of OuterClass
    Private ic As New InnerClass   ' Code that uses InnerClass

    Public Class InnerClass

        ' Body of InnerClass

    End Class

End Class
```

Description

- When two classes are closely related, it sometimes makes sense to code them in the same file, especially if the classes are relatively small. That way, the project consists of fewer files.
- One way to code two classes in a single file is to code them one after the other.
- Another way to code two classes in a single file is to *nest* one class within the other. This is useful when one class is used only within the context of another class.
- To refer to a nested class from another class, you must qualify it with the name of the class it's nested within like this:

```
OuterClass.InnerClass
```

Figure 20-1 How to code multiple classes in a single file

How to split a single class across multiple files

Figure 20-2 shows how to use *partial classes* to split a single class across multiple files. To do that, you just code the Partial keyword at the beginning of the Class statement to indicate that the members of the class are split across multiple source files. Then, when you build the solution, the compiler combines all the files that it finds for the partial classes to create the class. The resulting intermediate language produced by the compiler is the same as it would be if the entire class was coded in the same source file.

The first example in this figure illustrates how you code partial classes. Here, a Customer class is split across two files. You may want to use this technique if a class becomes too long or if you want to have different programmers work on different parts of the class. In most cases, though, it makes sense to store all the code for a class like this in a single file.

Even if you don't split the classes you create into partial classes, you should know that Visual Studio uses partial classes to separate the code that's generated for a Form class from the code that's entered by the programmer. This is illustrated in the second example in this figure. Here, the Form1.vb file contains the code that's added to the form by the programmer. Notice that the Class statement for this class doesn't include the Partial keyword. That's because Visual Basic lets you omit this keyword from one of the files that make up a partial class.

In contrast, the Class statement in the Form1.Designer.vb file does include the Partial keyword. This file contains the code that's generated by Visual Studio, as indicated by the attribute that appears at the beginning of the Class statement. Notice that this class inherits the System.Windows.Forms.Form class. Since this Inherits statement is included in the Form1.Designer.vb file, it's not necessary to include it in the Form1.vb file.

If you code your own partial classes, you should realize that the solution that contains them won't compile if the partial classes contain contradictory information. For example, if one partial class is declared as public and the other as private, you'll get a compile-time error.

A Customer class that's split into two files

The first file

```
Partial Public Class Customer

    ' Some members of the Customer class

End Class
```

The second file

```
Partial Public Class Customer

    ' The rest of the members of the Customer class

End Class
```

A Form class that's split into two files

The Form1.vb file

```
Public Class Form1

    ' The code for the Form1 class that's added
    ' by the programmer

End Class
```

The Form1.designer.vb file

```
<Global.Microsoft.VisualBasic.CompilerServices.DesignerGenerated()> _
Partial Class Form1
    Inherits System.Windows.Forms.Form

    ' The code for the Form1 class that's generated
    ' by Visual Studio

End Class
```

Description

- *Partial classes* can be used to split the code for a class across several files.
- To code a partial class, enter the Partial keyword at the beginning of the Class statement. Although you can omit the Partial keyword from one class declaration of a partial class, I don't recommend you do that.
- All partial classes must belong to the same namespace and the same assembly.
- If a class that you're working on becomes very long, or if you want to have different programmers work on different parts of a class, you can use partial classes to split the class across two or more files.
- Visual Studio uses partial classes to separate the code that's generated for a Form class from the code that's entered by the programmer.

Figure 20-2 How to split a class across multiple files

How to work with namespaces

As you know, a *namespace* is a container that's used to group related classes. For example, all the .NET Framework classes that are used for creating Windows forms are grouped in the System.Windows.Forms namespace, and all the classes for working with collections are grouped in the System.Collections and System.Collections.Generic namespaces.

When you create a project in Visual Basic, Visual Studio creates a *root namespace* for the project that has the same name as the project. Then, all of the classes you add to the project are stored in that namespace. In most cases, that's what you want. When you work with class libraries as shown later in this chapter, however, you may want to change the name of the root namespace. In addition, you may want to nest namespaces within other namespaces so the classes they contain are organized by function like the classes of the .NET Framework namespaces. When you refer to a class in the System.Collections namespace, for example, you're actually referring to a class in a namespace named Collections that's nested within a namespace named System.

The examples in figure 20-3 illustrate how to work with namespaces in code. The first example declares a namespace named Validation that contains a class named Validator. When you code a namespace like this, you should keep in mind that the namespace is nested within the root namespace for the project. If the root namespace is named Murach, for example, the name of the namespace shown in this example will be Murach.Validation.

You can also nest namespaces more than one level deep. To do that, you can use one of two techniques. First, you can code a Namespace statement within another namespace as shown in the second example in this figure. This example creates a namespace named Murach.Validation within the root namespace. The more common technique, however, is to simply name all of the nested namespaces on a single Namespace statement as shown in the third example.

To change the name of the root namespace for a project, you can display the Project Designer as described in this figure. Then, you can enter the name you want to use on the Application page.

Note that you can use the same root namespace for more than one project. For example, suppose you want to divide a namespace named Murach into two related namespaces named Validation and Data. Although you could include the Validation and Data namespaces in the same project, you're more likely to create a separate project for each namespace. Then, you can just change the name of the root namespace for both projects to Murach.

Although all of the classes of a project are typically stored in the same namespace, those classes use classes that are stored in other namespaces. For example, all Visual Basic applications use classes that are defined by the .NET Framework. To use a class in another namespace, you typically include an Imports statement for that namespace at the beginning of the class. Alternatively, you can qualify any reference to the class with the name of the namespace.

Code that declares a namespace

```
Namespace Validation

    Public Class Validator

        ' Body of Validator class

    End Class

End Namespace
```

Code that declares nested namespaces

```
Namespace Murach

    Namespace Validation

        ' Body of Validation namespace

    End Namespace

End Namespace
```

Another way to nest namespaces

```
Namespace Murach.Validation

    ' Body of Validation namespace

End Namespace
```

An Imports statement that specifies a namespace

```
Imports Murach.Validation
```

Description

- A *namespace* is a container that can be used to group related classes. By default, all of the classes that make up a Visual Basic project are part of a namespace that has the same name as the project. This namespace is called the *root namespace*.
- To change the root namespace for a project, double-click the My Project folder to display the Project Designer. Then, select the Application tab and enter the namespace name in the Root Namespace text box.
- To declare a namespace, code a Namespace statement at the beginning of a source file. Then, any code in that file is part of the namespace.
- When you declare a namespace in code, it is automatically nested within the namespace for the project. You can also nest a namespace within another namespace you declare in code by including a Namespace statement within the body of another namespace or by coding the fully-qualified name of the nested namespace in a Namespace statement.
- To use a class in a namespace other than the current namespace, you must either provide an Imports statement that names the other namespace, or you must qualify the class with the name of the namespace.

Figure 20-3 How to work with namespaces

How to document your classes

In the next topic, you'll learn how to add documentation to your classes. Then, you'll see how this documentation can make it easier for other programmers to use your classes.

How to add XML documentation to a class

As you already know, you can add general comments to any Visual Basic program by using comment statements that begin with a single quote. You can also use a documentation feature called *XML documentation* to create documentation for the classes and class members you create. XML documentation can make your classes easier for other programmers to use by providing information about the function of the class and its members. Then, this information appears in screen tips that are displayed when you work with the class in Visual Studio.

Figure 20-4 shows how to add XML documentation to a class. Although XML documentation is based on XML syntax, you don't have to know much about XML to use it. As you can see, XML documentation lines begin with three single quotes and appear immediately before the class or member they document.

The documentation for a class or member can contain one or more *documentation elements*. Each element begins with a *start tag*, such as <summary>, and ends with an *end tag*, such as </summary>. The contents of the element appear between the start and end tags. The table shown in this figure lists the most commonly used XML documentation elements.

The easiest way to create XML documentation is to type three single quotes on the line that immediately precedes a class or class member. Then, Visual Studio automatically generates skeleton XML documentation for you. This includes whatever tags are appropriate for the class or member you're documenting. For example, if you type three single quotes on the line before a method that includes a parameter list and has a return type, Visual Studio will generate a summary tag for the method, a param tag for each parameter, a returns tag for the method's return value, and a remark tag for any additional remarks. You can then type descriptive information between these tags to complete the documentation for the class.

Part of a Validator class that includes XML documentation

```
''' <summary>
''' Provides shared methods for validating data.
''' </summary>
''' <remarks></remarks>
Public Class Validator

    ''' <summary>
    ''' The title that will appear in dialog boxes.
    ''' </summary>
    ''' <remarks></remarks>
    Public Shared Title As String = "Entry Error"

    ''' <summary>
    ''' Checks whether the user entered data into a text box.
    ''' </summary>
    ''' <param name="textBox">The text box to be validated.</param>
    ''' <returns>True if the user has entered data.</returns>
    ''' <remarks>The Tag property of the text box must be set
    ''' to the name you want displayed for the field.</remarks>
    Public Shared Function IsPresent(textBox As TextBox) As Boolean
        If textBox.Text = "" Then
            MessageBox.Show(textBox.Tag.ToString &
                " is a required field.", Title)
            textBox.Select()
            Return False
        Else
            Return True
        End If
    End Function
```

Common XML elements used for class documentation

Element	Description
`<summary>`	Provides a general description of a class, property, method, or other element.
`<value>`	Describes the value that a property represents.
`<param name="name">`	Describes a parameter of a method.
`<returns>`	Describes the return value of a property or method.
`<remarks>`	Provides supplemental information about a class or member.

Description

- You can use special *XML tags* in Visual Basic source code to provide class documentation.
- An *XML documentation* line begins with three single quotes. Each *documentation element* begins with a *start tag*, such as <summary>, and ends with an *end tag*, such as </summary>. You code the description of the element between these tags.
- If you type three single quotes on the line immediately preceding a class or member declaration, Visual Studio automatically generates empty elements for you. Then, you just fill in the text that's appropriate for each element.

Figure 20-4 How to add XML documentation to a class

How to view the XML documentation

Once you add XML documentation, Visual Studio will use that documentation when it displays the screen tips that appear in the Visual Studio Code Editor window. This is illustrated in figure 20-5.

In the first example, when I typed the Validator class and a period, the IntelliSense feature displayed a list of the members of the Validator class. Then, I used the arrow keys to select the IsPresent method. When I did that, Visual Studio displayed a screen tip that included the signature of the IsPresent method along with the summary that's provided by the XML documentation shown in the previous figure.

In the second example, I typed the opening parenthesis for the IsPresent method. Then, Visual Studio displayed a screen tip that included the description of the TextBox parameter that's provided by the XML documentation shown in the previous figure.

A screen tip that displays the documentation for a method

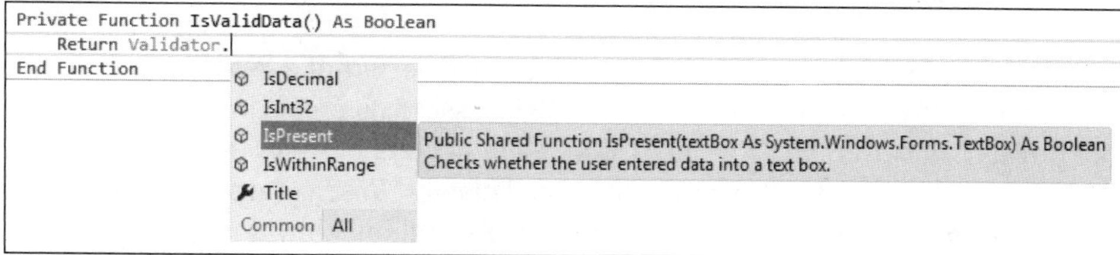

A screen tip that displays the documentation for a parameter

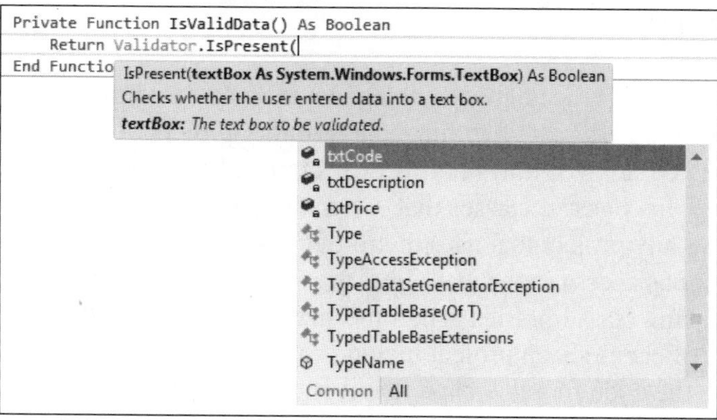

Description

- The XML documentation that you add to a class is visible in the screen tips that are displayed in the Code Editor.

Figure 20-5 How to view the XML documentation

How to create and use class libraries

So far, the classes you've seen have been created as part of a Windows Forms project. If you want to be able to use the classes you create in two or more projects, however, you'll want to store them in class libraries. Simply put, a *class library* consists of a collection of related classes. When you use a class library, you can use any of the classes in the library without copying them into the project.

How class libraries work

Figure 20-6 illustrates the difference between using classes created within a Windows Forms project and classes created within a class library project. As you can see, classes that are created in a Windows Forms project must be included in every project that uses them. In contrast, classes that are created in a class library project exist separately from any project that uses them. Because of that, they are available to any project that has access to the class library.

One of the benefits of using class libraries is that the size of each project that uses them is reduced. That's because each project includes only a reference to the class library rather than the code for each class that it needs. Also, because the classes in a class library are already compiled, Visual Studio doesn't have to compile them every time you build the application. This results in faster compile times.

Another benefit of using class libraries is that they simplify maintenance. If you must make a change to a class that's in a class library, you can change the class without changing any of the applications that use the library. When you're done, the modified library is immediately available to the projects that use it.

But probably the main benefit of using class libraries is that they let you create reusable code. If you design your classes carefully and place them in a library, you can reuse them in other projects that require similar functions. In most cases, you'll use the classes directly. However, you can also use them as base classes for the new classes that you add to your projects.

Two projects that use the Validator class

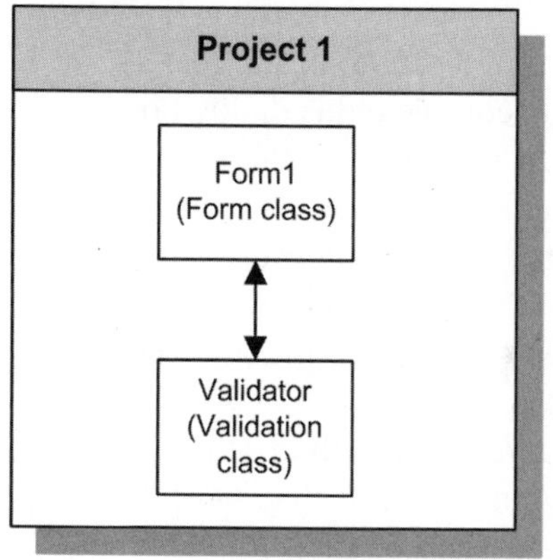

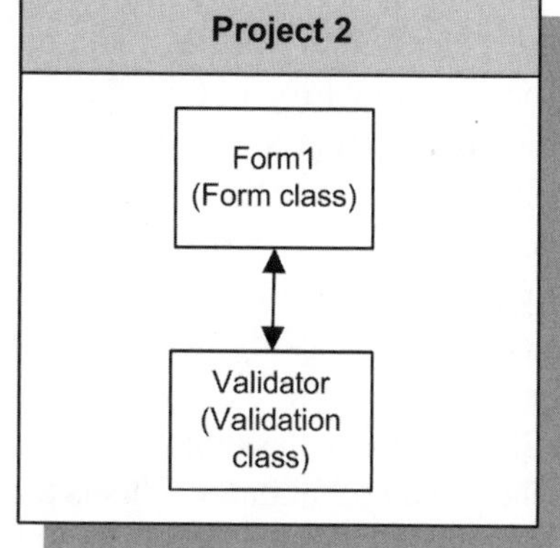

Two projects that access the Validator class via a class library

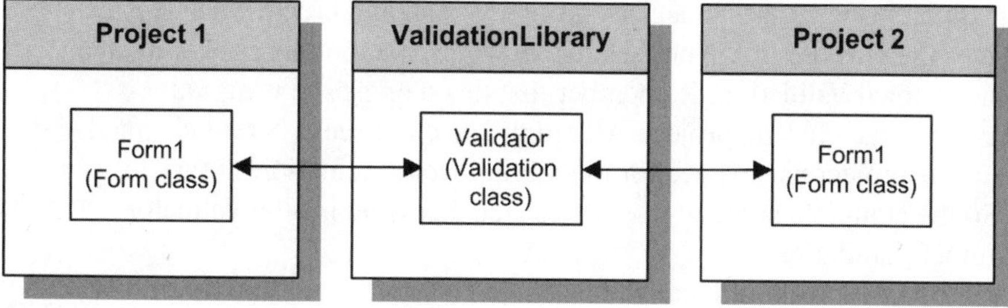

Description

- *Class libraries* provide a central location for storing classes that are used by two or more applications.
- When you store a class in a class library, you don't have to include the class in each application that uses it. Instead, you include a reference to the class library in those applications.
- When you modify a class in a class library, the changes are immediately available to all applications that use the library.
- To create a class library, you develop a class library project. Then, when you build the project, Visual Studio creates a *DLL file* for the class library. It's this *DLL* that you refer to from any application that needs to use the class library.

Figure 20-6 How class libraries work

How to create a class library project

To create a class library project, you use the Class Library template that's available from the New Project dialog box. After you complete this dialog box, Visual Studio creates a class library project that consists of a single class named Class1. Then, you can enter the code for this class and create additional classes using the techniques you've already learned. Or, if the classes you want to place in the library already exist in other projects, you can delete the Class1.vb file and use the Project→Add Existing Item command to copy the classes into the class library project.

Figure 20-7 shows a class library project named ValidationLibrary that includes a class named Validator. This is the same Validator class that was presented in chapter 11. In this case, though, the class is stored in a class library project instead of in the Windows Forms project that uses it.

Notice the Namespace statement at the beginning of the file for the Validator class. When you place classes in a class library, you should create a namespace that indicates the purpose of the classes in the namespace. In this case, I created a namespace named Validation. Remember that this namespace is nested within the namespace for the project. Although you can't see it here, I changed the name of the project namespace for this library from ValidationLibrary to Murach. So the complete name of the namespace that contains the Validator class is Murach.Validation.

Before I go on, you should realize that if the classes in your class library require access to classes in namespaces other than the System namespace, you'll need to add a reference to the assembly file that contains those classes. You'll learn the details of adding references in the next figure. For now, just realize that the Validator class uses the MessageBox and TextBox classes in the System.Windows.Forms namespace. Because of that, a reference to this namespace was added to the ValidationLibrary class library.

When you're done designing a class library, you build it to create an assembly. The assembly for a class library is a *DLL file*, or just *DLL*. This is a file with the *dll* extension that contains the executable code for the class library. By default, this file includes debugging information and is stored in the bin\Debug folder beneath the project folder for the project. Because you don't want the final version of a class library to include debugging information, though, you'll want to create a DLL file without this information when you're done testing the class library. To do that, you change the solution configuration from Debug to Release as described in this figure before you build the class library. Then, the DLL file is stored in the bin\Release folder, and you can include a reference to this file in other projects as described in the next topic.

As you're developing a class library, it's often useful to create the class library as a project in a solution that also has a Windows Forms project. That way, you can use the Windows Forms project to test the class library. To add a new class library project to an existing solution, right-click the solution in the Solution Explorer, then choose Add→New Project. You can also add an existing class library project to a solution by choosing Add→Existing Project. If you do that,

A class library project

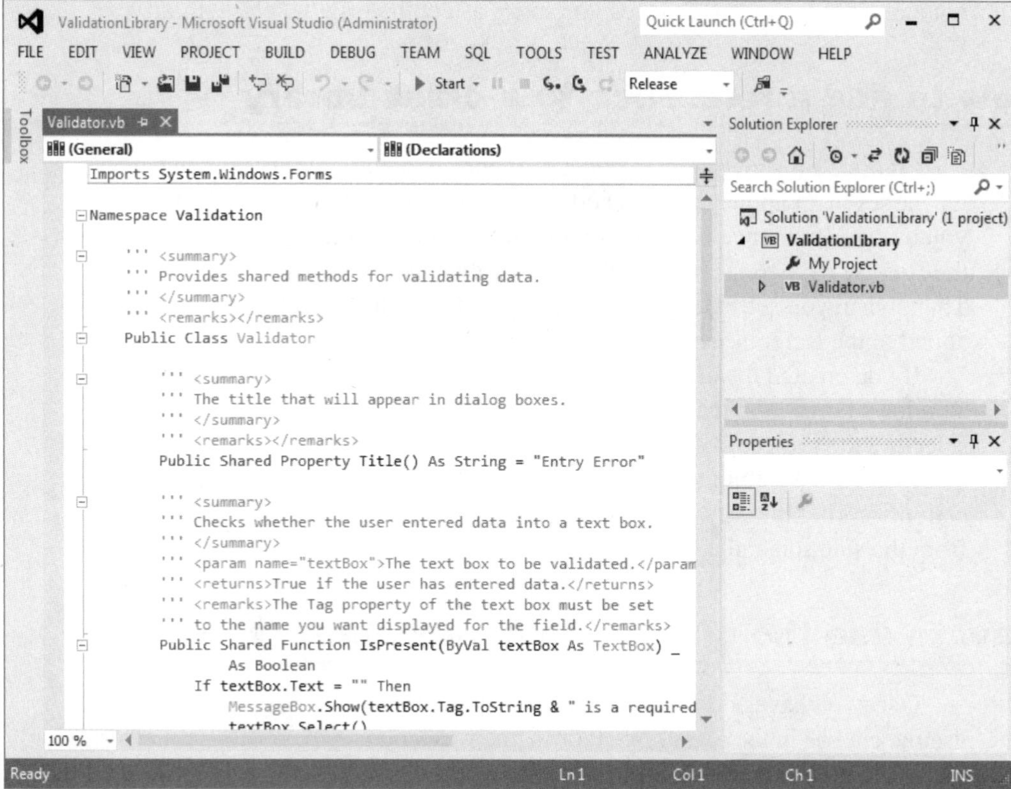

Description

- To create a class library project, display the New Project dialog box. Then, select the Class Library template and enter a name and location for the project.
- By default, a class library project includes a single class named Class1. You can modify this class any way you want or delete it from the project. You can also add new classes using the Project→Add Class command, and you can add classes from another project using the Project→Add Existing Item command.
- You should create a namespace for your class library that indicates the purpose of the classes contained in the library. In this example, the namespace is Validation. This namespace is nested within the root namespace for the project, which is named Murach.
- To compile a class library project, select the Release option from the Solution Configurations combo box in the Standard toolbar. Then, select the Build→Build Solution command. The class library is compiled into a DLL file that's stored in the bin\Release folder for the project.

Note

- The Validator class shown above requires the System.Windows.Forms namespace so it can use the MessageBox and TextBox classes. Because class libraries don't have access to this namespace by default, a reference to this namespace has been added to the project. See figure 20-8 for information on how to add a reference to a project.

Figure 20-7 How to create a class library project

though, keep in mind that you're working with the original class library project, not a copy of it. So any changes you make affect the original class library.

How to add a reference to a class library

Figure 20-8 shows how to add a reference to a class library so you can use its classes in an application. To add a reference to a class library to a project, you use the Reference Manager dialog box. From this dialog box, you can use the Browse page to locate the DLL file for the class library you want to refer to. Then, when you select that file and click the OK button, a reference to this file is added to the References folder in the Solution Explorer.

If you created the class library as a project in the same solution with a Windows Forms application, you can add a reference to the class library by selecting the project from the Solutions page of the Reference Manager dialog box instead of locating the DLL for the project. Then, when you have the application working the way you want it, you can remove the class library project from the solution and add a reference to the DLL file for this project.

How to use the classes in a class library

Once you have added a reference to a class library to your project, you can use the classes in the class library the same way you use the .NET Framework classes. First, you can add an Imports statement at the beginning of a Visual Basic class that identifies the namespace used by the class library to make it easier to refer to the classes it contains. The code example in figure 20-8, for example, shows an Imports statement for the Murach.Validation namespace.

After you add the Imports statement, you can use the classes in the library as if they were part of the same project. A complication arises, however, if the class you want to refer to in the class library has the same name as a class in another namespace in the project or has the same name as the namespace that contains the project (which is usually the same as the project name). In that case, you have to qualify the name of the class so Visual Basic knows where to look for it.

A project that includes a reference to a class library

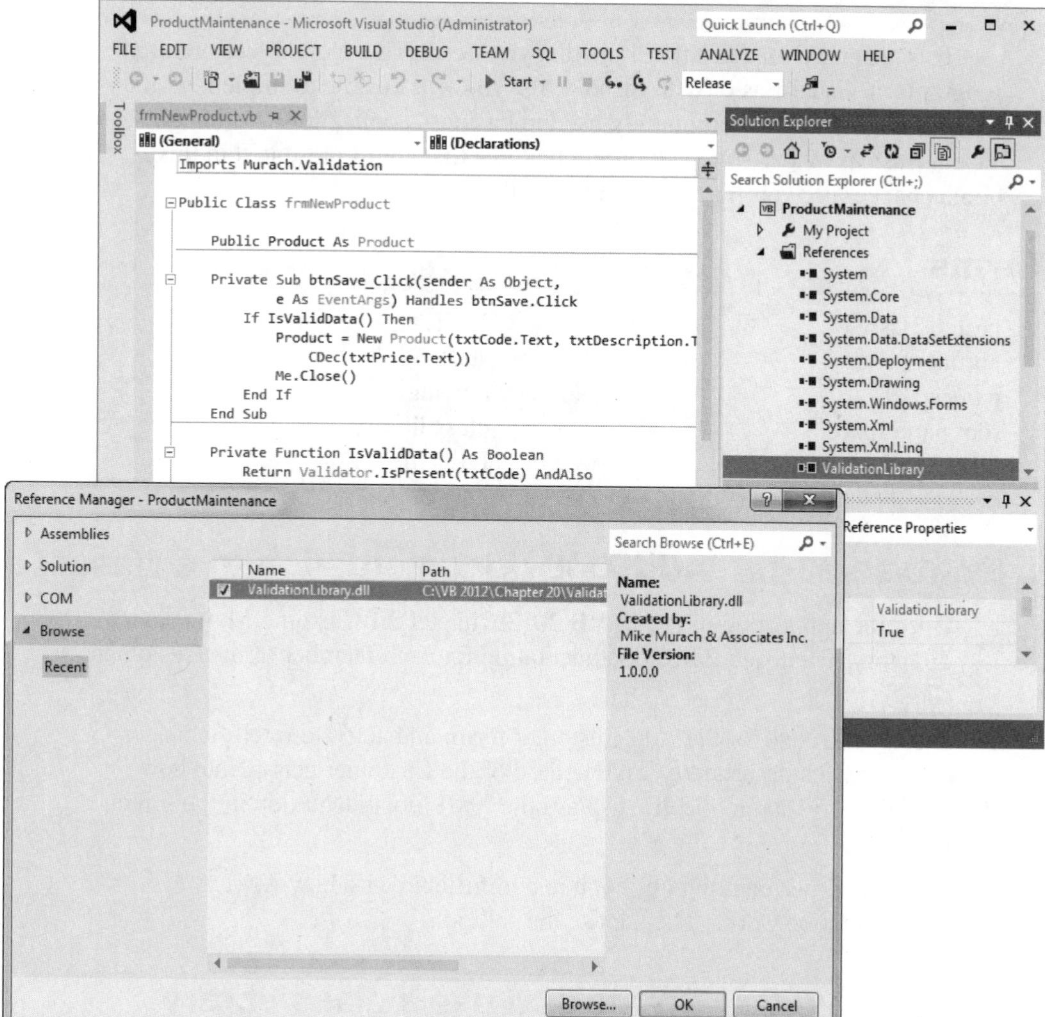

An Imports statement for the validation class library

```
Imports Murach.Validation
```

How to use a class library

- Add a reference to the class library using the Project→Add Reference command. In the Reference Manager dialog box, display the Browse page, click the Browse button, locate the DLL for the class library, select it, and click the OK button.
- If the class library project is included in the same solution as the client project, that project will appear in the list on the Solution page. Then, you can add a reference for the class library by double-clicking the project name.
- Once you have added a reference to the class library, you can include an Imports statement for the class library's namespace in any class that uses it. You can then use the classes in the class library without qualification. Alternatively, you can qualify the class names with the namespace name for the library.

Figure 20-8 How to use a class library

Perspective

This chapter completes the skills that you need to develop object-oriented programs in Visual Basic. With these skills, you will be able to implement the types of classes that are commonly used in business applications. Although Visual Basic provides some additional features that aren't presented in this book, chances are you'll never need to use them.

Terms

nested classes
partial classes
namespace
root namespace
XML documentation
documentation element
XML tag
start tag
end tag
class library
DLL file

Exercise 20-1 Add XML documentation to a class

1. Open the application in the C:\VB 2012\Chapter 20\CustomerMaintenance directory. Then, add XML documentation for each member of the Customer class.
2. Display the code for the Add Customer form, and activate IntelliSense for each constructor, property, and method of the Customer class. Note how Visual Studio automatically displays the XML documentation in the screen tip.
3. Continue experimenting until you're comfortable with how XML documentation works. Then, close the solution.

Exercise 20-2 Create and use a class library

In this exercise, you'll create a class library that contains the Validator class. Then, you'll use that class library with the CustomerMaintenance application.

1. Create a new Class Library project named ValidationLib. Then, delete the empty Class1.vb file, and add the Validator.vb file from the CustomerMaintenance project that you worked on in the previous exercise.
2. Change the name of the project namespace to Murach, change the name of the namespace in the Validator class to Validation, and add a reference to the System.Windows.Forms.dll assembly. Then, use the Build→Build Solution command to build the class library, and close the solution.
3. Open the application that you used in the previous exercise, delete the Validator.vb file, and add a reference to the ValidationLib assembly you created in step 2. Then, display the code for the Add Customer form and add an Imports statement for the Murach.Validation namespace.
4. Run the project and test it to make sure the validation works correctly.

Section 5

More skills for working with data

In the section 3 of this book, you learned how to use data sources and ADO.NET code to work with the data in databases. Now, the three chapters in this section present some additional skills for working with data. Since you won't need these skills for all your applications, you may want to just give these chapters a quick first reading. Then, you can return to these chapters for reference whenever you need the skills that they present.

In chapter 21, you'll learn how to read and write the data in two of the file types that are supported by .NET: text files and binary files. In chapter 22, you'll learn how to read and write the data in XML files, which will also prepare you for using XML in other contexts. And in chapter 23, you'll learn how to use LINQ to work with objects such as arrays and collections.

21

How to work with files and data streams

In section 3, you learned how to develop applications that store and retrieve data from a database. Because databases provide powerful features for working with data, databases are typically used for the data in most business applications. For some applications, though, you may need to save data in a file on disk and then read that data whenever it's needed. In this chapter, you'll learn how to do that with two different types of files: text and binary.

An introduction to the System.IO classes

The System.IO namespace provides a variety of classes for working with files and for managing directories, files, and paths. You'll be introduced to those classes in the topics that follow. In addition, you'll learn about the types of files and streams supported by the System.IO classes and how they're used to perform file I/O.

The classes for managing directories, files, and paths

Figure 21-1 summarizes the classes in the System.IO namespace that you can use to manage directories, files, and paths. As you can see, you can use the methods of the Directory class to create or delete a directory or determine if a directory exists. And you can use the methods of the File class to copy, delete, or move a file, or to determine if a file exists. Since the methods for both of these classes are shared methods, you call them directly from the class.

Before you begin working with any of the classes in the System.IO namespace, you typically code an Imports statement at the start of the class that you're developing, like the statement in the first example. Then, you can refer to the classes in this namespace without qualifying each reference with the namespace. If you want this namespace to be available to all of the classes in a project, though, you can double-click on My Project, select the References tab, and check the System.IO namespace in the Imported Namespaces list.

The second example shows how to use some of the methods of the Directory class. This code starts by declaring a string that holds the path to a directory that contains a file to be processed. Then, an If statement uses the Exists method of the Directory class to determine if this directory exists. If it doesn't, it uses the CreateDirectory method to create it.

The third example shows how to use some of the methods of the File class. This code declares a string that will hold the path to a file named Products.txt. Then, the If statement that follows uses the Exists method of the File class to determine if this file exists. If it does, it uses the Delete method to delete it.

System.IO classes used to work with drives and directories

Class	Description
Directory	Used to create, edit, delete, or get information on directories (folders).
File	Used to create, edit, delete, or get information on files.
Path	Used to get path information from a variety of platforms.

Common methods of the Directory class

Method	Description
Exists(path)	Returns a Boolean value indicating whether a directory exists.
CreateDirectory(path)	Creates the directories in a specified path.
Delete(path)	Deletes the directory at the specified path. The directory must be empty.
Delete(path, recursive)	Deletes the directory at the specified path. If True is specified for the recursive argument, any subdirectories and files in the directory are deleted. If False is specified, the directory must be empty.

Common methods of the File class

Method	Description
Exists(path)	Returns a Boolean value indicating whether a file exists.
Delete(path)	Deletes a file.
Copy(source, dest)	Copies a file from a source path to a destination path.
Move(source, dest)	Moves a file from a source path to a destination path.

A statement that simplifies references to the System.IO classes

```
Imports System.IO
```

Code that uses some of the Directory methods

```
Dim dir As String = "C:\VB 2012\Files\"
If Not Directory.Exists(dir) Then
    Directory.CreateDirectory(dir)
End If
```

Code that uses some of the File methods

```
Dim path As String = dir & "Products.txt"
If File.Exists(path) Then
    File.Delete(path)
End If
```

Description

- The classes for managing directories, files, and paths are stored in the System.IO namespace.
- To use the classes in the System.IO namespace, you should include an Imports statement. Otherwise, you have to qualify the references to its classes with System.IO.
- All of the methods of the Directory, File, and Path classes are shared methods.

Figure 21-1 The classes for managing directories, files, and paths

How files and streams work

When you use the System.IO classes to do *I/O operations* (or *file I/O*), you can use two different kinds of files: *text files* or *binary files*. To illustrate, figure 21-2 shows the contents of a text file and a binary file as they look when displayed in a text editor. Although both of these files contain the same data, they look quite different.

In a *text file*, all of the data is stored as text characters (or strings). Often, the *fields* in this type of file are separated by delimiters like tabs or pipe characters, and the *records* are separated by end of line characters. Although you can't see the end of line characters in this figure, you know they're there because each record starts at the beginning of a new line.

In contrast, the data in a *binary file* can include text characters as well as data types. Because of that, the data isn't always displayed properly within a text editor. For example, you can't tell what the value of the Price field is in each of these records because this field has a Decimal data type. Also, since the records in a binary file don't end with end of line characters, one record isn't displayed on each line in a text editor.

To handle I/O operations with text and binary files, the .NET Framework uses *streams*. You can think of a stream as the flow of data from one location to another. For instance, an *output stream* can flow from the internal memory of an application to a disk file, and an *input stream* can flow from a disk file to internal memory. When you work with a text file, you use a *text stream*. When you work with a binary file, you use a *binary stream*.

To work with streams and files using the System.IO namespace, you use the classes summarized in this figure. To create a stream that connects to a file, for example, you use the FileStream class. Then, to read data from a text stream, you use the StreamReader class. And to read data from a binary stream, you use the BinaryReader class. You'll learn how to use all of these classes later in this chapter.

Since you can store all of the built-in numeric data types in a binary file, this type of file is more efficient for applications that work with numeric data. In contrast, the numeric data in a text file is stored as characters, so each field must be converted to a numeric data type before it can be used in arithmetic operations.

When you save a text or binary file, you can use any extension you want for the file name. In this book, though, *txt* is used as the extension for all text files, and *dat* is used for all binary files. For instance, the text file in this figure is named Products.txt, and the binary file is named Products.dat.

A text file displayed in a text editor

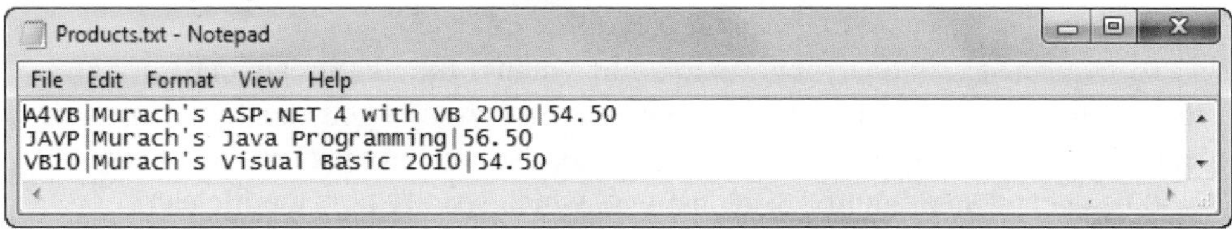

A binary file displayed in a text editor

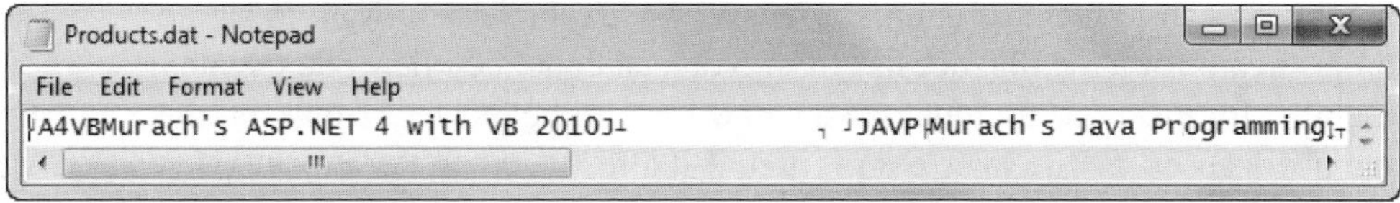

Two types of files

Type	Description
Text	A file that contains text (string) characters. The *fields* in each record are typically delimited by special characters like tab or pipe characters, and the *records* are typically delimited by new line characters.
Binary	A file that can contain a variety of data types.

Two types of streams

Stream	Description
Text	Used to transfer text data.
Binary	Used to transfer binary data.

System.IO classes used to work with files and streams

Class	Description
FileStream	Provides access to input and output files.
StreamReader	Used to read a stream of characters.
StreamWriter	Used to write a stream of characters.
BinaryReader	Used to read a stream of binary data.
BinaryWriter	Used to write a stream of binary data.

Description

- An *input file* is a file that is read by a program; an *output file* is a file that is written by a program. Input and output operations are often referred to as *I/O operations* or *file I/O*.
- A *stream* is the flow of data from one location to another. To write data, you use an *output stream*. To read data, you use an *input stream*. A single stream can also be used for both input and output.
- To read and write text files, you use *text streams*. To read and write binary files, you use *binary streams*.

Figure 21-2 How files and streams work

How to use the FileStream class

To create a stream that connects to a file, you use the FileStream class as shown in figure 21-3. In the syntax at the top of this figure, you can see its arguments. The first two, which specify the path for the file and the mode in which it will be opened, are required. The last two, which specify how the file can be accessed and shared, are optional.

To code the mode, access, and share arguments, you use the FileMode, FileAccess, and FileShare enumerations. If, for example, you want to create a file stream for a file that doesn't exist, you can code the FileMode.Create member for the mode argument and a new file will be created. However, this member causes the file to be overwritten if it already exists. As a result, if you don't want an existing file to be overwritten, you can use the CreateNew member for this argument. Then, if the file already exists, an exception is thrown.

For the access argument, you can code members that let you read records from the file, write records to the file, or both read and write records. If you omit this argument, the default is to allow both reading and writing of records.

For the share argument, you can code members that let other users read records, write records, or both read and write records at the same time that the first user is accessing the file. Or, you can code the None member to prevent sharing of the file. What you're trying to avoid is two users writing to a file at the same time, which could lead to errors. So if you code the access argument as ReadWrite or Write, you can code the share argument as Read or None. On the other hand, if you code the access argument as Read, you may want to code the share argument as Read or ReadWrite. However, when you set the share argument, additional permissions may be needed to share this file while it's being used by the current process. In that case, you can use the Close method to close the file when you're done with it to allow other processes to access the file.

The first example shows how to open a file stream for writing. Since this example uses the Write member to specify file access, this file stream can only be used to write the file, not to read it. And since this example uses the Create member for the mode argument, this code will create a new file if the file doesn't exist. Otherwise, it will overwrite the existing file. However, if the directory for this file doesn't exist, a DirectoryNotFoundException will be thrown.

The second example shows how to open a file stream for reading. This works similarly to opening a file stream for writing. However, the Open member is used to specify the mode argument. As a result, if the file doesn't exist, a FileNotFoundException will be thrown.

Incidentally, it sometimes makes sense to keep the file that an application processes in the project's directory instead of a separate directory. To do that, you can use dots to refer to the parent directory, as in:

```
"..\..\Products.txt"
```

This works because the current project is run from the bin\Debug subdirectory of the project directory.

The syntax for creating a FileStream object

```
New FileStream(path, mode[, access[, share]])
```

Members in the FileMode enumeration

Member	Description
`Append`	Opens the file if it exists and seeks to the end of the file. If the file doesn't exist, it's created. This member can only be used with Write file access.
`Create`	Creates a new file. If the file already exists, it's overwritten.
`CreateNew`	Creates a new file. If the file already exists, an exception is thrown.
`Open`	Opens an existing file. If the file doesn't exist, an exception is thrown.
`OpenOrCreate`	Opens a file if it exists, or creates a new file if it doesn't exist.
`Truncate`	Opens an existing file and truncates it so its size is zero bytes.

Members in the FileAccess enumeration

Member	Description
`Read`	Data can be read from the file but not written to it.
`ReadWrite`	Data can be read from and written to the file. This is the default.
`Write`	Data can be written to the file but not read from it.

Members in the FileShare enumeration

Member	Description
`None`	The file cannot be opened by other applications.
`Read`	Allows other applications to open the file for reading only. This is the default.
`ReadWrite`	Allows other applications to open the file for both reading and writing.
`Write`	Allows other applications to open the file for writing only.

Common method of the FileStream class

Method	Description
`Close()`	Closes the file stream and releases any resources associated with it.

Code that creates a FileStream object for writing

```
Dim path As String = "C:\VB 2012\Files\Products.txt"
Dim fs As New FileStream(path, FileMode.Create, FileAccess.Write)
```

Code that creates a new FileStream object for reading

```
Dim path As String = "C:\VB 2012\Files\Products.txt"
Dim fs As New FileStream(path, FileMode.Open, FileAccess.Read)
```

Note

- Operating system level permissions may limit which file access and file share options you can use.

Figure 21-3 How to use the FileStream class

How to use the exception classes for file I/O

In chapter 7, you learned the basic skills for handling exceptions. Now, figure 21-4 summarizes the exceptions that can occur when you perform I/O operations. Most of the time, you can write your code so these exceptions are avoided. For example, you can avoid a DirectoryNotFoundException by using the Exists method of the Directory class to be sure that the directory exists before you try to use it in the file path for a new file stream. Similarly, you can avoid a FileNotFoundException by using the Exists method of the File class.

However, I/O exceptions are often serious problems like hardware problems that an application can't do anything about. For example, if an application needs to open a file that's on a network drive that isn't available, an exception will be thrown. In that case, it's common to handle the exception by displaying an error message.

When handling I/O exceptions, it's common to use a Finally block. In this block, it's common to use the stream's Close method to close all streams that are open. This frees the resources that are used to access the file.

The code example shows how to handle some of the most common I/O exceptions. To start, the statement just before the Try block declares a variable for the stream. That way, this variable is available to the Catch blocks and the Finally block. In this case, the stream is a FileStream object, but you'll learn how to work with other types of streams later in this chapter.

Within the Try block, the first statement creates an instance of the stream. After this statement, the Try block will contain more code that uses the stream to read and write data. Later in this chapter, you'll learn how to write this type of code. For now, you can assume that there is more code in the Try block that uses the stream, and you can assume that this code may throw I/O exceptions, such as the exception that occurs when an application attempts to read beyond the end of the stream.

After the Try block, the Catch blocks are coded starting with the most specific type of exception and moving up the inheritance hierarchy towards the most general type of exception. In this case, both the DirectoryNotFoundException and FileNotFoundException classes inherit the IOException class. As a result, they must be coded before the Catch block for the IOException. All three of these Catch blocks display a message box that describes the type of exception to the user. This is a common way to handle I/O exceptions. However, in some cases, you may want to create a directory or file or allow the user to search for a directory or file.

Within the Finally block, an If statement is used to determine whether an exception was thrown before the stream was opened. If it was, the variable for the stream will be equal to Nothing. As a result, calling the Close method isn't necessary and would throw a NullPointerException. However, if an exception was thrown after the stream was opened, the variable won't be equal to Nothing. In that case, the Close method frees the resources used by the stream.

The exception classes for file I/O

Class	Description
IOException	The base class for exceptions that are thrown during the processing of a stream, file, or directory.
DirectoryNotFoundException	Occurs when part of a directory or file path can't be found.
FileNotFoundException	Occurs when a file can't be found.
EndOfStreamException	Occurs when an application attempts to read beyond the end of a stream.

Code that uses exception classes

```
Dim dirPath As String = "C:\VB 2012\Files\"
Dim filePath As String = dirPath & "Products.txt"
Dim fs As FileStream
Try
    fs = New FileStream(filePath, FileMode.Open)

    // code that uses the file stream
    // to read and write data from the file

Catch ex As FileNotFoundException
    MessageBox.Show(filePath & " not found.", "File Not Found")
Catch ex As DirectoryNotFoundException
    MessageBox.Show(dirPath & " not found.", "Directory Not Found")
Catch ex As IOException
    MessageBox.Show(ex.Message, "IOException")
Finally
    If fs IsNot Nothing Then
        fs.Close()
    End If
End Try
```

Description

- To catch any I/O exception, you can use the IOException class.
- To catch specific I/O exceptions, you can use the exception classes that inherit the IOException class such as the three shown in this figure.

Figure 21-4 How to use the exception classes for file I/O

How to use the My.Computer.FileSystem object

Before I go on, you should know that in addition to using the System.IO classes to work with files, you can use the My.Computer.FileSystem object that you learned about in chapter 3. Figure 21-5 summarizes some of the properties and methods that are available with this object. As you can see, some of these properties and methods duplicate the capabilities that are provided by the Directory and File classes. Because all of these capabilities are available from a single object, though, this feature can make it easier to find the properties and methods that you need to use.

By using the properties and methods of this object, you can more easily develop applications that manage the directories and files of a user's system. For instance, the example in this figure gets a directory path from a text box and then uses the GetFiles method to display the names of all the files in that directory in a list box. At that point, you could add code that lets the user delete, copy, or get more information about any of the files in the list box, and so on.

Since most business applications don't need that type of capability, you may never need to use the My.Computer.FileSystem object. On the other hand, you may want to use some of its methods like the DirectoryExists or FileExists method for the file handling that you do for typical business applications.

Properties of the My.Computer.FileSystem object

Property	Description
CurrentDirectory	Gets the current directory.
Drives	Gets information about the drives.
SpecialDirectories	Returns the My.Computer.FileSystem.SpecialDirectories object, which can be used to access special directories like Temp or MyDocuments.

Some of the methods of the My.Computer.FileSystem object

Method	Description
CopyDirectory	Copies a directory.
CopyFile	Copies a file.
CreateDirectory	Creates a directory.
DeleteDirectory	Deletes a directory.
DeleteFile	Deletes a file.
DirectoryExists	Returns a Boolean value indicating whether the directory exists.
FileExists	Returns a Boolean value indicating whether the file exists.
GetDirectories	Returns a String collection that holds the path names of the subdirectories within a directory.
GetDirectoryInfo	Returns a DirectoryInfo object for the specified path.
GetDriveInfo	Returns a DriveInfo object for the specified path.
GetFileInfo	Returns a FileInfo object for the specified path.
GetFiles	Returns a read-only String collection that holds the names of the files in a directory.
ReadAllBytes	Reads a binary file.
ReadAllText	Reads a text file.
WriteAllBytes	Writes a binary file.
WriteAllText	Writes a text file.

Code that displays a list of the files in a directory

```
Dim dir As String = txtDirectory.Text
If My.Computer.FileSystem.DirectoryExists(dir) Then
    For Each file As String In My.Computer.FileSystem.GetFiles(dir)
        lstFiles.Items.Add(file)
    Next
Else
    MessageBox.Show("Directory doesn't exist!", "Directory Error")
End If
```

Description

- The My.Computer.FileSystem object provides easy access to the properties and methods for handling files. In particular, it makes it easier to manage the drives, directories, and files of a system.
- When you use the My.Computer.FileSystem object, you don't need to import the System.IO namespace.

Figure 21-5 How to use the My.Computer.FileSystem object

How to work with text files

To read and write characters in a text file, you use the StreamReader and StreamWriter classes. When working with text files, you often need to use the techniques you learned in chapters 4 and 9 to build and parse strings.

How to write a text file

Figure 21-6 shows how to use the StreamWriter class to write data to a text file. This class lets you write any data to a text file by using the Write and WriteLine methods. When you use the WriteLine method, a line terminator is automatically added. Typically, a line terminator is used to end each record. However, the fields in a record are typically separated by special characters, such as tab or pipe characters, and you have to add those characters through code.

The example in this figure shows how this works. To start, this code creates a StreamWriter object that uses a FileStream object as its argument. This FileStream object specifies a file with write-only access.

Next, this code uses a For Each loop to write the three properties for each Product object in a List() collection named products to the file with pipe characters as separators. (In case you're not familiar with the pipe character, it's available from the same key as the backslash key on your keyboard.) For the last property, the WriteLine method is used to end the record with a line terminator. That way, each record will start on a new line. Finally, after all of the records have been written to the file by the For Each loop, the stream writer and file stream are closed.

Both the Write and WriteLine methods of the StreamWriter class are overloaded to accept any type of data. As a result, if you pass a non-string data type to either of these methods, the method converts the data type to a string that represents the data type and then it writes that string to the stream. To do that, these methods automatically call the ToString method of the data type. In other words, you can write the Decimal value that's stored in the Price property of a product to a text file like this:

```
textOut.WriteLine(product.Price)
```

This has the same effect as coding the statement like this:

```
textOut.WriteLine(product.Price.ToString)
```

The basic syntax for creating a StreamWriter object

```
New StreamWriter(stream)
```

Common methods of the StreamWriter class

Method	Description
`Write(data)`	Writes the data to the output stream.
`WriteLine(data)`	Writes the data to the output stream and appends a line terminator (usually a carriage return and a line feed).
`Close()`	Closes the StreamWriter object and the associated FileStream object.

Code that writes data from a collection of Product objects to a text file

```
Dim textOut As New StreamWriter(
    New FileStream(path, FileMode.Create, FileAccess.Write))

For Each product As Product In products
    textOut.Write(product.Code & "|")
    textOut.Write(product.Description & "|")
    textOut.WriteLine(product.Price)
Next

textOut.Close()
```

Description

- You can use the Write and WriteLine methods of a StreamWriter object to write data to a text file. If the data type that's passed to these methods isn't already a string, these methods will call the ToString method of the data type to convert it to a string before they write the data.
- If the fields that make up a record are stored in individual variables, you need to concatenate these variables to construct each record, and you need to add special characters to delimit each field. However, since the WriteLine method adds the line terminator automatically, you can use it to end each record.

Figure 21-6 How to write a text file

How to read a text file

Figure 21-7 shows how to use the StreamReader class to read data from a text file. To create a StreamReader object, you can use a FileStream object as the argument. Then, you can use the methods shown in this figure to work with the StreamReader object.

The three Read methods let you read a single character, a single line of data (a record), or all of the data from the current position to the end of the file. In most cases, though, you'll use the ReadLine method to read one record at a time. You can also use the Peek method to see if there is additional data in the file before you read from it, and you can use the Close method to close the stream reader and file stream when you're done with them.

The example shows how you can use a stream reader to read the data in a file one record at a time. After the file stream and stream reader are created, a Do loop is used to read the records in the file. The condition on this loop uses the Peek method to check that there is at least one more character. If there is, the ReadLine method reads the next record in the file into a string and that string is parsed into the individual fields. Then, each field is stored in one of the properties of a Product object, and each Product object is stored in a List() collection. When all of the records have been read, the Close method of the stream reader is used to close the StreamReader and FileStream objects.

Note in this example that the FileStream object is instantiated in OpenOrCreate mode. Then, if the file exists, it is opened. Otherwise, a new file is created with no records in it. In either case, the code that follows works because it peeks into the file before it tries to read the data. If the file is empty, no records are read.

The basic syntax for creating a StreamReader object

```
New StreamReader(stream)
```

Common methods of the StreamReader class

Method	Description
`Peek()`	Returns the next available character in the input stream without advancing to the next position. If no more characters are available, this method returns -1.
`Read()`	Reads the next character from the input stream.
`ReadLine()`	Reads the next line of characters from the input stream and returns it as a string.
`ReadToEnd()`	Reads the data from the current position in the input stream to the end of the stream and returns it as a string. This is typically used to read the contents of an entire file.
`Close()`	Closes both the StreamReader object and the associated FileStream object.

Code that reads data from a text file into a collection of Product objects

```
Dim textIn As New StreamReader(
    New FileStream(path, FileMode.OpenOrCreate, FileAccess.Read))

Dim products As New List(Of Product)

Do While textIn.Peek <> -1
    Dim row As String = textIn.ReadLine
    Dim columns() As String = row.Split(CChar("|"))
    Dim product As New Product
    product.Code = columns(0)
    product.Description = columns(1)
    product.Price = CDec(columns(2))
    products.Add(product)
Loop

textIn.Close()
```

Description

- You use a StreamReader object to read data from a text file. Because the records in most text files end with a line terminator (usually a carriage return and a line feed), you'll typically use the ReadLine method to read one record at a time.
- If the fields in a record are delimited by special characters, you need to parse the fields using the techniques of chapter 9.
- You can use the Peek method to determine if the input stream is positioned at the end of the stream.

Figure 21-7 How to read a text file

A class that works with a text file

In chapter 11, you learned how to develop an application that used a business class named Product. You also learned how to use two shared procedures in a database class named ProductDB to get the data for Product objects and to save the data for Product objects. However, you didn't learn how to code those database procedures.

Now, in figure 21-8, you can see a ProductDB class that implements those procedures using a text file. To start, the Imports statement specifies the System.IO namespace. Then, this class provides two constants that specify the path for the directory and the path for the text file. This makes those constants available to all of the procedures in the class.

The GetProducts method reads the product data from the file, stores that data in a List() of Product objects, and returns the List() collection. After the StreamReader object and the List() object are created, the Do loop reads the data in the file and stores the Product objects in the List() collection as described in the previous figure. When the loop ends, the StreamReader and FileStream objects are closed, and the method returns the List() object. At least that's the way this method works if the file already exists.

Note, however, that the GetProducts method also works if the directory or file doesn't exist when the method is executed. This situation could occur the first time an application is run. In that case, the method creates the directory if the directory doesn't exist, and it creates an empty file if the file doesn't exist. Then, the code that follows will still work, but it won't read any records.

In contrast, the SaveProducts method writes the data in the Product objects that are stored in the List() collection to the file. To start, this method accepts a List() of Product objects. Then, it writes each Product object to the file. Because the FileStream object is instantiated in Create mode, the Product objects will be written to a new file if the file doesn't already exist and they will overwrite the old file if it does exist.

To keep the emphasis on the code for file I/O, this class doesn't include exception handling. In a production application, though, you would probably add exception handling to a class like this. That way, the exceptions can be caught and handled close to their source, which often helps to reduce the amount of exception handling code that's necessary for an application.

A class that works with a text file

```
Imports System.IO

Public Class ProductDB

    Private Const Dir As String = "C:\VB 2012\Files\"
    Private Const Path As String = Dir & "Products.txt"

    Public Shared Function GetProducts() As List(Of Product)

        If Not Directory.Exists(Dir) Then
            Directory.CreateDirectory(Dir)
        End If

        Dim textIn As New StreamReader(
            New FileStream(Path, FileMode.OpenOrCreate, FileAccess.Read))

        Dim products As New List(Of Product)

        Do While textIn.Peek <> -1
            Dim row As String = textIn.ReadLine
            Dim columns() As String = row.Split(CChar("|"))
            Dim product As New Product
            product.Code = columns(0)
            product.Description = columns(1)
            product.Price = CDec(columns(2))
            products.Add(product)
        Loop

        textIn.Close()

        Return products

    End Function

    Public Shared Sub SaveProducts(products As List(Of Product))

        Dim textOut As New StreamWriter(
            New FileStream(Path, FileMode.Create, FileAccess.Write))

        For Each product As Product In products
            textOut.Write(product.Code & "|")
            textOut.Write(product.Description & "|")
            textOut.WriteLine(product.Price)
        Next

        textOut.Close()
    End Sub

End Class
```

Figure 21-8   A class that works with a text file

How to work with binary files

To read and write data in a binary file, you use the BinaryReader and BinaryWriter classes. You'll learn how to use these classes in the figures that follow, and you'll see a class that can be used to read and write a binary file.

How to write a binary file

Figure 21-9 shows how to use the BinaryWriter class to write data to a binary file. To start, you create a BinaryWriter object using the syntax at the top of this figure. To do that, you must supply a FileStream object as the argument for the constructor of the BinaryWriter class. This links the stream to the BinaryWriter object so it can be used to write to the file.

Once you create a BinaryWriter object, you can use its Write method to write data to the file. Like the Write method of the StreamWriter class, the Write method of the BinaryWriter class is overloaded, so you can use it with any type of data. However, the Write method of the BinaryWriter class doesn't convert the data to a string. Instead, it writes the data to the file without converting it. So, for example, if you pass a variable that contains a Decimal value to the Write method, this method will write the Decimal value to the file.

The example shows how this works. Here, a binary writer is created for a file stream that specifies a file that has write-only access. Since the mode argument has been set to Create, this will overwrite the file if it exists, and it will create the file if it doesn't exist. Then, a For Each loop is used to write the elements in a List() collection named products to the file. Since each element in the List() collection is an object of the Product class, each property of the Product object is written to the file separately using the Write method. After all of the elements in the List() collection have been written to the file, the Close method is used to close both the BinaryWriter and the FileStream objects.

The basic syntax for creating a BinaryWriter object

```
New BinaryWriter(stream)
```

Common methods of the BinaryWriter class

Method	Description
`Write(data)`	Writes the specified data to the output stream.
`Close()`	Closes the BinaryWriter object and the associated FileStream object.

Code that writes data from a collection of Product objects to a binary file

```
Dim binaryOut As New BinaryWriter(
    New FileStream(path, FileMode.Create, FileAccess.Write))

For Each product As Product In products
    binaryOut.Write(product.Code)
    binaryOut.Write(product.Description)
    binaryOut.Write(product.Price)
Next

binaryOut.Close()
```

Description

- You use a BinaryWriter object to write data to a binary file. In most cases, you'll write one field at a time in a prescribed sequence.
- Unlike the BinaryReader class, which provides several methods for reading fields that contain different types of data, the BinaryWriter class provides a single Write method for writing data to a file. This method determines the type of data being written based on the data type of the argument.

Figure 21-9 How to write a binary file

How to read a binary file

Figure 21-10 shows you how to use the BinaryReader class to read data from a binary file. Like the BinaryWriter class, the argument that you pass to the BinaryReader is the name of the FileStream object that connects the stream to a file.

In a binary file, there's no termination character to indicate where one record ends and another begins. Because of that, you can't read an entire record at once. Instead, you have to read one character or one field at a time. To do that, you use the Read methods of the BinaryReader class that are shown in this figure. In particular, you must use the appropriate method for the data type of the field that you want to read. To read a Boolean field, for example, you use the ReadBoolean method. To read a Decimal field, you use the ReadDecimal method.

The BinaryReader class provides methods to read most of the data types provided by the .NET Framework. However, this figure only shows the most common of these methods. For a complete list of methods, see the help information for the BinaryReader class.

Before you read the next character or field, you want to be sure that you aren't at the end of the file. To do that, you use the PeekChar method. Then, if there's at least one more character to be read, this method returns that character without advancing the cursor to the next position in the file. If there isn't another character, the PeekChar method returns a value of -1. Then, you can use the Close method to close the binary reader and the associated file stream.

This example shows how you can use some of these methods. Here, a FileStream object is created for a file that will have read-only access. Since the mode argument for the file stream specifies OpenOrCreate, this opens an existing file if one exists or creates a new file that's empty and opens it. Then, a new BinaryReader object is created for that file stream. Finally, the Do loop that follows is executed until the PeekChar method returns a value of -1, which means the end of the file has been reached.

Within the Do loop, the three fields in each record are read and assigned to the properties of a Product object. Because the first two fields in each record contain string data, the ReadString method is used to retrieve their contents. Because the third field contains Decimal data, the ReadDecimal method is used to retrieve its contents. Then, the Product object is added to the List() collection. When the Do loop ends, the Close method of the BinaryReader object is used to close both the BinaryReader and the FileStream objects.

The basic syntax for creating a BinaryReader object

```
New BinaryReader(stream)
```

Common methods of the BinaryReader class

Method	Description
`PeekChar()`	Returns the next available character in the input stream without advancing to the next position. If no more characters are available, this method returns -1.
`Read()`	Returns the next available character from the input stream and advances to the next position in the file.
`ReadBoolean()`	Returns a Boolean value from the input stream and advances the current position of the stream by one byte.
`ReadByte()`	Returns a byte from the input stream and advances the current position of the stream accordingly.
`ReadChar()`	Returns a character from the input stream and advances the current position of the stream accordingly.
`ReadDecimal()`	Returns a decimal value from the input stream and advances the current position of the stream by 16 bytes.
`ReadInt32()`	Returns a 4-byte signed integer from the input stream and advances the current position of the stream by 4 bytes.
`ReadString()`	Returns a string from the input stream and advances the current position of the stream by the number of characters in the string.
`Close()`	Closes the BinaryReader object and the associated FileStream object.

Code that reads data from a binary file into a collection of Product objects

```
Dim binaryIn As New BinaryReader(
    New FileStream(path, FileMode.OpenOrCreate, FileAccess.Read))

Dim products As New List(Of Product)

Do While binaryIn.PeekChar <> -1
    Dim product As New Product
    product.Code = binaryIn.ReadString
    product.Description = binaryIn.ReadString
    product.Price = binaryIn.ReadDecimal
    products.Add(product)
Loop

binaryIn.Close()
```

Description

- You use a BinaryReader object to read a single character or an entire field from a binary file. To read a single character, you use the Read method. And to read a field, you use the method that indicates the type of data the field contains.
- You can use the PeekChar method to determine if the input stream is positioned at the end of the stream.

Figure 21-10 How to read a binary file

A class that works with a binary file

Figure 21-11 presents the code for the ProductDB class that you saw in figure 21-8, but this time it uses a binary file instead of a text file. Because the methods in this class are similar to the ones for the text file, you shouldn't have any trouble understanding how they work.

Note, however, that the signatures for the two methods in this class are the same as the signatures for the methods in the ProductDB class in figure 21-8. As a result, either of these classes can be used with the Product Maintenance application presented in chapter 11. This clearly illustrates the benefit of encapsulation: the calling procedure doesn't know or care how the method is implemented. As a result, the programmer can change the way these methods are implemented without changing the rest of the application.

A class that works with a binary file

```
Imports System.IO

Public Class ProductDB

    Private Const Dir As String = "C:\VB 2012\Files\"
    Private Const Path As String = Dir & "Products.dat"

    Public Shared Function GetProducts() As List(Of Product)

        If Not Directory.Exists(Dir) Then
            Directory.CreateDirectory(Dir)
        End If

        Dim binaryIn As New BinaryReader(
            New FileStream(Path, FileMode.OpenOrCreate, FileAccess.Read))

        Dim products As New List(Of Product)

        Do While binaryIn.PeekChar <> -1
            Dim product As New Product
            product.Code = binaryIn.ReadString
            product.Description = binaryIn.ReadString
            product.Price = binaryIn.ReadDecimal
            products.Add(product)
        Loop

        binaryIn.Close()

        Return products

    End Function

    Public Shared Sub SaveProducts(products As List(Of Product))

        Dim binaryOut As New BinaryWriter(
            New FileStream(Path, FileMode.Create, FileAccess.Write))

        For Each product As Product In products
            binaryOut.Write(product.Code)
            binaryOut.Write(product.Description)
            binaryOut.Write(product.Price)
        Next

        binaryOut.Close()

    End Sub

End Class
```

Figure 21-11 A class that works with a binary file

Perspective

In this chapter, you learned how to read and write the data in text and binary files. These files can be used when you need a relatively easy way to store a limited number of records with a limited number of fields. However, when the data requirements for an application are more complex, it usually makes sense to use a database instead of text or binary files.

Terms

input file
output file
I/O operations
file I/O
text file
field
record
binary file
stream
output stream
input stream
text stream
binary stream

Exercise 21-1 Work with a text file

1. Open the project in the C:\VB 2012\Chapter 21\CustomerText directory. This is the Customer Maintenance application for exercise 11-1, but its CustomerDB class doesn't save or retrieve any data. To start, run this program to see how it works. Then, review the CustomerDB class.
2. In the CustomerDB class, add code to the GetCustomers and SaveCustomers methods so they use a text file to read and write a List() of Customer objects. Unless you moved it after downloading and installing the files for this book, the path for this file should be C:\VB 2012\Files\Customers.txt. Then, add code to the two methods so they read and write the text file.
3. Test the application by adding and deleting customers. To verify that the data is being saved to disk, stop the application and run it again. Or use a text editor like NotePad to open the file after a test run.

Exercise 21-2 Work with a binary file

1. Use Windows Explorer to copy the directory named CustomerText from the previous exercise and paste it within the chapter 21 directory. Then, rename that directory CustomerBinary, and open the project in that directory.
2. Modify the CustomerDB class so it uses a binary file named Customers.dat instead of a text file. Also, leave the signatures of the GetCustomers and SaveCustomers methods as they are so you won't need to modify the code in the form class that calls these methods. Then, test the application by adding and deleting customers.

22

How to work with XML files

XML is a standard way of storing data. Although XML is often used to exchange data between applications, particularly web-based applications, it can also be used to store structured data in a file. In this chapter, you'll learn the basics of creating XML documents, and you'll learn how to store those documents in a file.

An introduction to XML

This topic introduces you to the basics of XML. Here, you'll learn what XML is, how it is used, and the rules you must follow to create a simple XML document.

An XML document

XML (*Extensible Markup Language*) is a standard way to structure data by using tags that identify each data element. In some ways, XML is similar to HTML, the markup language that's used to format HTML documents on the World Wide Web. As a result, if you're familiar with HTML, you'll have no trouble learning how to create *XML documents*.

Figure 22-1 shows a simple XML document that contains data for three products. Each product has a code, description, and price. In the next two figures, you'll learn how the tags in this XML document work. But even without knowing those details, you can pick out the code, description, and price for each of the three products represented by this XML document.

XML was designed as a way to structure data that's sent over the World Wide Web. When you use .NET to develop web applications, though, you don't have to deal directly with XML. Instead, the .NET Framework classes handle the XML details for you.

Besides its use for web applications, XML is used internally throughout the .NET Framework to store data and to exchange data between various components of the Framework. In particular, the database features described in section 3 rely on XML. When you retrieve data from a database, for example, the .NET Framework converts the data to XML. However, since this is done automatically, the programmer doesn't have to deal with XML directly.

You can also use XML files as an alternative to the text and binary files described in chapter 21. Later in this chapter, for example, you'll learn how to create a ProductDB class for the Product Maintenance application that uses an XML file.

Data for three products

Code	Description	Price
A4VB	Murach's ASP.NET 4 with VB 2010	54.50
JAVP	Murach's Java Programming	56.50
VB10	Murach's Visual Basic 2010	54.50

An XML document that contains the data shown above

```
<?xml version="1.0" encoding="utf-8" ?>
<!--Product data-->
<Products>
  <Product Code="A4VB">
    <Description>Murach's ASP.NET 4 with VB 2010</Description>
    <Price>54.50</Price>
  </Product>
  <Product Code="JAVP">
    <Description>Murach's Java Programming</Description>
    <Price>56.50</Price>
  </Product>
  <Product Code="VB10">
    <Description>Murach's Visual Basic 2010</Description>
    <Price>54.50</Price>
  </Product>
</Products>
```

Description

- *XML*, which stands for *Extensible Markup Language*, provides a method of structuring data using special *tags*.
- The *XML document* in this figure contains data for three products. Each product has an *attribute* named Code and *elements* named Description and Price, which you'll learn more about in the next two figures.
- XML can be used to exchange data between different systems, especially via the Internet.
- Many .NET classes, particularly the database and web classes, use XML internally to store or exchange data.
- XML documents that are stored in a file can be used as an alternative to binary files, text files, or even database systems for storing data.
- When XML is stored in a file, the file name usually has an extension of xml.
- The .NET Framework includes several classes that let you read and write XML data. These classes are in the System.Xml namespace.

Figure 22-1 An XML document

XML tags, declarations, and comments

Figure 22-2 shows how XML uses tags to structure the data in an XML document. Here, each XML tag begins with the < character and ends with the > character. As a result, the first line in the XML document in this figure contains a complete XML tag. Similarly, the next three lines also contain complete tags. In contrast, the fifth line contains two tags, <Description> and </Description>, with a text value in between.

The first tag in any XML document is an *XML declaration*. This declaration identifies the document as an XML document and indicates which XML version the document conforms to. In this example, the document conforms to XML version 1.0. In addition, the declaration usually identifies the character set that's being used for the document. In this example, the character set is UTF-8, the most common one used for XML documents in English-speaking countries.

An XML document can also contain comments. These are tags that begin with <!-- and end with-->. Between the tags, you can type anything you want. For instance, the second line in this figure is a comment that indicates what type of data is contained in the XML document. It's often a good idea to include similar comments in your own XML documents.

XML elements

Elements are the building blocks of XML. Each element in an XML document represents a single data item and is identified by two tags: a *start tag* and an *end tag*. The start tag marks the beginning of the element and provides the element's name. The end tag marks the end of the element and repeats the name, prefixed by a slash. For example, <Description> is the start tag for an element named Description, and </Description> is the corresponding end tag.

It's important to realize that XML does not provide a pre-defined set of element names the way HTML does. Instead, you create your own element names to describe the contents of each element. Since XML names are case-sensitive, <Product> and <product> are not the same.

A complete element consists of the element's start tag, its end tag, and the *content* between the tags. For example, <Price>54.50</Price> indicates that the content of the Price element is 54.50. And <Description>Murach's Visual Basic 2010</Description> indicates that the content of the Description element is *Murach's Visual Basic 2010*.

Besides content, elements can contain other elements, known as *child elements*. This lets you add structure to a *parent element*. For example, a parent Product element can have child elements that provide details about each product, such as the product's description and price. In this figure, for example, you can see that the start tag, end tag, and values for the Description and Price elements are contained between the start and end tags for the Product element. As a result, Description and Price are children of the Product element, and the Product element is the parent of both the Description and Price elements.

As the XML document in figure 22-1 shows, an element can occur more than once within an XML document. In this case, the document has three

An XML document

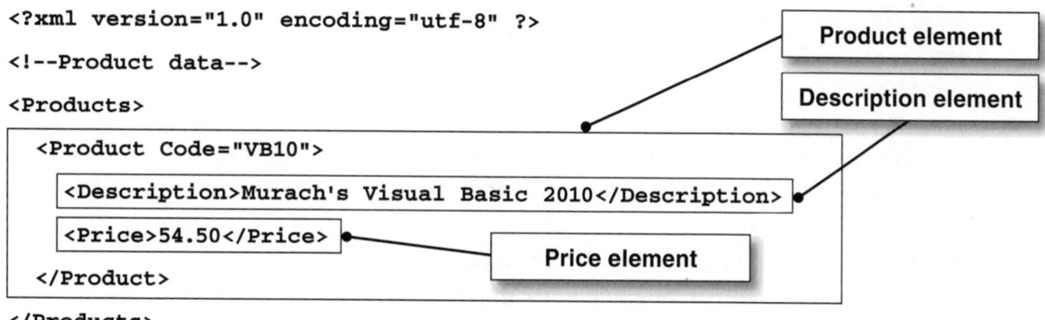
<?xml version="1.0" encoding="utf-8" ?>
<!--Product data-->
<Products>
<Product Code="VB10">
<Description>Murach's Visual Basic 2010</Description>
<Price>54.50</Price>
</Product>
</Products>
Product element
Description element
Price element

Tags, XML declarations, and comments

- Each XML tag begins with < and ends with >.
- The first line in an XML document is an *XML declaration* that indicates which version of the XML standard is being used for the document. In addition, the declaration usually identifies the standard character set that's being used. For documents in English-speaking countries, UTF-8 is the character set that's commonly used.
- You can use the <!-- and --> tags to include comments in an XML document.

Elements

- An *element* is a unit of XML data that begins with a *start tag* and ends with an *end tag*. The start tag provides the name of the element and contains any attributes assigned to the element (see figure 22-3 for details on attributes). The end tag repeats the name, prefixed with a slash (/). You can use any name you want for an XML element.
- The text between an element's start and end tags is called the element's *content*. For example, <Description>Murach's Visual Basic 2010</Description> indicates that the content of the Description element is the string *Murach's Visual Basic 2010.*
- Elements can contain other elements. An element that's contained within another element is known as a *child element*. The element that contains a child element is known as the child's *parent element*.
- Child elements can repeat within a parent element. For instance, in the example above, the Products element can contain more than one Product element. Similarly, each Product element could contain repeating child elements. For instance, each Product element could contain zero or more Category elements.
- The highest-level parent element in an XML document is known as the *root element*. An XML document can have only one root element.

Figure 22-2 XML tags, declarations, comments, and elements

Product elements, each representing a product. Since each of these Product elements contains Description and Price elements, these elements also appear three times in the document.

Although this example doesn't show it, a given child element can also occur more than once within a parent. For example, suppose you want to provide for products that have more than one category. You could do this by using a Category child element to indicate the category of a product. Then, for a product that belongs to multiple categories, you simply include multiple Category child elements within the Product element for that product.

The highest-level parent element in an XML document is known as the *root element*, and an XML document can have only one root element. In the examples in figures 22-1 and 22-2, the root element is Products. For XML documents that contain repeating data, it is common to use a plural name for the root element to indicate that it contains multiple child elements.

XML attributes

As shown in figure 22-3, *attributes* are a concise way to provide data for XML elements. In the products XML document, for example, each Product element has a Code attribute that provides an identifying code for the product. Thus, <Product Code="VB10"> contains an attribute named Code whose value is VB10.

Here again, XML doesn't provide a set of pre-defined attributes. Instead, you create attributes as you need them, using names that describe the content of the attributes. If an element has more than one attribute, you can list the attributes in any order you wish. However, you must separate the attributes from each other with one or more spaces. In addition, each attribute can appear only once within an element.

When you plan the layout of an XML document, you will often need to decide whether to use elements or attributes to represent the data items. In many cases, either one will work. In the products document, for example, I could have used a child element named Code rather than an attribute to represent each product's code. Likewise, I could have used an attribute named Description rather than a child element for the product's description.

Because attributes are more concise than child elements, it's often tempting to use attributes rather than child elements. Keep in mind, though, that an element with more than a few attributes soon becomes unwieldy. As a result, most designers limit their use of attributes to certain types of data, such as identifiers like product codes or customer numbers.

An XML document

```
<?xml version="1.0" encoding="utf-8" ?>
<!--Product data-->
<Products>
  <Product Code="VB10">
    <Description>Murach's Visual Basic 2010</Description>
    <Price>54.50</Price>
  </Product>
</Products>
```

Code attribute

Description

- You can include one or more *attributes* in the start tag for an element. An attribute consists of an attribute name, an equal sign, and a string value in quotes.
- If an element has more than one attribute, the order in which the attributes appear doesn't matter, but the attributes must be separated by one or more spaces.

When to use attributes instead of child elements

- When you design an XML document, you can use either a child element or an attribute to represent a data item for an element. The choice of whether to implement a data item as an attribute or as a separate child element is often a matter of preference.
- Two advantages of attributes are that they can appear in any order and they are more concise because they do not require end tags.
- Two advantages of child elements are that they are easier for people to read and they are more convenient for long string values.

Figure 22-3 XML attributes

How to work with the XML Editor

You can use the XML Editor that comes with Visual Studio to create or edit an XML document. The XML Editor is similar to the Code Editor that you use for working with Visual Basic code, but it includes features that make it easier to work with XML.

Of course, since an XML file is really just a text file with XML tags, you can open or create an XML file in any text editor. As a result, if you already have a text editor that you prefer, you can use that editor.

In addition, since XML is a standard format that's used on the web, you can use most web browsers to view an XML document. To do that, you can enter the path for the XML file in the browser's Address bar. Or, on most systems, you can double-click on the file in Windows Explorer.

How to create a new XML file

To create a new XML file and add it to your project, you can use the Project→Add New Item command as described in figure 22-4. This adds the file to your project, adds the XML declaration to the top of the file, and opens the file in the XML Editor. In this figure, for example, the XML declaration includes both the XML version attribute and the encoding attribute that indicates which character set the document uses. Unless you're working in a language other than English, you'll want to leave this attribute set to UTF-8.

How to open an existing XML file

To open an existing XML file that you've added to your project, you can just double-click on the file in the Solution Explorer. Before you can do that, though, you'll need to click the Show All Files button at the top of the Solution Explorer so you can see the file. You can also open an existing file that you haven't added to your project. To do that, you use the File→Open File command to display the Open File dialog box and select the file.

How to edit an XML file

When you work in the XML Editor, the task of editing XML files is simplified. For example, tags, content, attributes, values, and comments are color-coded so you can easily tell them apart. When you type a start tag, the XML Editor automatically adds the end tag and positions the cursor between the start and end tags. In addition, the XML Editor makes it easy to work with the indentation of the child elements, and it makes it easy to view data by expanding or collapsing elements. If you work with the XML Editor for a while, you'll quickly see how easy it is to use.

An XML document in the XML Editor

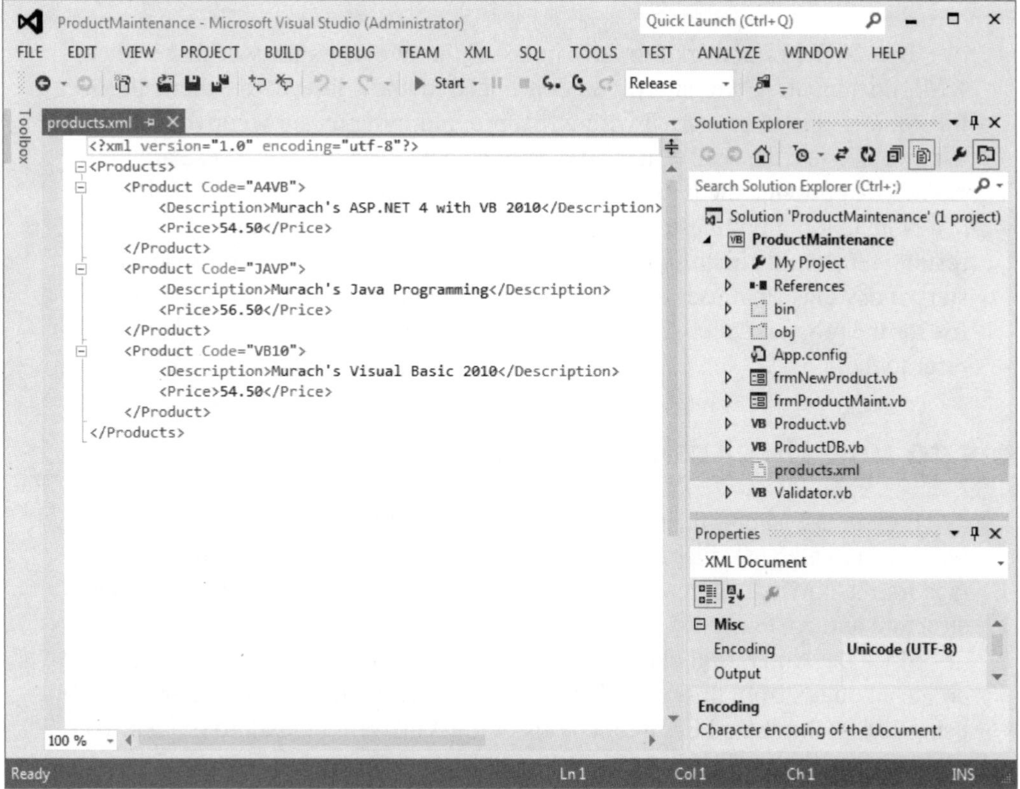

How to add a new XML file to a project

- Choose the Project→Add New Item command. In the Add New Item dialog box, select the XML File template; type a name for the XML file in the Name text box; and click Add. This adds an XML file to your project, adds the XML declaration for the document, and opens the document in the XML Editor.

How to open an existing XML file

- To open an existing XML file that's stored in the project, double-click on the file.
- To open an existing XML file without adding the file to your project, use the File→Open File command.

How to edit an XML file

- When you type a start tag, the XML Editor automatically adds an end tag for the element and positions the insertion point between the start and end tags so you can type the element's content.
- When you type an attribute, the XML Editor automatically adds a pair of quotation marks and positions the insertion point between them so you can type the attribute value.

Figure 22-4 How to work with the XML Editor

How to work with XML

The .NET Framework provides many different classes for working with XML documents. Fortunately, you don't need to know how to use them all. In this topic, I'll get you started with XML programming by showing you how to use two classes: the XmlWriter class and the XmlReader class. These are the classes that provide the basic services you need to write and read XML files.

Note that both of these classes reside in the System.Xml namespace. As a result, you should either include an Imports statement for this namespace at the start of any class that uses it or check System.Xml in the Imported Namespaces list for the project. Otherwise, you have to qualify the class names each time you refer to them.

How to use the XmlWriter class

Figure 22-5 shows the methods of the XmlWriter class that you can use to write data to an XML file. These methods make it easy to generate the XML tags for the XML document. As a result, you can concentrate on the document's structure and content.

Since the XmlWriter class is an abstract class, you can't use a constructor to create an object from this class. However, you can create an XmlWriter object by using one of the shared Create methods of the XmlWriter class. To do that, you typically supply a string variable that includes the path and file name of the file. Then, if the file you specify already exists, it's deleted and recreated. As a result, you can't use this technique to add XML to an existing file.

Before you code any statements that write XML to a file, you typically want to change some settings for the XmlWriter object so it uses spaces to indent child elements. This will make your XML files easier to read if they're opened in the XML Editor. To do that, you need to create an XmlWriterSettings object and set its Indent and IndentChars properties. Then, you pass this object to the Create method when you create an XmlWriter object.

To write XML data, you use one of the Write methods of the XmlWriter class. Although this class actually has over 50 Write methods, you can create basic XML documents using just the six Write methods in this figure.

When you use these methods, you need to use the WriteStartElement and WriteEndElement methods for elements that have children, such as the Products element. However, you don't need to use a WriteStartElement or WriteEndElement method to create an element that only contains content, such as the Description and Price elements. In this case, you can use the WriteElementString method to automatically write the start tag, the content, and the end tag.

Common methods of the XmlWriter class

Method	Description
Create(path)	A shared method that creates an XmlWriter object using the specified path or file name.
Create(path, settings)	A shared method that creates an XmlWriter object using the specified path or file name and the specified XmlWriterSettings object.
WriteStartDocument()	Writes an XML declaration line at the beginning of a document.
WriteComment(comment)	Writes a comment to the XML document.
WriteStartElement(elementName)	Writes a start tag using the element name you provide.
WriteAttributeString(attributeName, value)	Adds an attribute to the current element.
WriteEndElement()	Writes an end tag for the current element.
WriteElementString(elementName, content)	Writes a complete element including a start tag, content, and end tag.
Close()	Closes the XmlWriter object.

Common properties of the XmlWriterSettings class

Property	Description
Indent	Gets or sets a Boolean value that indicates whether to indent elements.
IndentChars	Gets or sets the string to use when indenting.

Description

- The XmlWriter class lets you write XML data to a file.
- When you create an XmlWriter object, you specify the name or path of the file where you want to write the XML. If the file already exists, it's deleted and then recreated.
- When you create an XmlWriter object, you can use an XmlWriterSettings object to specify the settings that will be used by the XmlWriter object.
- If you attempt to create an invalid XML document, an XmlException will be thrown. For example, an XmlException will be thrown if you try to write two XML declarations or if you try to write an end tag before you've written a start tag.

Figure 22-5 How to use the XmlWriter class

Code that writes an XML document

Figure 22-6 shows the code that creates an XML document like the one that's in figure 22-1. This code gets its data from a List() collection of Product objects named products where each product has three properties: Code, Description, and Price.

To start, this code defines a string variable that points to the Products.xml file that's stored in the C:\VB 2012\Files directory. Then, it creates an XmlWriterSettings object and sets the Indent and IndentChars properties so the XmlWriter object uses four spaces to indent each level of child elements. Finally, this code creates an XmlWriter object by passing the path and settings variables to the shared Create method of the XmlWriter class.

After this code creates the XmlWriter object, it uses the WriteStartDocument method to write the XML declaration for the document. In addition, it uses the WriteStartElement method to write the start tag for the root element of the document, which is the Products element.

The heart of this code is the For Each loop that writes a Product element for each Product object in the List() collection. To write a Product element, the loop uses the WriteStartElement method to write the start tag for the Product element, and then uses the WriteAttributeString method to add the Code attribute. Next, two WriteElementString methods are used to write the Description and Price elements. Finally, the WriteEndElement method is used to write the end tag for the Product element.

Since the For Each loop is preceded by a WriteStartElement method that writes the start tag for the document's root element, the For Each loop must be followed by a WriteEndElement method that writes the end tag for the root element. After that, the Close method is used to close the XmlWriter object.

In this code, the path of the XML document is coded as an absolute path like this:

```
Dim path As String = "C:\VB 2012\Files\Products.xml"
```

In this case, the XML file is stored in a directory other than the one where the rest of the files for the ProductMaintenance project are stored. However, if you want to use an XML file that's part of the project, you can specify a relative path like this:

```
Dim path As String = "..\..\Products.xml"
```

This works because the exe file for the application runs from the bin\Debug subdirectory of the project directory. As a result, you need to navigate back two directory levels to get to the directory that stores the files for the project.

Code that writes an XML document

```
Private Const Path As String = "C:\VB 2012\Files\Products.xml"

' create the XmlWriterSettings object
Dim settings As New XmlWriterSettings
settings.Indent = True
settings.IndentChars = ("    ")

' create the XmlWriter object
Dim xmlOut As XmlWriter = XmlWriter.Create(Path, settings)

' write the start of the document
xmlOut.WriteStartDocument()
xmlOut.WriteStartElement("Products")

' write each Product object to the XML file
For Each product As Product In products
    xmlOut.WriteStartElement("Product")
    xmlOut.WriteAttributeString("Code", product.Code)
    xmlOut.WriteElementString("Description", product.Description)
    xmlOut.WriteElementString("Price", product.Price.ToString)
    xmlOut.WriteEndElement()
Next

' write the end tag for the root element
xmlOut.WriteEndElement()

' close the XmlWriter object
xmlOut.Close()
```

Description

- This example saves a List() collection of Product objects as an XML document. The resulting XML document will be like the one in figure 22-1.
- To set the path for an XML file in the current project, you can use two dots to refer to the parent directory as in:

  ```
  "..\..\Products.xml"
  ```

  This works because the current project is run from the bin\Debug subdirectory of the project directory.

Figure 22-6 Code that writes an XML document

How to use the XmlReader class

To read an XML document, you can use the XmlReader class that's summarized in figure 22-7. Like the XmlWriter class, the XmlReader class is an abstract class. As a result, to create an object from this class, you must use the shared Create method that's available from the class. When you do that, you must supply the path of the XML file as a string. You can also supply an XmlReaderSettings object that contains any settings that you want to set for the XmlReader object.

For example, you typically want to set the IgnoreWhitespace property of the XmlReaderSettings object to indicate how you want to handle *white space*. White space refers to spaces, tabs, and return characters that affect the appearance but not the meaning of an XML document. To simplify the task of processing XML data, you typically set the IgnoreWhitespace property to True. That way, the XmlReader object will automatically skip white space in the XML document, and you won't have to write code to handle it.

Similarly, you typically want to set the IgnoreComments property of the XmlReaderSettings object to True. That way, the XmlReader object will automatically skip any comments in the XML document, and you won't have to write code to handle them.

To read data from an XML document, you can use the various Read methods of the XmlReader class. This class treats an XML document as a series of *nodes*, and you can use the basic Read method to read the next node from the file. Because the concept of nodes is so important to reading XML data, the next figure describes them in detail and walks you through the process of reading a simple XML document node by node. For now, you just need to know that every tag in an XML document is treated as a separate node, and each element's content is also treated as a separate node. Attributes, however, are not treated as nodes. Instead, an attribute is treated as part of a start tag node.

When you invoke the Read method, the XmlReader gets the next node from the XML document and makes that node the *current node*. Then, you can use the XmlReader's NodeType, Name, or Value property to retrieve the node's type, name, or value. If you read past the last node in the document, the EOF property is set to True. As a result, you can use this property to tell when you have reached the end of the file.

In fact, you can process an entire XML document by using just the Read method to read the document's nodes one at a time, by using the NodeType property to determine what type of node has just been read, and by taking appropriate action based on the node type.

However, the XmlReader has several other methods that simplify the task of parsing an XML document. For example, you can use the ReadToDescendant and ReadToNextSibling elements to read up to the element that you want to process. In addition, you can use the ReadElementContentAsString and ReadElementContentAsDecimal methods to read content from an element that contains content.

The ReadStartElement method starts by confirming that the current node is a start tag. If it is, the method checks to make sure that the name of the start

Common properties and methods of the XmlReader class

Property	Description
NodeType	Returns a member of the XmlNodeType enumeration that indicates the type of the current node.
Name	Gets the name of the current node, if the node has a name.
Value	Gets the value of the current node, if the node has a value.
EOF	Returns a True value if the reader has reached the end of the stream.
(name)	Gets the value of the specified attribute. If the current element does not have the attribute, this property returns an empty string.
Method	**Description**
Create(path)	A shared method that creates an XmlReader object using the specified path or file name.
Create(path, settings)	A shared method that creates an XmlReader object using the specified path or file name and the specified XmlReaderSettings object.
Read()	Reads the next node.
ReadStartElement(name)	Checks that the current node is a start tag with the specified name, then advances to the next node.
ReadEndElement()	Checks that the current node is an end tag, then advances to the next node.
ReadToDescendant(name)	If the specified descendant element is found, this method advances to it and returns a True value. Otherwise, it advances to the end tag of the current element and returns a False value.
ReadToNextSibling(name)	If the specified sibling element is found, this method advances to it and returns a True value. Otherwise, it advances to the end tag of the current element and returns a False value.
ReadElementContentAsString()	Reads the current element, returns the content as a string, and moves past the element's end tag.
ReadElementContentAsDecimal()	Reads the current element, returns the content as a Decimal value, and moves past the element's end tag.
Close()	Closes the XmlWriter and releases any resources.

Common properties of the XmlReaderSettings class

Property	Description
IgnoreWhitespace	Gets or sets a Boolean value that indicates whether to ignore white space. If set to False, white space is treated as a node.
IgnoreComments	Gets or sets a Boolean value indicating whether to ignore comments.

Description

- Some of these methods throw an XmlException if they encounter an unexpected situation, such as when the next element does not match the specified name.

Figure 22-7 How to use the XmlReader class

tag matches the name you supply as an argument. If both of these conditions are met, the method then reads the next node. Otherwise, an XmlException is thrown.

The ReadEndElement method is similar, but it checks to make sure the current node is an end tag rather than a start tag, and it doesn't check the element name. If the current node is an end tag, the ReadEndElement method reads the next node. Otherwise, it throws an XmlException.

The ReadElementContentAsString method reads a simple content element (an element that has content but no child elements) and returns its content node as a string. However, if the element contains child elements rather than simple content, an XmlException is thrown. After the element is read, the reader moves past the end tag so it's positioned to read the next element.

The ReadElementContentAsDecimal method works similarly. However, this method also converts the content that's stored in the element from a string to a Decimal value and returns that value. If this method isn't able to convert the content to a Decimal value, it throws an XmlException.

To read attributes, you can use the indexer of the XmlReader object. To do that, you code the name of the attribute as a string argument within brackets. Of course, this only works if the current node has an attribute with the specified name.

How the XmlReader class reads nodes

To use the XmlReader class properly, you need to understand exactly how it reads nodes. To help you with that, figure 22-8 presents a simple XML document and lists all of the nodes contained in that document. Even though this document contains just one Product element with two child elements, there are 12 nodes.

By studying this figure, you can see how the methods of the XmlReader class read the nodes. The first node is the XML declaration tag. The second node is the comment. The third node is the start tag for the Products element. And so on.

Notice that when the start tag for the Product element is reached, the Code attribute is available via the indexer. Also notice that the Description and Price child elements each use three nodes: one for the start tag, one for the content, and one for the end tag.

An XML document

```
<?xml version="1.0" encoding="utf-8" ?>
<!--Product data-->
<Products>
  <Product Code="VB10">
    <Description>Murach's Visual Basic 2010</Description>
    <Price>54.50</Price>
  </Product>
</Products>
```

The XML nodes in this document

NodeType	Name	Other properties
XmlDeclaration	xml	
Comment		Value = "Product data"
Element	Products	
Element	Product	("Code") = "VB10"
Element	Description	
Text		Value = "Murach's Visual Basic 2010"
EndElement	Description	
Element	Price	
Text		Value = "54.50"
EndElement	Price	
EndElement	Product	
EndElement	Products	

Description

- The XmlReader class lets you read the contents of an XML document one *node* at a time.
- For the XML declaration and each comment, the XmlReader class parses one node.
- For each element without content (usually, a parent element), the XmlReader class parses two nodes: an Element node for the start tag and an EndElement node for the end tag.
- For each element with content, the XmlReader class parses three nodes: an Element node for the element's start tag, a Text node for the element's text value, and an EndElement node for the element's end tag.
- If an element contains an attribute, the attribute is available via the indexer when the Element node is read.

Notes

- This example assumes that the IgnoreWhitespace property of the XmlReaderSettings object has been set to True, so white space is ignored.
- The NodeType, Name, Value, and indexer values shown in the table above correspond to the NodeType, Name, Value, and Item properties of the XmlReader class.

Figure 22-8 How the XmlReader class reads nodes

Code that reads an XML document

Figure 22-9 presents an example that reads the contents of the Products.xml file into a List() collection of Product objects. Here, the first statement specifies the path for the Products.xml file, which is in the C:\VB 2012\Files directory. The second statement creates a new List() collection to store the Product objects. The next three statements create an XmlReaderSettings object and set its IgnoreWhitespace and IgnoreComments properties so the reader will ignore any nodes for white space or comments. Then, this code creates an XmlReader object by passing the specified path and settings to the shared Create method of the XmlReader class.

After the XmlReader object has been created, the ReadToDescendant method is used to read past any nodes in the XML file that occur before the first Product element. If this method returns a True value, it indicates that a Product element was found. Then, a Do loop reads and processes the data for each Product element in the file. This loop begins by using the indexer to retrieve the value of the Code attribute. This works because the Do loop always begins with the reader positioned at the start tag for the Product element.

After the Code attribute has been retrieved and stored in the Product object, the loop uses the ReadStartElement method to advance to the next node, which is the Description element's start tag. Although it's also possible to use a Read method here, the ReadStartElement ensures that the reader is on the Product element.

After the reader has been positioned at the Description element, the next two statements use the ReadElementContentAsString and ReadElementContentAsDecimal methods to retrieve the contents of the Description and Price elements. Then, the last line adds the Product object to the List() collection.

Note that the ReadToNextSibling method is coded as the condition at the end of the Do loop. As a result, if the XML document contains another Product element, this method advances to the start tag for the next Product element and returns a True value so the loop will repeat. However, if the XML document doesn't contain another Product element, this method will return a False value and the loop won't repeat. In that case, the Close method is called to close the reader.

If the Products.xml file doesn't contain an XML document like the one shown in figure 22-1, one of the Read methods will throw an exception of the XmlException type. To catch this type of exception, you can code a Try...Catch statement just as you would for any other type of exception.

Code that reads an XML document

```
Private Const Path As String = "C:\VB 2012\Files\Products.xml"
Dim products As New List(Of Product)

' create the XmlReaderSettings object
Dim settings As New XmlReaderSettings
settings.IgnoreWhitespace = True
settings.IgnoreComments = True

' create the XmlReader object
Dim xmlIn As XmlReader = XmlReader.Create(Path, settings)

' read past all nodes to the first Product node
If xmlIn.ReadToDescendant("Product") Then

    ' create one Product object for each Product node
    Do
        Dim product As New Product
        product.Code = xmlIn("Code")
        xmlIn.ReadStartElement("Product")
        product.Description = xmlIn.ReadElementContentAsString
        product.Price = xmlIn.ReadElementContentAsDecimal
        products.Add(product)
    Loop While xmlIn.ReadToNextSibling("Product")
End If

' close the XmlReader object
xmlIn.Close()
```

Description

- This example loads the XML document in figure 22-1 into a List() collection of Product objects.
- To focus on the code that's used to read an XML file, this code doesn't include any exception handling. However, it's common to code a Try statement with Catch blocks that catch and handle any exceptions that this code might throw. In addition, it's common to include a Finally block that frees the resources being used by this code.

Figure 22-9 Code that reads an XML document

A class that works with an XML file

Figure 22-10 presents a ProductDB class that works with the data in an XML file. This shows how the code presented in this chapter can be used to implement the database class that's used by the Product Maintenance application that was presented in chapter 11.

As you can see, this class contains just two methods. The first is a Function procedure named GetProducts that gets the product data from an XML file and saves it in a List() of Product objects. The second is a Sub procedure named SaveProducts that receives a List() of Product objects and saves the data for each object in an XML file. Since all of this code has already been explained, you shouldn't have any trouble following it.

What's interesting is that the methods in this ProductDB class have the same names and signatures as the methods in the two ProductDB classes that were presented in chapter 21. That means that any one of these three classes could be used with the Product Maintenance application without changing any of the other classes in that application.

The code for the ProductDB class

```
Imports System.Xml

Public Class ProductDB

    Private Const Path As String = "C:\VB 2012\Files\Products.xml"

    Public Shared Function GetProducts() As List(Of Product)

        Dim products As New List(Of Product)

        Dim settings As New XmlReaderSettings
        settings.IgnoreWhitespace = True
        settings.IgnoreComments = True

        Dim xmlIn As XmlReader = XmlReader.Create(Path, settings)
        If xmlIn.ReadToDescendant("Product") Then
            Do
                Dim product As New Product
                product.Code = xmlIn("Code")
                xmlIn.ReadStartElement("Product")
                product.Description = xmlIn.ReadElementContentAsString
                product.Price = xmlIn.ReadElementContentAsDecimal
                products.Add(product)
            Loop While xmlIn.ReadToNextSibling("Product")
        End If

        xmlIn.Close()
        Return products

    End Function

    Public Shared Sub SaveProducts(products As List(Of Product))

        Dim settings As New XmlWriterSettings
        settings.Indent = True
        settings.IndentChars = ("    ")

        Dim xmlOut As XmlWriter = XmlWriter.Create(Path, settings)
        xmlOut.WriteStartDocument()
        xmlOut.WriteStartElement("Products")

        For Each product As Product In products
            xmlOut.WriteStartElement("Product")
            xmlOut.WriteAttributeString("Code", product.Code)
            xmlOut.WriteElementString("Description", product.Description)
            xmlOut.WriteElementString("Price", product.Price.ToString)
            xmlOut.WriteEndElement()
        Next

        xmlOut.WriteEndElement()
        xmlOut.Close()

    End Sub

End Class
```

Figure 22-10 A class that works with an XML file

Perspective

In this chapter, you learned the basics of reading and writing XML documents using the XmlReader and XmlWriter classes. With these skills, you should be able to incorporate simple XML documents into your applications. You should also have a better appreciation for the way XML is used internally by the database applications that you learned about in section 3.

However, this chapter is only an introduction to XML that omits some important features. For example, you can use *XML schemas* to define the layout for an XML document. Then, you can use .NET classes to make sure an XML document conforms to its schema. You can also use *DOM*, which stands for *Document Object Model*, to treat an entire XML document as a single XmlDocument object with property collections that represent the XML document's nodes. In short, there's a lot more to learn before you master XML.

Terms

XML (Extensible Markup Language)
tag
XML document
XML declaration
element
start tag
end tag
content
child element
parent element
root element
attribute
white space
node
current node

Exercise 22-1 Work with an XML file

1. Open the project in the C:\VB 2012\Chapter 22\CustomerXML directory. This application is the Customer Maintenance application for exercise 11-1, but it doesn't save or retrieve the data. To start, run the application and review the CustomerDB class.
2. Use Visual Studio to open the Customers.xml file that's stored in the C:\VB 2012\Files directory. This should open this file in the XML Editor so you can see how this data is structured. Then, close this file.
3. In the CustomerDB class, add code to the GetCustomers and SaveCustomers methods so they read the data from the Customers.xml file into a List() of Customer objects and write the data from a List() of Customer objects to the XML file.
4. Test the application by adding and deleting customers. To verify that the data is being saved to disk, you can stop the application and run it again. You can use Visual Studio to view the XML file in the XML Editor. Or you can double-click on the file in Windows Explorer. On most systems, this displays the XML file in your default web browser.

23

How to use LINQ

In this chapter, you'll learn the basic skills for using a feature of Visual Basic called LINQ. LINQ provides a way for you to query a data source using constructs that are built into the Visual Basic language. That way, you can use the same language to access a variety of data sources.

In this chapter, I'll focus on using LINQ with in-memory data structures such as arrays and generic lists. Keep in mind as you read this chapter, though, that you can also use the same skills to query datasets, relational databases, and XML files.

To give you an idea of how that works, I'll present two applications at the end of this chapter that perform the same function. The first one will use LINQ to query two generic lists, and the second one will use LINQ to query two tables in a typed dataset. Once you see how similar the queries for these applications are, you should begin to understand the real power of using LINQ.

Basic concepts for working with LINQ

As its name implies, *LINQ*, or *Language-Integrated Query*, lets you query a data source using the Visual Basic language. Before you learn how to code LINQ queries, you need to learn some concepts related to LINQ, such as how LINQ is implemented and what the three stages of a query operation are. In addition, you'll want to know the advantages you'll get from using LINQ so you can decide for yourself if it's a feature you want to use.

How LINQ is implemented

LINQ is implemented as a set of methods that are defined by the Enumerable class. Because these methods can only be used in a query operation, they're referred to as *query operators*. To make it easy to use the query operators, Visual Basic provides keywords that give you access to the operators. The keywords you're most likely to use are listed at the top of figure 23-1.

If you've ever coded a query using SQL, you shouldn't have any trouble understanding what each of these keywords does. For example, you use the From keyword to identify the data source for the query. You use the Where keyword to filter the data that's returned by the query. And you use the Select keyword to identify the fields you want to be returned by the query. You'll learn how to code queries that use all of these keywords later in this chapter.

Advantages of using LINQ

Figure 23-1 also lists several advantages of LINQ. Probably the biggest advantage is that it lets you query different types of data sources using the same language. As you'll see in this chapter, for example, you can use the same language to query an array and a generic list of objects. Keep in mind as you read this chapter, though, that you can use these same skills to query more sophisticated data sources such as datasets and databases.

The key to making this work is that the query language is integrated into Visual Basic. Because of that, you don't have to learn a different query language for each type of data source you want to query. In addition, as you enter your queries, you can take advantage of the IntelliSense features that are provided for the Visual Basic language. The compiler can catch errors in the query, such as a field that doesn't exist in the data source, so you don't get errors at runtime. And when a runtime error does occur, you can use the Visual Studio debugging features to determine its cause.

Finally, if you're working with a relational data source such as a SQL Server database, you can use designer tools provided by Visual Studio to develop an *object-relational mapping*. Then, you can use LINQ to query the objects defined by this mapping, and the query will be converted to the form required by the data source. This can make it significantly easier to work with relational data sources.

Some of the Visual Basic keywords for working with LINQ

Keyword	Description
`From`	Identifies the source of data for the query.
`Where`	Provides a condition that specifies which elements are retrieved from the data source.
`Order By`	Indicates how the elements that are returned by the query are sorted.
`Select`	Specifies the content of the returned elements.
`Join`	Combines data from two data sources.

Advantages of using LINQ

- Makes it easier for you to query a data source by integrating the query language with Visual Basic.
- Makes it easier to develop applications that query a data source by providing IntelliSense, compile-time syntax checking, and debugging support.
- Makes it easier for you to query different types of data sources because you use the same basic syntax for each type.
- Makes it easier for you to use objects to work with relational data sources by providing designer tools that create *object-relational mappings*.

Description

- *Language-Integrated Query* (*LINQ*) provides a set of *query operators* that are available as keywords from the Visual Basic language. You use these keywords to define a *query expression* that identifies the data you want to retrieve from the data source.
- To use LINQ with a data source, the data source must implement the IEnumerable(Of T) interface or another interface that implements IEnumerable(Of T) such as IQueryable(Of T). For more information on interfaces, see chapter 19.
- A data source such as an array or an array list that supports the non-generic IEnumerable interface can also be used with LINQ.

Note

- The LINQ operators are implemented as methods of the Enumerable class. Although you can execute these methods directly, you're more likely to use the keywords that are built into the Visual Basic language.

Figure 23-1 An introduction to LINQ

The three stages of a query operation

Figure 23-2 presents the three stages of a query operation and illustrates these stages using an array. The first stage is to get the data source. How you do that depends on the type of data source you're working with. For the array shown here, getting the data source means defining an array named numbers and assigning values to its elements. In this case, the array contains five integers with the values 0, 1, 2, 3, and 4.

The second stage is to define the *query expression*. This expression identifies the data source and the data to be retrieved from that data source. The query expression in this figure, for example, retrieves the even integers from the numbers array. It also sorts those integers in descending sequence. (Don't worry if you don't understand the syntax of this query expression. You'll learn how to code query expressions in the topics that follow.)

Notice here that the query expression is stored in a *query variable*. That's necessary because this query isn't executed when it's defined. Also notice that the query variable isn't declared with a type. Instead, it's given a type implicitly based on the type of elements returned by the query. In this case, because the query returns integers, the query variable is given the type IEnumerable(Of Integer).

For this to work, the data source must implement the IEnumerable or IEnumerable(Of T) interface. In case you're not familiar with interfaces, they consist of a set of declarations for one or more properties, methods, and events, but they don't provide implementation for those properties, methods, and events. If you want to learn more about interfaces, you can read chapter 19. For the example in this figure, however, all you need to know is that an array implements the IEnumerable interface.

The third stage of a query operation is to execute the query. To do that, you typically use a For Each statement like the one shown in this figure. Here, each element that's returned by the query expression is added to a string variable. Then, after all the elements have been processed, the string is displayed in a message box. As you can see, this message box lists the even numbers from 4 to 0 as defined by the query expression.

By the way, you may have noticed the two tab characters that I included in each line of the display in this example. They're needed to make the dialog box wide enough to accommodate the entire title. Without these characters, the title would be cut off.

When a query is defined and executed separately as shown here, the process is referred to as *deferred execution*. In contrast, queries that are executed when they're defined use *immediate execution*. Immediate execution typically occurs when a method that requires access to the individual elements returned by the query is executed on the query expression. For example, to get a count of the number of elements returned by a query, you can execute the Count method on the query expression. Then, the query will be executed immediately so the count can be calculated. Although LINQ provides several methods for returning these types of values, you won't learn about them in this book.

The three stages of a query operation

1. Get the data source. If the data source is an array, for example, you must declare the array and then assign values to its elements.
2. Define the query expression.
3. Execute the query to return the results.

A LINQ query that retrieves data from an array

Code that defines the array

```
Dim numbers(5) As Integer
For i As Integer = 0 To numbers.Length - 1
    numbers(i) = i
Next
```

A statement that defines the query expression

```
Dim numberList = From number In numbers
                 Where number Mod 2 = 0
                 Order By number Descending
                 Select number
```

Code that executes the query

```
Dim numberDisplay As String = ""
For Each number In numberList
    numberDisplay &= number & vbTab & vbTab & vbCrLf
Next
MessageBox.Show(numberDisplay, "Sorted Even Numbers")
```

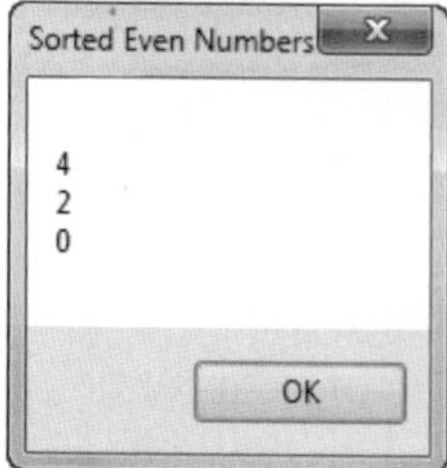

Description

- The process described above is called *deferred execution* because the query isn't executed when it's defined. Instead, it's executed when the application tries to access the individual elements returned by the query, such as when the query is used in a For Each statement.
- If a query isn't executed when it's defined, it's stored in a *query variable*. In that case, the query variable is implicitly typed as IEnumerable(Of T) where T is the type of each element. In the example above, the numberList variable is assigned the type IEnumerable(Of Integer) since the numbers array contains integers.
- If a query requires access to the individual elements identified by the query expression, *immediate execution* occurs. This typically happens when an aggregate value, such as the number of elements in the results, is requested. In that case, the query expression isn't saved in a query variable.

Figure 23-2 The three stages of a query operation

How to code a LINQ query

Now that you have a basic understanding of what a LINQ query is, you need to learn the syntax for coding query expressions. That's what you'll learn in the topics that follow.

How to identify the data source for a query

To identify the source of data for a query, you use the From clause shown in figure 23-3. As you can see, this clause declares a variable that will be used to iterate through the elements of the data source, and it names the data source, which must be a collection that implements the IEnumerable or IEnumerable(Of T) interface. It can also declare a type for the variable, although the type is usually omitted. If it is omitted, it's determined by the type of elements in the data source.

The first example in this figure shows how to use the From clause with an array of decimals named salesTotals. The first statement in this example declares the array and assigns values to its elements. Then, the second statement defines the query expression, which consists of just the From clause. This expression is stored in a query variable named salesList. Finally, a For Each statement loops through the values returned by the query and calculates a sum of those values.

At this point, you may be wondering why you would use a query expression like this. The answer is, you wouldn't. That's because you could just as easily use the For Each statement on the array itself. Because of that, you won't typically code the From clause by itself. It's shown by itself here to illustrate that it's the only required clause.

If you include other clauses in a query expression, the From clause must always be coded first. That way, Visual Basic knows what the source of data for the query is, and it can help you construct the rest of the query based on that data source.

The second example in this figure shows how to use the From clause with a generic list of invoices. Here, you can see that the Invoice class consists of a set of auto-implemented properties. Then, the statement that follows creates a list that's based on this class and loads invoices into it using the GetInvoices method of the InvoiceDB class. Note that it's not important for you to know how this method works. All you need to know is that it returns a List(Of Invoice) object. This object is then assigned to a variable named invoiceList.

The next statement defines the query expression, which consists of a From clause that identifies invoiceList as the data source. This expression is assigned to a query variable named invoices. Then, this variable is used in a For Each statement to calculate a sum of the InvoiceTotal fields in the invoices.

You may have noticed in both of the examples in this figure that the variable that's used in the query expression and the variable that's used in the For Each loop have the same name. That makes sense because they both refer to an element in the data source. However, you should know that you don't have to use

The syntax of the From clause

```
From elementName [As type] In collectionName
```

An example that uses an array of decimals

A statement that gets the data source

```
Dim salesTotals() As Decimal = {1286.45D, 2433.49D, 2893.85D, 2094.53D}
```

A statement that defines the query expression

```
Dim salesList = From sales In salesTotals
```

Code that executes the query

```
Dim sum As Decimal = 0
For Each sales In salesList
    sum += sales
Next
```

An example that uses a generic list of invoices as the data source

The Invoice class

```
Public Class Invoice
    Public Property InvoiceID As Integer
    Public Property CustomerID As Integer
    Public Property InvoiceDate As Date
    Public Property ProductTotal As Decimal
    Public Property SalesTax As Decimal
    Public Property Shipping As Decimal
    Public Property InvoiceTotal As Decimal
End Class
```

A statement that gets the data source

```
Dim invoiceList As List(Of Invoice) = InvoiceDB.GetInvoices
```

A statement that defines the query expression

```
Dim invoices = From invoice In invoiceList
```

Code that executes the query

```
Dim sum As Decimal = 0
For Each invoice In invoices
    sum += invoice.InvoiceTotal
Next
```

Description

- The From clause identifies the source of data for a query and declares a variable that's used to iterate through the elements of the data source.
- If the iteration variable you use in a query expression and the iteration variable you use in the For Each statement that executes the query refer to the same type of elements, you should give them the same name for clarity. Otherwise, you should give them different names to indicate the type of elements they refer to.
- The From clause is the only clause that's required in a query expression. In most cases, though, you'll include additional clauses in your query expressions. In that case, the From clause must be the first clause in the expression.

Figure 23-3 How to identify the data source for a query

the same names for these variables. In fact, when you code more sophisticated query expressions, you'll want to use different variable names to indicate the difference between the elements they refer to. That'll make more sense when you see the Select clause later in this chapter.

How to filter the results of a query

To filter the results of a query, you use the Where clause shown in figure 23-4. On this clause, you specify a condition that an element must meet to be returned by the query. The condition is coded as a Boolean expression like the ones you learned about in chapter 5. The two examples in this figure illustrate how this works.

The Where clause in the first example specifies that for an element to be returned from the salesTotals array, its value must be greater than 2000. Notice here that the iteration variable that's declared by the From clause is used in the Where clause to refer to the elements that are returned by the query. Then, the code that executes the query adds the returned values to a string, and the string is then displayed in a message box. If you compare the values that are listed in this message box to the values in the array shown in figure 23-3, you'll see that the value that is less than 2000 has been omitted.

The second example is similar, but it uses the generic list of invoices. Here, the Where clause indicates that only those invoices with invoice totals greater than 150 should be returned by the query. Notice again that the iteration variable that's declared by the From clause is used to refer to the elements that are returned by the query. This time, though, because each element is an Invoice object, the condition on the Where clause can refer to a member of that object.

The syntax of the Where clause

```
Where condition
```

An example that filters the salesTotals array

A query expression that returns only sales greater than $2000

```
Dim salesList = From sales In salesTotals
                Where sales > 2000
```

Code that executes the query

```
Dim salesDisplay As String = ""
For Each sales In salesList
    salesDisplay &= FormatCurrency(sales) & vbTab & vbTab & vbCrLf
Next
MessageBox.Show(salesDisplay, "Sales Over $2000")
```

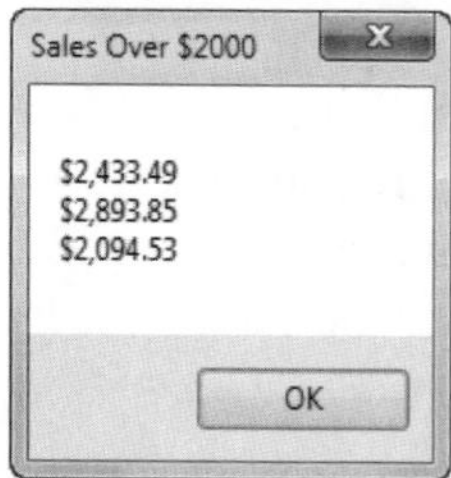

An example that filters the generic list of invoices

A query expression that returns invoices with totals over $150

```
Dim invoices = From invoice In invoiceList
               Where invoice.InvoiceTotal > 150
```

Code that executes the query

```
Dim invoiceDisplay As String = ""
For Each invoice In invoices
    invoiceDisplay &= FormatCurrency(invoice.InvoiceTotal) &
        vbTab & vbTab & vbCrLf
Next
MessageBox.Show(invoiceDisplay, "Invoices Over $150")
```

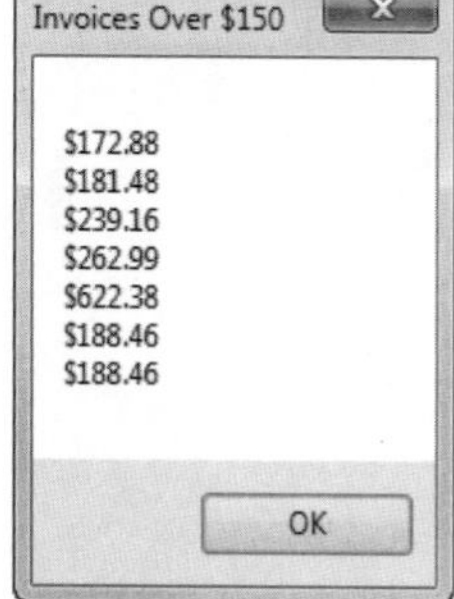

Description

- The Where clause lets you filter the data in a data source by specifying a condition that the elements of the data source must meet to be returned by the query.
- The condition is coded as a Boolean expression that can contain one or more relational and logical operators.

Figure 23-4 How to filter the results of a query

How to sort the results of a query

If you want the results of a query to be returned in a particular sequence, you can include the Order By clause in the query expression. The syntax of this clause is shown at the top of figure 23-5. This syntax indicates that you can sort by one or more expressions in either ascending or descending sequence.

To understand how this works, the first example in this figure shows how you might sort the salesTotals array. Here, the query expression includes an Order By clause that sorts the elements in this array in ascending sequence (the default). To do that, it names the iteration variable that is declared by the From clause. If you compare the results of this query with the results shown in the previous figure, you'll see how the sequence has changed.

The second example shows how you can sort query results by two expressions. In this case, the query will return invoices from the generic invoice list in descending invoice total sequence within customer ID sequence. If you look at the results of this query, you can see that the customer IDs are in ascending sequence. You can also see that the second and third invoices are for the same customer, and the invoice with the largest total is listed first.

The syntax of the Order By clause

```
Order By expression1 [Ascending|Descending]
       [, expression2 [Ascending|Descending]]...
```

An example that sorts the salesTotals array

A query expression that sorts the sales in ascending sequence

```
Dim salesList = From sales In salesTotals
                Where sales > 2000
                Order By sales
```

Code that executes the query

```
Dim salesDisplay As String = ""
For Each sales In salesList
    salesDisplay &= FormatCurrency(sales) & vbTab & vbTab & vbTab & vbCrLf
Next
MessageBox.Show(salesDisplay, "Sorted Sales Over $2000")
```

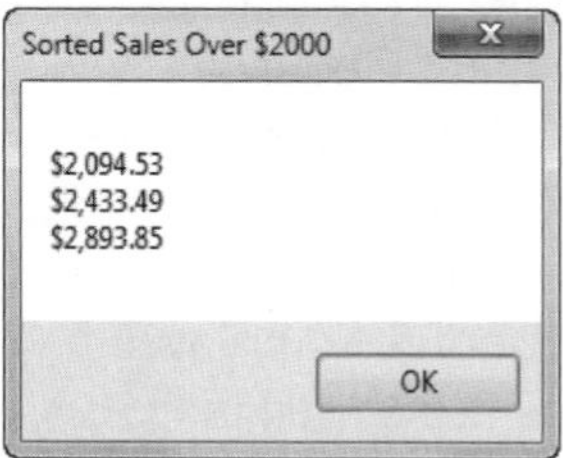

An example that sorts the generic list of invoices

A query expression that sorts the invoices by customer ID and invoice total

```
Dim invoices = From invoice In invoiceList
               Where invoice.InvoiceTotal > 150
               Order By invoice.CustomerID, invoice.InvoiceTotal Descending
```

Code that executes the query

```
Dim invoiceDisplay As String = "Cust ID" & vbTab & "Invoice amount" & vbCrLf
For Each invoice In invoices
    invoiceDisplay &= invoice.CustomerID & vbTab &
                      FormatCurrency(invoice.InvoiceTotal) & vbCrLf
Next
MessageBox.Show(invoiceDisplay, "Sorted Invoices Over $150")
```

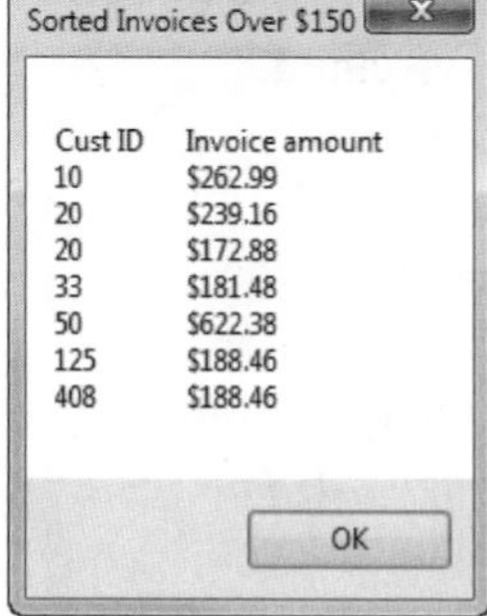

Description

- The Order By clause lets you specify how the results of the query are sorted. You can specify one or more expressions on this clause.

Figure 23-5 How to sort the results of a query

How to select fields from a query

So far, the queries you've seen in this chapter have returned entire elements of a data source. But you can also return selected fields of the elements. To do that, you use the Select clause shown in figure 23-6. This clause lets you identify one or more fields to be included in the query results. A query that returns something other than entire source elements is called a *projection*.

To illustrate how this works, the first example in this figure uses a sorted list named employeeSales. The keys for this list are employee names, and the values are sales totals. You can see the definition of this list and the data it contains at the beginning of this example.

The query expression that uses this list includes the From, Where, and Order By clauses. The Where clause indicates that only those elements with values (sales totals) greater than 2000 should be returned, and the Order By clause indicates that the returned elements should be sorted by the values in descending sequence. In addition, this query expression includes a Select clause. This clause indicates that only the key field (the employee name) should be returned.

The For Each statement that executes this query works like the others you've seen in this chapter. It creates a string that includes a list of the employee names. Notice, however, that the name of the iteration variable that's used in this statement is different from the name of the iteration variable used in the query expression. That's because the variable in the query expression refers to an element in the sorted list, but the variable in the For Each statement refers only to the employee names returned from the list by the query.

The second example in this figure shows another way to code the query you saw in the previous figure that retrieves data from the list of invoices. The only difference here is that a Select clause is included. This clause indicates that entire Invoice objects should be returned by the query. Although this clause isn't required when you want to return entire elements from the data source, it's often included for completeness.

The third example shows a query expression that returns selected fields from the Invoice objects. Specifically, it returns the CustomerID and InvoiceTotal fields. If you again look back at the example in the previous figure, you'll see that these are the only two fields that are used when the query is executed. Because of that, these are the only two fields that need to be retrieved.

Because this query returns selected fields, it's a projection just like the query in the first example. However, this query differs from the query in the first example because it returns more than one field. When a query returns a single field, the type of the query variable can be determined by the type of that field. When a query returns more than one field, however, an *anonymous type* is returned. This type is defined with properties that are based on the selected fields. Note that an anonymous type doesn't have a usable name, so you can't refer to it from anywhere in your code.

The basic syntax of the Select clause

```
Select columnExpression1 [, columnExpression2]...
```

An example that selects key values from a sorted list

The employee sales sorted list

```
Dim employeeSales As New SortedList(Of String, Decimal)
employeeSales.Add("Anderson", 1286.45D)
employeeSales.Add("Menendez", 2433.49D)
employeeSales.Add("Thompson", 2893.85D)
employeeSales.Add("Wilkinson", 2094.53D)
```

A query expression that selects the employee names from the list

```
Dim employeeList = From sales In employeeSales
       Where sales.Value > 2000
       Order By sales.Value Descending
       Select sales.Key
```

Code that executes the query

```
Dim employeeDisplay As String = ""
For Each employee In employeeList
    employeeDisplay &= employee & vbTab & vbTab & vbTab & vbCrLf
Next
MessageBox.Show(employeeDisplay, "Sorted Employees With Sales Over $2000")
```

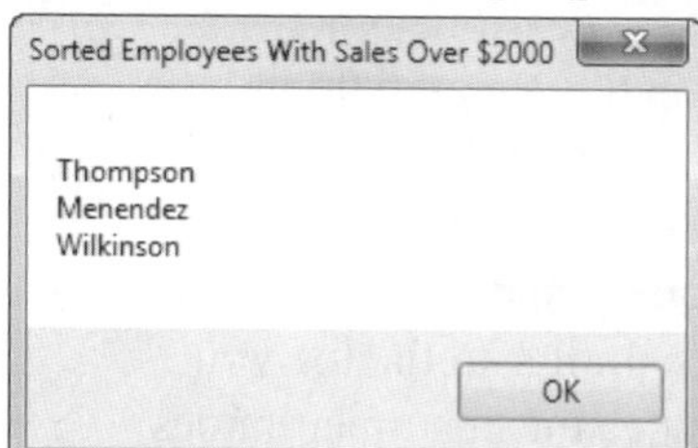

A query expression that selects Invoice objects from the list of invoices

```
Dim invoices = From invoice In invoiceList
               Where invoice.InvoiceTotal > 150
               Order By invoice.CustomerID, invoice.InvoiceTotal Descending
               Select invoice
```

A query expression that creates an anonymous type

```
Dim invoices = From invoice In invoiceList
               Where invoice.InvoiceTotal > 150
               Order By invoice.CustomerID, invoice.InvoiceTotal Descending
               Select invoice.CustomerID, invoice.InvoiceTotal
```

Description

- The Select clause indicates the data you want to return from each element of the query results.
- A query that returns anything other than entire source elements is called a *projection*. The first and third examples above illustrate projections.
- If a projection returns two or more fields, an *anonymous type* that contains those fields as its properties is created. This is illustrated by the third example above.

Figure 23-6 How to select fields from a query

How to join data from two or more data sources

Figure 23-7 shows how you can include data from two or more data sources in a query. To do that, you typically use the Join clause shown at the top of this figure. To start, this clause declares an iteration variable and names a data source just like the From clause does. Then, it indicates how the two data sources are related.

To illustrate, the first example in this figure joins data from the list of Invoice objects you've seen in the previous figures with a list of Customer objects. You can see the definition of the Customer class at the beginning of this example, along with the statements that declare and load the two lists. Like the invoice list, the customer list is loaded by calling a method of a database class.

The query expression that follows joins the data in these two lists. To do that, it names the invoice list on the From clause, and it names the customer list on the Join clause. Then, the On condition indicates that only customers in the customer list with customer IDs that match customer IDs in the invoice list should be included in the results.

Because both the invoice and customer lists are included as data sources in this query expression, the rest of the query can refer to fields in either data source. For example, the Order By clause in this query expression sorts the results by the InvoiceTotal field in the invoice list within the Name field in the customer list. Similarly, the Select clause selects the Name field from the customer list and the InvoiceTotal field from the invoice list.

The remaining code in this example executes the query and creates a list that includes the customer names and invoice totals. This is similar to the list you saw in figure 23-5. Because the list in figure 23-7 includes the customer names instead of the customer IDs, however, it provides more useful information.

You can also join data without using the Join clause. To do that, you list the data sources in the From clause, as shown in the second example in this figure. Then, you code the condition that indicates how the two data sources are related on the Where clause. For instance, the query expression in this example names both the invoice and customer lists on the From clause, and it indicates that the CustomerID fields in the two lists must be equal on the Where clause. The result of this query is the same as the result of the first query in this figure.

Although this figure only shows how to join data from two data sources, you can extend this syntax to join data from additional data sources. For example, suppose you have three data sources named invoiceList, lineItemList, and productList. Then, you could join the data in these lists using code like this:

```
From invoice In invoiceList
Join lineItem In lineItemList
  On invoice.InvoiceID Equals lineItem.InvoiceID
Join product In productList
  On lineItem.ProductCode Equals product.ProductCode
```

You could also perform this join by naming all three lists in the From clause and then coding both join conditions in the Where clause. In either case, you could then refer to fields from any of the three tables in the query expression.

The basic syntax of the Join clause

```
Join elementName In collectionName On keyName1 Equals keyName2
```

An example that joins data from two generic lists

The Customer class

```
Public Class Customer
    Public Property CustomerID As Integer
    Public Property Name As String
End Class
```

Code that gets the two data sources

```
Dim invoiceList As List(Of Invoice) = InvoiceDB.GetInvoices
Dim customerList As List(Of Customer) = CustomerDB.GetCustomers
```

A query expression that joins data from the two data sources

```
Dim invoices = From invoice In invoiceList
               Join customer In customerList
               On invoice.CustomerID Equals customer.CustomerID
               Where invoice.InvoiceTotal > 150
               Order By customer.Name, invoice.InvoiceTotal Descending
               Select customer.Name, invoice.InvoiceTotal
```

Code that executes the query

```
Dim invoiceDisplay As String = "Customer Name" & vbTab & vbTab &
                               "Invoice amount" & vbCrLf
For Each invoice In invoices
    invoiceDisplay &= invoice.Name & vbTab & vbTab &
                      FormatCurrency(invoice.InvoiceTotal) & vbCrLf
Next
MessageBox.Show(invoiceDisplay, "Joined Customer and Invoice Data")
```

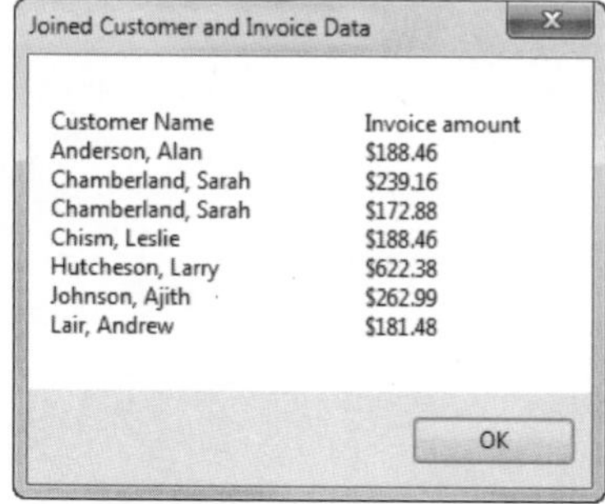

Another way to join the data in the two data sources

```
Dim invoices = From invoice In invoiceList, customer In customerList
               Where invoice.CustomerID = customer.CustomerID
                 And invoice.InvoiceTotal > 150
               Order By customer.Name, invoice.InvoiceTotal Descending
               Select customer.Name, invoice.InvoiceTotal
```

Description

- The Join clause lets you combine data from two or more data sources based on matching key values. The query results will include only those elements that meet the condition specified by the Equals operator.
- You can also join data without using the Join clause as illustrated by the second example above.

Figure 23-7 How to join data from two or more data sources

A Customer Invoice application that uses generic lists

The next two topics of this chapter present a simple application that uses a query to display customer and invoice information on a form. This will help you see how you can use a query from within a Visual Basic application.

The user interface

Figure 23-8 shows the user interface for the Customer Invoice application. As you can see, this interface consists of a single form that lists invoices by customer. This list is sorted by invoice total in descending sequence within customer name.

The list in this form is displayed in a ListView control. If you aren't familiar with this control, you may want to refer to Visual Studio help to find out how it works. For the purposes of this application, though, you just need to set the View property of this control to Details, and you need to define the column headings as described in this figure. In addition, you need to know how to load data into the control as shown in the next figure.

The Customer Invoice form

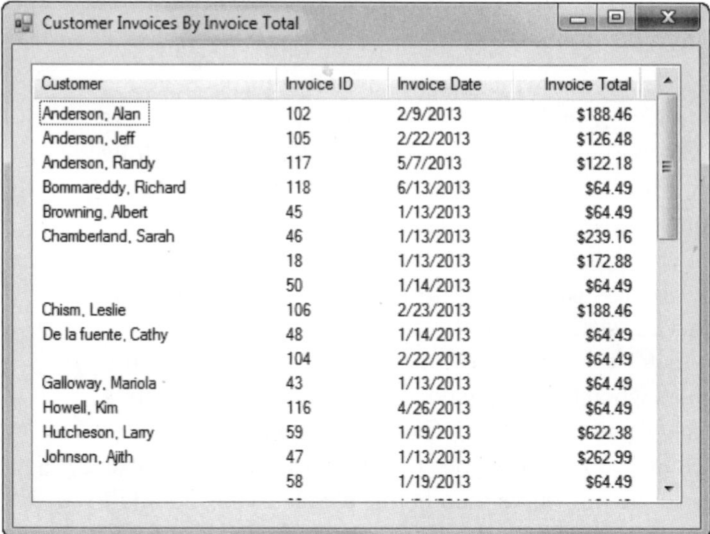

Description

- The Customer Invoice form uses a ListView control to display a list of invoices for each customer. The list is sorted by invoice total in descending sequence within customer name.
- To make this work, the View property of the ListView control is set to Details, which causes the data items to be displayed in columns. In addition, the column headers for the control were added using the ColumnHeader Collection Editor. To display this editor, you can select Edit Columns from the smart tag menu for the control. Then, you can set the Text, TextAlign, and Width properties for each column as necessary.

Figure 23-8 The user interface for the Customer Invoice application

The code for the form

Figure 23-9 shows the code for the Customer Invoice form. To start, you should know that the Customer and Invoice classes used by this code are the same as the classes shown earlier in this chapter, so I won't repeat them here. I also won't present the database classes that contain the methods for getting the customer and invoice data. That's because it doesn't matter where these methods get the data from or how they work. The only thing that matters is that the InvoiceDB class contains a method named GetInvoices that returns a List(Of Invoice) object, and the CustomerDB class contains a method named GetCustomers that returns a List(Of Customer) object.

All of the code for this form is placed within the Load event handler for the form so the list is displayed when the form is loaded. To start, this code uses the methods of the InvoiceDB and CustomerDB classes to load the invoice and customer lists. Then, the next statement defines the query expression. Because this expression is similar to others you've seen in this chapter, you shouldn't have any trouble understanding how it works. So I'll just summarize it for you.

First, notice that the query expression joins data from the invoice and customer lists. That's necessary because the customer name will be displayed on the form along with the invoice information. Second, notice that the query expression doesn't include a Where clause. Because of that, all of the invoices will be included in the results. Third, the results are sorted by invoice total within customer name so the invoices can be displayed as shown in the previous figure. And fourth, only the fields that are required by the form are included in the results.

To load data into the ListView control, this code uses a For Each statement that loops through the query results. But first, this code initializes two variables. The first one, customerName, will store the name of the current customer. This variable will be used to determine if the customer name is displayed for an invoice. The second variable, i, will be used as an index for the items that are added to the ListView control.

For each element in the query results, the For Each loop starts by checking if the Name field is equal to the customerName variable. If not, the Name field is added to the Items collection of the ListView control, which causes the name to be displayed in the first column of the control. In addition, the customerName variable is set to the Name field so the next element will be processed correctly. On the other hand, if the Name field and the customerName variable are equal, an empty string is added to the Items collection of the ListView control so the name isn't repeated.

The next three statements add the InvoiceID, InvoiceDate, and InvoiceTotal fields as subitems of the item that was just added. This causes these values to be displayed in the columns following the customer name column. Notice that these statements refer to the item by its index. Then, the last statement in the loop increments the index variable.

The code for the Customer Invoice form

```
Public Class Form1

    Private Sub Form1_Load(sender As Object,
            e As EventArgs) Handles MyBase.Load

        Dim invoiceList As List(Of Invoice) = InvoiceDB.GetInvoices
        Dim customerList As List(Of Customer) = CustomerDB.GetCustomers

        Dim invoices =
            From invoice In invoiceList Join customer In customerList
              On invoice.CustomerID Equals customer.CustomerID
            Order By customer.Name, invoice.InvoiceTotal Descending
            Select customer.Name, invoice.InvoiceID, invoice.InvoiceDate,
                   invoice.InvoiceTotal

        Dim customerName As String = ""
        Dim i As Integer = 0
        For Each invoice In invoices
            If invoice.Name <> customerName Then
                lvInvoices.Items.Add(invoice.Name)
                customerName = invoice.Name
            Else
                lvInvoices.Items.Add("")
            End If
            lvInvoices.Items(i).SubItems.Add(invoice.InvoiceID.ToString)
            lvInvoices.Items(i).SubItems.Add(
                CDate(invoice.InvoiceDate).ToShortDateString)
            lvInvoices.Items(i).SubItems.Add(
                FormatCurrency(invoice.InvoiceTotal))
            i += 1
        Next
    End Sub

End Class
```

Description

- The LINQ query used by this application makes it easy to include data from two generic lists. Without LINQ, you'd have to code your own procedure to get the customer name from the customer list.
- The LINQ query used by this application also makes it easy to sort the results based on two fields. Although you could sort a list by a single field in ascending sequence by implementing the IComparable() interface in the class that defines the objects in the list, it would be much more difficult to sort by two fields in one or more lists.

Notes

- The code for the Invoice and Customer classes is the same as shown earlier in this chapter.
- The invoice and customer data for this application is stored in text files. However, it could have been stored in any other type of data source, such as a binary file, an XML file, or a database.

Figure 23-9 The code for the Customer Invoice form that uses generic lists

A Customer Invoice application that uses a typed dataset

Now that you've seen an application that uses LINQ to query generic lists, you might want to compare this application to an application that uses LINQ to query a different type of data source. In the next two topics, then, you'll see an application that uses LINQ to query a typed dataset. If you aren't familiar with typed datasets, you might want to refer to chapter 14 to see how they work.

By the way, the user interface for the application presented here is identical to the interface shown in figure 23-8. So I won't show it again here.

The dataset schema

Figure 23-10 presents the dataset schema for the Customer Invoice application. As you can see, the dataset that this schema defines includes two tables: Customers and Invoices. In addition, the table adapter for each table contains a single query named Fill that can be used to load data into the dataset.

Although you can't tell from this figure, the Fill queries retrieve all the rows and columns from the Customers and Invoices tables in the MMABooks database (see figure 13-6 in chapter 13). To make this application more efficient, you could retrieve just the data it needs. In most cases, though, an application will perform more than just one function.

For example, an order entry application might let you list, select, add, and modify customers, list and add invoices, and so on. An application like that would need to include the data necessary to perform all these functions. So if you think of the function that the Customer Invoice application performs as just one part of a larger application, you can begin to see the power LINQ gives you for working with the data in a dataset.

The dataset schema

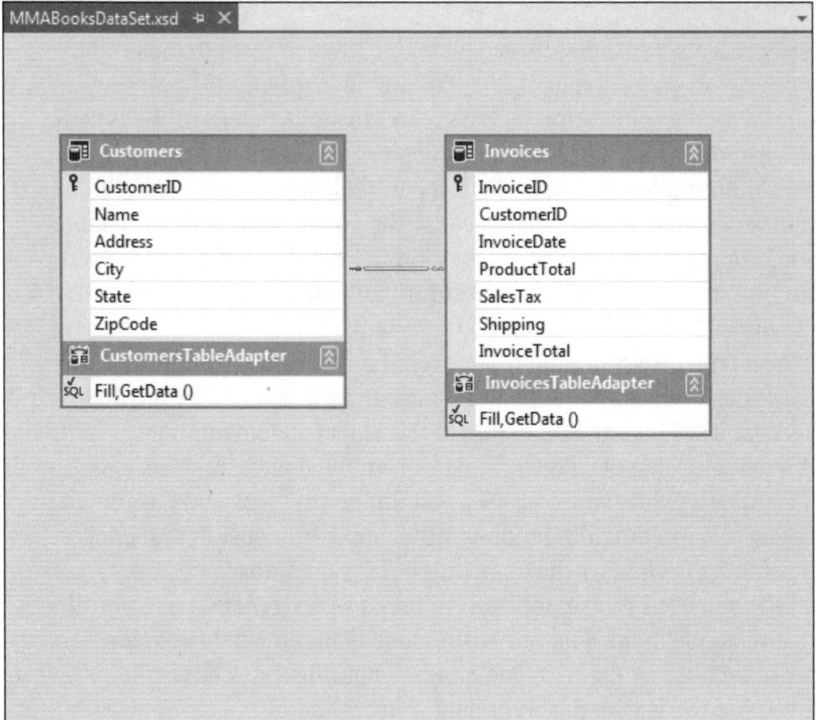

Description

- The dataset for this application includes all the columns from the Customers and Invoices tables in the MMABooks database.
- Because the Customer Invoice application doesn't use all the columns in these tables, the data source could have been defined so it includes only the required columns. It could also have been defined so the data is joined into a single table. However, this would give an application that performed additional functions less flexibility.
- The dataset used by this application was generated using the Data Source Configuration Wizard. For information on this wizard, please see chapter 14.

Figure 23-10 The dataset schema for the Customer Invoice application

The code for the form

Figure 23-11 presents the code for the Customer Invoice form that uses the typed dataset you saw in the previous figure. Unlike the applications you saw in chapters 14 and 15, this application uses code to create instances of the typed dataset and the Customers and Invoices table adapters that were generated by the Data Source Configuration Wizard. The three module-level variables used by this form store these instances. Note that because the classes that define the table adapters are stored in a separate namespace within the file that defines the typed dataset class, an Imports statement is included for that namespace. That makes it easier to refer to the table adapters in the variable declarations.

The first two statements within the Load event handler load data into the Invoices and Customers tables. To do that, they use the Fill method of the table adapters for these tables. This method executes the Select statement that's associated with the table adapter to retrieve data from the database.

After that, the query expression joins the data in the Invoices and Customers tables, sorts it by invoice total in descending sequence within customer name, and selects the columns needed by the application. If you compare this query expression with the one used by the application that queries generic lists, you'll see that they're almost identical. The only difference is that the data sources in this query expression name the two data tables. That illustrates how similar query expressions that work with different data sources can be.

* * *

Now that you've seen two applications that use LINQ with two types of data sources, you might want to consider how you would accomplish the same thing without using LINQ. If you do, I think you'll see that LINQ makes it quick and easy to select the data you need.

To join data from two generic lists without using LINQ, for example, you could include code that loops through one list looking for the object that's related to the object in the other list. And to join data from two tables of a dataset, you could use a relationship. In contrast, to join data from any two data sources using LINQ, you can simply code a Join clause.

Similarly, to sort the data in a generic list without using LINQ, you'd have to write code to implement the sort yourself. If you just needed to sort by a single field in ascending sequence, that would be manageable. If you needed to sort by more than one field, however, or you needed to sort by a field in descending sequence, it would be much more difficult. And if you needed to sort by fields in more than one data source, it would be extremely difficult. To sort the rows in a data table by one or more columns, you could use a data view. However, you couldn't sort by columns in two or more tables. In contrast, to sort by one or more fields using LINQ, you can simply code an Order By clause.

The bottom line is that LINQ provides concise language for querying data. So you should consider using it whenever you need to select data from one or more data sources.

The code for the Customer Invoice form

```
Imports CustomerInvoices.MMABooksDataSetTableAdapters

Public Class Form1

    Dim mmaBooksDataset As New MMABooksDataSet
    Dim invoicesTableAdapter As New InvoicesTableAdapter
    Dim customersTableAdapter As New CustomersTableAdapter

    Private Sub Form1_Load(sender As Object,
            e As EventArgs) Handles MyBase.Load
        invoicesTableAdapter.Fill(mmaBooksDataset.Invoices)
        customersTableAdapter.Fill(mmaBooksDataset.Customers)

        Dim invoices =
            From invoice In mmaBooksDataset.Invoices
            Join customer In mmaBooksDataset.Customers
              On invoice.CustomerID Equals customer.CustomerID
            Order By customer.Name, invoice.InvoiceTotal Descending
            Select customer.Name, invoice.InvoiceID, invoice.InvoiceDate,
                   invoice.InvoiceTotal

        Dim customerName As String = ""
        Dim i As Integer = 0
        For Each invoice In invoices
            If invoice.Name <> customerName Then
                lvInvoices.Items.Add(invoice.Name)
                customerName = invoice.Name
            Else
                lvInvoices.Items.Add("")
            End If
            lvInvoices.Items(i).SubItems.Add(invoice.InvoiceID.ToString)
            lvInvoices.Items(i).SubItems.Add(
                CDate(invoice.InvoiceDate).ToShortDateString)
            lvInvoices.Items(i).SubItems.Add(
                FormatCurrency(invoice.InvoiceTotal))
            i += 1
        Next
    End Sub

End Class
```

Description

- The query expression for this application is almost identical to the query expression in figure 23-9 that uses generic lists. The only difference is that the two data sources are tables in the dataset.
- LINQ makes it easy to join and sort the two tables used by this application. Although you can use a data view to filter and sort the data in a single table, and you can use a data relation to get data from a related table, it would involve considerably more code. In addition, you couldn't perform a sort that's based on columns in two tables.
- This application uses code to create an instance of the typed dataset that was generated by the Data Source Configuration Wizard. It also uses code to create instances of the two table adapters that were generated by this wizard.

Figure 23-11 The code for the Customer Invoice form that uses a typed dataset

Perspective

In this chapter, you learned the basic skills for coding and executing LINQ queries in Visual Basic. With these skills, you should be able to create simple queries that work with a variety of objects. However, there's a lot more to learn about LINQ than what's presented here.

For example, there are other clauses you can code in a query expression. In addition, there are special techniques you need to learn to use LINQ with other data sources, such as untyped datasets and databases. To learn about these features, you can refer to Visual Studio help, or you can get a separate book on LINQ.

Terms

Language-Integrated Query (LINQ)
object-relational mapping
query operator
query expression
deferred execution
query variable
immediate execution
projection
anonymous type

Exercise 23-1 Create the Customer Invoice application

In this exercise, you'll develop and test the Customer Invoice application that was presented in this chapter that uses generic lists.

Design the form

1. Open the project that's in the C:\VB 2012\Chapter 23\CustomerInvoices directory. In addition to the Customer Invoice form, this project contains the business and database classes needed by the application.
2. Add a ListView control to the Customer Invoice form, and set the View property of this control to Details.
3. Use the smart tag menu for the ListView control to display the ColumnHeader Collection Editor. Then, define the column headings for this control so they appear like the last three shown in figure 23-8. (You'll add the first column later.)

Add code to display the invoice data

4. Open the Invoice and InvoiceDB classes and review the code that they contain. In particular, notice that the GetInvoices method in the InvoiceDB class gets invoices from a text file named Invoices.txt and returns them in a List(Of Invoice) object.
5. Add an event handler for the Load event of the form. Then, use the GetInvoices method to get the list of invoices, and store this list in a variable.

6. Define a query expression that returns all the invoices from the invoice list and sorts them by invoice total in descending sequence. Include a Select clause in this query expression that selects entire invoices.
7. Use a For Each statement to execute the query and load the results into the ListView control.
8. Run the application to see how it works. Make any necessary corrections, and then end the application.
9. Modify the Select clause in the query expression so the query returns only the fields needed by the form. Then, run the application again to be sure it still works.

Enhance the application to include customer information

10. Open the Customer and CustomerDB classes and review the code they contain. Note that the GetCustomers method in the CustomerDB class gets customers from a text file named CustomersX23.txt and returns them in a List(Of Customer) object.
11. Add another column at the beginning of the ListView control for displaying the customer name. Then, add a statement to the Load event handler of the form that uses the GetCustomers method of the CustomerDB class to get a list of customers, and store the list in a variable.
12. Modify the query expression so it joins the data in the customer list with the data in the invoice list, so it sorts the results by invoice total within customer name, and so only the fields that are needed by the form are returned by the query.
13. Modify the For Each statement so it adds the customer name to the ListView control, but don't worry about not repeating the customer name.
14. Run the application to make sure it works correctly. When you're done, close the solution.

Section 6

Enhancement, deployment, and Windows 8

This section contains three chapters that present some additional skills you may need as you develop Windows applications in Visual Basic. To start, chapter 24 shows you how to enhance a Windows Forms application by using a multi-document interface and by adding features like menus, toolbars, and help to your forms. Then, chapter 25 shows you three ways to deploy a Windows Forms application.

Finally, chapter 26 introduces you to Windows 8 applications and presents the basic concepts and skills for developing Windows Store apps. Although you'll need to learn a lot more before you can start developing your own Windows Store apps, this chapter should give you a good idea of what these applications look like and how they work. Then, you can decide for yourself if you want to learn more.

24

How to enhance the user interface

In this chapter, you'll learn how to modify your applications so they can take advantage of two types of user interfaces. In addition, you'll learn how to add menus, toolbars, status bars, and help to your forms. And you'll learn how to use modules in your applications. When you're done with this chapter, you should be able to create a professional user interface that's easy and intuitive to use.

Two types of user interfaces

Figure 24-1 shows two versions of the Financial Calculations application that will be presented in this chapter. These applications use the Future Value form that you learned about earlier in this book, and they use a Depreciation form that's new to this chapter. In addition, both of these applications include a third form that provides a way for the user to access the other two forms.

A single-document interface (SDI)

The first version of the Financial Calculations application uses a *single-document interface* (*SDI*). In an SDI application, each form runs in its own application window, and this window is usually shown in the Windows taskbar. Then, if you're using a version of Windows before Windows 7, you can click the buttons in the taskbar to switch between the open forms.

If you're using Windows 7 or later, the buttons in the taskbar are grouped by application. Then, you can point to the button for an application to display thumbnails for all the open windows for that application. When I pointed to the button for the Financial Calculations application, for example, the seven thumbnails in this figure were displayed. Five of these thumbnails represent the windows that are displayed on the desktop, and the other two represent windows that have been minimized. You can click on any of these thumbnails to switch to that form.

When you use this interface, each form can have its own menus and toolbars. In addition, you can include a main form called a *startup form* that provides access to the other forms of the application. In this figure, for example, the startup form includes two buttons that the user can click to display the Future Value and Depreciation forms.

A multiple-document interface (MDI)

The second version of this application uses a *multiple-document interface* (*MDI*). In an MDI application, a container form called a *parent form* contains one or more *child forms*. Then, the menus and toolbars on the parent form contain the commands that let you open and view the child forms. In addition, you can include a status bar on the parent form that displays a variety of information, including information about the child forms. The main advantage of a multiple-document interface is that the parent form can make it easier to organize and manage multiple instances of the child forms.

Single-document interface (SDI)

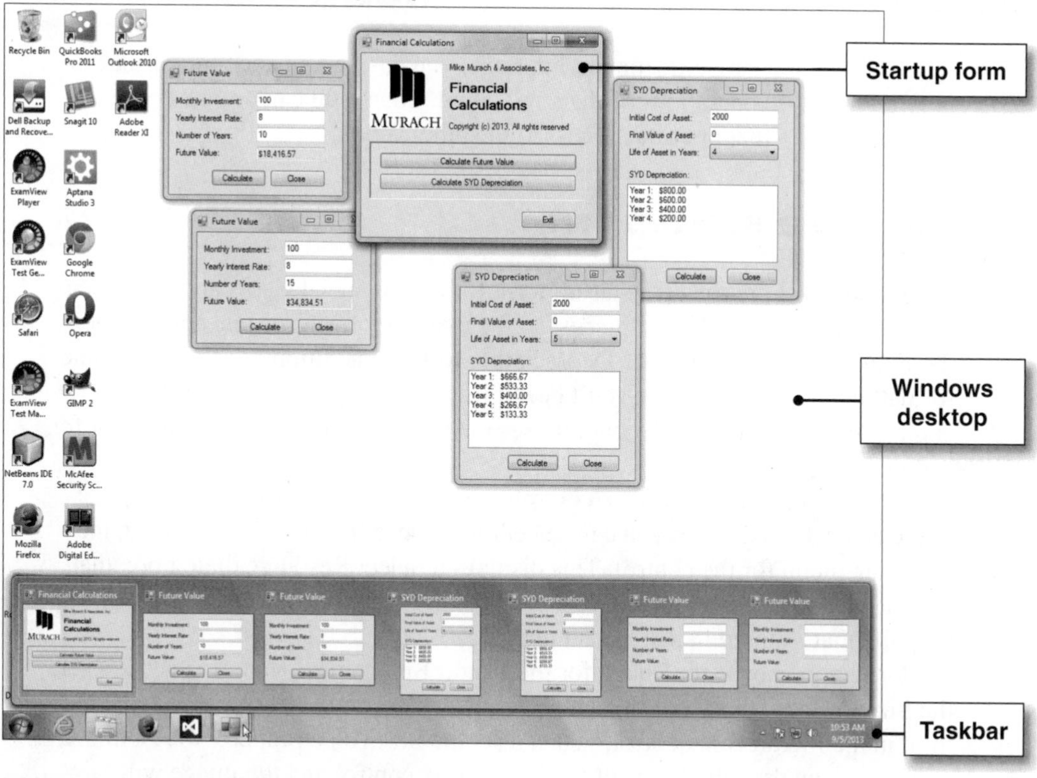

Multiple-document interface (MDI)

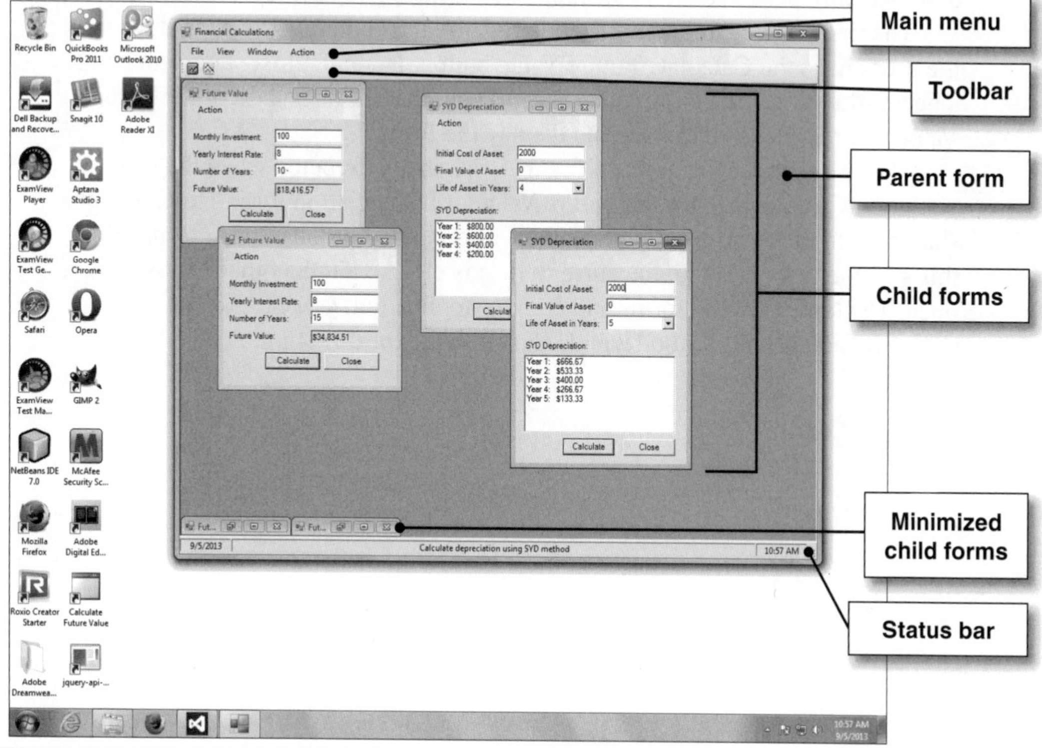

Figure 24-1 Single-document and multiple-document interfaces

How to develop SDI applications

To develop a single-document interface, you design and code the forms that provide the basic operations of the application. Then, you can design and code the startup form that provides access to the other forms.

How to use a startup form

Figure 24-2 presents the startup form for the Financial Calculations application. This form gives the user access to the two other forms of this application: the Future Value form and the Depreciation form. In addition, it illustrates some formatting techniques that haven't been presented yet. First, it uses a PictureBox control to include a logo. Second, it uses the Font property to change the font for some of the labels.

After you add a PictureBox control to a form, you need to add an image to the control. To do that, you can select the Choose Image command from the smart tag menu for the control. This displays a Select Resource dialog box that you can use to select an image. In this figure, for example, the company logo is a bmp file that's stored in the project directory.

Once you choose the image for the PictureBox control, you may need to set the SizeMode property so you can size it. If, for example, the image is too large to fit in the PictureBox control, you can set the SizeMode property to Zoom. Then, you can drag the edges of the PictureBox control and the image will automatically be resized to fit within the control.

The first code example in this figure shows the code that's executed when the user clicks the Calculate Future Value button. Here, the first statement creates a new instance of the Future Value form. Then, the Show method of the Future Value form is executed to load and display the form.

The second code example shows the code that's executed when the user clicks the Close button for the Future Value or Depreciation form. Here, the lone statement in the event handler calls the Close method of the current form. When this statement is executed, the current form is closed, but the other forms remain open. To close all of the forms and end the application, you can execute the Close method of the startup form as shown in the third example.

A startup form for the Financial Calculations application

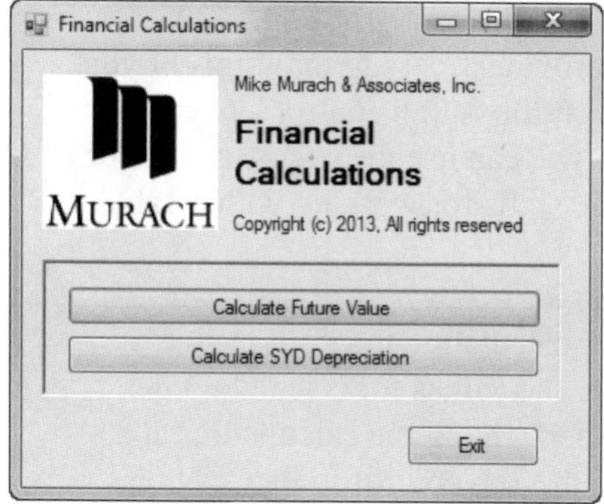

Code that displays a new instance of a form

```
Private Sub btnFutureValue_Click(sender As Object,
        e As EventArgs) Handles btnFutureValue.Click
    Dim futureValueForm As New frmFutureValue()
    futureValueForm.Show()
End Sub
```

Code that closes the current instance of a form

```
Private Sub btnClose_Click(sender As Object,
        e As EventArgs) Handles btnClose.Click
    Me.Close()
End Sub
```

Code in a startup form that closes all forms and ends the application

```
Private Sub btnExit_Click(sender As Object,
        e As EventArgs) Handles btnExit.Click
    Me.Close()
End Sub
```

Description

- An SDI application that consists of more than one form can begin with a *startup form* that directs the user to the other forms of the application.
- You can use the Font property of a control to change the font for the Text property of the control.
- You can use a PictureBox control to display an image on a form. To do that, you add the control to the form and select the Choose Image command from the control's smart tag menu. This opens a Select Resource dialog box that lets you select the file for the image. In addition, you may need to set the SizeMode property of the PictureBox control to Zoom so you can size the image by dragging the edges of the control.
- A form that's displayed from a startup form should contain a Close button rather than an Exit button to indicate that the button will close the form and not exit the application and close all open forms.

Figure 24-2 How to use a startup form

How to use a Tab control

One alternative to using a startup form to provide access to the forms of your application is to use a single form with a Tab control. A Tab control lets you create *tabs* that provide access to *pages*. Then, you can use the pages in place of individual forms. Figure 24-3 presents the basic skills for working with a Tab control.

As you can see, the form in this figure contains a Tab control with two pages. The first tab lets you enter the values for calculating the future value of an investment, and the second tab lets you enter the values for calculating the depreciation of an asset. Then, the buttons for performing the calculations and exiting from the application are placed outside the Tab control so they can be used regardless of which tab is displayed. Together, the Tab control and the two buttons provide functionality that's similar to the forms in figure 24-1.

When you work with a Tab control, you can use the SelectedIndex property to determine which tab is selected. For instance, when the user clicks the Calculate button, the first code example uses an If statement that checks this property. Then, it calls the appropriate procedure depending on which tab is selected.

The event you'll use most with a Tab control is the SelectedIndexChanged event. This event occurs when the SelectedIndex property of the control changes, which typically happens when a user clicks on another tab. For example, the event handler in the second example in this figure moves the focus to the appropriate control on a tab when that tab becomes the current tab. This event handler uses the SelectedIndex property to determine which tab is current.

A form that uses a Tab control with two tabs

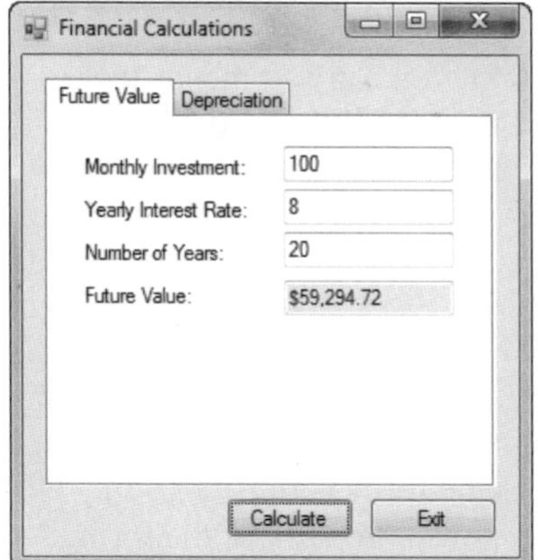

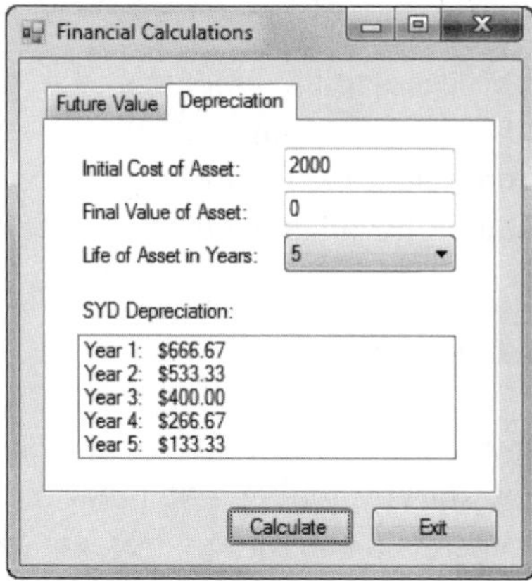

Code that uses the SelectedIndex property of the Tab control

```
Private Sub btnCalculate_Click(sender As Object,
        e As EventArgs) Handles btnCalculate.Click
    If tabCalculations.SelectedIndex = 0 Then
        Me.DisplayFutureValue()
    ElseIf tabCalculations.SelectedIndex = 1 Then
        Me.DisplayDepreciation()
    End If
End Sub
```

Code that uses the SelectedIndexChanged event of the Tab control

```
Private Sub tabCalculations_SelectedIndexChanged(
        sender As Object, e As EventArgs) _
        Handles tabCalculations.SelectedIndexChanged
    If tabCalculations.SelectedIndex = 0 Then
        txtMonthlyInvestment.Select()
    ElseIf tabCalculations.SelectedIndex = 1 Then
        txtInitialCost.Select()
    End If
End Sub
```

Description

- Each Tab control can contain two or more *tabs*. Each tab in a Tab control contains a *page* where you add the controls for the tab.
- To add a tab, use the Add Tab command in the smart tag menu for the Tab control. To delete the current tab, use the Remove Tab command.
- To set the text that's displayed in a tab, select the page and set the Text property.
- You can also add and remove tabs, reorder tabs, and work with tab properties by selecting the Tab control and using the TabPages property to display the TabPage Collection Editor.
- You can use the SelectedIndex property of the Tab control to determine which tab is currently selected.
- The SelectedIndexChanged event occurs when another tab is selected.

Figure 24-3 How to use a Tab control

How to add menus to a form

To provide access to the functions of an application, you can add menus to a form. Menus sometimes duplicate the functionality that's already available from the buttons and other controls of a form, but they can also provide access to functions that aren't available anywhere else.

How to create menus

Visual Studio provides an easy-to-use facility for adding *menus* to a form. To do that, you start by adding a MenuStrip control to the form as illustrated in figure 24-4. When you add this control, the MainMenuStrip property of the form is automatically set to the name of that control but the control isn't displayed on the form. Instead, it's displayed in the Component Designer tray at the bottom of the Form Designer.

After you add the MenuStrip control to the form, the Menu Designer is displayed at the top of the form. Then, you can add menus and *menu items* by typing the text you want to appear in the Menu Designer anywhere it says "Type Here." When you type the text for the first menu, additional areas open up below and to the right of that menu. As a result, it's easy to enter new menus, submenus, and menu items. As with other controls, you can use the ampersand character (&) to provide an access key when you enter the text for the menu item. In addition, you can create a separator bar by using a dash (-) for the menu item's text.

Once you've entered the menus and menu items for your application, you'll want to set the Name property of each menu item so you can refer to it from the code for the form. To do that, select the menu that contains the item. Then, select the menu item and use the Properties window to set the Name property.

When setting the names for each menu item, it's a common coding convention to use mnu as the prefix for each name. For example, you might use mnuClear or mnuActionClear as the name for the Clear item of the Action menu. Otherwise, you can accept the default name that's assigned by the Menu Designer. For example, the default name for the Clear item of the Action menu would be ClearToolStripMenuItem.

If you need to insert a new item in a menu, you can right-click on a menu item to display a shortcut menu. Then, you can select the MenuItem command from the Insert submenu to insert a new item. Or, you can select the Separator command from the Insert submenu to insert a separator bar. In addition, the shortcut menu for a menu item provides Cut, Copy, Paste, and Delete commands.

You can also use the Items Collection Editor to work with a menu. This editor lets you add, delete, and reorder menu items and set item properties. To display this editor, right-click on the menu and select the Edit DropDownItems command from the shortcut menu.

The beginning of the menu for the Future Value form

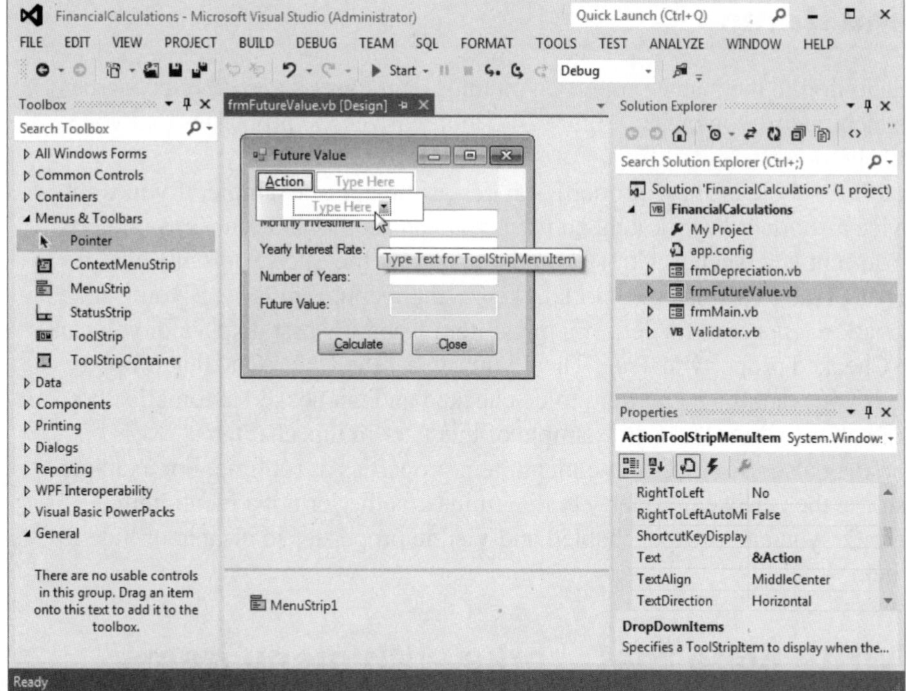

The complete Action menu

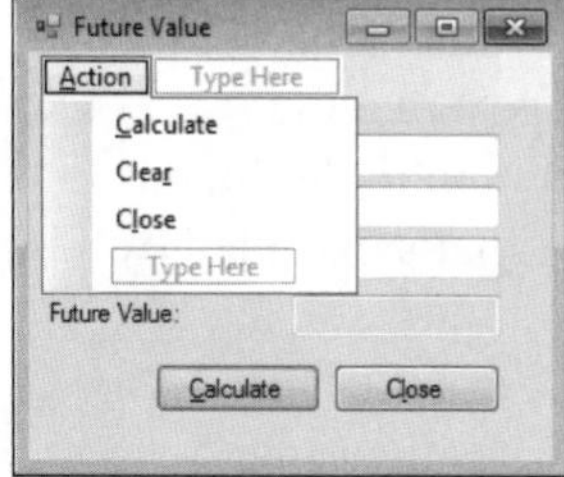

Description

- To add *menus* to a form, add a MenuStrip control to the form. This control will appear in the Component Designer tray at the bottom of the Form Designer window, and the MainMenuStrip property of the form will be set to the name of that control.
- To add items to the menu, click wherever it says "Type Here" in the Menu Designer. Then, type the text of the menu item and press the Enter key. Additional entry areas appear below and to the right of the entry.
- To edit the properties for a menu item, select the item and then use the Properties window. To insert a new item (including a separator bar), right-click on the menu item to display its shortcut menu and select a command from the Insert submenu. And to delete an item, select it and then press the Delete key.
- You can also use the Items Collection Editor to work with the items in a menu. To display this editor, right-click on the menu and select the Edit DropDownItems command.

Figure 24-4 How to create menus

How to set the properties that work with menu items

In addition to the Name property, you may want to set some other properties for the menu items you create. Figure 24-5 summarizes the properties that you're most likely to use.

You'll set some of these properties at design-time. For example, if you want to provide a shortcut key for a menu item, you can set the ShortcutKeys property to the shortcut key (such as Ctrl+C), and you can set the ShowShortcutKeys property to True to display the shortcut key in the menu. Similarly, if you want a check mark to appear to the left of a menu item when it's first displayed, you can set the Checked property to True. Then, you can set the CheckOnClick property to True if you want the menu item to be checked and unchecked automatically when it's clicked. You'll see an example of this later in this chapter.

You may also use some of the menu item properties at runtime. For example, you can use the Checked property to determine whether or not a menu item is checked. Or, you can use the Enabled and Visible properties to disable or hide a menu item.

How to write code that works with menu items

Figure 24-5 also shows some code examples for working with menu items. The first example is the event handler for the Click event of the Clear item in the Action menu. The Click event occurs when the user selects this menu item. Since this event is the default event for a menu item, you can generate the declaration for the event handler by double-clicking the menu item in the Menu Designer. Then, you can use the Code Editor to enter the code that's executed by the event handler.

The second example shows the event handler for the Click event of the Calculate item in the Action menu. Since this menu item provides the same functionality as the Calculate button, it simply calls the PerformClick method of that button. This causes the event handler for the Click event of the Calculate button to be executed.

The third example shows another way to handle the Click event of the Calculate item. Here, this event is included on the Handles clause of the event handler that handles the Click event of the Calculate button. To add this event to the Handles clause, you can display the list of events for the menu item just as you would for any other object. Then, you can set the Click event of the menu item to the event handler for the Click event of the Calculate button.

Common menu item properties

Property	Description
`Text`	The text that appears in the menu for the item. To provide an access key for a menu item, include an ampersand (&) in this property.
`Name`	The name that's used to refer to the menu item in code.
`CheckOnClick`	Determines if a menu item is automatically checked or unchecked when it's clicked.
`Checked`	Determines if a check mark appears to the left of the menu item.
`Enabled`	Determines if the menu item is available or grayed out. If a menu item is disabled or enabled, all items subordinate to it are disabled or enabled.
`Visible`	Determines if the menu item is displayed or hidden. If a menu item is hidden or displayed, all items subordinate to it are hidden or displayed.
`ShortcutKeys`	Specifies the shortcut key associated with the menu item.
`ShowShortcutKeys`	Determines if the shortcut key is displayed to the right of the menu item.

Code for the Click event of a menu item that clears four controls

```
Private Sub mnuClear_Click(sender As Object, e As EventArgs) _
        Handles mnuClear.Click
    txtMonthlyInvestment.Text = ""
    txtInterestRate.Text = ""
    txtYears.Text = ""
    txtFutureValue.Text = ""
End Sub
```

Code for the Click event of a menu item that calls another event handler

```
Private Sub mnuCalculate_Click(sender As Object, e As EventArgs) _
        Handles mnuCalculate.Click
    btnCalculate.PerformClick()
End Sub
```

Code that wires the Click event of a menu item to an existing event handler

```
Private Sub btnCalculate_Click(sender As Object, e As EventArgs) _
        Handles btnCalculate.Click, mnuCalculate.Click
    .
    .
End Sub
```

Notes

- The Click event is the default event for a menu item. You can code an event handler for this event just as you would for any other Click event.
- If a menu item executes the same code as another event handler, you can call that event handler instead of duplicating its code. You can use the PerformClick method of another button or menu item to cause its event handler to be executed. Or, you can use the Events list in the Properties window to wire the Click event to an existing event handler.

Figure 24-5 How to work with menu items

How to develop MDI applications

If the application you're developing requires multiple instances of one or more forms, you may want to use a multiple-document interface. That way, you can create a parent form that acts as a container for all of the child forms. Then, you can provide a Window menu to make it easier to display and manage the child forms.

How to create parent and child forms

Figure 24-6 shows the design of a parent form for the Financial Calculations application that provides File and Window menus to access its child forms. To create parent and child forms, you begin by adding standard Windows forms to your project. Then, to identify a form as a parent form, you set its IsMdiContainer property to True. In addition, in the code that displays a child form, you set the MdiParent property of the form to the parent form. You'll see code like this in the next figure, as well as code that uses the ActiveMdiChild property and the LayoutMdi method.

By the way, you can also create a parent form using the MDI Parent Form template in the Add New Item dialog box. When you create a form using this template, the IsMdiContainer property is set to True by default. In addition, the form includes standard menus, a toolbar, a status bar, and a ToolTip control, as well as starting code for implementing these items. Although this template provides more functionality than you'll need for most applications, you may want to experiment with it to see how it works.

An application with one parent form and two child forms

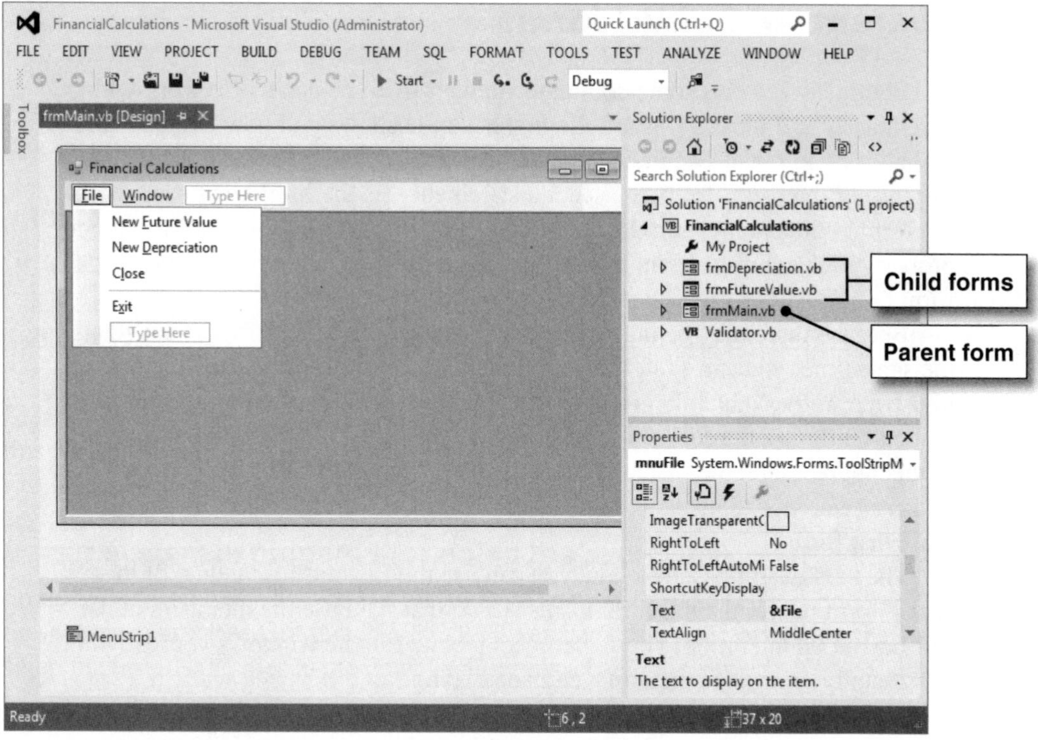

Properties and methods for a parent form

Property	Description
IsMdiContainer	At design time, you set this property to True to indicate that the form is a parent form.
ActiveMdiChild	At runtime, you can use this property to retrieve a reference to the active child form.
Method	**Description**
LayoutMdi(mdiLayout)	At runtime, you can use this method to arrange all child forms. To do that, you can specify one of the members of the MdiLayout enumeration: Cascade, TileVertical, TileHorizontal, and so on.

Typical property setting for a child form

Property	Description
MdiParent	At runtime, you can set this property to specify the parent form for a child form.

Note

- An MDI application can also include forms that aren't parent or child forms. These forms are typically modal forms like the ones that you learned about in chapter 10.

Figure 24-6 How to create parent and child forms

How to write code that works with parent and child forms

Figure 24-7 shows some coding techniques that you can use to work with parent and child forms. To start, the first example shows you how to create and display a child form. The first statement uses the New keyword to create a new instance of the form. Then, the second statement sets the MdiParent property of the form to the parent form. Here, the Me keyword is used to set the MdiParent property to the current form. Finally, the Show method is used to display the form.

Because there may be more than one instance of a child form displayed at the same time, you can't refer to an individual form by name. Instead, you need to use the ActiveMdiChild property of the parent form to refer to the child form that currently has the focus. You can see how this works in the second example in this figure. Here, the first statement uses the ActiveMdiChild property to return a reference to the active child form. Then, it uses the Close method to close that form.

The next example shows how you can use the LayoutMdi method of the parent form to arrange the child forms. To do that, you use the members of the MdiLayout enumeration. These members let you tile the windows vertically or horizontally or arrange them in a cascaded layout.

All of the code in this figure is executed in response to the Click event of a menu item, which occurs when the user selects the item. For example, the code that creates and displays a new instance of a child form is executed in response to the user selecting the New Future Value item from the File menu. The code that closes the active child form is executed in response to the user selecting the Close item from the File menu. And the code that arranges the child forms is executed in response to the user selecting the Tile Vertical item from the Window menu.

Whenever you need to display and organize the child forms of an MDI application, you can use menus in the parent form to do that. For example, it's common for a parent form to contain a File menu that lets the user display child forms, close the active child form, and exit the application, which closes all open child forms. Similarly, it's common for a parent form to contain a Window menu that lets the user cascade or tile all child forms. If you set the MdiWindowListItem property of the MenuStrip control to the name of the Window menu, this menu will also display a list of all the open child forms as shown in this figure.

You can also add menus to a child form that work directly with that form. For example, you could add a menu to a child form with a Clear menu item that clears all the text boxes on that form. Then, the menus for the active child form will be displayed to the right of the menus for the parent form. In this figure, for example, the Action menu that's displayed to the right of the Window menu is actually coded in the active child form, the Future Value form. As a result, when you run the Financial Calculations application and select a Future Value form, this Action menu is automatically appended to the parent form's menus.

An MDI application with three child forms arranged vertically

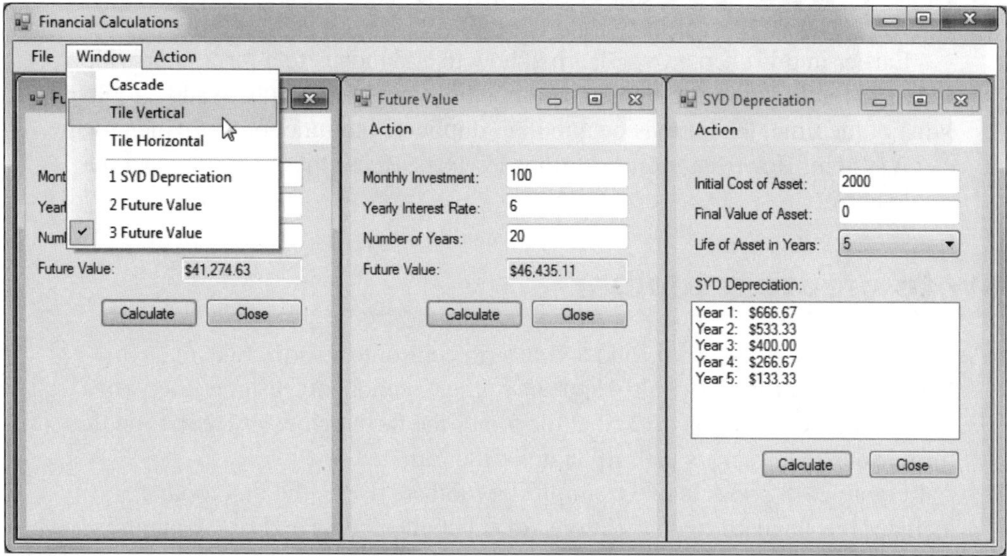

Code that creates and displays a new instance of a child form

```
Private Sub mnuNewFutureValue_Click(sender As Object,
        e As EventArgs) Handles mnuNewFutureValue.Click
    Dim futureValueForm As New frmFutureValue
    futureValueForm.MdiParent = Me
    futureValueForm.Show()
End Sub
```

Code that refers to the active child form

```
Private Sub mnuClose_Click(sender As Object,
        e As EventArgs) Handles mnuClose.Click
    Dim activeForm As Form = Me.ActiveMdiChild
    If activeForm IsNot Nothing Then
        activeForm.Close()
    End If
End Sub
```

Code that arranges the child forms vertically

```
Private Sub mnuTileVertical_Click(sender As Object,
        e As EventArgs) Handles mnuTileVertical.Click
    Me.LayoutMdi(MdiLayout.TileVertical)
End Sub
```

Description

- You can display a list of the open child forms in a menu by setting the MdiWindowListItem property of the menu strip to the name of the menu. A list like this is typically displayed in the Window menu.
- In this example, the Action menu is stored in the child form. This menu appears in the parent form when a child form that contains it is the active form.

Figure 24-7 How to write code that works with parent and child forms

How to add toolbars to a form

Earlier in this chapter, you learned how to add menus to a form to provide access to the functions of an application. Now, you'll learn how to add a toolbar. Most of the time, the buttons on a toolbar duplicate the functions provided by the menu system. However, toolbar buttons let users access these functions with a single click.

How to create a toolbar

To create a *toolbar*, you add a ToolStrip control to a form. Like the MenuStrip control, this control appears in the Component Designer tray. Then, by default, the toolbar is docked at the top of the form below any menus on the form and extends across the full width of the form.

Figure 24-8 presents two examples of toolbars. Here, the first toolbar includes the standard toolbar buttons for functions like Save, Print, Cut, and Paste. You can create a toolbar like this using the Insert Standard Items command in the toolbar's smart tag menu. The second toolbar has two custom buttons that let the user display a Future Value or Depreciation form. To add custom buttons, you can use the Items Collection Editor that's shown in this figure.

By default, each button you add to a toolbar displays a graphic image. To specify the image for the button, you can use the Image property of the button to display a dialog box that lets you select the image. In this figure, for example, the two buttons in the second toolbar use images that are stored in bmp files in the project directory. If you have experience working with computer graphics, you can create your own images. Or, you may be able to find images that you can use on the Internet.

Because it can be difficult to determine the function of a toolbar button from its image, you usually want descriptive text to be displayed when the user places the mouse pointer over the button. For example, you might want text like "Display a new Future Value form" and "Display a new Depreciation form" to be displayed for the two buttons on the second toolbar in this figure. To display text like this, called a *tool tip*, enter it for the ToolTipText property of the button.

By default, the items you add to a toolbar are displayed as standard push buttons. However, you can select other types of toolbar items from the combo box at the top of the Items Collection Editor. If, for example, you select DropDownButton from this combo box, you can create a menu that drops down from the button. With a little experimentation, you should be able to use this editor to add a variety of controls to a toolbar.

A ToolStrip control with the standard items

A ToolStrip control with two custom buttons

The Items Collection Editor for a ToolStrip control

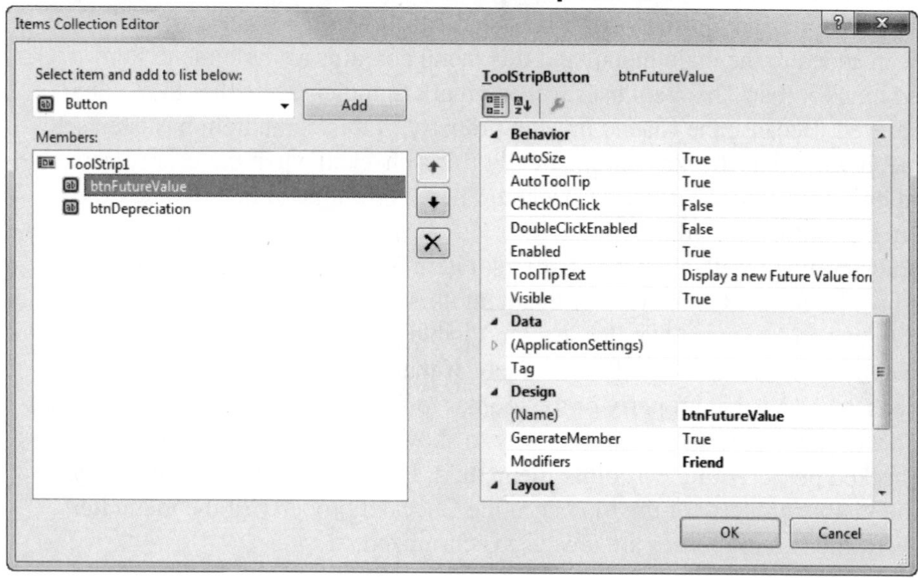

Description

- To create a *toolbar*, add a ToolStrip control to a form. By default, the toolbar is docked at the top of the form below the menus and fills the width of the form.
- To insert the standard items shown above, select the Insert Standard Items command from the toolbar's smart tag menu.
- To display the Items Collection Editor, select the Edit Items command from the toolbar's smart tag menu. You can use this editor to add controls to the toolbar and to set the properties for those controls.
- If you add a button to the toolbar, you can display an image on the button by using its Image property to display a dialog box that lets you select an image file. This dialog box works with most modern image file formats including gif, jpg, bmp, wmf, and png.
- To display text instead of an image on a button, set the DisplayStyle property of the button to Text and the Text property to the text you want displayed. You can also set the DisplayStyle property to ImageAndText to display both an image and text on the button.
- To specify the text that's displayed when the user points to a toolbar control with the mouse (called a *tool tip*), you can enter the text in the ToolTipText property of the control.
- By default, if all the controls you add to a toolbar don't fit in the allotted space, an overflow button appears at the right side of the toolbar. You can click this button to display the additional toolbar controls.

Figure 24-8 How to create a toolbar

How to write code that works with toolbars

After you create the toolbars for a form, you need to add the code that makes them work. To do that, you can code event handlers like those in figure 24-9.

The first example handles the Click event of the Future Value button on the toolbar. This event handler uses the PerformClick method of the New Future Value menu item to execute that event handler. That way, you don't have to duplicate the code that creates and displays the form.

The second example shows or hides a toolbar. In this case, a View menu has been added to the main menu, and this menu contains a single menu item named mnuToolbar. This item uses a check mark to indicate whether the toolbar is displayed. Because the CheckOnClick property of this menu item has been set to True, it will be unchecked automatically if it's checked when the user selects it, and it will be checked if it's unchecked. Then, you can use code to hide or display the toolbar accordingly.

To determine whether the Toolbar menu item is checked or unchecked, the event handler for the Click event of this item uses its Checked property. If the item is checked, the event handler sets the Visible property of the toolbar to True so the toolbar is displayed. Conversely, if the item is not checked, the event handler sets the Visible property of the toolbar to False so it's hidden.

The third example shows another way to show or hide the toolbar based on the Checked property of the Toolbar menu item. Here, the event handler simply sets the Visible property of the toolbar to the Checked property of the menu item. That way, the two properties are always synchronized.

Code for the Click event of a button on a ToolStrip

```
Private Sub btnFutureValue_Click(sender As Object,
        e As EventArgs) Handles btnFutureValue.Click
    mnuNewFutureValue.PerformClick()
End Sub
```

A View menu that shows or hides the toolbar

Code that shows or hides a toolbar depending on a menu selection

```
Private Sub mnuToolbar_Click(sender As Object,
        e As EventArgs) Handles mnuToolbar.Click
    If mnuToolbar.Checked Then
        tbMain.Visible = True
    Else
        tbMain.Visible = False
    End If
End Sub
```

Another way to show or hide the toolbar

```
Private Sub mnuToolbar_Click(sender As Object,
        e As EventArgs) Handles mnuToolbar.Click
    tbMain.Visible = mnuToolbar.Checked
End Sub
```

Description

- You use the Click event of a toolbar button to respond to the user clicking on that button.
- You can use the Checked property of a menu item to determine whether a check mark is displayed to the left of the item. This property is set automatically if the CheckOnClick property of the menu item is set to True, and it is set before the Click event handler of the item is executed.
- You can use the Visible property of a toolbar to show or hide the control.

Figure 24-9 How to write code that works with toolbars

How to create and use a status bar

In addition to menus and toolbars, you can include a status bar on the forms you create. A status bar is typically used to provide system information and general information about an application. Because of that, it's used most often on the parent form of an MDI application.

How to create a simple status bar

Figure 24-10 shows how to create a *status bar*. To start, you add a StatusStrip control to the form. This control appears in the Component Designer tray, and the status bar appears at the bottom of the form.

To display information in a status bar, you add a ToolStripStatusLabel to the status bar. If you're creating a simple status bar like the one in this figure that contains a single label, the easiest way to add the label is to use the drop-down list in the status bar as shown in this figure.

After you add a ToolStripStatusLabel to a status bar, you can determine the text that's displayed in the label when the form is first displayed by setting the Text property of the ToolStripStatusLabel at design time. You can also change the text that's displayed as the application executes by setting the Text property at runtime. This is illustrated in the code example in this figure.

The event handler in this example is executed when a Future Value child form becomes the active form. Then, the Text property of the status bar label is set to text that describes the function of this form. A similar event handler is included in the Depreciation form to describe its function. Notice that because the status bar is part of the parent form and its Text property is being set from a child form, the assignment statement starts by identifying the parent form and the status bar control. Then, it uses the Items property of the status bar with an index value of zero to identify the first label in the status bar.

A form with a simple status bar

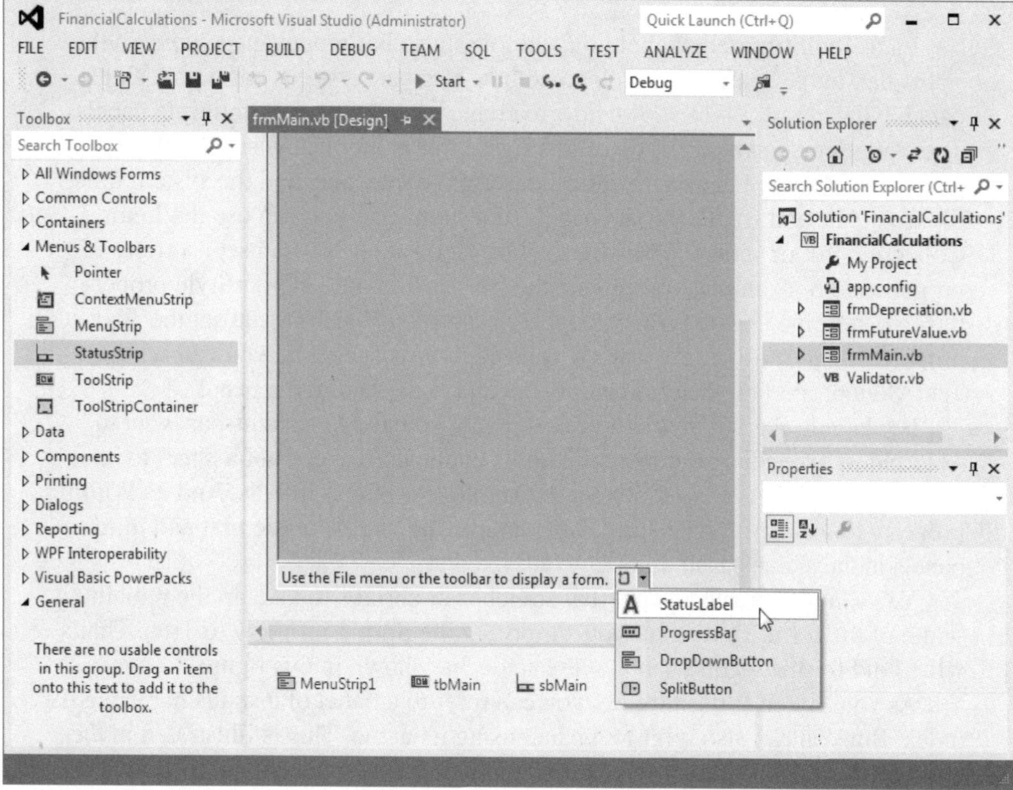

Code that displays descriptive text in the status bar

```
Private Sub frmFutureValue_Activated(sender As Object,
        e As EventArgs) Handles Me.Activated
    frmMain.sbMain.Items(0).Text =
        "Calculate the future value of a monthly investment."
End Sub
```

Description

- To create a *status bar*, add a StatusStrip control to a form. By default, the status bar is docked at the bottom of the form and fills the width of the form.
- To display text in a status bar, use the drop-down list that appears in the status bar to add a ToolStripStatusLabel control to the status bar. Then, set the Text property of this control to change the text that's displayed.
- The ToolStripStatusLabel control represents a *panel* in the status bar. See the next figure for more information on using panels in a status bar.

Figure 24-10 How to create a simple status bar

How to create a status bar with multiple panels

Each ToolStripStatusLabel you add to a status bar represents a *panel* in the status bar. In the last topic, you learned how to create a status bar with a single panel. Now, figure 24-11 shows how to create a status bar with multiple panels. The status bar shown at the top of this figure, for example, consists of three panels that display the system date, a descriptive message, and the system time.

To create and work with the panels of a status bar, you can use the Items Collection Editor shown in this figure. For each panel, you can set a variety of properties. For example, you can set the BorderSides and BorderStyle properties to determine how the panels appear in the status bar. You can set the Text property to the starting text that's displayed in the panel. And you can set the TextAlign property to determine how the text is aligned in the panel.

By default, the initial width of each panel you add to a status bar is set to 111, and its size changes depending on its contents. If you want a panel to have a fixed width, however, you can set its AutoSize property to False and its Width property to the appropriate size. For example, the widths of the first and third panels in the status bar in this figure are fixed at 75.

You can also create a panel that stretches or shrinks to take up the remaining width of the form. To do that, you simply set the Spring property to True. That's what I did for the second panel in the status bar shown in this figure.

As you saw in the last figure, you can refer to a panel of a status bar using its index. But you can also refer to a panel using its name. This is illustrated in the code example in this figure. Here, the ToolStripStatusLabel named lblDate that represents the first panel in the status bar is set to the current date. Similarly, the ToolStripStatusLabel named lblTime that represents the third panel is set to the current time.

Notice that this code is executed in response to the Tick event of a Timer control. The Timer control causes this event to occur at the interval you define in its Interval property. That way, you can update the information in the status bar periodically so it remains current.

A status bar that displays the date, time, and a descriptive message

8/29/2013 | Calculate the Future Value of monthly payments | 3:38 PM

The Items Collection Editor for a StatusStrip control

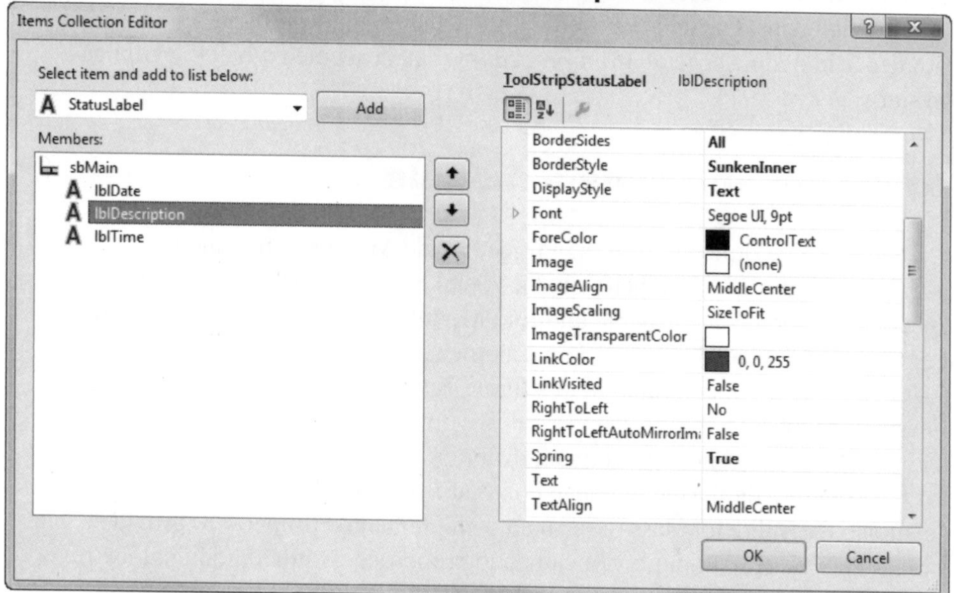

Code that changes the text in two status bar panels at regular intervals

```
Private Sub Timer1_Tick(sender As Object,
        e As EventArgs) Handles Timer1.Tick
    sbMain.Items("lblDate").Text = DateTime.Today.ToShortDateString
    sbMain.Items("lblTime").Text = DateTime.Now.ToShortTimeString
End Sub
```

Description

- The easiest way to create a status bar with multiple panels is to use the Items Collection Editor. To display this editor, select Edit Items from the smart tag menu for the control.
- To add a panel to the status bar, select StatusLabel from the drop-down list at the top of the editor and click the Add button. Then, set the properties for the panel.
- By default, the size of a panel changes depending on its contents. To create a panel with a fixed size, set the AutoSize property to False and set the Width property to the appropriate width. To size a panel so it takes up the remaining width of a form, set the Spring property to True.

How to use a Timer control to update information

- To update information in a status bar that changes periodically, use a Timer control. To do that, set the Interval property of the control to the number of milliseconds between updates, set the Enabled property to True, and then update the information in the event handler for the Tick event of the control.

Figure 24-11 How to create a status bar with multiple panels

How to work with modules

Besides the form, business, and database classes that you create for a project, you can create one or more *modules*. A module typically contains procedures, variables, and constants that are used by more than one form. In addition, a module can contain a special *Main procedure* that's executed when the application starts.

How to create and code a module

To create a module, you use the Project→Add Module command as described in figure 24-12. When you do, Visual Studio adds the module to the project and generates the Module and End Module statements. Then, you can enter the required code between these statements.

As you can see, the module in this figure is similar to the Validator class you saw in chapter 11 (figure 11-17). But if you compare this module with the Validator class, you'll notice two main differences. First, a public variable is used to store the title for the message box that's displayed if an entry is invalid. In contrast, the Validator class uses an auto-implemented property to provide access to this value. Although you can code properties within a module, they're not used as commonly as they are in classes.

Second, the Public and Shared keywords have been removed from the function declarations. The Public keyword has been removed because the procedures of a module are public by default. If you want to include this keyword for documentation, however, you can. Similarly, the Shared keyword has been removed because the procedures of a module are shared by default. Unlike the Public keyword, though, you can't code the Shared keyword on a procedure declaration or on a variable or constant declaration in a module.

When you code variables and procedures like the ones in this example in a module, they have *namespace scope* (also known as *project scope*) since all the classes in a project are typically in the same namespace. You can also code variables, constants, and procedures within a module using the Private keyword. In that case, they have module scope, which means that they can only be accessed from within the module.

You should also know that you can include a module in a class library. Then, the module is available to any project that includes a reference to that library. For this to work, however, you must include the Public keyword on the module declaration. See chapter 20 for more information on using class libraries.

At this point, you may be wondering when you should use a module instead of a class. Although there aren't any hard and fast rules, you can use modules for procedures, variables, and constants that apply to two or more forms within a project. You can also use them for code that relates just to the user interface of an application, not to any business processing that's done by the application. Another common use of a module is for a Main procedure, which you'll learn more about next.

A module with a Public variable and Public procedures

```
Module Validator

    Public Title As String = "Entry Error"

    Function IsPresent(textBox As TextBox) As Boolean
        If textBox.Text = "" Then
            MessageBox.Show(textBox.Tag.ToString &
                " is a required field.", Title)
            textBox.Select()
            Return False
        Else
            Return True
        End If
    End Function

    Function IsDecimal(textBox As TextBox) As Boolean
        Dim number As Decimal = 0
        If Decimal.TryParse(textBox.Text, number) Then
            Return True
        Else
            MessageBox.Show(textBox.Tag.ToString &
                " must be a decimal value.", Title)
            textBox.Select(0, textBox.Text.Length)
            Return False
        End If
    End Function

End Module
```

Description

- A *module* is typically used to define procedures, variables, and constants that are needed by more than one form in a project. A module should be considered part of the presentation layer of an application, and should not be used to define members that are directly related to a business or database object.
- You can also use a module to declare the Main procedure for the application as described in the next figure.
- By default, the procedures of a module have Public access, and the variables and constants have Private access.
- The Public members of a module are said to have *namespace scope* because they can be accessed by any class in the same namespace.
- To create a module, select the Project→Add Module command and enter a name for the module in the Add New Item dialog box that's displayed. Then, enter the code for the module between the Module and End Module statements that are generated.
- A module is similar to a class. The main difference between the two is that a module can't be instantiated.

Figure 24-12 How to create and code a module

How to use a Main procedure

In addition to using a module to store variables, constants, and procedures that are used by more than one form, a module can include a *Main procedure* that's executed when the application starts. This is particularly useful for getting information from the user before displaying the first form of the application or for deciding which form should be displayed first.

Figure 24-13 illustrates how you can use a Main procedure. In the code example in this figure, the Main procedure displays a custom dialog box that gets a password from the user. Notice that this code doesn't create a new instance of the dialog box before displaying it. That's because when you refer to a form by its class name, Visual Basic creates a default instance of the form with that name. In this example, the default instance of the frmLogin form is displayed.

If the password the user enters is valid, the procedure starts the application by executing the Run method of the Application class. This method accepts an object variable that contains an instance of the form you want to display. In this example, the Run method will display the default instance of the form named frmMain.

Notice that the Run method in this example is coded within the Try block of a Try…Catch statement. That way, you can handle any unexpected errors that occur as the application executes. Then, after the statements in the Catch block are executed, the program will end.

To indicate that you want to use the Main procedure as the starting point for an application, you set the project properties as shown in this figure. To display the project properties, just double-click on the My Project folder in the Solution Explorer. Then, display the Application page and remove the check mark from the Enable Application Framework option. When you do, the Startup Form label will change to Startup Object, and Sub Main will be included in the drop-down list. You select this item to start the application from the Main procedure.

The properties for starting a project from a Main procedure

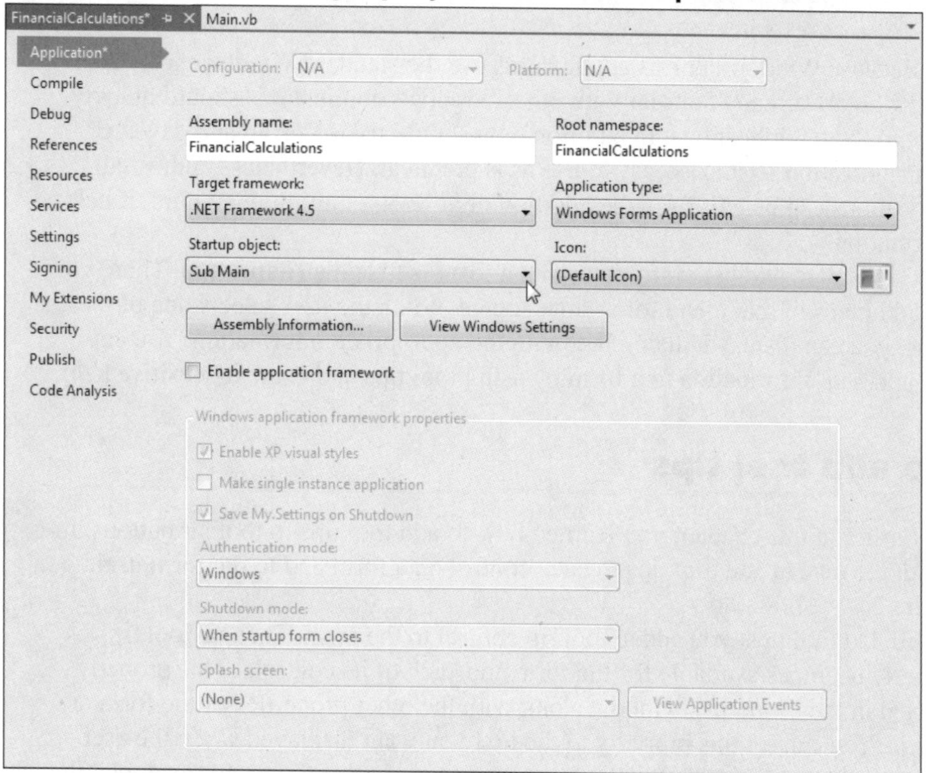

A module with a Main procedure and exception handling

```
Module Main
    Sub Main()
        If frmLogin.ShowDialog = DialogResult.OK Then
            Try
                Application.Run(frmMain)
            Catch ex As Exception
                MessageBox.Show(ex.Message, "Unexpected Error")
            End Try
        End If
    End Sub
End Module
```

Description

- To start an application by executing code rather than by displaying a form, you can use a *Main procedure*. A Main procedure is a procedure named Main that's typically coded within a module.
- To display the starting form for an application from within a Main procedure, you use the Run method of the Application class. If you code this method within a Try…Catch statement, you can catch any unhandled errors thrown by the application.
- To use a Main procedure as the starting point for an application, deselect the Enable Application Framework option for the project. Then, select Sub Main from the Startup Object drop-down list.

Figure 24-13 How to use a Main procedure

How to add help information

Because Windows Forms applications use the standard Windows interface, users who are already familiar with other Windows applications should quickly adapt to these applications. In addition, you should try to design and develop each application so it is as easy to use as is practical. Nevertheless, almost all applications can benefit from the addition of at least a minimum amount of help information.

One way to add help information to a form is to add a Help menu. Then, you can add items to that menu for various topics. When the user selects one of these items, you can display a dialog box with the appropriate information. You can also add help information to a form by using tool tips and context-sensitive help.

How to add tool tips

Earlier in this chapter, you learned how to add tool tips to toolbar buttons. In addition, you can add tool tips to each control on a form and to the form itself. Figure 24-14 shows how.

To add tool tips, you add a ToolTip control to the form. Then, a ToolTip property becomes available for the form and each of its controls. This property is listed in the Properties window along with the other properties of the form or control. You can set this property to the text you want displayed when the user places the mouse pointer over the form or control. In this figure, for example, the tool tip for the Initial Cost text box on the Depreciation form describes the value that should be entered.

How to add context-sensitive help

If you want to display help information that's more extensive than what you would normally display in a tool tip, you can use the HelpProvider control. This control lets you provide *context-sensitive help* for a form or control. Then, the user can display the help for the control that has the focus by pressing the F1 key. If help text isn't provided for that control, the help text for the form is displayed if it's provided.

To specify the help text for a form or control, you use the HelpString property that becomes available when you add a HelpProvider control to the form. In this figure, for example, the Depreciation form shows some context-sensitive help that describes the function of the form.

A tool tip

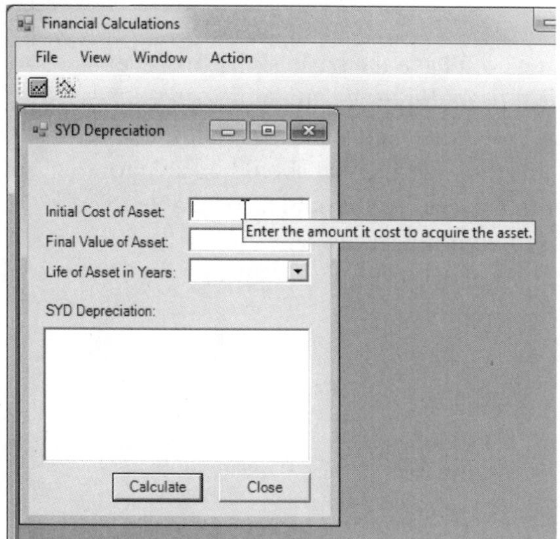

Context-sensitive help

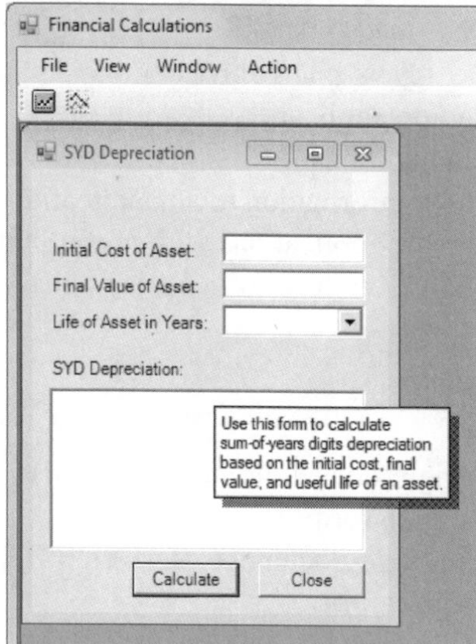

How to work with a tool tip

- A *tool tip* is a brief description of a control that's displayed automatically when you place the mouse pointer over that control.
- To create tool tips for a form, add a ToolTip control to the form. A control named ToolTip1 will appear in the Component Designer tray at the bottom of the window.
- The ToolTip control makes a property named "ToolTip on ToolTip1" available for each control on the form and for the form itself. You can enter the text for a tool tip in this property.

How to work with context-sensitive help

- To provide *context-sensitive help* for a form or control, add a HelpProvider control to the form. A control named HelpProvider1 will appear in the Component Designer tray at the bottom of the window. This control makes several additional properties available for the form and each control it contains.
- To display a text string when the user presses the F1 key for the control that has the focus, enter the text for the "HelpString on HelpProvider1" property of the control.
- You can also enter help text for the "HelpString on HelpProvider1" property of the form. Then, that text is displayed at the location of the mouse pointer if a help string isn't specified for the control that has the focus.
- When you enter text for the "HelpString on HelpProvider1" property, the "ShowHelp on HelpProvider1" property automatically changes from False to True.

Figure 24-14 How to work with tool tips and context-sensitive help

Perspective

Now that you've completed this chapter, you have the basic skills for developing applications that use single-document or multiple-document interfaces. In addition, you learned how to add menus, toolbars, status bars, modules, and help information to an application. With just those skills, you should be able to create applications with professional user interfaces. You should also be able to figure out how to add other enhancements to your interfaces.

Terms

single-document interface (SDI)
startup form
multiple-document interface (MDI)
parent form
child form
tab
page
menu
menu item
toolbar
tool tip
status bar
panel
module
namespace scope
project scope
Main procedure
context-sensitive help

Exercise 24-1 Create an SDI application

In this exercise, you'll create the SDI version of the Financial Calculations application that's presented in this chapter.

Open the project and adjust the startup form

1. Open the project in the C:\VB 2012\Chapter 24\FinancialCalculationsSDI directory. This project contains the beginning of a startup form named frmMain.
2. Open the Designer window for the startup form, select the PictureBox control, and note how the Image property in the Properties window is set. Then, delete this setting and note that the image in the PictureBox control is gone. To restore this image, select the Choose Image command from the PictureBox's smart tag menu to open the Select Resource dialog box. Then, find the file named Murach logo in the FinancialCalculationsSDI directory, and complete the dialog boxes.
3. Select the label that contains "Financial Calculations" in a larger than normal font size. Then, click on the plus sign before the Font property in the Properties window, and change the font name to Times New Roman, change the font size to 15, and turn italics on.

Add existing files from other projects

4. Use the Add Existing Item dialog box to add the frmFutureValue.vb and Validator.vb files in the C:\VB 2012\Chapter 24\FutureValue directory to your project.

5. Use the Add Existing Item dialog box to add the frmDepreciation.vb file in the C:\VB 2012\Chapter 24\Depreciation directory to your project.

Add the code for the startup form and fix other coding issues

6. Add code to the startup form that responds to the Click events of the three buttons. The event handlers for the two Calculate buttons should create an instance of the Future Value or Depreciation form and then display that form.
7. Change the Exit button on the Future Value form to a Close button.
8. Run and test the application. When the startup form is displayed, use it to display multiple versions of the Future Value and Depreciation forms. Make sure the Close button on each form works properly, and make sure the Exit button on the startup form closes all open forms.
9. Close this version of the Financial Calculations project.

Exercise 24-2 Create an MDI application

In this exercise, you'll create an MDI version of the Financial Calculations application that's similar to the one presented in this chapter.

Convert the SDI application to an MDI application

1. Create a copy of the FinancialCalculationsSDI directory from exercise 24-1, and store it in the C:\VB 2012\Chapter 24 directory. Rename this copied directory FinancialCalculationsMDI.
2. Display the form named frmMain in Design view and delete all controls from this form. Then, set the IsMdiContainer property of this form to True to identify it as the parent form, and resize the form so it's large enough to hold several child forms.

Add a File menu to the parent form

3. Add a MenuStrip control to the form, and note that it's displayed in the Component Designer tray at the bottom of the Form Designer. Also notice that a box with the words "Type Here" appears at the top of the form.
4. Use the Menu Designer to add a File menu with four menu items that will display a new Future Value form, display a new Depreciation form, close the active child form, and exit from the application. Include access keys if you like. Then, use the Menu Designer to name these menu items mnuNewFutureValue, mnuNewDepreciation, mnuClose, and mnuExit, and include a separator bar between the Close and Exit items.
5. Add an event handler for the Click event of each menu item as shown in figure 24-7. Then, delete any code that's left over from the SDI version of the application.
6. Run and test the application. You should be able to display and use multiple versions of either form, you should be able to close the active child form, and you should be able to exit the application, closing all child forms.

Add a Window menu to the parent form

7. Use the Menu Designer to add a Window menu to the right of the File menu. Then, add three items to this menu that will let the user arrange the forms in a cascaded, vertical, or horizontal layout.
8. Right-click in the Window menu and select the Edit DropDownItems command. Then, click on each menu item and enter an appropriate name for it.
9. Code an event handler for the Click event of each of the items in the Window menu. Each event handler should use the LayoutMdi method of the form to arrange the child forms using one of the members of the MdiLayout enumeration as shown in figure 24-7.
10. Set the MdiWindowListItem property of the menu strip to the name of the Window menu.
11. Run the application and display two or more instances of each form. Then, use the items in the Window menu to arrange the open forms and to move from one form to another.

Add an Action menu to one child form

12. Use the Menu Designer to add an Action menu to the Future Value form. Then, add Calculate and Clear items to this menu.
13. Code the event handlers for these items as described in figure 24-5.
14. Run the application and display two or more instances of each form. Note that the Action menu is only displayed when a Future Value form is the active child form, not when a Depreciation form is the active child form.

Add a toolbar to the parent form

15. Add a ToolStrip control to the parent form and add the Future Value and Depreciation buttons as described in figure 24-8. The two icons for the buttons are stored in the C:\VB 2012\Chapter 24 folder.
16. Add a View menu that has a checked Toolbar item. Set the CheckOnClick property of this item so it's checked and unchecked automatically when the user clicks on it. Then, write the code that uses this menu item to display and hide the toolbar as described in figure 24-9, and add the code that handles the Click event of the buttons on the toolbar.
17. Run the application and test it to be sure the toolbar and View menu work correctly.

Add a status bar to the parent form

18. Add a StatusStrip control to the parent form. Then, add three panels to the status bar as described in figure 24-11. All three panels should have a sunken appearance as shown in that figure but no initial text. In addition, the first and third panels should have a fixed width of 75 and the second panel should take up the remaining width of the form.

19. Open the Future Value form and start an event handler for the Activated event of that form. This event handler should contain code like that shown in figure 24-10 that sets the Text property of the second panel of the status bar. You can refer to the panel using either its index or name. Code a similar event handler for the Activated event of the Depreciation form.
20. Add a Timer control to the parent form and set its Enabled property to True. Then, add an event handler for the Tick event of this control that sets the Text property of the first panel in the status bar to the current date and the Text property of the third panel to the current time.
21. Run the application and note the current date and time in the first and third panels of the status bar. Then, display a Future Value form and notice the text that's displayed in the second panel of the status bar. Display a Depreciation form to see how this text changes. Now, notice the time in the third panel. Has it changed since you first displayed the form? If not, wait until it changes and then close the form.

Add a module with a Main procedure to the application

22. Add a module named Main to the Financial Calculations project. Then, add a procedure to this module named Main that displays this dialog box:

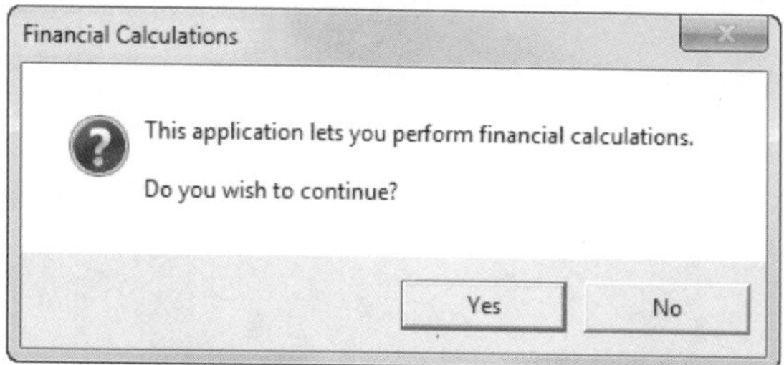

If the Yes button is clicked in this dialog box, the procedure should continue by displaying the parent form for the application as shown in figure 24-13.

23. Set the Main procedure as the starting object for the application as shown in figure 24-13.
24. Run the application. When the dialog box is displayed, click the No button to see that the application isn't run. Then, run the application again and click the Yes button to display the parent form.

Add help information

25. Add tool tips and context-sensitive help information for both the Future Value form and the Depreciation form as described in figure 24-14.
26. Run the application and test it to make sure that the help information is displayed properly and that the entire interface is "user friendly." When you're done, close the project.

25

How to deploy an application

At some point during the process of developing a Windows application, you need to deploy the application so you can test it on the target system, and ultimately so your users can run it. Since testing an application on the target system may help you discover issues that affect the design of the application, it often pays to deploy and test an application early in the development process.

In the past, most Windows applications were installed using a Setup program that was stored on a network server, CD, or DVD. In recent years, however, it has become possible for a Windows application to be installed from a web server, which makes it easier to update the application. Visual Studio 2012 makes it possible to deploy applications using either method.

An introduction to deploying Windows applications

Figure 25-1 lists three ways you can deploy a Windows application from Visual Studio 2012. Each of these ways has its advantages and disadvantages.

How XCopy works

The oldest and easiest way to deploy a Windows application is to copy the files that are required by the application to the user's computer. This method of deployment is known as *XCopy deployment* because you can use the DOS XCopy command to copy the files. However, you can also use Windows Explorer to copy the files.

Although XCopy deployment is adequate for simple applications with just a few users, it doesn't create a shortcut in the Start menu, it doesn't provide a way to automatically install prerequisite files (such as the .NET Framework 4.5), it doesn't provide an automatic way to update the application, and it doesn't provide a standard way to uninstall the application. As a result, you'll only want to use this type of deployment when you are prepared to copy the files onto the users system and are also prepared to update or delete these files as necessary.

How ClickOnce works

The second way to deploy an application is commonly called *ClickOnce deployment*. This type of deployment lets users install a Windows application from a network server or a web page.

Although it requires a little more work to set up ClickOnce deployment, the advantages of this deployment technique are usually worth the effort. That's because ClickOnce deployment creates a shortcut for the application in the Start menu, lets the user use the Control Panel to uninstall the application, and lets the user automatically update the application whenever new versions become available.

How a Setup program works

The third way to deploy an application is to create a *Setup program* for the application using a product called InstallShield Limited Edition. Then, you can run this program from each of the user's computers to install the application. Creating a Setup program with InstallShield typically requires more work than XCopy or ClickOnce deployment, and it doesn't have the automatic updating feature that's available from ClickOnce. As a result, you'll only want to create a Setup program when ClickOnce isn't adequate for your application. For example, you can use a Setup program if you need to modify the registry on the user's computer.

XCopy

- Installs the application by copying the directory for the application to the user's hard drive.
- Lets the user start the application by double-clicking on the exe file for the application. You can also create a shortcut for this file after you install the application.
- Lets the user remove the application by deleting the folder for the application.
- Works as long as all files required by the application are included in the folder for the application.
- Is adequate for some simple applications with just a few users.

ClickOnce

- Lets users install the application by running a setup.exe file from a network server or web page.
- Creates a shortcut for the application in the Start menu.
- Lets the user uninstall the application using the Uninstall or Change a Program window (Windows 8, Windows 7, and Windows Vista) or the Add or Remove Programs window (Windows XP) that can be accessed from the Control Panel.
- Provides a way to automatically check for and install any files needed by the application.
- Provides a way to automatically distribute updates to the application.
- Is adequate for many types of applications with multiple users.

Setup program

- Lets users install the application by running a Windows Setup program.
- Lets users specify the installation directory.
- Can create a shortcut for the application in the Start menu and on the desktop.
- Lets the user uninstall the application using the Uninstall or Change a Program window (Windows 8, Windows 7, and Windows Vista) or the Add or Remove Programs window (Windows XP) that can be accessed from the Control Panel.
- Provides a way to restrict an application from being installed on certain operating systems.
- Provides a way to automatically check for and install any files needed by the application.
- Can be used to modify the registry.
- Commonly used for commercial software that's installed from a CD.
- Is adequate for all but the most complex applications.

Note

- In Visual Studio 2012, you create a Setup program using a product developed by Flexera Software called InstallShield Limited Edition.

Figure 25-1 Three ways to deploy a Windows Forms application

How to use XCopy

You can use XCopy deployment to install an application just by copying its folder onto the user's hard drive. Then, if the files for all assemblies needed by the application are stored in that folder, the application should run correctly. The advantage of this approach is that no configuration or registration is required.

How to create a release build

Figure 25-2 shows how to use XCopy deployment to deploy an application. Before you begin copying files, you should decide whether you want to create a debug or release version of the application. By default, a debug version of the application is created and stored in the bin\Debug subdirectory of the project directory when you build the application. However, because the debug version contains symbolic debugging information that you don't typically need when you deploy an application, and because this version isn't optimized, you'll usually deploy a release version.

To create a release build, you select the Release option from the Solution Configurations combo box in the Standard toolbar. In addition, you'll want to remove the check mark from the Enable the Visual Studio Hosting Process option on the Debug page of the Project Designer so files that improve the performance of the debugger aren't generated. Then, when you build the application, the output is stored in the bin\Release subfolder of the project folder unless you change this folder on the Build page of the Project Designer.

How to copy the release build to the client

Once you've created the Release folder, you can use the XCopy command to copy that folder to the user's hard drive, often by way of a network drive. In this figure, for example, the XCopy command is used to copy all files in the bin\Release folder to a folder on a network drive named FutureValue1.0. Here, the first path specifies the source folder, the second path specifies the target folder, and the /S switch indicates that all files in the folders and subfolders of the source folder should be copied to the target location. Once this folder is on the network, you can use Windows Explorer to copy it to the hard drives of the clients that will use the application.

Unlike ClickOnce or Setup program deployment, XCopy deployment doesn't automatically check for dependencies. As a result, if the user's computer doesn't have all of the files required by the application, the application won't be able to run properly. If, for example, the user's computer doesn't have the .NET Framework 4.5 installed on it and the application uses features of this Framework, the application won't be able to run until you install the Framework.

The Debug page of the Project Designer

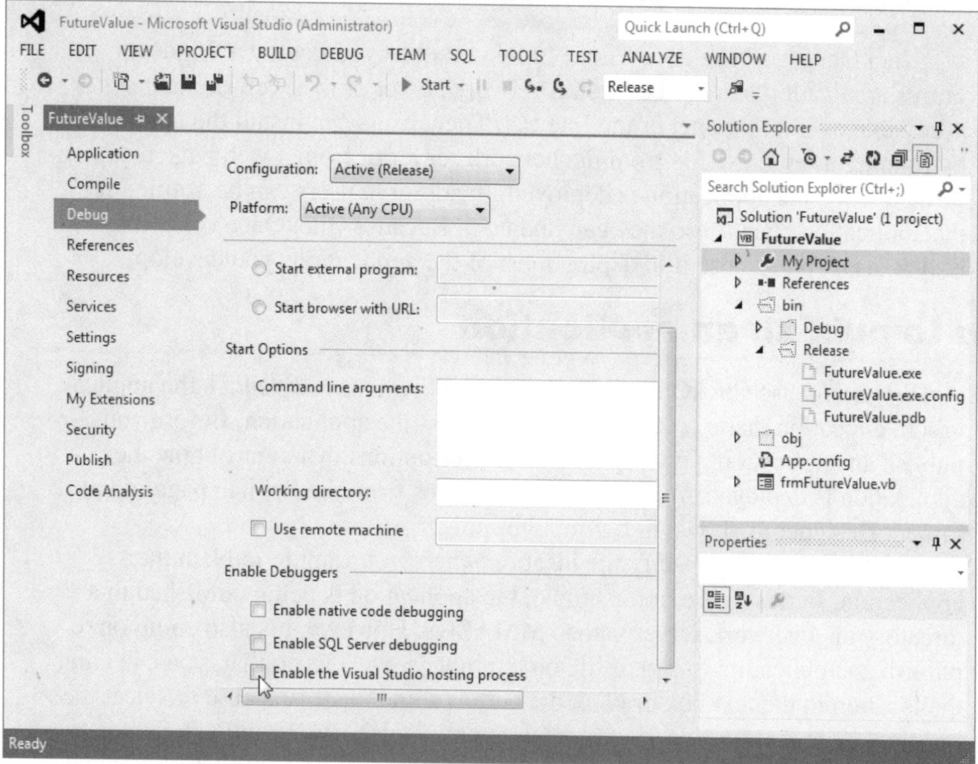

A procedure for using XCopy deployment

1. Select the Release option from the Solution Configurations combo box in the Standard toolbar.
2. Remove the check mark from the Enable the Visual Studio Hosting Process option on the Debug page of the Project Designer.
3. Build or run the project to create a bin\Release folder subordinate to the project folder.
4. Use the DOS XCopy command to copy the contents of the Release folder to the user's hard drive or a network drive.

An XCopy command that copies the release build to a network drive

```
C:\>xcopy "C:\VB 2012\FutureValue\bin\Release\*.*"
"M:\Murach\FutureValue1.0\" /S
C:\VB 2012\FutureValue\bin\Release\FutureValue.exe
C:\VB 2012\FutureValue\bin\Release\FutureValue.exe.config
C:\VB 2012\FutureValue\bin\Release\FutureValue.pdb
3 File(s) copied
```

Description

- If the files for all of the assemblies needed by the application are stored in the Release folder, the application should run without any configuration or registration.
- If you want to change the location of the Release folder, you can set the Build Output Path option on the Compile page of the Project Designer to any directory on the local drive.

Figure 25-2 How to use XCopy deployment

How to use ClickOnce

ClickOnce is a feature of Visual Studio that lets you deploy a Windows Forms application to a directory on a network server or to a web site that's accessible over an intranet or the Internet. Then, users can install the application by running a setup.exe file from the network server or from a web page that's created when the application is deployed. In addition, users can be notified if the application changes so they can update it. Because ClickOnce is flexible and easy to use, you can use it to deploy most of the applications you develop.

How to publish an application

When you use ClickOnce to deploy an application, you *publish* the application to a location that's accessible to the users of the application. Before you publish an application, you can set a variety of options that control how the application is deployed. You access these options from the Publish page of the Project Designer as shown in figure 25-3.

To start, you must specify the location where you want to publish the application. In this figure, for example, the application is being published to a directory on a network server named MMASBS. However, it's also common to publish an application to a web site on a remote server. To do that, you can enter the location in the text box or click the button with the ellipsis on it to select the location. Note that for this to work with a remote web site, FrontPage Server Extensions must be installed on the web server. You can also publish an application to a directory on your hard disk or to a directory on an FTP server, but that's not common.

If you publish an application to a remote web site, you may also need to specify an installation URL. That's the case if you publish the application to one server, such as a staging server, and the application is then moved to a web server. Then, the installation URL specifies the location where users go to install the application.

The two options in the Install Mode and Settings section of the Publish page let you specify whether the application will be available offline. By default, it is available offline. That means that the application will be installed on the user's hard drive, a shortcut will be added to the Start menu, and the application can be uninstalled using the Uninstall or Change a Program window (Windows 8, Windows 7, and Windows Vista) or the Add or Remove Programs window (Windows XP) that's available from the Control Panel.

However, it's also possible to create an application that's only available online. In that case, the user runs the application from the server where it's published. For this to work, of course, the user must be able to establish a connection to the server to run the application.

The four buttons in this section of the Publish page display dialog boxes that let you set various options. You'll see these dialog boxes in the next three figures.

The Publish page of the Project Designer

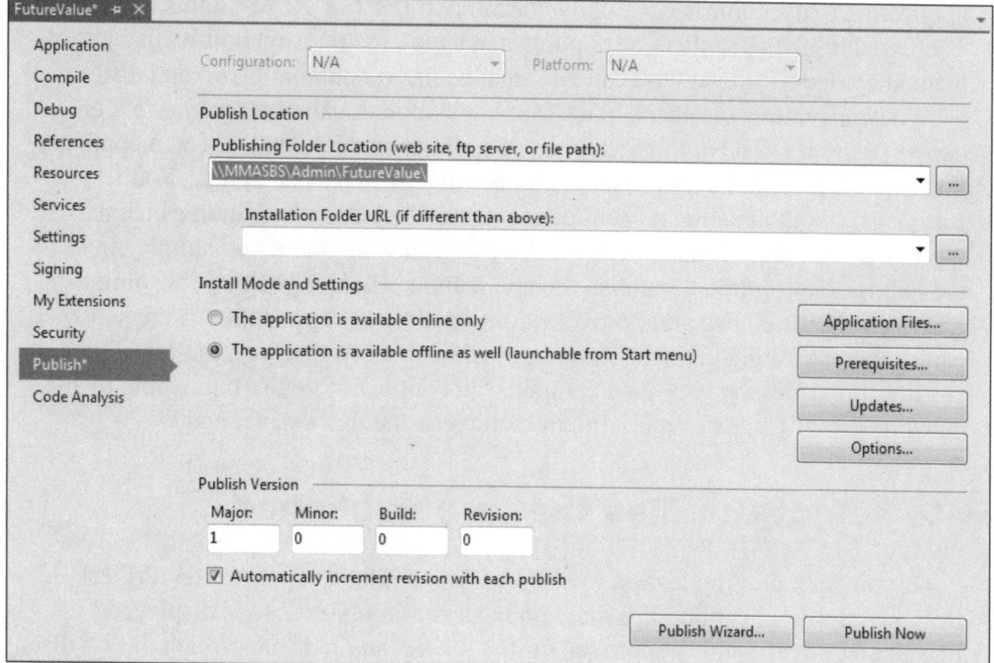

Description

- To publish an application, double-click My Project in the Solution Explorer to display the Project Designer and then display the Publish page. Enter the location where you want to publish the application, set the other options the way you want them, and click the Publish Now button.
- If the application will be installed from a location other than the location where it's published, you'll need to enter that location for the Installation Folder URL option.
- By default, the application is available offline, which means that it's installed on the user's hard drive. If that's not what you want, you can select the Online Only option. Then, the user will only be able to run the application from the server.
- By default, the version of an application is incremented automatically each time you publish it, and the initial version is set to 1.0.0.0. If that's not what you want, you can set the options in the Publish Version section of the Publish page.
- You can use the buttons in the Install Mode and Settings section of this page to set additional options. See figures 25-4, 25-5, and 25-6 for details.
- You can also use the Publish Wizard to publish an application. This wizard lets you specify where the application will be published and whether the application will be available offline. To start this wizard, select the Build→Publish command or click the Publish Wizard button on the Publish page.
- To publish an application to a remote web site, FrontPage Server Extensions must be installed on the web server.

Figure 25-3 How to publish an application

The options in the Publish Version section let you specify the version of the application that's published. Initially, the version is set as shown in this figure. Then, each time the application is published again, the revision number is incremented by one. However, you can also change the version number manually, and you can remove the check mark from the Automatically Increment Version option so the version isn't incremented automatically. Note that when an application is published with a new version number, it's treated as an update. You'll learn more about updating an application using ClickOnce later in this chapter.

Once you have all the options set the way you want them, you simply click the Publish Now button to publish the application. Then, if you're publishing to a web server, a web page that provides for installing the application is created as part of the publishing process. This page is then displayed so you can install and test the application on your own computer. In contrast, if you're publishing to a network server, you can simply run the setup.exe file that's generated.

How to select the files that are published

If you click the Application Files button on the Publish page of the Project Designer, the Application Files dialog box shown in figure 25-4 is displayed. This dialog box lists the output files for the project and indicates which ones will be published. By default, only the .exe, .exe.config, and .exe.manifest files will be published. If you want to publish the pdb and xml files as well, you can select the Include option from the Publish Status drop-down list.

How to select the prerequisites

If you click the Prerequisites button on the Publish page, the Prerequisites dialog box shown in figure 25-4 is displayed. This dialog box lets you select the components that must be installed for the application to work correctly. The target framework is selected by default, which is usually what you want.

In some cases, additional components will be required. If an application uses a SQL Server 2012 database that's installed on the user's computer, for example, the user must have SQL Server 2012 Express installed. You'll see an application like that later in this chapter.

By default, the components you select are downloaded from the vendor's web site and then installed by ClickOnce. For example, if the .NET Framework or SQL Server Express are needed, they're downloaded from Microsoft's web site. If the components are available from the computer where you're developing the application, though, you can publish them to the same location as the application. Then, if you select the second option in the Prerequisites dialog box, the components will be downloaded from the same location as the application. If you make the components available from another location, you can also use the third option to specify that location.

The Application Files and Prerequisites dialog boxes

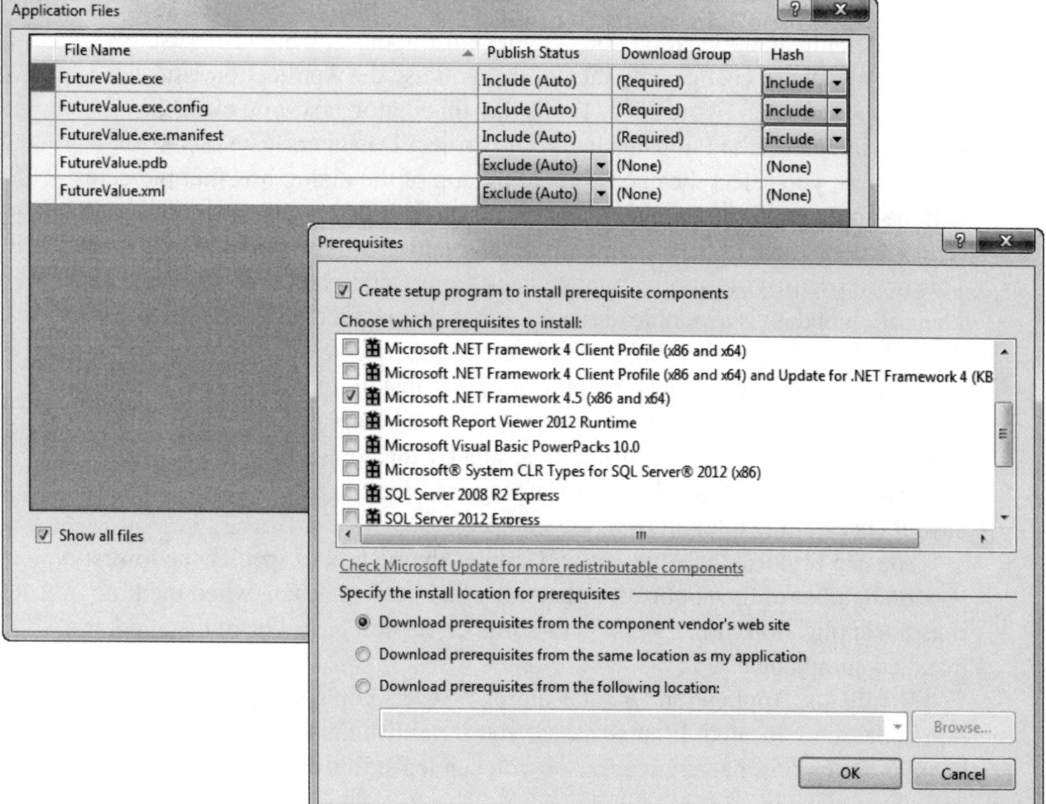

Description

- Only the .exe, .exe.config, and .exe.manifest files for an application are installed by default. If you want to include the .pdb or .xml file, you can display the Application Files dialog box, check the Show All Files option, and then change the publish status of these files.
- The target framework for the application is included as a prerequisite by default, which is usually what you want. Then, the installation program will download and install the .NET Framework from Microsoft's web site.
- If additional components, such as SQL Server 2012 Express, are required by an application, you can include them by selecting the appropriate options from the Prerequisites dialog box.

Notes

- The .exe.config file contains the configuration information that's stored in the application's App.config file.
- The .exe.manifest file contains the application manifest, which contains information about the application that's being deployed.

Figure 25-4 How to select the files that are published and the prerequisites

How to set the update options

By default, an application doesn't check for updates, which isn't usually what you want. To change how this works, you use the Application Updates dialog box shown in figure 25-5. To display this dialog box, you click the Updates button on the Publish page of the Project Designer.

To start, you select the check box at the top of the dialog box that indicates that the application should check for updates. When you do, the two options that follow will become available, and the second option will be selected by default. This option causes the application to check for updates each time the user runs it. Then, if an update is available, a dialog box is displayed that lets the user install the update. You'll see that dialog box in a minute.

You can also specify that an application not install updates until the next time it's run by selecting the After the Application Starts option. If you select this option, you can also specify how frequently the application checks for updates. By default, it checks for updates every time it's run, but you can also have it check at the interval of days you specify.

You can also use the Application Updates dialog box to specify the lowest version number of the application that must be installed. Then, when the user runs the application, if that version or a higher version hasn't been installed, it's installed automatically.

Finally, the Application Updates dialog box lets you specify where application updates are located. In most cases, you'll publish the updates to the same location as the original application, so you can leave this option blank.

The Application Updates dialog box

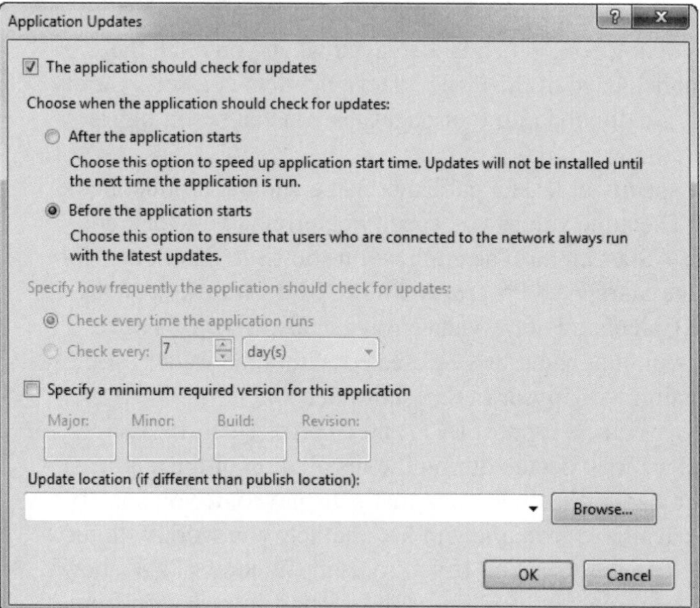

Description

- By default, an application doesn't check for updates. If that's not what you want, you can use the Application Updates dialog box to indicate when you want to check for updates.
- If you want an application to check for updates, select the check box at the top of the Application Updates dialog box. Then, by default, the application will check for updates each time it starts.
- You can also defer updates until the next time an application is run. In that case, you can specify whether the application checks for updates every time it's run or at a specified interval in days.
- The Application Updates dialog box also lets you specify a minimum version of an application that must be installed, and the location where it should be installed from if that location is different from the location where the application was published.

Figure 25-5 How to set the update options

How to set the publish options

The Publish Options dialog box, which is displayed when you click the Options button on the Publish page of the Project Designer, lets you set a variety of options. These options are divided into four pages, as you can see in figure 25-6.

In most cases, you'll specify at least a publisher name and the product name on the Description page. Then, the values you specify determine how the application appears in the user's Start menu. The application shown in this figure, for example, will appear in the Start→All Programs→Mike Murach & Associates, Inc. menu with the name Calculate Future Value. You can also specify a suite name. Then, a subfolder with that name will be created within the folder for the publisher, and the application will appear in that subfolder.

You may also want to specify a support URL and an error URL. If you specify an error URL and an error occurs during the installation of the application, the URL will be included in the dialog box that's displayed. If you specify a support URL, it will be available from the window that lets you work with the programs that are installed on your system. If you're using Windows 8, Windows 7, or Windows Vista, for example, you can access the support information from the Uninstall or Change a Program window. If you're using Windows XP, you can access the support information from the Add or Remove Programs window.

By default, the web page for installing an application from a web server isn't generated when you publish an application. This is appropriate if the application will be installed from a network server or a CD or DVD. If the application will be installed from a web server, however, you'll want to use the Deployment tab to provide information about the web page that's generated.

To start, you need to enter the name you want to use for the page in the text box. The name can be anything you want, but it must have an extension of htm or html. You can also specify whether this page is generated each time the application is published and whether it's displayed after the application is published. At the least, you'll want to select these options the first time you publish an application so the initial web page is generated and you can make sure it looks the way you want it to.

By the way, you can also modify the web page after it's generated. To do that, just open the page in any HTML editor and make the appropriate changes. In that case, you'll want to be sure not to generate the web page again the next time the application is published or you'll overwrite your changes.

In most cases, you'll leave the remaining options in the Publish Options dialog box at their default settings. If you publish your application to a CD or DVD, however, you may want to select the second to last option on the Deployment page. Then, the installation will start automatically when the CD or DVD is inserted. And if you want to create a shortcut on the user's desktop when the application is installed, you can select the last option on the Manifests page.

The four pages of the Publish Options dialog box

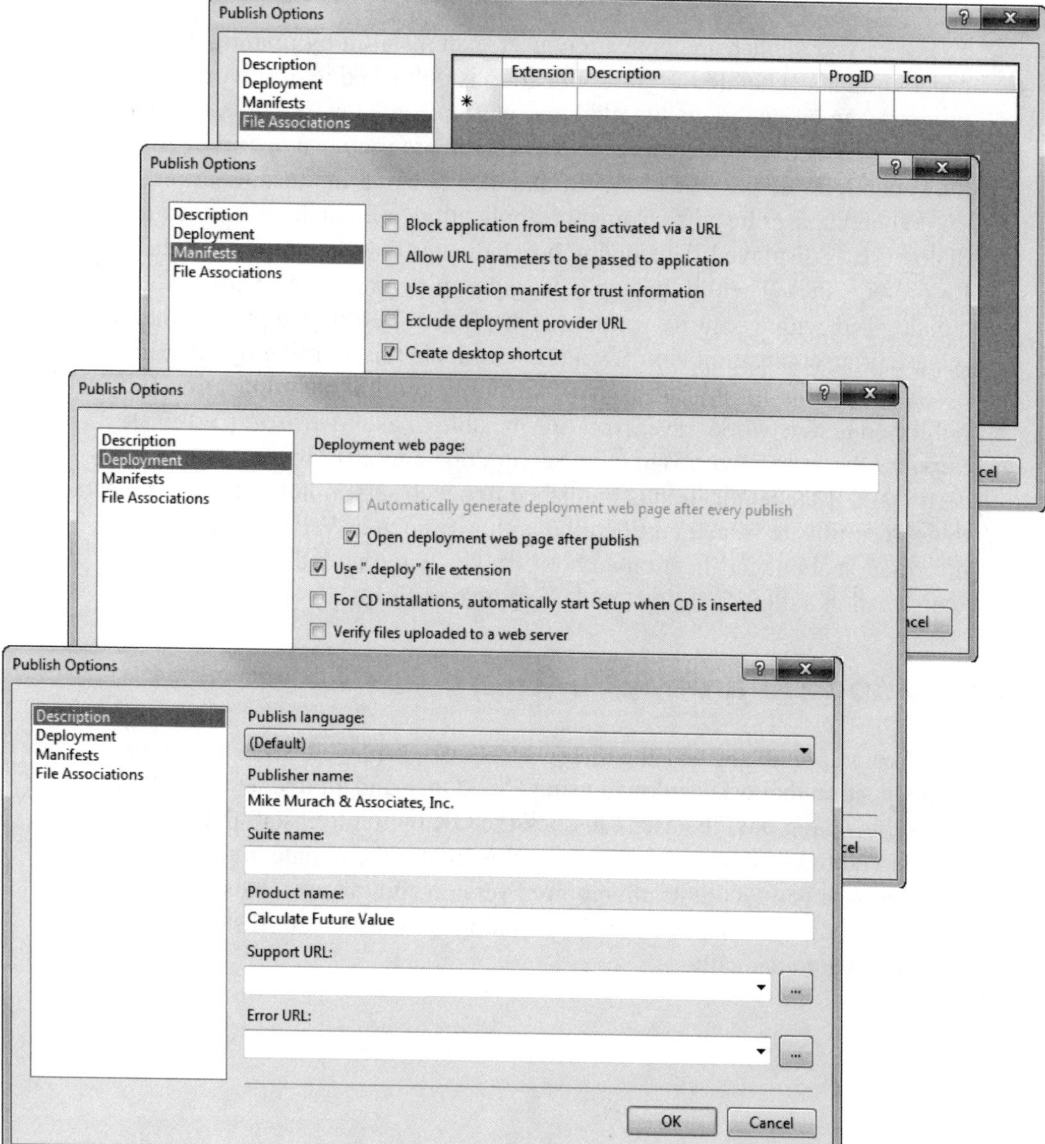

Description

- You can use the Publish Options dialog box to set a variety of options related to how an application is published.
- At the least, you should set the publisher name and product name on the Description page.
- If the application will be deployed from a web server, you will need to enter the name you want to use for the deployment web page on the Deployment page. You will also need to select the first check box on the Deployment page at least the first time you publish an application so a deployment web page is generated.

Figure 25-6 How to set the publish options

How to install an application

Once you publish an application, users can install it by running the setup.exe program that's generated. If the application is published to a network server, this program can be run by double-clicking on it in Windows Explorer. If the application is published to a web server, the setup.exe program can be run by displaying the generated web page in a browser and then clicking the Install button.

When the user installs or runs the application, a Launching Application dialog box is displayed. This dialog box indicates that the program is checking for prerequisites. Then, if the application doesn't come from a trusted source, a dialog box with a security warning is displayed. Before you publish the final release of an application, you'll want to eliminate this warning by installing a valid certificate for the publisher of the application. If the application is published to a network server, you may be able to use Microsoft Certificate Services that comes with Windows Server 2008 and 2012 to create your own certificate. If the application is published to a web server, however, you'll need to get a certificate from a certification authority such as VeriSign. For more information about certification authorities, you can search the Internet for "certification authorities" and "code signing certificate."

How to update an application

Figure 25-7 also shows the dialog box that's displayed when a user runs an application that was deployed using ClickOnce and an update is available. From this dialog box, the user can click the OK button to install the update or the Skip button to skip the installation. Note that if the update options for the application specify a minimum required version and the user doesn't have that version installed, the Update Available dialog isn't displayed. Instead, the update is installed automatically.

The dialog box for installing an application

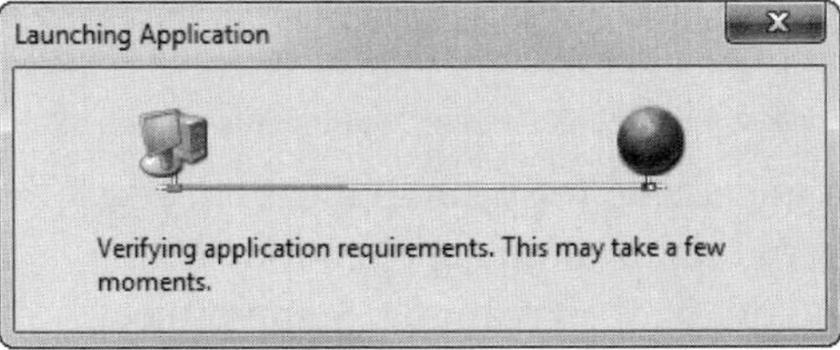

The dialog box that's displayed if an update is available

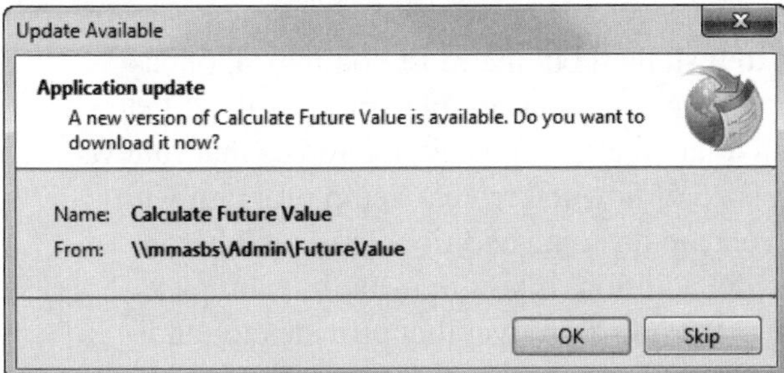

How to install an application from a network server

- To install an application along with any prerequisites, run the setup.exe program from the publish location.
- By default, the directory where an application is published is displayed in Windows Explorer after you publish the application. Then, you can run the setup program in this directory to test it on your own system.

How to install an application from a web server

- To install an application along with any prerequisites, open a web browser and navigate to the installation page that's created during publishing. Then, click the Install button to run the setup.exe program and install the application.

How to update an application

- If you run an application that's set to check for updates, the Update Available dialog box is displayed if a new version of the application is available. Then, you can click the OK button to update the application or the Skip button to skip the update.
- If a minimum version of the application is required and hasn't been installed, it's installed without displaying the Update Available dialog box.

Description

- Before an application is installed, a dialog box like the first one above is displayed to indicate that the setup program is checking for prerequisites. If any prerequisites need to be installed, they're installed before the application is installed.
- If an application doesn't come from a trusted source, a security warning will be displayed when you install the application. You can click the Install button in this dialog box to install the application.

Figure 25-7 How to install and update an application

How to create and use a Setup program

If XCopy or ClickOnce deployment isn't adequate for your application, you can create a *Setup program* that the user can run to install the application. With previous versions of Visual Studio, you could do that by creating a Setup project. This option is no longer available with Visual Studio 2012, however. Instead, you create a Setup program using a product developed by Flexera Software called *InstallShield Limited Edition*.

You can use a Setup program to install all but the most complex applications. However, creating a Setup program can be a complex process itself that varies widely from one application to another. As a result, the topics that follow are designed to give you a general idea of how to create a Setup program with InstallShield. Then, if necessary, you can do some additional research before creating your own Setup programs. In addition, if you're installing complex applications, you might consider purchasing a product that provides for additional functionality, such as the Express, Professional, or Premier Edition of InstallShield.

How to create an InstallShield project

Figure 25-8 shows how to create an InstallShield project for a Windows application. To do that, you start by opening the solution for the project that contains the Windows application that you want to deploy. Then, you use the Add New Project dialog box shown in this figure to add an InstallShield project for the application to that solution. In this example, I'm adding an InstallShield project named FutureValueSetup to a solution that contains the FutureValue project from chapter 7 .

Note that InstallShield isn't automatically installed with Visual Studio. Because of that, you will have to download and install it separately as described in this figure.

The Add New Project dialog box for an InstallShield project

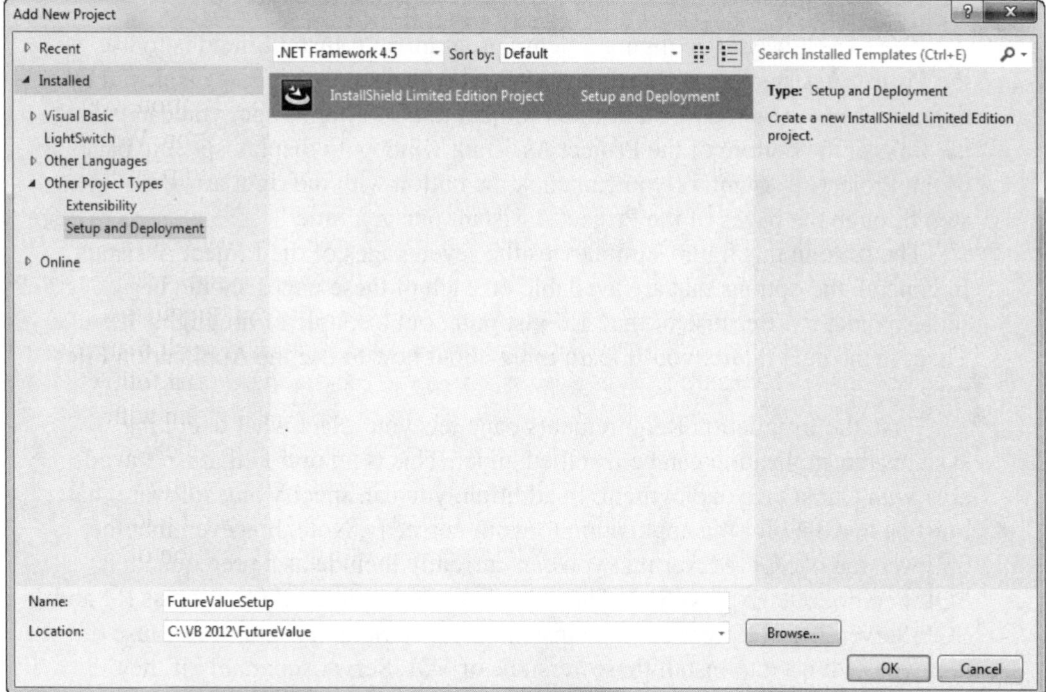

Description

- You can use InstallShield Limited Edition to create a *Setup program* that installs a Windows application. A Setup program is a type of Windows application that's used to install other Windows applications.
- To create an InstallShield project, open the solution that contains the Windows application that you want to deploy, and choose the File→Add→New Project command to display the Add New Project dialog box. Then, expand the Other Project Types group, select Setup and Deployment, select the InstallShield Limited Edition Project template, enter a name for the project, and click OK.
- When you create an InstallShield project, it is added to the solution that contains the Windows project that you want to create the Setup program for.
- Before you can use InstallShield, you must download and install it. To do that, select the Enable InstallShield Limited Edition option that's displayed in place of the InstallShield project template, click the OK button, and then follow the instructions on the web site that's displayed.

Express Edition limitation

- Visual Studio 2012 Express Edition doesn't provide for InstallShield projects.

Figure 25-8 How to create an InstallShield project

How to use the InstallShield Project Assistant

The easiest way to configure a Setup program with InstallShield is to use the Project Assistant shown in figure 25-9. The Project Assistant is displayed by default when you add an InstallShield project to a solution. Then, you can use the links at the bottom of the Project Assistant window to display specific pages of the Project Assistant, or you can click the button with the right arrow on it to step through the pages of the Project Assistant one at a time.

The table in this figure summarizes the seven pages of the Project Assistant. In general, the options that are available on each of these pages should be self-explanatory. Because of that, I'll just point out a couple of highlights here. Then, in the next figure, you'll learn more about how to use the Application Files page.

First, the Installation Requirements page lets you select what operating systems the application can be installed under. This is an option that isn't available with ClickOnce deployment. In addition, you can specify any software that must be installed for the application to work correctly. Note, however, that the only version of SQL Server that you can currently include as a prerequisite is SQL Server 2008 Express SP1. That's because SQL Server 2008 Express R2 and SQL Server 2012 Express can't be installed from a Setup program. Because of that, you will need to install these versions of SQL Server separately if they're required.

Second, by default, the Application Shortcuts page should include a shortcut for each executable file that's added to the project on the Application Files page. However, I have found that not to be the case. Worse yet, when I try to add a shortcut, an error message is displayed when the project is compiled. If you encounter the same error, then, you will need to manually add shortcuts to each user's computer after you install the application.

Before I go on, you should know that InstallShield lets you set configuration options in addition to those that are available from the Project Assistant. You can view these options by expanding the numbered nodes for the project in the Solution Explorer and then double-clicking on a subordinate node. For example, to customize the appearance of the dialog boxes that are displayed by the Setup program or to display additional dialog boxes, you can use the window that's displayed when you double-click the Dialogs node under the Customize the Setup Appearance node.

The InstallShield Project Assistant

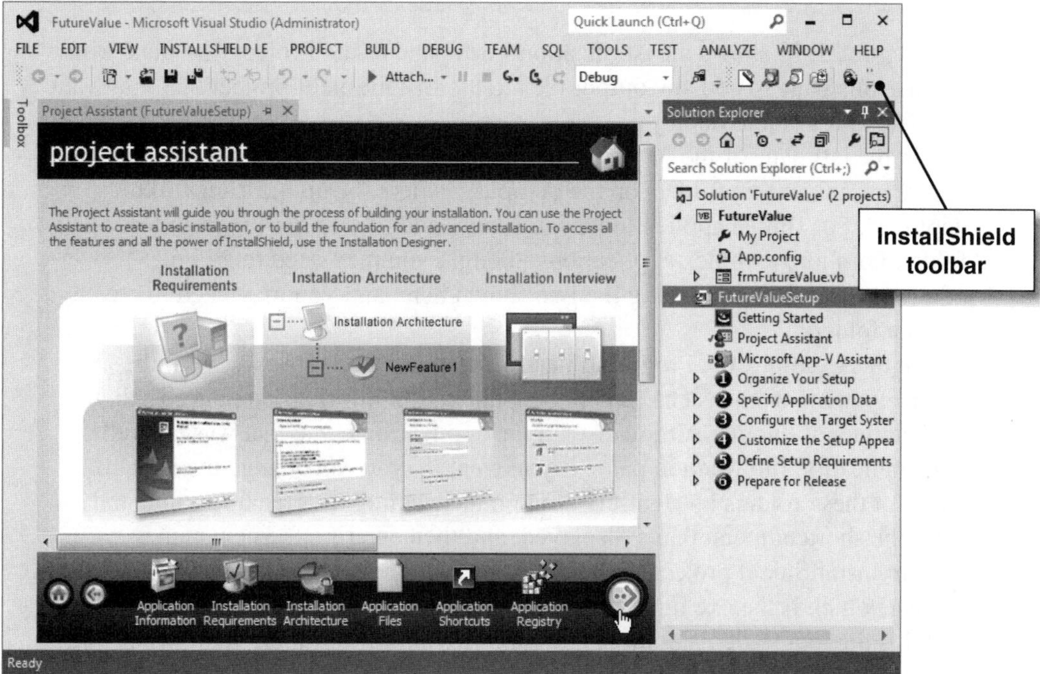

The seven pages of the Project Assistant

Page	Description
Application Information	Lets you specify a company name, application name, application version, and company web address.
Installation Requirements	Lets you restrict what operating systems the application can be installed under and specify prerequisite software.
Installation Architecture	These options aren't available with InstallShield Limited Edition.
Application Files	Lets you specify what files are installed and where they're installed. See figure 25-10 for more information.
Application Shortcuts	Lets you create shortcuts for the application.
Application Registry	Lets you specify entries that should be added to the Windows Registry.
Installation Interview	Lets you specify if a license agreement is displayed, if the user is prompted for a name and company, and if the user is given the option to launch the application when the installation is complete.

Description

- When you first create an InstallShield project, the Project Assistant is displayed. You can use the Project Assistant to configure the InstallShield project.
- To use the Project Assistant, you can click on the individual links at the bottom of the window, or you can click the button with the arrow on it in the lower right corner to step through the pages of the Project Assistant.
- To redisplay the Project Assistant after it's closed, just double-click on its node in the Solution Explorer.

Figure 25-9 How to use the InstallShield Project Assistant

How to add output files to an InstallShield project

Figure 25-10 shows the Application Files page of the Project Assistant. You can use this page to add any output files to the InstallShield project that you want the Setup program to deploy.

In the left pane of the Application Files page, you can see three folders that represent system folders on the computer where the application will be deployed. For simple applications, you'll only add files to the Program Files folder. For more complex applications, though, you may need to add files to other system folders including the two shown here, and you may need to create custom folders.

In this example, the Program Files folder contains a subfolder with the company name that was entered on the Application Information page. Then, this folder contains another subfolder with the application name that was entered on the Application Information page. If you want to, you can change the name of either of these folders by right-clicking on it, selecting the Rename command from the shortcut menu that's displayed, and then entering the new name.

An InstallShield project must include at least the primary output for the project, which is the exe file for a Windows application. In most cases, you'll add this file to a folder subordinate to the Program Files folder. Then, when you select this folder, the file will appear in the right pane of the Application Files page as shown in this figure. To add the primary output to a folder, select the folder, click the Add Project Outputs button, and use the Visual Studio Output Selector dialog box.

To add additional files to an InstallShield project, you can select the folder where you want to store the file, click the Add Files button, and then locate and select the file. For example, you might want to add a Readme file or a database file that's used by the application. You'll learn more about including database files later in this chapter. You can also add a folder and all of its contents to a project using the Add Folders button.

The Application Files page of the Project Assistant

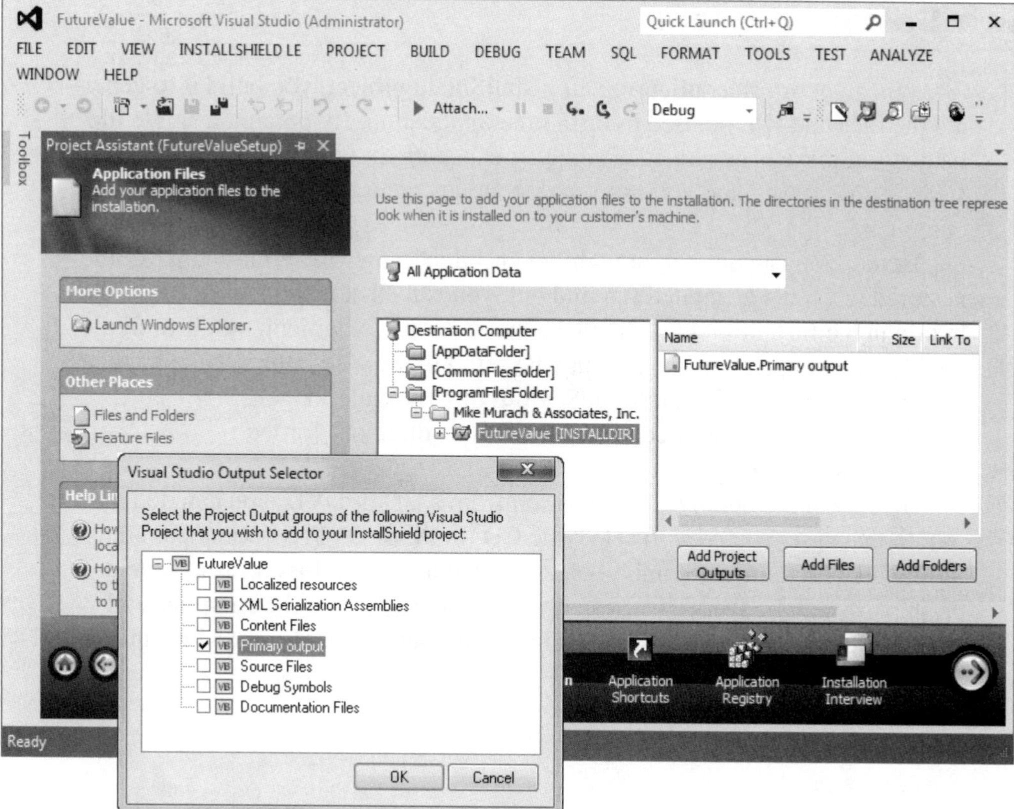

Description

- To add files to an InstallShield project, you use the Application Files page.
- To add project output such as the exe file for the application, select the appropriate folder in the directory tree for the destination computer and click the Add Project Outputs button to display the Visual Studio Output Selector dialog box. Then, select the output you want to include and click the OK button.
- To see what files will be added to the project when you select options from the Visual Studio Output Selector dialog box, right-click on the output item in the right pane of the Application Files page and select Resolve Project Output from the shortcut menu that's displayed.
- To add additional files, such as a Readme or database file, to the InstallShield project, select the appropriate folder in the directory tree, click the Add Files button, and then locate and select the file. You can also add entire folders and their contents using the Add Folders button.
- To add a new folder to the directory tree, right-click on the folder where you want to add the folder, select New Folder, and then enter a name for the folder.

Figure 25-10 How to add output files to an InstallShield project

How to create and view the installation files for a Setup program

When you finish configuring an InstallShield project, you build it to generate the files that will be used to install the application. By default, a single file named setup.exe is generated. Then, you can store that file in a central location such as on a server, and you can run it from any computer to install it on that computer.

Before you can do that, though, you need to know where the setup.exe file is stored when it's generated. To find out, you can click the Open Release Folder button in the InstallShield toolbar (the one with the folder icon on it). In figure 25-11, for example, you can see that the setup file for the Future Value application was stored in the FutureValueSetup\Express\SingleImage\DiskImages\DISK1 subdirectory of the project directory for the FutureValueSetup project.

If you want to deploy an application from a CD or DVD, you can do that too. In that case, you need to select the CD_ROM or DVD-5 option from the Solution Configurations combo box. (The default option for an InstallShield project is SingleImage.) Then, when you build the project, the compiler will generate all of the files you need, including the setup.exe file, and you can burn those files to a CD or DVD.

The installation file for the Future Value application

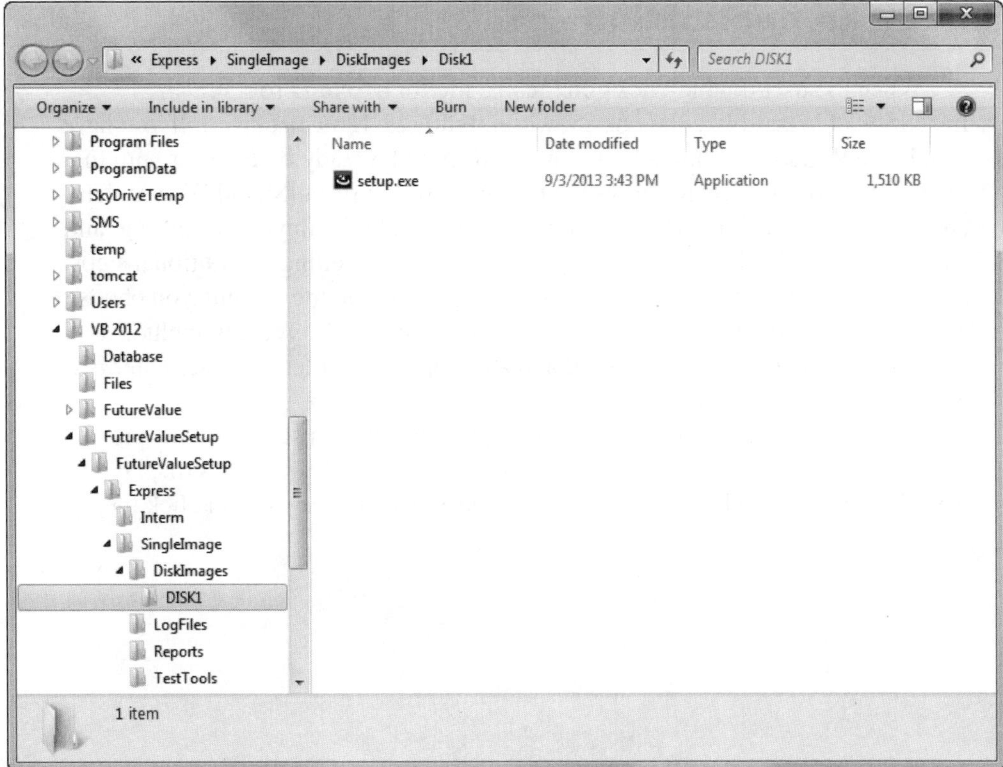

Description

- To create the installation files for a Setup program, select the InstallShield project in the Solution Explorer and choose the Build→Build *ProjectName* command.
- By default, a single file named setup.exe is generated when you build an InstallShield project as shown above. Then, you can execute that file to install the application.
- If you want to install an application from a CD or DVD, you can select the CD_ROM or DVD-5 option from the Solution Configurations combo box in the Standard toolbar. Then, you can burn the generated files to a CD or DVD.
- To view the installation files that are generated by an InstallShield project, click on the Open Release Folder button in the InstallShield toolbar.

Figure 25-11 How to create and view the installation files for a Setup program

How to use a Setup program to install an application

When the user double-clicks on the exe file for a Setup program, an InstallShield Wizard like the one shown in figure 25-12 is displayed. If you have installed a Windows application before, you should already be familiar with this type of wizard. This figure shows the two steps of the InstallShield Wizard that are displayed by default. The first step displays a default copyright warning, and the second step displays a summary of the installation settings. Additional steps may be displayed between these two steps depending on the options you choose when you configure the InstallShield project. For example, you can include a dialog box with a license agreement and a dialog box that lets the user enter his name and company name.

When the user clicks the Install button, the installation starts and the progress of the installation is displayed. Finally, a completion message is displayed when the application has been successfully installed. Then, you can click the Finish button to end the InstallShield Wizard.

The Welcome step of the InstallShield Wizard

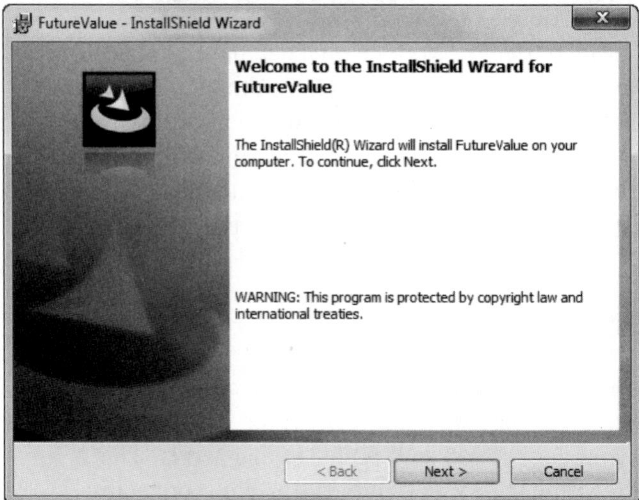

The Ready to Install step of the InstallShield Wizard

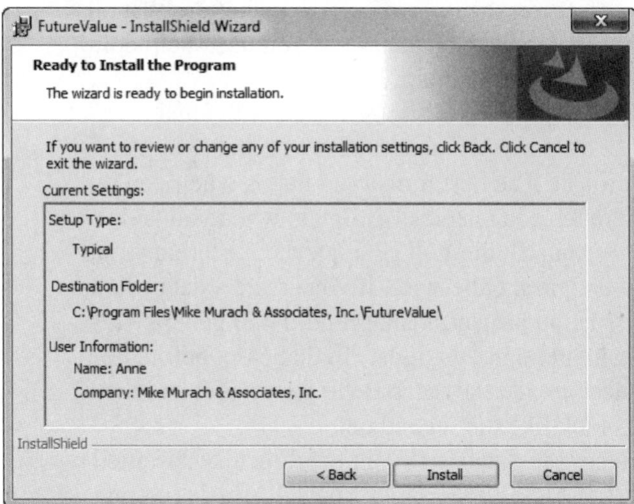

Description

- To start the installation, the user can run the setup.exe file. This displays a standard setup wizard that's similar to the setup wizard for most Windows applications.

Figure 25-12 How to use a Setup program to install an application

How to deploy database applications

If the application that you want to deploy works with a database, you need to make sure that each user has access to that database. The technique for doing that depends on where the database will be stored and which deployment technique you're using. In the two topics that follow, you'll learn how to deploy applications that work with databases on both network servers and local systems. And you'll learn how to do that using both ClickOnce deployment and a Setup program.

Using ClickOnce deployment

If you've developed an application for a group of users who are connected by a LAN, you'll want to store the database on a network server. Then, you need to set the connection string in your application so it points to that server. This is illustrated in the first connection string shown in figure 25-13. This connection string refers to a database named MMABooks that's running on a SQL Server Express database server on a network server named DBSERVER.

In addition to setting the connection string, you need to make sure that all users have adequate permissions to access the database. If you need help doing that, you should contact the network administrator.

If you've developed an application that's designed for an individual user, you'll want to store the database on the user's computer. To do that, you need to add the database file to the project. The best time to do that is when you're developing the project (see figure 14-2 in chapter 14). Then, when you create a data source from this database, Visual Studio will generate a connection string like the second one shown in this figure. Otherwise, if you create a data source for a database that's stored outside the project, Visual Studio will generate a connection string similar to the first one in this figure. In that case, before you deploy the application, you'll need to add the database to the project and then change the connection string to look like the second one.

This connection string attaches the database file in the directory specified by DataDirectory to the instance of SQL Server Express LocalDB that's running on the local computer. By default, DataDirectory points to the directory that contains the output file for the project, which is usually the bin\Debug folder within the project folder. You may remember from chapter 14 that Visual Studio copies the database file to this folder when you run the application. When you deploy the application, however, DataDirectory points to a special directory that's created to hold the database file.

If you add a database file to a project, that file is automatically included in the list of files that will be published. At the top of this figure, for example, you can see the Application Files dialog box for a version of the Customer Maintenance application that contains the MMABooks database. This dialog box includes the mdf file for the database as well as the ldf file that contains log information for the database. Because the publish status for these two files is set to Data File (Auto) and because the auto status for data files is to include them in the installation, these files are published by default.

The Application Files dialog box for a project that contains a database file

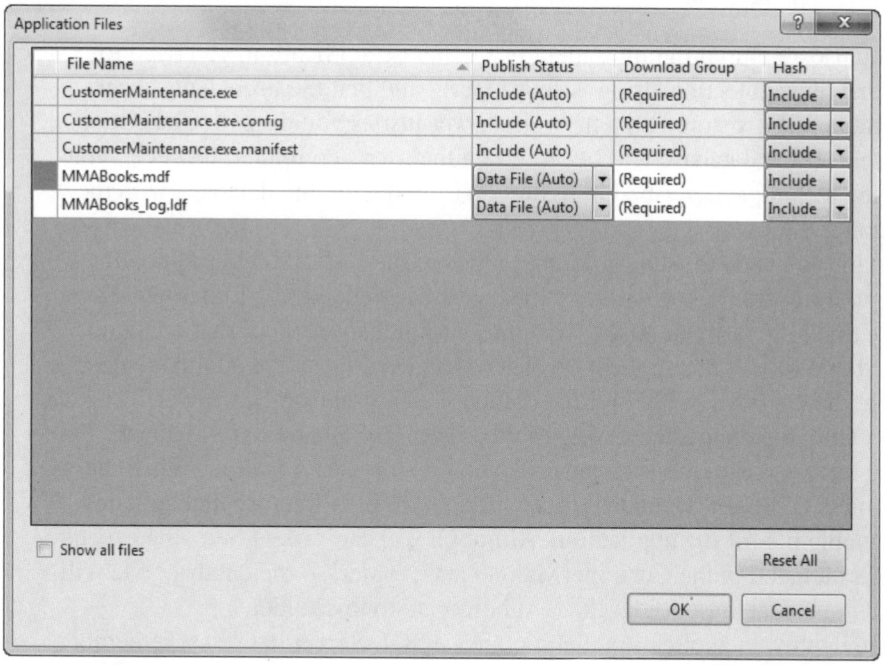

Application Files

File Name	Publish Status	Download Group	Hash
CustomerMaintenance.exe	Include (Auto)	(Required)	Include
CustomerMaintenance.exe.config	Include (Auto)	(Required)	Include
CustomerMaintenance.exe.manifest	Include (Auto)	(Required)	Include
MMABooks.mdf	Data File (Auto)	(Required)	Include
MMABooks_log.ldf	Data File (Auto)	(Required)	Include

Show all files

Reset All

OK Cancel

The connection string for a database that's on a network server

```
Data Source=DBSERVER\SqlExpress;Initial Catalog=MMABooks;Integrated
Security=True
```

The connection string for a database that's included in the project

```
Data Source=(LocalDB)\v11.0;AttachDbFilename=|DataDirectory|\MMABooks.mdf;
Integrated Security=True;Connect Timeout=30
```

Description

- To use a database that's available via a LAN, you need to make sure that the connection string is set correctly and that all users have proper permissions to access the database. To do that, you may need to make the application a full trust application.
- To deploy a database to the client along with the other files for the application, add the database file to the project. Then, that file and any related files are listed in the Application Files dialog box, and those files are published by default.
- When you add a database file to your project, the connection string is set as shown in the second example above. Then, when the application is deployed, the DataDirectory in this string points to a special directory that's created to hold the database file.
- When you add a database file to a project, the Data Source Configuration Wizard starts. If you've already created the data sources for the application, you'll want to cancel out of this wizard and then change the connection string so it looks like the second one above.

Figure 25-13 How to deploy a database application using ClickOnce deployment

Using a Setup program

If you use a Setup program to deploy a database application, you need to be sure that the connection string is set properly and that the users have access to the database if it's stored on a network server just as you do with ClickOnce deployment. If the database will be stored on the user's computer, however, you can use the technique described in figure 25-14 to deploy the database with the application.

To start, you need to add the database files to the InstallShield project. In this figure, for example, the database files have been added to a folder named Database that's subordinate to the Customer Maintenance folder that contains the executable file for the application. Then, you need to set the connection string that the application uses for the database so it points to this folder. This is illustrated in the connection string in this figure. Here, a directory named Database has been added following the DataDirectory specification. When the application is deployed, DataDirectory will point to the directory that contains the executable file for the application. Although you can't see it here, the executable file is included in the CustomerMaintenance folder, so the database file will be stored in the Database folder that's subordinate to this folder.

If you deploy an application that includes a SQL Server database, remember that InstallShield doesn't let you include SQL Server 2012 as a prerequisite. Because of that, you'll want to be sure that users who run the Setup program know that they will need to install SQL Server separately. In this case, though, only SQL Server 2012 Express LocalDB is required.

One way to let users know that they need to install SQL Server is to include a Readme dialog box in the InstallShield project. To do that, you can display the Dialogs window of the project as described earlier in this chapter. Then, you can enable the Readme option and specify the location of the Readme file in the Readme File property.

An InstallShield program that deploys an application with a database

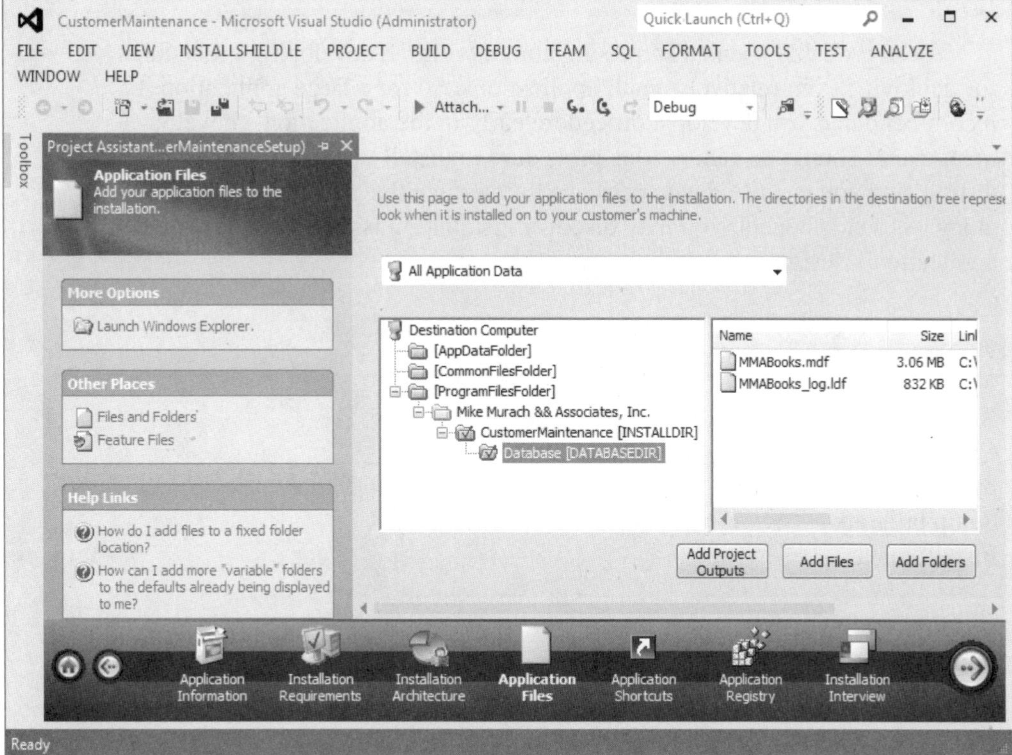

The connection string for the application

```
Data Source=(LocalDB)\v11.0;
AttachDbFilename=|DataDirectory|\Database\MMABooks.mdf;
Integrated Security=True;Connect Timeout=30
```

Description

- To use a database that's available via a LAN, you set the connection string and provide users with permissions to the database just as you do when you use ClickOnce deployment.
- To deploy a database to the user's computer along with the other files for an application, you use the Application Files page to add the database files to the folder where you want the database stored on the user's computer. In most cases, you'll add it to the Database folder that's subordinate to the folder that contains the executable file for the application.
- If you included the database file in the application you're deploying, the connection string that's generated includes a DataDirectory specification like the one you saw in the last figure. For Setup deployment, this is the directory that contains the executable file for the application.
- If you want to store the database files in a directory other than the one that contains the executable file, you'll need to modify the connection string as shown above.

Figure 25-14 How to deploy a database application using a Setup program

Perspective

You'll probably spend a surprising amount of time developing procedures for deploying even relatively small applications. So for a large application, I recommend that you develop a procedure early in the application's development cycle. Then, you can use this procedure to install the application during testing, and you can use that experience to fine-tune the procedure as you go along. As a side benefit, you may discover installation issues that affect the application's design.

Terms

XCopy deployment
ClickOnce deployment
publish an application
Setup program
InstallShield

26

An introduction to Windows 8 programming

Throughout this book, you've learned how to develop Windows Forms applications. As you learned in chapter 1, you can develop Windows Forms applications using Visual Studio 2012 running under Windows 7 or later operating systems. If you have Windows 8, though, you can also develop a new type of application called a Windows Store app that can run on a tablet as well as a desktop or laptop computer. This type of application is frequently referred to as just a Windows 8 application.

This chapter introduces you to Windows Store apps. Here, you'll learn about the design of these applications and how they work. You'll see some code from a sample Windows Store app to give you an idea of how this type of application is implemented. And you'll learn about some of the features that Visual Studio provides for developing Windows Store apps. When you're done, you should have a good foundation for learning more about developing Windows Store apps.

Windows 8 design concepts

The design of *Windows 8 applications* is considerably different from that of Windows Forms applications. In the topics that follow, you'll learn about some of the basic design concepts for Windows 8 applications so you can see these differences for yourself.

Microsoft design principles for Windows Store apps

Microsoft has developed a set of design principles that it recommends for *Windows Store apps*. If you read these design principles, you'll see that they are somewhat abstract. Because of that, figure 26-1 focuses on some of the ways you can apply these principles and presents the Bing Weather app to illustrate some of these principles.

One of the most important design principles is that the focus should be on the content. That means that you should remove unnecessary elements, such as the ones listed in this figure. Although that includes background images, you can see that the main portion of the page in this figure uses a background image. In this case, though, the image doesn't distract from the content of the page. That just shows you that these aren't hard and fast rules.

Another design principle is to use digital representations of objects to keep your apps simple and easy to use. If you want to include an icon that the user can click to go to the home page of an app, for example, you can use a digital representation of a house rather than a realistic-looking house. You'll see some icons like this in the next figure.

Windows Store apps should also use appropriate fonts, font sizes, colors, and white space. In the app shown in this figure, for example, you can see that all of the text is easy to read. In addition, the most important text is displayed in a larger font than the rest of the text, white space is used to visually separate the weather forecast for each day of the week, and color is used to divide different areas of the screen.

Next, you should use animation only if it serves a purpose and helps users understand the app. If the user clicks the right arrow at the right side of the weekly weather forecast, for example, animation is used to slide the display to the left so the forecast for the next week is displayed. This happens quickly so the user feels that the application is responsive to his actions.

When a page of a Windows Store app is first displayed, only the most frequently used functions should be available. All other functions should be placed in prescribed areas of the screen that can be displayed on command. You'll learn more about those areas of the screen in the next two figures.

Finally, because users can interact with Windows Store apps using touch input as well as mouse and keyboard input, these apps should use a prescribed set of gestures. For example, if a page extends beyond the bounds of the screen, it should be designed so the user can use a sliding gesture to display more of the page. Fortunately, the Windows 8 operating system and the Visual Studio

An app that follows the basic design principles

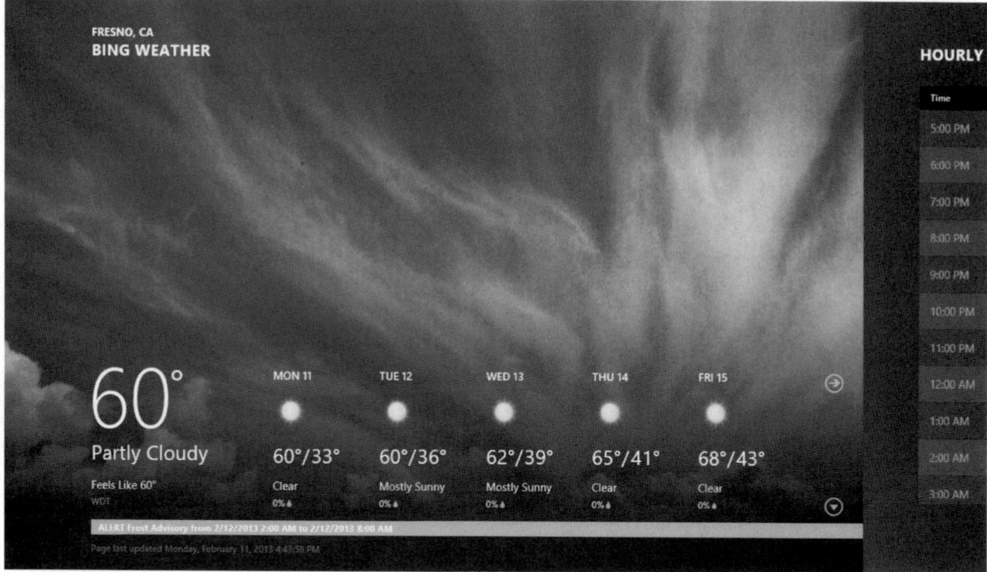

The basic design principles

- Focus on content by eliminating unnecessary elements such as borders, lines, background images, and graphical effects.
- Use digital representations of objects instead of ones that mimic the real world to keep your apps simple and easy to use.
- Display information in a readable format using appropriate fonts, font sizes, colors, and white space.
- Use animation that serves a purpose, helps the user understand the app, and is responsive to user interactions.
- Place commands that are related to the current context in prescribed areas of the screen that can be displayed on demand.
- Provide for manipulating content through touch using the prescribed set of gestures.

Description

- *Windows Store apps* run in a single, chromeless window that fills the entire screen by default.
- Windows Store apps work with touch input as well as traditional mouse and keyboard input.

Figure 26-1 Design principles for Windows Store apps

controls for Windows 8 style apps provide for all of the standard gestures by default.

Before I go on, you should notice that the Bing Weather app shown in figure 26-1 occupies the entire screen. All Windows 8 apps are displayed this way by default. Although they can be displayed in other view states as described later in this chapter, the window for a Windows 8 app never has any chrome such as a frame or header. Because of that, you have to use special touch, mouse, or keyboard input to interact with the windows. To close a window, for example, you can use your finger or the mouse to drag from the top of the window to the bottom of the window.

How to use the app bar

As I just mentioned, each page of a Windows Store app should display only its most frequently used functions by default. All other functions related to a page should be placed in an *app bar* at the bottom of the page. An app bar is a special type of Windows 8 control, and Microsoft provides guidelines for the organization and placement of the commands in an app bar.

In figure 26-2, you can see that the app bar for the Bing Weather app contains two buttons. The first one lets the user change the temperatures that are displayed to Celsius if they're currently displayed in Fahrenheit and to Fahrenheit if they're displayed in Celsius. In other words, the button that's displayed depends on the current context. The second button lets you refresh the display.

Notice that both buttons on the app bar include an icon that adheres to the Windows 8 design principles and text that makes the purpose of the button clear. Windows 8 provides a large variety of buttons you can use, but you can also create your own buttons if the standard buttons don't provide the function you need. For example, the Refresh button on the app bar in this figure is a standard button, but the Change to Celsius button isn't.

How to use the nav bar

A *nav bar* is a special type of app bar that's displayed at the top of a page. A nav bar is used to navigate directly to another page of an application. For example, the Bing Weather app shown in figure 26-2 includes a nav bar with three buttons. The first one displays the home page, which is the page that's currently displayed. The second one displays a page that lists all the places the user has selected to display weather for, lets the user select which place is displayed on the home page, and lets the user add new places. And the third one displays a world map that shows the weather in major cities and lets the user select a location to display on the home page.

Like the app bar for this application, the buttons in the nav bar include a digital icon. They also include text that makes it clear what page will be displayed when the user selects the button. Notice that the button for the home page has a light outline around it to indicate that the home page is currently displayed.

The app bar and nav bar for the Bing Weather app

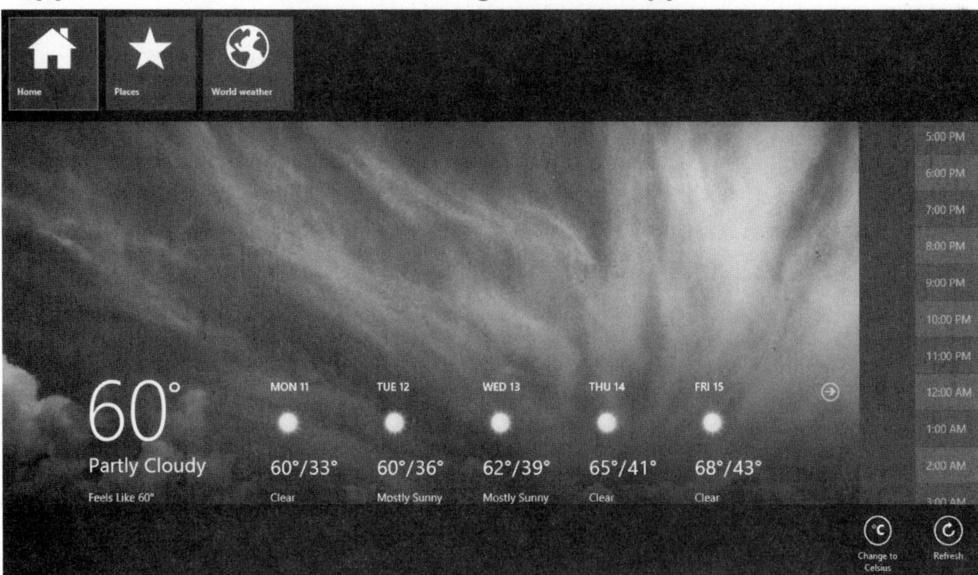

How to use the app bar

- You use the app bar for commands that you want users to be able to display on demand.
- The commands that are displayed in an app bar should be based on the current context. You can use Visual Basic code to determine what commands are visible and enabled.
- The commands in the app bar are typically buttons. However, an app bar can include other types of controls as well.
- Each button in an app bar includes an icon and a description. Windows 8 provides a variety of standard buttons you can use, but you can also create your own.

How to use the nav bar

- You use the nav bar to navigate directly to other pages of an application. The pages are typically represented by large icons, and the button for the current page is typically highlighted in some way.

Description

- The *application bar*, or *app bar*, is a special type of control that you can add to the pages of your applications. An app bar typically appears at the bottom of the page.
- When you create an app bar, you should follow the Microsoft guidelines for the organization and placement of commands.
- A *navigation bar*, or *nav bar*, is a special type of app bar that appears at the top of the page.
- The app bar and nav bar are displayed when the user swipes from the top or bottom edge of the screen, right-clicks on the screen, or presses Windows+Z.

Figure 26-2 How to use the app bar and the nav bar

How to use the charms

Figure 26-3 shows the *charm bar* that's provided by Windows 8 to access common operating system functions and settings. The table in this figure describes the purpose of each *charm* in the charm bar. For example, you can use the Search charm to search for applications, files, and settings with the text you enter, you can use the Start charm to switch between an application and the Windows 8 Start screen (this is the screen that lets you launch applications), and you can use the Settings charm to change a variety of computer and application settings.

When you develop your own app, you'll want to at least customize the Settings charm so it contains information about the app. For example, the Settings charm for the Bing Weather app lets you change options for the app, display information about the app, display credit information for the images used by the app, send feedback about the app, display terms of use, display a privacy statement, and display permissions for the app. The settings you provide depend on your app.

The charm bar for the Weather app

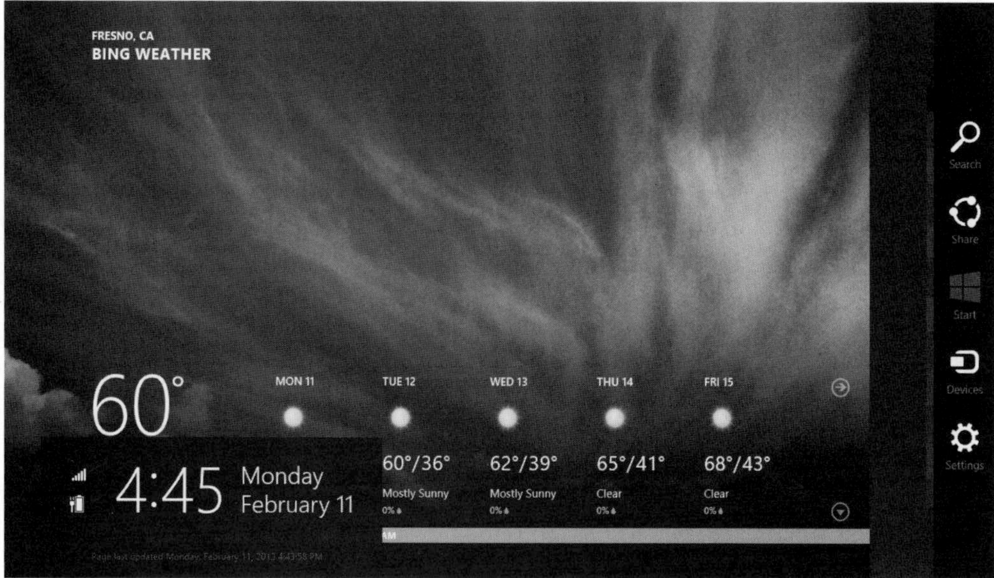

The charms in the Windows charm bar

Charm	Description
Search	Lets users search for apps, files, and settings with the text they enter. You can set up your own app so it can be searched.
Share	Lets users share data in your app with another app.
Start	Displays the Windows 8 Start screen if an app is displayed, or displays the last app you were using if the Start screen is displayed.
Devices	Lets you access and control external hardware devices.
Settings	Lets you control the network you're using, the volume of the speakers, the brightness of the screen, the power options, and a variety of other computer settings. You can also add custom settings for your own apps.

Description

- The *charm bar* provides access to common operating system functions and settings. The *charm* you're most likely to customize for your Windows Store apps is the settings charm.
- When you display the charm bar, an information box opens in the lower left corner of the screen. This box indicates the current date and time, the strength of your network signal, and the remaining battery power.

Figure 26-3 How to use the charms

The four application view states

Earlier in this chapter, I mentioned that a Windows 8 app occupies the entire screen by default. This is true whether the screen is in a horizontal, or landscape, orientation as you've seen so far in this chapter, or a vertical, or portrait, orientation. An application that occupies the entire screen in one of these orientations has one of the first two *view states* listed in figure 26-4: *full-screen landscape* or *full-screen portrait.*

If a screen is displayed in landscape orientation and has a resolution of at least 1366 pixels, it can also be used to display an application in a snapped or filled view state. In the *snapped view state*, an application occupies just 320 pixels at one side of the screen. In this figure, for example, the Bing Weather app is displayed in snapped view.

When one application is displayed in snapped view state, another application can be displayed in *filled view state*. In this view state, the application occupies the portion of the screen that isn't occupied by the application in snapped view state. In this figure, the Bing Maps app is displayed in filled view state.

Because an application can be displayed in any of these four view states, it may need to provide a different layout for each state. For example, if you compare the Bing Weather app in this figure to the ones shown in the previous figures, you'll see that its layout has changed so the weather forecast for the week is displayed in a vertical rather than a horizontal layout. In addition, some of the information, such as the hourly forecast, has been omitted.

To make it easy to provide for these different view states, Visual Studio can generate starting code for each of them. Then, you can make additional changes to the layout for each view state as necessary. You'll learn about the tools you use to do that later in this chapter.

One Bing app in snapped view and another in filled view

The four application view states

View state	Description
Full-screen landscape	The application occupies the entire screen and the screen is in landscape orientation.
Full-screen portrait	The application occupies the entire screen and the screen is in portrait orientation.
Snapped	The application occupies 320 pixels at the left or right side of the screen. An application can only be displayed in snapped view if the screen has landscape orientation with a resolution of at least 1366 pixels.
Filled	The application occupies the remaining width when another application is snapped to the screen.

Description

- When you design a Windows Store app, you need to provide for one or more of the four *application view states* shown above.
- When you create a new Windows Store app or add a page to an existing app, Visual Studio typically generates starting code for the four application view states. The generated code depends on the template you choose for the application or page. See figure 26-10 for more information on Windows Store app templates.

Figure 26-4 The four application view states

The Financial Calculations application for Windows 8

Now that you understand the basic design concepts for Windows 8 applications, you're ready to see the user interface and code for a simple application. Here, I'll use a Windows 8 version of the Financial Calculations application that was presented in chapter 24. Although the app shown here isn't a typical Windows Store app, it will make it easy for you to compare the implementations for Windows Forms and Windows Store apps.

The user interface

Figure 26-5 presents the user interface for the Financial Calculations app. This app consists of three pages that provide functions like the forms of the SDI version of this application that was presented in chapter 24. The Menu page lets the user display the other pages; the Future Value page lets the user calculate a future value of an investment given the monthly investment amount, the interest rate, and the number of years; and the Depreciation page lets the user calculate the depreciation for an asset given its initial cost, final value, and life.

As you can see, these pages use controls that are similar to Windows Forms controls. For example, the Menu page uses two buttons to display the Future Value and Depreciation pages. The Future Value page uses text boxes to accept the user entries, text blocks to identify the text boxes and to display the result, and a button that causes the result to be calculated and displayed. The Depreciation page also uses a combo box and a list box. When the user interacts with controls like these, an application can use event handlers to respond to the events that occur just like Windows Forms applications can.

Although you can't tell here, the Future Value and Depreciation pages use animation to display their results. When the user clicks the Calculate button on the Future Value form, the opacity of the text block that's used to display the result is changed so its value becomes visible, and the value slides down into view. And when the user clicks the Calculate button on the Depreciation page, the color of the text in the list box is changed from white to black so the results are visible. These animations happen over a short period of time so the results quickly fade into view. You'll see the code that implements these animations in just a minute, and you'll learn about a tool you can use to create animations later in this chapter.

The Future Value and Depreciation pages also include an app bar. This app bar contains a single button that lets the user clear the values from the page.

Notice that each of these pages includes a header with a title. The headers for the Future Value and Depreciation pages also include a back button that the user can click to return to the Menu page. Actually, the header for the Menu page includes this button too, but it's not displayed because this page is the first page of the application. The code for these headers is generated automatically when you use all but one of the Visual Studio templates that are available for creating a page. You'll learn more about these templates later in this chapter.

The Financial Calculations app

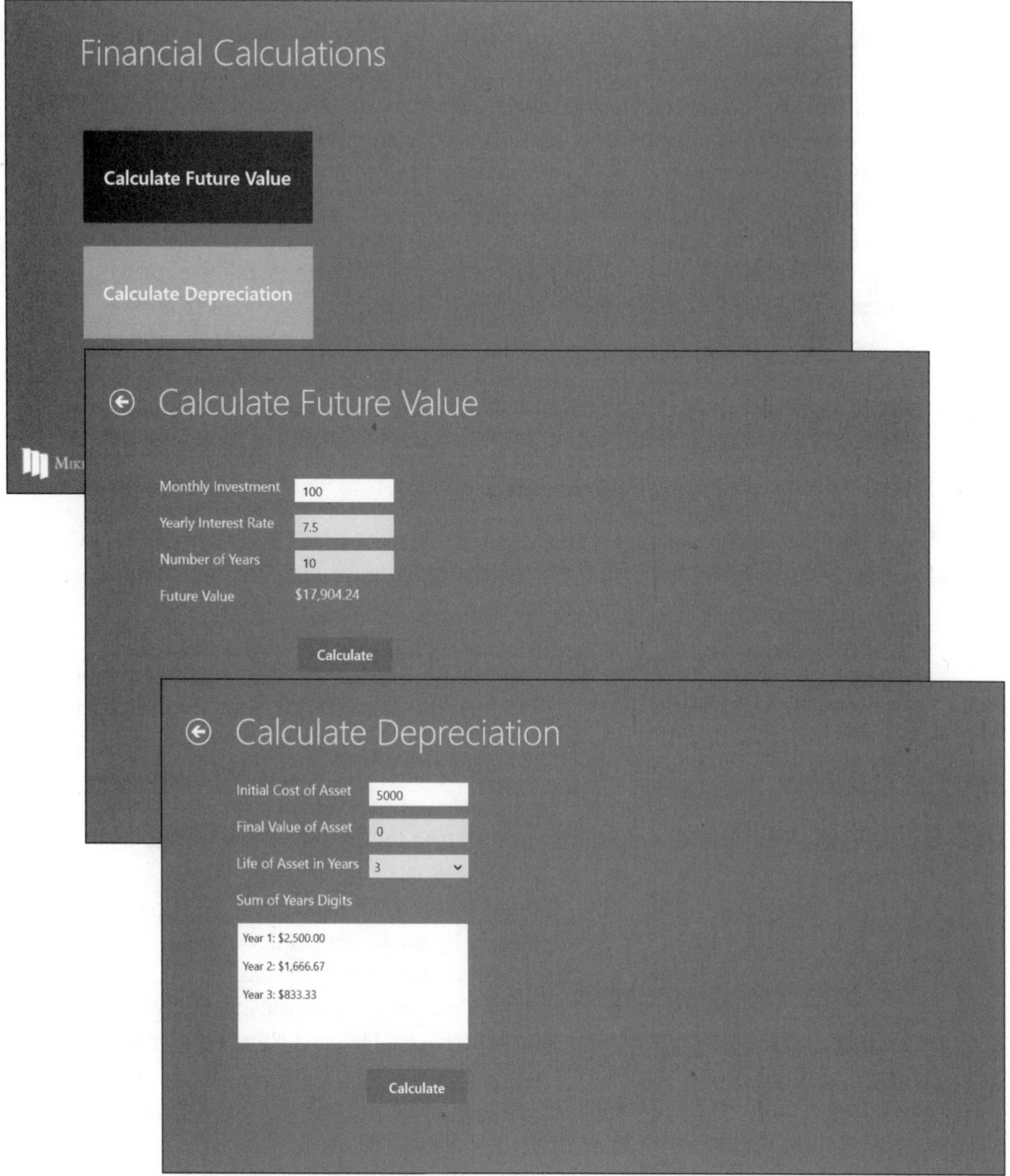

Description

- The Financial Calculations app consists of three pages. The Menu page lets the user click on one of two buttons to display the Future Value or Depreciation page. These pages work like forms you've seen in earlier chapters.
- All three forms include a header with a title and a back button that's displayed if the user can return to a previous page.
- The Future Value and Depreciation pages include an app bar with a button that lets the user clear the page, and they use animation to display their results.

Figure 26-5 The user interface for the Financial Calculations app

The XAML for the Menu page

When you develop Windows 8 apps using Visual Basic, the user interface is implemented using an XML-based declarative markup language called *XAML* (*Extensible Application Markup Language*). The main purpose of the XAML for an app is to define the pages and the objects they contain. To do that, the XAML consists of *elements* with *properties* that define the function and appearance of these objects. As you'll learn later in this chapter, you frequently work directly with the XAML for a page. Because of that, you need to understand this code to develop Windows 8 apps. In contrast, when you develop Windows Forms applications, the code that creates a form and its controls is hidden from you.

Figure 26-6 presents most of the XAML for the Menu page of the Financial Calculations app. Although this code may seem daunting, keep in mind that you can use Visual Studio to generate much of this code. Also keep in mind that you're not expected to understand all of this code, although I'll describe some of the details here.

To start, this code indicates that the page is layout aware. That means that it was generated from a template that provides for the four view states that you learned about in figure 26-4. It also provides a name for the page and identifies the class that contains the Visual Basic code for the page.

Although it's not shown here, the XAML for a page also includes some namespace declarations. These declarations are similar to the Imports statements you can add to your Visual Basic code to include namespaces that are used by a page.

Next, the Page.Resources element defines any resources used by the page. The resource shown here was generated automatically, and it provides a name for the page. Because this resource is referred to by the text block for the page title, I changed the default value so it's appropriate for this page.

Much of the code that follows defines the layout and format of the page and its controls. The layout of a page is defined by containers called *panels*. Then, these panels contain the controls that make up the user interface.

The root panel for the Menu page is a *grid*, which provides for a layout with rows and columns. This grid consists of two rows. The first row is defined with a height of 140 pixels and contains the back button and page title. The second row takes up the rest of the screen height (*) and contains the rest of the page. This grid was generated by default when the page was created.

Within the root panel is another grid that defines the layout of the back button and page title. This grid was also generated by default. Because the Grid element doesn't specify the row it applies to, it defines the layout of the first row (row 0). This grid defines two columns. The first one is for the back button, and its width is set so it will accommodate that button (Auto). The second column takes up the rest of the screen width and contains the page title.

Next are the declarations for the back button and title. Because the Button element doesn't specify the column it applies to, it's placed in the first column (column 0). In contrast, the text block that contains the title is placed in the second column. Notice that both of these controls include a Style property that identifies a static resource. These resources determine what the button and title

The XAML for the Menu page

Page 1

```
<common:LayoutAwarePage
  x:Name="pageRoot"
  x:Class="FinancialCalculations.MenuPage"
  ...
  <Page.Resources>
    <x:String x:Key="AppName">Financial Calculations</x:String>
  </Page.Resources>

  <!--
    This grid acts as a root panel for the page that defines two rows:
    * Row 0 contains the back button and page title
    * Row 1 contains the rest of the page layout
  -->
  <Grid Style="{StaticResource LayoutRootStyle}" Background="#FF5C7997">
    <Grid.RowDefinitions>
      <RowDefinition Height="140"/>
      <RowDefinition Height="*"/>
    </Grid.RowDefinitions>

    <!-- Back button and page title -->
    <Grid>
      <Grid.ColumnDefinitions>
        <ColumnDefinition Width="Auto"/>
        <ColumnDefinition Width="*"/>
      </Grid.ColumnDefinitions>

      <Button x:Name="backButton" Click="GoBack"
       IsEnabled="{Binding Frame.CanGoBack, ElementName=pageRoot}"
       Style="{StaticResource BackButtonStyle}"/>
      <TextBlock x:Name="pageTitle" Grid.Column="1"
       Text="{StaticResource AppName}"
       Style="{StaticResource PageHeaderTextStyle}"/>
    </Grid>

    <Grid Grid.Row="1">
      <Grid.RowDefinitions>
        <RowDefinition Height="Auto"/>
        <RowDefinition Height="*">
      </Grid.RowDefinitions>

      <StackPanel x:Name="stackPanel" HorizontalAlignment="Left"
       Height="Auto" Margin="120,60,0,0" VerticalAlignment="Top"
       Width="Auto">
        <Button x:Name="btnFutureValue"
         Content="Calculate Future Value" HorizontalAlignment="Left"
         Margin="0,0,0,30" VerticalAlignment="Top" FontSize="30" Padding="30"
         Background="#FF1F3759" BorderBrush="#FF1F3759" Height="150"
         Width="377"/>
        <Button x:Name="btnDepreciation" Content="Calculate Depreciation"
         HorizontalAlignment="Left" VerticalAlignment="Top" FontSize="30"
         Padding="30" Background="#FFEE9719" BorderBrush="#FFEE9719"
         Height="150"/>
     </StackPanel>

      <Image x:Name="image" HorizontalAlignment="Left" Height="50"
       Margin="20,0,0,20" Grid.Row="1" VerticalAlignment="Bottom"
       Source="Assets/MurachLogo.png"/>
    </Grid>
```

Figure 26-6 The XAML for the Menu page (part 1 of 2)

look like, and Windows 8 provides a number of standard style resources like this. These resources are defined in the StandardStyles.xaml file in the project's Common folder. You can also define your own custom resources.

The next Grid element defines the layout of the second row of the root panel. It consists of two rows. The first row will be sized to fit its content, and the second row will occupy the remaining height of the outer row.

The first row of this grid contains another type of panel called a *stack panel*. A stack panel is used to stack the controls it contains vertically or horizontally. Here, the stack panel contains the two buttons used to display the Future Value and Depreciation pages, and these two buttons are stacked vertically by default.

The last element on this page is for an image control. This image will be displayed near the bottom of the second row of the grid that contains it.

The stack panel at the top of page 2 of this listing defines the layout of the buttons and image when the page is displayed in snapped view. This stack panel occupies the two rows of the grid that's defined within the second row of the root panel. To do that, it sets the Grid.Row property to 1, and it sets the Grid.RowSpan property to 2.

Notice that the width of this stack panel is set to 320 since that's the width that an application occupies in snapped view. Also notice that the Visibility property of this stack panel is set to "Collapsed" so it's not displayed when the application starts. Then, the code for the controls within the stack panel is set so the controls are sized and positioned appropriately for this view.

The last element on this page is for the *Visual State Manager*, which defines the transitions that occur when the view state changes. The Visual State Manager contains a VisualStateGroup element that contains a VisualState element for each application view state. By default, a page that's displayed in full-screen landscape or filled view is displayed as defined by the root panel. That's why the VisualState elements for these views don't contain any code. In contrast, the VisualState element for full-screen portrait view changes the style for the back button so the left and right margins for the buttons are decreased. (This code isn't shown here.)

The VisualState element for snapped view also makes some changes by default. Specifically, it changes the styles for the back button and page title so these elements fit within the 320-pixel width. Notice that these changes are done using animations. However, because the KeyTime property of the DiscreteObjectKeyFrame element for each animation is set to zero, the changes occur immediately instead of gradually. Also notice that the animations are coded within a Storyboard element, which can be used to control multiple animations.

In addition to changing the back button and page title for the page, the Storyboard element is used to display the stack panel that was defined for snapped view. To do that, the Visibility property of this stack panel is changed to "Visible". Note that it isn't necessary to change the Visibility property of the grid that displays the buttons and image in the other views because the stack panel overlays this grid.

Although it's not shown here, the VisualState element for snapped view also reduces the height of the image control that's displayed at the bottom of the page. That way, the image will be displayed in an appropriate size within the 320-pixel width.

The XAML for the Menu page **Page 2**

```
<!-- StackPanel that's used in snapped view -->
<StackPanel x:Name="spSnappedDisplay" Grid.Column="0" Grid.Row="1"
 Grid.RowSpan="2" Height="500" Width="320" HorizontalAlignment="Left"
 VerticalAlignment="Top" Visibility="Collapsed" Background="#FF5C7997">
  <Button Content="Calculate Future Value" HorizontalAlignment="Center"
   VerticalAlignment="Top" Margin="0,40,0,0" FontSize="18" Padding="10"
   Background="#FF1F3759" BorderBrush="#FF1F3759" Height="75"
   Width="220"/>
  <Button Content="Calculate Depreciation" HorizontalAlignment="Center"
   VerticalAlignment="Top" Margin="0,30,0,0" FontSize="18" Padding="10"
   Background="#FFEE9719" BorderBrush="#FFEE9719" Height="75"
   Width="220"/>
</StackPanel>

<VisualStateManager.VisualStateGroups>
  <!-- Visual states reflect the application's view state -->
  <VisualStateGroup x:Name="ApplicationViewStates">
    <VisualState x:Name="FullScreenLandscape"/>
    <VisualState x:Name="Filled"/>

    <!-- The entire page respects the narrower 100-pixel margin
         convention for portrait -->
    <VisualState x:Name="FullScreenPortrait">...</VisualState>

    <!-- The back button and title have different styles when snapped -->
    <VisualState x:Name="Snapped">
      <Storyboard>
        <ObjectAnimationUsingKeyFrames Storyboard.TargetName="backButton"
         Storyboard.TargetProperty="Style">
          <DiscreteObjectKeyFrame KeyTime="0"
           Value="{StaticResource SnappedBackButtonStyle}"/>
        </ObjectAnimationUsingKeyFrames>
        <ObjectAnimationUsingKeyFrames
         Storyboard.TargetName="pageTitle"
         Storyboard.TargetProperty="Style">
          <DiscreteObjectKeyFrame KeyTime="0"
           Value="{StaticResource SnappedPageHeaderTextStyle}"/>
        </ObjectAnimationUsingKeyFrames>

        <!-- Make the alternate panel visible when snapped -->
        <ObjectAnimationUsingKeyFrames
         Storyboard.TargetProperty="(UIElement.Visibility)"
         Storyboard.TargetName="spSnappedDisplay">
          <DiscreteObjectKeyFrame KeyTime="0">
            <DiscreteObjectKeyFrame.Value>
              <Visibility>Visible</Visibility>
            </DiscreteObjectKeyFrame.Value>
          </DiscreteObjectKeyFrame>
        </ObjectAnimationUsingKeyFrames>
        ...
      </Storyboard>
    </VisualState>
  </VisualStateGroup>
 </VisualStateManager.VisualStateGroups>
</Grid>
</common:LayoutAwarePage>
```

Figure 26-6 The XAML for the Menu page (part 2 of 2)

The XAML for the Future Value page

Figure 26-7 shows some of the XAML for the Future Value page. To start, you should notice the Storyboard element that's defined in the Page.Resources element. This storyboard defines the animations that display the future value when the user clicks the Calculate button. Because the first animation moves the text block for the future value, this text block must be defined with a transformation as shown near the bottom of part 1 of this figure.

Like the Menu page, the second row of the grid that defines the root panel for this page contains another grid that defines the layout of that row. In this case, the grid is defined with two columns. The first column contains a stack panel that contains the text blocks that identify the data on the page. Then, the second column contains a stack panel with the text boxes that let the user enter the required data, a text block that displays the future value, and a button for calculating the future value.

At the top of page 2 of this listing, you can see some of the code that defines the animations that are used to implement snapped view. Unlike the Menu page, an alternate layout hasn't been defined for this page. Because of that, animation must be used to change a variety of properties so all the elements will fit on the page. This works because the contents of the page are narrow enough to be displayed in snapped view. If the content of a page is too wide to display in snapped view, though, you would typically simplify its content as illustrated by the Bing Weather app in figure 26-4.

The remainder of the code for this page defines the app bar for the page. The layout of this app bar is defined by a grid with two columns. These columns are given equal widths since no widths are specified. Each of these columns contains a stack panel, although the first stack panel is empty. This is the standard layout for an app bar so commands can be placed in both its left and right sides. Then, the right panel contains a single button that uses a standard resource for its style property.

The XAML for the Depreciation page

Some of the XAML for the Depreciation page is presented in figure 26-8. Like the Future Value page, it defines a resource that's used to animate the display of the results for the page. Then, the main portion of the page consists of a grid with two columns and two rows. The first column in the first row contains a stack panel with the text blocks that identify the entry fields, and the second column in this row contains a stack panel with the two text boxes and the combo box that are used to enter data.

The second row of the grid contains a stack panel that spans both columns. This panel contains the text block that identifies the contents of the list box, the list box where the results of the calculation are displayed, and the Calculate button.

Although it's not shown here, this page also contains code that defines the animations used to display the page in snapped view. In addition, it contains an app bar that's identical to the one for the Future Value page.

The XAML for the Future Value page

Page 1

```
<common:LayoutAwarePage
  ...
  <Page.Resources>
    <x:String x:Key="AppName">Calculate Future Value</x:String>

    <Storyboard x:Name="DropDownResult">
      <DoubleAnimationUsingKeyFrames Storyboard.TargetProperty=
       "(UIElement.RenderTransform).(CompositeTransform.TranslateY)"
       Storyboard.TargetName="tblkFutureValue">
        <EasingDoubleKeyFrame KeyTime="0" Value="-59.077"/>
        <EasingDoubleKeyFrame KeyTime="0:0:0.8" Value="0"/>
      </DoubleAnimationUsingKeyFrames>

      <DoubleAnimationUsingKeyFrames
       Storyboard.TargetProperty="(UIElement.Opacity)"
       Storyboard.TargetName="tblkFutureValue">
        <EasingDoubleKeyFrame KeyTime="0" Value="0.2"/>
        <EasingDoubleKeyFrame KeyTime="0:0:0.8" Value="1"/>
      </DoubleAnimationUsingKeyFrames>
    </Storyboard>
  </Page.Resources>

  <Grid Style="{StaticResource LayoutRootStyle}" Background="#FF1F3759">
    ...
    <!--  A Grid to hold the user input controls -->
    <Grid x:Name="grid" Grid.Row="1" HorizontalAlignment="Left" Height="Auto"
     Margin="120,60,0,0" VerticalAlignment="Top" Width="Auto">
      <Grid.ColumnDefinitions>
        <ColumnDefinition Width="Auto"/>
        <ColumnDefinition Width="Auto"/>
      </Grid.ColumnDefinitions>

      <!-- A stack panel to hold the descriptions -->
      <StackPanel x:Name="stackPanel1" HorizontalAlignment="Left"
       Height="Auto" Margin="0" VerticalAlignment="Top" Width="198">
        <TextBlock x:Name="textBlock" TextWrapping="Wrap"
         Text="Monthly Investment" FontSize="22"/>
        ...
      </StackPanel>

      <!-- A stack panel to accept user input and display the result -->
      <StackPanel x:Name="stackPanel" Grid.Column="1"...>
        <TextBox x:Name="txtMonthlyInvestment" TextWrapping="Wrap" Text=""
         FontSize="20" Height="36" Tag="Monthly Investment"/>
        ...
        <TextBlock x:Name="tblkFutureValue" TextWrapping="Wrap" Text=""
         Margin="0,20,0,0" FontSize="22" Height="36"
         RenderTransformOrigin="0.5,0.5">
          <TextBlock.RenderTransform>
            <CompositeTransform/>
          </TextBlock.RenderTransform>
        </TextBlock>
        <Button x:Name="btnCalculate" Content="Calculate".../>
      </StackPanel>
    </Grid>
    ...
```

Figure 26-7 The XAML for the Future Value page (part 1 of 2)

The XAML for the Future Value page — Page 2

```
    <VisualStateManager.VisualStateGroups>
      <!-- Visual states reflect the application's view state -->
      <VisualStateGroup x:Name="ApplicationViewStates">
        ...
        <VisualState x:Name="Snapped">
          <Storyboard>
            <!--Apply different styles to back button and page title -->
            ...
            <!--Apply different styles to other page controls -->
            <ObjectAnimationUsingKeyFrames
             Storyboard.TargetProperty="(FrameworkElement.Margin)"
             Storyboard.TargetName="grid">
              <DiscreteObjectKeyFrame KeyTime="0">
                <DiscreteObjectKeyFrame.Value>
                  <Thickness>10,61,0,0</Thickness>
                </DiscreteObjectKeyFrame.Value>
              </DiscreteObjectKeyFrame>
            </ObjectAnimationUsingKeyFrames>
            <DoubleAnimation Duration="0" To="18"
             Storyboard.TargetProperty="(TextBlock.FontSize)"
             Storyboard.TargetName="textBlock"/>
            ...
            <ObjectAnimationUsingKeyFrames
             Storyboard.TargetProperty="(FrameworkElement.Width)"
             Storyboard.TargetName="grid">
              <DiscreteObjectKeyFrame KeyTime="0">
                <DiscreteObjectKeyFrame.Value>
                  <x:Double>328</x:Double>
                </DiscreteObjectKeyFrame.Value>
              </DiscreteObjectKeyFrame>
            </ObjectAnimationUsingKeyFrames>
            <DoubleAnimation Duration="0" To="1"
             Storyboard.TargetProperty="(UIElement.Opacity)"
             Storyboard.TargetName="txtMonthlyInvestment"/>
             ...
          </Storyboard>
        </VisualState>
      </VisualStateGroup>
    </VisualStateManager.VisualStateGroups>
  </Grid>

  <Page.BottomAppBar>
    <AppBar>
      <Grid>
        <Grid.ColumnDefinitions>
          <ColumnDefinition/>
          <ColumnDefinition/>
        </Grid.ColumnDefinitions>
        <StackPanel Orientation="Horizontal"/>
        <StackPanel Grid.Column="1" HorizontalAlignment="Right"
         Orientation="Horizontal">
          <Button x:Name="btnClearAll" IsEnabled="True"
           Style="{StaticResource DeleteAppBarButtonStyle}"
           AutomationProperties.Name="Clear All" Visibility="Visible"/>
        </StackPanel>
      </Grid>
    </AppBar>
  </Page.BottomAppBar>
</common:LayoutAwarePage>
```

Figure 26-7 The XAML for the Future Value page (part 2 of 2)

The XAML for the Depreciation page

```
<common:LayoutAwarePage
  x:Name="pageRoot"
  x:Class="FinancialCalculations.DepreciationPage"
  ...
  <Page.Resources>

    <x:String x:Key="AppName">Calculate Depreciation</x:String>

    <Storyboard x:Name="ChangeListColor">
      <ColorAnimationUsingKeyFrames Storyboard.TargetProperty=
       "(Control.Foreground).(SolidColorBrush.Color)"
       Storyboard.TargetName="lstDepreciation">
        <EasingColorKeyFrame KeyTime="0" Value="White"/>
        <EasingColorKeyFrame KeyTime="0:0:1" Value="Black"/>
      </ColorAnimationUsingKeyFrames>
    </Storyboard>
  </Page.Resources>

  <Grid Style="{StaticResource LayoutRootStyle}" Background="#FF1F3759">
    ...
    <!--  A Grid to hold the user input controls -->
    <Grid x:Name="grid" Grid.Row="1" HorizontalAlignment="Left" Height="Auto"
     Margin="120,50,0,0" VerticalAlignment="Top" Width="Auto">
      <Grid.ColumnDefinitions>
        <ColumnDefinition Width="Auto"/>
        <ColumnDefinition Width="Auto"/>
      </Grid.ColumnDefinitions>
      <Grid.RowDefinitions>
        <RowDefinition Height="Auto"/>
        <RowDefinition Height="Auto"/>
      </Grid.RowDefinitions>
      ...
      <!-- A stack panel to hold the descriptions -->
      ...
      <!-- A stack panel to accept user input -->
      ...
      <!-- A StackPanel to display results-->
      <StackPanel x:Name="stackPanel1" Grid.Row="1" Grid.ColumnSpan="2"
       HorizontalAlignment="Left" Height="Auto" Margin="0,20,0,0"
       VerticalAlignment="Top" Width="375">
        <TextBlock x:Name="textBlock3" Text="Sum of Years Digits"
         FontSize="22"/>
        <ListBox x:Name="lstDepreciation" HorizontalAlignment="Left"
         Height="190" Margin="0,5,0,0" VerticalAlignment="Top" Width="Auto"
         Foreground="White" Background="White" FontSize="20"/>
        <Button x:Name="btnCalculate" Content="Calculate".../>
      </StackPanel>
    </Grid>

  <Page.BottomAppBar>
  ...
  </Page.BottomAppBar>
</common:LayoutAwarePage>
```

Figure 26-8 The XAML for the Depreciation page

The event handlers for the Menu page

Figure 26-9 presents the two event handlers for the Menu page. These event handlers are executed when the user clicks one of the buttons on this page. The first one causes the Future Value page to be displayed, and the second one causes the Depreciation page to be displayed. Here, *this* refers to the current page just like it does in a Windows Forms application. Then, the Framework property refers to the main content control for the page, which provides for navigation. Finally, the Navigate method is used to navigate to the appropriate page.

The event handlers for the Future Value page

The Future Value page includes two event handlers. The first one is executed when the user clicks the Calculate button, and the second one is executed when the user clicks the Clear All button in the app bar. The code for these event handlers is also shown in figure 26-9. Most of this code is identical to code you would use in a Windows Forms application. Because of that, I'll just focus on the major differences here.

To start, the last statement within the If block of the first event handler moves the focus to the Monthly Investment text box by calling the Focus method. This works like the Select method of a text box in a Windows Forms application. Notice here that when you call the Focus method, you must include an argument that indicates how the focus was set. In this case, the argument indicates that the focus was set programmatically.

The code that displays a dialog box if an error occurs is different as well. Here, instead of calling the static Show method of the MessageBox class, you have to create an instance of the MessageDialog class. The constructor for this class accepts two arguments for the text of the message and the caption for the dialog box. Then, the next statement displays this dialog box by calling its ShowAsync method. This method starts the display operation asynchronously and returns an object that represents the operation.

The last statement in this event handler causes the animation to start for the text block that displays the future value. Here, DropDownResult refers to the name of the resource that was defined for the animation in the XAML for the page. Then, the Begin method starts this animation.

The event handlers for the Menu page

```
Private Sub btnFutureValue_Click(sender As Object,
        e As RoutedEventArgs) Handles btnFutureValue.Click
    Me.Frame.Navigate(GetType(FutureValuePage))
End Sub

Private Sub btnDepreciation_Click(sender As Object,
        e As RoutedEventArgs) Handles btnDepreciation.Click
    Me.Frame.Navigate(GetType(DepreciationPage))
End Sub
```

The event handlers for the Future Value page

```
Private Sub btnCalculate_Click(sender As Object,
        e As RoutedEventArgs) Handles btnCalculate.Click
    Try
        If IsValidData() Then
            Dim monthlyInvestment As Decimal =
                CDec(txtMonthlyInvestment.Text)
            Dim yearlyInterestRate As Decimal =
                CDec(txtInterestRate.Text)
            Dim years As Integer = CInt(txtYears.Text)

            Dim monthlyInterestRate As Decimal =
                yearlyInterestRate / 12 / 100
            Dim months As Integer = years * 12

            Dim futureValue As Decimal = Me.FutureValue(
                monthlyInvestment, monthlyInterestRate, months)

            tblkFutureValue.Text = futureValue.ToString("c")
            txtMonthlyInvestment.Focus(FocusState.Programmatic)
        End If
    Catch ex As Exception
        Dim msg As New MessageDialog(ex.Message & vbCrLf & vbCrLf &
            ex.GetType.ToString & vbCrLf & ex.StackTrace, "Exception")
        Dim result = msg.ShowAsync
    End Try

    ' Call the XAML animation for the Future Value text block
    DropDownResult.Begin()
End Sub

Private Sub btnClearAll_Click(sender As Object,
        e As RoutedEventArgs) Handles btnClearAll.Click
    txtMonthlyInvestment.Text = ""
    txtInterestRate.Text = ""
    txtYears.Text = ""
    tblkFutureValue.Text = ""
End Sub
```

Figure 26-9 The event handlers for the Financial Calculations app (part 1 of 2)

The event handlers for the Depreciation page

Part 2 of figure 26-9 presents the three event handlers for the Depreciation page. The first one is executed when the page is loaded. It loads the combo box with the values the user can select for the life of an asset. Then, it sets the SelectedIndex property of the combo box to 4 so the fifth item in the list is displayed by default.

The second event handler is executed when the Calculate button is clicked. Like the Future Value page, the code for this page includes an argument on the Focus method that moves the focus to the Initial Cost text box. It also uses the MessageDialog class to display error messages. And it uses the Begin method of the ChangeListColor resource that's defined in the XAML for the page to start the animation for the list box.

The third event handler is executed when the Clear All button in the app bar is clicked. It simply resets the two text boxes, the combo box, and the list box to their original values.

The event handlers for the Depreciation page

```
Private Sub pageRoot_Loaded(sender As Object,
        e As RoutedEventArgs) Handles pageRoot.Loaded
    ' Populate the Life combo box with ints from 1 to 40
    For i As Integer = 1 To 40
        cboLife.Items.Add(i)
    Next i
    cboLife.SelectedIndex = 4
End Sub

Private Sub btnCalculate_Click(sender As Object,
        e As RoutedEventArgs) Handles btnCalculate.Click
    Try
        If IsValidData() Then
            Dim cost As Double = CDbl(txtInitialCost.Text)
            Dim finalValue As Double = CDbl(txtFinalValue.Text)
            Dim life As Integer = CInt(cboLife.SelectedItem)
            Dim dLife As Double = CDbl(life)

            lstDepreciation.Items.Clear()

            For i As Integer = 1 To life
                Dim period As Double = CDbl(i)
                Dim yearlyAllowance As Double =
                    Me.SYDDepreciation(cost, finalValue, dLife, period)
                lstDepreciation.Items.Add("Year " & i & ": " &
                    yearlyAllowance.ToString("c"))
            Next i
            txtInitialCost.Focus(FocusState.Programmatic)
        End If
    Catch ex As Exception
        Dim msg As New MessageDialog(ex.Message & vbLf & vbLf &
            ex.GetType.ToString & vbLf & ex.StackTrace, "Exception")
        Dim result = msg.ShowAsync
    End Try

    ' Call the XAML animation for the list box
    ChangeListColor.Begin()

End Sub

Private Sub btnClearAll_Click(sender As Object,
        e As RoutedEventArgs) Handles btnClearAll.Click
    txtInitialCost.Text = ""
    txtFinalValue.Text = ""
    cboLife.SelectedIndex = 4
    lstDepreciation.Items.Clear()
End Sub
```

Figure 26-9 The event handlers for the Financial Calculations app (part 2 of 2)

Visual Studio features for developing Windows Store apps

Visual Studio 2012 includes several features that can help you develop Windows Store apps. You'll learn about some of these features in the topics that follow. Note that these features are available with any of the full editions of Visual Studio 2012. In addition, they're available with Visual Studio 2012 Express for Windows 8.

The Windows Store app project templates

Figure 26-10 describes the three templates Visual Studio provides for creating Windows Store projects. You can use the Split App template to create a project with two pages like the ones shown at the top of this figure. Here, the first page includes a list of groups. Then, if the user selects a group, the second page displays the items in the group and the user can select an item to display its details.

The Grid App template is similar, but it provides for three pages. The first page uses a grid to display groups, along with the items in each group. Then, the user can select a group to display another page that provides the details for the group and a list of the items in the group. The third page displays the details for an individual item, and the user can display this page by selecting an item in one of the other two pages.

The Split App and Grid App templates are useful when you want to create an app that displays information by navigating among groups and the items in those groups. For all other apps, you'll want to use the Blank App template. This template creates a project with a single, blank page. In most cases, you'll delete this page and add the pages you want using the provided page templates. That includes templates for all of the pages of the Split App and Grid App project templates. It also includes a Basic Page template that includes the code for a back button and page title and the code that provides for layout awareness.

Before I go on, you should know that you have to have a developer license before you can create a Windows Store app. The first time you try to create a Windows Store app, you'll be prompted to get a license. This license is free, but it must be renewed every 30 days unless you have a developer account, which lets you submit your apps to the Windows Store. If you have a developer account, the license is good for 90 days. Visual Studio will prompt you to renew the license when it expires. You can also renew it before it expires using the Project→Store→Acquire Developer License command (or the Store→Acquire Developer License command from Visual Studio Express).

The two pages of the Split App template

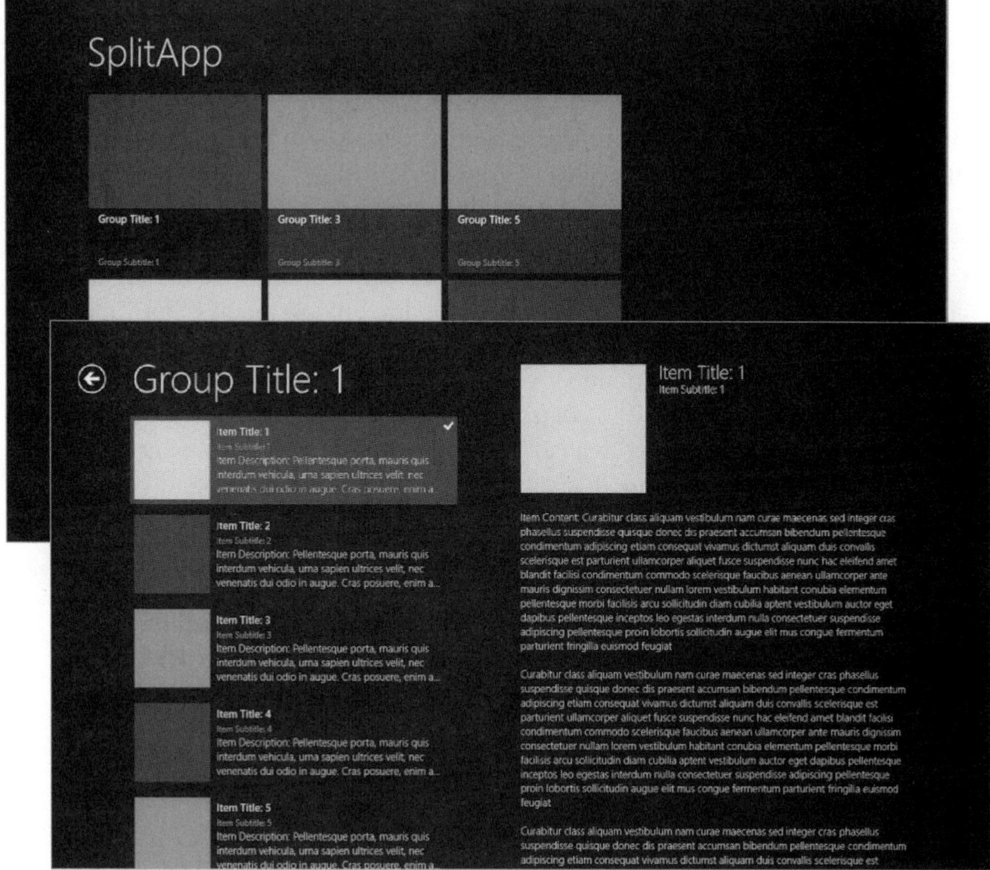

Three Windows Store app project templates

Template	Description
Blank App	Creates a single-page project with no predefined controls or layout.
Split App	Creates a two-page project that provides for navigating among grouped items displayed in a list. The first page lists the groups and lets the user select a group. The second page lists the items in the selected group and lets the user select an item to display its details.
Grid App	Creates a three-page project that provides for navigating among groups of items displayed in a grid. The first page displays the groups of items and lets the user select a group or an item. The second page displays the details for a selected group, along with a list of the items in that group, and lets the user select an item. The third page displays the details for an item.

Description

- The Split App and Group App templates generate code that provides for hierarchical navigation, moving between group and detail levels, and layout awareness.
- Visual Studio also provides individual page templates, including a Basic Page template that provides a page title, a back button, and layout awareness.

Figure 26-10 The Windows Store app project templates

How to use the XAML Designer

To design the user interface for a Windows Store app, you use the *XAML Designer* shown in figure 26-11. The main difference between this designer and the Form Designer is that the XAML Designer consists of two panes. The XAML pane displays the XAML for the page, and the Design pane shows the user interface that the XAML creates.

To add controls to a page, you can use the same basic skills you use to add controls to a form. For example, you can click on a control in the Toolbox and then click in the page where you want to place the control. Or, you can drag the control from the Toolbox to the page. When you develop a Windows Store app, you can also drag a control from the Toolbox to the XAML pane. Finally, you can enter the code for a control directly into the XAML pane.

To change the properties of a control, you can select it in the Design pane or place the cursor in the element that defines the control in the XAML pane. Then, the properties of the control are displayed in the Properties window and you can change them from there. You can also change properties directly in the XAML pane.

When you design a page for a Windows Store app, you typically start by designing the page that will be displayed in full-screen landscape view state. Then, when you have that view state the way you want it, you can provide code for displaying the page in the other view states. One way to do that is to use the Device tab that's shown in this figure.

To display a page in the various view states, you can use the View buttons at the top of the Device tab. To see how the page will look in snapped view state, for example, you can click the Snapped button. The first time you do that, the size of the back button and page title will be reduced if you started the page from a template that includes the code for making those changes. However, the rest of the elements will remain at their full size, and any portion of the page that extends beyond 320 pixels will be cut off.

At this point, you can make any changes you need for the page to fit in the allotted space. That includes resizing and repositioning elements as well as deleting elements. But first, you should select the Enable State Recording option on the Device tab. That way, any changes you make will be recorded in the Visual State Manager as you saw earlier in this chapter. When you're done, be sure to remove the check mark from this option.

As you develop a Windows Store app, you'll want to run and test it to be sure it works the way it should. You can run an app from Visual Studio on your local machine, on a remote machine, or in the simulator. To change the location, you select an option from the drop-down list to the right of the Run button. Then, you can click this button or press F5 to run the app in the selected location.

When you first run an app, it occupies the entire screen. If you want to see what the app looks like when it's displayed in snapped view, you can use the Windows+Period key combination. The first time you use this key combination, the app is displayed in snapped view at the right side of the screen. The second time, it's displayed in snapped view at the left side of the screen. And the third time, it's redisplayed in full-screen landscape view.

The Future Value page in the XAML Designer

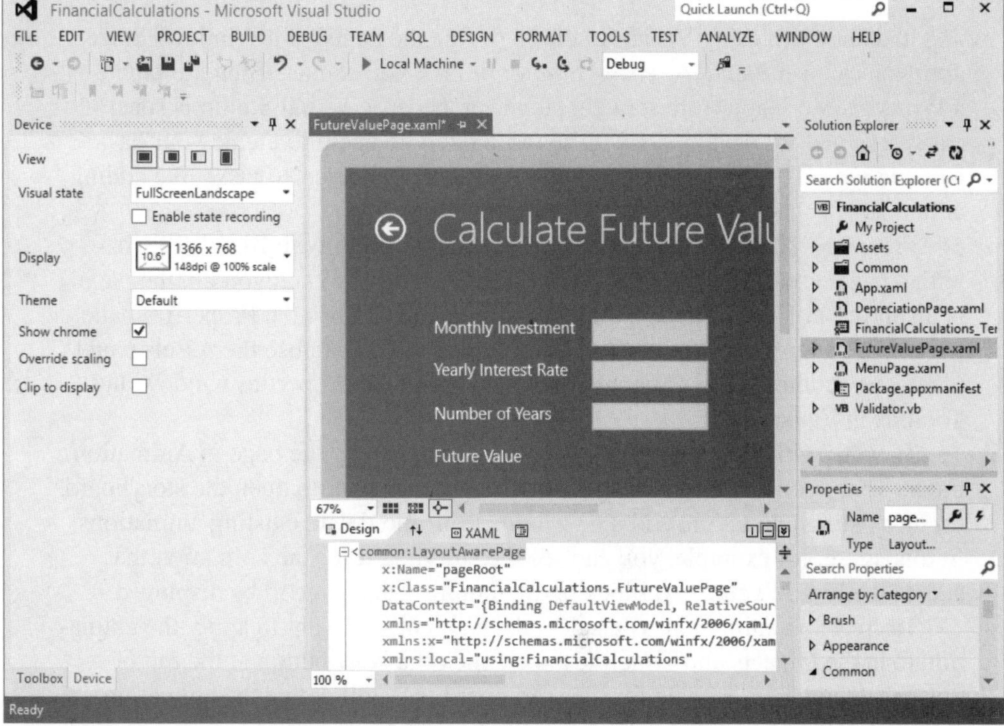

Description

- To define the user interface for a Windows Store app, you use the *XAML Designer*. This designer is divided into two panes. The Design pane shows the user interface for the page, and the XAML pane shows the XAML that defines the user interface.
- To add a control to a page and set its properties, you can use the same techniques you use for Windows Forms controls.
- You can also add a control by dragging it from the Toolbox to the location in the XAML pane where you want the control to appear or by entering the code for the control directly into the XAML pane.
- You can also set the properties of a control by entering them directly into the XAML pane.
- To define the user interface for different view states, you can use the Device window. This window is displayed in a tab that's grouped with the Toolbox and can be displayed using the Design→Device Window command.
- To work with a specific view state, click on the View button for that state. Then, to record the changes you make in the Visual State Manager, select the Enable State Recording option.

Figure 26-11 How to use the XAML Designer

How to use Blend for Visual Studio

In addition to using Visual Studio to design the pages of a Windows Store app, you can use *Blend for Visual Studio*. In fact, you can use Blend to create a Windows Store app from scratch. However, because Visual Studio is specifically designed for developers, you're more likely to use it to create your basic page designs. Then, you can use Blend for more sophisticated tasks like adding animation.

Figure 26-12 presents some basic skills for working with Blend. To work with a page, you start by displaying it on the *Artboard*. When you do, the page is displayed in Design mode by default. Then, you can use the Properties panel to change the properties of a selected control, and you can use the Assets panel to add new controls. These panels work much like the Properties window and Toolbox in Visual Studio.

To work with the animations for a page, you display the page in Animation mode. Then, you can use the Objects and Timeline panel to open the storyboard for an existing animation, add a new animation, and delete existing animations. In this figure, for example, you can see the storyboard for the animation that causes the Future Value text block on the Future Value page to be displayed.

To create an animation, you select the element you want to apply the animation to in the Objects and Timeline panel, click the New button at the top of this panel, and enter a name for the storyboard that will define the animation. Then, a timeline is displayed for the animation, and you can add markers called *keyframes* at points along the timeline where you want properties of the object to change. The position and length of a keyframe indicate when the animation will start and how long it will take.

To illustrate, consider the animation for the Future Value text block. This animation consists of two keyframes, both of which start at zero seconds on the timeline and take eight tenths of a second to complete. (You can't distinguish these two keyframes in this figure because they overlap.) One keyframe changes the vertical position of the text block from -59.077 at 0 seconds to 0 at .8 seconds. The other keyframe changes the opacity of the text block from .2 at 0 seconds to 1 at .8 seconds. If you look back to the beginning of the XAML code for the Future Value form in figure 26-7, you'll see how these animations were recorded. Note that the red circle to the left of the storyboard name in the Objects and Timeline panel indicates that recording mode is on. You can turn recording mode off and on by clicking on this circle.

You can also use Blend to change the layout of a page for any of the four application view states. To do that, you use the States panel shown in the lower left corner of this screen. When you select a view state from this panel, the page layout for that view is displayed on the Artboard, and the objects on the page are listed in the Objects and Timeline panel. Then, you can select a control on the Artboard or in the object list and change its property values in the Properties panel to record the changes in the Visual State Manager. When you're done, be sure to turn recording mode off so you don't make any unintended changes.

The Future Value page in Blend for Visual Studio

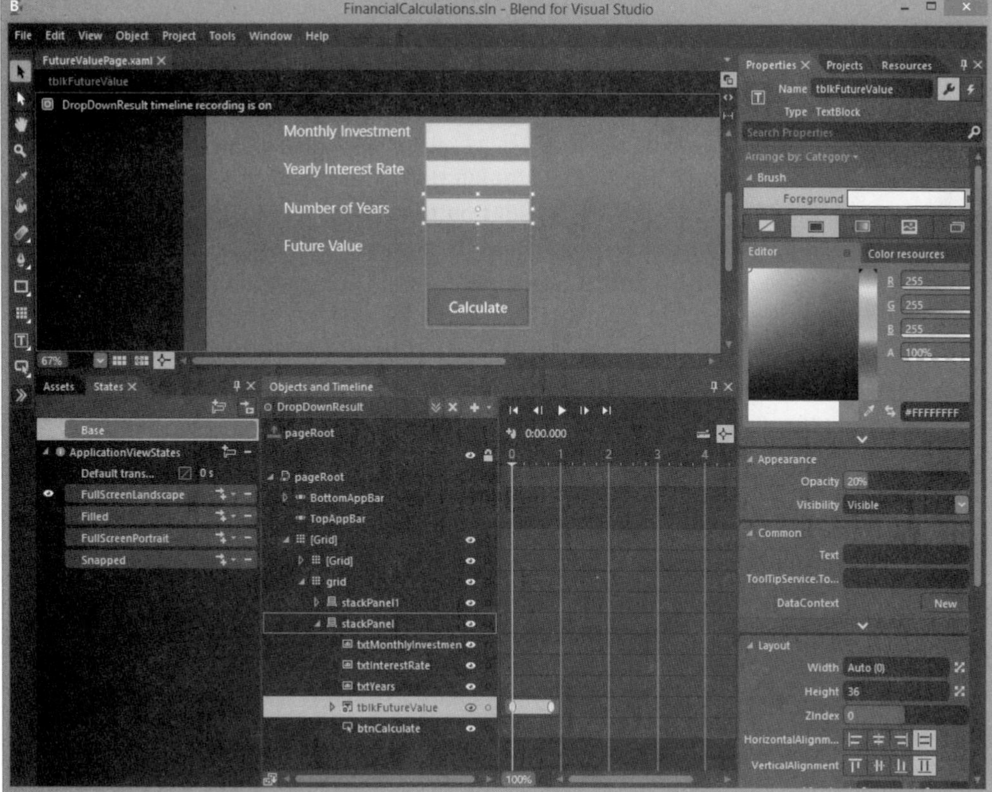

Description

- To open the current project in Blend for Visual Studio, right-click on the project name in the Solution Explorer and select the Open in Blend command.
- To display a page on the *Artboard*, double-click on it in the Projects panel.
- To work with animations, use the Window→Workspaces→Animations command to display the workspace in Animation mode.
- To animate an object, you use the Objects and Timeline panel. This panel lets you add *keyframes* that mark specific points along the timeline of the animation.
- An animation can cause one or more properties of a control to change along a keyframe. You can change the height, width, and position of a control by dragging in the Artboard. You can change other properties in the Properties panel.
- When an animation runs, the properties of the control will change gradually from their previous state to the state that's set in the keyframe.
- You can also work with the design of a page by displaying the workspace in Design mode (Window→Workspaces→Design). From this mode, you can add controls using the Assets panel, and you can change properties using the Properties panel.
- The States panel lets you change the layout of a page for any of the four application view states. This works much like the state recording feature of Visual Studio.

Figure 26-12 How to use Blend for Visual Studio

How to use the Visual Studio simulator

If a Windows Store app you develop will run on a tablet like a Microsoft Surface, you'll want to test the app in a similar environment before you deploy it. To do that, you can use the Visual Studio simulator. Figure 26-13 shows how this simulator works.

Before you can run an app in the simulator, you must select the Simulator option from the drop-down list on the Start button. Then, when you click this button, the app is displayed in the simulator as shown in this figure. Here, the Future Value page of the Financial Calculations app is displayed.

By default, the simulator is displayed in mouse mode so you can use the mouse to interact with it. However, you can also use the simulator to test an application using touch gestures even if you don't have a touch screen. To do that, you use the second, third, and fourth buttons in the second group of buttons at the right side of the simulator. (This first button is for mouse mode.)

The second button lets you emulate touch gestures that require a single finger. When you click this button, a pointer that consists of a circle with a plus sign on it is displayed as shown in this figure. Then, you can use the mouse to move this pointer, you can click the mouse to emulate a tap, and you can press and hold the left mouse button to drag or swipe.

The third and fourth buttons let you emulate pinch and zoom gestures and touch rotation. When you click one of these buttons, two pointers appear. Then, you can use the scroll wheel to move the pointers closer or farther apart, and you can press and hold the left mouse button and use the scroll wheel to zoom in or out or rotate the screen. Note that you can use these gestures only if your application explicitly provides for them. In contrast, the touch gestures that require a single finger are provided by default.

The two buttons in the next group let you change the orientation of the screen. The first button rotates the simulator 90 degrees clockwise, and the second button rotates the simulator 90 degrees counterclockwise. That way, you can test the application in both landscape and portrait orientation.

The button in the next group lets you set the screen size and resolution. When you click this button, a list is displayed that lets you select the size and resolution you want to use. That's important because the size and resolution of different tablets vary. This list also includes two standard sizes and resolutions for PC monitors.

The button in the next group is useful if the app you're testing is location-aware. When you click this button, a dialog box is displayed that lets you set a latitude, longitude, altitude, and margin of error. Then, you can change these values to test the app using different locations.

The two buttons in the next group let you take a screenshot of the page that's displayed in the simulator and change settings related to the screenshots, such as where they're saved. Finally, the last button displays online help information for using the simulator.

The Future Value page displayed in the simulator

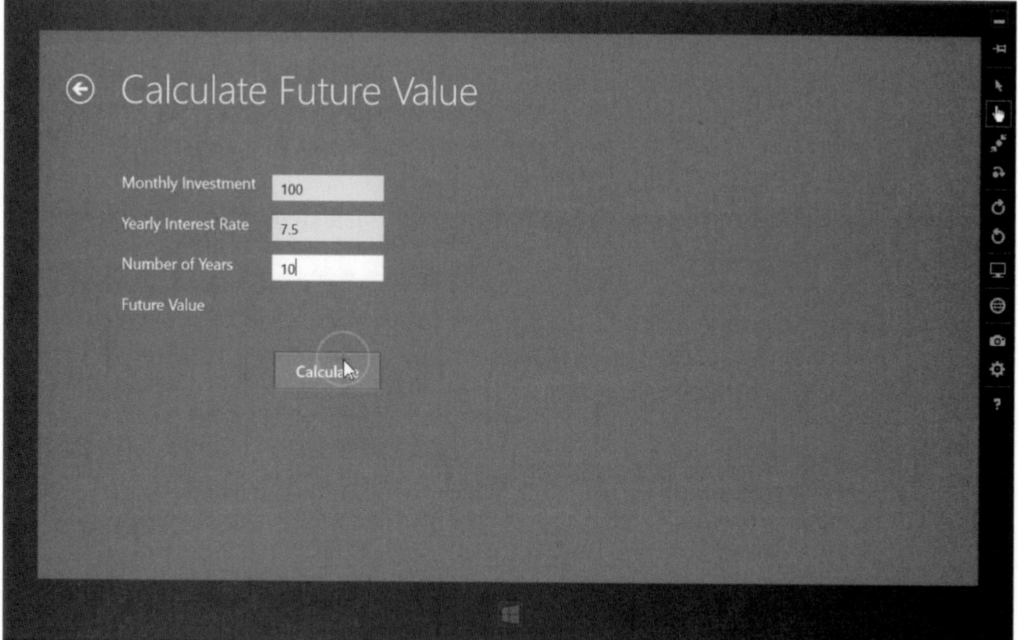

Description

- The Visual Studio simulator lets you test Windows Store apps as if they're being run on a tablet.
- To run an app in the simulator, select the Simulator option from the drop-down list on the Start button and then click this button.
- The buttons on the right side of the simulator let you use standard mouse gestures to interact with the app, emulate various touch gestures, change the orientation of the tablet, and change the screen size and resolution.
- The simulator is particularly useful for testing touch gestures on screens that don't provide for touch. It's also useful for testing an app in portrait orientation and in different screen resolutions.
- You can also display an app in snapped view in the simulator. To do that, use the Windows+Period key combination to switch between snapped view displayed at the right side of the simulator, snapped view displayed at the left side of the simulator, and full-screen view.
- To exit from the simulator, press Ctrl+Alt+F4.

Note

- The simulator must have focus before you can use the keyboard shortcuts to switch between snapped view and full-screen view or to exit from the simulator. To make sure it has the focus, you can interact with the application or press one of the simulator's buttons.

Figure 26-13 How to use the Visual Studio simulator

How to submit an app to the Windows Store

Once you've thoroughly tested your app, you're ready to deploy it so your users have access to it. In this topic, I'll summarize the procedure for making an app available from the Windows Store. Keep in mind, though, that if you're developing an app for use by a single company, you may want to deploy the app to the company's server instead of to the Windows Store. Then, you can use a feature of the operating system called Windows PowerShell to install the app on any PC or tablet that has access to the server.

Figure 26-14 presents the basic steps you must complete to submit an app to the *Windows Store*, which is an online store from which users can download apps. To start, you must open a developer account. Then, you can reserve a name for your app. This name must be unique within the Windows Store, and it is good for up to one year. If you don't submit an app with this name within a year of reserving the name, the name is released and you will have to reserve it again.

Before you can upload an app to the Windows Store, you must create a *splash screen* that's displayed when the app starts. In addition, you must create at least three logos. The store logo is displayed along with a description of the app in the results of a search in the Windows Store. The logo is displayed on the square tile for the app on the Start screen after the app is installed. And the small logo is displayed in the results of a search from the Start screen and in the list of searchable apps when the Start screen is zoomed out. These items are typically stored in the project's Assets folder and must be a predetermined size.

The next step is to modify the *application manifest* so it contains the information necessary to submit your app. Then, you can associate the app with the Windows Store. This downloads some required values from the Windows Store to the application manifest.

When you submit an app to the Windows Store, you must include at least one screenshot of the app. To create this screenshot, you can use the Capture Screenshots command to build the project and display it in the simulator. Or, you can just start the app in the simulator as described in the previous figure. Then, you can use the Copy Screenshot button to create from one to eight screenshots.

The last step before submitting the app is to create a *package* for the app, which includes all the instructions and resources a user needs to run the app. To do that, you will need to log in to your developer account and then complete the steps of the Create App Packages wizard.

Finally, you're ready to upload your app to the Windows Store. Before you do that, though, you might want to check that the app meets Microsoft's requirements for a Windows Store app. To do that, you can use the Windows App Certification Kit that's installed with Visual Studio.

To start the upload process, you need to log in to your developer account. Then, if you've already reserved a name for your app, you can use the dashboard that's displayed to edit the existing information for the app and upload its package. Otherwise, you can click the Submit a New App button and then follow the instructions to upload the package.

Basic steps for submitting an app to the Windows Store

- Open a developer account that lets you upload your apps to the Windows Store. To do that from Visual Studio, use the Project→Store→Open Developer Account command.
- Reserve a name for your app. To do that from Visual Studio, use the Project→Store→Reserve App Name command. You can reserve a name up to a year before you submit the app.
- If you haven't already done so, create a splash screen and application logos for the app, and add them to the project.
- Modify the application manifest for the project as necessary, including identifying the splash screen and logos. To display the application manifest, double-click on the Package.appxmanifest file in the Solution Explorer or use the Project→Store→Edit App Manifest command.
- Associate the app with the Windows Store using the Project→Store→Associate App with the Store command.
- Use the Visual Studio simulator to capture a copy of from one to eight screen images of the app.
- Create a package for the app using the Project→Store→Create App Packages command.
- Upload the package for your app to the Windows Store using the Project→Store→Upload App Packages command.

Description

- The *application manifest* contains information that identifies and describes your app, specifies what system features and devices it can use, declares customizations made to Windows 8 features, and identifies and describes your app when it's deployed.
- A *package* is a container that contains instructions and resources related to your app. A user who downloads an app from the Windows Store gets the app package.
- When you submit an app to the Windows Store, it's checked to be sure it meets the requirements for all Windows Store apps. To be sure your app passes this certification process, you can use the Windows App Certification Kit that's installed with Visual Studio.

Express Edition difference

- The commands for submitting an app are on the Store menu rather than the Project→Store menu.

Figure 26-14 How to submit an app to the Windows Store

Perspective

The purpose of this chapter was to introduce you to Windows Store apps and some of the tools you can use to develop them. Now that you've finished this chapter, we hope you'll see that Windows 8 and Visual Studio 2012 provide an exciting new way to develop modern applications that can be run on PCs and tablets. Keep in mind, though, that there's a lot more you need to know before you can begin developing your own Windows Store apps. In particular, you need to learn the details of using XAML to define a user interface. To get those skills, we recommend that you purchase a book specifically about developing Windows Store apps with Visual Basic and XAML.

Terms

Windows 8 application
Windows Store app
app bar
nav bar
charm bar
charm
view state
full-screen landscape view state
full-screen portrait view state
snapped view state
filled view state
XAML (Extensible Application Markup Language)
element
property
panel
grid
stack panel
Visual State Manager
XAML Designer
Blend for Visual Studio
Artboard
keyframe
Windows Store
splash screen
application manifest
package

Appendix A

How to install and use the software for this book

To develop the applications presented in this book, you need to have Visual Studio 2012 or Visual Studio Express 2012 for Windows Desktop installed on your system. In addition, if you're going to develop database applications that use databases that are stored on your own PC rather than on a remote server, you need to install SQL Server on your PC. The easiest way to do that is to install SQL Server 2012 Express LocalDB. In fact, this edition of SQL Server is installed by default when you install any edition of Visual Studio 2012.

This appendix describes how to install Visual Studio 2012 or Visual Studio 2012 Express. In addition, this appendix describes what you need to do to use the database for this book. But first, this appendix describes the files for this book that are available for download from our web site and shows you how to download, install, and use them.

How to use the downloadable files

Throughout this book, you'll see complete applications that illustrate the skills that are presented in each chapter. To help you understand how these applications work, you can download these applications from our web site. Then, you can open these applications in Visual Studio, view the source code, and run them.

These applications come in a single download that also includes the starting points and solutions for the exercises that are at the end of each chapter. Figure A-1 describes how you can download, install, and use these files. When you download the single setup file and execute it, it will install all of the files for this book in the C:\Murach\VB 2012 directory.

The Book Applications directory contains all of the Windows applications that are presented in this book. If you like, you can use Visual Studio to open these applications. Then, you can view the source code for these applications, and you can run them to see how they work.

The Exercise Starts directory contains all of the starting points for the exercises presented in this book. When you execute the setup file, the subdirectories of this directory are copied to the C:\VB 2012 directory (creating this directory if necessary). This makes it easy to locate the exercise starts as you work through the exercises. For example, you can find the exercise start for chapter 1 in the C:\VB 2012\Chapter 01 directory. In addition, if you make a mistake and want to restore a file to its original state, you can do that by copying it from the directory where it was originally installed.

The Exercise Starts directory also contains Database and Files subdirectories that are copied to C:\VB 2012. The Database subdirectory contains the files for the MMABooks database that are used by the exercises for the chapters in section 3 of this book. The Files subdirectory contains all the text, binary, and XML files used by the exercises for the chapters in sections 4 and 5 as well as for chapter 11.

The Exercise Solutions directory contains the source code for the solutions to the exercises. If you have trouble doing the exercises, you can use Visual Studio to open these applications. Then, you can compare the solutions to your applications to solve any problems that you encountered while attempting to do the exercises.

The Database directory contains another copy of the files for the MMABooks database that's used in section 3. In addition, it contains two files that you can use to create the MMABooks database if you want to use SQL Server Express instead of SQL Server Express LocalDB. You'll learn more about using all of these files in figure A-3.

What the downloadable files for this book contain

- All of the applications presented in this book
- The starting points for all of the exercises in this book
- The solutions for all of the exercises in this book
- The data files and database for the applications and exercises

How to download and install the files for this book

- Go to www.murach.com, and go to the page for *Murach's Visual Basic 2012.*
- Click the link for "FREE download of the book applications." Then, select the "All book files" link and respond to the resulting pages and dialog boxes. This will download a setup file named vb12_allfiles.exe onto your hard drive.
- Use Windows Explorer to find the setup file on your hard drive. Then, double-click this file and respond to the dialog boxes that follow. This installs the files in directories that start with C:\Murach\VB 2012.

How your system is prepared for doing the exercises

- Some of the exercises have you start from existing projects. The source code for these projects is in the C:\Murach\VB 2012\Exercise Starts directory. After the setup file installs the files in the download, it runs a batch file named exercise_starts_setup.bat that copies all of the subdirectories of the Exercise Starts directory to the C:\VB 2012 directory. Then, you can find all of the starting points for the exercises in directories like C:\VB 2012\Chapter 01 and C:\VB 2012\Chapter 04.

How to view the source code for the applications

- The source code for the applications presented in this book can be found in the C:\Murach\VB 2012\Book Applications directory. You can view this source code by opening the project or solution in the appropriate directory.

How to view the solutions to the exercises

- The exercise solutions can be found in the C:\Murach\VB 2012\Exercise Solutions directory. You can view these applications by opening the project or solution in the appropriate directory.

How to prepare your system for using the database

- If you will be using SQL Server 2012 Express LocalDB, no preparation is required. If you will be using SQL Server 2012 Express, however, you will need to install this product and then run the batch file we provide to create the database and attach it to the database server as described in figure A-3.

Figure A-1   How to use the downloadable files for this book

How to install Visual Studio 2012

If you've installed Windows applications before, you shouldn't have any trouble installing Visual Studio 2012. You simply insert the DVD and the setup program starts automatically. This setup program will lead you through the steps for installing Visual Studio as summarized in figure A-2.

After you accept the license terms and click the Next button on the first page of the setup program, the program lets you select the optional features you want to install. This includes features like Blend for Visual Studio, LightSwitch, and developer tools for Microsoft Office, Microsoft SharePoint, and Microsoft Web. If you're sure you won't need some of these features, you can uncheck them. Then, when you click the Install button, all the features you selected, along with the .NET Framework 4.5 and SQL Server 2012 Express LocalDB, are installed.

The procedure for installing Visual Studio Express 2012 for Windows Desktop is similar. Before you can install this edition, though, you have to download the setup program from Microsoft's web site. Then, when you run the setup program, no optional features are installed. However, the .NET Framework 4.5 and SQL Server 2012 Express LocalDB are installed just as they are for other editions of Visual Studio.

The Visual Studio 2012 setup program

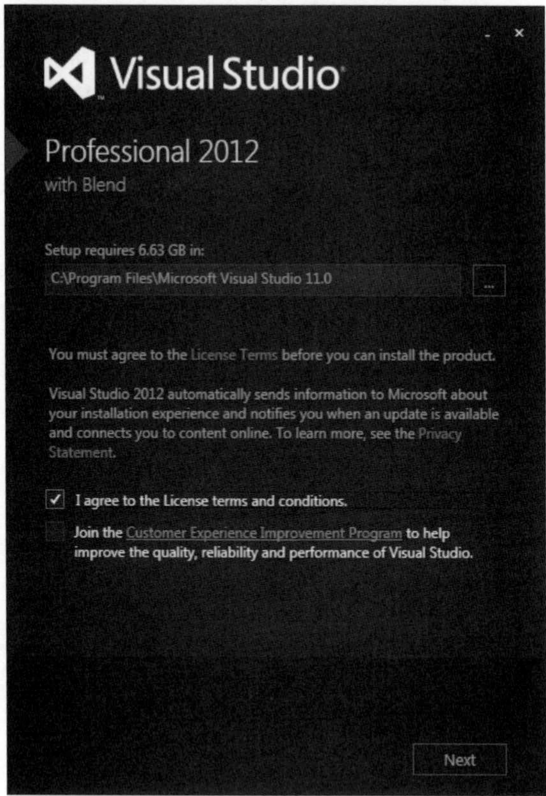

How to install Visual Studio 2012

1. Insert the DVD and the setup program will start automatically.
2. Review and then agree to the license terms by checking the appropriate box. Then, click the Next button.
3. When the Optional Features page is displayed, you can uncheck any features you don't need and then click the Install button.
4. When the Setup Successful page is displayed, you can click the Restart Now button to restart your computer and finish the installation.

How to install Visual Studio Express 2012 for Windows Desktop

1. Go to the page on Microsoft's web site for the download of the Visual Studio Express 2012 editions, and follow the directions to download the setup program for the Windows Desktop edition.
2. Run the setup program. It works similarly to the setup program for Visual Studio 2012, but no optional features are available.

Note

- The Visual Studio 2012 setup programs install not only Visual Studio, but also the .NET Framework 4.5 and SQL Server 2012 Express LocalDB.

Figure A-2 How to install Visual Studio 2012

How to use the MMABooks database

In section 3 of this book, you learned how to develop applications that work with the data in a database. The book applications in that section use a database named MMABooks with an edition of SQL Server 2012 called SQL Server 2012 Express LocalDB. This edition of SQL Server is designed specifically for developers and doesn't require any management. It lets you create applications that automatically start the database engine and attach the database to the server when an application is run. In addition, it is automatically installed with all editions of Visual Studio 2012.

Figure A-3 summarizes the techniques for using the MMABooks database with SQL Server Express LocalDB. To do that, you can simply add the MMABooks.mdf file to a project. Then, when the Data Source Configuration Wizard starts, you can complete the wizard to create a data source with a connection string that points to the included database as shown in chapter 14. Or, you can cancel out of this wizard if you're writing your own data access code as shown in chapter 16.

Of course, you can also use the MMABooks database with other editions of SQL Server 2012. If you already have SQL Server 2012 Express installed on your PC, for example, you can use the database with that server. Otherwise, you can install and work with SQL Server Express as described in this figure. The Express Edition of SQL Server 2012 is free, and it provides all of the features of the full editions of SQL Server 2012.

Although you don't need to know much about how SQL Server Express works to use it, you should know that when you run the setup program, it creates an instance of SQL Server with the same name as your computer appended with SQLEXPRESS. For example, the copy of SQL Server on my system is named ANNE-PC\SQLEXPRESS. After this server is installed and started, you can create databases that are managed by the server. Then, you can connect to those databases from your Visual Basic applications using the generated server name or the name localhost\SqlExpress. Here, *localhost* indicates that the database server is running on the same PC as the application.

To create the MMABooks database, you can run the batch file named create_database.bat that's stored in the C:\Murach\VB 2012\Database directory when you download and install the files for this book as described in figure A-1. This batch file runs a SQL Server script named create_database.sql that creates the MMABooks database and attaches it to the SQL Server Express database server that's running on your computer.

Note, however, that if the database server on your system has a name other than the computer name appended with SQLEXPRESS, the batch file we provide won't work. But you can easily change it so it will work. To do that, just open the file in a text editor such as NotePad. When you do, you'll see a single command with this server specification:

```
sqlcmd -S localhost\SqlExpress -E /i create_database.sql
```

Then, you can just change this specification to the name of your server.

How to use the database with SQL Server 2012 Express LocalDB

- The MMABooks database files (MMABooks.mdf and MMABooks_log.ldf) are included in each application for this book that uses this database.
- To use the MMABooks database in your own applications, you can add the MMABooks.mdf file to your project as described in figure 14-2 in chapter 14. This will automatically add the MMABooks_log.ldf file and start the Data Source Configuration Wizard.
- If you're writing your own data access code for an application as described in chapter 16, you can cancel out of the Data Source Configuration Wizard that starts when you add the MMABooks.mdf file to the project.
- The MMABooks.mdf and MMABooks_log.ldf files are stored in the C:\Murach\VB 2012\Database and C:\VB 2012\Database directories when you download and install the files for this book as described in figure A-1.

How to use the database with SQL Server 2012 Express

- To use the MMABooks database with SQL Server Express, you must first create it. To do that, you can use Windows Explorer to navigate to the C:\Murach\VB 2012\Database directory and double-click the create_database.bat file. This runs the create_database.sql file that creates the database objects and inserts the rows into each table.
- The create_database.sql file starts by deleting the MMABooks database if it already exists. That way, you can use it to recreate the database and restore the original data if you ever need to do that.
- When you create the MMABooks database, the MMABooks.mdf and MMABooks_log.ldf files are created and stored in the default data directory for your instance of SQL Server. For SQL Server 2012, that directory is C:\Program files\Microsoft SQL Server\MSSQL11.SQLEXPRESS\MSSQL\DATA.
- To define a connection to the MMABooks database, you can use the server name localhost\SqlExpress or a name that consists of your computer name followed by \SqlExpress.

How to install and work with SQL Server 2012 Express

- To install SQL Server 2012 Express, you can download its setup file from Microsoft's web site for free and then run that file.
- After you install SQL Server Express, it will start automatically each time you start your PC. To start or stop this service or change its start mode, start the SQL Server Configuration Manager (Start→All Programs→Microsoft SQL Server 2012→Configuration Tools→SQL Server Configuration Manager), select the server in the right pane, and use the buttons in the toolbar.

Note

- SQL Server 2012 Express LocalDB is automatically installed with all editions of Visual Studio 2012, so no setup is required to use it.

Figure A-3 How to use the MMABooks database

Index

B

C

D

E

F

G

H

I

J

K

L

M

N

O

P

S

T

U

V

W

X

Y

Z

What software you need for this book

- Any of the full editions of Microsoft Visual Studio 2012 or Visual Studio Express 2012 for Windows Desktop.
- If you want to store databases on your PC and you don't want to use SQL Server 2012 Express LocalDB, which is installed with Visual Studio, you can install SQL Server 2012 Express.
- For information about downloading and installing these products, please see appendix A.

The downloadable files for this book

- All of the applications presented in this book including source code and data.
- Starting points for the exercises in the book so you can get more practice in less time.
- Solutions for all of the exercises in this book so you can check your work on the exercises.
- The files for the MMABooks database that's used by this book, along with files for creating this database if you're using an edition of SQL Server 2012 other than SQL Server 2012 Express LocalDB.

How to download the files for this book

- Go to www.murach.com, and go to the page for ***Murach's Visual Basic 2012***.
- Click the link for "FREE download of the book applications." Then, select the "All book files" link and respond to the resulting pages and dialog boxes. This will download a setup file named vb12_allfiles.exe onto your hard drive.
- Use Windows Explorer to find this exe file on your hard drive. Then, double-click this file and respond to the dialog boxes that follow. This installs the files in directories that start with C:\Murach\VB 2012, and then runs a batch file that copies the subdirectories of the C:\Murach\VB 2012\Exercise Starts directory to the C:\VB 2012 directory.